THE NEW HAMLYN

CROSSWORD

DICTIONARY

THE NEW HAMLYN

CROSSWORD

DICTIONARY

GENERAL EDITOR: JOHN BAILIE

BCA

LONDON NEW YORK SYDNEY TORONTO

First published in 1932
Revised 1963, 1978

Published in 1983 and in 1988 by Reed Consumer Books Limited
under the title *Hamlyn Crossword Dictionary*

This revised and updated edition published in 1992
by BCA by arrangement with
Reed Consumer Books Limited
Michelin House, 81 Fulham Road, London SW3 6RB
and Auckland, Melbourne, Singapore and Toronto

Reprinted 1993, 1994 (twice), 1995 (twice)

CN 8128

Printed in England by Clays Ltd, St Ives plc

Contents

Introduction

The New Hamlyn Crossword Dictionary is an extensively revised and updated edition of the immensely popular *Hamlyn Crossword Dictionary*. It is the ideal guide for the crossword enthusiast, presenting in a convenient form a collection of over 75,000 carefully selected and classified words which will prove invaluable in solving and compiling crosswords.

It is really very simple to use. In crossword puzzles the number of letters in the required word is known and usually also the subject. The aim of *The Hamlyn Crossword Dictionary* is to enable the reader to quickly find the word he wants. For this reason it has been systematically divided into a number of main subject categories, including *Armed Forces, Business, Professions and Occupations, Geography, Literature and the Arts, Natural History,* and *Science and Technology,* each of which is split up into subdivisions. In these subdivisions all the relevant words will be found under the number of letters required, in lists of words of from two to fifteen (and sometimes more) letters, each list being set out in alphabetical order.

The New Hamlyn Crossword Dictionary is not only the indispensable companion for the crossword-puzzle fan but the encyclopedic coverage of its contents makes it a most useful general reference book as well. Among the many valuable sections in the book are the comprehensive lists of animals, birds, fish, coins, plants, etc., and characters from mythology and literature.

ARMED FORCES
Air force ranks and appellations: British and U.S.

2 – 4
A.C.1
A.C.2
F.O.
L.A.C.
W.A.A.F.

5
major (U.S.)
pilot

6
airman
fitter
rigger

7
aviator
captain (U.S.)

colonel (U.S.)
general (U.S.)
private (U.S.)

8
armourer
corporal
mechanic
observer
sergeant

9
air gunner
bomb aimer
drum-major
navigator

10
air marshal
apprentice

balloonist
bombardier (U.S.)
nose gunner
rear gunner
tail gunner

11
aircraftman
belly gunner
second pilot

12
air commodore
group captain
major general (U.S.)
pilot officer

13
flying officer
sergeant major (U.S.)

staff sergeant (U.S.)
wing commander

14
air vice marshal
flight engineer
flight mechanic
flight sergeant
master sergeant (U.S.)
squadron leader
warrant officer

15
air chief marshal
first lieutenant (U.S.)

16
flight lieutenant
second lieutenant (U.S.)

Battles and sieges

3 AND 4
Acre
Aden
Agra
Alma (The)
Amoy
Caen
Gaza
Ivry
Jena
Kut
Laon
Loos
Lys (The)
Maas
Mons
Nile (The)
Taku
Tet
Ulm

Yser (The)
Zama

5
Aisne (The)
Alamo (The)
Arcot
Arras
Basra
Boyne (The)
Bulge (The)
Cadiz
Cairo
Crécy
Crete
Delhi
El Teb
Eylau
Genoa

Herat
Issus
Kabul
Kandy
Liège
Ligny
Maida
Malta
Marne (The)
Meuse
Miami
Paris
Pusan
Rhine
Sedan
Selle
Somme (The)
Tagus (The)
Texel (The)
Tours
Valmy

Ypres

6
Actium
Amiens
Arbela
Argaon
Armada (The)
Arnhem
Assaye
Atbara (The)
Bagdad
Barnet
Bataan
Berlin
Burgos
Busaco
Calais
Camden

Cannae
Chusan
Coruña
Dargai
Delium
Dunbar
Ferrol
Guarda
Gujrat
Havana
Isonzo (The)
Jattoo
Jhansi
Lutzen
Madras
Madrid
Majuba
Malaga
Manila
Mantua
Midway
Mileto
Minden
Moscow
Nagpur
Narvik
Naseby
Oporto
Orthez
Ostend
Peking
Plevna
Quebec
Rhodes
Rivoli
Rocroi
Sadowa
Saints (The)
Shiloh
Tarifa
Tobago
Tobruk
Toulon
Tudela
Tugela (The)
Ushant
Verdun
Vienna
Wagram
Warsaw

7

Aboukir
Abu Klea
Alamein
Albuera
Almansa

Almeida
Antwerp
Badajoz
Baghdad
Bapaume
Bautzen
Bousaco
Brienne
Bull Run
Cambrai
Cape Bon
Cassino
Chalons
Coimbra
Colenso
Cordova
Coronel
Corunna
Dresden
Dunkirk
Edghill
El Obeid
Falkirk
Flodden
Granada
Gwalior
Iwo Jima
Jutland
La Hogue
Leipzig
Lemberg
Lepanto
Leuthen
Lucknow
Magdala
Magenta
Marengo
Matapan
Minorca
Moselle
Moskowa (The)
Nations (The)
Newbury
Nivelle (The)
Okinawa
Orleans
Plassey
Poltava
Preston
St. Kitts
St. Lucia
Salamis
Salerno
Sobraon
Solebay
Vimiera
Vitoria

8

Ardennes
Atlantic (The)
Bastille (The)
Beresina (The)
Blenheim
Bhurtpur
Borodino
Bosworth
Calcutta
Carthage
Cawnpore
Culloden
Edgehill
Flanders
Flushing
Fontenoy
Fort Erie
Granicus
Hastings
Hydaspes
Inkerman
Kandahar
Khartoum
Lake Erie
Le Cateau
Mafeking
Malakoff (The)
Marathon
Maubeuge
Medellin
Messines
Metaurus
Montreal
Navarino
Nieuport
Normandy
Omdurman
Philippi
Poitiers
Potidaea
Pretoria
Przemysl
St. Mihiel
St. Pierre
Salsette
Saratoga
Spion Kop
Stirling
Suvla Bay
Syracuse
Talavera
Tiberias
Toulouse
Valencia
Waterloo
Yorktown
Zaragoza

9

Agincourt
Algeciras
Arginusai
Balaclava
Belle Isle
Caporetto
Chaeronea
Champagne
Charleroi
Ctesiphon
Dettingen
El Alamein
Falklands (The)
Festubert
Friedland
Gallipoli
Gaugamela
Gibraltar
Hyderabad
Kimberley
Ladysmith
Laing's Nek
Leningrad
Leyte Gulf
Louisburg
Mauritius
Melagnano
Mobile Bay
Oudenarde
Pharsalus
Port Mahon
Ramillies
Rodriguez
Saragossa
St. Quentin
St. Vincent
Salamanca
Sedgemoor
Solferino
Stormberg
Stromboli
Tarragona
Tourcoing
Trafalgar
Vicksburg
Walcheren
Worcester
Zeebrugge

10

Adrianople
Ahmednagar
Alexandria
Appomattox
Austerlitz

Brandywine
Brownstown
Bunker Hill
Camperdown
Chevy-chase
Copenhagen
Corregidor
Dogger Bank
Fort George
Gettysburg
Gravelotte
Guadeloupe
Heligoland
Imjin River
Kut-el-Amara
La Rochelle
Les Saintes
Malplaquet
Martinique
Montevideo
Montfaucon
New Orleans
Nördlingen
Paardeburg
Petersburg
Port Arthur
Porto Praya
Quatre Bras
River Plate
Sevastopol
Shrewsbury
Stalingrad
Tannenberg
Tel-el-Kebir
Tewkesbury
Tinchebray

11

Albuquerque
Bannockburn
Breitenfeld
Chattanooga
Chilianwala
Dardanelles (The)
Dien Bien Phu
Fort Niagara
Guadalcanal
Hohenlinden
Isandhlwana
Jameson Raid (The)
Marston Moor
Pearl Harbor
Philiphaugh
Philippines (The)
Pieter's Hill
Pondicherry
Port Stanley

Prestonpans
Quiberon Bay
Rorke's Drift
Schoneveldt
Thermopylae
Ticonderoga

12 AND OVER

Antietam Creek (13)
Battle of Britain (15)
Bloemfontein (12)
Cape St. Vincent (13)
Ciudad Rodrigo (13)
Constantinople (14)
Delville Wood (12)

Falkland Islands (15)
Flodden Field (12)
Lake Champlain (13)
Little Bighorn (12)
Magersfontein (13)
Messines Ridge (13)
Neuve Chapelle (13)
Neville's Cross (13)
Passchendaele (13)

Plains of Abraham (15)
San Sebastian (12)
Seringapatam (12)
Spanish Armada (The) (13)
Stamford Bridge (14)
Trichinopoly (12)
Tsushima Strait (14)
White Mountain (13)

Military ranks and appellations

2 AND 3

A.D.C.
A.T.S.
C.O.
C.S.M.
G.I.
N.C.O.
O.C.
R.S.M.
R.T.O.
S.A.S.

4

goum
koul
lewa
naik
para
peon

5

cadet
fifer
Jäger
major
miner
piper
poilu
pongo
scout
sepoy
sowar
spahi
Tommy
Uhlan

6

archer
askari
batman
bomber
bowman
bugler
cornet
driver
ensign
gunner
Gurkha
hetman
hussar
lancer
marine
ranger
ranker
sapper
sutler
yeoman
Zouave

7

ancient
Arnaout
captain
colonel
Cossack
dragoon
drummer
estafet
farrier
general
hobbler
hoplite
janizar
jemadar
lancers
marines

marshal
militia
officer
orderly
pikeman
pioneer
private
recruit
redcoat
regular
reserve
saddler
samurai
sappers
soldier
subadar
trooper
vedette
veteran
warrior

8

adjutant
armourer
bandsman
cavalier
chasseur
commando
corporal
daffadar
decurion
deserter
doughboy
dragoons
fencible
fugelman
fusilier
havildar
infantry
janizary
Landwehr

marksman
messmate
muleteer
mutineer
partisan
rifleman
risaldar
sentinel
sergeant
spearman
turncoat
waterman

9

beefeater
berserker
brigadier
cannoneer
cannonier
centurion
combatant
commander
conductor
conscript
drum-major
estafette
field rank
fife-major
fort-major
grenadier
guardsman
guerrilla
Home Guard
irregular
Janissary
lance-naik
lifeguard
man-at-arms
musketeer
paymaster
pensioner

11

pipe-major
signaller
subaltern
tactician
town-major
trumpeter
tradesman
vexillary
voltigeur
volunteer

10

aide-de-camp
bandmaster
bombardier
campaigner
carabineer
cavalryman
commandant
cuirassier
drummer-boy
file-leader
footguards
halberdier
instructor
Lansquenet
lieutenant
Life Guards
militiaman
other ranks
paratroops
roughrider
strategist

11

arquebusier
artillerist
auxiliaries
bashi-bazook
bersaglieri
condottiere
crack troops
crossbowman
gendarmerie
horse guards
infantryman
Landsknecht
moss-trooper
parachutist
paratrooper
rangefinder
top sergeant
Tommy Atkins

12

armour-bearer
artilleryman
brigade-major
camp-follower
ensign-bearer
field marshal
field officer
horse soldier
jemadar-major
major-general
master gunner

officer cadet
P.T. instructor
Royal Marines
Royal Signals
staff officer
storm-trooper
subadar-major
sub-conductor
territorials

13

army commander
barrack-master
brevet-colonel
bugle-corporal
color-sergeant
corporal-major
dispatch-rider
drill sergeant
first sergeant
generalissimo
lance-corporal
lance-daffadar
lance-sergeant
lifeguardsman
light infantry
machine-gunner
marine officer
mounted rifles
prisoner of war
quartermaster
risaldar major
sergeant major
staff-sergeant

14

citizen-soldier
colonel-in-chief
colour-havildar
colour-sergeant
liaison officer
master sergeant
medical officer
military police
orderly officer
provost-marshal
Royal Artillery
Royal Engineers
Royal Tank Corps
second corporal
signals officer
standard bearer
warrant officer

15

adjutant-general
corporal-of-horse
first lieutenant
gentleman-at-arms
honorary colonel
household troops
mounted infantry
orderly corporal
orderly sergeant
ordnance officer
provost sergeant

Military terms (including fortifications)

2 – 4

aim
ally
ammo
anfo
arm
arms
army
A.W.O.L.
band
base
bawn
belt
berm
blip
camp
defy

draw
duck
duel
dun
fife
file
fire
flag
flak
foe
foot
form
fort
foss
gas
gun
halt
host

hut
jam
jeep
kern
kit
lay
levy
line
loot
man
map
mess
mine
moat
N.A.T.O.
O.C.T.U.
out
pa

pah
park
P.I.A.T.
plan
post
P.O.W.
push
raid
ramp
rank
raze
rear
rout
ruse
sack
sap
shot
slay

slug
spot
spur
star
take
tank
tent
tilt
trap
turn
unit
van
war
ward
wing
zero

5

abort
agent
alarm
alert
annex
A.N.Z.A.C.
armed
armor
array
baton
beret
berme
beset
booty
boyau
busby
butts
cadre
cavin
cells
clean
corps
decoy
depot
depth
ditch
dogra
draft
drawn
dress
drill
enemy
enrol
equip
feint
field
fight
flank
flare
foray
fosse
fours
front
gazon
gorge
guard
guide
gurry
herse
horse
khaki
lance
lines
march
medal
mêlée
mount

mufti
onset
order
party
peace
pivot
poilu
pouch
prime
radar
rally
range
ranks
redan
relay
repel
rifle
round
route
royal
sally
salvo
scale
scarp
S.E.A.T.O.
seize
S.H.A.E.F.
shako
shell
shift
shock
shoot
siege
snipe
sonar
sonic
spoil
squad
staff
stand
storm
strap
talus
T.E.W.T.S.
track
troop
truce
unarm
vexil
wheel
wound
yield

6

abatis
ack-ack
action

affray
allies
ambush
archer
armour
assail
attack
bailey
banner
barbed
battle
beaten
billet
blinds
blow up
bonnet
bouche
brevet
bunker
cartel
castle
centre
charge
clayes
cohort
colour
column
combat
convoy
cordon
corral
curfew
dagger
débris
decamp
defeat
defend
defier
defile
deploy
desert
detach
detail
disarm
donjon
double
dugout
embark
embody
encamp
engage
enlist
enmity
ensign
epaule
escape
escarp
escort
Fabian

fanion
firing
fleche
foeman
forted
fraise
gabion
glacis
guards
guides (the)
guidon
hawhaw
helmet
hurter
impact
inroad
invade
invest
inwall
kitbag
legion
limber
merlon
mining
mobile
muster
mutiny
number
obsess
occupy
oppose
orders
orgues
outfit
parade
parley
parole
patrol
pennon
permit
picket
plonge
pompom
pompon
primer
pursue
raider
ransom
rapine
rappel
ration
ravage
rebuff
recall
recoil
reduce
relais
relief

report
resist
retake
retire
review
riddle
rideau
roster
saddle
salute
sconce
sensor
signal
sketch
sortie
square
stores
strife
strike
stripe
stroke
subdue
submit
supply
target
tattoo
tenail
thrust
trench
trophy
umpire
vallum
valour
victor
volley
walled
warcry
zareba
zigzag

7

abattis
advance
aid-post
air-raid
airlift
archery
armoury
arsenal
assault
baggage
barrack
barrage
basenet
bastion
battery
battled

besiege
bivouac
bombard
brigade
bulwark
caltrop
canteen
carbine
caserne
cavalry
chamade
charger
chevron
citadel
cold war
colours
command
company
conquer
counter
coupure
crusade
curtain
debouch
defence
defiant
degrade
destroy
détente
detrain
disband
dismiss
dispart
drawn up
draw off
dungeon
echelon
ecoutes
enguard
enomoty
entrain
envelop
environ
epaulet
fallout
fanfare
fascine
fatigue
flanker
fortify
fortlet
forward
fourgon
foxhole
fraised
gallery
guérite
gunfire
gunnery

gun-shot
half-pay
harness
holster
hostage
hostile
hutment
jamming
Kremlin
landing
leaguer
liaison
looting
lunette
madrier
maniple
marquee
martial
megaton
moineau
mounted
neutral
nuclear
on guard
outpost
outwing
outwork
overawe
overrun
parados
parapet
pennant
phalanx
pillbox
pitfall
platoon
plongée
postern
priming
protect
provost
prowess
pursuit
quarter
rampart
rations
ravelin
redoubt
refugee
regular
remblai
remount
repulse
reserve
retaken
retreat
reverse
Riot Act
salient

sand-bag
section
service
sniping
spurred
stand-by
subvert
support
tactics
tambour
tenable
tilting
trailer
triumph
unarmed
uncased
uniform
valiant
van-foss
venture
victory
ward off
warfare
wargame
war-hoop
warlike
warpath
warsong
warworn
wheeler
windage
wounded

8

accoutre
advanced
airborne
air force
alarm gun
alliance
armament
armature
armorial
arms race
Army List
baldrick
barbette
barbican
barracks
bartizan
bawdrick
bearskin
billeted
blockade
bull's eye
camisade
camisado

campaign
casemate
casualty
chivalry
civil war
collapse
conquest
cornetcy
crusader
decimate
decisive
defended
defender
defiance
demi-lune
demolish
despatch
detonate
disarray
disenrol
dismount
dispatch
distance
division
doubling
drumhead
duelling
earth-bag
embattle
embodied
enceinte
enfilade
ensigncy
entrench
equipage
escalade
escouade
estacade
eyes left
fastness
field day
fighting
flagpost
flanking
footband
fortress
fourneau
furlough
garrison
gauntlet
gendarme
gonfalon
guerilla
half-moon
hang-fire
hedgehog
herisson
hillfort
horn-work

intrench
invasion
knapsack
last post
lay siege
lay waste
limber up
lodgment
loophole
magazine
majority
Mameluke
mantelet
marching
mark time
matériel
mess bill
militant
military
mobilize
movement
muniment
musketry
mutinous
on parade
on parole
opponent
ordnance
orillion
outflank
outguard
outlying
overcome
overkill
palisade
paradrop
passport
password
pavilion
pay corps
petronel
pipe-clay
prisoner
punitive
quarters
railhead
ramparts
rear line
rear rank
rearward
recharge
re-embark
re-embody
regiment
remounts
reprisal
resalute
retirade
retrench

reveille
ricochet
rifle-pit
roll-call
sabotage
saboteur
saluting
scout-car
security
sentry-go
services (the)
shabrack
shelling
shooting
shot-belt
siege-war
skirmish
soldiery
spotting
squadron
stampede
standard
star-fort
stockade
stoppage
storming
straddle
strategy
strength
struggle
supplies
support
surprise
surround
sword arm
tactical
tenaille
time-fuse
tortoise
training
transfer
traverse
trooping
   (the colour)
unallied
unbeaten
unlimber
uprising
valorous
vanguard
vanquish
vexillar
victuals
vigilant
vincible
warfarer
warhorse
warpaint
war-plume

war-whoop
watch-box
wheeling
yeomanry
zero hour

9

aggressor
alarm post
ambuscade
ambuscado
armistice
armouries
army corps
artillery
assailant
atomic war
attrition
ballistic
bandolier
banquette
barricade
barricado
battalion
batteries
battle-cry
beachhead
beleaguer
bellicose
billeting
bodyguard
bombproof
bugle call
bulldozer
cannonade
caponiere
captaincy
cashiered
cavalcade
ceasefire
challenge
chevalier
colonelcy
combatant
comitadji
conqueror
covert-way
crossfire
crown-work
crow's foot
defection
defensive
defiatory
demi-gorge
desertion
devastate
discharge

disembody
disengage
dismantle
earthwork
elevation
embattled
embrasure
encompass
encounter
enfiladed
enrolment
epaulette
equipment
espionage
esplanade
eyes front
eyes right
fencibles
field rank
fire-drill
flagstaff
forage-cap
form fours
fortalice
fortifier
fortilage
fusillade
gabionade
gas attack
gladiator
guardroom
guerrilla
haversack
heliostat
hersillon
homograph
hostility
housewife
incursion
interdict
invalided
irregular
land force
Landsturm
legionary
lifeguard
logistics
loopholed
Luftwaffe
majorship
manoeuvre
mechanist
mercenary
militancy
musketoon
Mutiny Act
objective
offensive
officiate

onsetting
onslaught
operation
overpower
overshoot
overthrow
overwhelm
packdrill
pack train
palladium
parachute
predictor
pregnable
pressgang
projector
promotion
protector
provender
rearguard
rebellion
reconquer
red ensign
re-enforce
refortify
reinforce
rencontre
reprimand
revetment
revictual
safeguard
sally-port
scrimmage
semaphore
sentry-box
sham-fight
slaughter
slope arms
slow-march
stack arms
stand-fast
stand fire
stand-firm
stratagem
strategic
subaltern
subjugate
surrender
sword-knot
taskforce
tenaillon
terrorist
train-band
transport
treachery
tricolour
unbridged
undaunted
undrilled
unguarded

unhostile
uniformed
unopposed
unordered
unscathed
unsheathe
unstormed
unwarlike
unwounded
vigilance
war office
watchword
Wehrmacht
white flag
withstand
zigzagged

10

action left
aggressive
air-defence
ammunition
annexation
annihilate
arbalister
armipotent
arrière-ban
attackable
battlement
blitzkrieg
blockhouse
breastwork
brevet rank
bridgehead
camel corps
camouflage
cantonment
capitulate
ceremonial
challenger
color guard
commandeer
commissary
commission
contraband
crenulated
dead ground
decampment
defendable
defensible
defilading
demobilize
demolition
deployment
desolating
desolation
despatches

detachment
detonation
direct fire
dismounted
dispatches
divisional
dragonnade
drawbridge
embodiment
encampment
enfilading
engagement
engarrison
enlistment
epaulement
epauletted
escalation
escarpment
expedition
fieldworks
flying camp
garrisoned
glasshouse
ground fire
guardhouse
hand-to-hand
heliograh
indecisive
Indian file
inspection
investment
invincible
leadership
light-armed
light horse
limited war
line of fire
manoeuvres
map-reading
martial law
militarism
musketeers
muster book
muster roll
night-watch
no man's land
nuclear war
occupation
odd-numbers
operations
opposition
outgeneral
over the top
patrolling
point blank
portcullis
presidiary
prison camp
projectile

protection
provision
quartering
quick-march
raking fire
reconquest
recruiting
re-entering
regimental
rencounter
rendezvous
reorganize
reparation
resistance
respirator
retirement
revolution
rifle range
route march
sabretache
sentry beat
sentry duty
sentry post
shell-proof
siege-train
signal-fire
signalling
skirmisher
slit trench
soldiering
squad drill
state of war
sticky bomb
stronghold
subjection
subsection
submission
submissive
subversion
surrounded
sword-fight
table money
terreplein
tirailleur
trajectory
triumphant
undecisive
undefended
unequipped
unlimbered
unmolested
unsheathed
vanquisher
victorious
volunteers
vulnerable
war-council
watchtower

11

action front
action right
aides-de-camp
assaultable
barackroom
battle-array
battledress
battlefield
battle-royal
belligerent
besiegement
bombardment
bridge-train
bulletproof
button-stick
castellated
colour party
conquerable
co-operation
countermine
defenceless
demi-bastion
devastation
disarmament
disbandment
disgarrison
double-march
drawn swords
dress parade
embarkation
emplacement
envelopment
even numbers
fatigue duty
firing party
firing squad
flag of truce
flying party
flying squad
foot-soldier
forced march
forlorn hope
form two deep
fortifiable
generalship
germ warfare
guerilla war
impregnable
indefensive
machicoulis
mobile force
orderly room
penetration
postern gate
present arms
protagonist
range-finder

rank-and-file
reconnoitre
recruitment
redoubtable
review order
royal salute
running-fire
safe conduct
searchlight
shock-troop
skirmishing
smokescreen
stand-to-arms
supply depot
trous-de-loup
trumpet call
unconquered
unfortified
unprotected
unsoldierly
unsupported
vincibility
war memorial

12

advanced base
advance guard
annihilation
anti-aircraft
Bailey bridge
barking-irons
battlemented
bush-fighting
capitulation
civil defence
commissariat
commissioned
conscription
counterguard
countermarch
court-martial
covering fire
demi-distance
disaffection
dropping fire
fatigue party
field colours
field-kitchen
flying column
foot-barracks
garrison town
guerrilla war
headquarters
heavy brigade
hollow square
horse-and-foot
indefensible

indirect fire
intelligence
intrenchment
invulnerable
irresistible
landing party
light brigade
light cavalry
line-of-battle
machicolated
Maltese cross
mobile column
mobilization
outmanoeuvre
platoon drill
plunging fire
protectorate
quarter-guard
remount depot
retrenchment
running fight
ruse-de-guerre
shock tactics
saluting base
shoulder-belt
shoulder-knot
siege tactics
siege warfare
staff college
surveillance
truce-breaker
ungarrisoned
unintrenched
unobstructed
unvanquished
vanquishable
white feather
working party

13

accoutrements
advanced guard
carrier pigeon
cheval-de-frise
circumvallate
co-belligerent
column-of-route
counterattack
counter-parole
counterstoke
disembodiment
encompassment
fatigue parade
field equipage
field of battle
fighting force
flying colours

fortification
guards' brigade
interior lines
invincibility
lorry workshop
machicolation
martello tower
mass formation
mounted police
mushroom cloud
order of battle
ordnance depot
pontoon-bridge
radiolocation
rallying point
re-embarkation
re-enforcement
regular troops
reinforcement
sapper officer
shoulder-strap
splinter-proof
squadron drill
storming-party
strategically
swordsmanship
trench warfare
unarmed combat
unconquerable
unsoldierlike
unsurrendered
urban guerila
Victoria Cross
vitrified fort
war department

14

ammunition dump
auxiliary force
blockade-runner
castrametation
chevaux-de-frise
demobilization
field allowance
general reserve
mechanized army
military school
miniature-range
medical officer
musketry course
musketry school
nuclear warfare
Pyrrhic victory
reconnaissance
reinforcements
reorganization
standing orders

16

supreme command	*15*	dressing-station	military railway
trooping-season		flying artillery	non-commissioned
unvanquishable	auxiliary forces	guerilla warfare	observation post
urban guerrilla	casualty station	intrenching tool	operation orders
volunteer force	circumvallation	invulnerability	submarine-mining
winter quarters	clearing station	married quarters	substantive rank
	contravallation	military academy	turning movement
	counter-approach	military college	
	discharge papers	military funeral	

Naval (British and U.S.), Fleet Air Arm, Merchant Navy (Merchant Marine) ranks and appellations

4	fireman	navigator	port officer	fourth officer
	greaser	paymaster	post captain	harbourmaster
cook	jack-tar	powder-boy	rating pilot	leading seaman
Easy	look-out	ropemaker	rear-admiral	leading stoker
mate	messman	sailmaker	vice-admiral	marine officer
wren	recruit	ship's cook	watchkeeper	privateersman
	shipman	signalman		quartermaster
	sideboy	tugmaster		quarter rating
5	skipper		*12*	radio operator
	steward			sailing master
bosun	surgeon	*10*	boy artificer	second officer
cadet	trimmer		cabin steward	ship's corporal
diver	wireman	able seaman	chief officer	signal officer
middy		apprentice	chief skipper	stern-sheetman
pilot		coastguard	chief steward	sub-lieutenant
	8	gun captain	first officer	third engineer
		instructor	master-at-arms	torpedo-gunner
6	armourer	lieutenant	master gunner	
	cabinboy	midshipman	officers' cook	
cooper	chaplain	range-taker	petty officer	*14 AND 15*
ensign	coxswain	shipmaster	photographer	
lascar	engineer	ship's baker	powder monkey	boarding officer
marine	flag rank	shipwright	P.T. instructor	boatswain's mate
master	gun-layer	torpedoman	schoolmaster	first lieutenant
purser	helmsman	wardmaster	seaman-bugler	flag-lieutenant
rating	leadsman		seaman-gunner	fourth engineer
reefer	messmate		second master	half-pay officer
seaman	motorman	*11*	senior purser	leading steward
snotty	ship's boy		ship's butcher	lieut.-commander
stoker	winchman	air mechanic	ship's caulker	officer's steward
topman		branch pilot	ship's surgeon	ordinary seaman
writer	*9*	chief stoker	supply rating	rating observer
yeoman		electrician	telegraphist	sailmaker's mate
	air-fitter	extra master	third officer	second engineer
	artificer	flag captain		ship's carpenter
7	boatswain	flag officer	*13*	torpedo coxswain
	commander	foremastman		warrant officer
admiral	commodore	gunner's mate	armourer's mate	
armorer	cook's mate	leading wren	captain's clerk	
artisan	donkeyman	master's mate	chief armourer	
captain	engineman	mechanician	chief engineer	
deckboy		port admiral		

Weapons and armour

3 AND 4

ABM
ammo
arm
arms
axe
ball
bill
bola
bolt
bomb
bow
bren
butt
cane
club
colt
cosh
da
dag
dah
dart
dirk
egg
epée
flak
foil
gade
gaff
gas
goad
gun
helm
ICBM
jack
jet
kris
mace
mail
mere
meri
mine
nike
pike
ram
shot
sten
tace
tank
tuck
VTOL
wad
whip
Z-gun

5

A-bomb
aegis
armet
armor
arrow
bilbo
birch
clean
crest
curat
estoc
fusee
fusil
grape
H-bomb
hobit
knife
knout
kukri
lance
lasso
lathi
Luger
Maxim
panga
poker
pouch
rifle
royal
sabre
saker
salvo
shaft
shell
skean
skene
sling
spear
staff
stick
sword
targe
tasse
tawse
visor
vizor

6

ack-ack
air-gun
anlace
armlet
armour
barrel
basnet
bodkin
Bofors
bonnet
buffer
bullet
cannon
carrel
casque
cruise
cudgel
cuisse
dagger
dragon
dualin
dumdum
espada
Exocet
feltre
glaive
gorget
hanger
hanjar
heaume
helmet
homing
jezail
kreese
lariat
lassoo
lorica
mailed
mauser
minnie
morion
mortar
musket
muzzle
napalm
petard
pistol
pom-pom
popgun
powder
primer
quarry
rapier
recoil
salade
sallet
saturn
scutum
shield
sickle
sparth
sparke
stylet
swivel
target
tonite
tuille
tulwar
umbril
waster
weapon
Webley
zipgun

7

anelace
arblast
assagai
assegai
ataghan
bar-shot
baslard
bayonet
bazooka
brasset
Bren gun
buckler
bundook
caestus
carbine
calibre
cordite
couteau
cuirass
curtana
curtein
cutlass
djerrid
dualine
dudgeon
ejector
elf-bolt
espadon
firearm
fire-pot
gantlet
gasmask
Gatling
greaves
grenade
gunshot
hackbut
halberd
halbert
handgun
handjar
harpoon
hatchet
hauberk
holster
javelin
langrel
longbow
long tom
lyddite
machete
megaton
missile
morglay
murrion
nuclear
oil-bomb
panoply
poitrel
polaris
priming
pole-axe
poniard
puldron
quarrel
rabinet
roundel
shotgun
side-arm
sjambok
Skybolt
Spandau
sparthe
Sten gun
teargas
tocemma
torpedo
trident
trisula
twibill
vamplet
ventail
warhead
wind-gun

8

aerodart
amusette
arbalist
armalite
arquebus
atom bomb
attaghan
balister
ballista
bascinet
basilisk
birdbolt
blowpipe
bludgeon
brassart
broad-axe
Browning
burganet
burgonet
canister
carabine
case-shot
catapult
cavalier
chamfron
charfron
chausses
claymore
corselet
crossbow
culettes
culverin
damaskin
dynamite
eel-spear
elf-arrow
enforcer
falchion
falconet
field-gun
firearms
fire-ball
firelock
fireship
fougasse
gadlings
gauntlet
gavelock
gunsight
half-pike
hand-pike
haquebut
howitzer
jazerant
langrage
Lewis gun
linstock
magazine
mangonel
mantelet
Maxim gun
munition
naval gun

oerlikon
ordnance
palstaff
paravane
partisan
paterero
pectoral
pederero
petronel
pistolet
plastron
port-fire
pyroxyle
revolver
ricochet
ringmail
scabbard
scimitar
scorpion
shrapnel
siege-gun
skeandhu
spadroon
spontoon
springal
steam-gun
stiletto
stinkpot
stonebow
Thompson
tomahawk
Tommy gun
umbriere
vambrace
vamplate
whin-yard
whitearm
yataghan

9

angel-shot
arquebuse
arrowhead
artillery
automatic
aventaile
backpiece
ballistic
bastinado
battleaxe
Big Bertha
blackjack
Blue Water
boar-spear
Bofors gun
bomb-chest
bombshell

boomerang
brandiron
Brown Bess
brownbill
carronade
cartouche
cartridge
chain-mail
chain-shot
chassepot
columbiad
defoliant
demi-lance
derringer
deterrent
detonator
equaliser
equalizer
espringal
face-guard
fish-spear
flintlock
garde-bras
gelignite
grapeshot
guncotton
gunpowder
habergeon
half-track
hand-staff
headpiece
heavy tank
heelpiece
light tank
matchlock
Mills bomb
munitions
musketoon
needle-gun
poison gas
quaker-gun
sarbacane
shillalah
slow-match
slung-shot
smallarms
smallbore
smoke-bomb
spring-gun
starshell
stinkbomb
sword-cane
teeth arms
troop ship
truncheon
turret gun
vantbrace
vant-brass
ward staff

welsh-hook
xyloidine
zumbooruk

10

ammunition
arcubalist
battery gun
blind shell
Blue Streak
bowie-knife
brigandine
broadsword
burrel-shot
cannonball
cannon-shot
cataphract
coat armour
coat of mail
cross-arrow
demi-cannon
field-piece
fire-barrel
Gatling gun
grainstaff
harquebuse
knobkerrie
Lee-Enfield
machine-gun
medium tank
Minie rifle
mustard-gas
paixhan-gun
pea-shooter
powder horn
projectile
pyroxyline
recoilless
safety-fuse
sidewinder
six-shooter
skeneoccle
snickersee
sticky bomb
sword-stick
touchpaper
Winchester

11

antitank gun
armoured car
basket sword
blunderbuss
bow and arrow
breastplate

contact-mine
cruiser tank
Dahlgren gun
depth-charge
grande-garde
gun carriage
gun-howitzer
hand-grenade
harping-iron
Jacob's-staff
Lochaber axe
morgenstern
morning-star
mountain-gun
powder-chest
powder flask
safety-catch
scale-armour
Snider rifle
stern-chaser
Thompson gun

12

Armstrong gun
battering ram
boarding pike
bombing plane
breech-loader
cartridge-box
conventional
cross-bar-shot
demi-culverin
double-charge
flame-thrower
fowling-piece
Lancaster gun
landing craft
Mills grenade
mitrailleuse
muzzle-loader
quarterstaff
rocket-mortar
spigot mortar
Stokes mortar
sword-bayonet
tracer bullet
trench mortar
wheel-lock dag

13

aerial torpedo
armor-piercing
ball-cartridge
cartridge-case
cat-o'-nine-tails

Damocles sword	submarine-mine	blank cartridge (a.) (14)
guided missile	thermonuclear	Brennan torpedo (14)
high-explosive	two-edged sword	flame-projector (14)
knuckleduster		incendiary bomb (a.) (14)
life preserver		lachrymatory gas (15)
percussion cap	**14 – 16**	miniature rifle (14)
poisoned arrow		nitroglycerine (a.) (14)
scalping-knife	anti-aircraft-gun (15)	nuclear weapons (14)
shrapnel shell	armour-piercing (14)	powder-magazine (14)
submachine-gun	ballistic missile (16)	small-bore rifle (14)

BUSINESS, PROFESSIONS AND OCCUPATIONS
Business, trade and commerce

2 AND 3	boom	loss	bid up	offer	*6*
	bull	mart	block	order	
A 1	call	mint	board	owing	accept
bid	cash	nett	bonds	panic	accrue
B.O.T.	cess	note	bonus	paper	advice
buy	chip	owed	brand	payee	agency
C.A	coin	paid	bribe	payer	amount
C.O.D.	cost	P.A.Y.E.	bulls	pound	assets
cut	deal	poll	buyer	price	assign
dun	dear	pool	buy in	proxy	at cost
E.C.U.	debt	post	buy up	quota	avails
E.E.C.	deed	puff	by-law	quote	bailee
fee	dole	punt	cargo	rally	bailor
F.O.B.	dues	ramp	cheap	rates	banker
G.N.P	dump	rate	check	remit	barter
H.P.	duty	rent	chips	repay	bearer
I.O.U.	earn	ring	clear	rider	borrow
job	easy	risk	clerk	score	bought
lot	E.F.T.A.	sale	costs	scrip	bounce
Ltd	even	scot	cover	share	bounty
net	fine	sell	crash	shark	bourse
owe	firm	sink	cycle	short	branch
par	fisc	sold	debit	sight	broker
pay	free	spot	draft	slump	bubble
r.d.	fund	stag	entry	stock	budget
rig	gain	tare	ex cap.	talon	burden
S.E.T.	G.A.T.T.	term	ex div.	taxes	buying
sum	gild	turn	float	teind	buy out
tax	gilt	vend	folio	tight	by-laws
tip	giro	wage	funds	tithe	cartel
V.A.T.	glut		gilts	token	cheque
	gold		goods	trade	change
	good	*5*	gross	trend	charge
4	hire		hedge	trust	client
	idle	agent	'House'	usury	corner
agio	I.O.U.S.	angel	index	value	coupon
back	kite	asset	issue	wages	credit
bail	lend	at par	labor	worth	crisis
bank	levy	audit	lease	yield	cum. div.
bear	lien	award	limit		dealer
bill	loan	batch	money		deal in
bond	long	bears	notes		debtor

defray
demand
dicker
docket
drawee
drawer
equity
estate
excise
expend
export
factor
figure
fiscal
freeze
godown
growth
hammer
holder
honour
import
in cash
income
in debt
indent
insure
jobber
job lot
labour
ledger
lender
liable
Lloyd's
lock-up
margin
market
mark-up
mature
merger
minute
nem. con.
notice
octroi
office
on call
oncost
option
one off
outbid
outlay
outlet
output
packet
parity
pay-day
paying
pay-off
pay out
pledge

plunge
policy
profit
public
punter
quorum
racket
rating
realty
rebate
recoup
redeem
refund
remedy
rental
rentes
report
resale
retail
return
salary
sample
save up
saving
sell in
sell up
set off
settle
shares
shorts
silver
simony
specie
spiral
spread
staple
stocks
strike
supply
surety
surtax
syndic
tariff
taxman
teller
tender
ticket
tithes
trader
tycoon
unload
unpaid
usance
usurer
valuta
vendor
vendue
volume
wampan

wealth
wind up

7

account
actuary
advance
allonge
annuity
arrears
at sight
auction
auditor
average
backing
bad debt
balance
banking
bargain
bidding
bonanza
bullion
buy back
cambist
capital
cashier
ceiling
certify
charter
company
consols
convert
crossed
customs
cut-rate
damages
day book
dealing
declare
default
deficit
deflate
deposit
douceur
draw out
dumping
duopoly
economy
embargo
endorse
engross
entrust
ex bonus
expense
exploit
exports
factory

failure
fall due
feedback
finance
flutter
forward
freight
funding
futures
gearing
haulage
hedging
holding
imports
imprest
indorse
inflate
in funds
insured
interim
invoice
jobbers
jobbing
kaffirs
killing
lay days
leasing
lending
limited
lockout
lottery
lump sum
manager
mint par
minutes
name day
nest egg
net gain
no funds
on offer
on order
package
partner
payable
pay cash
payment
pay rise
payroll
pay slip
pension
per cent
pre-empt
premium
prepaid
pricing
product
profits
promote
pro rata

pyramid
realize
receipt
reissue
renewal
reserve
returns
revenue
rigging
royalty
salvage
selling
sell-out
service
sold out
solvent
spinoff
squeeze
stipend
storage
subsidy
surplus
swindle
takings
tax free
tonnage
trade in
trading
traffic
trustee
utility
vending
venture
war bond
war loan
warrant
way bill
wound up
write up

8

above par
acceptor
accounts
act of God
after tax
agiotage
amortize
ante-date
appraise
assignee
assigner
auditing
back bond
bailment
bank bill
bankbook

bank giro
bank loan
banknote
bank rate
bankrupt
barratry
basic pay
below par
berthage
blue chip
book debt
borrower
bottomry
business
buying in
carriage
cashbook
cash down
cash sale
clearing
commerce
consumer
contango
contract
creditor
credit to
cum bonus
currency
customer
cut-price
dealings
defrayed
delivery
director
disburse
discount
dividend
drawings
dry goods
earnings
embezzle
employee
employer
emporium
endorsee
endorser
entrepot
equities
estimate
evaluate
exchange
expenses
exporter
ex gratia
ex rights
finances
fine gold
flat rate
gold pool

goodwill
gratuity
hallmark
hammered
hard cash
hard sell
hot money
importer
in arrear
increase
indebted
industry
interest
in the red
investor
lame duck
manifest
mark down
markings
maturing
maturity
merchant
monetary
monopoly
mortgage
net price
novation
on credit
on demand
on strike
operator
ordinary
overhead
overtime
par value
passbook
pin money
poundage
price cut
price war
proceeds
producer
property
purchase
quit rent
rack rent
receipts
receiver
recovery
reinvest
reserves
retailer
retainer
scarcity
schedule
security
shipment
sinecure
solvency

spending
spot cash
sterling
straddle
supertax
swindler
takeover
taxation
tax dodge
taxpayer
trade gap
transfer
Treasury
turnover
undercut
unquoted
wage rate
warranty
windfall
write off

9

actuarial
ad valorem
aggregate
allotment
allowance
annuitant
ante-dated
anti-trust
appraisal
appraiser
arbitrage
arrearage
assurance
averaging
bank stock
blank bill
book value
bordereau
borrowing
brokerage
by-product
call money
call price
carry over
certified
chartered
charterer
clearance
closing bid
commodity
cost price
cum rights
death duty
debenture
debit note

deck cargo
deduction
defaulter
deflation
demurrage
depletion
depositor
directors
dishonour
easy money
easy terms
economics
economies
economize
emolument
exchequer
executive
extortion
face value
fair price
fair trade
fiat money
fiduciary
financial
financier
fine paper
firm offer
firm price
first call
first cost
flotation
franchise
free trade
fully paid
garnishee
gilt-edged
going rate
guarantee
guarantor
hard money
import tax
in arrears
incentive
income tax
indemnity
indenture
inflation
insolvent
insurance
inventory
leasehold
liability
liquidate
liquidity
list price
long-dated
mail order
marketing
middleman

mortgagee
mortgagor
near money
negotiate
net income
order book
outgoings
overdraft
overdrawn
overheads
packaging
pari passu
paymaster
pecuniary
petty cash
piecework
portfolio
preferred
price list
price ring
price rise
prime cost
principal
profiteer
promotion
purchaser
put option
quittance
quotation
ratepayer
ready cash
recession
redundant
reflation
reimburse
repayable
repayment
resources
restraint
reversion
royalties
sell short
shift work
short bill
shortfall
short time
sideline
sight bill
sold short
speculate
spot price
stamp duty
statement
stock list
stockpile
subscribe
subsidize
surcharge
syndicate

tax return
ticket day
trade fair
trademark
trade name
tradesman
traveller
treasurer
undersell
unit trust
utilities
valuation
vendition
viability
wage claim
warehouse
wealth tax
wholesale
winding up
work force
work sheet
work study
World Bank

10

acceptance
accountant
account day
accounting
accumulate
active bond
adjustment
advice note
appreciate
assessment
assignment
attachment
auctioneer
automation
average out
bank credit
bank return
bankruptcy
bear market
bearer bond
bill broker
bill of sale
block grant
bondholder
bonus issue
bonus share
bookkeeper
bucket shop
bulk buying
bull market
calculator
call option

capitalism
capitalist
capitalize
capitation
chain store
chequebook
closed shop
collateral
colporteur
commercial
commission
compensate
consortium
contraband
conversion
credit bank
credit card
credit note
credit slip
cumulative
defalcator
del credere
depreciate
depression
direct cost
dirty money
drawn bonds
elasticity
encumbered
engrossing
ergonomics
evaluation
excise duty
ex dividend
first offer
fiscal year
fixed charge
fixed costs
fixed price
fixed trust
free market
floor price
forwarding
funded debt
gross value
ground rent
growth area
honorarium
import duty
income bond
industrial
insolvency
instalment
investment
joint stock
lighterage
liquidator
living wage
long period

loss leader
management
marked down
marketable
mass market
mercantile
money order
monopolist
monopolize
moratorium
negotiable
nonpayment
no par value
note of hand
obligation
open cheque
open credit
opening bid
open market
open policy
option rate
overcharge
paper money
pawnbroker
percentage
plough back
pre-emption
preference
prepayment
price index
price level
production
profitable
profits tax
prospector
prospectus
prosperity
prosperous
provide for
purchasing
pure profit
pyramiding
quarter day
ready money
real estate
real income
recompense
redeemable
redemption
redundancy
remittance
remunerate
rock bottom
sales force
scrip issue
second-hand
securities
selling out
settlement

serial bond
share index
short bonds
short-dated
sole agency
speculator
statistics
stockpiles
stock split
subscriber
tape prices
tax evasion
ticker tape
tight money
trade cycle
trade price
trade union
ultra vires
underwrite
unemployed
upset price
wage freeze
Wall Street
wholesaler
working day
work to rule
written off

11

account book
accountancy
acquittance
advance note
advertising
arbitration
asking price
auction ring
auction sale
average bond
bank account
bank balance
bank holiday
bank of issue
bear squeeze
beneficiary
big business
bill of entry
billionaire
bimetallism
black market
blank cheque
bonded goods
bonus scheme
book-keeping
budget price
businessman
capital gain
cash account

central bank
certificate
circulation
commitments
competition
comptometer
commodities
common stock
competitive
consignment
consumption
co-operative
corporation
counterfeit
cum dividend
customs duty
days of grace
defence bond
demand curve
demand draft
deposit rate
deposit slip
devaluation
discounting
dishonoured
distributor
dividend tax
double entry
down payment
economic law
economic man
endorsement
expenditure
fixed assets
fixed charge
fixed income
fluctuation
foreclosure
free on board
freight note
Gresham's Law
gross income
high finance
hypothecate
income stock
indemnified
indirect tax
industrials
job analysis
joint return
legal tender
liquidation
loan capital
manufacture
market overt
market price
mass-produce
merchandise
middle price

millionaire
minimum wage
money-lender
negotiation
net interest
net receipts
open account
option price
outstanding
overpayment
overtrading
package deal
partnership
pay on demand
physiocrats
point of sale
postal order
poverty line
premium bond
price fixing
price freeze
property tax
purchase tax
Queer Street
raw material
realization
reinsurance
reserve bank
revaluation
rights issue
risk capital
safe deposit
sales ledger
savings bank
seigniorage
sell forward
selling day
shareholder
single entry
sinking fund
small trader
sold forward
speculation
stockbroker
stockjobber
stock market
stockpiling
stocktaking
subsistence
supermarket
syndicalism
take-home pay
takeover bid
time deposit
transaction
undercharge
undervalued
underwriter
with profits

12

above the line
account payee
ad valorem tax
amalgamation
amortization
appreciation
assembly line
balance sheet
banker's draft
banker's order
bargain price
below the line
bill of lading
board meeting
Board of Trade
bond creditor
bonded stores
bottomry bond
branch office
bridging loan
buyer's market
callable bond
capital gains
capital goods
capital stock
carrying over
carry-over day
cash and carry
caveat emptor
charter party
clearing bank
closing price
common market
compensation
consumer goods
contract note
cost of living
credit rating
current price
current ratio
customs union
Defence Bonds
denomination
depreciation
differential
direct labour
disbursement
discount rate
disinflation
distribution
Dutch auction
earned income
embezzlement
econometrics
economy drive
entrepreneur
exchange rate

export credit
first refusal
fiscal policy
fixed capital
floating debt
frozen assets
going concern
gold standard
hard currency
hire purchase
indirect cost
interest rate
invoice clerk
irredeemable
joint account
keep accounts
labour market
laissez-faire
life interest
liquid assets
manufacturer
marginal cost
mass-produced
maturity date
mercantilism
merchant bank
mixed economy
monetization
money changer
national bank
national debt
nearest offer
nominal price
nominal value
official list
opening price
overcapacity
pay as you earn
pay in advance
paying-in-slip
policy holder
present worth
price ceiling
price control
price current
price rigging
productivity
profiteering
profit margin
profit motive
profit taking
public sector
rate of growth
raw materials
redeployment
remuneration
remunerative
reserve price
rig the market

rising prices
running costs
sale or return
sales manager
salesmanship
severance pay
share capital
shareholding
sliding scale
social credit
soft currency
specie points
statistician
sterling area
stock in trade
stockjobbery
stockjobbing
surplus value
tax avoidance
tax collector
tax exemption
terms of trade
trade balance
trading stamp
transfer deed
treasury bill
treasury bond
treasury note
trial balance
trustee stock
underwriting
valued policy
welfare state
works council

13

acceptilation
allotment note
appropriation
articled clerk
average clause
backwardation
bank statement
blank transfer
bullion market
business cycle
clearing house
contract curve
credit account
credit control
credit squeeze
crossed cheque
current assets
discount house
dividend yield
dollar premium
Dow-Jones index

exchequer bill
free trade area
futures market
gross receipts
guarantee fund
incomes policy
interim report
issued capital
livery company
Lombard Street
long-dated bill
making-up price
non-cumulative
not negotiable
ordinary share
outside broker
overhead price
paid-up capital
par of exchange
participating
premium income
private sector
profitability
profit sharing
public company
quota sampling
rateable value
sales forecast
settlement day
share transfer
specification
Stock Exchange
switch selling
taxable income
trade discount
value added tax
vendor's shares
wasting assets
wheeler-dealer
works councils

14

account current
advance freight
apprenticeship
balance of trade
bearer security
bill of exchange
blocked account
break-even point
bureau de change
capital account
capital gearing
capitalization
consumer credit
convertibility
corporation tax

current account
current balance
debenture stock
decimalization
deferred rebate
deferred shares
deposit account
discount market
economic growth
featherbedding
fiduciary issue
finance company
floating charge
founders' shares
fringe benefits
full employment
garnishee order
general average
general manager
half-commission
holder for value
holding company
hyperinflation
infrastructure

inscribed stock
invisible trade
joint stock bank
letter of credit
limited company
liquidity ratio
Lloyd's Register
loan conversion
macro-economics
managing agents
market research
micro-economics
monthly account
mortgage broker
new issue market
nominal capital
option dealings
ordinary shares
oversubscribed
preferred stock
progress chaser
promissory note
quality control
random sampling

rate of exchange
rate of interest
receiving order
revenue account
short-term gains
social secunty
superannuation
surrender value
trading account
uberrimae fidei
unearned income
working capital

15

average adjuster
bonded warehouse
building society
capital employed
commission agent
consignment note
dividend warrant
exchange control

ex-gratia payment
foreign exchange
interim dividend
investment trust
labour-intensive
liquidity ratios
marine insurance
nationalization
non-contributory
political science
preference bonds
preference share
preferred shares
preference stock
public ownership
public relations
purchasing power
rationalization
redemption yield
reducing balance
secured creditor
sleeping partner
sterling balance
unissued capital

Journalism, printing and publishing

2

ad
em
en
o.p.
pi
s.c.
w.f.

3

ads
bed
box
cub
cut
die
imp
mat
out
pie
pot
run
set
sub
web

4

back
body
bold
bulk
caps
comp
copy
cyan
dash
demy
edit
etch
face
film
flap
font
grid
lead
limp
news
open
page
pica
puff
pull
quad
ream
ruby
rule
sewn
sink
slug
stet
take
trim
type

5

beard
black
bleed
block
blurb
cameo
canon
caret
cased
chase
chill
cloth
clump
crown
daily
Didot
draft
dummy
flong
folio
forme
fount
gloss
index
leads
libel
linen
litho
metal
pearl
plate
point
print
proof
punch
quire
quote
Ralph
recto
reset
roman
rough
royal
run-on
scoop
serif
sigla
solid
sorts
spine
stone
story
tilde
title
verso
xerox

6

back-up
banner
boards
ceriph
cliché
coated
cock-up
column
delete
editor
flimsy
format
galley
indent
italic
jacket
keep up
layout
leader
linage
lock up
makeup
marked
masked
matrix
minion
morgue
offset
ozalid
punch
quotes
random
review
revise
rotary
screen
serial
series

set-off
sketch
spiked
splash
umlaut
weekly
weight

7

article
artwork
binding
bled off
brevier
bromide
bumping
capital
caption
cast off
cedilla
clicker
diamond
display
edition
English
engrave
etching
feature
Fraktur
full out
gravure
gripper
imprint
justify
leading
literal
masking
measure
monthly
mortice
net sale
overrun
overset
preface
prelims
printer
publish
release
reprint
rewrite
sits vac
subedit
tabloid
typeset
woodcut

8

art board
ascender
bleeding
boldface
colophon
cut flush
dateline
deadline
designer
endpaper
footnote
fudge box
hairline
halftone
hardback
headband
headline
hot metal
imperial
intaglio
keyboard
linotype
monotype
obituary
paginate
photoset
print run
register
reporter
slipcase
streamer
tailband
turnover
type area
verbatim
vignette
woodpulp

9

art editor
bookplate
bourgeois
box number
brilliant
broadside
casebound
co-edition
collating
columnist
copypaper
copyright
crossword
descender
editorial
exclusive

facsimile
freelance
furniture
idiot tape
laminated
lineblock
lower case
make ready
newpaper
newsprint
nonpareil
overprint
pageproof
paperback
paragraph
photocopy
photostat
pseudonym
publisher
quarterly
sans serif
signature
small pica
stonehand
subeditor
symposium
tear sheet
the morgue
title verso
upper case
watermark
web-offset
woodblock
wrong font

10

assembling
annotation
blockmaker
body matter
broadsheet
casting box
casting-off
catch title
city editor
compositor
copyholder
copytaster
copywriter
dead matter
dirty proof
feuilleton
film critic
four colour
imposition
impression
imprimatur

interleave
journalese
journalism
journalist
lamination
leader page
lithograph
long primer
monochrome
news agency
news editor
nom-de-plume
overmatter
pagination
paraphrase
periodical
plagiarism
press agent
reverse out
separation
short story
stereotype
supplement
syndication
title verso
trade paper
typesetter
typography
vignetting
wrong fount
xerography

11

advance copy
advertising
agony column
circulation
copyfitting
crown octavo
cub reporter
display type
galley proof
great primer
half measure
letterpress
line drawing
lithography
night editor
platemaking
proofreader
running head
section-sewn
unjustified

12

block letters
book reviewer
cross heading
facing matter
feature story
illustration
keep standing
leader writer
London editor
magazine page
perfect bound
sports editor
telegraphese
works manager

13

advertisement
composing room
editor-in-chief
foreign editor
justification
literary agent
photogravure
spiral binding
stop press news
wire stitching

14 – 16

banner headline (14)
calendered paper (15)
colour separation (16)
dramatic critic (14)
features editor (14)
literary editor (14)
managing editor (14)
offset printing (14)
perfect binding (14)
personal column (14)
photolithography (16)
running headine (15)

Officials (including titles and religious designations)

2 – 4

abbé
aga
agha
aide
amir
amma
babu
beak
beg
bey
cadi
cham
cid
curé
czar
dean
dey
doge
don
duce
duke
earl
emir
foud
graf
head
imam
inca
jam
J.P.
khan
king
lady
lama
lord

miss
M.C.
M.P.
naib
naik
page
papa
peer
pope
rani
rank
ras
rex
shah
sir
sire
tsar
tzar
ward
whip
zaim

5

abbot
agent
ameer
baboo
baron
bedel
begum
board
boyar
canon
chief
Clare

count
dewan
divan
donna
doyen
edile
elder
emeer
envoy
ephor
friar
hakam
imaum
judge
junta
junto
jurat
kalif
laird
laity
liege
macer
mahdi
mayor
mufti
nabob
nawab
nizam
noble
pacha
pasha
padre
porte
prior
queen
rabbi
rajah

ranee
reeve
ruler
sagan
sahib
sheik
sophi
staff
state
suite
synod
thane
title
vakil
vicar
wazir

6

abbess
aedile
alcade
archon
ataman
avener
avenor
bailie
barony
bashaw
beadle
begaum
bigwig
bishop
brehon
bursar
caesar

caliph
cantor
censor
cherif
childe
consul
curate
custos
datary
deacon
deputy
despot
donzel
duenna
dynast
eparch
ephori
exarch
fecial
Führer
gauger
harman
herald
hetman
judger
kaiser
kavass
keeper
knight
legate
lictor
mikado
misses
mister
mullah
notary
nuncio

police
préfet
pretor
primus
prince
puisne
rabbin
ranger
rector
regent
sachem
satrap
sbirro
senate
sexton
sheikh
shogun
sirdar
squire
sultan
syndic
tanist
umpire
verger
vestry
vizier
warden
warder

7

alcalde
apostle
armiger
asiarch
attaché

bailiff	mahatma	antistes	lay elder	zemindar
baronet	majesty	archduke	legation	
bellman	marquis	autocrat	licenser	
bencher	marshal	banneret	life peer	**9**
burgess	monarch	baroness	lordling	
cacique	muezzin	baronial	lordship	ale-conner
caloyer	navarch	Black Rod	maharaja	ale-taster
cazique	nomarch	blazoner	manciple	archdruid
commère	notable	blindman	mandarin	archducal
compère	officer	brevetcy	margrave	archduchy
consort	orderer	burgrave	marquess	authority
coroner	padisha	canoness	marquise	baronetcy
council	paladin	cardinal	martinet	beglerbeg
curator	paritor	carnifex	mayoress	bodyguard
custode	peerage	caudillo	minister	bretwalda
custrel	peeress	chafewax	ministry	bumbledom
czarina	podesta	chairman	monarchy	burggrave
dapifer	pontiff	chaplain	monocrat	caliphate
dauphin	praetor	cicerone	myriarch	captaincy
dogeate	prefect	co-bishop	myrmidon	carmelite
donship	prelate	cofferer	nobility	cartulary
dowager	premier	consular	nobleman	castellan
duchess	primacy	co-regent	noblesse	catchpole
dukedom	primate	cursitor	official	celebrant
duumvir	proctor	czarevna	oligarch	cellarist
dynasty	prophet	deaconry	optimacy	centurion
earldom	provost	deanship	overlord	chevalier
effendi	questor	deemster	overseer	chieftain
elector	referee	delegate	palatine	chief whip
embassy	regency	diaconal	placeman	chiliarch
emperor	retinue	dictator	pontifex	commander
empress	royalty	diocesan	princess	commodore
enactor	sea-king	diplomat	priorate	constable
eparchy	sea-lord	director	prioress	cordelier
equerry	senator	douanier	provisor	court fool
equites	senatus	dukeling	quaestor	cupbearer
esquire	shereef	dukeship	recorder	custodian
estafet	sheriff	duumviri	regality	Dalai Lama
exactor	signior	emeritus	register	darbyites
fidalgo	skipper	emissary	resident	deaconess
Fuehrer	speaker	enthrone	sagamore	decemviri
gabeler	steward	ethnarch	seigneur	despotism
gaekwar	subadar	genearch	seignior	diaconate
Gestapo	sub-dean	guardian	squireen	dictatrix
grandee	sultana	head girl	summoner	dignitary
hangman	supremo	headship	suzerain	diplomate
head boy	Tammany	headsman	synarchy	directory
headman	toparch	heptarch	talukdar	dominator
hidalgo	tribune	hierarch	tetrarch	drum major
infanta	tsarina	highness	tipstaff	eldership
infante	tzarina	hospodar	treasury	electress
jemadar	vavasor	imperial	triarchy	envoyship
jerquer	viceroy	imperium	tribunal	ephoralty
justice	vaivode	interrex	triumvir	escheator
khalifa	voivode	kingling	tsarevna	estafette
khedive		ladyship	tzarevna	exarchate
kinglet	**8**	laureate	verderer	exciseman
maestro		lawgiver	viscount	executive
magnate	alderman	lawmaker	wardmote	exequatur

ex-officer
fort major
goldstick
grand duke
high court
incumbent
inspector
Jack Ketch
judgeship
justiciar
knightage
landgrave
lifeguard
liveryman
lord mayor
magnifico
maharajah
majordomo
mandatary
mandatory
matriarch
mayoralty
moderator
monocracy
monsignor
oligarchy
ombudsman
Orangeman
palsgrave
patriarch
patrician
pendragon
pentarchy
policeman
polyarchy
polycracy
portfolio
portreeve
potentate
precentor
presbyter
president
pretender
princedom
principal
proconsul
registrar
reichsrat
rural dean
sacristan
secretary
seneschal
seraskier
sovereign
statesman
sub-beadle
sub-deacon
suffragan
sultaness

timocracy
town clerk
town crier
treasurer
vestryman
viscounty
vizierate
waldgrave
whipper-in
zemindari

10

agonothete
aide-de-camp
ambassador
appanagist
archbishop
archdeacon
archflamen
archimagus
archpriest
areopagite
autocrator
bergmaster
borsholder
bumbailiff
bursarship
camerlengo
carabineer
catechumen
catholicos
censorship
chancellor
chaplaincy
chartulary
chatellany
cimeliarch
cloisterer
cloistress
commandant
commissary
consulship
controller
corporator
corregidor
coryphaeus
councillor
councilman
covenanter
crown agent
czarevitch
dauphiness
deaconship
delegation
designator
dock-master
doorkeeper

enomotarch
enumerator
episcopate
excellency
fire-master
headmaster
heraldship
high master
high priest
Home Office
incumbency
inquisitor
institutor
justiciary
king-at-arms
knighthood
lay brother
legateship
legislator
lieutenant
lower house
mace-bearer
magistracy
magistrate
margravine
marquisate
mayor-elect
midshipman
ministrant
mint-master
monarchism
noblewoman
ochlocracy
officially
oligarchal
opposition
parliament
plutocracy
postmaster
prebendary
presbytery
presidency
proclaimer
procurator
prolocutor
proscriber
proveditor
pursuivant
rectorship
regentship
ringmaster
sachemship
sea captain
sextonship
shrievalty
sign manual
squirehood
squireship
statecraft

state paper
sultanship
suzerainty
tithing-man
unofficial
upper house
vice-consul
vicegerent
vice-master
vice-regent
war council
whiggarchy

11

adelantado
archdapifer
archduchess
archdukedom
aristocracy
assay-master
autocratrix
burgess-ship
burgomaster
cardinalate
catercousin
chamberlain
chieftaincy
comptroller
corporation
country court
court jester
cross-bearer
crossbowman
crown lawyer
crown prince
diplomatist
directorate
directorial
earl-marshal
ecclesiarch
electorship
executioner
flag officer
functionary
good templar
grand master
grand vizier
gymnasiarch
headborough
intercessor
internuncio
justiceship
landgravine
legislatrix
legislature
lieutenancy
lord provost

marchioness
marshalship
ministerial
monarchical
monseigneur
officialdom
officiating
papal legate
papal nuncio
policewoman
pontificate
pound-keeper
praepositor
premiership
primateship
prince royal
preconsular
proctorship
protocolist
protonotary
provostship
puisne judge
queen-mother
questorship
referendary
school board
senatorship
speakership
squirearchy
stadtholder
stratocracy
subordinate
sword-bearer
tax assessor
tax gatherer
thesmothete
town council
tribuneship
triumvirate
vestry clerk
vice-regency
viceroyalty
viscountess
wreckmaster

12

agent-general
ambassadress
armour-bearer
avant-courier
bound-bailiff
carpet-knight
chairmanship
chief justice
chief of staff
churchwarden
civil servant

civil service
commendatory
commissioner
constabulary
crown-equerry
dictatorship
ecclesiastic
enfranchiser
enthronement
field officer
guardianship
headmistress
heir apparent
House of Lords
inspectorate
internuncius
jack-in-office
laureateship
legislatress
lord-temporal
maid of honour
mastersinger
metropolitan
muster-master
notary-public
office-bearer
parish priest
peace officer
poet laureate
prince-bishop
Privy Council
quaestorship
queen-consort
queen-dowager
queen-regnant
quindecemvir

recordership
remembrancer
sheriff-clerk
staff officer
tax collector
Trinity house
unauthorized
uncovenanted
vicar-general
viscountship
water-bailiff
witenagemote

13

administrator
archidiaconal
archimandrite
archpresbyter
archtreasurer
army commander
barrack-master
borough-master
chieftainship
chorepiscopus
color sergeant
consul-general
count palatine
county council
district judge
generalissimo
grand-seigneur
gubernatorial
high constable
inspectorship

judge-advocate
lord-spiritual
mounted police
parliamentary
prime minister
Prince of Wales
Princess Royal
public trustee
state function
states-general
statesmanship
vice-president
vigintivirate

14

archchancellor
archiepiscopal
auditor-general
chancellorship
chief constable
colour sergeant
crown solicitor
dowager-duchess
lord of the manor
gentleman-usher
high court judge
House of Commons
king's messenger
lord chancellor
lord lieutenant
lords-spiritual
medical officer
parochial board
political agent

provost-marshal
revenue officer
superintendent
town councillor
vicar-apostolic
vice-chancellor

15

advocate-general
archchamberlain
archiepiscopacy
archiepiscopate
astronomer-royal
attorney-general
cabinet minister
chamberlainship
chargé d'affaires
district officer
election-auditor
governor-general
heir-presumptive
lords lieutenant
messenger-at-arms
parliamentarian
plenipotentiary
privy councillor
queen's messenger
sheriff's officer
suffragan bishop
surveyor-general
vice-chamberlain
vice-chancellors

People

2 AND 3

A.B.
ace
ass
B.A.
bov
B.Sc.
cad
cit
dab
dad
D.D.
deb

dux
elf
fag
fan
fop
fub
G.I.
gun
guy
hag
ham
imp
kid
kin

lad
lob
M.A.
ma
man
me
men
mob
M.P.
Mr.
Mrs.
mug
mum
N.C.O.

nun
oaf
pa
pal
pet
Ph.D.
pig
rat
rip
R.S.M.
she
sir
spy
son

sot
tar
us
wag
we
wit
ye
yob
you

4

ally

aunt	kith	vamp	do-all	knave
babe	lass	waif	donce	lazar
baby	liar	ward	donor	leper
band	loon	whig	doter	limey
bard	lout	wife	dozer	local
bear	lush	wino	droll	locum
beau	magi	yogi	drone	loser
bevy	mald	zany	dummy	lover
bird	male		dunce	madam
blue	mama		duper	maker
boor	mate	*5*	dwarf	mamma
bore	mess		eater	mater
boss	mime	adept	enemy	mimic
brat	minx	adult	exile	minim
buck	miss	aider	extra	minor
bull	mite	airer	fakir	miser
chap	mome	alien	felon	moron
chum	monk	angel	fence	mouse
clan	muff	argus	fiend	mover
colt	mute	aunty	fifer	mower
cove	mutt	bairn	filer	mummy
crew	nizy	beast	firer	muser
dame	ogre	being	flier	namer
dear	papa	belle	flirt	nanny
demy	peer	bigot	flock	Negro
doer	peon	biter	fogey	niece
doll	pimp	black	fraud	ninny
dolt	prig	blade	freak	noddy
doxy	rake	blood	freer	nomad
drip	roué	booby	gamin	nymph
duck	runt	bride	gaper	odist
dude	sage	broad	gazer	ogler
dupe	salt	brute	genii	owner
feed	sect	bully	ghost	pacer
folk	seer	cadet	giant	pagan
fool	self	carle	giber	party
funk	sept	cheat	gipsy	pater
gaby	serf	child	giver	patsy
gang	shot	choir	goose	payee
gawk	silk	chuff	grass	payer
girl	sire	chump	groom	peach
goer	slut	churl	guest	pigmy
goth	snob	clare	guide	piler
grub	soak	clown	hater	pin-up
gull	star	co-aid	heavy	piper
haji	swot	couch	hewer	porer
heel	tart	crank	hider	poser
heir	team	crone	hiker	posse
herd	them	crony	hodge	proxy
hero	thug	crook	hunks	prude
hick	tike	crowd	hussy	pryer
hobo	toff	cynic	idiot	puker
host	tony	dandy	idler	punch
idol	tool	darky	in-law	pupil
jack	tory	decoy	issue	puppy
jade	twin	deist	jingo	pygmy
jill	tyke	devil	joker	quack
jilt	tyro	dicer	Judas	queen
jury	user	diver	juror	queer

31

racer	whore	client	female	humbug
raker	whoso	clique	fencer	hummer
raver	widow	co-ally	Fenian	hunter
rebel	wight	coaxer	fiancé	hurler
rider	wiper	codder	fibber	hussar
rival	witch	codger	filler	hymner
rogue	women	co-heir	finder	iceman
rough	wooer	coolie	foeman	infant
rover	yahoo	copier	foiler	inmate
rower	yobbo	co-star	forcer	ironer
sahib	yokel	cottar	friend	jeerer
saint	youth	cotter	gadder	jerker
saver		cousin	gaffer	jester
scamp		coward	gagger	Jesuit
scion	*6*	craven	gainer	jet set
scold		creole	gammer	jilter
scout	abaser	cretin	gasbag	jogger
screw	abider	cueist	genius	jolter
shark	abuser	damsel	gentry	jumper
shrew	admass	dancer	getter	junior
sider	adored	darner	geezer	junker
silly	adorer	dauber	giglot	junkie
siren	agnate	debtor	gigman	keeper
sizar	albino	defier	gigolo	kicker
skier	allies	delver	gillie	kidder
snail	alumna	denier	glider	killer
sneak	amazon	deputy	godson	kisser
sorry	ambler	digger	golfer	knower
sower	angler	dipper	gossip	lacker
spark	apache	dodger	granny	lagger
sport	auntie	doodle	grazer	lancer
squab	au pair	dotard	griper	lander
squaw	backer	double	grouch	lapper
staff	bandit	dragon	grower	lasher
stoic	barfly	drawee	guiser	lassie
stray	batman	drawer	guller	layman
sumph	bayard	drazel	gulper	leader
swain	beater	driver	gunman	league
swell	beauty	drudge	gunner	leaper
taker	beldam	dry-bob	gusher	leaser
tenor	better	ducker	halter	leaver
thief	bettor	duffer	harlot	lecher
toady	bibber	dyvour	healer	legist
tommy	bidder	earwig	hearer	lender
toper	bilker	egoist	heater	lessee
toyer	blacks	elator	heaver	lessor
tramp	blonde	envier	hector	letter
trier	bomber	eraser	hedger	lifter
troop	boozer	escort	helper	limner
trull	bowler	eunuch	hermit	lisper
trump	buster	expert	hinter	lister
twins	cadger	fabler	hippie	loafer
uncle	caller	faggot	hoaxer	lobber
urger	camper	family	holder	lodger
vexer	captor	fanner	hooter	looker
vixen	carper	father	hopper	loonie
voter	carver	fawner	howler	looter
wader	casual	feeler	hoyden	lubber
wench	chaser	fellow	huffer	lurker

lyrist	outlaw	rascal	slider	victor
madcap	pandit	rating	sloven	viewer
madman	panter	reader	smiler	Viking
maiden	papist	reaper	smiter	virago
maniac	parent	relict	smoker	virgin
marine	pariah	relier	snarer	votary
marker	parter	rhymer	sniper	voyeur
maroon	patron	rifter	snorer	wafter
marrer	pauper	ringer	snudge	walker
martyr	pawnee	rinker	soaker	wanton
masher	pawner	rinser	solver	warmer
masker	paynim	rioter	sparer	warner
master	pecker	ripper	spouse	washer
matron	pedant	risker	squire	waster
medium	pedlar	roamer	square	wearer
melter	peeler	roarer	stager	weeder
member	peeper	rocker	starer	weeper
menial	pelter	Romany	stayer	wet-bob
mentor	penman	rookie	stoner	whiner
mestee	penpal	rotter	stooge	wincer
midget	person	rouser	stroke	winder
minion	piecer	rubber	sucker	winker
misses	pigeon	ruiner	suitor	winner
missis	pinner	runner	surety	wisher
missus	placer	rusher	tacker	wizard
mister	player	rustic	talker	wittol
mocker	poller	sadist	tartar	worker
modist	Pommie	sailer	tasker	worthy
mohawk	poseur	santon	taster	wretch
mohock	poster	savage	tatler	writer
moiler	pourer	savant	tearer	yapper
monkey	pouter	scaler	teaser	yeoman
mooter	prater	scorer	teller	yonker
moppet	prayer	scouse	tenant	zealot
mortal	preyer	scrimp	Teuton	zombie
mother	proser	second	theist	
mugger	prover	seeker	thrall	
mulier	public	seizer	throng	7
mummer	puffer	selves	tilter	
myself	puller	sender	toiler	abactor
nagger	pumper	senior	tomboy	abetter
nation	pundit	sentry	tooter	abettor
native	punter	shadow	tosser	acceder
needer	puppet	shaker	truant	accuser
nephew	purger	shaman	tutrix	adapter
nipper	purist	sharer	tyrant	admirer
nitwit	pusher	shaver	umpire	adviser
nobody	quaker	sheila	undoer	agamist
nodder	quoter	shover	uniter	aircrew
noodle	rabbit	shower	urchin	also-ran
novice	rabble	shrimp	vamper	alumnus
nudist	racist	sigher	vandal	amateur
ogress	racker	sinner	vanner	amorosa
ord boy	ragtag	sipper	varlet	amoroso
old man	raider	sister	vendee	anybody
opener	railer	sitter	vendor	ascetic
oracle	rammer	skater	vestal	assizer
orator	ranter	slayer	viator	assumer
orphan	rapist	slicer	victim	atheist

athlete	consort	dreamer	flouter	hipster
avenger	convert	drifter	foister	hoarder
averter	convict	driller	fondler	hobbler
babbler	copycat	drinker	fopling	homager
ballboy	co-rival	droller	forager	hoodlum
bastard	Cossack	drowner	founder	hostage
batsman	coterie	drubber	freeman	hostess
beatnik	counter	dualist	freezer	hothead
bedmate	courser	dueller	frisker	huddler
bedouin	courter	dullard	frowner	humbler
beldame	coxcomb	dweller	frumper	hurrier
beloved	crawler	edifier	fuddler	husband
best man	creator	egghead	fumbler	hustler
bigshot	creeper	egotist	gabbler	hymnist
blabber	cringer	ejector	gallant	imagist
blender	cripple	elector	gambler	imbiber
boarder	croaker	elegist	garbler	impeder
boaster	crooner	elogist	general	imposer
boggler	crusher	elohist	gentile	imputer
bookman	cry baby	empiric	giggler	inciter
bouncer	cuckold	emptier	glutton	inducer
bounder	culprit	enactor	gobbler	infidel
breeder	curioso	endower	goodman	infuser
brother	cyclist	endurer	gormand	ingrate
bucolic	dabbler	engager	gossoon	inhaler
buffoon	dabster	enjoyer	gourmet	injurer
bumpkin	dallier	enticer	gownman	insured
bungler	damosel	entrant	grandam	insurer
burgher	dangler	epicure	grandma	invader
bushman	darling	erecter	grantee	invalid
bustler	dastard	eremite	granter	inviter
cackler	dawdler	escapee	grantor	invoker
caitiff	daysman	escaper	grasper	jackass
captain	debaser	exactor	griffin	jack-tar
captive	debater	exalter	groupie	jacobin
casuist	defacer	exciter	grouser	jangler
caveman	defamer	exegete	growler	Jezebel
changer	defiler	exposer	grown-up	Joe Soap
chanter	defunct	failure	grubber	jostler
Charlie	delator	fair sex	grudger	juggler
charmer	deluder	fall-guy	grunter	jumbler
cheater	denizen	fanatic	guesser	juryman
checker	derider	fancier	guildry	juvenal
Chindit	desirer	fantast	guzzler	Kantist
citizen	devisee	fascist	gymnast	killjoy
clapper	deviser	fathead	habitué	kindler
cleaver	devisor	faulter	haggler	kindred
climber	devotee	favorer	half-wit	kingpin
clipper	diarist	feaster	handler	kinsman
clubman	dibbler	feoffee	has-been	kneeler
cockney	diehard	feoffor	hatcher	knocker
cognate	dilator	fiancée	haunter	knoller
colleen	divider	fiddler	heathen	know-all
colonel	diviner	fielder	heckler	laggard
combine	dizzard	filcher	heiress	landman
commons	doubter	flapper	hell-hag	laugher
company	dowager	flasher	hellier	leaguer
compère	dragoon	fleecer	heretic	learner
comrade	dreader	floater	heroine	legatee

34

liberal	papoose	reducer	shutter	stooper
limiter	paragon	referee	shyster	stopper
loather	partner	refugee	sibling	strayer
lobcock	parvenu	refuser	skimmer	striker
lookout	patcher	refuter	skipper	striver
lorette	patient	regular	skulker	stroker
lounger	patriot	relater	slacker	student
lowbrow	Paul Pry	remover	slammer	studier
lunatic	peasant	renewer	slasher	stumper
lurcher	peruser	repiner	sleeper	stylist
magnate	pervert	replier	slinger	subduer
mangler	piercer	rescuer	slipper	subject
manikin	pilgrim	reserve	slitter	suicide
mankind	pincher	retaker	smasher	suspect
marcher	pioneer	retinue	snapper	swagman
marplot	plaiter	reverer	snarler	swinger
meddler	planner	reviver	sniffer	swearer
menacer	playboy	rhymist	snipper	sweater
mestino	pleadee	riddler	snoozer	sweeper
mestizo	pleader	roadhog	snorter	swiller
milksop	pleaser	royalty	snuffer	swimmer
mingler	plenist	ruffian	society	swinger
minikin	plodder	ruffler	soloist	tarrier
misdoer	plotter	rumbler	someone	tattler
mobster	plucker	runaway	soother	taunter
modiste	plumper	rustler	sophist	templar
monitor	plunger	saluter	soprano	tempter
moulder	pounder	sandman	spaniel	text-man
mounter	praiser	saviour	spanker	thinker
mourner	pranker	scalder	spanner	thriver
mouther	presser	scalper	speaker	thrower
mudlark	pricker	sceptic	speeder	thumper
mugwump	prinker	schemer	speller	tickler
mulatto	private	scholar	spender	tippler
mumbler	prodigy	scoffer	spiller	toaster
Negress	progeny	scolder	spitter	toddler
Negrita	protégé	scooper	spoiler	tomfool
nettler	prowler	scorner	sponger	toppler
nibbler	puncher	scraper	sponsor	tosspot
niggard	punster	scraple	sporter	tourist
niggler	puritan	scrooge	spotter	trainee
nithing	pursuer	scroyle	spouter	trainer
nominee	puzzler	sculler	sprayer	traitor
oarsman	quaffer	seceder	spurner	treader
obligee	queller	sectary	spurrer	treater
obliger	querent	securer	stabber	tricker
obligor	querist	seducer	stand-by	trifler
oddball	quieter	seminar	stand-in	tripper
offerer	quitter	service	starlet	trollop
old fogy	radical	settler	starter	trooper
old girl	rambler	shammer	stealer	tropist
old maid	ravener	sharker	stentor	trouper
old salt	reacher	sharper	stepson	trudger
oppidan	realist	shedder	sticker	trustee
opposer	rebuker	shifter	stiller	truster
orderer	reciter	shooter	stinger	tumbler
outcast	recluse	shopper	stinker	twirler
Oxonian	redhead	shouter	stinter	twister
paddler	redskin	show-off	stirrer	twitter

35

upstart	adherent	braggart	deceased
usurper	adjutant	brethren	deceiver
utopian	adulator	brunette	defector
utterer	advocate	busybody	defender
vacuist	aesthete	cabalist	deferrer
vagrant	agitator	caballer	democrat
vampire	agnostic	callgirl	demoniac
vaulter	alarmist	canaille	departer
vaunter	allottee	cannibal	deponent
veteran	allotter	canoeist	depraver
villain	alter ego	carouser	depriver
villein	altruist	castaway	derelict
visitor	ancestor	catamite	deserter
vouchee	ancestry	Catholic	deserver
voucher	anchoret	caviller	despiser
voyager	antihero	celibate	detainee
vulture	antipope	cenobite	detainer
waddler	apostate	champion	detector
wagerer	appellee	chaperon	devourer
wakener	appellor	children	diffuser
waltzer	approver	chiliast	digester
want-wit	arranger	chuckler	diner-out
warbler	aspirant	cicerone	dirty dog
warlock	assassin	cicisbeo	disciple
wastrel	assembly	civilian	disponee
watcher	assertor	claimant	disponer
waterer	assignee	clansman	disposer
waverer	assignor	classman	disputer
weigher	assuager	clincher	ditheist
welcher	attacker	clodpoll	diverter
wencher	attestor	cognizee	divorcée
whipper	audience	cognizor	divorcer
whisker	aularian	colonial	divulger
widower	awakener	colonist	do-gooder
wielder	bachelor	combiner	dogsbody
windbag	balancer	commando	drencher
wise guy	bankrupt	commoner	dribbler
witling	banterer	commuter	drunkard
witness	baritone	complier	duellist
wolf cub	barrator	computer	duettist
worrier	beadsman	consumer	dullard
wounder	beginner	convener	effector
wrapper	beguiler	conveyer	elegiast
wrecker	believer	coquette	elevator
wrester	bellower	corporal	embracer
wringer	benedict	co-surety	emigrant
yielder	bestower	cottager	emulator
younker	betrayer	courtier	enchanter
Zionist	bigamist	co-worker	encloser
	big noise	crackpot	enforcer
	blackleg	creditor	enhancer
8	blazoner	criminal	enjoiner
	blighter	customer	enlarger
abdicant	bluecoat	crusader	enricher
abductor	bohemian	dalesman	enslaver
absentee	bookworm	daughter	ensnarer
academic	borderer	deadhead	ephesian
accepter	borrower	deaf-mute	erastian
achiever	boy scout	debutant	eschewer

espouser
esteemer
eulogist
euphuist
Eurasian
everyman
everyone
evildoer
evocator
examinee
examiner
exceeder
exceptor
executor
expiator
expirant
exploder
explorer
exponent
extender
extoller
fanfaron
fatalist
favourer
feminist
ferreter
figurant
finalist
finisher
flaunter
flincher
folk-hero
follower
fomenter
fondling
foregoer
foreseer
forgiver
fourling
franklin
freedman
freshman
fribbler
frizzler
front man
fugitive
fusilier
futurist
gadabout
galloper
gamester
gaolbird
garroter
gatherer
genearch
geometer
getter-on
giantess
godchild

goodwife	innocent	malapert	opponent	quadroon
gourmand	inquirer	malaprop	oppugner	quaverer
gownsman	insister	maligner	optimist	quencher
graduate	insnarer	mandarin	oratress	quibbler
grandson	inspirer	man-hater	outliver	quidnunc
grisette	insulter	mannikin	outsider	quietist
grumbler	intended	marauder	pacifier	Quisling
habitant	intender	marksman	pacifist	rakehell
hanger-on	intimate	martinet	paleface	ransomer
harasser	intruder	may-queen	palterer	ratifier
hardener	investor	medalist	pamperer	ravisher
harridan	islander	mediator	panderer	reasoner
harrower	jabberer	merryman	Papalist	rebutter
hastener	jackaroo	mesmeree	paramour	recaptor
hazarder	Jacobite	messmate	parasite	receiver
hectorer	jailbird	mimicker	parcener	reckoner
hedonist	Jehovist	mislayer	pardoner	recliner
helpmate	jingoist	mistress	parodist	recoiler
helpmeet	John Bull	modalist	partaker	recorder
highbrow	Jonathan	modifier	partisan	recreant
hijacker	joy-rider	molester	passer-by	redeemer
hinderer	Judaizer	monodist	patentee	reformer
homicide	juvenile	monsieur	pelagian	refunder
honourer	kinsfolk	moon-calf	penitent	regicide
hooligan	lady-love	moonling	perjurer	rejecter
horseman	lame duck	moralist	pesterer	rejoicer
huckster	lamenter	Moravian	pharisee	relapser
Huguenot	landsman	motorist	picaroon	relation
humanist	landsmen	murderer	pilferer	releasee
humorist	latinist	murmurer	pillager	releaser
humpback	launcher	mutineer	plagiary	reliever
idealist	layabout	mutterer	playgoer	remarker
idolater	lay-clerk	namesake	playmate	reminder
idolizer	layer-out	narrator	plebeian	remitter
idyllist	laywoman	narrower	poisoner	renderer
imaginer	legalist	naturist	polluter	renegade
imbecile	levanter	neophyte	poltroon	repealer
imitator	leveller	nepotist	ponderer	repeater
immortal	libellee	neurotic	popinjay	repeller
impairer	libeller	new broom	populace	reporter
imparter	liegeman	newcomer	prattler	reprover
impeller	linesman	nihilist	preparer	repulser
implorer	lingerer	nuisance	presager	reseizer
impostor	linguist	numberer	presbyte	resenter
improver	listener	numskull	presumer	reserver
impugner	literate	nursling	prisoner	resident
inceptor	literati	objector	prize-man	resigner
incloser	litigant	obscurer	prodigal	resister
indictee	livewire	observer	producer	resolver
indicter	logician	obtainer	profaner	resorter
indigene	loiterer	obtruder	promisee	restorer
inductee	looker-on	occupant	promiser	retarder
inductor	loyalist	occupier	promoter	retorter
indulger	luminary	offender	proposer	returner
infecter	lunarian	old-timer	protégée	revealer
inferior	lutanist	old woman	provoker	reveller
inflamer	luxurist	onlooker	punisher	revenger
informer	lyricist	operator	purifier	revolter
initiate	macaroni	opificer	Puseyite	rewarder

riffraff
rifleman
rigorist
rodomont
romancer
Romanist
romantic
rotarian
royalist
runagate
ruralist
saboteur
satanist
saucebox
sciolist
scorcher
scourger
scrawler
scuffler
seafarer
searcher
seconder
selector
sentinel
sergeant
shortner
shrieker
shrimper
shrinker
shuffler
sidekick
sidesman
simoniac
simperer
skeleton
sketcher
slattern
slugabed
sluggard
slyboots
small fry
snatcher
snuffler
sodomite
softener
softling
solecist
solitary
somebody
songster
son-in-law
sorcerer
spinster
spitfire
splitter
spreader
springer
sprinter
squaller

squasher
squatter
squeaker
squealer
squeezer
squinter
squireen
squirter
stancher
stickler
stinkard
stitcher
stowaway
stranger
stripper
stroller
strutter
stumbler
suborner
suckling
sufferer
superior
superman
supposer
surmiser
survivor
sybarite
tacksman
talesman
tartuffe
taxpayer
teddy boy
teenager
telltale
tenantry
testator
theorist
thrasher
threader
thruster
thurifer
thwarter
tightwad
top brass
torturer
townsman
traditor
traducer
trampler
trappist
trembler
triplets
truckler
truelove
turncoat
twaddler
twitcher
two-timer
underdog

unionist
upholder
upper ten
vagabond
vanguard
vapourer
venturer
verifier
vilifier
villager
violator
visitant
votaress
votarist
wallower
wanderer
wayfarer
waylayer
waymaker
weakener
weanling
welcomer
Wesleyan
wheedler
whistler
whitener
whizz-kid
wiseacre
wonderer
wrangler
wrestler
wriggler
yeomanry
yodeller
yokemate
yourself

9

abecedary
aborigine
absconder
abstainer
academist
accessory
acclaimer
addressee
addresser
admiralty
adulterer
adversary
affirmant
aggressor
alcoholic
analogist
anarchist
anchoress
anchorite

annuitant
apologist
appellant
applauder
applicant
appraiser
arch-enemy
assailant
associate
augmenter
authority
automaton
bacchanal
backbiter
banqueter
barbarian
bargainee
bargainer
battleaxe
bedfellow
bedlamite
beggarman
bel esprit
biblicist
bicyclist
blockhead
bluebeard
blunderer
blusterer
bolsterer
bon vivant
bourgeois
boy friend
bridesman
brigadier
bystander
cabin crew
Calvinist
candidate
canvasser
careerist
carnalist
celebrity
chain-gang
chantress
character
charlatan
charterer
chatterer
chiseller
Christian
churchman
clatterer
clientele
coadjutor
coalition
cocklaird
co-heiress
colleague

collegian
combatant
comforter
commander
committee
committer
committor
commodore
communist
community
compacter
companion
concubine
confessor
confidant
conformer
Confucian
co-nominee
conqueror
conscript
consenter
consignee
consignor
conspirer
constable
consulter
contemner
contender
continuer
contralto
contriver
converter
co-patriot
corrector
corrupter
covergirl
crack shot
creatress
creditrix
cricketer
crookback
cut-throat
daredevil
dark horse
debauchee
débutante
declaimer
declarant
defaulter
defeatist
defendant
defrauder
deliverer
demagogue
demandant
demi-monde
dependant
depositor
depressor

depurator	expositor	guest star	ladies' man	occultist
designate	expounder	guineapig	landowner	offspring
desperado	exquisite	half-breed	law-monger	old master
despoiler	extractor	half-caste	lay reader	oppressor
destinist	extravert	haranguer	lazybones	organizer
destroyer	extrovert	harbinger	libellant	ourselves
detractor	extremist	harbourer	liberator	pacemaker
dialector	falsifier	harnesser	libertine	palaverer
dialogist	family man	hearkener	lionheart	panellist
disburser	favourite	hell-hound	lip-reader	paralytic
discerner	fetishist	highflier	liturgist	paranymph
discloser	find-fault	hillbilly	lost sheep	parricide
disgracer	fire-eater	Hottentot	loud-mouth	part-owner
disguiser	first born	household	lowlander	passenger
dispeller	flatterer	housewife	magnifier	patricide
disperser	flay-flint	hunchback	makepeace	patroness
displayer	fleshling	hylozoist	malthorse	peasantry
disprover	forbidder	hypocrite	mammonist	Pecksniff
disputant	forebears	ignoramus	mannerist	peculator
disseizor	foreigner	immigrant	masochist	pen-friend
dissenter	forfeiter	immolator	matricide	pen-pusher
dissident	forgetter	impeacher	meanderer	pensioner
disturber	formalist	impleader	medallist	perceiver
disuniter	fortifier	inamorata	mediatrix	perfecter
divinator	forwarder	inamorato	messieurs	performer
dogmatist	fossicker	increaser	Methodist	permitter
dolly bird	foster-son	incurable	metrician	personage
do-nothing	foundling	indicator	middleman	personnel
driveller	foundress	indweller	millenary	persuader
dyspeptic	fratricide	inebriate	miscreant	perturber
early bird	free agent	inflicter	mitigator	perverter
earthling	freelance	informant	moderator	pessimist
eccentric	free-liver	infractor	modernist	pilgarlic
Edwardian	freemason	infringer	modulator	pinchfist
emendator	fulfiller	inhabiter	monitress	pin-up girl
enchanter	furtherer	inheritor	moonraker	plaintiff
encomiast	gainsayer	initiator	moralizer	platonist
energizer	garnishee	innovator	mortgagee	plunderer
energumen	garnisher	in-patient	mortgagor	plutocrat
enfeebler	garreteer	inscriber	mortifier	plutonist
engrosser	garrotter	insolvent	Mrs. Grundy	poetaster
enlivener	gathering	instiller	multitude	portioner
entangler	gentleman	insurgent	muscleman	possessor
entourage	girl guide	intestate	mutilator	posterity
entreater	Girondist	intriguer	mythmaker	postponer
epicurean	go-between	introvert	Narcissus	postulant
epileptic	godfather	inveigher	neglecter	pot-hunter
epistoler	godmother	inveigler	neighbour	practiser
evacuator	Gothamite	Jansenist	neogamist	precursor
everybody	grandpapa	jay-walker	Neptunian	predicant
exactress	grandsire	jitterbug	next of kin	predictor
examinant	gratifier	joculator	nominator	preferrer
excusator	great-aunt	joint-heir	nonentity	prelatist
executant	greenhorn	journeyer	non-smoker	presbyope
executrix	grenadier	jovialist	nourisher	presentee
exhauster	greybeard	justifier	novitiate	presenter
exhibiter	groomsman	kidnapper	nullifier	preserver
exhibitor	groveller	kinswoman	numerator	pretender
exploiter	guerrilla	lackbrain	observant	preventer

proceeder
profferer
profiteer
projector
prolonger
promissor
promulger
proselyte
prosodist
protector
protester
protruder
punctuist
purchaser
purloiner
pussyfoot
Quakeress
quickener
rabbinist
racketeer
raconteur
rainmaker
ransacker
rapturist
ratepayer
recipient
recordist
recoveree
recoverer
rectifier
redresser
reflector
refresher
regulator
rehearser
reinsurer
renouncer
renovator
represser
reprobate
requester
respecter
rhymester
ridiculer
ritualist
roisterer
Romanizer
roughneck
routinist
rubrician
ruminator
Samaritan
Sassenach
satellite
satisfier
Saturnist
saunterer
scapegoat
scarecrow

scavenger
scholiast
schoolboy
scoundrel
scrambler
scratcher
scribbler
scrutator
sea-lawyer
sectarian
separator
serenader
sermonist
sexualist
shaveling
shortener
shoveller
sightseer
simpleton
skin-diver
skinflint
skylarker
slanderer
slobberer
slowcoach
slumberer
smatterer
sniveller
socialist
socialite
sojourner
solicitor
solitaire
son-of-a-gun
sophister
sophomore
spadassin
spectator
Spinozist
spiritist
spokesman
sportsman
sprinkler
sputterer
squabbler
stammerer
stargazer
star pupil
stigmatic
straggler
strangler
stretcher
stripling
strongman
struggler
stutterer
subaltern
submitter
subverter

succeeder
successor
succourer
suggester
sundowner
suppliant
supporter
surfeiter
susceptor
suspecter
suspender
sustainer
swaggerer
swallower
sweetener
sycophant
symbolist
syncopist
tactician
Talmudist
targumist
temptress
termagant
terminist
terrorist
testatrix
testifier
theorizer
thickskin
thunderer
toad-eater
tormentor
townsfolk
traitress
trapanner
traveller
traverser
trepanner
tribesman
trickster
trigamist
tritheist
truepenny
underling
unitarian
valentine
venerator
verbalist
versifier
Victorian
vigilante
visionary
volunteer
vulcanist
warmonger
wassailer
whosoever
womanizer
womankind

womenfolk
worldling
wrongdoer
xenophobe
yachtsman
young lady
youngling
youngster

10

aboriginal
aborigines
Abraham man
absolutist
accomplice
admonisher
adulterant
adulteress
adventurer
aficionado
alcoranist
allegorist
alms people
ambidexter
ambodexter
anabaptist
ancestress
anecdotist
anglophile
anglophobe
Anglo-Saxon
antagonist
antecedent
antecessor
antecursor
antichthon
antiscians
apologizer
aristocrat
assemblage
assentient
babe-in-arms
baby-sitter
bamboozler
beautifier
bed-presser
bedswerver
Belgravian
belswagger
benefactor
Benthamite
Bethlemite
better half
big brother
blackamoor
blackguard
black sheep

blasphemer	deprecator	extenuator	importuner
bobbysoxer	depredator	extirpator	imprisoner
bogtrotter	deputation	eye-witness	incendiary
bold spirit	descendant	fabricator	individual
bootlicker	diatribist	factionist	inhabitant
borstal boy	dilettante	fagot-voter	inheritrix
bridegroom	diminisher	fashionist	inquisitor
bridesmaid	directress	federalist	insinuator
bureaucrat	discharger	fire-raiser	instigator
bushranger	discourser	flagellant	interceder
campaigner	discoverer	flourisher	interferer
capitalist	discursist	fly-by-night	interloper
caravanner	disheritor	footballer	interposer
card-player	disparager	footlicker	intervener
cavalryman	dispraiser	forefather	introducer
centralist	dispreader	foreleader	Ishmaelite
changeling	disquieter	foremother	jackadandy
chatterbox	dissembler	forerunner	jackanapes
chauvinist	distracter	forswearer	jobbernowl
cheesecake	distruster	fosterling	job-hunter
churchgoer	divineress	foxhunter	jolterhead
Cinderella	divisioner	fraternity	kith and kin
clodhopper	dogmatizer	freeholder	lady-killer
cloisterer	dominicide	free-trader	land-holder
cloistress	dramatizer	frequenter	landlubber
coadjutant	Drawcansir	fuddy-duddy	languisher
coadjutrix	drug addict	fund-holder	lawbreaker
cohabitant	drug pusher	fund-raiser	left-winger
coloratura	dunderpate	Gasconader	legitimist
commonalty	dunderhead	gastronome	liberty man
competitor	Dutch uncle	gentlefolk	licentiate
complainer	dynamitard	girl friend	lieutenant
confessant	early riser	glacialist	literalist
confessary	ear-witness	goal keeper	loggerhead
confidante	elaborator	gold-digger	lotus-eater
considerer	electorate	goodfellow	lower class
contendent	electoress	grandchild	Lychnobite
contestant	elucidator	grand juror	machinator
controller	emboldener	grandmamma	magnetizer
co-operator	empiricist	grandniece	maiden aunt
coparcener	empoisoner	grand-uncle	maiden lady
copyholder	emulatress	grass widow	malefactor
co-relation	encourager	great-uncle	malingerer
councillor	encroacher	half-sister	manoeuvrer
counsellor	engenderer	harmonizer	man of straw
countryman	Englishman	hatchet man	married man
crackbrain	enigmatist	head hunter	marshaller
cringeling	enthusiast	heliolater	mastermind
criticizer	enumerator	heresiarch	matchmaker
crosspatch	enunciator	highjacker	merrymaker
curmudgeon	epitaphist	highlander	metaphrast
daggle-tail	epitomizer	hitch-hiker	methuselah
daydreamer	equestrian	human being	middlebrow
day-tripper	eternalist	iconoclast	militarist
declaimant	evangelist	identifier	mindreader
deforciant	exhortator	ideologist	misogamist
delinquent	expatiator	idolatress	misogynist
demoiselle	explicator	impenitent	monarchist
depositary	expurgator	impoisoner	moneyed man

monogamist
monologist
monomaniac
monopolist
monotheist
mountebank
mouthpiece
muddied oaf
multiplier
namby-pamby
ne'er-do-well
neutralist
nincompoop
nominalist
non-starter
notability
obstructer
occasioner
old soldier
opinionist
opium-eater
originator
orthoepist
out-patient
overrunner
overturner
painstaker
pall-bearer
panegyrist
paraphrast
past master
patronizer
peacemaker
pedestrian
Peeping Tom
pensionary
persecutor
persifleur
personator
petitioner
phenomenon
philistine
pinchpenny
plagiarist
polo player
polygamist
polyhistor
polytheist
population
positivist
pragmatist
preadamite
procreator
profligate
progenitor
prohibiter
promenader
pronouncer
propagator

prophesier
propounder
proprietor
prosecutor
prostitute
Protestant
psychopath
pulverizer
pyrrhonist
quarreller
questioner
rabblement
ragamuffin
rascallion
Rechabites
recidivist
reclaimant
recognizer
recognitor
reconciler
reimburser
relinquent
rememberer
reproacher
reprobater
reproducer
republican
repudiator
restrainer
restricter
retributer
reverencer
revivalist
rhapsodist
ringleader
sacrificer
scrapegrace
Scaramouch
schematist
schismatic
scrutineer
secularist
sensualist
separatist
sermonizer
seventh son
shoplifter
shanghaier
sinecurist
slammerkin
smart aleck
snuff-taker
solemnizer
solicitant
solifidian
solitarian
son and heir
songstress
soothsayer

Sorbonnist
speculator
spoilsport
squanderer
starveling
stepfather
stepmother
stepsister
stimulator
stipulator
strategist
street arab
strokesman
subscriber
substitute
subtracter
sugar daddy
supplanter
supplicant
suppressor
surmounter
suscipient
sweetheart
sworn enemy
syllogizer
syncopater
syncretist
synonymist
tale-bearer
tale-teller
tantalizer
taskmaster
tea-drinker
televiewer
temporalty
temporizer
tenderfoot
tenderling
textualist
textuarist
themselves
thickskull
third party
threatener
timeserver
tramontane
transferee
transferer
transmuter
trespasser
troglodyte
troubadour
tub-thumper
tweedledee
tweedledum
tuft-hunter
unbeliever
undertaker
unemployed

upper class
upper crust
utopianist
vacillator
vanquished
vanquisher
Vaticanist
vegetarian
vindicator
voluptuary
wallflower
well-wisher
white friar
whomsoever
widow-maker
wine-bibber
wirepuller
withdrawer
withholder
woman-hater
worshipper
yoke-fellow
young blood
yourselves

11

abbreviator
abecedarian
academician
accompanier
accumulator
adventuress
animal lover
aristocracy
association
bandy-player
beauty queen
belligerent
beneficiary
Bible reader
bibliolater
bibliophile
bird's-nester
blackmailer
bloodsucker
blue-eyed boy
blunderhead
bourgeoisie
braggadocio
breadwinner
brotherhood
calumniator
catabaptist
cave-dweller
centenarian
chance-comer
cheer leader

cheese parer
chucklehead
clairvoyant
coalitioner
cognoscenti
co-inheritor
collitigant
commentator
complainant
condisciple
confamiliar
confiscator
conjecturer
connoisseur
conspirator
constituent
continuator
contributor
co-ordinator
deliberator
denominator
denunciator
depopulator
depreciator
detractress
devotionist
dilapidator
diluvialist
dipsomaniac
discipliner
discourager
dishonourer
dissentient
dissertator
distributor
disunionist
doctrinaire
domestician
double agent
draggle-tail
dram-drinker
drug peddler
eager beaver
electioneer
emancipator
embellisher
embroiderer
enchantress
encounterer
endeavourer
enlightener
enlisted man
enterpriser
entertainer
epigenesist
epistolizer
equilibrist
equivocator
establisher

euphemerist
exaggerator
exasperater
father-in-law
fault-finder
femme fatale
fifth column
fighting man
first cousin
flat dweller
flying squad
foot soldier
forestaller
foster-child
francophile
francophobe
freethinker
frothblower
fustilarian
galley slave
gallows bird
gatecrasher
gentlefolks
gentlewoman
ginger group
god-daughter
gormandizer
grandfather
grandmother
grandnephew
grandparent
gull-catcher
guttersnipe
half brother
hard drinker
harum-scarum
helping hand
high society
hobbledehoy
holder-forth
homo sapiens
hyperbolist
hypercritic
ideopraxist
imperialist
inaugurator
infantryman
inhabitress
inheritress
interceptor
intercessor
interrupter
interviewer
intimidater
joint-tenant
knucklehead
leaseholder
libertarian
lickspittle

lilliputian
littérateur
living image
lycanthrope
manipulator
marrying-man
masquerader
materialist
matinee idol
maxim-monger
merry Andrew
metaphorist
middle class
millenarian
millionaire
misanthrope
misbeliever
misinformer
monopolizer
moonlighter
mother-in-law
mountaineer
mouth-friend
Mrs. Malaprop
name dropper
nationalist
necessarian
neutralizer
night-walker
nondescript
non-resident
nosey-parker
opportunist
owner-driver
pacificator
panic-monger
parishioner
participant
pearly queen
pedobaptist
peripatetic
perpetrator
personality
perturbator
phenomenist
philosopher
physicalist
predecessor
prize-winner
probabilist
probationer
prodigal son
proletarian
proletariat
promulgator
propitiator
prosecutrix
protagonist
protectress

protestator
Punchinello
punctualist
purgatorian
questionist
rank and file
rapscallion
rationalist
reactionary
recommender
recompenser
religionist
replenisher
reprehender
resuscitant
reversioner
right-winger
Rosicrucian
royal family
rugby player
sabbatarian
sacrilegist
sans-culotte
scaremonger
scatterling
scoutmaster
scripturist
scrutinizer
search party
shareholder
simple Simon
singularist
sister-in-law
sleepwalker
spectatress
speculatist
speech-maker
speed-skater
spendthrift
spindlelegs
stepbrother
stockholder
stonewaller
stool pigeon
story teller
stump-orator
subordinate
suffragette
surrenderee
surrenderer
sword player
sworn friend
sympathizer
systematist
system-maker
tautologist
teetotaller
teleologist
telepathist

thanksgiver
theosophist
time-pleaser
Tommy Atkins
torch-bearer
town-dweller
traditioner
transmitter
trencherman
trend setter
undersigned
undervaluer
undesirable
Walter Mitty
war criminal
wastethrift
weathercock
wholehogger
withstander

12

abolitionist
acquaintance
advance party
antediluvian
anticourtier
appropriator
artful dodger
assassinator
awkard squad
bachelor girl
backwoodsman
barber-monger
benefactress
bible-thumper
bibliomaniac
blood brother
bluestocking
bond-creditor
bottle-friend
bottle-washer
brother-in-law
bounty hunter
carpet-knight
chief mourner
church-member
coalitionist
collaborator
Colonel Blimp
commiserator
committeeman
communicator
competitress
complimenter
compossessor
conservative
consignatory

conquistador
contemplator
contemporary
controverter
convalescent
conventicler
conventioner
convivialist
co-respondent
corporealist
cosmopolitan
cousingerman
defectionist
demimondaine
demonstrator
determinator
dialectician
disciplinant
discommender
discontinuer
disenchanter
disorganizer
dispossessor
disseminator
doppelgänger
double-dealer
eavesdropper
educationist
elocutionist
encumbrancer
enfranchiser
equestrienne
exclusionist
excursionist
exhibitioner
experimenter
expostulator
exserviceman
extemporizer
extensionist
exterminator
extinguisher
featherbrain
filibusterer
firstnighter
foster father
foster mother
foster parent
foster sister
foundationer
gastronomist
gesticulator
globe-trotter
gospel-gossip
grey eminence
guest speaker
hair-splitter
headshrinker
heir-apparent

holidaymaker
humanitarian
impersonator
impoverisher
improvisator
inseparables
intellectual
intercipient
interlocutor
intermeddler
intermediary
interpolator
interrogator
investigator
irregularist
kleptomaniac
knight-errant
landed gentry
leading light
legacy-hunter
letter-writer
longshoreman
lounge lizard
mademoiselle
man-about-town
married woman
melancholist
mercurialist
mezzo soprano
misconstruer
misinformant
modest violet
morris dancer
natural child
near relation
neoplatonist
noctambulist
nonagenarian
obscurantist
octogenarian
old gentleman
pantophagist
participator
peace-breaker
penitentiary
perambulator
peregrinator
persona grata
philosophist
pillion-rider
poor relation
postdiluvian
postgraduate
pot-companion
precipitator
prevaricator
primogenitor
proprietress
proselytizer

public figure
quater-cousin
recriminator
redemptioner
relinquisher
remonstrator
residentiary
resolutioner
resuscitator
roller-skater
rolling stone
salvationist
scatterbrain
schoolfellow
second cousin
second fiddle
sequestrator
sexagenarian
significator
single person
sister-german
sole occupant
somnambulist
somniloquist
spiritualist
spirit-rapper
stepdaughter
stormtrooper
straightener
street-urchin
stuffed shirt
sub-committee
sublapsarian
subpurchaser
Sunday driver
swashbuckler
sworn enemies
systematizer
system-monger
tennis player
testificator
theologaster
transgressor
transmigrant
transvestite
troublemaker
truce-breaker
truncheoneer
ugly customer
ugly duckling
ultramontane
undermanager
unemployable
universalist
velocipedist
versificator
village idiot
way passenger
wicket keeper

wool gatherer
working class

13

adminiculator
administrator
anagrammatist
Anglo-American
Anglo-Catholic
annexationist
anthropophagi
antisocialist
apothegmatist
bibliophilist
blood relation
brother-german
bureaucratist
castle-builder
chamber-fellow
comprovincial
conceptualist
concessionist
conspiratress
conventionist
co-religionist
correspondent
daughter-in-law
deck passenger
deuterogamist
devotionalist
discriminator
distinguisher
exhibitionist
experimentist
fashion-monger
first offender
foot passenger
fortune-hunter
foster brother
fresh-air fiend
grand-daughter
hard bargainer
high churchman
hypochondriac
immaterialist
irreligionist
Job's comforter

laughing stock
life-annuitant
machiavellian
millennialist
miracle-monger
miracle-worker
misanthropist
mischief-maker
multiplicator
necessitarian
nonconformist
paterfamilias
perfectionist
philhellenist
philosophizer
predestinator
protectionist
proverbialist
reprobationer
revolutionary
sophisticator
speed merchant
spindleshanks
spiritualizer
state criminal
state prisoner
strike-breaker
tranquillizer
transmigrator
undergraduate
understrapper

14

antiaristocrat
armchair critic
billiard-player
corpuscularian
destructionist
disciplinarian
disenchantress
foster daughter
galactophagist
good-for-nothing
grammaticaster
ichthyophagist
improvisatrice
indifferentist

latitudinarian
ministerialist
misinterpreter
obstructionist
paragrammatist
philanthropist
procrastinator
prognosticator
progressionist
prohibitionist
promise-breaker
psilanthropist
quadragenarian
quodlibetarian
requisitionist
restorationist
sabbath-breaker
sacramentarian
sensationalist
sentimentalist
septuagenarian
skittles-player
squandermaniac
stamp-collector
superior person
tatterdemalion
trencher-friend
ultramontanist
undergraduette
valetudinarian
waifs-and-strays
weather prophet
whippersnapper

15

antitrinitarian
autograph hunter
circumnavigator
constitutionist
conversationist
emancipationist
experimentalist
heir-presumptive
insurrectionary
insurrectionist
intellectualist
supernaturalist
Tom, Dick and Harry

Professions, occupations, trade, etc.

2 – 4

alma
ayah
babu
bard
boss
char
chef
cook
crew
diva
doc
don
dyer
gang
G.P.
gyp
hack
hand
head
herd
hind
lead
magi
maid
mali
mate
mime
M.D.
M.O.
P.A.
page
peon
P.M.
poet
pro
P.R.O.
rep
ryot
seer
serf
spy
syce
thug
tout
vet
ward
whip

5

actor
ad-man
agent

augur
avoué
baker
bonze
boots
bosun
caddy
choir
clerk
clown
coach
comic
crier
crimp
curer
daily
egger
envoy
extra
fakir
fence
fifer
filer
finer
flier
gager
gipsy
gluer
groom
guard
guide
guild
hakim
harpy
helot
hirer
hiver
hoppo
lamia
leech
luter
mason
medic
miner
navvy
nurse
oiler
owler
pilot
piper
plyer
pupil
quack
quill
rabbi
rater

reeve
runer
scout
sewer
shoer
slave
smith
sower
staff
swami
sweep
tamer
tawer
taxer
thief
tiler
tuner
tutor
tyler
usher
valet
viner

6

airman
archer
artist
aurist
author
bagman
bailee
bailer
bailor
balker
bandit
banker
barber
bargee
barker
barman
batman
bearer
beggar
binder
boffin
bookie
bowman
brewer
broker
bugler
bursar
busker
butler
cabbie

cabman
calker
canner
carman
carter
carver
casual
censor
clergy
cleric
codist
coiner
comber
conder
con man
coolie
cooper
copper
co-star
coster
cowboy
cowman
critic
cutler
cutter
dacoit
dancer
dealer
digger
docker
doctor
dowser
draper
drawer
driver
drover
editor
fabler
factor
farmer
fellah
feller
fictor
fisher
fitter
flayer
forger
fowler
framer
fuller
gaffer
ganger
gaoler
gaucho
gauger
gigolo

gilder
gillie
glazer
glover
graver
grocer
guider
guidon
gunman
gunner
harper
hatter
hawker
healer
heaver
hodman
hooper
horner
hosier
hunter
intern
issuer
jailer
jailor
jobber
jockey
joiner
jowter
jurist
keeler
keeper
killer
lackey
lander
lascar
lawyer
lector
lender
loader
logman
lumper
magian
marker
master
matron
medico
mender
menial
mentor
mercer
milker
miller
minter
monger
morisk
mummer

mumper	seizor	waller	buttons	flesher
mystic	seller	warden	callboy	florist
nailer	server	warder	cambist	flunkey
notary	setter	warper	carrier	flutist
nurser	sexton	washer	caseman	footboy
oboist	shroff	weaver	cashier	footman
oilman	singer	weeder	cateran	footpad
orator	sircar	welder	caterer	foreman
ostler	skivvy	whaler	caulker	founder
packer	slater	worker	cellist	friseur
parson	slaver	wright	chanter	frogman
pastor	slavey	writer	chapman	fueller
patrol	sleuth		chemist	furrier
pavier	snarer		chorist	gateman
pavior	socman	*7*	cleaner	girdler
pedant	sorter		clicker	glazier
pedlar	souter	abacist	clippie	gleaner
penman	spicer	abigail	co-agent	gleeman
picker	squire	acolyte	coalman	glosser
pieman	stager	acolyth	cobbler	graffer
pirate	stoker	acrobat	cockler	grafter
pitman	storer	actress	collier	grainer
plater	sutler	actuary	co-pilot	granger
player	tabler	alewife	copyist	grantee
porter	tailor	almoner	coroner	grantor
potboy	tamper	alnagar	corsair	grazier
potter	tanner	alnager	counsel	grinder
priest	tasker	analyst	courier	gymnast
pruner	taster	ancient	cowherd	hackler
purser	teller	apposer	cowpoke	harpist
querry	termer	Arabist	crofter	haulier
rabbin	tester	arbiter	cropper	helotry
ragman	tiller	artisan	curator	herbist
ranger	tinker	artiste	currier	herdman
ratter	tinman	assayer	custode	heritor
reader	tinner	assizer	danseur	higgler
reaper	toller	assured	dentist	hogherd
reaver	touter	assurer	dialist	hostler
rector	toyman	auditor	dietist	indexer
regent	tracer	aviator	ditcher	inlayer
relief	trader	awarder	dominie	ironist
renter	troupe	bailiff	doorman	janitor
rigger	tubman	bandman	dragman	juggler
ringer	turner	barmaid	drapier	junkman
robber	tycoon	bedeman	drawboy	juryman
roofer	typist	bellboy	drayman	keelman
rooter	usurer	bellhop	dredger	knacker
sacker	vacher	birdman	dresser	knitter
sailor	valuer	blaster	drogman	laborer
salter	vamper	blender	drummer	laceman
salvor	vanman	boatman	dustman	linkboy
sapper	vassal	bondman	exegete	linkman
sartor	vender	bookman	famulus	lockman
sawyer	vendor	bottler	farrier	lombard
scribe	verger	bouncer	fascist	mailman
sea-dog	verser	brigand	faunist	maltman
sealer	viewer	builder	fiddler	manager
seaman	waiter	burglar	fireman	mangler
seiner	walker	butcher	fish-fag	marbler

47

marcher	shopboy	**8**	cow-leech	handmaid
mariner	shopman		coxswain	handyman
marshal	showman	adscript	croupier	hatmaker
matador	shunter	aeronaut	cutpurse	haymaker
matelot	silkman	algerine	dairyman	headsman
mealman	simpler	analyser	danseuse	head cook
meatman	skinner	annalist	deckhand	helmsman
metayer	skipper	aphorist	defender	henchman
metrist	slipper	apiarist	designer	herdsman
midwife	smelter	apron-man	director	hired man
milkman	snipper	arborist	dog-leech	hireling
modiste	socager	armourer	domestic	histrion
moneyer	soldier	armorist	doughboy	home help
monitor	soloist	arrester	dragoman	hotelier
mootman	spencer	arrestor	druggist	houseboy
moulder	spinner	assessor	editress	huckster
newsboy	spotter	attorney	educator	huntsman
oculist	stainer	bagmaker	embalmer	importer
officer	stamper	bagpiper	emissary	improver
orderer	stapler	ballader	employee	inkmaker
orderly	statist	bandsman	employer	inventor
packman	steerer	bargeman	engineer	japanner
pageboy	steward	bearherd	engraver	jet pilot
painter	surgeon	bearward	enroller	jeweller
palmist	swabber	bedesman	epic poet	jongleur
pantler	sweeper	bedmaker	essayist	kipperer
peddler	taborer	bit-maker	essoiner	labourer
pianist	tallier	bleacher	exorcist	landgirl
picador	tapster	boatsman	explorer	landlady
planner	taxi-man	bondmaid	exporter	landlord
planter	teacher	bondsman	fabulist	lapidary
pleader	tipster	boniface	factotum	larcener
plumber	tracker	botanist	falconer	larderer
poacher	trainer	bowmaker	famulist	Latinist
poetess	trapper	boxmaker	farmhand	leadsman
postboy	trawler	brewster	ferryman	lecturer
postman	trimmer	broacher	figurant	linesman
presser	trucker	busheler	filmstar	lumberer
prestor	trustee	cabin boy	finisher	magician
printer	tumbler	cellarer	fishwife	magister
puddler	turnkey	ceramist	flatfoot	maltster
rancher	vintner	chandler	flautist	manciple
realtor	violist	choirboy	fletcher	masseuse
refiner	wagoner	co-author	fodderer	measurer
riveter	waister	ciderist	forester	mechanic
roadman	warrior	claqueur	forgeman	medalist
roaster	waterer	clothier	fugleman	melodist
rustler	webster	coachman	gangster	mercator
sacrist	weigher	codifier	gardener	merchant
saddler	wheeler	coistril	gavelman	messager
sampler	whetter	collator	gendarme	metal -man
samurai	wireman	comedian	glassman	milkmaid
scourer	woodman	compiler	goatherd	millgirl
scraper	woolman	composer	godsmith	millhand
servant	workman	conclave	gossiper	milliner
settler	wrapper	conjurer	governor	minister
sharper		conveyor	guardian	minstrel
shearer		coryphée	gunsmith	mistress
shipper		courtier	hammerer	modeller

muleteer
muralist
musician
neatherd
newshawk
novelist
onion-man
operator
optician
ordainer
ordinand
organist
outrider
overseer
pargeter
parodist
penmaker
perfumer
peterman
pewterer
picaroon
picklock
pinmaker
plagiary
plougher
polisher
portress
postiler
potmaker
preacher
prefacer
preluder
pressman
probator
procurer
promoter
prompter
prosaist
provider
psalmist
publican
pugilist
purveyor
quarrier
raftsman
ranchero
rapperee
receiver
recorder
regrater
relessee
relessor
repairer
reporter
resetter
restorer
retailer
retainer
reviewer

rewriter
rivetter
romancer
rugmaker
rumourer
salesman
satirist
sawbones
scullion
sculptor
seamster
sea-rover
seasoner
seedsman
sempster
servitor
shearman
shepherd
ship's boy
shipmate
shopgirl
showgirl
sidesman
simplist
sketcher
smuggler
soldiery
spaceman
spearman
speedcop
spurrier
starcher
stitcher
stockman
storeman
stripper
strummer
stuntman
supplier
surveyor
swindler
tabourer
tallyman
taverner
teamster
thatcher
thespian
thresher
tin miner
tinsmith
tipstaff
torturer
toymaker
tripeman
truckman
turncock
turnspit
tutoress
unionist

valuator
vintager
virtuoso
vocalist
volumist
waitress
walker-on
wardress
warrener
watchman
waterman
wet nurse
whaleman
whitener
whitster
wigmaker
winnower
wool-dyer
workfolk
workhand
wrestler

9

alchemist
alluminor
anatomist
annotator
announcer
arbitress
arborator
archeress
architect
archivist
art critic
art dealer
artificer
astronaut
attendant
authoress
balladeer
balladist
ballerina
bank agent
barrister
barrow boy
beefeater
beekeeper
beemaster
berserker
biologist
boanerges
boatswain
bodyguard
boilerman
bondslave
bondwoman
bookmaker

bootblack
bootmaker
buccaneer
bus driver
burnisher
cab driver
café owner
cameraman
car driver
caretaker
carpenter
casemaker
catechist
cellarman
chanteuse
charwoman
chauffeur
cheapjack
chorister
clarifier
clergyman
clinician
clogmaker
coalminer
coalowner
collector
columnist
colourist
comprador
concierge
conductor
conserver
cosmonaut
cost clerk
costumier
courtesan
couturier
cowfeeder
cowkeeper
cracksman
craftsman
crayonist
cymbalist
dactypist
daily help
dairymaid
decorator
decretist
desk clerk
detective
dice-maker
die-sinker
dietetist
dietitian
directrix
dispenser
dissector
distiller
doctoress

draftsman
dramatist
drawlatch
drum major
drum-maker
drysalter
ecologist
embezzler
enameller
engineman
engrosser
epitomist
errand boy
estimator
examinant
excavator
excerptor
exchanger
executive
exercitor
exciseman
exorciser
eye doctor
fabricant
fandancer
fashioner
felt-maker
figurante
financier
film actor
film extra
film-maker
fire-eater
fish-curer
fisherman
fish-woman
flag-maker
flax-wench
flyfisher
freelance
freighter
fripperer
fruiterer
furbisher
furnisher
galvanist
gasfitter
gazetteer
gem-cutter
geologist
gladiator
gluemaker
goldsmith
gondolier
gospeller
governess
groundman
guardsman
guerrilla

49

10

guitarist	man-at-arms	precentor	stagehand	able seaman
gun-runner	mannequin	predicant	stationer	accomptant
harlequin	mechanist	preceptor	stay-maker	accoucheur
harmonist	medallist	prelector	steersman	accountant
harpooner	memoirist	priestess	stevedore	acolothist
harvester	mendicant	privateer	subeditor	adelantado
Hellenist	mercenary	professor	subworker	advertiser
herbalist	mesmerist	profilist	succentor	aerologist
herbarian	messenger	provedore	sur-master	agrologist
herborist	metallist	publicist	swan-upper	agronomist
herb-woman	metrician	publisher	swineherd	air hostess
hired hand	middleman	pulpiteer	switchman	air steward
hired help	mill-owner	puppeteer	swordsman	algebraist
homeopath	modelgirl	pythoness	syndicate	amanuensis
historian	mortician	qualifier	synoptist	apothecary
hog-ringer	muffin-man	quarryman	tablemaid	apple-woman
hop-picker	musketeer	quirister	tactician	apprentice
hosteller	musketoon	racketeer	tailoress	arbalister
housemaid	myologist	railmaker	tap dancer	arbitrator
housewife	navigator	recruiter	teataster	astrologer
hygienist	negotiant	reformist	tentmaker	astronomer
hypnotist	neologian	rehearser	test pilot	atmologist
incumbent	neologist	ribbonman	therapist	auctioneer
ingrafter	newsagent	roadmaker	theurgist	audit clerk
innholder	nursemaid	romancist	throwster	ballet girl
innkeeper	odd job man	ropemaker	timberman	balloonist
inscriber	office boy	roundsman	toolsmith	ballplayer
inspector	operative	ruddleman	top sawer	bandmaster
intendant	orchestra	rum-runner	town clerk	bank robber
ironsmith	ordinator	sacristan	towncrier	baseballer
itinerant	osteopath	safemaker	tire-woman	bassoonist
jack-smith	otologist	sailmaker	tradesman	beadswoman
job-master	outfitter	scarifier	tragedian	beautician
kennel-man	pantaloon	scavenger	traveller	bell-hanger
lacemaker	part-timer	scenarist	treasurer	bell-ringer
lacquerer	pasquiler	scholiast	trepanner	bibliopole
lady's maid	paymaster	schoolman	tributary	bill-broker
lampooner	pedagogue	scientist	trumpeter	billposter
land agent	performer	scrivener	tympanist	biochemist
landreeve	physician	scytheman	usherette	biographer
larcenist	physicist	sea-robber	varnisher	blacksmith
launderer	pitsawyer	secretary	versifier	bladesmith
laundress	planisher	ship's mate	vetturino	blockmaker
law writer	plasterer	shipowner	vexillary	bluejacket
legionary	ploughboy	shoeblack	violinist	bombardier
librarian	ploughman	shoemaker	volcanist	bondswoman
linotyper	pluralist	sightsman	voltigeur	bonesetter
liontamer	poetaster	signalman	wadsetter	bookbinder
liveryman	pointsman	sinologue	warrantee	bookholder
loan agent	policeman	soapmaker	warranter	bookkeeper
lockmaker	pontonier	solicitor	washerman	bookseller
locksmith	pop artist	sonneteer	waxworker	bootlegger
log-roller	porteress	sopranist	whitester	bricklayer
lumberman	portrayer	sorceress	winemaker	brickmaker
machinist	portreeve	soubrette	wood-reeve	brushmaker
magnetist	postilion	space crew	workwoman	bureaucrat
majordomo	postwoman	spiderman	zookeeper	butterwife
male model	poulterer	stableboy	zoologist	
male nurse	practiser	stableman	zootomist	

caravaneer	dramaturge	horse-leech	pantrymaid	shipwright
career girl	dressmaker	house agent	park-keeper	shopfitter
cartoonist	drummer-boy	huckstress	park-ranger	shopkeeper
cartwright	dry cleaner	husbandman	pasquilant	shopwalker
cash-keeper	emblazoner	inoculator	pastry-cook	signwriter
cat breeder	emboweller	institutor	pathfinder	silentiary
cat burglar	enamellist	instructor	pawnbroker	silk-mercer
ceramicist	ephemerist	interagent	pearl-diver	silk-weaver
chair-maker	epitaphist	ironmonger	pediatrist	sinologist
chargehand	epitomizer	ironworker	pedicurist	skirmisher
charioteer	evangelist	journalist	peltmonger	slop seller
chirurgeon	examinator	journeyman	penologist	sneak thief
chorus girl	explorator	lady doctor	perruquier	soap-boiler
chronicler	eye-servant	land holder	pharmacist	specialist
chucker-out	fell-monger	land jobber	philologer	staff nurse
circuiteer	fictionist	land waiter	piano tuner	steersmate
claim agent	file-cutter	land worker	pickpocket	stewardess
clapper boy	fillibuster	laundryman	platelayer	stipulator
clockmaker	film editor	law officer	playwright	stocktaker
clog dancer	firemaster	legislator	politician	stone-borer
cloth maker	fire-worker	librettist	portionist	stonemason
coachmaker	fishmonger	lighterman	postillion	strategist
coal-backer	flight crew	lime-burner	postmaster	street-ward
coal-fitter	flowergirl	linotypist	prescriber	supercargo
coalheaver	fluvialist	liquidator	prima donna	superviser
coal-master	folk-dancer	lobsterman	private eye	surcharger
co-assessor	folk-singer	lock-keeper	procurator	surface-man
coastguard	forecaster	lumberjack	programmer	swan-keeper
collocutor	frame-maker	magistrate	pronouncer	symphonist
colloquist	freebooter	management	proprietor	tally clerk
colporteur	fund raiser	manageress	prospector	taskmaster
comedienne	fustianist	manicurist	protractor	taxi-dancer
compositor	gamekeeper	manservant	proveditor	taxi-driver
compounder	game warden	matchmaker	puncturist	tea-blender
concordist	geisha girl	meat-hawker	pyrologist	tea planter
contractor	gear-cutter	medical man	quiz-master	technician
controller	geneticist	militiaman	railwayman	technocrat
copyholder	geographer	millwright	rat catcher	theogonist
copywriter	glee-singer	mineralist	recitalist	theologian
cordwainer	glossarist	ministress	researcher	theologist
cotton lord	glue-boiler	mintmaster	ringmaster	threnodist
counsellor	gold-beater	missionary	roadmender	timekeeper
crow-keeper	gold-digger	moonshiner	ropedancer	tractarian
cultivator	gold-washer	naturalist	roughrider	trade union
customs man	governante	nautch girl	safeblower	traffic cop
cytologist	grammarian	negotiator	sales force	trafficker
delineator	gunslinger	news editor	saleswoman	tram-driver
directress	hackney-man	newscaster	schoolmarm	transactor
disc jockey	hall porter	newsvendor	scrutineer	translator
discounter	handmaiden	newswriter	sculptress	trawlerman
discoverer	harvestman	night nurse	sea-captain	treasuress
dishwasher	hatcheller	nosologist	seamstress	troubadour
dispatcher	head porter	nurseryman	second mate	typesetter
distrainer	head waiter	obituarist	seminarist	undertaker
distrainor	hierophant	oil painter	serving-man	veterinary
dockmaster	highwayman	orchardist	sexologist	victualler
dog breeder	horn player	osteologer	ship-broker	vinegrower
dog-fancier	horologist	overlooker	ship-holder	vivandiere
doorkeeper	horsecoper	panegyrist	shipmaster	vocabulist

wage-earner
wainwright
warrioress
watchmaker
waterguard
wharfinger
wholesaler
whitesmith
winegrower
wine-waiter
wireworker
woodcarver
woodcutter
wood-monger
woodworker
wool-carder
wool-comber
wool-driver
wool-grower
wool-sorter
wool-trader
wool-winder
wool-worker
work-fellow
working man
workmaster
work people
yardmaster
zinc-worker
zoographer
zymologist

11

accompanist
accoucheuse
acoustician
adjudicator
allopathist
annunciator
antiquarian
apple-grower
arbitratrix
army officer
arquebusier
artillerist
audio typist
auscultator
bag-snatcher
ballad-maker
bank cashier
bank manager
bargemaster
basketmaker
batti-wallah
battologist
beachcomber
bell-founder

Benedictine
bill-sticker
bird-catcher
bird-fancier
bird-watcher
boatbuilder
body servant
boilermaker
boilersmith
bondservant
boot-catcher
broadcaster
bullfighter
businessman
butter-woman
candlemaker
car salesman
cattle thief
cat's-meat-man
chair-mender
chalk-cutter
chambermaid
chiffonnier
chirologist
chiromancer
chiropodist
choirmaster
chronologer
cinder-wench
cinder-woman
clock-setter
cloth-worker
coal-whipper
coffin-maker
cognoscente
collar-maker
common-crier
condisciple
condottiere
conductress
confederate
congressman
consecrator
conservator
constituent
conveyancer
coppersmith
cosmogonist
cosmologist
crane driver
crimewriter
cub reporter
cypher clerk
day-labourer
delivery man
demographer
dispensator
draughtsman
duty officer

electrician
emblematist
embroiderer
entertainer
estate agent
ethnologist
etymologist
executioner
extortioner
face-painter
factory hand
faith healer
fancy-monger
field worker
figure-maker
filing clerk
finestiller
fire brigade
fire insurer
flax-dresser
flesh-monger
fourbisseur
fringe-maker
fruit picker
funambulist
galley-slave
genealogist
ghostwriter
glass-bender
glass-blower
glass-cutter
glass-worker
grass-cutter
grave-digger
greengrocer
haberdasher
hagiologist
hairdresser
hair stylist
hardwareman
harvest lord
head foreman
head workman
hedge-priest
hedge-writer
hierologist
histologist
horse doctor
horse jockey
horse-keeper
horse trader
hospitaller
hotel-keeper
housekeeper
housemaster
housemother
hymnologist
illuminator
illusionist

illustrator
infantryman
institutist
interpreter
interviewer
iron-founder
ivory-carver
ivory-turner
ivory-worker
kennelmaid
kitchenmaid
lamplighter
land steward
laundrymaid
leading lady
ledger clerk
lifeboatman
lightkeeper
linen draper
lithologist
lithotomist
lorry driver
madrigalist
maidservant
mammalogist
master baker
mechanician
medicine man
merchantman
memorialist
metal worker
miniaturist
money-broker
money-lender
monographer
mule-spinner
music critic
music master
myographist
mysteriarch
mythologist
necrologist
necromancer
needlewoman
neurologist
neurotomist
night porter
night sister
nightworker
nomenclator
numismatist
office staff
onion-seller
opera singer
ophiologist
orientalist
orthopedist
osteologist
pamphleteer

panel-beater
pantomimist
paperhanger
parish clerk
parlourmaid
pathologist
pattenmaker
pearlfisher
pedobaptist
penny-a-liner
petrologist
pettifogger
philatelist
philologist
piece worker
phytologist
phonologist
polyphonist
pork butcher
portraitist
preceptress
print-seller
probationer
promulgator
proofreader
property man
proprietrix
quacksalver
questionary
radiologist
rag merchant
representer
republisher
rhetorician
roadsweeper
safebreaker
sandwich man
Sanscritist
saxophonist
scoutmaster
scrapdealer
scrip-holder
secret agent
seditionary
servant girl
serving-maid
share-broker
sheepfarmer
shepherdess
shipbreaker
shipbuilder
ship's master
shopsteward
silk-thrower
silversmith
slaughterer
slave-driver
slave-holder
smallholder

sociologist
stage-driver
stage-player
stake-holder
steeplejack
stereotyper
stipendiary
stockbroker
stockjobber
stonecutter
storekeeper
stripteaser
sundriesman
system-maker
taxidermist
telegrapher
telephonist
ticket agent
toastmaster
tobacconist
tooth-drawer
topographer
torch-bearer
town planner
toxophilite
tragedienne
train-bearer
transcriber
transporter
travel agent
type-founder
typographer
underbearer
underletter
underwriter
upholsterer
versemonger
vine-dresser
waiting-maid
washerwoman
watchkeeper
water-doctor
water-gilder
wax-chandler
wheel-cutter
wheelwright
whitewasher
witch-doctor
wool-stapler
xylophonist
zoographist

12

accordionist
actor manager
ambulance man
anaesthetist

animalculist
archeologist
artilleryman
artist's model
bagpipe-maker
ballad singer
ballet dancer
ballet master
bantamweight
bellows-maker
bibliologist
bibliopegist
bibliopolist
body-snatcher
booking clerk
bus conductor
cabinet-maker
calligrapher
caricaturist
carpet-bagger
carpet-fitter
cartographer
cataclysmist
cerographist
cheesemonger
chief cashier
chimney-sweep
chiropractor
chronologist
churchwarden
circuit rider
civil servant
clarinettist
clerk of works
cloth-shearer
coach-builder
coleopterist
commissioner
conchologist
confectioner
corn chandler
cosmographer
costermonger
crafts-master
craniologist
cryptogamist
dance hostess
deep-sea diver
demonologist
demonstrator
dendrologist
dramaturgist
ecclesiastic
Egyptologist
elecutionist
engastrimuth
engine-driver
entomologist
entomotomist

entrepreneur
escapologist
ethnographer
experimenter
family doctor
farm labourer
film director
film producer
first officer
flying doctor
footplateman
geometrician
geriatrician
glass-grinder
glossologist
greasemonkey
guild brother
gymnosophist
gynecologist
hagiographer
haliographer
harness-maker
head gardener
headshrinker
homeopathist
horse-breaker
horse-courser
horse-knacker
hotel manager
housebreaker
housepainter
house steward
house surgeon
hydrographer
hydropathist
hypothecator
immunologist
instructress
invoice clerk
jerry-builder
joint-trustee
jurisconsult
juvenile lead
king's counsel
knife-grinder
knife-thrower
labouring man
land surveyor
lath-splitter
leader-writer
legal adviser
lexicologist
lithographer
longshoreman
loss adjuster
lumber-dealer
maitre d'hotel
make-up artist
malacologist

man of letters
manual worker
manufacturer
mass producer
meat-salesman
mezzo soprano
metallurgist
microscopist
mineralogist
miscellanist
money-changer
monographist
morris-dancer
mosaic-artist
mosaic-worker
mythographer
newspaperman
notary public
nutritionist
obstetrician
office junior
oneirocritic
orchestrator
organ-builder
organ-grinder
orthodontist
orthographer
ovariotomist
paper-stainer
papyrologist
pattern-maker
pediatrician
phonographer
photographer
phrenologist
physiologist
plant manager
ploughwright
plumber's mate
plyer-for-hire
postmistress
practitioner
press officer
prestigiator
prison warder
prize-fighter
professional
propagandist
proprietress
psychiatrist
psychologist
publicity man
pupil-teacher
puppet-player
pyrotechnist
quarry master
racing driver
radiographer
receptionist

remembrancer
restaurateur
riding-master
right-hand man
rubber-grader
sales manager
scene-painter
scene-shifter
schoolmaster
screenwriter
scriptwriter
scullery-maid
seafaring man
seed-merchant
seismologist
sharecropper
sharpshooter
ship chandler
ship's husband
shoe-repairer
silver-beater
slaughterman
snake-charmer
social worker
soil mechanic
special agent
speechwriter
spice-blender
sportscaster
sportswriter
stage manager
statistician
steel erector
stenographer
stonebreaker
stonedresser
stonesquarer
street-trader
street-walker
sugar-refiner
tax-collector
technologist
telegraph boy
telegraphist
test engineer
therapeutist
thief-catcher
ticket-porter
timber trader
toll-gatherer
tourist agent
toxicologist
tradespeople
transplanter
trichologist
undermanager
underservant
veterinarian
waiting-woman

water diviner
warehouseman
wine merchant
wood-engraver
woollen-draper
works manager
zincographer

13

administrator
agriculturist
antique dealer
arachnologist
archaeologist
arithmetician
articled clerk
Assyriologist
barber-surgeon
bibliographer
calico-printer
campanologist
cartographist
chartographer
chicken-farmer
chirographist
choreographer
chronographer
civil engineer
clearstarcher
coffee-planter
cometographer
contrabandist
contortionist
cotton-spinner
counter-caster
counterfeiter
cranioscopist
cryptographer
dancing master
deipnosophist
dermatologist
diagnostician
diamond-cutter
draughtswoman
drawing-master
dress designer
drill sergeant
electroplater
electrotypist
emigrationist
encyclopedist
entozoologist
epigrammatist
estate manager
exhibitionist
family butcher
fencing-master

fortune-teller
freight-broker
galvanologist
game-preserver
gastriloquist
glossographer
glyphographer
ground-balliff
gynaecologist
harbour master
hieroglyphist
horse-milliner
hospital nurse
ichthyologist
industrialist
intelligencer
joint-executor
letter-carrier
letter-founder
lexicographer
lighthouse-man
maid-of-all-work
master-builder
master mariner
mathematician
melodramatist
metaphysician
meteorologist
metoposcopist
music mistress
night-watchman
old-clothes-man
ornithologist
orthographist
park attendant
periodicalist
pharmaceutist
physiognomist
physiographer
posture-master
poultry farmer
privateersman
process-server
psalmographer
psychoanalyst
pteridologist
public speaker
queen's counsel
racing-tipster
revolutionary
revolutionist
rubber-planter
sailing master
schoolteacher
science master
shop assistant
silk-throwster
singing-master
station-master

stenographist
stereoscopist
stethoscopist
street-sweeper
sub-contractor
superintender
supernumerary
thaumaturgist
thimble-rigger
toll collector
trade unionist
tram conductor
tramcar-driver
ventriloquist
violoncellist
window-cleaner
window-dresser
writing-master

14

administratrix
anthropologist
autobiographer
bacteriologist
ballet mistress
billiard-marker
billiard-player

chamber-counsel
chimney-sweeper
citizen-soldier
classics master
colour sergeant
commissionaire
dancing partner
discount-broker
educationalist
ecclesiologist
encyclopaedist
exchange-broker
grammaticaster
handicraftsman
heresiographer
horticulturist
house decorator
house furnisher
language master
leather-dresser
manual labourer
market-gardener
medical officer
merchant-tailor
miscellanarian
money-scrivener
mother-superior
music publisher
naval pensioner

painter-stainer
pharmacologist
pneumatologist
psalmographist
reception clerk
representative
schoolmistress
ship's-carpenter
siderographist
spectacle-maker
spectroscopist
superintendent
systems analyst
tallow chandler
water-colourist
weather prophet

15

arboriculturist
assistant master
Bow Street runner
crossing-sweeper
crustaceologist
dancing mistress
diamond merchant
domestic servant
forwarding agent

gentleman-farmer
hackney coachman
heart specialist
helminthologist
hierogrammatist
historiographer
instrumentalist
insurance broker
jack-of-all-trades
musical director
numismatologist
ophthalmologist
palaeontologist
platform-speaker
portrait-painter
professional man
programme seller
provision dealer
railway engineer
resurrectionist
scripture-reader
sleeping partner
stretcher-bearer
ticket collector
tightrope walker
tonsorial artist

DOMESTIC
Clothes and materials

3	rep	cony	jute	repp
	sox	cope	képi	robe
aba	tam	cowl	kilt	ruff
abb	tie	cuff	lace	sack
alb	wig	down	lamé	sari
bag	zip	drab	lawn	sark
bib		drag	leno	sash
boa		duck	list	shag
bra	4	duds	maud	shoe
bur		felt	maxi	silk
cap	abba	frog	mesh	slip
fez	band	garb	midi	sock
fur	baft	gear	mini	spur
hat	batt	geta	mink	stud
hem	belt	gimp	mitt	suit
jam	boot	gown	moff	toga
kid	brim	gros	muff	togs
kit	burr	haik	mule	tutu
lap	capa	harn	mull	vamp
mac	cape	hide	pelt	veil
net	clog	hood	poke	vest
PVC	coat	hose	pulu	wool
rag	coif	inro	pump	wrap

55

yarn	inkle	stays	bowler	fillet
	jabot	stock	bow tie	flares
	jasey	stola	braces	fleece
5	jeans	stole	briefs	foxfur
	jippo	stuff	brogan	frieze
abaya	jupon	suede	brogue	fringe
action	jussi	surah	buckle	gaiter
amice	kamik	tabby	burlap	garter
amict	kapok	tails	burnet	girdle
apron	khaki	talma	buskin	gloria
baize	lacet	tammy	bustle	grogan
batik	lapel	tanga	button	guimpe
beige	Levis	toile	byssus	gurrah
benjy	linen	terai	cabeca	gusset
beret	liner	terry	caftan	hankie
bezan	lisle	topee	calash	helmet
boots	middy	toque	calico	humhum
braid	mitre	train	camlet	insole
budge	mitts	trews	canvas	jacket
busby	moiré	tulle	capoch	jerkin
camis	mufti	tunic	capote	jersey
capoc	mungo	tweed	chimer	joseph
caxon	mutch	twill	chinos	jubbah
chaps	ninon	vamps	chintz	jumper
chino	nubia	V-neck	chiton	juppon
cloak	nylon	voile	cilice	kabaya
clogs	orlon	weeds	cloche	kaftan
cloth	orris	welly	coatee	kersey
clout	pants		collar	kimono
cotta	parka		collet	kirtle
crape	pique	**6**	corset	lappet
crash	plaid		cossas	linlng
crêpe	pleat	abolla	cotton	linsey
cuban	plume	achkan	cravat	livery
denim	plush	alpaca	crepon	madras
dhoti	pumps	angola	cyprus	mantle
dicky	quoif	angora	dacron	mantua
dress	rayon	anorak	damask	marmot
drill	romal	aridas	diadem	merino
ephod	ruche	baftas	diaper	mitten
ermin	rumal	banian	dickey	mobcap
fanon	sable	barege	dimity	mohair
fichu	sabot	barret	dirndl	moreen
finos	sagum	basque	dolman	mundil
floss	satin	beaver	domett	muslin
fogle	sayon	bengal	domino	nutria
foule	scarf	berlin	dornic	nylons
frill	serge	bikini	dorsel	panama
frock	shako	biggin	dowlas	patten
gauze	shash	blazer	duffel	peltry
get-up	shawl	blouse	ear-cap	peplum
gilet	shift	boater	edging	peruke
glove	shirt	bob-wig	ermine	pleats
guimp	simar	bodice	fabric	pompon
gunny	skirt	bolero	fag-end	poncho
habit	slops	bonnet	faille	pongee
haick	smock	bonten	fedora	poplin
heels	snood	bootee	ferret	puttee
imrah	spats	bouclé	fibule	PVC mac

raglan	wimple	cut-away	Mae West	tabaret
ratine	wincey	delaine	malines	tabinet
rebato	woolly	djibbah	maniple	taffeta
reefer	zonnar	doeskin	mantlet	taffety
riband		dogskin	matting	tatting
ribbon		dollman	mechlin	textile
rigout	**7**	dornock	minever	ticking
rochet		doublet	miniver	tiffany
ruffle	abb wool	drabbet	montero	top coat
russet	acrilan	drawers	morocco	top-knot
samite	alamode	drip-dry	muffler	tricorn
sandal	alepine	egrette	nacarat	tunicle
sarong	apparel	epaulet	nankeen	turn-ups
satara	art-silk	ermelin	necktie	tussore
sateen	bandana	faconné	nightie	twinset
sendal	bandeau	fallals	oilskin	uniform
sequin	batiste	falsies	organza	vandyke
serape	bay-yarn	felt hat	orleans	velours
sheath	beveren	felting	orphrey	vesting
shoddy	biretta	filibeg	overall	vesture
shorts	blanket	flannel	paisley	webbing
slacks	blucher	flat hat	paletot	wellies
sleeve	bocking	floroon	pallium	wetsuit
smalls	bottine	flounce	panties	whittle
soneri	brocade	foulard	parasol	wiggery
stamin	brogans	frislet	partlet	woollen
sunhat	buckram	frounce	pattens	worsted
tabard	burnous	fur coat	pelisse	yashmak
tamine	bycoket	fustian	periwig	
tartan	byssine	gaiters	petasus	
thibet	cagoule	galloon	pigskin	**8**
ticken	calotte	gantlet	pugaree	
tights	camblet	garment	purflew	aigrette
tippet	cambric	gaskins	puttees	appliqué
tissue	capuche	genappe	pyjamas	babouche
tobine	cantoon	gingham	raiment	baffetas
toison	cassock	grogram	rompers	baldrick
top-hat	casuals	guipure	rosette	barathea
toquet	challis	G-string	sacking	barracan
torque	chamois	gymslip	sarafan	bathrobe
toupee	chapeau	handbag	sarsnet	baudekin
toupet	chechia	hat-band	satinet	bearskin
tricot	chemise	hessian	scarlet	bed linen
trilby	chenille	hoggers	silesia	bedsocks
trunks	chimere	hogskin	singlet	biggonet
T-shirt	chlamys	holland	ski-boot	blancard
tucker	chopine	homburg	slip-ons	bloomers
turban	chrisom	hopsack	slipper	bluchers
tussah	civvies	hosiery	soutane	boat-neck
tuxedo	clobber	jaconet	spattee	body-belt
tweeds	clothes	lasting	spencer	bombasin
ulster	coating	latchet	sporran	bonelace
velure	cockade	layette	stammel	bootikin
velvet	coronet	leather	stetson	bottines
visite	corsage	legging	suiting	breeches
waders	costume	leghorn	sunsuit	brocatel
wampum	cow-hide	leotard	surcoat	brodekin
weeper	crochet	loafers	surtout	buckskin
whites	crounet	lockram	sweater	Burberry

burnoose
bycocket
cameline
camisole
capeline
cardigan
carlisle
cashmere
Celanese
chagreen
chaperon
chasuble
chausses
chenille
chesible
cloaking
cloth cap
clothing
coiffure
collaret
corduroy
cordwain
corporal
corselet
cracowes
cretonne
culottes
dagswain
deerskin
diamanté
dress tie
drilling
dungaree
earmuffs
ensemble
eolienne
Fair Isle
fatigues
fillibeg
fingroms
flannels
florence
fontange
footwear
frilling
frippery
frontlet
froufrou
furbelow
gabarage
galoshes
gambeson
gambroon
gauntlet
glad rags
gold lace
gold lamé
gold wire
gossamer

gumboots
gymshoes
half-hose
headband
hipsters
homespun
jackboot
Jacquard
jodhpurs
jump suit
kerchief
knickers
knitwear
lambskin
leggings
lingerie
lustring
mackinaw
mantelet
mantilla
marcella
material
menswear
moccasin
moleskin
moquette
muffetee
muslinet
musquash
nainsook
neckband
négligée
nightcap
oilcloth
opera hat
organdie
osnaburg
overalls
overcoat
overshoe
pabouche
paduasoy
pelerine
piccadil
pinafore
playsuit
plumelet
polo-neck
ponyskin
prunella
prunello
pullover
raincoat
rose-knot
sandshoe
sarsenet
sealskln
scapular
shagreen

shalloon
Shantung
sheeting
shirring
shirting
shoelace
shot silk
skiboots
skipants
skullcap
slippers
smocking
sneakers
snowshoe
sombrero
soutache
stitchel
stocking
straw hat
sundress
sunshade
surplice
swanskin
swimsuit
tabbinet
taglioni
tailcoat
tapestry
tarboosh
tarlatan
terai-hat
Terylene
Thai silk
trimming
trousers
two-piece
umbrella
valentia
vallancy
vestment
wardrobe
whipcord
woollens
wristlet

9

alpargata
Alice band
ankle-boot
astrakhan
baby linen
balaclava
bandolier
beachwear
bedjacket
billycock
blond lace

blue jeans
bombazine
bowler hat
brassiere
broadbrim
bushshirt
calamanco
camelhair
caparison
cassimere
cerecloth
chantilly
charmeuse
chaussure
cheongsam
clump boot
cocked hat
comforter
Courtelle
crinoline
Cuban heel
dalmatica
décolleté
dog collar
dress coat
dress suit
duffle bag
dungarees
epaulette
fermillet
fingering
fleshings
flipflops
floss silk
forage cap
frockcoat
full dress
full skirt
fur collar
gaberdine
galoshes
gambadoes
garibaldi
gauntlets
georgette
Glengarry
greatcoat
grenadine
grosgrain
haircloth
hairshift
hairpiece
headdress
headscarf
high heels
hoop skirt
horsehair
housecoat
huckaback

Inverness
jack boots
jockey cap
justi-coat
kid gloves
knee socks
lambswool
levantine
linen mesh
loincloth
longcloth
long dress
long skirt
long socks
macintosh
millinery
miniskirt
moiré silk
muffette
nightgown
nightwear
neckcloth
organzine
overdress
overshoes
panama hat
pantalets
pantaloon
paramatta
patchwork
pea jacket
peaked cap
percaline
petersham
petticoat
pina cloth
pixie hood
plimsolls
plus-fours
point lace
polonaise
pourpoint
polyester
press stud
quoiffure
redingote
round-neck
sackcloth
sack dress
safety pin
sailcloth
sailor cap
sailor hat
sanbenito
satinette
scapulary
school cap
scoop-neck
separates

sharkskin
sheepskin
shovel hat
shower cap
silk serge
sloppy joe
slouch hat
snowshoes
sou'wester
spun rayon
stockinet
stockings
stomacher
strapless
strouding
suede coat
sunbonnet
swansdown
sweatband
sword belt
tarpaulin
towelling
track suit
trilby hat
trousseau
underwear
velveteen
vestments
waistband
waistcoat
wedge heel
wide-awake
wristband
zucchetto

10

angora wool
ankle socks
balbriggan
ballet shoe
bathing cap
beaverteen
Berlin wool
bishop's-cap
blanketing
bobbin lace
bobbysocks
boiler suit
bombazette
broadcloth
brocatello
bushjacket
buttonhole
candlewick
canonicals
cassinette
chatelaine

chemisette
chinchilla
court dress
court shoes
coverchief
crepe soles
cricket cap
cummerbund
diving suit
drainpipes
dress shoes
embroidery
epauletted
Eton collar
Eton jacket
fancy dress
fearnought
feather boa
florentine
foot mantle
foresleeve
fustanella
gold thread
grass cloth
grass skirt
habiliment
halterneck
Havana pelt
hodden-gray
hodden-grey
horsecloth
Irish linen
jersey silk
jersey wool
kerseymere
khaki drill
lounge suit
mackintosh
mess jacket
middy skirt
mock velvet
mousseline
needlecord
new clothes
nightdress
nightshirt
old clothes
opera cloak
overblouse
Oxford bags
pantalettes
pantaloons
party dress
persiennes
piccadilly
pillow lace
pilot-cloth
pith helmet
plastic mac

print dress
rabbitskin
riding-hood
roquelaure
sailorsuit
scratch wig
seersucker
shoebuckle
shoe string
slingbacks
sportscoat
suspenders
sweatshirt
tablecloth
table linen
thrown silk
toilinette
trench coat
trousering
turtle-neck
tussah silk
underpants
waterprcof
windjammer
wing collar
wraparound

11

Aran sweater
battledress
bellbottoms
best clothes
black patent
candystripe
canvas shoes
cap and bells
cheesecloth
clodhoppers
cloth-of-gold
crash-helmet
deerstalker
diving dress
Dolly Varden
dreadnought
farthingale
flannelette
flared skirt
football cap
hammer cloth
hand-me-downs
Harris tweed
herringbone
Honiton lace
Kendal green
leather coat
leatherette
leopardskin

mechlin lace
morning coat
mortarboard
neckerchief
netherlings
nettlecloth
Norfolk suit
panty girdle
Phrygian cap
pilot jacket
pinstripes
ready-to-wear
regimentals
riding habit
shoe leather
shoulder bag
slumberwear
stiff collar
stockinette
suede jacket
tam-o'-shanter
tennis dress
tennis skirt
torchon lace
trencher cap
trouser suit
tussore silk
watered silk
wellingtons
widow's weeds
windcheater
yachting cap

12

antigropelos
asbestos suit
bathing dress
billycock hat
body stocking
bolting cloth
business suit
cardinal's hat
cavalry twill
chastity belt
circassienne
chesterfield
collar and tie
college scarf
crêpe-de-chine
dinner jacket
divided skirt
donkey jacket
dress clothes
dressing gown
Easter bonnet
evening dress
football boots

galligaskins
handkerchief
Indian cotton
knee breeches
leather skirt
lumber jacket
moiré antique
monkey jacket
morning dress
plain clothes
pleated skirt
service dress
shirtwaister
sleeping suit
sportsjacket
stockingette
underclothes
wedding dress
Welsh flannel

13

Anthony Eden
Bermuda shorts
cashmere shawl
chinchilla fur
football scarf
leather jacket
Norfolk jacket
patent leather
pinafore dress
platform soles
Russia leather
spatterdashes
swaddling band
underclothing

14

artificial silk
bathing costume
chamois leather
Fair Isle jumper
knickerbockers
Morocco leather
riding breeches
Shetland jumper
shoulder strap
swaddling cloth
undress uniform

15

maribou feathers
mourning clothes
ostrich feathers
tarpaulin jacket

Dances

3

bop
fan
hay
hop
jig
pas

4

ball
clog
giga
hula
jive
jota
juba
juke
kola
polk
polo
reel
step

5

bebop
caper
conga
fling
galop
gigue
limbo
loure
mambo
pavan
pavin
polka
rondo
rumba
samba
stomp
tango
twist
valse
waltz

6

Almain
Apache
bolero
boston
bourée
branle
cancan
cha-cha
chassé
corant
gallop
lavolt
minuet
morisk
morris
oberek
pavane
redowa
reigen
rhumba
rondel
shimmy
valeta
watusi

7

beguine
bourree
boutade
choctaw
cachuca
coranto
esardos
farruca
forlana
fox-trot
gavotte
hoedown
lancers
ländler
la volta
madison
mazurka
measure
morisco
one-step
planxty
rondeau

roundel
tsardar
sardana
two-step
ziganka

8

bunny-hug
cachucha
cake-walk
capriole
chaconne
cotillon
courante
danseuse
excuse-me
fandance
fandango
flamenco
galliard
habanera
hay-de-guy
hoolican
hornpipe
hulahula
murciana
rigadoon
saraband
tap-dance

9

allemande
arabesque
barndance
bossa nova
cha-cha-cha
clog dance
cotillion
écossaise
eightsome
farandole
folkdance
gallopade
jitterbug
paso doble
passepied
Paul Jones
pirouette

polonaise
poussette
quadrille
quickstep
rock 'n' roll
Siciliana

10

boston reel
charleston
hey-de-guize
hokey-pokey
pooka-pooka
saltarello
strathspey
sword-dance
tambourine
tarantella
torch dance
turkey-trot
tripudiary

11

contra-dance
jolly miller
morris dance
rock and roll
square-dance
schottische
varsovienne

12

country dance
maypole dance
palais-glide
state-lancers
tripudiation

13 AND 14

eightsome reel
Helston flurry
Highland fling
light fantastic

Drink (wines, spirits, non-alcoholic beverages, etc.)

3

ale
ara
bub
cha
dop
fix
gin
jar
kat
kir
mum
nip
nog
rum
rye
sip
sup
tea
tot
vat
vin

4

arak
asti
Bass
beer
bock
bols
brut
bual
café
char
coke
cola
dram
fine
fizz
flip
grog
Hine
hock
kava
krug
lush
marc
mate
mead
mild
milk
moët

mumm
ouzo
port
raki
reid
rosé
sack
sake
saki
slug
soda
stum
swig
tape
tent
wine
wort

5

arack
assai
ayala
biddy
bohea
bowle
broth
bumbo
byrrh
capri
chica
cider
cocoa
congo
cream
cuppa
daisy
evian
glass
haoma
hogan
hogen
hooch
hyson
Irish
irroy
joram
julep
kefir
kvass
lager
Maçon
Médoc
mobby

mocha
morat
nantz
negus
noyau
padra
pekoe
perry
pinta
plonk
punch
purre
quass
rumbo
salep
shrub
sirop
sling
smash
snort
soave
staws
stout
swats
tafia
toddy
Tokay
tonic
vichy
vodka
water
winox
Xeres
Yerba

6

alegar
amrita
apozem
arrack
Barsac
Beaune
bishop
bitter
Bovril
brandy
bubbly
bumper
canary
cassis
caudle
chicha
claret

coffee
Cognac
congou
Cooper
crusta
double
egg-nog
elixir
entire
geneva
Gibson
gimlet
gloria
grappa
Graves
hootch
junora
kephir
kirsch
kummel
liquor
Lisbon
lotion
Malaga
masdeu
mastic
muscat
nectar
noggin
oolong
oulong
pastis
Pernod
pimint
plotty
poison
pontac
porter
posset
poteen
potion
ptisan
pulque
Ribena
rickey
saloop
Saumur
Scotch
shandy
sherry
simkin
spirit
squash
stingo
Strega

strunt
swipes
tiffin
tipple
tisane
treble
volnay
wallop
wherry
whisky

7

absinthe
alcohol
ale-gill
alicant
amoroso
aquavit
Bacardi
bitters
bourbon
Campari
catawba
Chablis
Chandon
Chianti
cobbler
collins
cordial
curaçao
draught
egg-flip
Falerno
gin fizz
gin sour
goodies
koumiss
limeade
liqueur
low-wine
mace ale
Madeira
Malmsey
Marsala
martini
mineral
molotov
Moselle
negroni
oloroso
Orvieto
pale ale
perrier

pilsner
pink gin
plottie
Pomerol
Pommard
Pommery
potable
Pouilly
pulchra
ratafia
red wine
retsina
samshoo
Sangria
sherbet
sidecar
simkin
sloe-gin
snifter
spirits
spunkie
stinger
tequila
tintara
twankay
vibrona
vouvray
whiskey

8

Adam's ale
absinthe
Advocaat
alkermes
anisette
aperitif
Assam tea
bees'-wing
beverage
block tea
bock-beer
Bordeaux
brick tea
Burgundy
champers
charneco
China tea
cider cup
ciderkin
Clicquot
coca-cola
cocktail
dog's nose

Drambuie
dry wines
Dubonnet
eau-de-vie
espresso
florence
Frascati
gin-sling
green tea
Guinness
herb-beer
highball
hockclip
Hollands
Horlick's
hydromel
lemonade
montilla
muscadel
muscatel
near beer
nightcap
oopak tea
padra tea
pekoe tea
pilsener
Pol Roger
pouchong
prasites
punt y mes
ramboose
red biddy
red wines
roederer
rosoglio
ruby port
rum-punch
rum-shrub
St. Julien
sangaree
Sauterne
schnapps
sillabub
skim-milk
small-ale
souchong
sour milk
spritzer
syllabub
tia maria
tincture
verjuice
vermouth
vin blanc
wish-wash

9

Adam's wine
altar wine
angostura
Anjou wine
applejack
aqua vitae
Badminton
barley-pop
birch wine
bitter ale
black beer
Bollinger
brut wines
Buck's fizz
Budweiser
Carlsberg
Ceylon tea
champagne
chocolate
claret cup
Cointreau
copa de oro
cuba libre
demitasse
elder wine
Falernian
febrifuge
firewater
ginger-ale
ginger-pop
grenadine
gunpowder
Hall's wine
hermitage
Heidsieck
hippocras
iced water
Indian tea
lager beer
lamb's wool
limejuice
lollshrob
Manhattan
metheglin
milk-punch
milk-shake
mint julep
moonshine
mulled ale
muscadine
oolong-tea
orangeade
orange-gin
St. Emilion
St. Raphael
salutaris
Scotch ale

slivovica
slivovitz
small-beer
soda water
soft drink
still-hock
sundowner
tarragona
tawny port
vodkatini
white lady
white port
white wine
Wincarnis

10

Beaujolais
bitter beer
black-strap
bloody mary
café-au-lait
calcavella
cappuccino
chartreuse
clary-water
constantia
dry martini
frontiniac
genevrette
ginger beer
ginger wine
goldwasser
horse's neck
iced drinks
Jamaica rum
lime-squash
malt liquor
malted milk
malt whisky
maraschino
Mateus Rosé
mickey finn
Moselle cup
mulled wine
Munich beer
pale sherry
raisin wine
Rhine wines
Rhône wines
rye whiskey
sack posset
shandygaff
soft drinks
spruce beer
still wines
sweet wines
tanglefoot
Tom Collins

tonic water
usquebaugh
twankay tea
vichy water
white capri
white wines

11

aguardiente
amontillado
apollinaris
apple brandy
barley broth
barleywater
benedictine
black velvet
Bristol milk
cider-brandy
citron water
Courvoisier
cowslip wine
doch-an-doris
dry monopole
Irish coffee
Irish whisky
John Collins
lemon squash
montefiasco
mountain-dew
Niersteiner
orange-pekoe
peach brandy
Plymouth gin
potash water
pouchong tea
Saint Julien
screwdriver
scuppernong
soda and mllk
souchong tea
spring water
tomato juice
vin de Graves
vintage wine

12

champagne cup
cherry brandy
crème de cacao
crème-de-menthe
Cyprus sherry
Fernet-Branca
ginger brandy
Grand Marnier
humpty dumpty
ice-cream soda
India pale ale

Irish whiskey
kirschwasser
Malvern water
marcobrunner
mulled claret
old fashioned
orange brandy
orange squash
peach bitters
Perrier-Jouet
red wine punch
Rhenish wines
Saint Emilion
Saint Raphael
sarsaparilla
Scotch whisky
seltzer water
still Moselle
Suffolk punch
supernaculum
treacle water
vin ordinaire

13

aerated waters
aperitif wines

apricot brandy
bijou cocktail
bronx cocktail
Château-Lafite
Contrexéville
dandelion wine
Darjeeling tea
Falernian wine
ginger cordial
Liebfraumilch
liqueur brandy
liqueur whisky
mineral waters
Möet et Chandon
orange bitters
pink champagne
planters' punch
prairie oyster
seidlitz water
sherry cobbler
sparkling hock
sparkling wine
Touraine wines
Veuve Clicquot

14

bamboo-cocktail
blended whiskey
champagne cider
champagne punch
Château-Margaux
French vermouth
Johannisberger
Piper-Heidsieck
Rob Roy cocktail
sparkling-wines
vermouth cassis
white wine punch

15

cascade-cocktail
champagne-cognac
duchess-cocktail
green chartreuse
Italian vermouth
martini-cocktail
molotov cocktail
sacramental wine
sparkling waters
tintara burgundy

Food

3 AND 4

bap, bean, beef, blin, bran, brie, bun, cake, cate, chop, chou, curd, Edam, egg, fare, fat, fish, flan, fool, fowl, game, ghee, grub

gur, ham, hare, hash, herb, ice, jam, jowl, junk, kai, kale, lamb, lard, lean, loaf, loin, lung, meal, meat, milk, mint, mush, naan, nan, oxo

pâté, pie, poi, pork, puff, rice, rob, roe, roll, roti, roux, rusk, sago, snow, soup, soy, stew, suet, tart, veal, whey, yolk

5

aioli, aspic, bacon, blini, blood, board, bombe, borsh, brawn, bread, brose, broth, candy, cakes, cheer, chili, clove, cream, crêpe, crust, curds, curry, dough

dulse, filet, flour, fruit, fudge, gigot, glaze, Gouda, gravy, gruel, gumbo, heart, honey, icing, jelly, joint, juice, kebab, liver, lolly, lunch, manna, matzo, melba, melts

mince	comfit	potage	chutney	rhubarb
mocha	congee	potato	cobloaf	rice bun
pasta	cookie	quiche	compote	ricotta
paste	course	rabbit	confect	risotto
pasty	crowdy	ragout	corn cob	rissole
patty	crumbs	raisin	cracker	sapsago
pilaf	cutlet	rasher	crumble	sausage
pilau	dainty	relish	crumpet	savarin
pilaw	dinner	salami	currant	saveloy
pitta	dragée	samosa	custard	savoury
pizza	éclair	sea-pie	dariole	seafood
prune	eggnog	simnel	dessert	sherbet
pulse	entrée	sinker	faggots	sirloin
roast	faggot	sorbet	falafel	soufflé
salad	fillet	sowens	fig cake	Stilton
salmi	flitch	sponge	fritter	strudel
sauce	fodder	squash	galette	succado
scoff	fondue	staple	game pie	sucrose
scone	fumado	sundae	gelatin	tapioca
shape	gammon	supper	giblets	tartlet
snack	garlic	sweets	glucose	teacake
syrup	gâteau	tiffin	gnocchi	treacle
spice	gelato	tit-bit	goulash	truffle
split	ginger	toffee	gristle	venison
steak	grease	tongue	gruyère	vinegar
stock	greens	trifle	haricot	windsor
sugar	grouse	viands	haslets	yoghurt
sushi	haggis	waffle	houmous	
sweet	hot dog	walnut	jam roll	
syrup	hot-pot	yogurt	jam tart	
table	humbug		ketchup	**8**
taffy	hummus		lasagne	
tansy	jujube	**7**	Madeira	allspice
toast	jumble		madzoon	ambrosia
tripe	junket	aliment	Marmite	aperitif
viand	kelkel	bannock	matzoon	apple jam
wafer	kidney	banquet	meat pie	apple pie
yeast	leaven	bath bun	mustard	bath chap
	lights	beef tea	oatcake	béchamel
	mousse	biltong	oatmeal	biscotin
6	muffin	biscuit	olycook	bouillon
	mutton	bloater	pancake	chestnut
almond	noodle	blossom	papmeat	chop suey
batter	nougat	borscht	paprika	chow mein
biffin	noyeau	botargo	pickles	coleslaw
blintz	nut oil	bouilli	plum jam	confetti
bonbon	oliver	brisket	plum pie	conserve
borsch	omelet	broiler	polenta	consommé
Bovril	oxtail	brownie	popcorn	couscous
brains	paella	bull's eye	potargo	cracknel
brunch	panada	cabbage	pottage	cream bun
burger	parlein	calipee	poultry	cross bun
butter	pastry	caramel	praline	dainties
canapé	pepper	catchup	pretzel	date roll
casein	pickle	caviare	pudding	déjeuner
caviar	pilaff	cheddar	ramekin	delicacy
cereal	pillau	chicken	rarebit	dog's-meat
cheese	polony	chicory	ratafia	doughnut
collop	posset	chowder	ravioli	dripping

dumpling
escalope
fishmeal
flapjack
flummery
frumenty
frosting
fruit pie
hardbake
hazelnut
hotchpot
hung beef
ice cream
iced cake
Julienne
kedgeree
kickshaw
lamb chop
loblolly
lollipop
luncheon
macaroni
macaroon
marzipan
meatball
meatloaf
meringue
mince pie
mishmash
molasses
moussaka
mushroom
napoleon
olive oil
omelette
parmesan
pastrami
pemmican
peperoni
poppadum
porridge
preserve
racahout
raisinée
ramequin
rice cake
rollmops
roly poly
ryebread
salad oil
salpicon
salt fish
salt junk
salt pork
sandwich
scrag-end
seedcake
sillabub
skim milk

slapjack
soda cake
sparerib
squab pie
steak pie
stuffing
tortilla
turnover
undercut
victuals
whitepot
yoghourt

9

antipasti
appetizer
arrowroot
beefsteak
breakfast
bridecake
bubblegum
Camembert
cassareep
casserole
cassonade
chipolata
chocolate
chump-chop
comfiture
condiment
confiture
corn bread
corn salad
crackling
cream cake
croquette
drop scone
Easter egg
enchilada
entremets
forcemeat
fricassee
fried eggs
fried fish
fruit cake
fruit tart
galantine
Genoa cake
giblet pie
gravy soup
gustation
hamburger
hard sauce
honeycomb
Irish stew
lemon curd
loafsugar

lobscouse
lump sugar
macedoine
madeleine
margarine
marmalade
mincemeat
mint sauce
mousetrap
mutton ham
mutton pie
nutriment
picalilli
pigeon pie
potato pie
potpourri
pound cake
provelone
provender
puff paste
raised pie
rillettes
Roquefort
rumpsteak
schnitzel
scotch egg
seasoning
shellfish
shortcake
sour cream
sourdough
spaghetti
stirabout
succotash
sugarloaf
sugar-plum
sweetmeat
swiss roll
tipsy cake
vegetable
white meat
whole meal
wild honey
Yorkshire

10

apple sauce
apricot jam
bath oliver
beefburger
bêche-de-mer
blancmange
blanquette
Bombay duck
bosh butter
breadstuff

bridescake
brown bread
buttermilk
cannelloni
capillaire
cheesecake
chelsea bun
comestible
confection
corned beef
cornflakes
cottage pie
currant bun
delicacies
dog biscuit
estouffade
fig pudding
flesh broth
frangipane
French loaf
fricandeau
fruit salad
giblet soup
ginger cake
girdle cake
gloucester
gorgonzola
grape sugar
ground rice
guava jelly
ham and eggs
hodge-podge
hotch-potch
ice pudding
indian corn
jugged hare
lamb cutlet
maple sugar
marrow bone
mayonnaise
minced meat
minestrone
mock turtle
montelimar
mutton chop
pepper cake
peppermint
poached egg
Pontefract
potted fish
potted meat
provisions
pudding pie
puff pastry
raisin loaf
rhubarb pie
rolled oats
saccharine
salmagundi

salmagundy
salt butter
sauerkraut
shortbread
shortcrust
simnel cake
sponge cake
stale bread
stewed meat
sugar candy
sustenance
sweetbread
tea biscuit
temse bread
tenderloin
tortellini
tinned food
turtle soup
vermicelli
water gruel
white bread
white sauce

11

baked Alaska
Banbury cake
barley sugar
bonne bouche
cassava cake
chiffon cake
comestibles
cream cheese
coulommiers
curry powder
frankfurter
French bread
gingerbread
golden syrup
green turtle
griddle cake
ham sandwich
hors d'oeuvre
hot cross bun
iron rations
jam sandwich
meat biscuit
meat pudding
medlar jelly
milk pudding
olla podrida
oyster patty
peppermints
plum pudding
raisin bread
refreshment
rice biscuit
rice pudding

sago pudding
sausage roll
short pastry
stewed fruit
suet pudding
tagliatelle
vichyssoise
wedding cake
Welsh mutton
Welsh rabbit
Wensleydale
wheaten loaf
wine biscuit

12

apfel strudel
apple fritter
birthday cake
burnt amonds
butterscotch
chip potatoes
clotted cream
Cornish pasty
corn-on-the-cob
curds and whey
Danish pastry
dunmow flitch

eggs and bacon
finnan haddie
guarana-bread
hasty pudding
Julienne soup
liver sausage
lobster patty
maid of honour
marshmallow
merry thought
mullagatawny
mulligatawny
nutmeg butter
peanut butter
pease pudding
plum porridge
pumpernickel
quartern loaf
refreshments
shepherd's pie
ship's biscuit
steak pudding
sweet and sour
taramasalata
tripe de roche
Welsh rarebit

13

apple dumpling
béchamel sauce
bouillabaisse
cheddar cheese
chili con carne
Christmas cake
confectionery
cottage cheese
custard-coffin
flitch of bacon
German sausage
gigot de mouton
ginger pudding
gruyère cheese
Oxford sausage
roll and butter
salad dressing
scotch collops
sirloin of beef
sponge pudding
Stilton cheese
toad-in-the-hole
veal-and-ham pie

14

almond hardbake
apple charlotte
bologna sausage
bread and butter
bread and cheese
caramel custard
charlotte russe
haunch of mutton
household bread
mashed potatoes
mock-turtle soup
parmesan cheese
Pontefract cake
saddle of mutton
toasted teacake
turkish delight
wholemeal bread

15

bakewell pudding
black-cap pudding
bubble and squeak
chocolate éclair
Devonshire cream
haunch of venison

Furniture, fittings and personal effects
See also **Kitchen utensils and requisites**

3

bag
bar
bed
bin
can
cot
fan
hod
ink
mat
nib
nog
pad
ped
pen
pew
pin
rug
urn
vat

4

ambo
bath
bowl
bunk
butt
case
cask
cist
comb
cott
crib
desk
door
etui
form
gong
hi-fi
lamp
mull
oven
poke

rack
sack
safe
seal
seat
sofa
tank
tape
till
trap
tray
trug
vase
wick

5

apron
arras
basin
bench
besom

bidet
blind
board
broom
chair
chest
china
cigar
clock
cloth
coign
coppy
couch
cover
crate
creel
crock
cruet
cruse
diota
divan
doily
dosel

doser
duvet
flask
flisk
glass
globe
grill
guard
jesse
joram
jorum
label
laver
leash
light
linen
mural
paper
paten
patin
piano
pouch
purse

quill	drawer	shower	commode	samovar
quilt	duster	siphon	compact	sampler
radio	fender	sponge	costrel	sand-box
razor	fly-net	starch	counter	satchel
scrip	forfex	string	cue-rack	scraper
shade	fridge	syphon	cutlery	shelves
shelf	geyser	tablet	curtain	shoebox
skeel	goblet	teapot	cushion	show-box
slate	goglet	tea set	door-mat	skimmer
spill	hamper	tea urn	down-bed	soap-box
stand	hat-box	thread	drapery	sofa-bed
stool	hearth	throne	dresser	steamer
stoup	heater	tiller	drugget	stopper
strop	hookah	tin box	dustbin	stopple
suite	hoppet	tinder	dust-pan	syringe
swing	hussif	toy box	epergne	tallboy
table	ink-pot	trevet	flacket	tambour
tache	ice-box	tripod	flasket	tankard
tapis	ladder	trivet	fly-rail	tea-cosy
tongs	keeler	trophy	fuse-box	tea-tray
tools	kit-bag	tureen	gas-fire	tent-bed
torch	kurkee	valise	gas ring	thermos
towel	locker	wallet	goggles	thimble
traps	log bin	window	griddle	tin-case
trunk	loofah	wisket	hair-oil	toaster
twine	lowboy	zip-bag	hammock	tobacco
vesta	mangle		hassock	tool kit
watch	mirror		hip bath	trammel
	mobile	**7**	holdall	trolley
	napery		horn-cup	truckle
6	napkin	adaptor	ink-horn	tumbler
	needle	aerator	knocker	tun-dish
air bed	noggin	almirah	lagging	valance
ash-bin	oilcan	amphora	lantern	wardian
ash-can	pallet	andiron	lectern	wash-tub
awning	patera	armoire	lighter	what-not
basket	patine	ash-tray	matches	whisket
beaker	pelmet	baggage	matting	wine-bag
bicker	pencil	bath mat	monocle	woodcut
bucket	piggin	bathtub	netsuke	work-bag
bunker	pillow	bedding	oil-lamp	workbox
bureau	plaque	beeswax	ottoman	wringer
camera	pomade	bellows	padlock	yule-log
carafe	posnet	blanket	pannier	
carboy	pottle	blotter	percher	
carpet	pouffe	bolster	pianino	**8**
carver	punkah	brasier	pianola	
casket	punnet	brazier	picture	ale bench
castor	red ink	broiler	pillion	angel bed
cheval	rocker	bunk bed	pin-case	armchair
chowry	saddle	cabinet	playpen	baluster
coffer	salver	camp bed	pomatum	banister
consol	scales	canteen	pottager	barbecue
cooker	sconce	chalice	pot-hook	bassinet
cradle	scovel	chamois	roaster	bed cover
day-bed	screen	chopper	rundlet	bed linen
dishes	settee	cistern	rush-mat	bed quilt
dosser	settle	cobiron	saccule	bedstaff
drapet	shovel	coir-mat	sadiron	bedstead

bed-straw
bird-bath
bird-cage
bookcase
bookends
borachio
camp-bath
card-case
cashbook
cathedra
causeuse
cellaret
chair-bed
chattels
clay pipe
coat-hook
colander
coverlet
credenza
crockery
cupboard
curtains
cuspidor
decanter
demi-john
ditty-box
dog-chain
doorbell
doorknob
door-step
egg-timer
endirons
eyeglass
fauteuil
field-bed
firewood
flock-bed
fly paper
foot-bath
fuse wire
gallipot
gasalier
handbell
hangings
hat-brush
hatstand
heirloom
hip flask
holdfast
inkstand
jalousie
knapsack
lamp-wick
lanthorn
latchkey
linoleum
lipstick
loo table
love seat

matchbox
mattress
nail-file
note-book
oak chest
oilcloth
ornament
penknife
pianette
pipe-rack
postcard
press-bed
quill-pen
radiator
reticule
road-book
saddlery
scissors
sea chest
shoehorn
shoelace
show-case
sink unit
sitz-bath
slop bowl
slop pail
snuffbox
snuffers
soap dish
speculum
spittoon
stair-rod
standish
steel pen
suitcase
sun-blind
table-mat
tabouret
tantalus
tape-line
tapestry
tea-board
tea-caddy
tea-chest
tea-cloth
tea-table
trencher
tridarne
triptych
tweezers
umbrella
vestiary
vestuary
wall-safe
wardrobe
watch-key
water-can
water-pot
water tap

wax cloth
wax light
wineskin
wireless

9

barometer
bathtowel
bedspread
black-jack
bookshelf
book-stand
boot-brush
bric-à-brac
cakestand
camp-chair
camp-stool
cane-chair
cantharus
card-table
carpet-bag
carpeting
case-knife
casserole
china bowl
chinaware
cigarette
clack-dish
clasplock
club chair
coffee-cup
coffee-pot
comb-brush
container
corkscrew
crumb-tray
cullender
cushionet
davenport
deck chair
devonport
directory
dishcloth
dish-clout
dish-cover
dog-basket
dog-collar
dog-kennel
dust-brush
dust-sheet
Dutch oven
easy chair
egg boiler
elderdown
equipment
face towel
faldstool

fire-board
fire-brush
fire-grate
fire-guard
fire-irons
fireplace
fish-knife
fish-plate
flower-pot
food-mixer
foot-board
footstool
frying-pan
gas-burner
gas-cooker
gas-geyser
girandole
gold-plate
gout-stool
hairbrush
hair tonic
hall table
hand-towel
haversack
high chair
horsewhip
housewife
ink-bottle
ink-holder
inventory
jack-towel
jewel case
kitchener
lamp-shade
lampstand
letter-box
light bulb
loving-cup
marquetry
master-key
mouse-trap
muffineer
music book
nail brush
newspaper
nick-nacks
nipperkin
notepaper
ornaments
paillasse
palliasse
paper clip
paper-rack
parchment
pepper-pot
perdonium
pewter pot
pier-glass
pier-table

piggy-bank
plate-rack
porringer
portfolio
port glass
pot-hanger
pot-pourri
pounce-box
powder-box
punchbowl
punkah-fan
quail-pipe
radiogram
rush-light
safety-pin
scrutoire
secretary
serviette
shakedown
shoe-brush
shower-cap
sideboard
side-light
side-table
slop-basin
spin-drier
sponge-bag
sprinkler
stair rods
stamp-case
steel wool
stopwatch
string-box
sword-cane
table bell
table hook
table lamp
tableware
tea-kettle
telephone
timepiece
timetable
tinder-box
tin-opener
toothpick
underfelt
vanity-box
wall-clock
wallpaper
wall-light
wash-basin
wash-board
wash-stand
water-butt
water-tank
wax candle
wax polish
window-box
wine glass

work table

10

air-cushion
alarm clock
alarm watch
bedclothes
biscuit-box
boot polish
broomstick
brown paper
buck-basket
cabbage net
calefactor
candelabra
canterbury
ceiling fan
chandelier
chessboard
chiffonier
chopsticks
clamp-irons
clothes peg
clothes pin
coal bucket
coal bunker
coat hanger
crumb-brush
crumb cloth
curtain rod
dandy-brush
deep-freeze
disfurnish
dishwasher
down pillow
dumb-waiter
elbow-chair
escritoire
featherbed
finger-bowl
fire-basket
fire-bucket
fire-escape
firescreen
fire-shovel
fish-basket
fish-carver
fish-kettle
fish-trowel
flesh-brush
floor-cloth
flower-bowl
fly-catcher
fly-swotter
foot-warmer
fourposter
garbage-can

gas-bracket
gas-lighter
gramophone
grand piano
hair lotion
hair pomade
jardinière
knife-board
langesettle
lead pencil
letter-rack
loose cover
marking ink
musical box
music-stand
music-stool
napkin ring
needle-book
needle-case
needlework
night-light
nutcracker
opera glass
overmantel
pack-saddle
pack-thread
paper-knife
paper-stand
pencil-case
peppermill
persian mat
persian rug
pewter dish
photograph
pianoforte
piano stool
pile carpet
pillowcase
pillowslip
pincushion
plate-glass
pocket-book
prayer-book
rattan-cane
razor-strop
riding-whip
rolling-pin
saddle-bags
salt-cellar
scatter rug
sealing-wax
secretaire
shower-bath
soda syphon
spectacles
spirit lamp
stamp-album
stationery
step-ladder

strip light
tablecloth
table linen
tablespoon
television
time-keeper
time-switch
tobacco-jar
toilet roll
toothbrush
toothpaste
truckle-bed
trug-basket
trundlebed
typewriter
upholstery
vapour-bath
warming-pan
wash basket
wassail-cup
watch-chain
watch-glass
watch-guard
watch-light
watch-stand
window-seat
wine-bottle
wine-cooler
work basket
wrist-watch

11

account book
address book
airing horse
alarum clock
alarum watch
attaché case
basket chair
bed-hangings
billiard-cue
bolster-case
book matches
boot-scraper
braising-pan
butter-print
butter-stamp
button-stick
candelabrum
candlestick
centrepiece
chafing-dish
cheese board
cheval-glass
chiffonnier
clothes-hook
clothes-line

coal-scuttle
coffee table
coir-matting
counterpane
curtain hook
curtain rail
curtain ring
despatch-box
dining-table
dinner-table
dispatch-box
dredging-box
dripping-pan
Dutch carpet
finger-glass
fire-lighter
first-aid box
floor polish
flour-dredge
footcushion
foot-scraper
fountain-pen
gaming-table
garden chair
hearth brush
knick-knacks
lamp-chimney
leather case
linen basket
minute glass
minute watch
mosquito-net
nut-crackers
ormolu clock
paper-basket
paperweight
picture-rail
pipe-lighter
pocket flask
pocket-glass
pocket-knife
porridge-pot
portmanteau
primus stove
pumice-stone
reading lamp
roll-top desk
saddle-cloth
safety-razor
scuttle-cask
shopping bag
siphon-stand
slate-pencil
stair-carpet
straw pillow
syphon-stand
table napkin
table-runner
tape-measure

tea-canister
thermometer
tin-lined box
tissue paper
tobacco pipe
toilet-cover
toilet-table
tooth-powder
vacuum flask
vinaigrette
waffle-irons
washing line
wash-leather
wassail-bowl
waste-basket
water heater
watering-can
watering-pot
window blind
writing-desk

12

adhesive tape
antimacassar
bedside light
bedside table
blotting book
bottle-opener
bucking stool
camp-bedstead
candleholder
candle-sconce
carpet beater
chaise longue
chesterfield
churchwarden
clothes-brush
clothes drier
clothes-horse
console table
cottage piano
cup and saucer
despatch-case
dessert-spoon
dispatch-case
dressing-case
drinking-horn
Dutch dresser
electric bulb
electric fire
electric iron
electric lamp
fan regulator
field-glasses
fish-strainer
flour-dredger
flower-basket

folding stool
gate-leg table
gladstone bag
hot-water tank
hubble-bubble
ironing board
ironing table
judgment-seat
kitchen table
kneehole desk
knife-cleaner
looking-glass
lucifer match
nail-scissors
nutmeg-grater
opera-glasses
packing cloth
packing paper
packing sheet
paraffin lamp
picnic basket
picnic hamper
playing cards
porridge-bowl
postage stamp
reading glass
record-player
refrigerator
roasting-rack
rocking chair
rocking horse
standard lamp
straw bolster
sweating-bath
table lighter
table service
tallow-candle
tape recorder
thermos flask
tin-lined case
toasting fork
tobacco pouch
toilette case
trestle table
turkey carpet
visitors' book
upright piano
walking-staff
walking stick
washing board
water pitcher
Welsh dresser
wicker basket
Windsor chair
wine decanter
writing table
writing paper

13

billiard balls
billiard table
blotting paper
carpet sweeper
chopping block
chopping knife
cribbage board
dressing-table
electric clock
electric stove
feather pillow
feeding bottle
filing cabinet
florence flask
folding screen
medicine glass
netting needle
newspaper rack
packing needle
persian blinds
persian carpet
petrol-lighter
ping-pong table
quizzing-glass
razor-stropper
roulette table
sewing-machine
smoothing-iron
sounding-board
straw mattress
styptic pencil
turnover table
umbrella stand
vacuum cleaner
visiting-cards
washhand-stand
window curtain
witney blanket

14

anglepoise lamp
billiard marker
chamber-hanging
chest-of-drawers
cocktail-shaker
eiderdown quilt
electric cooker
electric geyser
electric kettle
feather bolster
glove-stretcher
hot water bottle
kitchen dresser
meerschaum pipe
tobacco stopper

Venetian blinds	*15*	gate-legged table	photograph album
washing machine		Japanese lantern	photograph frame
	electric blanket	knitting needles	pneumatic pillow
	feather mattress	mosquito curtain	
	garden furniture	pestle and mortar	

Games, sports and pastimes

2 AND 3	*4*	polo	basto	mount
		pool	batik	music
ace	arts	punt	bingo	ombre
art	bait	quiz	bogey	opera
bat	ball	race	boule	paced
bet	bias	ride	bowls	pacer
bob	bite	ring	boxer	party
bow	boat	rink	caddy	piste
box	brag	ruff	capot	pitch
bye	club	shot	cards	point
cue	crib	sice	chase	poker
cup	dice	side	cheat	prize
die	dive	skip	chess	queen
eo	draw	slam	clubs	quits
fun	epée	slip	craps	racer
gym	faro	snap	dance	rafia
hux	foil	solo	darts	reins
jeu	fore	spar	Derby	relay
lap	foul	suit	deuce	revel
l.b.w.	gala	swim	dicer	rider
lie	game	team	diver	rifle
lob	goal	toss	dormy	rodeo
lov	golf	tote	drama	roque
nap	grab	trap	drawn	rugby
oar	hunt	trey	drive	rummy
out	I-spy	trip	dummy	samba
pam	jack	trot	extra	score
peg	jazz	turf	field	skate
put	judo	vint	fives	skier
rod	king	vole	fluke	slice
set	knar	volt	glaze	slide
ski	knur	walk	halma	slosh
sod	love	whip	hobby	spade
tag	ludo	wide	joker	spoon
taw	luge	xyst	joust	sport
tie	main	yoga	kayle	spurt
tig	mate	yo-yo	kendo	stalk
tir	meet		knave	start
top	mime		lasso	stump
toy	miss	*5*	links	stunt
win	mora		lists	swing
won	Oaks	amuse	loser	tarot
	odds	arena	lotto	throw
	pace	baign	lucky	touch
	pawn	bails	match	track
	play	bandy	monte	train

trial	hockey	skater	checker	may-pole
trump	hoopla	skiing	chicane	misdeal
vault	hunter	slalom	codille	montant
veney	hurdle	slider	collage	mosaics
wager	huxing	soccer	concert	netball
whist	jetton	soirée	contest	oarsman
yacht	jigger	squash	cookery	oarsmen
	jigsaw	stroke	cooking	off-side
	jockey	stumps	cooncan	old-maid
6	karate	T'ai chi	cricket	origami
	kicker	tarocs	crochet	outdoor
aikido	knight	tarots	croquet	outride
archer	kung-fu	tenace	curling	pageant
ballet	lariat	tennis	cycling	pallone
banker	leg-bye	tierce	cyclist	pastime
basset	loader	tip-cat	dancing	pat ball
battue	lobber	toss-up	decider	pharaoh
bewits	manege	travel	diabolo	picquet
bowler	marker	trophy	dice-box	pitcher
bowman	mashie	umpire	discard	play day
boxing	masque	unfair	doddart	playing
bridge	maying	venery	doubles	play off
caddie	no-ball	victor	drawing	pontoon
casino	not-out	vigaro	dribble	pottery
cinque	outing	wicket	driving	potting
clumps	outrun	winner	etching	primero
cobnut	pacing	xystos	fencing	pushpin
cockal	paddle	yorker	fielder	putting
course	peg-top		fishery	rackets
crafts	pelota	**7**	fishing	reading
crambo	piquet		fluking	referee
crease	pistol	agonism	forward	regatta
cup tie	player	agonist	fowling	reversi
dealer	poetry	allonge	fox hunt	ringtaw
defeat	punter	amateur	gambler	rinking
discus	putter	ambs-ace	glasses	roadhog
diving	puzzle	ames-ace	glazing	running
domino	quoits	angling	gliding	sailing
driver	rabbit	archery	golf bag	saltant
dyeing	racing	athlete	gunning	scooter
ecarté	racket	auction	gymnast	scoring
euchre	raffle	average	hunting	scratch
falcon	rattle	bathing	hurling	sculler
finish	recite	batsman	innings	sea trip
fluker	record	batting	javelin	shuffle
flying	revoke	beagles	joy-ride	singing
gambit	riddle	benefit	ju-jitsu	singles
gamble	riding	bezique	jumping	skating
gammon	rowing	bicycle	keep fit	ski jump
gillie	rubber	boating	last lap	sliding
gobang	rugger	bone ace	leaping	snooker
go-kart	runner	bowling	loggats	St. Leger
googly	savate	bran-pie	lottery	stadium
gully	scorer	bruiser	love all	starter
gymnic	second	canasta	love set	sub-aqua
hammer	see-saw	carving	low bell	surfing
hazard	shinny	cassino	macramé	tilting
header	shinty	century	mahjong	tinchel
hiking	single	charade	marbles	tombola

top spin
tourney
trained
trainer
trapeze
'vantage
vaulter
wagerer
walking
wargame
weaving
weights
whip top
winning
wrestle
writing

8

all-fours
antiques
appliqué
aquatics
baccarat
baseball
biathlon
bost race
boundary
canoeing
carnival
carolina
catapult
ceramics
champion
charades
cheating
chessmen
climbing
commerce
contract
counters
coursing
cribbage
cup final
dead heat
deck golf
dominoes
doublets
drag-hunt
draughts
duelling
eurythme
eventing
exercise
face card
fair play
falconry
fielding

flat race
football
foot race
forfeits
fox chase
full back
game laws
gin rummy
goal line
golf ball
golf club
gymkhana
handball
handicap
harriers
high jump
hurdling
jiu-jitsu
jousting
juggling
knitting
korfball
lacrosse
leapfrog
long jump
long stop
love game
lucky-dip
marathon
may games
monopoly
motoring
movement
napoleon
natation
ninepins
olympiad
olympics
out-field
outsider
painting
palestra
pall-mall
patience
petanque
ping-pong
pinochle
pole jump
pony race
pope Joan
printing
proverbs
pugilism
pugilist
pyramids
quatorze
racquets
rambling
roulette

rounders
sack race
scrabble
sculling
shooting
sing-song
skipping
skittles
sledding
softball
somerset
spadille
sparring
sporting
stalking
stumping
swimming
teamwork
teetotum
third-man
tiny golf
toboggan
training
tray-trip
trial run
tricycle
trotting
tumbling
turf club
umpiring
vaulting
vauntlay
walkover
wall-game
woodwork
yachting

9

advantage
adventure
agonistes
agonistic
amusement
archeress
athletics
aunt-sally
babyhouse
badminton
bagatelle
ball games
bandalore
bicycling
bilboquet
billiards
blackjack
bob cherry
breakdown

broad jump
bull board
bull feast
bullfight
camelling
challenge
checkmate
cherry pit
chicanery
clock golf
close time
cockfight
cockmatch
conqueror
court-card
cricketer
cup winner
decathlon
deck games
decoy duck
dirt track
dog racing
drawn game
dumbbells
embrocado
engraving
entertain
equitancy
fairy tale
fancy ball
fish spear
frivolity
gardening
gate money
goal posts
golf clubs
grand slam
gymnasium
gymnastic
hatha yoga
hopscotch
horseplay
horserace
ice hockey
joy riding
lampadist
lob bowler
make merry
marooning
marquetry
megaphone
merrimake
merriment
merriness
motorboat
newmarket
night club
nine holes
novelette

overmatch
pacemaker
pageantry
palestric
palmistry
parcheesi
pedalling
philately
plaything
pole vault
potholing
prize-ring
programme
promenade
quadrille
racehorse
racestand
reception
relay race
repasture
revelment
revel rout
river trip
rolly poly
scorching
scorecard
scrapbook
sculpture
showplace
shrimping
ski runner
skylarker
sleighing
smock race
solitaire
spectacle
sportsman
springing
square-leg
stalemate
stool ball
stopwatch
storybook
stroke oar
summerset
symposiac
symposium
tablegame
tabletalk
test match
tie dyeing
tip and run
torch race
touch line
trap stick
trial game
trial race
trump card
untrained

victoress
vingt-et-un
wandering
water jump
water polo
whipper-in
whirligig
whistling
woodcraft
wrestling
yacht-race
yachtsman

10

acrobatics
agonistics
agonothete
backgammon
ballooning
basket-ball
bat-fowling
battledoor
battledore
bear garden
blind harry
challenger
chessboard
collecting
competitor
conundrums
cover-point
cricket-bat
cup-and-ball
deck quoits
deck tennis
derby sweep
doll's house
dumb crambo
eel fishing
embroidery
enamelling
equitation
fancy dress
fast bowler
feathering
feuilleton
field gmes
fishing net
fishing rod
fisticuffs
fives court
flat racing
flop-dragon
fly-fishing
fox-hunting
goalkeeper
goalkicker

grandstand
greasy pole
groundbait
gymnastics
handspring
handy-dandy
hippodrome
hobby horse
hockey ball
hockey club
hotcockles
hucklebone
humming-top
hunting box
hurdle race
ice dancing
ice sailing
ice skating
kettle pin
lace making
lampadrome
landing net
lansquenet
lawn tennis
ledger line
lob bowling
masquerade
midget golf
Monte Carlo
needlework
opposition
palestrian
pancratist
pancratium
paper chase
pentathlon
philopoena
pony racing
pot hunting
prison base
prize fight
put-and-take
racecourse
raceground
recreation
relaxation
riding pony
riding whip
rollicking
rotary club
roundabout
rowing club
saturnalia
scoreboard
scratch man
sea bathing
shovepenny
shuffle cap
silk screen

ski running
skylarking
slow bowler
snapdragon
somersault
spillikins
stirrup cup
strokesman
surf riding
sweepstake
switchback
table bowls
tap dancing
tarantella
tauromachy
team spirit
tennis ball
thimblerig
tomfoolery
tournament
travelling
trial match
trick track
tricycling
trivia quiz
troumadame
victorious
volley ball
vulnerable
weighing-in
whirlabout
word making

11

agonistical
athleticism
barley-brake
bear baiting
bull baiting
bumblepuppy
calligraphy
chariot race
chess player
competition
competitive
county match
cricket ball
croquet ball
deck cricket
Derby winner
dicing house
disportment
diving board
fast bowling
field sports
fishing line
five hundred

flaconnade
fleet-footed
fluking-iron
folk dancers
free fishery
garden party
general post
grand circle
grass skiing
gymnasiarch
hang gliding
happy family
heavyweight
hide-and-seek
high jumping
high pitched
hockey stick
horse racing
horse riding
hunt counter
hunting horn
ice yachting
indian club
inter-county
lawn bowling
lightweight
lithography
long jumping
magic square
make-believe
masquerader
merrymaking
minute watch
oarsmanship
open-air life
picnic party
pillow fight
pole jumping
prawning net
prize giving
prizewinner
promenading
protagonist
public stand
regatta card
riding horse
river sports
rouge-et-noir
rough riding
sand sailing
schottische
shovel board
show jumping
shuttlecock
sightseeing
single stick
skateboard
skating club
skating rink

skittle pool
slot machine
slow bowling
snowballing
soap bubbles
span-counter
spelling bee
springboard
stirrup lamp
stonewaller
summersault
sweepstakes
sword player
table tennis
tale telling
tennis court
tent pegging
theatre-goer
tobogganing
top-spinning
totalisator
toxophilite
trap-and-ball
trick riding
trolmydames
trout-stream
uncontested
unexercised
water skiing
whipping-top
wild fowling
winning crew
winning side
winning team
wood cutting
world record
yacht racing

12

bantamweight
billiard ball
bird's nesting
bobsleighing
bowling alley
brass rubbing
bullfighting
butterfly net
calisthenics
championship
club swinging
cockfighting
competitress
consequences
cricket match
curling stone
deer stalking
draughtboard
drinking bout

field glasses
figure skater
first-nighter
flower making
glass blowing
googly bowler
hoodman-blind
horsemanship
housewarming
hunting-horse
huntsmanship
jigsaw puzzle
losing hazard
magic lantern
marathon race
marking board
medicine ball
merry-go-round
miss milligan
mixed bathing
mixed doubles
nimble footed
novel reading
obstacle race
Olympic games
opera glasses
parallel bars
parlour games
pitch-and-toss
pleasure trip
point-to-point
pole vaulting
professional
prize fighter
prize winning
pyrotechnics
Pythian games
racing stable
rock climbing
roller skater
rope climbing
rope spinning
rope throwing
sand yachting
scotch-hopper
shrimping net
skipping rope
skittle alley
span farthing
speed skating
starting post
state lottery
steeplechase
stilt walking
stirrup strap
storytelling
swimming gala
table croquet
table turning

tennis player
tennis racket
theatre-going
thoroughbred
tiddley-winks
tittle-tattle
wicket keeper
wlnning horse
winter sports

13

alectoromachy
alectryomachy
aquatic sports
auction bridge
ballad singing
blindman's buff
bubble blowing
camera obscura
Christmas tree
chuck farthing
cribbage board
cricket ground
cricket stumps
croquet mallet
deck billiards
divertisement
double or quits
entertainment
featherweight
figure skating
fishing tackle
googly-bowling
ground-angling
hare-and-hounds
horizontal bar
international
Isthmian games
jisaw puzzles
jollification
kiss-in-the-ring
machine junket
model yachting
motor cruising
musical chairs
Olympian games
parlour tricks
pillion riding
prisoner's base
prize fighting
record breaker
roller skating
roulette table
speed merchant
spirit rapping
sportsmanshlp
squash rackets

stalking horse
starting point
steeplechaser
sword fighting
ten-pin bowling
track and field
vantage ground
vaulting horse
victor ludorum
weight lifting
wicket keeping
winning hazard

14

all-in wrestling
billiard marker
billiard player
bladder angling
children's party
coin collecting
contract bridge
discus-throwing
divertissement
double patience
downhill skiing
driving licence
ducks-and-drakes
hunt-the-slipper
hunt-the-thimble
long-arm balance
mountaineering
record breaking
rubicon bezique
shove-halfpenny
steeplechasing
thimblerigging
weight training

15

ballroom dancing
cinderella dance
consolation race
crossword puzzle
Derby sweepstake
dirt track racing
greyhound racing
javelin throwing
king-of-the-castle
Old English bowls
public enclosure
short-arm balance
stamp collecting
talking pictures
three-legged race
unsportsmanlike
youth hostelling

Jewellery, gems, etc.

3 AND 4

bead
clip
gaud
gem
jade
jet
onyx
opal
ring
ruby
sard
stud
torc
unio
ural

5

agate
aglet
amber
badge
beads
beryl
bezel
bijou
brait
bugle
cameo
carat
clasp
coral
crown
ivory
jewel
lapis
links
nacre
paste
pearl
tiara
topaz
union
watch

6

albert
amulet
anklet
armlet

augite
bangle
bauble
brooch
corals
diadem
enamel
fibula
garnet
gewgaw
iolite
ligure
locket
olivet
pearls
pyrope
quartz
signet
sphere
spinel
telesm
tiepin
torque
turkis
wampum
zircon

7

abraxas
adamant
annulet
armilla
asteria
axinite
cat's eye
chaplet
coronet
crystal
diamond
eardrop
earring
emerald
espinel
euclase
faceted
filigree
jacinth
jewelry
olivine
pendant
peridot
regalia
ringlet

rubicel
sardine
sardius
sceptre
smaragd
spangle
telesia
trinket
yu-stone

8

adularia
aigrette
amethyst
armillet
bracelet
carcanet
cardiace
corundum
diopside
gemmeous
hallmark
hyacinth
intaglio
liginite
necklace
pectoral
rock ruby
sapphire
sardonyx
scarf-pin
shirt-pin
sparkler
sunstone
topazine

9

balas ruby
black onyx
black opal
breast-pin
brilliant
carbuncle
carnelian
cornelian
cufflinks
foil-stone
gold watch
jadestone
jewellery
marcasite

medallion
moonstone
morganite
moss-agate
paillette
phenacite
press stud
pyreneite
rubellite
seed pearl
solitaire
starstone
thumbring
trinketry
turquoise
uvarovite

10

adderstone
amber beads
andalusite
aquamarine
black pearl
bloodstone
chalcedony
chrysolite
coral beads
glass beads
madrepearl
Mocha stone
rhinestone
signet ring
topazolite
tourmaline
watch-chain
watchstrap
water opal
wristwatch

11

aiguillette
alexandrite
bostrychite
cameo brooch
chalcedonyx
chrysoberyl
chrysophrase
colophonite
crocidolite
lapis lazuli
slave bangle
wedding-ring

12 AND OVER

bead necklace (12)
chain bracelet (13)
coral necklace (13)
crystal necklace (15)

engagement ring (14)
eternity ring (12)
grossularite (12)
link bracelet (12)
mother-of-pearl (13)
mourning brooch (14)

mourning ring (13)
pearl necklace (13)
precious stone (13)

Kitchen utensils and requisites

3

bin
can
cup
hob
jar
jug
lid
mop
mug
pan
pot
tap
tin
tub
urn
wok

4

bowl
coal
cosy
dish
ewer
fork
grid
hook
iron
lard
oven
pail
peel
rack
salt
sink
soap
soda
spit
suet
trap
tray

5

airer
basin
besom
broom
broth
brush
caddy
china
cover
crock
cruet
doily
dough
drier
flour
glass
grate
grill
gruel
hatch
herbs
jelly
joint
knife
ladle
match
mixer
mould
paste
plate
poker
range
sauce
scoop
shelf
sieve
spice
spoon
steel
stock
stove
sugar

table
timer
tongs
towel
whisk
wiper
yeast

6

ash-pan
beaker
beater
boiler
bottle
buckct
burner
butter
candle
carver
caster
cooker
cupful
drawer
duster
eggbox
eggcup
fender
filter
flagon
funnel
gas-jet
geyser
grater
grease
haybox
heater
ice-box
jugful
juicer
kettle
larder
mangle

mincer
pantry
pastry
pepper
pickle
polish
pot-lid
posnet
primus
recipe
salver
saucer
scales
shovel
sifter
skewer
slicer
starch
tea-cup
tea-pot
tea-urn
trivet
tureen
vessel

7

basting
blender
bluebag
broiler
butlery
cake-tin
cambrel
canteen
chopper
coal-bin
coal-box
cuisine
cutlery
dishmat
dishmop
drainer

dresser
dust-bin
dust-pan
freezer
griller
grinder
infuser
kneader
kneeler
milk-jug
panikin
pie-dish
pitcher
platter
potager
sapples
saltbox
scuttle
seether
skillet
spatula
steamer
stew-pan
tea-cosy
tea-tray
terrine
toaster
tumbler
vinegar
wash-tub

8

bread bin
canister
cauldron
clapdish
colander
covercle
cream-jug
crockery
cupboard
dish rack

77

egg-slice
eggspoon
eggwhisk
fish fork
flan ring
flat-iron
gas stove
gridiron
hotplate
matchbox
meatsafe
oilcloth
oilstove
patty pan
saucepan
scissors
shoe box
slop bowl
stockpot
strainer
tea caddy
teacloth
teaplate
teaspoon
water jug

9

bain-marie
can opener
casserole
chinaware
coffee-cup
coffee pot
corkscrew
crumb tray
dishcloth
dish cover
egg beater
egg boiler
firegrate

fire-irons
fireplace
fish-knife
fish-plate
fish-slice
flue brush
frying-pan
gas burner
gas cooker
gas geyser
gravy boat
muffineer
pepper-box
pepper-pot
plate-rack
porringer
slop basin
soupspoon
sugar bowl
tea kettle
tin opener
wineglass

10

apple corer
biscuit box
bread board
bread knife
broomstick
butter dish
coffee mill
cook's knife
dishwasher
egg poacher
fish carver
fish kettle
floor cloth
flour crock
gas lighter
ice freezer

jelly mould
knife board
liquidizer
milk boiler
pan scourer
pepper mill
percolator
rolling pin
rotisserie
salamander
salt cellar
tablecloth
tablespoon
waffle iron

11

baking sheet
bread grater
butter knife
coalscuttle
dinner plate
dripping pan
flour dredge
meat chopper
paring knife
porridge pot
pudding bowl
sugar dredge
tea canister
water filter

12

breakfast-cup
carving knife
dessertspoon
double boiler
fishstrainer
flour dredger

hot cupboard
ironing board
kitchen range
knife cleaner
knife machine
measuring cup
nutmeg grater
porridge bowl
potato masher
potato peeler
pudding basin
pudding cloth
refrigerator
thermos flask
toasting fork

13

chopping board
coffee grinder
lemon squeezer
microwave oven
saucepan brush
water softener

14

crockery washer
fuelless cooker
galvanized pail
knife sharpener
mincing machine
pressure cooker
scrubbing brush

15

vegetable cutter

EDUCATION
Educational terms

2 AND 3		4	form	swot	bedel
	G.C.E.		gate	term	class
B.A.	gyp	bump	gown	test	coach
cap	M.A.	crib	hall		D.Phil.
C.S.E.	Ph.D.	dean	head		gaudy
D.E.S.	Pop	demy	hood	5	grant
don		digs	I.L.E.A.		house
fag		exam	poly	backs	lines

pupil
scout
sizar
study
tawse
tutor

6

A-level
beadle
bodley
bursar
course
day boy
degree
eights
fellow
Hilary
incept
locals
locker
master
matron
O-level
optime
reader
rector
regent
school
sconce
senate
tripos
warden

7

academy
battels
Bodley's
bull-dog
burgess
bursary
captain
college
crammer
diploma
dominie
faculty
gestalt
head boy
honours
lecture
monitor
nursery
prefect
proctor

project
provost
reading
scholar
seminar
student
teacher
teach-in
the high
torpids
Trinity
tuition

8

academic
ad eundem
backward
emeritus
encaenia
examinee
famulist
graduate
guidance
head girl
homework
learning
lecturer
little-go
maniple
May races
mistress
red-brick
research
roll-call
semester
seminary
send down
statutes
textbook
tuck-shop
tutorial
vacation
viva voce
wrangler

9

art master
art school
bilateral
classroom
collegian
day school
dormitory
great hall
pedagogue

playgroup
preceptor
prelector
president
principal
professor
refectory
registrar
scale post
scholarly
schoolboy
selection
speech day
streaming
sub-rector
trimester

10

blackboard
chancellor
collegiate
commonroom
day release
dining-hall
eleven-plus
exhibition
extra-mural
fellowship
fives court
form-master
headmaster
illiteracy
imposition
instructor
laboratory
Michaelmas
sabbatical
schooldays
schoolgirl
schoolmarm
schoolmate
schoolroom
school year
Sheldonian
university
vicegerent

11

convocation
examination
games master
head teacher
holiday task
housemaster
matriculate

mortarboard
music master
polytechnic
responsions
scholarship
school hours

12

aptitude test
congregation
exhibitioner
headmistress
kindergarten
master of arts
night-classes
public orator
pupil-teacher
regent master
schoolfellow
schoolmaster
Sunday school

13

adult learning
co-educational
comprehension
comprehensive
doctor of music
grammar school
matriculation
mature student
schoolteacher
science master
supply teacher
unergraduate
vice-principal

14

bachelor of arts
common entrance
junior wrangler
language master
Open University
schoolmistress
senior wrangler
vice-chancellor

15

doctor of science
master of science
school inspector
secondary modern

Oxford and Cambridge colleges

(C.) = Cambridge; (m.) = mixed;
(O.) = Oxford; (p.p.h.) = permanent private hall; (w.) = women.

3 – 5

B.N.C. (O.) (Brasenose)
Caius (C.) (Gonville and)
Clare (C.) (m.)
Green (O.)
Hall (C.) (Trinity Hall)
House (O.) (Christ Church)
Jesus (C. and O.)
Keble (O.)
King's (C.) (m.)
New (O.)
Oriel (O.)

6

Darwin (C.) (m.)
Exeter (O.)
Girton (C.) (w.)
Merton (O.)
Queens' (C. and O.)
Selwyn (C.) (m.)
Wadham (O.)

7

Balliol (O.)
Christ's (C.)
Downing (C.)
Linacre (O.)
Lincoln (O.)
New Hall (C.) (w.)
Newnham (C.) (w.)

St. Anne's (O.)
St. Cross (O.)
St. Hugh's (O.) (w.)
St. John's (C. and O.)
Trinity (C. and O.)
Wolfson (C. and O.)

8

All Souls (O.)
Emmanuel (C.)
Hertford (O.)
Magdalen (O.)
Nuffield (O.)
Pembroke (C. and O.)
Robinson (C.)
St. Hilda's (O.) (w.)
St. Peter's (O.)

9 AND 10

Brasenose (O.) (9)
Churchill (C.) (m.) (9)
Clare Hall (C.) (m.) (9)
Greyfriars (O.) (p.p.h.) (10)
Hughes Hall (C.) (w.) (10)
Magdalene (C.) (9)
Mansfield (O.) (p.p.h.) (9)
Osler House (O.) (10)
Peterhouse (C.) (10)
St. Antony's (O.) (9)
Saint Hugh's (O.) (w.) (10)
Saint John's (C. and O.) (10)

Somerville (O.) (w.) (10)
Templeton (O.) (9)
University (O.) (10)
Worcester (O.) (9)

11 AND 12

Campion Hall (O.) (p.p.h.) (11)
Christ Church (O.) (12)
Fitzwilliam (C.) (11)
Regent's Park (O.) (p.p.h.) (11)
Rewley House (O.) (11)
St. Benet's Hall (O.) (p.p.h.) (12)
St. Catharine's (C.) (12)
St. Catherine's (O.) (12)
St. Edmund Hall (O.) (12)
Saint Hilda's (O.) (w.) (11)
Saint Peter's (O.) (11)
Sidney Sussex (C.) (m.) (12)
Trinity Hall (C.) (11)

13 AND OVER

Corpus Christi (C. and O.) (13)
Gonville and Caius (C.) (16)
Lady Margaret Hall (O.) (w.) (16)
Lucy Cavendish (C.) (w.) (13)
Saint Benet's Hall (O.)
    (p.p.h.) (15)
Saint Catharine's (C.). (15)
Saint Catherine's (O.) (15)
Saint Edmund Hall (O.) (15)
St. Edmund's House (C.) (14)

Some boys' schools

(c.) = "College", as distinct from "School", in title.

4 – 6

Douai (5)
Dover (c.) (5)
Durham (6)
Eltham (c.) (6)
Epsom (c.) (5)
Eton (c.) (4)
Exeter (6)

Fettes (c.) (6)
Harrow (6)
Leys (The) (4)
Oakham (6)
Oundle (6)
Radley (c.) (6)
Repton (6)
Rugby (5)
St. Bees (6)

Stowe (5)
Trent (c.) (5)

7

Bedales
Bedford
Bloxham

Clifton (c.)
Dulwich (c.)
Felsted
Lancing (c.)
Loretto
Malvern (c.)
Mercers'
Oratory
Rossall

St. Paul's
Taunton
The Leys
Warwick

8

Abingdon

Ardingly (c.)
Beaumont (c.)
Blue Coat
Brighton (c.)
Denstone (c.)
Downside
Highgate
Mill Hill
St. Albans
St. Olave's
Sedbergh
Whitgift

Sherborne
Tonbridge
Uppingham
Wakefield

10

Ampleforth (c.)
Birkenhead
Bromsgrove
Cheltenham (c.)
Eastbourne (c.)
Greyfriars
Haileybury (c.)
Royal Naval (c.)
Shrewsbury
Stoneyhurst (c.)
Summerhill
Wellington (c.)
Winchester (c.)

11

Berkhamsted
Eton College
Framlingham (c.)
Giggleswick
Gordonstoun
Leatherhead
 (St. John's)
Marlborough (c.)
Westminster

12

Charterhouse
City of London
King's College (School)
Monkton Combe

13

Bedford Modern
Bedford School
Wolverhampton

14

Blue Coat School
Hurstpierpoint (c.)
Wellingborough

15

Christ's Hospital
Imperial Service (c).
King's, Canterbury
Magdalen College
 (School)
Merchant Taylors'

9

Blundell's
Bradfield (c.)
Bryanston
Cranbrook
Cranleigh
Dean Close
Liverpool (c.)

FAMOUS PEOPLE
Admirals

3 – 5

Anson (Lord)
Bacon
Blake
Boyle
Brand
Brock
Broke
Byng
Cowan
Dewar
Dewey
Drake
Field
Hawke
Hood (Lord)
Hope
Howes (Lord)
James
Jones
Keith
Kerr
Keyes (Lord)
Mahan
May
Milne
Moore
Noble

Rooke
Scott
Sims
Stark
Togo
Tovey
Tromp
Tryon

6

Beatty (Lord)
Bridge
Brueys
Calder
Colomb
Darlan
Dönitz
Duncan
Fisher (Lord)
Fraser
Halsey
Horton
Howard (Lord)
Jerram
Jervis
Keppel
Madden

Nelson (Lord)
Nimitz
Oliver
Parker
Popham
Porter
Raeder
Ramsay
Rawson
Rodney (Lord)
Rupert (Prince)
Ruyter
Scheel
Scheer
Shovel

7

Burnaby
Burnett
Dampier
de Chair
Doenitz
Exmouth (Lord)
Hopkins
Jackson
Markham
Rainier

Raleigh
Ronarch
Seymour
Sturdee
Tirpitz
von Spee
Watkins

8

Berkeley
Boscawen
Caldwell
Cochrane (Lord)
Cockburn
Colville
Craddock
Custance
de Robeck
de Ruyter
Fanshawe
Farragut
Jellicoe (Lord)
Mark Kerr
Muselier
Richmond
Saunders
Saumarez

Tyrwhitt
Villaret
van Tromp
Yamamoto

Frobisher
St. Vincent (Lord)
von Hipper
Warrender

von Tirpitz

11 AND *12*

Collingwood (11)
Culme-Seymour (12)
Elphinstone (11)
Mountbatten (Lord) (11)
Wester-Wemyss (Lord) (12)

9

Albemarle
Arbuthnot
Beresford (Lord)
Callaghan
Chatfield (Lord)
Duckworth
Effingham
Fremantle

10

Codrington
Cunningham
Evan-Thomas
Kempenfelt
Mountevans (Lord)
Somerville
Troubridge
Villeneuve

13 AND OVER

Cork and Orrery (Lord) (13)
Rozhdestvensky (14)

Celebrities

1. The World of Entertainment: theatre, opera, ballet, films, the circus, television, radio, music (classical, jazz, folk, pop, etc.).

3 AND *4*

Baez, Joan
Bass, Alfie
Bilk, Acker
Bron, Eleanor
Cash, Johnny
Coco (the clown)
Cole, George
Cole, Nat King
Cook, Peter
Day, Doris
Day, Sir Robin
Dean, James
Dors, Diana
Ford, John
Fry, Stephen
Fury, Billy
Getz, Stan
Gish, Lillian
Hall, Henry
Hall, Sir Peter
Hess, Dame Myra
Hope, Bob
Joad, Prof. Cyril
John, Elton
Kean, Edmund
Kerr, Deborah
Lean, David
Lee, Christopher
Lee, Peggy
Lunt, Alfred
Lynn, Vera
Marx brothers

Monk, Thelonious
More, Kenneth
Muir, Frank
Nunn, Trevor
Peck, Gregory
Piaf, Edith
Ray, Satyajit
Reed, Sir Carol
Reid, Beryl
Rix, Lord
Ross, Annie
Sim, Alistair
Swan, Donald
Tati, Jacques
Took, Barrie
Tree, Sir Herbert
Wise, Ernie
Wise, Robert
Wood, Sir Henry
York, Michael
York, Susannah

5

Adler, Larry
Allen, Chesney
Allen, Dave
Allen, Woody
Arden, John
Askey, Arthur
Baker, Dame Janet
Baker, Richard
Baker, Sir Stanley

Basie, Count
Bates, Alan
Benny, Jack
Black, Cilla
Blair, David
Boult, Sir Adrian
Bowie, David
Brain, Dennis
Bream, Julian
Brice, Fanny
Brook, Peter
Bryan, Dora
Clark, Lord
Clark, Petula
Cooke, Alistair
Costa, Sam
Cukor, George
Davis, Bette
Davis, Sir Colin
Davis, Miles
Davis, Sammy
Dench, Dame Judi
Dolan, Anton
Dyall, Valentine
Dylan, Bob
Evans, Dame Edith
Faith, Adam
Felix, Julie
Finch, Peter
Flynn, Errol
Fonda, Henry
Fonda, Jane
Frost, David
Gable, Clark

Gabor, Zsa Zsa
Garbo, Greta
Gigli, Beniamino
Gobbi, Tito
Gould, Elliot
Grade, Lord
Grant, Cary
Greco, Juliette
Green, Hughie
Haley, Bill
Handl, Irene
Hines, Earl
Holly, Buddy
Horne, Kenneth
Horne, Lena
James, Clive
James, Sid
Jones, Tom
Kazan, Elia
Kelly, Barbara
Kelly, Grace
Kempe, Rudolf
Korda, Alexander
La Rue, Danny
Leigh, Vivien
Lloyd, Harold
Losey, Joseph
Magee, Patrick
Marks, Alfred
Mason, James
Melba, Dame Nellie
Melly, George
Miles, Lord
Mills, Bertram

Mills, Mrs
Moore, Dudley
Moore, Gerald
Mount, Peggy
Negus, Arthur
Niven, David
Ogdon, John
Pears, Sir Peter
Quinn, Anthony
Reith, Lord
Scott, Terry
Smith, Bessie
Smith, Dame Maggie
Somes, Michael
Sousa, John
Starr, Ringo
Stern, Isaac
Swann, Sir Michael
Sykes, Eric
Tatum, Art
Teyte, Dame Maggie
Terry, Ellen
Tynan, Kenneth
Vitti, Monica
Wayne, John
Welch, Raquel
Welsh, Alex
Worth, Irene

6

Adrian, Max
Ashton, Sir Frederick
Bacall, Lauren
Barber, Chris
Bardot, Brigitte
Barnet, Lady (Isobel)
Barnum, P. T.
Bassey, Shirley
Baylis, Lilian
Bechet, Sidney
Bogart, Humphrey
Boulez, Pierre
Braden, Bernard
Brando, Marlon
Burney, Fanny
Burton, Richard
Callas, Maria
Caruso, Enrico
Casals, Pablo
Cleese, John
Colyer, Ken
Cooper, Gary
Coward, Sir Noel
Crosby, Bing
Curran, Sir Charles
Curzon, Sir Clifford
Cusack, Cyril

Cushing, Peter
de Sica, Vittorio
Disney, Walt
Dowell, Anthony
Duncan, Isadora
Fields, Gracie
Fields, W. C.
Finney, Albert
Greene, Sir Hugh
Garson, Greer
Godard, Jean-Luc
Goring, Marius
Groves, Sir Charles
Harlow, Jean
Heston, Charlton
Hiller, Dame Wendy
Hobson, Harold
Howard, Frankie
Howard, Trevor
Ingrams, Richard
Irving, Sir Henry
Jacobs, David
Jagger, Mick
Joplin, Scott
Keaton, Buster
Kemble, Fanny
Kramer, Stanley
Lennon, John
Lidell, Alvar
Lillie, Beatrice
Miller, Glenn
Miller, Jonathan
Mingus, Charlie
Monroe, Marilyn
Moreau, Jeanne
Morley, Robert
Morton, Jelly Roll
Mostel, Zero
Nerina, Nadia
Newman, Nanette
Newman, Paul
Norden, Dennis
Oliver, King
O'Toole, Peter
Parker, Charlie
Parker, Dorothy
Powell, Dilys
Previn, André
Quayle, Sir Anthony
Renoir, Jean
Robson, Dame Flora
Roger, Ginger
Rooney, Mickey
Savile, Sir Jimmy
Seegar, Peggy
Seegar, Pete
Sibley, Antoinette
Sinden, Donald
Snagge, John

Talbot, Godfrey
Tauber, Richard
Taylor, Elizabeth
Temple, Shirley
Waller, Fats
Waring, Eddie
Warner Brothers
Warner, David
Welles, Orson
Wilder, Billy
Wilder, Gene
Winters, Shelley
Wogan, Terry
Wolfit, Sir Donald

7

Andrews, Eamonn
Andrews, Julie
Astaire, Fred
Baillie, Isobel
Beecham, Sir Thomas
Bennett, Alan
Bennett, Jill
Bentine, Michael
Bentley, Dick
Bergman, Ingmar
Bergman, Ingrid
Blondin, Charles
Bogarde, Dirk
Branagh, Kenneth
Brubeck, Dave
Chaplin, Sir Charles
Chester, Charlie
Cocteau, Jean
Collins, Joan
Connery, Sean
Corbett, Harry
Domingo, Plácido
Donegan, Lonnie
Donovan
Dougall, Robert
Douglas, Kirk
Douglas, Michael
Edwards, Jimmy
Feldman, Marty
Fellini, Federico
Ferrier, Kathleen
Fonteyn, Dame Margot
Freeman, John
Garland, Judy
Garnett, Alf
Garrick, David
Gielgud, Sir John
Goldwyn, Sam
Goosens, Léon
Goodman, Benny
Guiffre, Jimmy

Guthrie, Sir Tyrone
Guthrie, Woody
Hammond, Joan
Hancock, Sheila
Hancock, Tony
Handley, Tommy
Harding, Gilbert
Hawkins, Jack
Hendrix, Jimi
Hepburn, Audrey
Hepburn, Katherine
Hoffman, Dustin
Holiday, Billie
Hopkins, Antony
Houdini, Harry
Jackson, Glenda
Jackson, Mahalia
Jackson, Michael
Jacques, Hattie
Karloff, Boris
Kendall, Kenneth
Kennedy, Ludovic
Kubrick, Stanley
Lympany, Moira
MacColl, Ewan
Markova, Dame Alicia
McQueen, Steve
Menuhin, Sir Yehudi
Montand, Yves
Monteux, Pierre
Murdoch, Richard
Novello, Ivor
Nureyev, Rudolf
Olivier, Lord
Pavlova, Anna
Pickles, Wilfred
Rambert, Dame Marie
Rantzen, Esther
Redford, Robert
Richard, Cliff
Roberts, Rachel
Rodgers, Richard
Rushton, William
Russell, Jane
Russell, Ken
Sargent, Sir Malcolm
Secombe, Sir Harry
Sellers, Peter
Seymour, Lynn
Shankar, Ravi
Shearer, Moira
Sherrin, Ned
Siddons, Mrs Sarah
Simmons, Jean
Sinatra, Frank
Stevens, Cat
Stewart, James
Swanson, Gloria
Ulanova, Galina

Ustinov, Sir Peter
Vaughan, Frankie
Vaughan, Sarah
Whicker, Alan
Wheldon, Sir Huw
Withers, Googie

8

Anderson, Lindsay
Anderson, Marian
Ashcroft, Dame Peggy
Beerbohm, Sir Max
Brambell, Wilfred
Bygraves, Max
Campbell, Mrs Pat
Chisholm, George
Christie, Julie
Clements, Sir John
Coltrane, John
de Valois, Dame Ninette
Dietrich, Marlene
Dimbleby, Richard
Eastwood, Clint
Flanagan, Bud
Flanders, Michael
Fletcher, Cyril
Grenfell, Joyce
Guinness, Sir Alec
Harrison, George
Harrison, Sir Rex
Helpmann, Sir Robert
Hoffnung, Gerard
Holloway, Stanley
Horowitz, Vladimir
Laughton, Charles
Lawrence, Gertrude
Liberace
Matthews, Jessie
Milligan, Spike
Mitchell, Joni
Mulligan, Gerry
Nijinski, Vaslav
Oistrakh, David
Oistrakh, Igor

Paganini, Niccolò
Pickford, Mary
Polanski, Roman
Redgrave, Sir Michael
Redgrave, Vanessa
Robinson, Edward G.
Robinson, Eric
Robinson, Robert
Scofield, Paul
Stephens, Robert
Streeter, Fred
Truffaut, François
Visconti, Luchino
Williams, Andy
Williams, John
Williams, Kenneth
Zeppelin, Led

9

Antonioni, Michelangelo
Armstrong, Louis
Ashkenazy, Vladimir
Barenboim, Daniel
Barrymore, John
Belafonte, Harry
Bernhardt, Sarah
Brannigan, Owen
Cardinale, Claudia
Chevalier, Maurice
Christoff, Boris
Courtenay, Tom
Dankworth, John
Davenport, Bob
Diaghilev, Serge
Ellington, Duke
Gillespie, Dizzy
Grisewood, Freddy
Engelmann, Franklin
Fairbanks, Douglas
Hampshire, Susan
Hitchcock, Alfred
Humphries, Barry
Klemperer, Otto
Leadbelly

Lyttelton, Humphrey
McCartney, Paul
Monkhouse, Bob
Morecambe, Eric
Pavarotti, Luciano
Pleasence, Donald
Plowright, Joan
Preminger, Otto
Reinhardt, Django
Reinhardt, Max
Sternberg, Joseph von
Streisand, Barbra
Thorndike, Dame Sybil

10

Barbirolli, Sir John
Eisenstein, Sergei
Fitzgerald, Ella
Littlewood, Joan
Michelmore, Cliff
Muggeridge, Malcolm
Richardson, Sir Ralph
Rubinstein, Artur
Rutherford, Dame Margaret
Sutherland, Dame Joan

11 AND OVER

Attenborough, Sir David (12)
Attenborough, Sir Richard
  (12)
Beiderbecke, Bix (11)
Chipperfield, Mary (12)
Fischer-Dieskau, Dietrich
  (14)
Granville-Barker, Harley
  (15)
Hammerstein, Oscar (11)
Springfield, Dusty (11)
Stradivarius, Antonio (12)
Terry, Thomas (11)

2. Sports and Games

ath. = athletics; *box.* = boxing; *ch.* = chess; *crc.* = cricket; *fb.* = football; *gf* = golf;
gym. = gymnastics; *hr.* = horseracing; *mr.* = motor-racing; *mt.* = mountaineering;
sj. = showjumping; *sw.* = swimming; *ten.* = tennis; *yt.* = yachting

3 AND 4

Ali, Muhammed *box.*
Amis, Dennis, *crc.*
Ashe, Arthur *ten.*
Best, George *fb.*
Borg, Bjorn *ten.*
Cash, Pat *ten.*
Clay, Cassius *box.*
Cobb, Ty *baseball*
Coe, Sebastian *ath.*
Endo, Yukio *gym.*
Fox, Uffa *yt.*
Graf, Steffi *ten.*
Hill, Graham *mr.*
Hoad, Lew *ten.*
Hunt, James *mr.*
Hunt, Sir John *mt.*
John, Barry *rugby*
Khan, Imran *crc.*
Kim, Nellie *gym.*
King, Billie Jean *ten.*
Law, Denis *fb.*
Lock, Tony *crc.*
May, Peter *crc.*
Moss, Stirling *mr.*
Read, Phil *motor-cycling*
Ruth, 'Babe' *baseball*
Snow, John *crc.*
Wade, Virginia *ten.*
Webb, Capt. M. *sw.*

5

Banks, Gordon *fb.*
Brown, Joe *mt.*
Bruno, Frank *box.*
Bueno, Maria *ten.*
Busby, Sir Matthew *fb.*
Clark, Jim *mr.*
Close, Brian *crc.*
Court, Margaret *ten.*
Curry, John *skating*
Davis, Joe *billiards*
Evans, Godfrey *crc.*
Evert, Chris *ten.*
Grace, Dr W. G. *crc.*
Greig, Tony *crc.*
Hobbs, Sir John *crc.*
Hogan, Ben *gf*
Irwin, Hale *gf*

Jones, Ann *ten.*
Keino, Kip *ath.*
Knott, Alan *crc.*
Kodes, J. *ten.*
Laker, Jim *crc.*
Lauda, Niki *mr.*
Laver, Rod *ten.*
Lendl, Ivan *ten.*
Lloyd, Chris *ten.*
Lloyd, Clive *crc.*
Louis, Joe *box.*
Moore, Ann *sj.*
Moore, Bobby *fb.*
Ovett, Steve *ath.*
Perry, Fred, *ten.*
Pirie, Gordon *ath.*
Revie, Don *fb.*
Roche, Tony *ten.*
Scott, Sheila *aviation*
Sloan, James *hr.*
Smith, Harvey *sj.*
Smith, Stan *ten.*
Spitz, Mark *sw.*
Tyson, Mike *box.*
Wills, Helen *ten.*

6

Barker, Sue *ten.*
Becker, Boris *ten.*
Bedser, Alec *crc.*
Benaud, Richard *crc.*
Botham, Ian *crc.*
Broome, David *sj.*
Bugner, Joe *box.*
Casals, Rosemary *ten.*
Cooper, Henry *box.*
Dexter, Ted *crc.*
Drobny, Jaroslav *ten*
Edberg, Stefan *ten.*
Edrich, John *crc.*
Fangio, Juan *mr.*
Foster, Brendan *ath.*
Fraser, Dawn *sw.*
Gibson, Althea *ten.*
Hadlee, Sir Richard *crc.*
Hutton, Sir Len *crc.*
Kanhai, Rohan *crc.*
Karpov, Anatoly *ch.*
Keegan, Kevin *fb.*
Korbut, Olga *gym.*

Lillee, Dennis *crc.*
Liston, Sonny *box.*
Merckx, Eddy *cycling*
Palmer, Arnold *gf*
Peters, Mary *ath.*
Player, Gary *gf*
Ramsey, Sir Alf *fb.*
Sobers, Sir Gary *crc.*
Smythe, Pat *sj.*
Stolle, Fred *ten.*
Taylor, Roger *ten.*
Thoeni, G. *skiing*
Titmus, Fred *crc.*
Turpin, Randolph *box.*
Wilkie, David *sw.*
Willis, Bob *crc.*

7

Boycott, Geoffrey *crc.*
Brabham, Jack *mr.*
Bradman, Sir Don *crc.*
Compton, Denis *crc.*
Connors, Jimmy *ten.*
Cowdrey, Colin *crc.*
Dempsey, Jack *box.*
Elliott, Herb *ath.*
Emerson, Roy *ten.*
Ferrari, Enzio *mr.*
Fischer, Bobby *ch.*
Foreman, George *box.*
Frazier, Joe *box.*
Greaves, Jimmy *fb.*
Hillary, Sir Edmund *mt.*
Hopkins, Thelma *ath,*
　hockey
Jacklin, Tony *gf*
Johnson, Amy *aviation*
Lineker, Gary *fb.*
McEnroe, John *ten.*
Mottram, Buster *ten.*
Nastase, Ilie *ten.*
Piggott, Lester *hr.*
Spassky, Boris *ch.*
Stewart, Jackie *mr.*
Surtees, John *mr.*
Tabarly, Eric *yt.*
Tensing, Sherpa *mt.*
Thomson, Jeff *crc.*
Trevino, Lee *gf*
Trueman, Freddie *crc.*
Worrell, Sir Frank *crc.*

8

Alekhine, Alexander *ch.*
Brinkley, Brian *sw.*
Chappell, Greg *crc.*
Chappell, Ian *crc.*
Charlton, Bobby *fb.*
Charlton, Jack *fb.*
Comaneci, Nadia *gym.*
Connolly, Maureen *ten.*
Cordobés, El *bullfighting*
Cousteau, Jacques-Yves
  diving
Docherty, Tommy *fb.*
Elvstrom, Paul *yt.*
Gligorić, Svetozar *ch.*
Graveney, Tom *crc.*
Kasparov, Gary *ch.*
Latynina, Larissa *gym.*
Marciano, Rocky *box.*
Matthews, Sir Stanley *fb.*

McClaren, Bruce *mr.*
Mortimer, Angela *ten.*
Newcombe, John *ten.*
Nicklaus, Jack *gf*
Phillips, Capt. Mark *sj.*
Richards, Sir Gordon *hr.*
Rosewall, Ken *ten.*
Weiskopf, Tom *gf*

9

Bannister, Sir Roger *ath.*
Bonington, Chris *mt.*
D'Oliveira, Basil *crc.*
Goolagong, Evonne *ten.*
Johansson, Ingemar *box.*
Lindbergh, Charles *aviation*
Patterson, Floyd *box.*
Pattisson, Rodney *yt.*
Underwood, Derek *crc.*

10 AND OVER

Barrington, Jonah *squash* (10)
Blanchflower, Danny *fb.* (12)
Capablanca, José *ch.* (10)
Chichester, Sir Francis *yt.* (10)
Constantine, Sir Leary *crc.* (11)
Fittipaldi, Emerson *mr.* (10)
Fredericks, Roy *crc.* (10)
Illingworth, Ray *crc.* (11)
Lonsbrough, Anita *sw.* (10)
Navratilova, Martina *ten.* (11)
Oosterhuis Peter *gf* (10)
Schockemohle, Alwin *sj.* (12)
Turischeva, Ludmila *gym.* (10)
Weissmuller, Johnny *sw.* (11)

3. Other prominent people

3 AND 4

Beit, Alfred (S. African financier)
Cid, The (Spanish hero)
Eddy, Mrs Mary Baker (U.S. founder of Christian Science)
Fox, George (Eng. preacher)
Fry, Elizabeth (Eng. social reformer)
Hus, Jan (Bohemian religious reformer)
Hall, Marshall (Eng. physiologist)
Hill, Octavia (Eng. social reformer)
Hill, Sir Rowland (Eng. pioneer in postal services)
Jung, Carl Gustav (Swiss psychoanalyst)
Kant, Immanuel (Ger. philosopher)
Kidd, Capt. William (Sc. pirate)
Knox, John (Sc. religious reformer)
Kun, Bela (Communist leader in Hungary)
Lee, Ann (Eng. founder of Society of Shakers)

Low, David (N.Z.-born cartoonist)
Luce, Henry Robinson (U.S. publisher)
Marx, Karl (Ger. Socialist)
Mond, Ludwig (Ger.-born chemist)
Nash, Beau (Eng. social arbiter)
Penn, William (Eng. Quaker, founder of Pennsylvania)
Polo, Marco (It. explorer)
Salk, Jonas Edward (U.S. scientist)

5

Acton, John Dalberg, Lord (Eng. historian)
Adams, Henry (U.S. historian)
Adler, Alfred (Austrian psychologist)
Amati, Nicolò (Italian violin-maker)
Astor, John Jacob (U.S. millionaire)
Astor, Nancy, Viscountess (first woman in Br. House of Commons)
Bacon, Roger (philosopher)

Baird, John Logie (Sc. pioneer in TV)
Banks, Sir Joseph (Eng. naturalist)
Barth, Karl (Swiss theologian)
Booth, William (founder of the Salvation Army)
Botha, General Louis (Boer leader)
Clive, Robert (Indian Empire pioneer)
Freud, Sigmund (Austrian pioneer psychoanalyst)
'Grock' (Adrien Wettach) (Swiss clown)
Hegel, Georg Wilhelm Friedrich (Ger. philosopher)
Herzl, Theodor (Hung.-born founder of Zionism)
Karsh, Yousuf (Armenian-born photographer)
Keble, John (Eng. divine)
Zeiss, Carl (Ger. optical instrument maker)

6

Alcock, Sir John William (pioneer aviator)
Attila (King of the Huns)
Barker, Sir Herbert Atkinson (Eng. specialist in manipulative surgery)
Baruch, Bernard Mannes (U.S. financier)
Beeton, Isabella (Eng. cookery writer)
Besant, Mrs Anne (Eng. theosophist)
Boehme, Jakob (Ger. theosophist)
Butler, Mrs Josephine (Eng. social reformer)
Calvin, John (Fr. theologian)
Capone, Al (U.S. gangster)
Caslon, William (Eng. typefounder)
Cavell, Nurse Edith (Eng. patriot)
Caxton, William (first Eng. printer)
Cicero, Marcus Tullius (Roman statesman and writer)
Diesel, Rudolf (Ger. engineer)
Dunant, Henri (Swiss founder of International Red Cross)
Euclid (Greek mathematician)
Fawkes, Guy (Eng. conspirator)
Fokker, Anton (Dutch aviation pioneer)
Graham, Billy (U.S. evangelist)
Halley, Edmond (Eng. astronomer)
Hearst, William Randolph (U.S. newspaper publisher)
Keynes, John Maynard (Eng. economist)
Luther, Martin (Ger. church reformer)
Mellon, Andrew William (U.S. financier)
Mesmer, Friedrich Franz (Ger. hypnotist)
Morgan, John Pierpont (U.S. financier)
Petrie, William Flinders (Eng. archaeologist)
Pitman, Sir Isaac (Eng. inventor of shorthand)
Planck, Max (Ger. physicist – formulated quantum theory)
Sandow, Eugene (Ger. strong man)
Stopes, Dr Marie (Eng. pioneer in family planning)
Tagore, Rabindranath (Indian poet and philosopher)
Turpin, Dick (Eng. highwayman)
Wesley, John (founder of Methodism)
Wright, Orville (U.S. pioneer aviator)
Wright, Wilbur (U.S. pioneer aviator)
Wyclif, John (Eng. religious reformer)

7

Abelard, Peter (Fr. philosopher)
Aga Khan (Ismaili leader)
Atatürk, Kemal (Turkish soldier and statesmen)
Bleriot, Louis (Fr. aviator)
Blondin, Charles (Fr. acrobat)
Boyd-Orr, John, Baron (Sc. nutritionist)
Buchman, Frank (U.S. founder of Moral Rearmament)
Cassini, Giovanni Domenico (It. astronomer)
Celsius, Anders (Sw. inventor of Centigrade thermometer)
Ehrlich, Paul (Ger. bacteriologist)
Erasmus, Desiderius (Dutch religious reformer and theologian)
Haeckel, Ernest Heinrich (Ger. naturalist)
Houdini, Harry (Erich Weiss) (Hung.-born magician and conjurer)
Leblanc, Nicolas (Fr. chemist)
Lesseps, Ferdinand de (Fr. engineer and diplomat)
Linacre, Thomas (Eng. founder of Royal College of Physicians)
Lumière, August and Louis (Fr. pioneers of cinematography)
MacEwen, Sir William (Sc. surgeon)

Scribner, Charles (U.S. publisher)
Spinoza, Benedict (Dutch philosopher)
Steiner, Rudolf (Hung.-born philosopher and educationalist)
Tussaud, Mme Marie (Swiss-born modeller in wax)

8

Avicenna (Arab philosopher)
Bancroft, George (U.S. historian)
Berkeley, George (Irish philosopher)
Carnegie, Andrew (Sc.-born philanthropist)
Earheart, Amelia (U.S. aviator)
Grimaldi, Joseph (Eng. clown)
Larousse, Pierre Athanase (Fr. encyclopaedist)
Mercator, Geradus (Flemish geographer)
Negretti, Enrico (It.-born instrument-maker)
Nuffield, William Richard Morris, Viscount (motor manufacturer and philanthropist)
Sheraton, Thomas (Eng. cabinet-maker)
Socrates (Gr. philosopher)
Wedgwood, Josiah (Eng. potter)

9

Arbuthnot, Alexander (printer of first bible, 1579, in Scotland)
Aristotle (Greek philosopher)
Arkwright, Sir Richard (inventor)
Blackwell, Dr. Elisabeth (first Eng. registered woman doctor)
Blavatsky, Madame Helena (Russian-born theosophist)
Courtauld, Samuel (Eng. silk manufacturer)
Descartes, René (Fr. philosopher)
Gutenberg, Johannes (Ger. founder of movable type)

Heidegger, Martin (Ger. philosopher)
Macgregor, Robert ('Rob Roy') (Sc. rebel)
Nietzsche, Friedrich (Ger. philosopher)
Pankhurst, Mrs. Emmeline (Eng. suffragette leader)

10

Bernadotte, Jean Baptiste (Fr. general and king of Sweden)
Cagliostro, Alessandro (Guiseppe Balsamo) (It. alchemist)
Flammarion, Camille (Fr. astronomer)
Guggenheim, Meyer (U.S. financier)
Macpherson, Aimée Semple (U.S. evangelist)
Max-Müller, Friedrich (Ger.-born philologist and orientalist)
Montessori, Maria (It. founder of Montessori educational method)

Rothermere, Harold Sidney Harmsworth, Viscount (Eng. newspaper publisher)
Rothschild, Meyer Amschel (Ger. financier)
Rutherford, Daniel (Sc. discoverer of nitrogen)
Schweitzer, Dr. Albert (Alsatian musician and medical missionary)
Stradivari, Antonio (It. violin-maker)
Swedenborg, Emanuel (Sw. theologian)
Vanderbilt, Cornelius (U.S. financier)

11

Beaverbrook, William Maxwell Aitken, 1st Baron (Canadian-born newspaper publisher)
Chippendale, Thomas (Eng. furniture designer)
Hippocrates (Greek physician)
Machiavelli (It. political reformer)

Nightingale, Florence (Eng. pioneer in training nurses)
Northcliffe, Alfred Harmsworth, Viscount (Irish-born newspaper owner)
Shaftesbury, Anthony Ashley Cooper, 7th Earl (Eng. philanthropist)
Wilberforce, Samuel (Eng. divine)
Wilberforce, William (Eng. abolitionist)

12

Krishnamurti, Jiddu (Indian mystic)
Schopenhauer, Arthur (Ger. philosopher)
Wittgenstein, Ludwig (Austrian-born philosopher)

Explorers

3 AND 4

Back
Beke
Bird
Byrd
Cam
Cook
Diaz
Gama
Gann
Hore
Leif
Park
Polo
Rae
Ross
   (Sir John)
Rut

5

Anson
   (Lord George)
Baker
Brown
   (Lady)
Bruce
   (General)
Burke
Cabot
Clark
Davis
Drake
   (Sir Francis)
Dyatt
Dyott
   (Commander)
Evans (Capt.)
Fuchs
Gomez
Hanno
Hedin
Lewis
Mosto
Nares
   (Sir George)
Necho
Nuyts
Oates (Capt.)
Ojeda
Parry
   (Admiral)
Peary
   (Admiral)
Penny (Capt.)
Prado
Scott (Capt.)
Smith (Capt.)
Speke (Capt.)
Terry
Welzl
Wills

6

Andrée
Austin (Capt.)
Baffin
Balboa
Barnes
Barrow
   (Sir John)
Bellot
Bering
Burton
   (Sir Richard)
Cabral

Conway
   (Sir Martin)
Cortes
Da Gama
de Soto
Dr. Gann
Duguid
Duluth
Eannes
Forbe (Rosita)
Fraser
Hanway
Hartog
Hedges
Henday
Hobson
Hudson
Hurley (Capt.)
Joliet
Kellas

Landor
Marcks
Mawson
Morton
Nansen
Nobile
   (General)
Osborn
Philby
Philip
Pocok (Capt.)
Siemel
Smythe
Tasman
Thomas
   (Bertram)
Torres
Treatt

7

Abruzzi
Almeida
Behring
Belzoni
Bullock
Cameron
Cartier
Charcot
Colbeck
Dampier (William)
de Ojeda
de Piano
de Prado (Albert)
de Windt
Doughty
Fawcett (Col.)
Francke
Fremont
Gilbert
Hawkins (Sir John)
Hillary (Sir Edmund)
Houtman
John Rae
Kearton
Kellett (Capt.)
Kennedy (William)
Kosloff
La Salle
McClure (Sir Robert)
Markham (Albert)
Mendana
Pizzaro
Raleigh (Sir Walter)
Shippee (Robert)
Stanley (Sir H. M.)
Stewart (Capt.)
Tristam
Tweedie (Mrs.)
Watkins
Wegener
Wilkins
Workman

8

Agricola
Amundsen
Bee-Mason
Champion
Clifford
Columbus
Coronado
de Torres
Diego Cam
Etherton
Filchner
Flinders
Franklin (Sir John)
Grenfell
Hovgaard
Humboldt
Jan Welzl
Johansen
Johnston
Kingsley
Lawrence
McGovern
Magellan
Ommanney
Radisson
Sverdrup
Thompson (David)
Vespucci
William (Sir Hubert)

9

Africanus
Cadamosto
Champlain
Cockerill
de Almeida
de Filippi
de Houtman
de Mendana
Emin Pasha
Frobisher (Sir Martin)
Gonsalvez
Grenville
Jenkinson

John Cabot
John Davis
John Smith (Capt.)
Kropotkin (Prince)
Lancaster
Mackenzie
M'Clintock
Marco Polo
Mrs. Marcks
Mungo Park
Sven Hedin
Vancouver
Van Diemen
Velasquez

10

Abel Tasman
Bransfield
Chancellor
Clapperton
Diego Gomez
Dirk Hartog
Dr. McGovern
Eric the Red
Herjulfson
Inglefield
Kohl-Larsen
Leichhardt
Leigh Smith
Lewis Cabot
McClintock
Mandeville
Prjevalsky
Richardson (Sir James)
Schliemann
Shackleton
Stefansson
Thomas Gann
Willoughby (Sir Hugh)

11

Admiral Byrd
Albuquerque
Captain Bird

Captain Cook
Court-Treatt
Dr. Sven Hedin
Dyhrenfurth
Jean Charcot
Kingdon-Ward
La Vérendrye
Leif Ericson
Livingstone
Nuno Tristam
Pieter Nuyts
Prince Henry
Roger Pocock
Vasco da Gama

12

Bougainville
Cabeza de Vaca
Cressy-Marcks (Mrs.)
Friar Oderico
Nordenskjöld
Piano Carpini
St. John Philby
Sascha Siemel
Savage Landor
Younghusband

13

Bellinghausen
Cherry Kearton
de Albuquerque
Hunter Workman
Louis de Torres
Richmond Brown (Lady)

14

Antam Gonsalvez
Bullock-Workman
Diego Velasquez
Fridtjof Nansen
Pierre de Brazza
Sebastian Cabot

Generals, field marshals, air marshals, etc.

3 – 5

Adam
Baird
Blood
Bock
Bols
Botha
Bruce
Byng
Clark
Clive
Condé
Craig
Dawes
Dayan
de Wet
Duff
Dyer
Foch
Giap
Gort
Gough
Grant
Haig
Hart
Horne
Ismay
Jacob
Jodl
Junot
Kleist
Kluge
Lee
Leese
Maude
Milne
Model
Monro
Moore
Munro
Murat
Neill
Ney
Nye
Paget
Parma
Patch
Peck
Pile
Raban

Robb
Saxe
Shea
Slim
Smuts
Soult
Sulla
Tojo
Tully
Weeks
White
Wolfe
Wood

6

Barrow
Buller
Butler
Caesar
Capper
Creagh
Crerar
Cronje
Daxout
Dundas
Eugene
French
Giraud
Gordon
Göring
Graham
Harris
Hunter
Joffre
Keitel
Koniev
Mangin
Marius
Moltke
Murray
Napier
Newall
Outram
Patton
Pétain
Plumer
Pompey
Portal
Raglan

Rommel
Rundle
Rupert (Prince)
Scipio
Spaatz
Tedder
Trajan
Wilson
Zhukov

7

Allenby
Blücher
Bradley
Cadorna
Capello
Dempsey
Douglas
Fairfax
Gamelin
Gaselee
Gatacre
Gonzalo
Gourand
Haldane
Joubert
Leclerc
Lyautey
McMahon
MacMunn
Masséna
Maurice
Maxwell
Methuen
Mortier
Nivelle
O'Connor
Roberts
Salmond
Sherman
Simpson
Stewart
Turenne
Weygand
Wingate

8

Birdwood
Brancker
Browning
Campbell
Chetwode
Cromwell
De Gaulle
Freyberg
Galliéni
Gleichen
Guderian
Hamilton
Hannibal
Havelock
Ironside
Lockhart
Manstein
Napoleon
Pershing
Radetsky
Saunders
Skobelev
Townsend
Urquhart
von Bülow
von Kluck
Wolseley

9

Alexander
Berthelot
Boulanger
Cambridge
Chermside
Connaught
Dundonald
Garibaldi
Harington
Higginson
Kitchener
Lyttelton
Ludendorf
Macarthur
Macdonald
Miltiades
Nicholson
Rawlinson

Robertson
Rundstedt
Trenchard
Wellesley
Willcocks

10

Alanbrooke
Auchinleck
Bernadotte
Chelmsford
Cornwallis
Eisenhower
Falkenhayn
Hindenburg
Kesselring
Kuropatkin
Montgomery
Timoshenko
Voroshilov
Wellington

11

Abercrombie
Baden-Powell
Brackenbury
de Castelnau
Marlborough
Ochterlonie
Strathnairn
Wallenstein

12 AND 13

Hunter-Weston (12)
Smith-Dorrien (12)
von Mackensen (12)
von Rundstedt (12)
Younghusband (12)

14 AND 15

Forestier-Walker (15)
Garnet-Wolseley (14)
Napier of Magdala (15)

Politicians and statesmen:

a selection

3 AND 4

Amin
Blum
Burr
Cato
Chou
Clay
Foot
Fox
Grey
Hess
Hull
Meir
Pitt
Pym
Rhee
Root
Rusk
Tito

5

Banda
Benés
Bevan
Bevin
Burke
Ciano
Cleon
Desai
Hiero
Hoare
Hoxha
Husak
Jagan
Kadar
Laval
Lenin
Marat
Nehru
Perón
Sadat
Simon
Smith
Smuts
Solon
Sulla

6

Bhutto
Borgia
Brandt
Bright
Caesar
Castro
Cavour
Chiang
Cicero
Cobden
Cripps
Cromer
Curzon
Danton
Dubcek
Dulles
Franco
Gadafy
Gandhi
Hitler
Horthy
Kaunda
Marcos
Marius
Mobutu
Mosley
Nasser
Pétain
Powell
Rhodes
Samuel
Stalin

7

Acheson
Allende
Batista
Bolivar
Bormann
Giscard
Gomulka
Halifax
Hampden
Himmler
Kennedy
Kosygin
Kreisky
Lumumba
Masaryk
Menies
Mintoff

Molotov
Nkrumah
Nyerere
Parnell
Pearson
Ptolemy
Redmond
Reynaud
Salazar
Sukarno
Trotsky
Trudeau
Vorster
Webster
Yeltsin

8

Adenauer
Augustus
Ayub Khan
Bismarck
Brezhnev
Bulganin
Cromwell
Daladier
De Gaulle
De Valera
Dollfuss
Duvalier
Goebbels
Hamilton
Kenyatta
Lycurgus
Makarios
Montfort
Morrison
Napoleon
O'Higgins
Pericles
Pinochet
Podgorny
Poincaré
Pompidou
Ulbricht
Verwoerd
Welensky

9

Alexander
Ben Gurion
Bonaparte

Bourguiba
Chou En-Lai
Churchill
Clarendon
Dionysius
Garibaldi
Gorbachev
Ho Chi Minh
Mussolini
Richelieu
Salisbury
Strafford

10

Clemenccau
Hindenburg
Khrushchev
Lee Kuan-Yew
Mao Tse Tung
Metternich
Ribbentrop
Sekou Touré
Talleyrand

11

Boumédienne
Castlereagh
Chamberlain
Cleisthenes
Robespierre
Shaftesbury

12

Bandaranaike
Hammarskjöld
Kemal Atatürk
Mendès-France
Themistocles

13 AND OVER

Chiang Kai-Shek (13)
Giscard d'Estaing (15)
Hailé Selassié (13)

Presidents of the United States

4 AND 5

Adams, John
Adams, John Quincy
Bush, George
Ford, Gerald
Grant, Ulysses S.
Hayes, Rutherford B.
Nixon, Richard M.
Polk, James K.
Taft, William
Tyler, John

6

Arthur, Chester A.
Carter, Jimmy
Hoover, Herbert
Munroe, James
Pierce, Franklin
Reagan, Ronald
Taylor, Zachary
Truman, Harry
Wilson, Woodrow

7

Harding, Warren G.
Jackson, Andrew
Johnson, Andrew
Johnson, Lyndon B.
Kennedy, John F.
Lincoln, Abraham
Madison, James

8

Buchanan, James
Coolidge, Calvin
Fillmore, Millard
Garfield, James A.
Harrison, Benjamin

Harrison, William
McKinley, William
Van Buren, Martin

9

Cleveland, Grover
Jefferson, Thomas
Roosevelt, Franklin D.
Roosevelt, Theodore

10

Eisenhower, Dwight
Washington, George

Prime ministers of Great Britain

4 AND 5

Bute, Lord
Derby, Lord
Eden, Sir Anthony
Grey, Lord
Heath, Edward
Major, John
North, Lord
Peel, Sir Robert
Pitt, William (the Younger)

6

Attlee, Clement
Pelham, Henry
Wilson, Sir Harold

7

Asquith, Herbert
Baldwin, Stanley
Balfour, Arthur
Canning, George

Chatham, Lord (Wm Pitt
  the Elder)
Grafton, Duke of
Russell, Lord John
Walpole, Sir Robert

8

Aberdeen, Lord
Bonar Law, Andrew
Disraeli, Benjamin
Goderich, Lord
Perceval, Spencer
Portland, Duke of
Rosebery, Lord
Thatcher, Margaret

9

Addington, Henry
Callaghan, James
Churchill, Sir Winston
Gladstone, William
Grenville, George

Grenville, Lord
Liverpool, Lord
MacDonald, Ramsay
Macmillan, Harold
Melbourne, Lord
Newcastle, Duke of
Salisbury, Marquis of
Shelburne, Lord

10

Devonshire, Duke of
Palmerston, Lord
Rockingham, Marquis of
Wellington, Duke of
Wilmington, Lord

11 AND OVER

Beaconsfield, Lord (12)
Campbell-Bannerman, Sir
  Henry (17)
Chamberlain, Neville (11)
Douglas-Home, Sir Alec (11)
Lloyd George, David (11)

Scientists, engineers and mathematicians

3 AND 4

Aird
Ball
Bell
Bohr
Bose
Coué
Davy
Ford
Gall
Gibb
Gold
Hahn
Hale
Hero
Hess
Howe
Koch
Low
Ohm
Paré
Ray
Reed
Swan
Watt
Wren

5

Bacon
Banks
Barry
Bondi
Boole
Boyle
Bragg
Brahe
Crick
Curie
Debye
Euler
Ewing
Fermi
Galen
Gamow
Gauss
Haber

Hardy
Henri
Hertz
Hooke
Hoyle
Jacob
Jeans
Joule
Klein
Krebs
Lodge
Maxim
Monod
Morse
Pauli
Pliny
Segrè
Smith
Volta
White

6

Ampère
Boffin
Brunel
Bunsen
Calvin
Cantor
Cardew
Dalton
Darwin
Dawson
Edison
Euclid
Froude
Fulton
Galois
Halley
Harvey
Hubble
Hughes
Hutton
Huxley
Jenner
Kekulé
Kelvin
Kepler

Kulper
Liebig
Lister
Mendel
Morgan
Napier
Nernst
Newton
Pascal
Pavlov
Perutz
Planck
Ramsay
Rennie
Roscoe
Stokes
Thales
Turing
Watson

7

Andrews
Banting
Charles
Compton
Coulomb
Coulson
Crookes
Dalmler
Da Vinci
Doppler
Faraday
Fleming
Galileo
Galvani
Hilbert
Huggins
Huygins
Kapitsa
Kendrew
Lamarck
Leibniz
Lockyer
Lorentz
Marconi
Maxwell
Medawar

Moseley
Newmann
Pasteur
Pauling
Peierls
Piccard
Ptolemy
Röntgen
Rumford
Seaborg
Siemens
Spinoza
Thomson
Tyndall
Venturi
Virchow
Wallace
Whitney

8

Agricola
Avogadro
Bessemer
Blackett
Chadwick
Crompton
De Forest
Einstein
Foucault
Franklin
Goodyear
Harrison
Herschel
Humboldt
Lawrence
Leibnitz
Linnaeus
Malpighi
Mercator
Millikan
Poincaré
Rayleigh
Thompson
Van Allen
Van't Hoff
Zeppelin

9

Aristotle
Armstrong
Arrhenius
Becquerel
Bernoulli
Cavendish
De Broglie
Descartes
Eddington
Fibonacci
Gay-Lussac
Heaviside
Kirchhoff
Lankester
Mendeleev
Michelson
Priestley
Ramanujan

10

Archimedes
Cannizzaro
Copernicus
Fahrenheit
Heisenberg
Hipparchus
Littlewood
Paracelsus
Rutherford
Stephenson
Torricelli

11 AND OVER

Grosseteste (11)
Le Châtelier (11)
Leeuwenhoek (11)
Oppenheimer (11)
Schrödinger (11)
Szent-Györgyi (12)
Van der Waals (11)

GEOGRAPHY
References for geographical lists

Adr. Adriatic Sea	Eth. Ethiopia	Nor. Norway
Aeg. Aegean Sea	Eur. Europe	N.Z. New Zealand
Af. Africa	Fin. Finland	Pac. Pacific Ocean
Afghan. Afghanistan	Fr. France	Pak. Pakistan
Alg. Algeria	Geo. Georgia	Papua Papua New Guinea
Am. America	Ger. Germany	Philip. Philippines
Antarc. Antarctic (Ocean)	Gr. Greece	Pol. Poland
Arab. Arabia	Him. Himalayas	Port. Portugal
Arabian Sea	Hung. Hungary	Pyr. Pyrenees
Arc. Arctic (Ocean)	Ind. India	Rom. Romania
Arg. Argentina	Indian Ocean	Rus. Russia
Arm. Armenia	Indo. Indonesia	S.A. South Africa
Asia M. Asia Minor	Ire. Ireland	S. Am. South America
Atl. Atlantic Ocean	Republic of Ireland	Sard. Sardinia
Aust. Austria	Isr. Israel	Saudi Saudi Arabia
Austral. Australia	It. Italy	Scot. Scotland
Azer. Azerbaijan	Jap. Japan	Sib. Siberia
Balt. Baltic (Sea)	Jord. Jordan	Sic. Sicily
Bangla. Bangladesh	Kaz. Kazakhstan	Slov. Slovenia
Belg. Belgium	Kir. Kirghizia	Sp. Spain
Belo. Belorussia	Lat. Latvia	Sri Sri Lanka
Boliv. Bolivia	Lith. Lithuania	Swed. Sweden
Braz. Brazil	Mad. Madagascar	Swit. Switzerland
Bulg. Bularia	Malay. Malaysia	Tadz. Tadzhikistan
Bur. Burundi	Med. Mediterranean (Sea)	Tanz. Tanzania~
C. Am. Central America	Mex. Mexico	Tas. Tasmania
Can. Canada	Mold. Moldavia	Thai. Thailand
Cen. Af. Rep. Central	Mon. Mongolia	Trin. Trinidad
African Republic	Moroc. Morocco	Turk. Turkey
Ch. Is. Channel Islands	Moz. Mozambique	Turkmen. Turkmenistan
Cors. Corsica	N. Af. North Africa	Ukr. Ukraine
Cze. Czechoslovakia	N. Am. North America	Uzbek. Uzbekistan
Den. Denmark	Nep. Nepal	Venez. Venezuela
E. Af. East Africa	N. Guin. New Guinea	Viet. Vietnam
E . I . East Indies	Neth. Netherlands	W. Af. West Africa
Eng. England	N.I. Northern Ireland	W.I. West Indies
Est. Estonia	Nig. Nigeria	Yug. Yugoslavia

Bays, bights, firths, gulfs, sea lochs, loughs and harbours

B. = Bay. Bi. = Bight. F. = Firth. Fi. = Fiord. G. = Gulf.
Har. = Harbour. L. = Loch (Scottish). Lou = Lough (Irish) S. = Sea.

2 – 4

Acre, B. of (Isr.)	Fyne, L. (Scot.)	Ob, G. of (Rus.)	Wash, The (Eng.)
Aden, G. of (Arab.)	Gilp, L. (Scot.)	Riga, G. of (Lat.)	
Awe, L. (Scot.)	Goil, L. (Scot.)	Siam, G. of (Asia)	### 5
Clew, B. (Ire.)	Kiel, B. (Ger.)	Suez, G. of (Red S.)	
Ewe, L. (Scot.)	Long, L. (Scot.)	Tay, F. of (Scot.)	Aqaba, G. of (Arab.)
	Luce, B. (Scot.)	Tees, B. (Eng.)	Algoa, B. (S.A.)
	Lyme, B. (Eng.)	Tor, B. (Eng.)	Benin, Bi. of (W. Af.)

Blind, B. (N.Z.)
Broom, L. (Scot.)
Chi-Li, G. of (China)
Clyde, F. of (Scot.)
Cutch, G. of (Ind.)
Enard B. (Scot.)
Evans B. (N.Z.)
False B. (S.A.)
Forth, F. of (Scot.)
Foyle, Lou. (Ire.)
Fundy, B. of (Can.)
Genoa, G. of (It.)
Hawke B. (N.Z.)
Izmir, G. of (Turk.)
James B. (Can.)
Leven, L. (Scot.)
Lions, G. of (Med.)
Lorne, F. of (Scot.)
Moray F. (Scot.)
Otago Har. (N.Z.)
Papua, G. of (N. Guin.)
Paria, G. of (S. Am.)
Table B. (S.A.)
Tunis, G. of (N. Af.)

6

Aegina, G. of (Gr.)
Aylort, L. (Scot.)
Baffin B. (Can.)
Bantry B. (Ire.)
Bengal, B . of (Ind.)
Biafra, Bi. of (W. Af.)
Biscay, B. of (Fr.)
Botany B. (Austral.)
Broken B. (Austral.)
Cambay, G. of (Ind.)
Cloudy B. (N.Z.)
Colwyn B. (Wales)
Danzig G. of (Pol.)
Darien G. of (S. Am.)
Denial B. (Austral.)
Dingle B. (Ire.)
Drake's B. (U.S.A.)
Dublin B. (Ire.)
Galway B. (Ire.)
Guinea, G. of (W. Af.)
Hervey B. (Austral.)
Hudson B. (Can.)
Ijssel S. (Neth.)
Linnhe, L. (Scot.)
Lübeck B. (Ger.)
Manaar, G. of (Ind.)
Mexico, G. of (Mex.)
Mounts B. (Eng.)
Naples, B. of (It.)
Panama, G. of (C. Am.)
Plenty B. of (N.Z.)

St. Malo, G. of (Fr.)
Sharks B. (Austral.)
Smyrna, G. of (Turk.)
Solway F. (Scot.)
Sunart, L. (Scot.)
Swilly, Lou. (Ire.)
Sydney Har. (Austral.)
Tasman B. (N.Z.)
Tonkin, G. of (S. China S.)
Venice, G. of (It.)
Walvis B. (S.A.)
Zuider S. (Neth.)

7

Aboukir B. (Med.)
Argolis, G. of (Gr.)
Baffin's B. (Can.)
Belfast Lou. (N.I.)
Boothia, G. of (Can.)
Bothnia, G. of (Swed.)
Bustard B. (Austral.)
Chaleur B. (Can.)
Delagoa B. (S.A.)
Donegal B. (Ire.)
Dornoch F. (Scot.)
Dundalk B. (Scot.)
Finland, G. of (Eur.)
Fortune B. (Can.)
Halifax B. (Austral.)
Hudson's B. (Can.)
Kaipara Har. (N.Z.)
Lepanto, G. of (Gr.)
Moreton B. (Austral.)
Pe-Chi-Li, G. of (China)
Pegasus B. (N.Z.)
Persian G. (Asia)
Salerno, G. of (It.)
Snizort, L. (Scot.)
Taranto, G. of (It.)
Tarbert, L. (Scot.)
Trieste, G. of (Adr.)
Trinity B. (Can.)
Volcano B. (Jap.)

8

Cagliari, G. of (It.)
Campeche, B. of (Mex.)
Cardigan B. (Wales)
Cromarty F. (Scot.)
Delaware B. (U.S.A.)
Georgian B. (Can.)
Hammamet, G. of (N. Af.)
Hang-Chow B. (China)
Honduras, G. of (C. Am.)
Liau-Tung, G. of (China)

Martaban, G. of (Burma)
Pentland F. (Scot.)
Plymouth Har. (Eng.)
Portland B. (Austral.)
Portland Har. (Eng.)
Quiberon B. (Fr.)
Salonika, G. of (Gr.)
San Jorge, G. of (S. Am.)
San Pablo B. (U.S.A.)
Spencer's G. (Austral.)
Thailand, G. of (Asia)
Tongking, G. of (S. China S.)
Tremadoc B. (Wales)
Weymouth Bay (Eng.)

9

Admiralty B. (N.Z.)
Broughton B. (Austral.)
Buzzard's B. (U.S.A.)
Cambridge G. (Austral.)
Discovery B. (Austral.)
Encounter B. (Austral.)
Frobisher B. (Can.)
Galveston B. (U.S.A.)
Geographe B. (Austral.)
Hermitage B. (Can.)
Inverness F. (Scot.)
Mackenzie B. (Can.)
Morecambe B. (Eng.)
Notre Dame B. (Can.)
Placentia B. (Can.)
St. Bride's B. (Wales)
St. George's B. (Can.)
St. George's B. (S. Am.)
Saint Malo, G. of (Fr.)
San Matias, G. of (S. Am.)
St. Vincent G. (Austral.)
Van Diemen G. (Austral.)
Venezuela, G. of (S. Am.)

10 *AND OVER*

Barnstaple B. (Eng.) (10)
Bridgwater B. (Eng.) (10)
California, G. of (Mex.) (10)
Canterbury Bi. (N.Z.) (10)
Camarthen B. (Wales) (10)
Carpentaria, G. of (Austral.) (11)
Chesapeake B. (U.S.A.) (10)
Christiania Fi. (Nor.) (11)
Conception B. (Can.) (10)
Great Australian Bi. (Austral.) (15)
Heligoland B. (Ger.) (10)
Pomeranian B. (Baltic S.) (10)
Port Jackson B. (Austral.) (11)
Port Philip B. (Austral.) (10)

95

Portsmouth Har. (Eng.) (10)   Saint Bride's B.(Wales) (11)   San Francisco B. (U.S.A.) (12)
Princess Charlotte B. (Austral.) (17)   St. Lawrence, G. of (Can.) (10)   Southampton Water (Eng.) (16)
Ringkøbing Fi. (Den.) (10)   Saint Lawrence G. of (Can.) (13)   Tehuantepec, G. of (Mex.) (12)
Robin Hood's B. (Eng.) (10)   Saint Vincent G. of (Austral.) (12)

Capes, headlands, points, etc.

C. = Cape. Hd. = Head, or Headland. N. = Ness. Pt. = Point.

3 AND 4

Aird Pt. (Scot.)
Ann, C. (U.S.A.)
Ayre Pt. (Eng.)
Baba, C. (Turk.)
Bon, C. (N Af.)
Busa, C. (Crete)
Cod, C. (U.S.A.)
Cruz, C. (S. Am.)
East C. (N Z.)
East Pt. (Can.)
Farr Pt. (Scot.)
Fear, C. (U.S.A.)
Fife N. (Scot.)
Fogo, C. (Can.)
Frio, C. (Braz.)
Frio, C. (W. Af.)
Hoe Pt. (Scot.)
Horn, C. (S. Am.)
Howe, C. (Austral.)
Icy C. (Can.)
King, C. (Jap.)
Krio, C. (Crete)
Loop Hd. (Ire.)
May, C. (U.S.A.)
Nao, C. (It.)
Naze (The) (Eng.)
Naze (The) (Nor.)
Nord, C. (Nor.)
Noss Hd. (Scot.)
Nun, C. (W. Af.)
Race, C. (Can.)
Roxo, C. (Can.)
Sima, C. (Jap.)
Slea Hd. (Ire.)
Soya, C. (Jap.)
Sur Pt. (S. Am.)
Toe Hd. (Scot.)
Turn N. (Scot.)
York, C. (Austral.)

5

Adieu, C. (Austral.)
Amber, C. (E. Af.)
Aniva, C. (Rus.)

Bauer, C. (Austral.)
Brims N. (Scot.)
Byron, C. (Austral.)
Clark Pt. (Can.)
Clare, C. (Ire.)
Corso, C. (Cors.)
Creus, C. (Sp.)
Dunge N. (Eng.)
Gallo, C. (Gr.)
Gaspé C. (Can.)
Lopez C. (W. Af.)
Malia, C. (Gr.)
Mirik, C. (W. Af.)
Negro, C. (W. Af.)
North C. (N.Z.)
North C. (Nor.)
Orme's Hd. (Wales)
Otway, C. (Austral.)
Quoin Pt. (S.A.)
Roray Hd. (Scot.)
Sable, C. (Can.)
Sable, C. (U.S.A.)
Sandy C. (Austral.)
San Ho, C. (Viet.)
Sheep Hd. (Ire.)
Slade Pt. (Austral.)
Sleat Pt. (Scot.)
Slyne Hd. (Ire.)
South C. (China)
Spurn Hd. (Eng.)
Start Pt. (Eng.)
Tavoy Pt. (Burma)
Troup Hd. (Scot.)
Verde, C. (W. Af.)
Wiles, C. (Austral.)
Worms Hd. (Wales)
Wrath, C. (Scot.)
Yakan, C. (Sib.)

6

Andres Pt. (S. Am.)
Bantam, C. (Indo.)
Barren, C. (Austral.)
Beachy Hd. (Eng.)
Blanco, C. (N. Af.)
Blanco, C. (S. Am.)

Branco, C. (S. Am.)
Breton, C. (Can.)
Buddon N. (Scot.)
Burrow Hd. (Scot.)
Burrow Pt. (Scot.)
Carmel, C. (Isr.)
Castle Pt. (N.Z.)
Comino, C. (Sard.)
Cuvier, C. (Austral.)
De Gata, C. (Spain)
De Roca, C. (Port)
Dodman Pt. (Eng.)
Dunnet Hd. (Scot.)
Egmont, C. (N.Z.)
Formby Hd. (Eng.)
Friars Pt. (U.S.A.)
Galley Hd. (Ire.)
Gallon Hd. (Scot.)
Glossa, C. (Turk.)
Lizard (The) (Eng.)
Orford N. (Eng.)
Palmas, C. (W. Af.)
Prawle Pt. (Eng.)
Recife, C. (S.A.)
Rhynns Pt. (Scot.)
St. Abb's Hd. (Scot.)
St. Bees Hd. (Eng.)
St. Mary, C. (Can.)
St. Paul, C. (W. Af.)
Sambro, C. (Can.)
Sanaig Pt. (Scot.)
Sidero, C. (Crete)
Sorell, C. (Austral.)
Tarbat, N. (Scot.)
Tarifa, C. (Sp.)
Tolsta Hd. (Scot.)
Wad Nun, C. (N. Af.)
Whiten Hd. (Scot.)
Yerimo, C. (Jap.)

7

Agulhas, C. (S.A.)
Arisaig Pt. (Scot.)
Bengore Hd. (N I.)
Bismark, C. (Green.)
Bizzuto, C. (It.)

Blanche C. (Austral.)
Charles C. (U.S.A.)
Clogher Hd. (Ire.)
Colonna, C. (Gr.)
Comorin, C. (Ind.)
De Palos, C. (Sp.)
De Penas, C. (Sp.)
De Sines C. (Port.)
Formosa C. (W. Af.)
Gregory, C. (Can.)
Gris-Nez, C. (Fr.)
Haytian, C . (W. I.)
Icy Cape (Can.)
Kataska, C. (Jap.)
Kennedy, C. (U.S.A.)
La Hague, C. (Fr.)
Leeuwin, C. (Austral.)
Matapan, C. (Gr.)
Milazzo, C. (Sic.)
Mondego, C. (Port.)
Mumbles Hd. (Wales)
Needles, The (Eng.)
Negrais, C. (Burma)
Orlando, C. (Sic.)
Ortegal, C. (Sp.)
Rattray Hd. (Scot.)
Romania, C. (Malay.)
Runaway C. (N.Z.)
St. Lucia C. (S.A.)
San Blas, C. (U.S.A.)
São Tomé, C. (Braz.)
Spartel, C. (N. Af.)
Strathy Pt. (Scot.)
Tegupan Pt. (Mex.)
Teulada, C. (Sard.)
The Horn (S. Am.)
The Naze (Eng.)
The Naze (Nor.)
Toe Head (Scot.)
Upstart, C. (Austral.)
Vincent, C. (U.S.A.)
Yang-tsi, C. (China)

8

Bathurst, C. (Can.)
Cambodia Pt. (Thai.)

East Cape (N.Z.)
Espicher, C. (Port.)
Fairhead, C. (N.I.)
Farewell, C. (Green.)
Farewell, C. (N.Z.)
Fife Ness (Scot.)
Flattery, C. (U.S.A.)
Foreland (The) (Eng.)
Gallinas Pt. (S. Am.)
Good Hope, C. of (S.A.)
Greenore Pt. (Ire.)
Hangklip, C. (S.A.)
Hartland Pt. (Eng.)
Hatteras, C. (U.S.A.)
Kaliakra, C. (Bulg.)
Kinnaird Hd. (Scot.)
Land's End (Eng.)
Loop Head (Ire.)
Maranhao, C. (Braz.)
Melville, C. (Austral.)
Palliser, C. (N.Z.)
Palmyras Pt. (Ind.)
Patience, C. (Jap.)
St. Albans Hd. (En.)
St. David's Hd. (Wales)
St George, C. (Can.)
St. Gowan's Hd. (Wales)
San Diego, C. (S. Am.)
San Lucas, C. (Mex.)
São Roque, C. (Braz.)
Sidmouth, C. (Austral.)
Slea Head (Ire.)
Sordwana Pt. (S.A.)
Strumble Hd. (Wales)
Sumburgh Hd. (Scot.)
Sur Point (U.S.A.)
Thorsden, C. (Arc.)
Turn Ness (Scot.)
Vaticano, C. (It.)

9

Bonavista, C. (Can.)
Brims Ness (Scot.)
Canaveral, C. (U.S.A.)
Carvoeira, C. (Port.)
Claremont Pt. (Austral.)
De Talbert Pt. (Fr.)
Dungeness (Eng.)
East Point (Can.)
Esquimaux, C. (Can.)
Farr Point (Scot.)
Girardeau, C. (U.S.A.)
Granitola, C. (Sic.)
Guardafin, C. (E. Af.)
Inishowen Hd. (Ire.)
Mendocino C. (U.S.A.)
Murchison C . (Can.)
Nash Point (Wales)

North Cape (N.Z.)
North Cape (Nor.)
Ormes Head (Wales)
Roray Head (Scot.)
Saint Abbs Hd. (Scot.)
Saint Bees Hd. (Eng.)
St. Francis, C. (Can.)
Saint Mary, (C. Can.)
Saint Paul, C. (W. Af.)
St. Vincent, C. (Port.)
Sand Patch Pt. (Austral.)
Sandy Cape (Austral.)
Sandy Cape (Tas.)
Santo Vito, C. (Sic.)
Sheep Head (Ire.)
Slyne Head (Ire.)
South Cape (China)
Spurn Head (Eng.)
Streedagh Pt. (Ire.)
The Lizard (Eng.)
Trafalgar, C. (Sp.)
Troup Head (Scot.)
Vaternish Pt. (Scot.)
Worms Head (Wales)

10

Beachy Head (Eng.)
Breakheart Pt. (Can.)
Buddon Ness (Scot.)
Burrow Head (Scot.)
Clark Point (Can.)
Conception Pt. (U.S.A.)
Duncansbay Hd. (Scot.)
Dunnet Head (Scot.)
Finisterre, C. (Sp.)
Galley Head (Ire.)
Gallon Head (Scot.)
Great Ormes Hd. (Wales)
Greenstone Pt. (Scot.)
Orford Ness (Eng.)
Palmerston, C. (Austral.)
Quoin Point (S.A.)
Rayes Point (S. Am.)
Saint Lucia, C. (S.A.)
St. Margaret Pt. (Can.)
St. Matthieu Pt. (Fr.)
San Antonio Pt. (Mex.)
San Lorenzo, C. (S. Am.)
Santa Maria, C. (Port.)
Selsey Bill (Eng.)
Slade Point (Austral.)
Sleat Point (Scot.)
Snettisham Pt. (Can.)
Start Point (Eng.)
Tarbat Ness (Scot.)
Tavoy Point (Burma)
The Needles (Eng.)
Tolsta Head (Scot.)

Walsingham, C. (Can.)
Washington, C. (Arc.)
Whiten Head (Scot.)

11

Andres Point (S. Am.)
Bengore Head (N.I.)
Bridewater, C. (Austral.)
Castle Point (N.Z.)
Catastrophe, C. (Austral.)
Clogher Head (Ire.)
De San Adrian, C. (Sp.)
Dodman Point (Eng.)
Downpatrick Hd. (N.I.)
Flamborough Head (Eng.)
Friars Point (U.S.A.)
Little Ormes Hd. (Wales)
Lizard Point (Eng.)
Mumbles Head (Wales)
Murraysburg, C. (S.A.)
Prawle Point (Eng.)
Rattray Head (Scot.)
Rhynns Point (Scot.)
Saint Albans Hd. (Eng.)
Saint David's Hd. (Wales)
Saint Gilda's Pt. (Fr.)
Saint Gowan's Hd. (Wales)
Sanaig Point (Scot.)
The Foreland (Eng.)
Three Points, C. (W. Af.)
Tribulation, C. (Austral.)

12 AND OVER

Ardnamurchan Pt. (Scot.) (12)
Arisaig Point (Scot.) (12)
Breakheart Point (Can.) (15)
Cape of Good Hope (S.A.) (14)
Cayenne Point (E. Af.) (12)
Claremont Point (Austral.) (14)
Conception Point (U.S.A.) (15)
Downpatrick Head (N.I.) (15)
Duncansbay Head (Scot.) (14)
Flamborough Head (Eng.) (15)
Gracias a Dios, C. (C. Am.) (12)
Inishowen Head (Ire.) (13)
North Foreland (Eng.) (13)
Northumberland, C. (Austral.) (14)
Palmuras Point (Ind.) (13)
Portland Bill (Eng.) (12)
Saint Margaret Pt. (Can.) (13)
Sand Patch Point (Austral.) (14)
San Francisco, C. (S. Am.) (12)
Strumble Head (Wales) (12)
Sumburgh Head (Scot.) (12)
Tegupan Point (Mex.) (12)
Vaternish Point (Scot.) (14)

Capital cities of the world

3 AND 4

Aden (Yemen)
Apia (W. Samoa)
Baku (Azer.)
Bern (Swit.)
Bonn (Ger.)
Doha (Qatar)
Kiev (Ukr.)
Lima (Peru)
Lomé (Togo)
Male (Maldives)
Oslo (Nor.)
Riga (Latvia)
Rome (It.)
San'a (Yemen)
Suva (Fiji)

5

Abuja (Nig.)
Accra (Ghana)
Agana (Guam)
Ajman (Ajman)
Amman (Jordan)
Berne (Swit.)
Cairo (Egypt)
Dacca (Bangla.)
Dakar (Senegal)
Delhi (India)
Dubai (Dubai)
Hanoi (Viet.)
Kabul (Afghan.)
Lagos (Nig.)
La Paz (Boliv.)
Macao (Macao)
Minsk (Belo.)
Paris (Fr.)
Praia (Cape Verde Is.)
Quito (Ecuador)
Rabat (Moroc.)
Sanaa (Yemen)
Saria (Yemen)
Seoul (S. Korea)
Sofia (Bulg.)
Sucre (Boliv.)
Tokyo (Jap.)
Tunis (Tunisia)
Vaduz (Liechtenstein)
Zomba (Malawi)

6

Ankara (Turk.)

Athens (Gr.)
Bagdad (Iraq)
Bamako (Mali)
Bangui (Cen. Af. Rep.)
Banjul (Gambia)
Beirut (Lebanon)
Belice] (Belice)
Belize] (Belize)
Berlin (Ger.)
Bissau (Guinea-Bissau)
Bogotá (Colombia)
Brunei (Brunei)
Dublin (Ire.)
Habana] (Cuba)
Havana]
Harare (Zimbabwe)
Hobart (Tasmania)
Kigali (Rwanda)
Kuwait (Kuwait)
Lisbon (Port.)
London (U.K.)
Luanda (Angola)
Lusaka (Zambia)
Madrid (Sp.)
Malabo (Equatorial
  Guinea)
Manama (Bahrain)
Maputo (Mozambique)
Maseru (Lesotho)
Masqat (Oman)
Mexico (Mexico)
Monaco (Monaco)
Moroni (Comoro Is.)
Moscow (Russia)
Muscat (Oman)
Nassau (Bahamas)
Niamey (Niger)
Ottawa (Can.)
Panama (Panama)
Peking (China)
Prague (Cze.)
Riyadh (Saudi)
Roseau (Dominica)
Saigon (Viet.)
Taipei (Taiwan)
Tehran (Iran)
Thimbu] (Bhutan)
Thimpu]
Tirana (Albania)
Vienna (Aust.)
Warsaw (Pol.)
Zagreb (Croatia)

7

Abidjan (Ivory Coast)
Algiers (Alg.)
Alma-Ata (Kaz.)
Andorra (Andorra)
Baghdad (Iraq)
Bangkok (Thai.)
Belfast (N. Ire.)
Bishkek (Kir.)
Caracas (Venez.)
Colombo (Sri)
Conakry (Guinea)
Cotonou (Benin)
Douglas (Isle of Man)
El Aaiun (W. Sahara)
Gangtok (Sikkim)
Jakarta (Indo.)
Kampala (Uganda)
Managua (Nicaragua)
Mbabane (Swaziland)
Nairobi (Kenya)
Nicosia (Cyprus)
Rangoon (Burma)
St. John's (Antigua)
San José (Costa Rica)
São Tomé (São Tomé
  and Principé)
Sharjah (Sharjah)
Stanley (Falkland Is.)
Tallinn (Est.)
Teheran (Iran)
Tbilisi (Geo.)
Tripoli (Libya)
Valetta (Malta)
Vatican (Vatican)
Vilnius (Lithuania)
Yaoundé (Cameroun)
Yerevan (Arm.)

8

Abu Dhabi (U.A.E.)
Asunción (Paraguay)
Belgrade (Yug.)
Brasilia (Braz.)
Brussels (Belg.)
Budapest (Hung.)
Canberra (Austral.)
Cape Town (S.A.)
Castries (St. Lucia)
Damascus (Syria)
Djibouti (Djibouti)
Dushanbe (Tadz.)
Freetown (Sierra Leone)

Fujairah (Fujairah)
Gaborone (Botswana)
Hamilton (Bermuda)
Helsinki (Fin.)
Katmandu (Nep.)
Khartoum (Sudan)
Kingston (Jamaica)
Kinshasa (Zaïre)
Kishinev (Mold.)
Lilongwe (Malawi)
Monrovia (Liberia)
N'Djamena (Chad)
New Delhi (Ind.)
Plymouth (Montserrat)
Pretoria (S.A.)
St. Helier (Jersey)
Santiago (Chile)
Tashkent (Uzbek.)
Valletta (Malta)
Victoria (Hong Kong)
Victoria (Seychelles)
Windhoek (Namibia)

9

Amsterdam (Neth.)
Ashkhabad (Turkmen.)
Bucharest (Rom.)
Bujumbura (Burundi)
Edinburgh (Scot.)
Gaberones (Botswana)
Grand Turk (Turks and
  Caicos Is.)
Guatemala (Guatemala)
Islamabad (Pak.)
Jamestown (St. Helena)
Jerusalem (Isr.)
Kingstown (St. Vincent)
Ljubliana (Slov.)
Mogadishu (Somalia)
Nukualofa (Tonga)
Phnom Penh (Cambodia)
Port Louis (Mauritius)
Porto Novo (Benin)
Pyongyang (N. Korea)
Reykjavik (Iceland)
St. George's (Grenada)
San Marino (San Marino
Singapore (Singapore)
Stockholm (Swed.)
The Valley (Anguilla)
Ulan Bator (Mon.)
Vientiane (Laos)

10

Addis Ababa (Eth.)
Basseterre (St. Christopher-
Nevis-Anguilla)
Bridgetown (Barbados)
Copenhagen (Den.)
Georgetown (Cayman Is.)
Georgetown (Guyana)
Kuwait City (Kuwait)
Libreville (Gabon)
Luxembourg (Luxembourg)
Mexico City (Mexico)
Montevideo (Uruguay)
Nouakchott (Mauritania)
Ougadougou (Burkina)
Paramaribo (Surinam)
Quezon City (Philip.)

Tananarive (Mad.)
Washington (U.S.A.)
Wellington (N.Z.)

11 AND OVER

Brazzaville (Congo) (11)
Buenos Aires (Arg.) (11)
Dar es Salaam (Tanz.) (11)
Guatemala City
(Guatemala) (13)
Kuala Lumpur (Malay.) (11)
Luang Prabang (Laos) (12)
Medina as-Shaab (Yemen) (13)
Port-au-Prince (Haiti) (12)
Port Moresby (Papua) (11)
Port of Spain (Trinidad and
Tobago) (11)

Ras al-Khaimah (Ras
al-Khaimah) (12)
St. Peter Port (Guernsey)
(11)
San Salvador (El Salvador)
(11)
Santa Isabel (Equatorial
Guinea) (11)
Santo Domingo (Dominican
Rep.) (12)
Tegucigalpa (Honduras)
(11)
Uaboe District (Nauru) (13)
Umm al-Qaiwain (Umm
al-Qaiwain) (12)
Vatican City (Vatican) (11)

Channels, passages, sounds and straits

Ch. = Channel. P. = Passage. Sd. = Sound. St.(s). = Strait(s).
Note - The land references are to give a general idea as to location.

3 AND 4

Bass St. (Austral.)
Coll, P. of (Scot.)
Cook St. (N.Z.)
Fox Ch. (Can.)
Jura Sd. (Scot.)
Mona P. (W.I.)
Nore (The) (Eng.)
Palk St. (Ind.)

5

Cabot St. (Can.)
Davis St. (Can.)
Dover, Sts. of (Eng.)
Downs (The) (Eng.)
Korea St. (Jap.)
Menai Sts. (Wales)
Minch (The) (Scot.)
North Ch. (Scot.)
Ormuz, St. of (Iran)
Puget Sd. (U.S.A.)
Sleat, Sd. of (Scot.)
Smith Sd. (Can.)
Sound (The) (Swed.)
Sunda, St. of (E.I.)

6

Achill Sd. (Ire.)
Barrow St. (Can.)

Bering St. (Pac.)
Biscay (Fr.)
Denmark St. (Green.)
Harris, St. of (Scot.)
Hecate St. (Can.)
Hudson St. (Can.)
Nootka Sd. (Can.)
Panama Canal (C. Am.)
Queen's Ch. (Austral.)
Solent (The) (Eng.)
Torres St. (Austral.)
Tromsø Sd. (Nor,)

7

Behring St. (Sib.)
Bristol Ch. (Eng.)
Cuillin Sd. (Scot.)
Dolphin St. (Can.)
English Ch. (Eng.)
Florida St. (U.S.A.)
Formosa St. (China)
Foveaux St. (N.Z.)
Georgia, St. of (Can.)
Le Maire St. (S. Am.)
Malacca St. (Malaya)
Messina, St. of (It.)
Molucca P. (E.I.)
Otranto, St. of (It.)
Pamlico Sd. (U.S.A.)
The Nore (Eng.)
Yucatan Ch. (Mex.)

8

Cattegat (The) (Den.)
Colonsay, P. of (Scot.)
Kattegat (The) (Den.)
Magellan St. (S. Am.)
Plymouth Sd. (Eng.)
Spithead (Eng.)
The Downs (Eng.)
The Minch (Scot.)
The Sound (Swed.)
Windward P. (W.I.)

9

Bonifacio, St. of (Med.)
Bosphorus (The) (Turk.)
Gibraltar, Sts. of (Spain)
Great Belt (The) (Den.)
Lancaster Sd. (Can.)
St. George's Ch. (Eng.)
Scapa Flow (Scot.)
Skagerrak (Nor. and
Den.)
Suez Canal (Af.)
The Solent (Eng.)
Van Diemen St. (Jap.)

10

Dogger Bank (N. Sea)
Golden Gate (U.S.A.)

Golden Horn (Turk.)
Kilbrennan Sd. (Scot.)
King George Sd.
(Austral.)
Little Belt (The) (Den.)
Mozambique Ch. (E. Af.)

11 AND OVER

Bab-el-Mandeb St. (Red
S.) (11)
Caledonian Canal (Scot.)
(15)
Dardanelles (The)
(Turk.) (11)
Goodwin Sands (Eng.)
(12)
Hampton Roads (U.S.A.)
(12)
Northumberland St.
(Can.) (14)
Pas de Calais (Fr.) (11)
Queen Charlotte Sd.
(Can.) (14)
Saint George's Ch. (Eng.)
(12)
The Bosphorus (Turk.)
(12)
The Dardanelles (Turk.)
(14)
The Great Belt (Den.) (12)
The Little Belt (Den.) (13)

Counties: United Kingdom and Republic of Ireland

(E.) = England. (Ire.) = Republic of Ireland. (N.I.) = Northern Ireland. (S.) = Scotland. (W.) = Wales.

Note.—As the names of some counties are commonly used in shortened form, both full and shortened names are given in this list. It also includes county names no longer officially in use.

3 AND 4

Avon (E.)
Ayr (S.)
Beds (E.)
Bute (S.)
Cork (Ire.)
Down (N.I.)
Fife (S.)
Kent (E.)
Leix (Ire.)
Mayo (Ire.)
Oxon (E.)
Ross (S.)
York (E.)

5

Angus (S.)
Banff (S.)
Berks (E.)
Bucks (E.)
Cavan (Ire.)
Clare (Ire.)
Clwyd (W.)
Derby (E.)
Devon (E.)
Dyfed (W.)
Elgin (S.)
Essex (E.)
Flint (W.)
Gwent (W.)
Hants (E.)
Herts (E.)
Hunts (E.)
Kerry (Ire.)
Lancs (E.)
Louth (Ire.)
Meath (Ire.)
Moray (S.)
Nairn (S.)
Notts (E.)
Perth (S.)
Powys (W.)
Salop (E.)
Sligo (Ire.)
Wilts (E.)

6

Antrim (N.I.)
Argyll (S.)
Armagh (N.I.)
Brecon (W.)
Carlow (Ire.)
Dorset (E.)
Dublin (Ire.)
Durham (E.)
Forfar (S.)
Galway (Ire.)
Lanark (S.)
London (E.)
Offaly (Ire.)
Orkney (S.)
Oxford (E.)
Radnor (W.)
Staff (E.)
Surrey (E.)
Sussex (E.)
Tyrone (N.I.)

7

Bedford (E.)
Berwick (S.)
Cumbria (E.)
Denbigh (W.)
Donegal (Ire.)
Gwynedd (W.)
Kildare (Ire.)
Kinross (S.)
Leitrim (Ire.)
Lincoln (E.)
Norfolk (E.)
Peebles (S.)
Renfrew (S.)
Rutland (E.)
Selkirk (S.)
Suffolk (E.)
Warwick (E.)
Wexford (Ire.)
Wicklow (Ire.)
Wigtown (S.)

8

Aberdeen (S.)
Anglesey (W.)
Ayrshire (S.)
Cardigan (W.)
Cheshire (E.)
Cornwall (E.)
Cromarty (S.)
Dumfries (S.)
Hereford (E.)
Hertford (E.)
Kilkenny (Ire.)
Limerick (Ire.)
Longford (Ire.)
Monaghan (Ire.)
Monmouth (E.)
Pembroke (W.)
Roxburgh (S.)
Somerset (E.)
Stafford (E.)
Stirling (S.)

9

Berkshire (E.)
Caithness (S.)
Cambridge (E.)
Cleveland (E.)
Connaught (Ire.)
Dunbarton (S.)
Edinburgh (S.)
Fermanagh (N.I.)
Glamorgan (W.)
Hampshire (E.)
Inverness (S.)
Leicester (E.)
Merioneth (W.)
Middlesex (E.)
Northants (E.)
Roscommon (Ire.)
Tipperary (Ire.)
Waterford (Ire.)
Westmeath (Ire.)
Wiltshire (E.)
Worcester (E.)
Yorkshire (E.)

10

Banffshire (S.)
Buckingham (E.)
Caernarvon (W.)
Carmarthen (W.)
Cumberland (E.)
Derbyshire (E.)
Devonshire (E.)
East Sussex (E.)
Flintshire (W.)
Gloucester (E.)
Haddington (S.)
Humberside (E.)
Huntingdon (E.)
Kincardine (S.)
Lancashire (E.)
Linlithgow (S.)
Merseyside (E.)
Midlothian (S.)
Montgomery (W.)
Nottingham (E.)
Perthshire (S.)
Shropshire (E.)
Sutherland (S.)
West Sussex (E.)

11 AND 12

Argyllshire (S.) (11)
Bedfordshire (E.) (12)
Berwickshire (S.) (12)
Clackmannan (S.) (11)
Denbighshire (W.) (12)
Dorsetshire (E.) (11)
East Lothian (S.) (11)
Forfarshire (S.) (11)
Isle of Wight (E.) (11)
King's County (Ire.) (11)
Lanarkshire (S.) (11)
Lincolnshire (E.) (12)
Londonderry (N.I.) (11)
Mid Glamorgan (W.) (12)
Northampton (E.) (11)
Oxfordshire (E.) (11)
Queen's County (Ire.) (12)
Radnorshire (W.) (11)
Renfrewshire (S.) (12)
Rutlandshire (E.) (12)
Tyne and Wear (E.) (11)
Warwickshire (E.) (12)

West Lothian (S.) (11)
West Midlands (E.) (12)
Westmorland (E.) (11)

13 AND 14

Aberdeenshire (S.) (13)
Brecknockshire (W.) (14)
Cambridgeshire (E.) (14)
Cardiganshire (W.) (13)
Dunbartonshire (S.) (14)
Dumfriesshire (S.) (13)
Glamorganshire (W.) (14)
Herefordshire (E.) (13)

Hertfordshire (E.) (13)
Inverness-shire (S.) (14)
Kircudbright (S.) (13)
Leicestershire (E.) (14)
Merionethshire (W.) (14)
Monmouthshire (E.) (13)
Northumberland (E.) (14)
North Yorkshire (E.) (14)
Pembrokeshire (W.) (13)
Somersetshire (E.) (13)
South Glamorgan (W.) (14)
South Yorkshire (E.) (14)
Staffordshire (E.) (13)
West Glamorgan (W.) (13)
West Yorkshire (E.) (13)

Worcestershire (E.) (14)

15 AND 16

Buckinghamshire (E.) (15)
Caenarvonshire (W.) (15)
Carmarthenshire (W.) (15)
Gloucestershire (E.) (15)
Huntingdonshire (E.) (15)
Montgomeryshire (W.) (15)
Northamptonshire (E.) (16)
Nottinghamshire (E.) (15)
Ross and Cromarty (S.) (15)

Countries and continents

Note.—This list includes names of former countries.

3 AND 4

Anam (Asia)
Asia
Bali (Asia)
Chad (Af.)
C.I.S. (Asia, Eur.)
Cuba (W.I.)
D.D.R. (E. Ger.)
Eire (Eur.)
Fiji (S. Pac.)
G.D.R. (E. Ger.)
Guam (Pac.)
Iran (Asia)
Iraq (Asia)
Java (Asia)
Laos (Asia)
Mali (Af.)
Nejd (Asia)
Oman (Asia)
Peru (S. Am.)
Siam (Asia)
Togo (Af.)
U.A.R. (Af.)
U.S.A. (N. Am.)
U.S.S.R. (Asia, Eur.)

5

Annam (Asia)
Assam (Asia)
Benin (Af.)
Burma (Asia)
Chile (S. Am.)
China (Asia)
Congo (Af.)

Egypt (Af.)
Fiume (Eur.)
Gando (Af.)
Ghana (Af.)
Haiti (W.I.)
India (Asia)
Italy (Eur.)
Japan (Asia)
Kandy (Asia)
Kenya (Af.)
Khmer (Asia)
Korea (Asia)
Libya (Af.)
Lydia (Asia)
Malta (Med.)
Natal (Af.)
Nauru (Pac.)
Nepal (Asia)
Niger (Af.)
Papua (E.I.)
Qatar (Asia)
Spain (Eur.)
Sudan (Af.)
Syria (Asia)
Tchad (Af.)
Tibet (Asia)
Timor (E.I.)
Tonga (Pac.)
Tunis (Af.)
Wales (Eur.)
Yemen (Asia)
Zaïre (Af.)

6

Africa

Angola (Af.)
Arabia (Asia)
Azores (Atl.)
Belice }
Belize } (C. Am.)
Bhutan (Asia)
Brazil (S. Am.)
Brunei (E.I.)
Canada (N. Am.)
Cathay (Asia)
Ceylon (Asia)
Cyprus (Med.)
Epirus (Eur.)
Europe
France (Eur.)
Gambia (Af.)
Greece (Eur.)
Guinea (Af.)
Guyana (S. Am.)
Hawaii (Pac.)
Israel (Asia)
Johore (Asia)
Jordan (Asia)
Kuwait (Asia)
Latvia (Eur.)
Malawi (Af.)
Malaya (Asia)
Mexico (N. Am.)
Monaco (Eur.)
Muscat (Asia)
Norway (Eur.)
Panama (S. Am.)
Persia (Asia)
Poland (Eur.)
Ruanda (Af.)
Russia (Eur., Asia)
Rwanda (Af.)

Serbia }
Servia } (Eur.)
Sicily (Eur.)
Sikkim (Asia)
Soudan (Af.)
Sweden (Eur.)
Taiwan (Asia)
Tobago (W.I.)
Turkey (Eur., Asia)
Ulster (Eur.)
Uganda (Af.)
Urundi (Af.)
Zambia (Af.)

7

Albania (Eur.)
Algeria (Af.)
Andorra (Eur.)
Antigua (W.I.)
America
Armenia (Asia)
Ashanti (Af.)
Assyria (Asia)
Austria (Eur.)
Bahamas (W.I.)
Bahrain (Arab.)
Bavaria (Eur.)
Belgium (Eur.)
Belarus (Eur.)
Bermuda (Atl.)
Bohemia (Eur.)
Bolivia (S. Am.)
Britain (Eur.)
Burkina (Af.)
Burundi (Af.)

Croatia (Eur.)
Dahomey (Af.)
Denmark (Eur.)
Ecuador (S. Am.)
England (Eur.)
Eritrea (Af.)
Estonia (Eur.)
Faeroes (Atl.)
Finland (Eur.)
Formosa (Asia)
Georgia (Asia)
Germany (Eur.)
Grenada (W.I.)
Holland (Eur.)
Hungary (Eur.)
Iceland (Eur.)
Ireland (Eur.)
Jamaica (W.I.)
Lebanon (Asia)
Lesotho (Af.)
Liberia (Af.)
Livonia (Eur.)
Macedon (Eur.)
Moldova (Eur.)
Morocco (Af.)
Namibia (Af.)
Nigeria (Af.)
Prussia (Eur.)
Romania }
Rumania } (Eur.)
St. Kitts (W.I.)
São Tomé (Atl.)
Sarawak (Asia)
Senegal (Af.)
Slovenia (Eur.)
Somalia (Af.)
Sumatra (E.I.)

Sumeria (Asia)
Surinam (S. Am.)
Tangier (Af.)
Tartary (Asia)
Tripoli (Af.)
Tunisia (Af.)
Ukraine (Eur.)
Uruguay (S. Am.)
Vatican (Eur.)
Vietnam (Asia)

8

Barbados (W.I.)
Bielarus (Eur.)
Botswana (Af.)
Bulgaria (Eur.)
Burgundy (Eur.)
Cambodia (Asia)
Cameroun (Af.)
Colombia (S. Am.)
Djibouti (Af.)
Dominica (W.I.)
Ethiopia (Af.)
Honduras (S. Am.)
Hong Kong (Asia)
Malagasy (Af.)
Malaysia (Asia)
Maldives (Ind.)
Moldavia (Eur.)
Mongolia (Asia)
Pakistan (Asia)
Paraguay (S. Am.)
Portugal (Eur.)
Rhodesia (Af.)
Roumania (Eur.)
St. Helena (Atl.)
Salvador (C. Am.)
Sardinia (Med.)
Scotland (Eur.)
Sri Lanka (Asia)
Tanzania (Af.)
Tasmania (Austral.)
Thailand (Asia)
Togoland (Af.)
Trinidad (W.I.)
Zanzibar (Af.)
Zimbabwe (Af.)
Zululand (Af.)

9

Abyssinia (Af.)
Argentina (S. Am.)
Argentine, The (S. Am.)
Australia
Babylonia (Asia)

Caledonia (Eur.)
Cameroons (Af.)
Costa Rica (C. Am.)
Gibraltar (Eur.)
Greenland (Arc.)
Guatemala (C. Am.)
Hindustan (Asia)
Indochina (Asia)
Indonesia (E.I.)
Kampuchea (Asia)
Kirghizia (Asia)
Lithuania (Eur.)
Luxemburg (Eur.)
Macedonia (Eur.)
Manchuria (Asia)
Mauritius (Ind.)
New Guinea (E.I.)
Nicaragua (C. Am.)
Nyasaland (Af.)
Palestine (Asia)
Pondoland (Af.)
San Marino (Eur.)
Singapore (Asia)
Swaziland (Af.)
The Gambia (Af.)
Transvaal (Af.)
Venezuela (S. Am.)

10

Antarctica
Azerbaijan (Asia)
Bangladesh (Asia)
Basutoland (Af.)
Belorussia (Eur.)
California (N. Am.)
Cape Colony (Af.)
Damaraland (Af.)
El Salvador (C. Am.)
Ivory Coast (Af.)
Kazakhstan (Asia)
Luxembourg (Eur.)
Madagascar (Af.)
Mauretania ⎫
Mauritania ⎭ (Af.)
Montenegro (Eur.)
Montserrat (W.I.)
Mozambique (Af.)
New Zealand (Pac.)
North Korea (Asia)
Seychelles (Ind.)
Shan States (Asia)
Somaliland (Af.)
South Korea (Asia)
South Yemen (Asia)
Tanganyika (Af.)
Upper Volta (Af.)
Uzbekistan (Asia)

Yugoslavia (Eur.)

11

Afghanistan (Asia)
Australasia
Baluchistan (Asia)
Byelorussia (Eur.)
Cochin China (Asia)
Cook Islands (Pac.)
Dutch Guiana (S. Am.)
East Germany (Eur.)
French Congo (Af.)
Malay States (Asia)
Mashonaland (Af.)
Mesopotamia (Asia)
Namaqualand (Af.)
Netherlands (Eur.)
New Hebrides (Pac.)
Philippines (Asia)
Saudi Arabia (Asia)
Sierra Leone (Af.)
South Africa
Soviet Union (Asia, Eur.)
Switzerland (Eur.)
Transjordan (Asia)
Vatican City (Eur.)
West Germany (Eur.)

12

Bechuanaland (Af.)
Belgian Congo (Af.)
Cocos Islands (Ind.)
Faroe Islands (Atl.)
French Guiana (S. Am.)
Great Britain (Eur.)
Guinea-Bissau (Af.)
Indian Empire (Asia)
Matabeleland (Af.)
Newfoundland (N. Am.)
North America
North Vietnam (Asia)
Ruanda-Urundi (Af.)
South America
South Vietnam (Asia)
Tadzhikistan (Asia)
Turkmenistan (Asia)
The Argentine (S. Am.)
United States (N. Am.)

13

Afars and Issas (Af.)
Barbary States (Af.)
Cayman Islands (W.I.)

Comoro Islands (Af.)
Khmer Republic (Asia)
Liechtenstein (Eur.)
Norfolk Island (Pac.)
Trucial States (Asia)
United Kingdom (Eur.)

14

Cape of Good Hope (Af.)
Congo Free State (Af.)
Czecholovakia (Eur.)
Gilbert Islands (Pac.)
Irish Free State (Eur.)
Maldive Islands (Ind.)
Mariana Islands (Pac.)
Papua-New Guinea (E.I.)
Pitcairn Island (Pac.)
Society Islands (Pac.)
Solomon Islands (Pac.)

15

British Honduras (C. Am.)
Caroline Islands (Pac.)
Christmas Island (Pac.)
Falkland Islands (Atl.)
Holy Roman Empire (Eur.)
Northern Nigeria (Af.)
Northern Ireland (Eur.)
Orange Free State (Af.)
Southern Nigeria (Af.)
South-West Africa (Af.)

16 AND OVER

Cape Verde Islands (Af.) (16)
Congolese Republic (Af.) (17)
Dominican Republic (W.I.) (17)
Equatorial Guinea (Af.) (16)
Malagasy Republic (Af.) (16)
São Tomé and Principé (Af.) (18)
United Arab Emirates (Asia) (18)
United Arab Republic (Af., Asia) (18)
Vatican City State (Eur.) (16)

Geographical terms

2 AND 3

ait
alp
as
bay
ben
bog
cay
col
cwm
dam
dun
ea
fen
geo
lea
lin
map
nek
ria
sea
tor
voe

4

aber
bank
beck
berg
bill
burn
cape
city
comb
cove
crag
croy
dale
dell
dene
dike
doab
dune
east
eyot
ford
gapo
glen
gulf
hill
holm
holt

inch
isle
kaim
kame
lake
land
lane
linn
loam
loch
lock
marl
mead
mere
mesa
moor
mull
naze
ness
pass
peak
pole
pond
port
race
reef
reen
rill
road
rock
sike
sima
spit
sudd
syke
tarn
town
tump
vale
vega
wadi
weir
west
wind
wold
wood
wynd
zone

5

abyss
alley
atlas

atoll
Banat
bayou
bight
brook
canal
chart
chasm
chine
cliff
clime
coast
combe
copse
creek
crest
croft
delta
donga
downs
drift
duchy
esker
fault
field
fiord
fjord
firth
fieet
ghaut
glade
globe
gorge
grove
haven
heath
hithe
hurst
hythe
inlet
islet
karoo
kloof
kopje
knoll
lande
llano
loess
lough
marsh
monte
mound
mount
mouth
north

oasis
ocean
plain
point
polar
poles
reach
rhine
ridge
river
sands
scarp
shelf
shire
shoal
shore
slade
sound
south
speos
state
swale
swamp
swang
sward
weald
yarfa

6

alpine
arctic
boreal
cañada
canton
canyon
circar
clough
colony
colure
common
county
cranny
crater
cuesta
defile
desert
diapir
dingle
divide
domain
empery
empire
eyalet

forest
geyser
glacis
hamlet
harbor
inland
inning
island
isobar
jungle
karroo
lagoon
maidan
meadow
morass
nullah
orient
pampas
parish
polder
rapids
ravine
region
riding
rillet
runlet
runnel
seaway
sierra
skerry
spinny
spruit
steppe
strait
strath
stream
street
suburb
summit
talook
tropic
tundra
upland
valley
warren
yarpha

7

airport
alluvia
austral
bogland
channel

clachan
commune
compass
contour
country
cutting
deltaic
drought
eastern
enclave
eparchy
equator
estuary
euripus
exclave
georama
glacier
habitat
harbour
highway
hillock
hilltop
hommock
hornito
hummock
hundred
iceberg
ice-floe
insular
isthmus
kingdom
lakelet
lowland
midland
new town
oceanic
plateau
polders
prairie
rivulet
rosland
satrapy
savanna
seaport
seaside
spurway
straits
thicket
torrent
tropics
village
volcano
western

8

affluent
alluvial
alluvium
altitude
brooklet
cantonal
cataract
crevasse
currents
district
dominion
downland
easterly
eastward
eminence
eminency
environs
foreland
frontier
headland
highland
high road
hillside
home-park
interior
isthmian
landmark
latitude
littoral
lowlands
mainland
midlands
moorland
mountain
neap-tide
northern
occident
oriental
post-town
province
quagmire
republic
salt lake
seaboard
seacoast
seashore
sheading
snow-line
southern
sub-polar
toparchy
township
tropical
volcanic
westerly
westward
wild land

woodland

9

antarctic
antipodal
antipodes
backwater
backwoods
cadastral
capricorn
catchment
cisalpine
coastline
continent
coral reef
fleet-dike
foothills
heathland
highlands
landslide
longitude
marshland
monticule
north-east
northerly
northward
north-west
peninsula
precipice
rockbound
salt-marsh
sandbanks
shore-line
south-east
southerly
southmost
southward
south-west
stewartry
streamlet
sub-alpine
tableland
territory
tetrarchy
trade wind
tributary
wapentake
waterfall
watershed
waterside
westwards

10

co-latitude
county town

equatorial
escarpment
fluviatile
frigid zone
garden city
geographer
Gulf Stream
hemisphere
interfluve
land-locked
margravate
market town
meridional
metropolis
mountainet
no-man's-land
occidental
palatinate
peninsular
plantation
polar-angle
population
presidency
projection
promontory
quicksands
sandy beach
south downs
spring tide
table-shore
tidal creek
torrid zone
water table
wilderness

11

archipelago
bergschrund
circumpolar
cisatlantic
continental
conurbation
coral island
countryside
equinoctial
morningland
mountainous
northwardly
polar circle
polar region
river course
septentrion
subtropical
territorial
tetrarchate
tidal waters
transalpine

transmarine
trout stream
ultramarine
watercourse

12

equatorially
landgraviate
magnetic pole
northeastern
northwestern
principality
protectorate
southeastern
southernmost
southwestern
stratosphere
ultramontane
virgin forest

13

deltafication
extratropical
intertropical
magnetic north
Mediterranean
mother country
neighbourhood
northeasterly
northeastward
northwesterly
northwestward
polar distance
septentrional
southeasterly
southeastward
southwesterly
southwestward
temperate zone
transatlantic
virgin country
watering place

14 AND 15

acclimatization (15)
circummeridian (14)
circumnavigate (14)
irrigation canal (15)
magnetic equator (15)
Mercator's chart (14)
north frigid zone (15)
south frigid zone (15)
tropic of cancer (14)

Islands

Arch = Archipelago I. = Island. Is. = Islands. (v.) = volcanic.

2 – 4

Adi (Pac.)
Amoy (China)
Aran (Ire.)
Arru Is. (Indo.)
Bali (Indo.)
Bay Is. (C. Am.)
Bere (Ire.)
Bua (Adr.)
Buru (Indo.)
Bute (Scot.)
Ceos (Gr.)
Coll (Scot.)
Cook Is. (Pac.)
Cos (Gr.)
Cuba (W.I.)
Dago (Fin.)
Dogs, I. of (Eng.)
Eigg (Scot.)
Elba (Med.)
Ewe (Scot.)
Farn Is. (Eng.)
Faro (Balt.)
Fiji Is. (Pac.)
Fohr (Ger.)
Gozo (Med.)
Guam (Pac.)
Hall Is. (Pac.)
Herm (Ch. Is.)
High I. (Ire.)
Holy I. (Scot.)
Hoy (Scot.)
Idra (Gr.)
Iona (Scot.)
Java (Indo.)
Jura (Scot.)
Kei Is. (Indo.)
Long I. (U.S.A.)
Low Arch. (Pac.)
Man, I. of (Eng.)
May, I. of (Scot.)
Milo (Gr.)
Moen (Den.)
Muck (Scot.)
Mull, I. of (Scot.)
Oahu (Pac.)
Paxo (Gr.)
Rat Is. (Pac.)
Ré (Fr.)
Rum (Scot.)
Saba (W.I.)
Sark (Ch. Is.)
Scio (Gr.)
Skye (Scot.)

Sulu Is. (Indo.)
Sylt (Ger.)
Syra (Gr.)
Tory (Ire.)
Uist (Scot.)
Ulva (Scot.)
Unst (Scot.)
Yap (Pac.)
Yell (Scot.)
Yezo (Jap.)
Zea (Gr.)
Zebu (Indo.)

5

Abaco (W.I.)
Aland Is. (Balt.)
Albay (Indo.)
Arran (Scot.)
Banca (Malay)
Banda (Indo.)
Banks (S. Pac.)
Barra (Heb.)
Bonin Is. (Pac.)
Caldy (Wales)
Canna (Scot.)
Capri (It.)
Ceram (Indo.)
Cheja (Korea)
Chios (Gr.)
Clare (Ire.)
Clear (Ire.)
Cocos Is. (Ind.)
Corfu (Gr.)
Corvo (Atl.)
Crete (Med.)
Dabaz (Scot.)
Delos (Gr.)
Disco (Arc.)
Disko (Arc.)
Eagle I. (Ire.)
Ellis (U.S.A.)
Farne Is. (Eng.)
Fayal (Atl.)
Ferro (Atl.)
Foula (Scot.)
Funen (Den.)
Goree (Atl.)
Gozzo (Med.)
Haiti (W.I.)
Hart's I. (U.S.A.)
Hatia (Ind.)
Hondo (Jap.)
Hydra (Gr.)

Ibiza (Med.)
Inyak (S.A.)
Islay (Scot.)
Ivica (Med.)
Leros (Gr.)
Lewis (Scot.)
Leyte (Philip.)
Lissa (Adr.)
Lobos Is. (S. Am.)
Lundy I. (Eng.)
Luzon (Philip.)
Malta (Med.)
Matsu (China)
Melos (Gr.)
Milos (Gr.)
Nauru (Pac.)
Naxos (Gr.)
Nevis (W.I.)
Oesel (Balt.)
Ormuz (Iran)
Papua (E.I.)
Parry Is. (Arc.)
Pearl Is. (Pac.)
Pelew Is. (E.I.)
Pelew Is. (Pac.)
Pemba (Af.)
Perim (Af.)
Pines, I. of (Pac. and W.I.)
Pinos (S. Am.)
Rhode I. (U.S.A.)
Rugen (Ger.)
Sable I. (Can.)
Samoa (Pac.)
Samos (Gr.)
Skyro (Gr.)
Spice Is. (Indo.)
Sunda Is. (Indo.)
Texel (Neth.)
Thera (Gr.)
Timor (Malay)
Tiree (Scot.)
Tonga (Pac.)
Turk's I. (W.I.)
Voorn (Neth.)
Wight, I. of (Eng.)
Zante (Gr.)

6

Achill (Ire.)
Aegina (Gr.)
Alban (Austral.)
Anamba Is. (Indo.)
Andros (Gr.)

Azores (Atl.)
Baffin (Can.)
Bahama Is. (W.I.)
Banana Is. (Atl.)
Bissao (Atl.)
Borkum (Ger.)
Borneo (Indo.)
Bounty Is. (N.Z.)
Brazza (Adr.)
Burray (Scot.)
Caicos I. (W.I.)
Calamo (Gr.)
Candia (Med.)
Canary Is. (Atl.)
Cayman Is. (W.I.)
Cerigo (Med.)
Cherso (It.)
Chiloe (S. Am.)
Chusan (China)
Comoro Is. (Af.)
Crozet Is. (Ind.)
Cyprus (Med.)
Dursey (Ire.)
Easter I. (Pac.)
Ellice Is. (Pac.)
Euboea (Aeg.)
Faroes (Atl.)
Flores (Atl.)
Flores (Indo.)
Gilolo (Indo.)
Gomera (Can.)
Hainan (China)
Harris (Scot.)
Hawaii (Pac.)
Honshu (Jap.)
Imbros (Aeg.)
Inagua (W.I.)
Ionian Is. (Med.)
Ischia (It.)
Ithaca (Med.)
Iturup (Jap.)
Jaluit (Pac.)
Jersey (Ch. Is.)
Jethou (Ch. Is.)
Kishni (Iran)
Kodiak (Pac.)
Kurile Is. (Pac.)
Kyushu (Jap.)
Labuan (Malay.)
Lambay (Ire.)
Lemnos (Aeg.)
Lerins Is. (Fr.)
Lesbos (Aeg.)
Lesina (Adr.)
Limmos (Aeg.)

Lipari Is. (Med.)
Lombok (Malay.)
Marajo (S. Am.)
Marken (Neth.)
Negros (Indo.)
Oleron (Fr.)
Orkney Is. (Scot.)
Patmos (Med.)
Penang (Malay.)
Philae (Nile)
Pomona (Scot.)
Puffin I. (Wales)
Quemoy (China)
Rhodes (Med.)
Robben (S.A.)
Rottum (Neth.)
St. John (W.I.)
St. Paul (Ind.)
Samsoe (Den.)
Sangir Is. (Indo.)
Savage I. (Pac.)
Scarba (Scot.)
Scilly Is. (Eng.)
Sicily (Med.)
Skyros (Gr.)
Staffa (Scot.)
Staten I. (U.S.A.)
Stroma (Scot.)
Tahiti (Pac.)
Taiwan (China)
Thanet, I. of (Eng.)
Tholen (Neth.)
Tobago (W.I.)
Trömso (Nor.)
Tubugi Is. (Pac.)
Usedom (Ger.)
Ushant (Fr.)
Vaigen (Indo.)
Virgin Is. (W.I.)

7

Aegades Is. (Med.)
Aeolian Is. (v.) (Med.)
Amboina (Indo.)
Ameland (Neth.)
Andaman Is. (Ind.)
Antigua (W.I.)
Bahamas (W.I.)
Bahrain (Arab.)
Balleny Is. (Antarc.)
Behring Is. (Pac.)
Bermuda (Atl.)
Bernera (Scot.)
Bourbon (Ind.)
Cabrera (Med.)
Capraja (Med.)
Caprera (Med.)

Celebes (Indo.)
Channel Is. (Eng.)
Chatham Is. (Pac.)
Chincha Is. (S. Am.)
Comoros (Af.)
Corisco (Af.)
Corsica (Med.)
Cumbrae (Scot.)
Curaçao (W.I.)
Curzola (Adr.)
Dampier Is. (Austral.)
Dinding Is. (Malay.)
Diomede Is. (Arc.)
Domingo (W.I.)
Eriskay (Scot.)
Faeroes (Atl.)
Falster (Balt.)
Fanning (Pac.)
Fehmeru (Balt.)
Flannan Is. (Scot.)
Formosa (China)
Frisian Is. (Neth.)
Gambier Is. (Pac.)
Gilbert Is. (Pac.)
Gotland (Balt.)
Grenada (W.I.)
Hayling I. (Eng.)
Iceland (v.) (Atl.)
Ichaboe (Af.)
Ireland
Jamaica (W.I.)
Johanna (Af.)
Kamaran (Red S.)
Kandava (Pac.)
Keeling Is. (Ind.)
Kolonev (Rus.)
Laaland (Den.)
Leeward Is. (W.I.)
Liakhov Is. (Arc.)
Lofoten Is. (Nor.)
Loo Choo Is. (China)
Loyalty Is. (Pac.)
Madeira (Atl.)
Mageroe (Arc.)
Majorca (Med.)
Maldive Is. (Ind.)
Massowa (Red S.)
Mayotte (Af.)
Minicoy (Ind.)
Minorca (Sp.)
Molokai (Pac.)
Molucca Is. (Indo.)
Mombasa (Af.)
Mykonos (Gr.)
Nicobar Is. (Ind.)
Norfolk I. (Austral.)
Nossi Be (v.) (Af.)
Oceania (Pac.)
Orkneys (Scot.)

Phoenix Is. (Pac.)
Portsea I. (Eng.)
Princes Is. (Turk.)
Purbeck, I. of (Eng.)
Rathlin (N.I.)
Reunion (Ind.)
Roanoke (U.S.A.)
Rockall (Atl.)
Rotumah (Pac.)
St. Agnes (Eng.)
St. Kilda (Scot.)
St. Kitts (Pac.)
St. Lucia (W.I.)
St. Marie (Af.)
Salamis (Gr.)
São Tomé (Af.)
Serifos (Gr.)
Sheppey, I. of (Eng.)
Sherbro (Af.)
Shikoka (Jap.)
Society Is. (Pac.)
Socotra (Ind.)
Solomon Is. (Pac.)
Stewart I. (N.Z.)
Sumatra (Indo.)
Sumbawa (Indo.)
Tenedos (Med.)
Ternate (Indo.)
Tortola (W.I.)
Tortuga (W.I.)
Tuamotu (Pac.)
Watling I. (W.I.)
Whalsay (Scot.)

8

Alderney (Ch. Is.)
Aleutian Is. (Pac.)
Amirante Is. (Ind.)
Andamans (Ind.)
Anglesey (Wales)
Antilles Is. (W.I.)
Auckland Is. (N.Z.)
Balearic Is. (Med.)
Barbados (Is.) (W.I.)
Bermudas (Is.) (Atl.)
Berneray (Scot.)
Billiton (Indo.)
Bismark Arch. (Pac.)
Bissagos Is. (Af.)
Bornholm (Balt.)
Campbell (N.Z.)
Canaries (Atl.)
Caribbee Is. (W.I.)
Caroline Is. (Pac.)
Colonsay (Scot.)
Copeland Is. (Ire.)
Cyclades Is. (Gr.)

Desertas (Atl.)
Desirade (W.I.)
Dominica (W.I.)
Fair Isle (Scot.)
Falkland Is. (Atl.)
Flinders (Austral.)
Friendly Is. (Pac.)
Furneaux Is. (Austral.)
Guernsey (Ch. Is.)
Hebrides (Scot.)
Hokkaido (Jap.)
Hong Kong (China)
Inchcolm (Scot.)
Jan Mayen (Arc.)
Kangaroo Is. (Austral.)
Kermadec Is. (Pac.)
Krakatoa (v.) (Indo.)
Ladrones (Pac.)
Leucadia (Med.)
Lord Howe Is.
  (Austral.)
Magdalen Is. (Can.)
Malicolo (Pac.)
Mallorca (Med.)
Manihiki Is. (Pac.)
Marianne Is. (Pac.)
Marshall Is. (Pac.)
Melville (Am. and
  Austral.)
Mindanao (Philip.)
Miquelon (Can.)
Mitylene (Gr.)
Moluccas (Indo.)
Otaheite (Pac.)
Pitcairn Is. (Pac.)
Portland, I. of (Eng.)
Pribilof Is. (Pac.)
Pribylov Is. (Pac.)
Quelpart (Korea)
Rothesay (Scot.)
St. Helena (Atl.)
St. Martin (W.I.)
St. Thomas (Af.
  and W.I.)
Sakhalin (Rus.)
Salsette (Ind.)
Sandwich Is. (Pac.)
Sardinia (Med.)
Scillies (Eng.)
Seriphos (Gr.)
Shetland Is. (Scot.)
Skopelos (Gr.)
Sri Lanka (Asia)
Starbuck (Pac.)
Tasmania (Austral.)
Tenerife (Atl.)
Thousand Is. (N. Am.)
Thursday I. (Austral.)
Tortugas Is. (U.S.A.)

Trinidad (W.I.)
Unalaska (U.S.A.)
Valentia (Ire.)
Victoria (Can.)
Viti-Levu (Fiji)
Vlieland (Neth.)
Windward Is. (W.I.)
Zanzibar (Af.)

9

Admiralty Is. (Pac.)
Anticosti (Can.)
Arranmore (Ire.)
Ascension (Atl.)
Belle Isle (Fr.)
Benbecula (Scot.)
Beverland (Neth.)
Buccaneer Arch.
  (Ind.)
Cape Verde Is. (Atl.)
Cerigotto (Med.)
Christmas I. (Pac.
  and Ind.)
Dordrecht (Neth.)
Elephanta (Ind.)
Eleuthera (W.I.)
Ellesmere (N. Am.)
Erromanga (Scot.)
Falklands (Atl.)
Galapagos Is. (v.)
  (Pac.)
Greenland (Arc.)
Halmahera (Indo.)
Inchkeith (Scot.)
Inishturk (Ire.)
Isle of Man (Eng.)
Isle of May (Scot.)
Lampedusa (Med.)
Langeland (Den.)
Louisiade Arch (E.I.)
Manhattan (U.S.A.)
Margarita (W.I.)
Marquesas Is. (Pac.)
Mauritius (Ind.)
Melanesia (Pac.)
Nantucket (U.S.A.)
Negropont (Gr.)
New Guinea (E.I.)
Norderney (Ger.)
Polynesia (Pac.)
Porto Rico (W.I.)
Raratonga (Pac.)
Rodrigues (Ind.)
Saghalien (Rus.)
Saint John (W.I.)
St. Michael (Atl.)
St. Nicolas (Atl.)

Saint Paul (Ind.)
St. Vincent (W.I.)
Santa Cruz (W.I.)
Santorini (v) (Gr.)
Scarpanto (Med.)
Shetlands (Scot.)
Singapore (Asia)
Stromboli (v.) (Med.)
Timor Laut Is. (Pac.)
Vancouver (Can.)
Vanua Levu (Fiji)
Walcheren (Neth.)
Wellesley Is. (Austral.)

10

Ailsa Craig (Scot.)
Bay Islands (C. Am.)
Calamianes (Indo.)
Cape Barren I.
  (Austral.)
Cape Breton I. (Can.)
Cephalonia (Gr.)
Dirk Hartog (Austral.)
Dodecanese (Med.)
Fernando Po (Af.)
Formentera (Med.)
Fortune Bay I. (Can.)
Friendlies (Pac.)
Grenadines (W.I.)
Guadeloupe (W.I.)
Heligoland (N. Sea)
Holy Island (Scot.)
Inchgarvie (Scot.)
Inishshark (Ire.)
Isle of Dogs (Eng.)
Isle of Skye (Scot.)
Isle of Mull (Scot.)
Kuria Muria Is. (Arab.)
Laccadives (Arab.)
Long Island (U.S.A.)
Madagascar (Af.)
Manitoulin Is. (Pac.)
Martinique (W.I.)
Micronesia (Pac.)
Montserrat (W.I.)
Navigators' I. (Pac.)
New Britain (Pac.)
New Siberia (Arc.)
New Zealand (Pac.)
North Devon (Arc.)
Nova Zembla (Arc.)
Philippine Is. (Asia)
Puerto Rico (W.l.)
Rat Islands (Pac.)
Ronaldshay (Scot.)
Saint Agnes (Eng.)
Saint Kilda (Scot.)

Saint Kitts (W.I.)
Saint Lucia (W.I.)
Saint Marie (Af.)
Sandlewood I. (Malay.)
Seychelles (Ind.)
Skerryvore (Scot.)
West Indies (Atl.)

11

Cook Islands (Pac.)
Eagle Island (Ire.)
Grand Canary (Atl.)
Guadalcanal (Pac.)
Hall Islands (Pac.)
Hart's Island (U.S.A.)
Isle of Pines (Pac. and
  W.I.)
Isle of Wight (Eng.)
Isola Grossa (Adr.)
Lindisfarne (Scot.)
Lundy Island (Eng.)
Mascarenene Is. (Ind.)
Monte Cristo (It.)
New Hebrides (Pac.)
North Island (N.Z.)
Pantellaria (Med.)
Philippines (Asia)
Rhode Island (U.S.A.)
Sable Island (Can.)
Saint Helena (Atl.)
Saint Martin (W.I.)
Saint Thomas (W.I.)
Scilly Isles (Eng.)
Southampton (Can.)
South Island (N.Z.)
Spitsbergen (Arc.)

12

Baffin Island (N. Am.)
Bougainville (Pac.)
British Isles
Easter Island (Pac.)
Great Britain (U.K.)
Great Cumbrae (Scot.)
Inaccesible I. (Atl.)
Isle of Thanet (Eng.)
Mariagalante (W.I.)
Melville Land (Arc.)
New Caledonia (Pac.)
Newfoundland (Can.)
Novaya Zemlya (Arc.)
Prince Albert (Can.)
Prince Edward I. (Can.)
Puffin Island (Wales)
Saint Michael (Atl.)

Saint Nicolas (Atl.)
Saint Vincent (W.I.)
Savage Island (Pac.)
South Georgia (Al.)
Staten Island (U.S.A.)
Turks' Islands (W.I.)

13 AND OVER

D'Entrecastreaux Is.
  (Austral.) (15)
Isle of Portland
  (Eng.) (14)
Isle of Purbeck
  (Eng.) (13)
Isle of Sheppey
  (Eng.) (13)
Juan Fernandez
  (Pac.) (13)
Kerguelen Land
  (Pac.) (13)
Little Cumbrae
  (Scot.) (13)
Martha's Vineyard
  (U.S.A.) (15)
Norfolk Island
  (Pac.) (13)
North Somerset
  (Arc.) (14)
Prince of Wales I.
  (Malay.) (13)
Queen Charlotte I.
  (Can.) (14)
St. Bartholomew
  (W.I.) (13)
St. Christopher
  (W.I.) (13)
South Shetlands
  (Atl.) (14)
Stewart Island
  (N.Z.) (13)
Thursday Island
  (Austral.) (14)
Tierra del Fuego
  (Chile) (14)
Tristan da Cunha
  (Atl.) (14)
Watling Island
  (Atl.) (13)
West Spitsbergen
  (Arc.) (15)

Lakes, inland lochs, etc.

3 AND 4

Aral (Kaz./Uzbek.)
Ard (Scot.)
Awe (Scot.)
Bala (Wales)
Bear (U.S.A.)
Biwa (Jap.)
Chad (Af.)
Como (It.)
Derg (Ire.)
Dore (Can.)
Earn (Scot.)
Eil (Scot.)
Erie (Can. and U.S.A.)
Erne (N.I.)
Ewe (Scot.)
Eyre (Austral.)
Ha Ha (Can.)
Iseo (It.)
Key (Ire.)
Kivu (Af.)
Long (Scot.)
Mead (U.S.A.)
Ness (Scot.)
Oahu (N.Z.)
Ree (Ire.)
Ryan (Scot.)
Shin (Scot.)
Tana (Eth.)
Tay (Scot.)
Thun (Swit.)
Utah (U.S.A.)
Van (Turk.)
Voil (Scot.)
Zug (Swit.)

5

Abaya (Eth.)
Allen (Ire.)
Baker (Can.)
Camm (Can.)
Elton (Rus.)
Enara (Fin.)
Etive (Scot.)
Frome (Austral.)
Garda (It.)
Garry (Can.)
Ghana (Can.)
Hamun (Afghan.)
Honey (U.S.A.)
Huron (Can. and U.S.A.)
Ilmen (Rus.)

Kossu (Af.)
Leven (Scot.)
Lochy (Scot.)
Loyal (Scot.)
Malar (Swed.)
Maree (Scot.)
Minto (Can.)
Mjøsa (Nor.)
Moero (Af.)
Morar (Scot.)
Mweru (Af)
Neagh (N.I.)
Moore (Austral.)
Nevis (Scot.)
Nyasa (Af.)
Onega (Rus.)
Payne (Can.)
Rainy (Can.)
Shiel (Scot.)
Talka (Can.)
Taupo (N.Z.)
Tchad (Af.)
Tsano (Eth.)
Tumba (Af.)
Urmia (Iran)
Volta (Ghana)
Wener (Swed.)
Yssel (Neth.)

6

Albert (Af.)
Arkaig (Scot.)
Assynt (Scot.)
Austin (Austral.)
Baikal (Sib.)
Buloke (Austral.)
Chilka (Ind.)
Edward (Af.)
Ennell (Ire.)
Geneva (Swit.)
George (Af. and Austral.)
Indian (U.S.A.)
Itasca (U.S.A.)
Kariba (Af.)
Khanka (Asia)
Ladoga (Rus.)
Lomond (Scot.)
Lugano (Swit.)
Mahood (Can.)
Malawi (Af.)
Nasser (Egypt)
Nyanza (Bur.)
Oneida (I.A.)

Peipus (Est. Rus.)
Placid (U.S.A.)
Quoich (Scot.)
Rideau (Can.)
Rudolf (Af.)
St. John (Can.)
Shasta (U.S.A.)
Shirwa (Af.)
Simcoe (Can.)
Stuart (Can.)
Te Anau (N.Z.)
Tuz Gol (Turk.)
Vanern (Swed.)
Viedma (S. Am.)
Vyrnwy (Wales)
Wanaka (N.Z.)
Wenham (U.S.A.)
Wetter (Swed.)
Zürich (Swit.)

7

Abitibi (Can.)
Balaton (Hung.)
Balkash (Asia)
Benmore (N.Z.)
Blanche (Austral.)
Caillou (U.S.A.)
Caspian (Asia)
Chapala (Mex.)
Dead Sea (Asia)
Etawney (Can.)
Fannich (Scot.)
Galilee (Asia)
Hirakud (Ind.)
Hjelmar (Swed.)
Idi Amin (Af.)
Katrine (Scot.)
Koko Nor (China)
Lachine (Can.)
Leopold (Af.)
Loch Eil (Scot.)
Loch Tay (Scot.)
Lucerne (Swit.)
Muskoka (Can.)
Nipigon (Can.)
Okhrida (Turk.)
Ontario (Can. and U.S.A.)
Perugia (It.)
Quesnal (Can.)
Rannoch (Scot.)
Rosseau (Can.)
Rybinsk (Rus.)
Seistan (Afghan.)

Sempach (Swit.)
Sheelin (Ire.)
Tarbert (Scot.)
Texcoco (Mex.)
Tezcuco (Mex.)
Torrens (Austral.)
Tyrrell (Austral.)

8

Akamyara (Af.)
Balkhash (Asia)
Bear Lake (U.S.A.)
Chowilla (Austral.)
Cooroong (Austral.)
Drummond (U.S.A.)
Gairdner (Austral.)
Grasmere (Eng.)
Hirfanli (Turk.)
Humboldt (Austral.)
Issyk-Kul (Asia)
Kakhovka (Ukr.)
Kawarthi (Can.)
Kootenay (Can.)
La Crosse (U.S.A.)
Loch Ness (Scot.)
Loch Ryan (Scot.)
Luichart (Scot.)
Maggiore (It.)
Manipuri (N.Z.)
Manitoba (Can.)
Mareotis (Egypt)
Menteith (Scot.)
Menzaleh (Egypt)
Michigan (U.S.A.)
Reindeer (Can.)
Seaforth (Scot.)
Sese Soko (Af.)
Stefanie (Af.)
Superior (U.S.A.)
Tarawera (N.Z.)
Titicaca (Peru)
Tungting (China)
Victoria (Af.)
Wakatipu (N.Z.)
Winnipeg (Can.)
Xaltocan (Mex.)

9

Argentino (S. Am.)
Athabaska (Can.)
Bangweolo (Af.)

108

Champlain (N. Am.)
Constance (Swit.)
Ennerdale (Eng.)
Eucumbene (Austral.)
Great Bear (Can.)
Great Salt (U.S.A.)
Hindmarsh (Austral.)
Honey Lake (U.S.A.)
Killarney (Ire.)
Kuibyshev (Rus.)
Lochinvar (Scot.)
Loch Leven (Scot.)
Loch Maree (Scot.)
Loch Nevis (Scot.)
Maracaibo (Venez.)
Maravilla (S. Am.)
Neuchâtel (Swit.)
Nicaragua (Am.)
Nipissing (Can.)
Playgreen (Can.)
Tengri-Nor (Tibet)
Thirlmere (Eng.)
Trasimeno (It.)
Ullswater (Eng.)
Wastwater (Eng.)

Wollaston (Can.)
Yssel Lake (Neth.)

10

Brokopondo (S. Am.)
Buttermere (Eng.)
Great Slave (Can.)
Hawes Water (Eng.)
Ijsselmeer (Neth.)
Indian Lake (U.S.A.)
Lackawanna (U.S.A.)
Loch Lomond (Scot.)
Lough Neagh (N.I.)
Michikamau (Can.)
Mistassini (Can.)
Roguaguado (Boliv.)
Rotomahana (N.Z.)
Rydal Water (Eng.)
Serpentine (Eng.)
Tanganyika (Af.)
Windermere (Eng.)
Xochimilco (Mex.)

11 AND OVER

Albert Edward Nyanza (Af.) (18)
Albert Nyanza (Af.) (12)
Bitter Lakes (Egypt) (11)
Cabora Bassa (Af.) (11)
Coniston Water (Eng.) (13)
Derwentwater (Eng.) (12)
Diefenbaker (Can.) (11)
Grand Coulee (U.S.A.) (11)
Great Salt Lake (U.S.A.) (13)
Great Slave Lake (Can.) (14)
Lake of the Woods (Can. and U.S.A.) (14)
Lesser Slave Lake (Can.) (15)
Loch Katrine (Scot.) (11)
Loch Tarbert (Scot.) (11)
Pontchatrain (U.S.A.) (12)
The Cooroong (Austral.) (11)
Timiskaming (Can.) (11)
Victoria Nyanza (Af.) (14)
Virginia Water (Eng.) (13)
Winnipegosis (Can.) (12)
Yellowstone (U.S.A.) (11)

Mountains

H. = Hill.   Hs. = Hills.   M. = "Mountain," commonly used *after* name.   Ms. = Mountains.   Mt = "Mount," "Monte," or "Mont," commonly used *before* name.   (v.) = volcanic.

2 – 4

Abu, Mt. (Ind.)
Aboo, Mt. (Ind.)
Alps Ms. (Eur.)
Blue Ms. (Austral. and U.S.A.)
Caha Ms. (Ire.)
Cook M. (N.Z.)
Ebal, Mt. (Jord.)
Elk Ms. (U.S.A.)
Etna, Mt. (v.) (Sic.)
Fuji, Mt. (v.) (Jap.)
Harz Ms. (Ger.)
Ida, Mt. (Crete)
Iron M. (U.S.A.)
Jura Ms. (Eur.)
K2 (Him.)
Kea (v.) (Hawaii)
Kibo, Mt. (Tanz.)
Kong Ms. (Af.)
Naga Hs. (Ind.)
Ossa, Mt. (Gr., Tas.)
Qara Ms. (Arab.)
Rigi, Mt. (Swit.)

Rosa, Mt. (Alps)
Ural Ms. (Rus.)
Zug M. (Ger.)

5

Adams M. (U.S.A.)
Altai Ms. (Him.)
Andes Ms. (S. Am.)
Aripo M. (Trin.)
Athos, Mt. (Gr.)
Atlas Ms. (Af.)
Baker (v.) (U.S.A.)
Barry Ms. (Austral.)
Black Ms. (U.S.A. and Wales)
Blanc, Mt. (Alps)
Brown M. (N. Am.)
Cenis, Mt. (Alps)
Eiger (Swit.)
Djaja, Mt. (Indo.)
Downs, The (Hs.) (Eng.)
Ghats, The (Ms.) (Ind.)
Green Ms. (U.S.A.)
Hecla (v.) (Iceland)

Kamet, Mt. (Him.)
Kenia, Mt. (E. Af.)
Kenya, Mt. (E. Af.)
Logan, Mt. (Yukon)
Maipu (v.) (Arg.)
Mönch, (Swit.)
Ochil Hs. (Scot.)
Ophir, Mt. (Malay.)
Overo (v.) (S. Am.)
Pelée (v) (W.I.)
Rocky Ms. (N. Am.)
Sinai, Mt. (Arab.)
Table M. (S.A.)
Tabor, Mt. (Isr.)
Vinta, Mt. (U.S.A.)
White Ms. (U.S.A.)
Wolds, The (Hs.) (Eng.)

6

Ararat, Mt. (Turk.)
Averno, Mt. (v.) (It.)
Balkan Ms. (Eur.)
Beluha (Him.)
Bogong, Mt. (Austral.)

Carmel Mt. (Isr.)
Darwin, Mt. (S. Am.)
Elbruz (Rus./Geo.)
Erebus (v.) (Antarc.)
Galtee Ms. (Ire.)
Hayden, Mt. (U.S.A.)
Hermon, Mt. (Asia)
Hooker, M. (Can.)
Hoosac Ms. (U.S.A.)
Juncal (v.) (S. Am.)
Kazbek, Mt. (Geo.)
Lennox Hs. (Scot.)
Lhotse, Mt. (Him.)
Makalu, Mt. (Him.)
Masaya (v.) (C. Am.)
Mendip Hs. (Eng.)
Mourne Ms. (Ire.)
Nelson, Mt. (Tas.)
Nuptse, Mt. (Him.)
Olives, Mt. of (Isr.)
Pamirs (Asia)
Pelion, Ms. (Gr.)
Pindus Ms. (Gr.)
Robson (Can.)
Sahama (v.) (S. Am.)
Sangay (v.) (S. Am.)

Scafel, Mt. (Eng.)
Sidlaw Hs. (Scot.)
Sorata (2 Ms.) (S. Am.)
Taunus Ms. (Ger.)
Terror (v.) (Antarc.)
Tolima (v.) (S. Am.)
Vosges Ms. (Fr.)

7

Balkans Ms. (Eur.)
Ben More (Scot.)
Bernima, Mt. (Alps)
Big Horn Ms. (U.S.A.)
Bow Fell, Mt. (Eng.)
Brocken, Mt. (Ger.)
Cascade Ms. (N. Am.)
Cazambe, Mt. (S. Am.)
Cheviot Hs. (Eng.)
Dapsang, Mt. (Him.)
Darling, Mt. (Austral.)
El Potra, Mt. (S. Am.)
Everest, Mt. (Him.)
Hoffman, Mt. (U.S.A.)
Illampa, Mt. (Boliv.)
Jaintia Ms. (Assam)
Jonsong, Mt. (Him.)
Jorullo (v.) (Mex.)
Kilauea (v.) (Pac.)
La Pelée (v.) (W.I.)
Lebanon, Mt. (Leb.)
Lookout M. (U.S.A.)
Malvern Hs. (Eng.)
Mamturk Ms. (Ire.)
Mendips Hs. (Eng.)
Milanji, Mt. (Af.)
Miltsin, Mt. (Af.)
M'Kinley (Alaska)
Nilgiri Hs. (Ind.)
Olympus, Mt. (Gr.)
Orizaba (Mex.)
Pennine Ms. (Eng.)
Peteroa (v.) (S. Am.)
Pilatus, Mt. (Swit.)
Quizapu (v.) (S. Am.)
Rainier, Mt. (U.S.A.)
Rhodope, Mt. (Turk.)
Rockies Ms. (N. Am.)
Roraima, Mt. (S. Am.)
Ruahine, Mt. (N.Z.)
San José (v.) (S. Am.)
San Juan Ms. (U.S.A.)
Simplon, Mt. (Swit.)
Siwalik Hs. (Ind.)
Skiddaw, Mt. (Eng.)
Snowdon, Mt. (Wales)
St. Elias, Mt. (Can. and Gr.)

Sudetes Ms. (Eur.)
Tomboro (v.) (Jap.)
Vindhya Ms. (Ind.)
Vulcano (v.) (It.)
Wenchow, Mt. (China)
Whitney, Mt. (U.S.A.)

8

Anapurna (Him.)
Aravalli Ms. (Ind.)
Auvergne Ms. (Fr.)
Ben Nevis (Scot.)
Ben Venue (Scot.)
Ben Wyvis (Scot.)
Ben-y-Gloe (Scot.)
Catskill Ms. (U.S.A.)
Caucasus Ms. (Eur.)
Cheviots (Hs.) (Eng.)
Chiltern Hs. (Eng.)
Cotopaxi (v.) (Ecuad.)
Cotswold Hs. (Eng.)
Demavend, Mt. (Iran)
Edgehill (H.) (Eng.)
Estrelle, Mt. (Port.)
Flinders Ms. (Austral.)
Fujiyama (v.) (Jap.)
Goatfell, Mt. (Scot.)
Haramokh, Mt. (Him.)
Hualalai (v.) (Pac.)
Illimani, Mt. (Bol.)
Jungfrau, Mt. (Swit.)
Katahdin, Mt. (U.S.A.)
Kinabalu (v.) (Born.)
Koh-i-Baba (Afghan.)
Krakatoa (v.) (Indo.)
Kuenluiv Ms. (Asia)
McKinley, Mt. (Alaska)
Moorfoot Hs. (Scot.)
Mulhacén, Mt. (Sp.)
Nilgiris Hs. (Ind.)
Pennines (Hs.) (Eng.)
Pentland Hs. (Scot.)
Preseley Ms. (Wales)
Pyrenees Ms. (Eur.)
Quantock Hs. (En.)
Rajmahal Hs. (Ind.)
Rushmore, Mt. (U.S.A.)
Scawfell, Mt. (Eng.)
Snaefell, Mt. (I. of Man)
Sulaiman Ms. (Ind.)
Tarawera, Mt. (N.Z.)
The Downs (Hs.) (Eng.)
The Ghats (Ms.) (Ind.)
The Wolds (Hs.) (Eng.)
Tien Shan Ms. (Asia)
Townsend, Mt. (Austral.)

Vesuvius (v.) (It.)
Wrangell, Mt. (Can.)
Yablonoi Ms. (Asia)

9

Aconcagua (v) (Arg.)
Adam's Peak (Sri)
Allegheny Ms. (U.S.A.)
Annapurna (Him.)
Apennines (It.)
Ben Lawers (Scot.)
Ben Lomond (Scot.)
Black Dome (U.S.A.)
Blue Ridge Ms. (U.S.A.)
Breithorn (Alps)
Cairntoul (Scot.)
Carstensz (Indo.)
Chilterns (Hs.) (Eng.)
Chumalari, Mt. (Him.)
Communism (Tadz.)
Cotswolds (Hs.) (Eng.)
Cuchullin Hs. (Skye)
Dardistan, Mt. (Ind.)
Faucilles Ms. (Fr.)
Grampians (Ms.) (Scot.)
Helvellyn, Mt. (Eng.)
Himalayas (Ms.) (Asia)
Hindu-Kush Ms. (Asia)
Itaculomi, Mt. (S. Am.)
Karakoram, Mt. (Asia)
Koseiusko, Mt. (Austral.)
Lafayette, Mt. (U.S.A.)
Las Yeguas (v.) (Chile)
Lenin Peak (Tadz./Kir.)
Licancaur, Mt. (Chile)
Liverpool (Austral.)
Maladetta, Mt. (Pyr.)
Mont Blanc (Alps)
Mont Cenis (Alps)
Mont Perdu (Pyr.)
Monte Rosa (Alps)
Naga Hills (Ind.)
Nanga-Devi (Him.)
Parnassus, Mt. (Gr.)
Pic du Midi (Pyr.)
Pike's Peak (U.S.A.)
Rakaposhi (Him.)
Ruwenzori Ms. (Uganda and Zaïre)
Solfatara (v.) (It.)
St. Bernard (Pass) (Swit.)
St. Gothard, Mt. (Swit.)
Stromboli (v.) (Med.)
Thian-Shan Ms. (Asia)
Tongariro (v.) (N.Z.)

Tupungato (v.) (S. Am.)
Wind River Ms. (U.S.A.)

10

Adirondack Ms. (U.S.A.)
Ben Macdhui (Scot.)
Cairngorms (Scot.)
Cantabrian Ms. (Sp.)
Carpathian Ms. (Eur.)
Cedar Berge, Mt. (S.A.)
Chimborazo (v.) (Ecuad.)
Chumallari, Mt. (Him.)
Dent du Midi (Swit.)
Dhaulagiri, Mt. (Him.)
Diablerets, Mt. (Swit.)
Erzgebirge (Ger.)
Graian Alps (Eur.)
Khyber Pas (Afghan., Pak.)
Koshtan Tau (Rus.)
Kuh-i-Taftan (v.) (Iran)
Kwathlamba, Mt. (S.A.)
Lammermuir Hs. (Scot.)
Laurentian Ms. (Can.)
Matterhorn, The (Alps)
Moel Fammau, Mt. (Wales)
Monte Corno (It.)
Ochil Hills (Scot.)
Pinlimmon, Mt. (Wales)
Saint Elias (Can. and Gr.)
Wellington, Mt. (Tas.)
Wetterhorn, The (Swit.)

11

Appalachian Ms. (U.S.A.)
Bernese Alps (Swit.)
Carpathians (Ms.) (Eur.)
Citlaltepec, Mt. (Mex.)
Descapezado (v:) (Chile)
Dinaric Alps (Eur.)
Drachenfels, Mt. (Ger.)
Drakensberg Ms. (S.A.)
Drakenstein, Mt. (S.A.)
Hochstetter, Mt. (N.Z.)
Kilimanjaro, Mt. (Tanz.)
La Sonfrière (v.) (W.I.)
Lennox Hills (Scot.)
Livingstone Ms. (Af.)
Mendip Hills (Eng.)
Nanga Parbat (Him.)
Ortler Spitz (Aust.)

Owen Stanley Ms. (Papua)
Pennine Alps (Eur.)
Schreckhorn (Swit.)
Sidlow Hills (Scot.)
Sierra Madre Ms. (Mex.)
Splugen Pass (Swit.)
Stelvio Pass (It.)
Swabian Alps (Ger.)
Vatnajökull (Iceland)

12

Bougainville, Mt. (Papua)
Cheviot Hills (Eng.)
Godwin Austen, Mt. (Him.)
Ingleborough, Mt. (Eng.)
Jaintia Hills (Ind.)
Kanchenjunga, Mt. (Him.)
Kinchinjunga, Mt. (Him.)

Llullaillaco (v.) (Chile)
Malvern Hills (Eng.)
Maritime Alps (Fr., It.)
Nilgiri Hills (Ind.)
Peak District (Eng.)
Popocatepetl (v.) (Mex .)
Roncesvalles (v) (Pyr.)
Saint Gothard, Mt. (Swit.)
Schiehallion, Mt. (Scot.)
Sierra Morena, Mt. (Sp.)
Sierra Nevada Ms. (Sp.)
Siwalik Hills (Ind.)
Tinguiririca (v.) (Chile)
Zoutpansberg, Mt. (S.A.)

13 AND OVER

Black Dome Peak (U.S.A.)
 (13)

Carrantuohill, Mt. (Ire.)
 (13)
Chiltern Hills (Eng.) (13)
Cotswold Hills (Eng.) (13)
Fichtelgebirge (Ger.) (14)
Finsteraahorn, Mt. (Swit.) (13)
Grossglockner, Mt. (Alps)
 (13)
Knockmealdown, Mt. (Ire.)
 (13)
Mont Aux Sources (Lesotho)
 (14)
Mount of Olives (Isr.) (13)
Pentland Hills (Scot.) (13)
Pidurutalagala (Sri) (14)
Riesengebirge Ms. (Eur.)
 (13)
Skaptarjökull (v.) Iceland (13)
Table Mountain (S.A.) (13)
Tabor Mountain (Isr.) (13)

Oceans and seas

3 AND 4

Aral S. (Kaz., Uzbek.)
Azov, S. of (Ukr./Rus.)
Dead S. (Jord., Isr.)
Java S. (Indo.)
Kara S. (Rus.)
Red S. (Egypt, Arab.)
Ross S. (Antarc.)
Sava S. (Indo.)
Sulu S. (Philip.)

5

Banda S. (Indo.)
Black S. (Eur., Turk.)
Ceram S. (Indo.)
China S. (China)
Coral S. (Indo.)
Irish S. (Brit. Isles)
Japan, S. of (Jap.)
Malay S. (Malay.)
North S. (Eur.)
Timor S. (Indo.)
White S. (Rus.)

6

Aegean S. (Gr., Turk.)
Arctic O.

Baltic S. (N. Eur.)
Bering S. (Pac.)
Flores S. (Indo.)
Gaelic S. (Brit. Isles)
Indian O.
Ionian S. (Gr.)
Laptev S. (Rus.)
Scotia S. (Antarc.)
Tasman S. (Austral.)
Yellow S. (China)

7

Andaman S. (Indo.)
Arabian S. (Ind.)
Arafura S. (Austral.)
Barents S. (Rus.)
Behring S. (Pac.)
Caspian S. (Eur., Asia)
Celebes S. (Indo)
Marmora, S. of (Turk.)
Molucca S. (Indo.)
Okhotsk, S. of (Rus.)
Pacific O.
Weddell S. (Antarc.)

8

Adriatic S. (Med.)
Amundsen S. (Antarc.)

Atlantic O.
Beaufort S. (Can.)
Ligurian S. (It.)
Macassar S. (Indo.)
McKinley S. (Green.)
Sargasso S. (Atl.)

9

Antarctic O.
Caribbean S. (Am.)
East China S. (China)
Greenland S. (Green.)
Norwegian S. (Nor.)
Zuider Zee ⎱ (Neth.)
Zuyder Zee ⎰

10 AND OVER

Bellingshausen S. (Antarc.)
 (13)
East Siberian S. (Rus.)
 (12)
King Haakon VIII S.
 (Antarc.) (14)
Mediterranean S. (Eur., Af.)
 (13)
South China S. (China) (10)
Tyrrhenian S. (W. Med.) (10)

Ports

3 AND 4

Acre (Isr.)
Aden (Yemen)
Akko (Isr.)
Amoy (China)
Baku (Azer.)
Bar (Yug.)
Bari (It.)
Cebu (Philip.)
Cobh (Ire.)
Cork (Ire.)
Deal (Eng.)
Elat (Isr.)
Erie (U.S.A.)
Hull (Eng.)
Ilo (Peru)
Kiel (Ger.)
Kobe (Jap.)
Okha (Rus.)
Oran (Alg.)
Oslo (Nor.)
Para (Braz.)
Pula (Yu.)
Riga (Latvia.)
Rye (Eng.)
Safi (Moroc.)
Suez (Egypt)
Tain (Scot.)
Tema (Ghana)
Wick (Scot.)

5

Akyab (Burma)
Arica (Chile)
Barry (Wales)
Basra (Iraq)
Beira (Moz.)
Belem (Braz.)
Brest (Fr.)
Cadiz (Sp.)
Canea (Gr.)
Ceuta (Moroc.)
Colon (Panama)
Corfu (Gr.)
Dakar (Senegal)
Delft (Neth.)
Dover (Eng.)
Dubai (Dubai)
Eilat (Isr.)
Emden (Ger.)
Gaeta (It.)
Galle (Sri.)

Genoa (It.)
Haifa (Isr.)
Havre (Le) (Fr.)
Izmir (Turk.)
Kerch (Ukr.)
Kochi (Jap.)
Kotor (Yug.)
Lagos (Nig.)
Larne (N. Ire.)
Leith (Scot.)
Lulea (Swed.)
Mahon (Minorca)
Malmö (Swed.)
Mocha (Yemen)
Osaka (Jap.)
Ostia (It.)
Palma (Sp.)
Palos (Sp.)
Poole (Eng.)
Pusan (S. Korea)
Rabat (Moroc.)
Reval (Est.)
Scapa (Scot.)
Split (Yug.)
Trani (It.)
Tunis (Tun.)
Turku (Fin.)
Varna (Bulg.)
Wisby (Swed.)
Yalta (Ukr.)
Ystad (Swed.)

6

Agadir (Moroc.)
Ahmedi (Yemen)
Ancona (It.)
Ashdod (Isr.)
Balboa (Panama)
Bastia (Cors.)
Beirut (Lebanon)
Bergen (Nor.)
Bilbao (Sp.)
Bombay (Ind.)
Boston (U.S.A.)
Bremen (Ger.)
Calais (Fr.)
Callao (Peru)
Cannes (Fr.)
Chalna (Pak.)
Chefoo (China)
Cochin (Ind.)
Dairen (China)
Danzig (Pol.)

Darwin (Austral.)
Dieppe (Fr.)
Douala (Cameroun)
Dunbar (Scot.)
Dundee (Scot.)
Durban (S.A.)
F'derik (Mauritania)
Ferrol (Sp.)
Gdansk (Pol.)
Gdynia (Pol.)
Haldia (Ind.)
Hankow (China)
Hobart (Tas.)
Izmail (Ukr.)
Jeddah (Saudi)
Kalmar (Swed.)
Kandla (Ind.)
Kuwait (Kuwait)
Larvik (Nor.)
Lisbon (Port.)
Lobito (Angola)
London (Eng.)
Madras (Ind.)
Malaga (Sp.)
Manila (Philip.)
Matadi (Zaïre)
Mtwara (Tanz.)
Naples (It.)
Narvik (Nor.)
Nelson (N Z.)
Odense (Den.)
Odessa (Ukr.)
Oporto (Port.)
Ostend (Belg.)
Padang (Indo.)
Patras (Gr.)
Penang (Malay.)
Ramsey (I. of Man)
Recife (Braz.)
Rhodes (Gr.)
Rijeka (Yug.)
Santos (Braz.)
Sittwe (Burma)
Skikda (Alg.)
Smyrna (Turk.)
Suakin (Sudan)
Swatow (China)
Sydney (Austral.)
Tainan (Taiwan)
Tetuán (Moroc.)
Toulon (Fr.)
Tromsø (Nor.)
Venice (It.)
Weihai (China)
Wismar (Ger.)

7

Aalborg (Den.)
Abidjan (Ivory Coast)
Ajaccio (Cors.)
Algiers (Alg.)
Antwerp (Belg.)
Bangkok (Thai.)
Belfast (N.I.)
Bushire (Iran)
Cardiff (Wales)
Cattaro (Yug.)
Cayenne (Fr. Guiana)
Chatham (Eng.)
Colombo (Sri)
Corunna (Sp.)
Cotonou (Benin)
Dampier (Austral.)
Detroit (U.S.A.)
Donegal (Ire.)
Dundalk (Ire.)
Dunkirk (Fr.)
Foochow (China)
Funchal (Sp.)
Geelong (Austral.)
Grimsby (Eng.)
Guaymas (Mex.)
Halifax (Can.)
Hamburg (Ger.)
Harwich (Eng.)
Hodeida (Yemen)
Horsens (Den.)
Houston (U.S.A.)
Jakarta (Indo.)
Karachi (Pak.)
Keelung (Taiwan)
Kitimat (Can.)
Kowloon (Hong Kong)
La Plata (Arg.)
Larnaca (Cypru)
Leghorn (It.)
Le Havre (Fr.)
Marsala (It.)
Melilla (Moroc.)
Messina (It.)
Mogador (Moroc.)
Mombasa (Kenya)
New York (U.S.A.)
Norfolk (U.S.A.)
Okhotsk (Rus.)
Palermo (It.)
Piraeus (Gr.)
Rangoon (Burma)
Rosario (Arg.)
Rostock (Ger.)

Salerno (It.)
San Juan (Puerto Rico)
Seattle (U.S.A.)
Stettin (Pol.)
Swansea (Wales)
Tallinn (Est.)
Tangier (Moroc.)
Tilbury (Eng.)
Tobarao (Braz.)
Trapani (It.)
Trieste (It.)
Tripoli (Libya)
Yingkow (China)
Youghal (Ire.)

8

Abu Dhabi
Adelaide (Austral.)
Alicante (Sp.)
Arrecife (Sp.)
Auckland (N.Z.)
Benghazi (Libya)
Bordeaux (Fr.)
Boulogne (Fr.)
Brindisi (It.)
Brisbane (Austral.)
Budapest (Hung.)
Calcutta (Ind.)
Cape Town (S.A.)
Cocanada (Ind.)
Coquimbo (Chile)
Cuxhaven (Ger.)
Damietta (Egypt)
Djibouti (Djibouti)
Dunleary (Ire.)
Elsinore (Den.)
Europort (Neth.)
Falmouth (Eng.)
Flushing (Neth.)
Freetown (Sierra Leone)
Gisborne (N.Z.)
Göteborg (Swed.)
Greenock (Scot.)
Hakodate (Jap.)
Halmstad (Swed.)
Helsinki (Fin.)
Holyhead (Wales)
Honfleur (Fr.)
Hong Kong
Honolulu (Hawaii)
Istanbul (Turk.)
Kakinada (Ind.)
Kingston (Jam.)
La Guiara (Venez.)
La Coruña (Sp.)
Llanelli (Wales)
Macassar (Indo.)

Makassar (Indo.)
Matarini (Peru)
Montreal (Can.)
Moulmein (Burma)
Murmansk (Rus.)
Nagasaki (Jap.)
Nakhodka (Rus.)
Navarino (Gr.)
Newhaven (Eng.)
New Haven (U.S.A.)
Nyköping (Swed.)
Paradeep (Indo.)
Pechenga (Rus.)
Pembroke (Wales)
Penzance (Eng.)
Plymouth (Eng.)
Portland (Eng.)
Port Said (Egypt)
Rosslare (Ire.)
St. Helier (Ch. Is.)
Sandwich (Eng.)
Szczecin (Pol.)
Shanghai (China)
Taganrog (Rus.)
Takoradi (Ghana)
Tamatave (Mad.)
Tientsin (China)
Tiksi Bay (Rus.)
Vera Cruz (Mex.)
Weymouth (Eng.)
Yokohama (Jap.)

9

Algeciras (Sp.)
Amsterdam (Neth.)
Archangel (Rus.)
Ardrossan (Scot.)
Avonmouth (Eng.)
Baltimore (U.S.A.)
Barcelona (Sp.)
Cartagena (Sp. and
  Colombia)
Cherbourg (Fr.)
Churchill (Can.)
Cristobal (Panama)
Devonport (Eng.)
Dubrovnik (Croatia)
Esquimalt (Can.)
Essaouira (Moroc.)
Fishguard (Wales)
Flensburg (Ger.)
Fos-sur-Mer (Fr.)
Fremantle (Austral.)
Galveston (U.S.A.)
Gibraltar (Med.)
Gravesend (Eng.)
Guayaquil (Equador)

Helsingör (Den.)
Hiroshima (Jap.)
Kagoshima (Jap.)
Kaohsiung (Taiwan)
King's Lynn (Eng.)
Kolobrzeg (Pol.)
Las Palmas (Sp.)
Leningrad (Rus.)
Liverpool (Eng.)
Lyttelton (N.Z.)
Mbuji-Mayi (Zaïre)
Melbourne (Austral.)
Mossel Bay (S.A.)
Nantucket (U.S.A.)
Newcastle (Eng. and
  Austral.)
Owen Sound (Can.)
Port Arzew (Alg.)
Pensacola (U.S.A.)
Port Klang (Malay.)
Port Louis (Mauritius)
Portmadoc (Wales)
Port Mahon (Sp.)
Port Natal (S.A.)
Porto Novo (Benin)
Port Royal (Jam.)
Port Sudan (Sudan)
Rotterdam (Neth.)
Scapa Flow (Scot.)
Sheerness (Eng.)
Singapore
Stavangar (Nor.)
Stockholm (Swed.)
Stornaway (Scot.)
Trondheim (Nor.)
Vancouver (Can.)
Zeebrugge (Belg.)

10

Alexandria (Egypt)
Barnstaple (Eng.)
Bridgeport (U.S.A.)
Casablanca (Moroc.)
Charleston (U.S.A.)
Chittagong (Ind.)
Colchester (Eng.)
Constantsa (Rom.)
Copenhagen (Den.)
East London (S.A.)
Felixstowe (Eng.)
Folkestone (Eng.)
George Town (Malay.)
Gothenburg (Swed.)
Hammerfest (Nor.)
Hartlepool (Eng.)
Hermopolis (Gr.)
Jersey City (U.S.A.)

La Rochelle (Fr.)
Los Aneeles (U.S.A.)
Marseilles (Fr.)
Montego Bay (Jam.)
Montevideo
  (Uruguay)
New Bedford (U.S.A.)
New Orleans (U.S.A.)
Nouadhibou
  (Mauritania)
Pernambuco (Braz.)
Perth Amboy (U.S.A.)
Port Arthur (China)
Portsmouth (Eng.
  and U.S.A.)
Rock Harbour
  (U.S.A.)
San Juan Bay (Peru)
Simonstown (S.A.)
Sunderland (Eng.)
Teignmouth (Eng.)
Travemünde (Ger.)
Valparaiso (Chile)
Vlissingen (Neth.)
Whitstable (Eng.)

11

Bremerhaven (Ger.)
Buenos Aires (Arg.)
Christiana (Nor.)
Cinque Ports (Eng.)
Dar es Salaam
  (Tanz.)
Dun Laoghaire (Ire.)
Grangemouth (Scot.)
Helsingborg (Swed.)
Hermoupolis (Gr.)
Masulipatam (Ind.)
Pearl Harbor
  (Hawaii)
Pondicherry (Ind.)
Port Glasgow (Scot.)
Port Jackson
  (Austral.)
Port Moresby
  (Papua)
Port of Spain
  (Trinidad)
Richard's Bay (S.A.)
Saint Helier (Ch. Is.)
St. Peter Port (Ch. Is.)
Shimonoseki (Jap.)
Southampton (Eng.)
Three Rivers (Can.)
Trincomalee (Ind.)
Vladivostok (Rus.)

113

12

Barranquilla (Colombia)
Buenaventura (Colombia)
Kotakinabalu (Malay.)
Masulipatnam (Ind.)
Mina al-Ahmadi (Kuwait)
Milford Haven (Wales)
North Shields (Eng.)
Port Adelaide (Austral.)
Port Harcourt (Nig.)

Port Sunlight (Eng.)
Puerto Hierro (Venez.)
Rio de Janeiro (Braz.)
San Francisco (U.S.A.)

13 AND 14

Christiansund (Nor.) (13)
Constantinople (Turk.) (14)

Frederikshavn (Den.) (13)
Middlesbrough (Eng.) (13)
Mina Hassan Tani (Moroc.) (14)
Petropavlovsk (Rus.) (13)
Port Elizabeth (S.A.) (13)
Puerto Cabello (Venez.) (13)
Santiago de Cuba (Cuba) (14)
Wilhelmshaven (Ger.) (13)

Provinces, cantons, districts, regions, dependent states, etc.

3 AND 4

Ain (Fr.)
Aube (Fr.)
Aude (Fr.)
Bari (It.)
Bern (Swit.)
Cher (Fr.)
Diu (Ind.)
Eure (Fr.)
Fars (Iran)
Gard (Fr.)
Gaza (Isr.)
Gers (Fr.)
Goa (Ind.)
Ica (Peru)
Iowa (U.S.A.)
Jaen (Sp.)
Jura (Fr.)
Kano (Nig.)
Kum (Iran)
Leon (Sp.)
Lima (Peru)
Lot (Fr.)
Lugo (Sp.)
Nord (Fr.)
Ohio (U.S.A.)
Oise (Fr.)
Orne (Fr.)
Oudh (Ind.)
Pale (The) (Ire.)
Para (Braz.)
Pegu (Burna)
Pisa (It.)
Rome (It.)
Saar (Ger.)
Sind (Pak.)
Sus (Moroc.)
Tarn (Fr.)
Uri (Swit.)
Utah (U.S.A.)

Var (Fr.)
Vaud (Swit.)
Zug (Swit.)

5

Achin (Indo.)
Adana (Turk.)
Aisne (Fr.)
Anjou (Fr.)
Assam (Ind.)
Baden (Ger.)
Bahia (Braz.)
Banat (Eur.)
Basel (Swit.)
Béarn (Fr.)
Beira (Port.)
Berne (Swit.)
Berry (Fr.)
Bihar (Ind.)
Cadiz (Sp.)
Ceara (Braz.)
Doubs (Fr.)
Drome (Fr.)
Eifel (Ger.)
Eupen (Belg.)
Fayum (Egypt)
Genoa (It.)
Goiás (Braz.)
Hamar (Nor.)
Hejaz (Saudi)
Herat (Afghan.)
Hesse (Ger.)
Honan (China)
Hopeh (China)
Hunan (China)
Hupeh (China)
Idaho (U.S.A.)
Indre (Fr.)
Isère (Fr.)

Judea (Aia)
Jujuy (Arg.)
Kansu (China)
Khiva (Asia)
Kirin (China)
Kwara (Nig.)
Lagos (Nig.)
La Paz (Boliv.)
Lecce (It.)
Liège (Belg.)
Loire (Fr.)
Lucca (It.)
Maine (U.S.A. and
    Fr.)
Marne (Fr.)
Meuse (Fr.)
Milan (It.)
Morea (Gr.)
Namur (Belg.)
Nubia (Sudan)
Ojaca (Mex.)
Oruro (Boliv.)
Otago (N.Z.)
Padua (It.)
Parma (It.)
Pavia (It.)
Perak (Malay.)
Posen (Pol.)
Rhône (Fr.)
Sabah (Malay.)
Sahel (Af.)
Salta (Arg.)
Savoy (It.)
Seine (Fr.)
Simla (Ind.)
Sivas (Turk.)
Somme (Fr.)
Surat (Ind.)
Tacna (Chile)
Tavoy (Burma)
Tepic (Mex.)

Terai (Ind.)
Texas (U.S.A.)
Tibet (China)
Tigre (Eth.)
Tokay (Hung.)
Tomsk (Rus.)
Tyrol (Aust.)
Vizeu (Port.)
Weald (The) (Eng.)
Yonne (Fr.)
Yukon (Can.)

6

Aargau (Swit.)
Alaska (U.S.A.)
Alisco (Mex.)
Allier (Fr.)
Alsace (Fr.)
Anhwei (China)
Apulia (It.)
Aragon (Sp.)
Ariège (Fr.)
Artois (Fr.)
Bashan (Asia)
Basque Prov.
Bengal (Ind.)
Bergen (Nor.)
Biscay (Sp.)
Bombay (Ind.)
Bosnia (Yug.)
Cachar (Ind.)
Creuse (Fr.)
Crimea (Ukr.)
Dakota (U.S.A.)
Darfur (Sudan)
Emilia (It.)
Epirus (Gr.)
Faenza (It.)
Fukien (China)
Geneva (Swit.)

Gerona (Sp.)
Ghilan (Iran)
Glarus (Swit.)
Guiana (S. Am.)
Hawaii (U.S.A.)
Hedjaz (Saudi)
Huelva (Sp.)
Huesca (Sp.)
Iloilo (Philip.)
Johore (Ind.)
Judaea (Asia)
Kansas (U.S.A.)
Karroo (S.A.)
Kaspan (Iran)
Kerala (Ind.)
Kerman (Iran)
Kielce (Pol.)
Ladakh (Ind.)
Landes (Fr.)
Latium (It.)
Lerida (Sp.)
Levant (Asia)
Loiret (Fr.)
Loreto (Port.)
Lozère (Fr.)
Lublin (Pol.)
Madras (Ind.)
Málaga (Sp.)
Manche (Fr.)
Mantua (It.)
Marico (S.A.)
Mercia (Eng.)
Mergui (Burma)
Modena (It.)
Molise (It.)
Murcia (Sp.)
Mysore (Ind.)
Nelon (N.Z.)
Nevada (U.S.A.)
Nièvre (Fr.)
Novara (It.)

Oaxaca (Mex.)
Oregon (U.S.A.)
Orense (Sp.)
Orissa (Ind.)
Oviedo (Sp.)
Pahang (Malay.)
Pampas (S. Am.)
Paraná (Braz.)
Poitou (Fr.)
Potosi (Boliv.)
Punjab (Ind. and Pak.)
Quebec (Can.)
Rivers (Nig.)
Sahara (Af.)
St. Gall (Swit.)
Sarthe (Fr)
Saxony (Ger.)
Scania (Swed.)
Schwyz (Swit.)
Scinde (Ind.)
Serbia (Yug.)
Shansi (China)
Shensi (China)
Sicily (It.)
Sokoto (Nig.)
Sonora (Mex.)
Soudan (Af.)
Styria (Aust.)
Swabia (Ger.)
Sylhet (Ind.)
Thrace (Gr.)
Ticino (Swit.)
Toledo (Sp.)
Tromsø (Nor.)
Ulster (N.I.)
Umbria (It.)
Upsala (Swed.)
Valais (Swit.)
Vendée (Fr.)
Veneto (It.)
Viborg (Den.)
Vienne (Fr.)
Vosges (Fr.)
Wessex (Eng.)
Yunnan (China)
Zamora (Sp.)
Zurich (Swit.)

7

Abruzzi (It.)
Alabama (U.S.A.)
Alagoas (Braz.)
Alberta (Can.)
Algarve (Port.)
Almeria (Sp.)
Antwerp (Belg.)
Arizona (U.S.A.)

Aveyron (Fr.)
Bavaria (Ger.)
Bohemia (Cze.)
Bokhara (Asia)
Brabant (Belg.)
Caceres (Sp.)
Castile (Sp.)
Chiapas (Mex.)
Corrèze (Fr.)
Côte-d'Or (Fr.)
Drenthe (Neth.)
Durango (Mex.)
Eritrea (Eth.)
Ferrara (It.)
Finmark (Nor.)
Florida (U.S.A.)
Galicia (Pol. and Sp.)
Galilee (Isr.)
Gascony (Fr.)
Georgia (U.S.A.)
Granada (Sp.)
Grisons (Swit.)
Guienne (Fr.)
Gujarat (Ind.)
Hanover (Ger.)
Haryana (Ind.)
Hérault (Fr.)
Hidalgo (Mex.)
Holland (Neth.)
Huanuco (Peru)
Indiana (U.S.A.)
Iquique (Chile)
Jalisco (Mex.)
Jutland (Den.)
Karelia (Rus.)
Kashmir (Ind. and Pak.)
Kiangsi (China)
Lapland (Eur.)
Leghorn (It.)
Liguria (It.)
Limburg (Neth.)
Linares (Chile)
Logroño (Sp.)
Lucerne (Swit.)
Malacca (Malay.)
Manipur (Ind.)
Marches (It.)
Mayenne (Fr.)
Mendoza (Arg.)
Montana (U.S.A.)
Moravia (Cze.)
Munster (Ire.)
Navarre (Sp.)
New York (U.S.A.)
Ontario (Can.)
Orléans (Fr.)
Paraíba (Braz.)
Perugia (It.)
Picardy (Fr.)

Potenza (It.)
Prussia (Ger.)
Ravenna (It.)
Riviera (The) (Fr., It.)
Samaria (Asia)
Santa Fé (Arg.)
Sarawak (Malay.)
Segovia (Sp.)
Sennaar (Sudan)
Sergipe (Braz.)
Seville (Sp.)
Siberia (Rus.)
Silesia (Pol.)
Simaloa (Mex.)
Sondrio (It .)
Tabasco (Mex.)
Tafilet (Moroc.)
Tanjore (Ind.)
Teheran (Iran)
Thurgau (Swit.)
Tripura (Ind.)
Tucuman (Arg.)
Tuscany (It.)
Utrecht (Neth.)
Venetia (It.)
Vermont (U.S.A.)
Waldeck (Ger.)
Western (Nig.)
Wyoming (U.S.A.)
Yucatan (Mex.)
Zealand } (Neth.)
Zeeland }

8

Alentejo (Port.)
Alicante (Sp.)
Amazonas (Braz.)
Anatolia (Turk.)
Ardennes (Fr.)
Arkansas (U.S.A.)
Asturias (Sp.)
Auckland (N.Z.)
Brittany (Fr.)
Bukovina (Eur.)
Burgundy (Fr.)
Calabria (It.)
Calvados (Fr.)
Campania (It.)
Campeche (Mex.)
Carniola (Aust.)
Carolina (U.S.A.)
Caucasia (Rus., Geo., Azer. or Asia)
Charente (Fr.)
Chekiang (China)
Coahuila (Mex.)
Colorado (U.S.A.)

Columbia (U.S.A.)
Dalmatia (Yug.)
Dauphiné (Fr.)
Delaware (U.S.A.)
Dordogne (Fr.)
Ferghana (Turk.)
Flanders (Belg.)
Florence (It.)
Fribourg (Swit.)
Girgenti (It.)
Gothland (Swed.)
Guerrero (Mex.)
Hainault (Belg.)
Hannover (Ger.)
Haut Rhin (Fr.)
Hawke Bay (N.Z.)
Holstein (Ger.)
Illinois (U.S.A.)
Kandahar (Afghan.)
Kentucky (U.S.A.)
Korassan (Iran)
Kordofan (Sudan)
Kweichow (China)
Labrador (Can.)
Leinster (Ire.)
Liaoning (China)
Limousin (Fr.)
Lombardy (It.)
Lorraine (Fr.)
Lothians (The) (Scot.)
Lowlands (Scot.)
Luristan (Iran)
Lyonnais (Fr.)
Macerata (It.)
Manitoba (Can.)
Maranhao (Braz.)
Maryland (U.S.A.)
Michigan (U.S.A.)
Missouri (U.S.A.)
Moldavia (Rom.)
Morbihan (Fr.)
Nagaland (Ind.)
Nebraska (U.S.A.)
Normandy (Fr.)
Norrland (Swed.)
Oberland (Swit.)
Oklahoma (U.S.A.)
Palencia (Sp.)
Parahiba (Braz.)
Peshawar (Ind.)
Piacenza (It.)
Piedmont (It.)
Provence (Fr.)
Roumelia (Turk.)
Ruthenia (Eur.)
Saarland (Ger.)
Salonika (Gr.)
Salzburg (Aust.)
Sardinia (It.)

Shantung (China)
Sinkiang (China)
Slavonia (Eur.)
Slovakia (Cze.)
Syracuse (It.)
Szechwan (China)
Taranaki (N.Z.)
Tarapaca (Chile)
Thessaly (Gr.)
Tiaxcala (Mex.)
Tongking (Asia)
Trentino (It.)
Tsinghai (China)
Valdivia (Chile)
Valencia (Sp.)
Vaucluse (Fr.)
Vera Cruz (Mex.)
Victoria (Austral.)
Virginia (U.S.A.)
Wallonia (Belg.)
Westland (N.Z.)
Wimmeria (Austral.)

9

Alto Adige (It.)
Andalusia (Sp.)
Appenzell (Swit.)
Aquitaine (Fr.)
Asia Minor (Asia)
Astrakhan (Rus.)
Carinthia (Aust.)
Catalonia (Sp.)
Champagne (Fr.)
Chihuahua (Mex.)
Connaught (Ire.)
Dakahlieh (Egypt)
Entre Rios (Arg.)
Franconia (Ger.)
Friesland (Neth.)
Groningen (Neth.)
Guipuzcoa (Sp.)
Hadramaut (Arab.)
Highlands (Scot.)
Kamchatka (Rus.)
Karnataka (Ind.)
Khuzestan (Iran)
Kwangtung (China)
Languedoc (Fr.)
Linköping (Swed.)
Louisiana (U.S.A.)
Macedonia (Gr. and
   Yug.)
Meghalaya (Ind.)
Melanesia (Pac.)
Michoacan (Mex.)
Minnesota (U.S.A.)
Neuchâtel (Swit.)

New Forest (Eng.)
New Jersey (U.S.A.)
New Mexico (U.S.A.)
Nivernais (Fr.)
Nuevo León (Mex.)
Oedenburg (Hung.)
Oldenburg (Ger.)
Overyssel (Neth.)
Palestine (Asia)
Patagonia (S. Am.)
Polynesia (Pac.)
Pomerania (Ger. and
   Pol.)
Potteries (The) (Eng.)
Queretaro (Mex.)
Rajasthan (Ind.)
Rajputana (Ind.)
Rhineland (Ger.)
Saint Gall (Swit.)
Salamanca (Sp.)
Samarkand (Asia)
Saragossa (Sp.)
Schleswig (Ger.)
Southland (N.Z.)
Tamil Nadu (Ind.)
Tarragona (Sp.)
Tennessee (U.S.A.)
Thayetmyo (Burma)
Thuringia (Ger.)
Transvaal (S.A.)
Trebizond (Turk.)
Trondheim (Nor.)
Turkestan (Asia)
Turkistan (Asia)
Turkmenia (Asia)
Villareal (Port.)
Wallachia (Rom.)
Wisconsin (U.S.A.)
Zacatecas (Mex.)

10

Adrianople (Turk.)
Baffinland (Can.)
Basilicata (It.)
Bessarabia (Ukr., Mold.)
Burgenland (Aust.)
California (U.S.A.)
Canterbury (N.Z.)
East Africa
East Anglia (Eng.)
Eure-et-Loir (Fr.)
Gelderland (Neth.)
Griqualand (S.A.)
Guanajuato (Mex.)
Haute-Loire (Fr.)
Haute-Marne (Fr.)
Haute-Saône (Fr.)

Kermanshah (Iran)
Lambayeque (Peru)
Loir-et-Cher (Fr.)
Mazandaran (Iran)
Micronesia (Pac.)
Mid-Western (Nig.)
Montenegro (Yug.)
New Castile (Sp.)
Nova Scotia (Can.)
Old Castile (Sp.)
Overijssel (Neth.)
Palatinate (Ger.)
Pernambuco (Braz.)
Pontevedra (Sp.)
Queensland (Austral.)
Rawalpindi (Pak.)
Rohilkhand (Ind.)
Roussillon (Fr.)
Senegambia (Af.)
Slave Coast (Af.)
Tamaulipas (Mex.)
Tavastehus (Fin.)
Tenasserim (Burma)
Valladolid (Sp.)
Valparaiso (Chile)
Vorarlberg (Aust.)
Washington (U.S.A.)
Waziristan (Pak.)
West Africa
West Bengal (Ind.)
West Indies (Carib.)
Westphalia (Ger.)

11

Baluchistan (Pak.)
Bourbonnais (Fr.)
Brandenburg (Ger.)
Connecticut (U.S.A.)
Côtes-du-Nord (Fr.)
East-Central (Nig.)
Estremadura (Port. and
   Sp.)
Great Karroo (S.A.)
Guadalajara (Sp.)
Guelderland (Neth.)
Hautes-Alpes (Fr.)
Haute-Savoie (Fr.)
Haute-Vienne (Fr.)
Herzegovina (Yug.)
Hesse-Nassau (Ger.)
Ile-de-France (Fr.)
Lower Saxony (Ger.)
Maharashtra (Ind.)
Matto Grosso (Braz.)
Mecklenburg (Ger.)
Minas Gerais (Braz.)
Mississippi (U.S.A.)

North Africa
North Dakota (U.S.A.)
Northumbria (Eng.)
Pas de Calais (Fr.)
Peloponnese (Gr.)
Quintana Roo (Mex.)
Rhode Island (U.S.A.)
Schwarzwald (Ger.)
South Dakota (U.S.A.)
Sudetenland (Ger.)
The Lothians (Scot.)
Unterwalden (Swit.)
Valle d'Aosta (It.)
West Prussia (Pol.)
White Russia
Württemberg (Ger.)

12

Benue-Plateau (Nig.)
British Isles (Eur.)
Franche-Comté (Fr)
Haute-Garonne (Fr.)
Heilungkiang (China)
Hohenzollern (Ger.)
Huancavelica (Peru)
Indre-et-Loire (Fr.)
Latin America
Little Russia
Lot-et-Garonne (Fr.)
Lower Austria (Aust.)
New Brunswick (Can.)
Newfoundland (Can.)
New Hampshire (U.S.A
North Brabant (Neth.)
North-Central (Nig.)
North-Eastern (Nig.)
North Holland (Neth.)
North-Western (Nig.)
Pennsylvania (U.S.A.)
Rio de Janeiro (Braz.)
Saskatchewan (Can.)
Schaffhausen (Swit.)
Schleswig-Holstein
   (Ger.)
Seine-et-Marne (Fr.)
South-Eastern (Nig.)
South Holland (Neth.)
The Potteries (Eng.)
Transylvania (Rom.)
Upper Austria (Aust.)
Uttar Pradesh (Ind.)
West Virginia (U.S.A.)

13

Andhra Pradesh (Ind.)

Canary Islands (Sp.)
Christiansand (Nor.)
Emilia-Romagna (It.)
Espirito Santo (Braz.)
Ille-et-Vilaine (Fr.)
Inner Mongolia (China)
Madhya Pradesh (Ind.)
Massachusetts (U.S.A.)
New South Wales (Austral.)
North Carolina (U.S.A.)
Rhondda Valley (Wales)
Romney Marshes (Eng.)
San Luis Potosi (Mex.)
Santa Catarina (Braz.)
Saxe-Altenberg (Ger.)
Saxe-Meiningen (Ger.)
South Carolina (U.S.A.)
Tarn-et-Garonne (Fr.)
Transbaikalia (Rus.)
Witwatersrand (S.A.)

14 AND OVER

Alpes-Maritimes (Fr.) (14)
Alsace-Lorraine (Fr.) (14)
Baden-Württemberg (Ger.) (16)
Basque Provinces (Sp.) (14)
Bihar and Orissa (Ind.) (14)
British Columbia (Can.) (15)
Central America (14)
Channel Islands (U.K.) (14)
District of Columbia (U.S.A.) (18)
Entre-Douro-e-Minho (Port.) (16)
Griqualand West (S.A.) (14)
Hautes-Pyrénées (Fr.) (14)
Himachal Pradesh (Ind.) (15)
Loire-Atlantique (Fr.) (15)
Lower California (Mex.) (15)
Northern Ireland (U.K.) (15)
North Rhine-Westphalia (Ger.) (20)

North-West Frontier (Pak.) (17)
Orange Free State (S.A.) (15)
Rhenish Prussia (Ger.) (14)
Rio Grande do Sul (Braz.) (14)
Santa Catharina (Braz.) (14)
Saxe-Coburg-Gotha (Ger.) (15)
Schaumberg-Lippe (Ger.) (15)
South Australia (Austral.) (14)
Southern Africa (14)
United Provinces (Ind.) (15)
Western Australia (Austral.) (16)

Rivers

R. = River, and is inserted where "River" commonly follows the name.

1 – 3

Aar (Swit.)
Ain (Fr.)
Aln (Eng.)
Axe (Eng.)
Bug (Pol., Ukr.)
Cam (Eng.)
Dee (Eng.)
Don (Scot.)
Ems (Ger.)
Esk (Scot.)
Exe (Eng.)
Fal (Eng.)
Fly (Papua)
Hex R. (S.A.)
Hsi (China)
Hue (Asia)
Ili (Asia)
Ill (Fr.)
Inn (Aust.)
Ket (Sib.)
Kur (Rus.)
Kwa (Af.)
Lea (Eng.)
Lee (Ire.)
Lek (Neth.)
Lot (Fr.)
Lys (Fr. and Belg.)
Nen (Eng.)
Ob (Sib.)

Oka (Rus.)
Po (It.)
Red R. (U.S.A.)
Rur (Eur.)
Rye (Eng.)
Sid (Eng.)
Sow (Eng.)
Syr (Kaz.)
Taw (Eng.)
Tay (Scot.)
Tom (Sib.)
Ure (Eng.)
Usa (Rus.)
Usk (Wales)
Var (Fr.)
Wey (Eng.)
Wye (Eng.)
Wye (Wales)
Y (Neth.)
Yeo (En.)
Zab (Turk.)

4

Adda (It.)
Adur (Eng.)
Aire (Eng.)
Aire (Scot.)
Alma (Ukr.)
Amur (Asia)

Anio (It.)
Arno (It.)
Arun (Eng.)
Avon (Eng.)
Bann (N.I.)
Beas (Ind.)
Bure (Eng.)
Cart (Scot.)
Cher (Fr.)
Cole (Eng.)
Coln (Eng.)
Dart (Eng.)
Doon (Scot.)
Dora (It.)
Dove (Eng.)
Earn (Scot.)
Ebro (Sp.)
Eden (Eng.)
Eden (Scot.)
Elbe (Ger.)
Enns (Aust.)
Erne (Ire.)
Fall (U.S.A.)
Geba (W. Af.)
Gila (U.S.A.)
Gota (Swed.)
Ha Ha (Can.)
Isar (Ger.)
Isis (Eng.)
Juba (E. Af.)
Kama (Rus.)

Kusi (Ind.)
Kwai (Thai)
Lahn (Ger.)
Lech (Ger.)
Lena (Sib.)
Loir (Fr.)
Lune (Eng.)
Lynd (Austral.)
Maas (Neth.)
Main (Ger.)
Main (Ire.)
Mole (Eng.)
Mooi (S.A.)
Naze (Eng.)
Neva (Rus.)
Nida (Pol.)
Nile (Af.)
Nith (Scot.)
Oder (Cze, Ger., Pol.)
Ohio (U.S.A.)
Oise (Fr.)
Ouse (Eng.)
Oxus (Asia)
Peel (Austral.)
Peel (Can.)
Prah (Af.)
Ravi (Ind.)
Rede (Eng.)
Roer (Eur.)
Ruhr (Ger.)

Saar (Fr., Ger.)
Salt R. (U.S.A.)
Save (Fr.)
Spey (Scot.)
Styr (Sp.)
Suck (Ire.)
Suir (Ire.)
Swan (Austral.)
Taff (Wales)
Tana (E. Af.)
Tara (Sib.)
Tarn (Fr.)
Tawe (Wales)
Tees (Eng.)
Test (Eng.)
Thur (Swit.)
Tons (Ind.)
Towy (Wales)
Tyne (Eng.)
Umea (Swed.)
Ural (Rus., Kaz.)
Vaal (S. Af.)
Vire (Fr.)
Waag (Hung.)
Waal (Neth.)
Wash (Eng.)
Wear (Eng.)
Yana (Sib.)
Yare (Eng.)

5

Abana (Syr.)
Adige (It.)
Adour (Fr.)
Agout (Fr.)
Aisne (Fr.)
Alice (Autral.)
Allan (Scot.)
Allen (Scot.)
Aller (Ger.)
Annan (Scot.)
Avoca (Austral.)
Benue (W. Af.)
Black R. (U.S.A.)
Blood R. (S. A.)
Bober (Ger.)
Bogie (Scot.)
Boyne (Ire.)
Brent (Eng.)
Bride (Ire.)
Camel (Eng.)
Clyde (Scot.)
Colne (Eng.)
Congo (Af.)
Deben (Eng.)
Desna (Rus.)
Devon (Scot.)
Douro (Port., Sp.)
Dovey (Wales)
Drave (Hung.)
Drina (Yug.)
Dunay (Rus.)
Eider (Ger.)
Etive (Scot.)
Feale (Ire.)
Fleet (Eng.)
Forth (Scot.)
Foyle (Ire.)
Frome (Eng.)
Gogra (Ind.)
Green R. (U.S.A.)
Gumti (Ind.)
Habra (N. Af.)
Havel (Ger.)
Huang (China)
Hugli (Ind.)
Hunza (Ind.)
Ikopa (E. Af.)
Indus (Ind.)
Isère (Fr.)
Ishim (Kaz.)
James R. (U.S.A.)
Jelum (Ind.)
Jumna (Ind.)
Kabul R. (Afghan.)
Kafue (Af.)
Karun (Iran)
Katun (Sib.)

Koros (Hung.)
Kowie (S.A.)
Kuram (Afghan.)
Lagan (N. Ire.)
Leven (Scot.)
Liard (Can.)
Loire (Fr.)
Marne (Fr.)
Maroo (Rom.)
Memel (Ger.)
Menam (China)
Meuse (Belg.)
Miami (U.S.A.)
Minho (Port. and Sp.)
Moose (Can.)
Neath (Wales)
Neuse (U.S.A.)
Niger (Af.)
Oglio (It.)
Onega (Rus.)
Otter (Eng.)
Peace R. (Can.)
Pecos (U.S.A.)
Pei Ho (China)
Perak (Malay.)
Plate (S. Am.)
Pruth (Rom.)
Purus (S. Am.)
Rance (Fr.)
Reuss (Swit.)
Rhine (Ger., Neth., Swit.)
Rhone (Fr., Swit.)
Saale (Ger.)
Saone (Fr.)
Seine (Fr.)
Shari (E. Af.)
Sheaf (Eng.)
Shiel (Scot.)
Shire (Af.)
Snake R. (U.S.A.)
Somme (Fr.)
Spree (Ger.)
Stour (Eng.)
Sugar (U.S.A.)
Sulir (Swit.)
Swale (Eng.)
Tagus (Port.)
Tamar (Eng.)
Tapti (Ind.)
Tarim (China)
Teffe (S. Am.)
Teifi (Wales)
Teign (Eng.)
Teith (Scot.)
Temes (Hung.)
Tiber (It.)
Tisza (Hung.)
Traun (Aust.)

Trent (Can.)
Trent (Eng.)
Tweed (Scot.)
Usuri (Asia)
Volga (Rus.)
Volta (W. Af.)
Warta (Pol.)
Welle (Af.)
Werra (Ger.)
Weser (Ger.)
Xiugo (S. Am.)
Yonne (Fr.)
Yssel (Neth.)
Yukon (Can.)
Zaïre (Af.)
Zenta (Hung.)

6

Agogno (It.)
Aguada (Sp.)
Alagon (Sp.)
Albany (Can.)
Albert (Austral.)
Allier (Fr.)
Amazon (S. Am.)
Angara (Rus.)
Arinos (S. Am.)
Atbara (Af.)
Barrow (Ire.)
Barwon (Austral.)
Beauly (Scot.)
Bolsas (Mex.)
Brazos (U.S.A.)
Buller (N Z.)
Calder (Eng.)
Canton R. (China)
Caroni (S. Am.)
Carron (Scot.)
Chenab (Ind.)
Coquet (Eng.)
Crouch (Eng.)
Danube (Eur.)
Dihong (Ind.)
Draava (Hung.)
Elster (Ger.)
Foyers (Scot.)
Fraser (Can.)
French (Can.)
Gambia (Af.)
Gandak (Ind.)
Ganges (Ind.)
Grande (S. Am.)
Grande (U.S.A., Mex.)
Grande (W. Af.)
Hamble (Eng.)
Hawash (E. Af.)
Hudson (U.S.A.)

Humber (Eng.)
Irtish (Rus.)
Irwell (Eng.)
Itchen (Eng.)
Japura (Braz.)
Jhelum (Ind.)
Jordan
  (Isr., Jord., Syria)
Kagera (Af.)
Kaveri (Ind.)
Kennet (Eng.)
Komati (E. Af.)
Kwanza (W. Af.)
Lehigh (U.S.A.)
Leitha (Hung.)
Liffey (Ire.)
Loddon (Eng.)
Loddon (Austral.)
Lomami (Af.)
Medina (Eng.)
Medway (Eng.)
Mekong (Asia)
Mersey (Eng.)
Mincio (It.)
Mobile (U.S.A.)
Modder R. (S.A.)
Mohawk (U.S.A.)
Moldau (Cze.)
Monnow (Eng.)
Morava (Cze.)
Moskva (Rus.)
Murray R. (Austral.)
Neckar (Ger.)
Neisse (Ger.)
Nelson (Can.)
Neutra (Hung.)
Niemen (Belo., Lith.)
Ogowai (Af.)
Oneida (U.S.A.)
Orange (S.A.)
Orwell (Eng.)
Ottawa (Can.)
Paraná (S. Am.)
Parima (Braz.)
Parret (Eng.)
Platte (U.S.A.)
Porali (Ind.)
Pungwe (E. Af.)
Pungwe (S.A.)
Racket (U.S.A.)
Ribble (Eng.)
Roding (Eng.)
Rother (Eng.)
Rovuma (E. Af.)
Rufiji (E. Af.)
Sabine (U.S.A.)
Sarthe (Fr.)
St. Paul (W. Af.)
Salwin (Burma)

Sambre (Belg., Fr.)
Santee (U.S.A.)
Scioto (U.S.A.)
Seneca (U.S.A.)
Sereth (Rom.)
Severn (Can.)
Severn (Eng., Wales)
Slaney (Ire.)
Stroma (Balkans)
Sunday (S.A.)
Sutlej (Ind.)
Sutluj (Ind.)
Swilly (Ire.)
Tamega (Port.)
Tanaro (It.)
Teviot (Scot.)
Thames (Can.)
Thames (Eng.)
Thames (N.Z.)
Theiss (Hung.)
Ticino (Swit.)
Tigris (Iraq, Turk.)
Tormes (Sp.)
Tornio (Fin.)
Tugela (S.A.)
Tummel (Scot.)
Ubangi (Af.)
Viatka (Rus.)
Vienne (Fr.)
Vltava (Cze.)
Wabash (U.S.A.)
Waihou (N.Z.)
Wandle (Eng.)
Warthe (Pol.)
Weaver (Eng.)
Wensum (Eng.)
Wharfe (Eng.)
Wipper (Ger.)
Witham (Eng.)
Yarrow (Scot.)
Yavari (S. Am.)
Yellow R. (China)
Zarang (Iran)
Zontag (S.A.)

7

Abitibi (Can.)
Alabama (U.S.A.)
Big Blue R. (U.S.A.)
Buffalo (S.A.)
Calabar (Af.)
Catawba (U.S.A.)
Cauvery (Ind.)
Chambal (Ind.)
Chelmer (Eng.)
Chumbal (Ind.)
Darling (Austral.)

Derwent (Eng.)
Deveron (Scot.)
Dnieper (Rus., Belo.,
 Ukr.) or (Asia)
Dunajec (Pol.)
Durance (Fr.)
Ettrick (Scot.)
Feather (U.S.A.)
Fitzroy (Austral.)
Gamtoos (S.A.)
Garonne (Fr.)
Gauritz (S.A.)
Genesee (U.S.A.)
Gilbert (Austral.)
Glenelg (Austral.)
Glommen (Nor.)
Guapore (S. Am.l
Heri Rud (Afghan.)
Hoang Ho (China)
Hooghli (Ind.)
Hwangho (China)
Juniata (U.S.A.)
Kanawha (Ind.)
Kubango (Af.)
Lachlan (Austral.)
La Plata (S. Am.)
Limpopo (S.A.)
Lualaba (Af.)
Luangwa (Af.)
Lugendi (Af.)
Madeira (S. Am.)
Marañón (S. Am.)
Maritza (Gr.)
Mattawa (Can.)
Mayenne (Fr.)
Meklong (Thail.)
Moselle (Eur.)
Muluyar (N. Af.)
Murghab (Afghan.)
Narbuda (Ind.)
Niagara (N. Am.)
Niagara (U.S.A.)
Olifant (S.A.)
Orinoco (S. Am.)
Orontes (Syria)
Paraiba (S. Am.)
Paraná (Braz.)
Parsnip (Can.)
Passaic (U.S.A.)
Pechora (Rus.)
Potomac (U.S.A.)
Rubicon (It.)
San Juan (S. Am.)
Sankuru (Af.)
St. Johns (U.S.A.)
Salween (Burma)
Schelde (Belg., Neth.)
Scheldt (Belg., Neth.)
Selenga (Asia)

Semliki (Af.)
Senegal (Af.)
Shannon (Ire.)
Spokane (U.S.A.)
Sungari (Asia)
Surinam (S. Am.)
Suwanee (U.S.A.)
Tampico (Mex.)
Tapajos (S. Am.)
Thomson (Austral.)
Tobique (Can.)
Torridge (Eng.)
Trinity (U.S.A.)
Ucayali (S. Am.)
Uruguay (S. Am.)
Vistula (Pol.)
Walkato (N.Z.)
Warrego (Austral.)
Washita (U.S.A.)
Waveney (Eng.)
Welland (Eng.)
Wichita (U.S.A.)
Yangtse (China)
Yarkand (Asia)
Yenesei (Sib.)
Ystwith (Wales)
Yuruari (S. Am.)
Zambezi (Af.)

8

Amu Darya (Asia)
Arkansas (U.S.A.)
Beaulieu (Eng.)
Beresina (Belo.)
Big Black R. (U.S.A.)
Blue Nile (Af.)
Brisbane R. (Austral.)
Campaspe (Austral.)
Cape Fear R. (U.S.A.)
Chambezi (Af.)
Cherwell (Eng.)
Chindwin (Burma)
Clarence (Austral.)
Colorado R. (U.S.A.)
Columbia (N. Am.)
Delaware (U.S.A.)
Demerara (S. Am.)
Dniester (Ukr., Mold.)
Evenlode (Eng.)
Gallinas (W. Af.)
Gatineau (Can.)
Georgina (Austral.)
Godavari (Ind.)
Goulburn (Austral.)
Great Kei (S.A.)
Guadiana (Sp.)
Hankiang (China)

Huallaga (S. Am.)
Humboldt (U.S.A.)
Itimbiri (Af.)
Kankakee (U.S.A.)
Kelantan (Malay.)
Kennebec (U.S.A.)
Klondyke R. (Can.)
Kootenay (N. Am.)
Mahanadi (Ind.)
Mazaruni (S. Am.)
Merrimac (U.S.A.)
Missouri (U.S.A.)
Mitchell (Austral.)
Nebraska (U.S.A.)
Ob Irtish (Rus.)
Paraguay (S. Am.)
Parahiba (S. Am.)
Putumayo (S. Am.)
Red River (U.S.A.)
Richmond (Austral.)
Rimouski (Can.)
Rio Negro (S. Am.)
Rio Tinto (Sp.)
Saguenay (Can.)
St. Claire (Can.)
Santiago (S. Am.)
Savannah (U.S.A.)
Syr Daria (Kaz.)
Tunguska (Sib.)
Umvolosi (S.A.)
Wanganui (N.Z.)
Wansbeck (Eng.)
Windrush (Eng.)
Winnipeg (Can.)

9

Abbitibee (Can.)
Churchill (Can.)
Crocodile R. (S.A.)
East River (U.S.A.)
Esmeralda (S. Am.)
Essequibo (S. Am.)
Euphrates (Iraq., Turk.,
 Syria)
Gala Water (Scot.)
Great Fish R. (S.A.)
Great Ouse (Eng.)
Guadalete (Sp.)
Indigirka (Rus.)
Irrawaddy (Burma)
Kalamazoo (U.S.A.)
Kizil Uzen (Iran)
Mackenzie (Can.)
Mallagami (Can.)
Miramichi (Can.)
Mirimichi (Can.)
Missimabi (Can.)

Nipisquit (Can.)
Paranaíba (S. Am.)
Penobscot (U.S.A.)
Pilcomayo (S. Am.)
Rede River (Eng.)
Rio Branco (S. Am.)
Rio Grande (Braz.)
Rio Grande (U.S.A., Mex.)
Rio Grande (W. Af.)
Saint John (Can.)
Saint Paul (W. Af.)
Salt River (U.S.A.)
Tennessee (U.S.A.)
Tocantins (S. Am.)
Toombudra (Ind.)
Umsimvubu (S.A.)
Umsimkulu (S.A.)
White Nile (Af.)
Wisconsin (U.S.A.)
Zarafshan (Asia)

Blood River (S.A.)
Great Slave R. (Can.)
Green River (U.S.A.)
Hawkesbury (Austral.)
Kizil Irmak (Turk.)
Lackawanna (U.S.A.)
Macquarrie (Austral.)
Manzanares (Sp.)
Monagahela (U.S.A.)
Paranahiba (S. Am.)
Parramatta (Austral.)
Sacramento (U.S.A.)
San Joaquin (U.S.A.)
Saint John's (U.S.A.)
St. Lawrence (Can.)
Shat-el-Arab (Asia)
Shenandoah (U.S.A.)
Snake River (U.S.A.)
White River (U.S.A.)
Yarra Yarra (Austral.)

Big Sandy River (U.S.A.)
   (13)
Big Sioux River (U.S.A.)
   (13)
Bonaventure (Can.) (11)
Brahmaputra (Ind.) (11)
Desaguadero (S. Am.) (11)
Ettrickwater (Scot.) (12)
Great Kanawka (U.S.A.)
   (12)
Guadalquivir (Sp.) (12)
Misissippi (U.S.A.) (11)
Modder River (S.A.) (11)
Murray-Darling (Austral.)
   (13)
Rappahannock (U.S.A.) (12)
Restigouche (Can.) (11)
Rio del Norte (Mex.) (11)
Saint Claire (Can.) (11)
Saint Lawrence (Can.) (13)
São Francisco (Braz.) (12)
Saskatchewan (Can.) (12)
Shubenacadia (Can.) (12)
Susquehanna (U.S.A.) (11)
Upper Paraná (S. Am.) (11)
Yangtse Kiang (China) (12)
Yarrowwater (Scot.) (11)
Yellow River (China) (11)

10

Allenwater (Scot.)
Black River (U.S.A.)
Blackwater (Eng.)
Blackwater (Ire.)

11 AND OVER

Big Black River (U.S.A.)
   (13)
Big Blue River (U.S.A.) (12)
Big Horn River(U.S.A.) (12)

States of the USA (Abbreviations)

Ala (Alabama)
Alas (Alaska)
Ariz (Arizona)
Ark (Arkansas)
Cal (California)
Colo (Colorado)
Conn/CT (Connecticut)
D.C. (District of
   Columbia)
Del (Delaware)
Fla (Florida)
Ga (Georgia)
Ia (Iowa)

Id/Ida (Idaho)
Ill (Illinois)
Ind (Indiana)
Kan (Kansas)
Ky/Ken (Kentucky)
La (Louisiana)
Md (Maryland)
Me (Maine)
Mass (Massachusetts)
Mich (Michigan)
Minn (Minnesota)
Miss (Mississippi)
Mo (Missouri)

Mont (Montana)
N.C. (North Carolina)
N.D. (Norh Dakota)
Neb (Nebraska)
Nev (Nevada)
N.H. (New Hampshire)
N.J. (New Jersey)
N.M. (New Mexico)
N.Y. (New York)
O. (Ohio)
Okla (Oklahoma)
Ore/Oreg (Oregon)
Penn (Pennsylvania)

R.I. (Rhode Island)
S.C. (South Carolina)
S. Dak (South Dakota)
Tenn (Tennessee)
Tex (Texas)
Ut (Utah)
Va (Virginia)
Wash (Washington)
W.Va (West Virginia)
Wis (Wisconsin)
Wyo (Wyoming)
Hawaii

Towns and cities: United Kingdom

(E.) = England.   (N.I.) = Northern Ireland.   (S.) = Scotland.   (W.) = Wales

3 AND 4

Alva (S.)
Ayr (S.)
Bala (W.)
Barr (S.)
Bath (E.)
Bray (E.)
Bude (E.)
Bury (E.)
Clun (E.)
Deal (E.)
Diss (E.)
Duns (S.)
Elie (S.)
Ely (E.)
Eton (E.)
Eye (E.)
Holt (E.)
Holt (W.)
Hove (E.)
Hull (E.)
Hyde (E.)
Ince (E.)
Kirn (S.)
Leek (E.)
Looe (E.)
Luss (S.)
Lydd (E.)
Mold (W.)
Nigg (S.)
Oban (S.)
Pyle (W.)
Reay (S.)
Rhyl (W.)
Rona (S.)
Ross (E.)
Ryde (E.)
Rye (E.)
Shap (E.)
Stow (S.)
Uig (S.)
Usk (E.)
Ware (E.)
Wark (E.)
Wem (E.)
Wick (S.)
Yarm (E.)
York (E.)

5

Acton (E.)
Alloa (S.)

Alton (E.)
Annan (S.)
Appin (S.)
Avoch (S.)
Ayton (S.)
Bacup (E.)
Banff (S.)
Beith (S.)
Blyth (E.)
Bourn (E.)
Brora (S.)
Bunaw (S.)
Busby (S.)
Calne (E.)
Ceres (S.)
Chard (E.)
Cheam (E.)
Chirk (W.)
Clova (S.)
Clune (S.)
Colne (E.)
Cowes (E.)
Crail (S.)
Crewe (E.)
Cupar (S.)
Denny (S.)
Derby (E.)
Doagh (N.I.)
Downe (S.)
Dover (E.)
Egham (E.)
Elgin (S.)
Ellon (S.)
Epsom (E.)
Errol (S.)
Filey (E.)
Flint (W.)
Fowey (E.)
Frome (E.)
Fyvie (S.)
Glynn (N.I.)
Goole (E.)
Govan (S.)
Grays (E.)
Hawes (E.)
Hedon (E.)
Hurst (E.)
Hythe (E.)
Insch (S.)
Islay (S.)
Keady (N.I.)
Keiss (S.)
Keith (S.)
Kelso (S.)
Lairg (S.)

Largo (S.)
Larne (N.I.)
Leeds (E.)
Leigh (E.)
Leith (S.)
Lewes (E.)
Louth (E.)
Luton (E.)
March (E.)
Nairn (S.)
Neath (W.)
Nevin (W.)
Newry (N.I.)
Olney (E.)
Omagh (N.I.)
Otley (E.)
Perth (S.)
Poole (E.)
Reeth (E.)
Ripon (E.)
Risca (E.)
Rugby (E.)
Salen (S.)
Sarum (E.)
Selby (E.)
Stoke (E.)
Stone (E.)
Tebay (E.)
Tenby (W.)
Thame (E.)
Toome (N.I.)
Towyn (W.)
Tring (E.)
Troon (S.)
Truro (E.)
Wells (E.)
Wigan (E.)

6

Aboyne (S.)
Alford (E.)
Alford (S.)
Alston (E.)
Amlwch (W.)
Antrim (N.I.)
Ashton (E.)
Augher (N.I.)
Bangor (W.)
Barnet (E.)
Barrow (E.)
Barton (E.)
Barvas (S.)
Batley (E.)

Battle (E.)
Bawtry (E.)
Beauly (S.)
Bedale (E.)
Belcoo (N.I.)
Belper (E.)
Beragh (N.I.)
Bervie (S.)
Biggar (S.)
Bodmin (E.)
Bognor (E.)
Bolton (E.)
Bo'ness (S.)
Bootle (E.)
Boston (E.)
Brecon (W.)
Bruton (E.)
Buckie (S.)
Builth (W.)
Bungay (E.)
Burton (E.)
Buxton (E.)
Carron (S.)
Castor (E.)
Cawdor (S.)
Cobham (E.)
Comber (N.I.)
Comrie (S.)
Conway (W.)
Crieff (S.)
Cromer (E.)
Cullen (S.)
Culter (S.)
Darwen (E.)
Dollar (S.)
Drymen (S.)
Dudley (E.)
Dunbar (S.)
Dundee (S.)
Dunlop (S.)
Dunnet (S.)
Dunoon (S.)
Durham (E.)
Dysart (S.)
Ealing (E.)
Eccles (E.)
Edzell (S.)
Epping (E.)
Exeter (E.)
Findon (S.)
Forfar (S.)
Forres (S.)
Girvan (S.)
Glamis (S.)
Goring (E.)

Hanley (E.)
Harlow (E.)
Harrow (E.)
Havant (E.)
Hawick (S.)
Henley (E.)
Hexham (E.)
Howden (E.)
Huntly (S.)
Ilford (E.)
Ilkley (E.)
Ilsley (E.)
Irvine (S.)
Jarrow (E.)
Kendal (E.)
Killin (S.)
Kilmun (S.)
Lanark (S.)
Lauder (S.)
Leslie (S.)
Leyton (E.)
Linton (S.)
Lochee (S.)
London (E.)
Ludlow (E.)
Lurgan (N.I.)
Lynton (E.)
Lytham (E.)
Maldon (E.)
Malton (E.)
Marlow (E.)
Masham (E.)
Meigle (S.)
Moffat (S.)
Morley (E.)
Naseby (E.)
Nelson (E.)
Neston (E.)
Newark (E.)
Newent (E.)
Newlyn (E.)
Newton (E.)
Norham (E.)
Oakham (E.)
Oldham (E.)
Ormsby (E.)
Ossett (E.)
Oundle (E.)
Oxford (E.)
Penryn (E.)
Pewsey (E.)
Pinner (E.)
Pladda (S.)
Pudsey (E.)
Putney (E.)

Ramsey (E.)
Redcar (E.)
Reston (S.)
Rhynie (S.)
Ripley (E.)
Romney (E.)
Romsey (E.)
Rosyth (S.)
Rothes (S.)
Ruabon (W.)
Rugely (E.)
Ruthin (W.)
St. Ives (E.)
Seaham (E.)
Seaton (E.)
Selsey (E.)
Settle (E.)
Shotts (S.)
Snaith (E.)
Strood (E.)
Stroud (E.)
Sutton (E.)
Thirsk (E.)
Thorne (E.)
Thurso (S.)
Tongue (S.)
Totnes (E.)
Walmer (E.)
Walton (E.)
Watton (E.)
Welwyn (E.)
Weston (E.)
Whitby (E.)
Widnes (E.)
Wigton (E.)
Wilton (E.)
Wishaw (S.)
Witham (E.)
Witney (E.)
Wooler (E.)
Yarrow (S.)
Yeovil (E.)

7

Airdrie (S.)
Alnwick (E.)
Andover (E.)
Appleby (E.)
Arundel (E.)
Ashford (E.)
Aylsham (E.)
Balfron (S.)
Balloch (S.)

8

Bampton (E.)
Banavie (S.)
Banbury (E.)
Barking (E.)
Beccles (E.)
Bedford (E.)
Belfast (N.I.)
Belford (E.)
Belleek (N.I.)
Berwick (E.)
Bewdley (E.)
Bexhill (E.)
Bickley (E.)
Bilston (E.)
Bourton (E.)
Bowfell (E.)
Bowmore (S.)
Braemar (S.)
Brandon (E.)
Brechin (S.)
Bristol (E.)
Brixham (E.)
Brodick (S.)
Bromley (E.)
Burnham (E.)
Burnley (E.)
Burslem (E.)
Caistor (E.)
Caledon (N.I.)
Canobie (S.)
Cantyre (S.)
Carbost (S.)
Carbury (W.)
Cardiff (W.)
Cargill (S.)
Carluke (S.)
Carrick (N.I.)
Catford (E.)
Cawston (E.)
Charing (E.)
Chatham (E.)
Cheadle (E.)
Cheddar (E.)
Chesham (E.)
Chester (E.)
Chorley (E.)
Clacton (E.)
Clifton (E.)
Clogher (N.I.)
Crathie (S.)
Crawley (E.)
Croydon (E.)
Culross (S.)
Cumnock (S.)
Cwmbran (W.)
Darsley (E.)
Datchet (E.)
Dawlish (E.)
Denbigh (W.)

Denholm (S.)
Dervock (N.I.)
Devizes (E.)
Dorking (E.)
Douglas (E.)
Douglas (S.)
Dundrum (N.I.)
Dunkeld (S.)
Dunmore (N.I.)
Dunning (S.)
Dunster (E.)
Elstree (E.)
Enfield (E.)
Evanton (S.)
Everton (E.)
Evesham (E.)
Exmouth (E.)
Fairlie (S.)
Falkirk (S.)
Fareham (E.)
Farnham (E.)
Feltham (E.)
Fintona (N.I.)
Galston (S.)
Gifford (S.)
Gilford (N.I.)
Glasgow (S.)
Glenarm (N.I.)
Glencoe (S.)
Glossop (E.)
Golspie (S.)
Gosport (E.)
Gourock (S.)
Granton (S.)
Grimsby (E.)
Guthrie (S.)
Halifax (E.)
Halkirk (S.)
Hampton (E.)
Harwich (E.)
Haworth (E.)
Helston (E.)
Heywood (E.)
Hitchin (E.)
Honiton (E.)
Hornsea (E.)
Hornsey (E.)
Horsham (E.)
Ipswich (E.)
Ixworth (E.)
Kenmore (S.)
Kessock (S.)
Keswick (E.)
Kilmory (S.)
Kilmuir (S.)
Kilsyth (S.)
Kinross (S.)
Kington (E.)
Kintore (S.)

Lamlash (S.)
Lancing (E.)
Langton (E.)
Larbert (S.)
Ledbury (E.)
Leyburn (E.)
Lincoln (E.)
Lisburn (N.I.)
Lybster (S.)
Macduff (S.)
Maesteg (W.)
Malvern (E.)
Margate (E.)
Matlock (E.)
Maybole (S.)
Meldrum (S.)
Melrose (S.)
Melvich (S.)
Methven (S.)
Molesey (E.)
Monikie (S.)
Moreton (E.)
Morpeth (E.)
Mossley (E.)
Muthill (S.)
Newbury (E.)
Newport (E.)
Newport (W.)
Newport (S.)
Newtown (W.)
Norwich (E.)
Oldbury (E.)
Overton (E.)
Padstow (E.)
Paisley (S.)
Peebles (S.)
Penrith (E.)
Polmont (S.)
Poolewe (S.)
Portree (S.)
Portsoy (S.)
Poulton E.)
Prescot (E.)
Preston (E.)
Rainham (E.)
Reading (E.)
Redhill (E.)
Redruth (E.)
Reigate (E.)
Renfrew (S.)
Retford (E.)
Romford (E.)
Rossall (E.)
Royston (E.)
Runcorn (E.)
Saddell (S.)
St. Asaph (W.)
St. Neots (E.)
Salford (E.)

Saltash (E.)
Sandown (E.)
Sarclet (S.)
Saxelby (E.)
Scourie (S.)
Seaford (E.)
Selkirk (S.)
Shifnal (E.)
Shipley (E.)
Shipton (E.)
Silloth (E.)
Skipton (E.)
Spilsby (E.)
Staines (E.)
Stanley (S.)
Stilton (E.)
Strathy (S.)
Sudbury (E.)
Sunbury (E.)
Swanage (E.)
Swansea (W.)
Swindon (E.)
Swinton (E.)
Tarbert (S.)
Tarland (S.)
Taunton (E.)
Tayport (S.)
Telford (E.)
Tenbury (E.)
Tetbury (E.)
Thaxted (E.)
Tilbury (E.)
Torquay (E.)
Tranent (S.)
Turriff (S.)
Tundrum (S.)
Twyford (E.)
Ullster (S.)
Ventnor (E.)
Walsall (E.)
Waltham (E.)
Wantage (E.)
Wareham (E.)
Warwick (E.)
Watchet (E.)
Watford (E.)
Weobley (E.)
Wickwar (E.)
Windsor (E.)
Winslow (E.)
Winster (E.)
Wisbeck (E.)
Worksop (E.)
Wrexham (W.)
Yetholm (S.)

Aberavon (W.)
Aberdare (W.)
Aberdeen (S.)
Abergele (W.)
Aberlady (S.)
Abingdon (E.)
Abington (S.)
Ahoghill (N.I.)
Alfreton (E.)
Alnmouth (E.)
Amesbury (E.)
Ampthill (E.)
Arbroath (S.)
Arrnadale (S.)
Arrochar (S.)
Auldearn (S.)
Axbridge (E.)
Aycliffe (E.)
Bakewell (E.)
Ballater (S.)
Banchory (S.)
Barmouth (W.)
Barnsley (E.)
Barrhill (S.)
Beattock (S.)
Berkeley (E.)
Beverley (E.)
Bicester (E.)
Bideford (E.)
Blantyre (S.)
Bolsover (E.)
Brackley (E.)
Bradford (E.)
Brampton (E.)
Bridgend (W.)
Bridport (E.)
Brighton (E.)
Bromyard (E.)
Broseley (E.)
Burghead (S.)
Caerleon (E.)
Camborne (E.)
Canisbay (S.)
Cardigan (W.)
Carlisle (E.)
Carnwath (S.)
Caterham (E.)
Chepstow (E.)
Chertsey (E.)
Clevedon (E.)
Clovelly (E.)
Coventry (E.)
Crediton (E.)
Creetown (S.)
Cromarty (S.)
Dalkeith (S.)
Dalmally (S.)

Dartford (E.)
Daventry (E.)
Debenham (E.)
Dedworth (E.)
Deptford (E.)
Dewsbury (E.)
Dingwall (S.)
Dirleton (S.)
Dolgelly (W.)
Dufftown (S.)
Dumfries (S.)
Dunbeath (S.)
Dunblane (S.)
Dungiven (N.I.)
Dunscore (S.)
Earlston (S.)
Egremont (E.)
Eversley (E.)
Eyemouth (S.)
Fakenham (E.)
Falmouth (E.)
Findhorn (S.)
Fortrose (S.)
Foulness (E.)
Glenluce (S.)
Grantham (E.)
Grantown (E.)
Greenlaw (S.)
Greenock (S.)
Hadleigh (E.
Hailsham (E.)
Halstead (E.)
Hamilton (S.)
Hastings (E.)
Hatfield (E.)
Hawarden (W.)
Helmsley (E.)
Hereford (E.)
Herne Bay (E.)
Hertford (E.)
Hilltown (N.I.)
Hinckley (E.)
Holbeach (E.)
Holyhead (W.)
Holywell (W.)
Hunmanby (E.)
Ilkeston (E.)
Inverary (S.)
Inverury (S.)
Jeantown (S.)
Jedburgh (S.)
Keighley (E.)
Kidwelly (W.)
Kilbride (S.)
Kilniver (S.)
Kilrenny (S.)
Kinghorn (S.)
Kingston (E.)
Kirkwall (S.)

Knighton (W.)
Lampeter (W.)
Langholm (S.)
Latheron (S.)
Lavenham (E.)
Lechlade (E.)
Leuchars (S.)
Liskeard (E.)
Llanelly (W.)
Llanrwst (W.)
Loanhead (S.)
Longtown (E.)
Lynmouth (E.)
Markinch (S.)
Marykirk (S.)
Maryport (E.)
Midhurst (E.)
Minehead (E.)
Moniaive (S.)
Monmouth (E.)
Montrose (S.)
Monymusk (S.)
Muirkirk (S.)
Nantwich (E.)
Neilston (S.)
Newburgh (S.)
Newhaven (E.)
Newmilns (S.)
Nuneaton (E.)
Ormskirk (E.)
Oswestry (E.)
Pembroke (W.)
Penicuik (S.)
Penzance (E.)
Pershore (E.)
Peterlee (E.)
Petworth (E.)
Pevensey (E.)
Pitsligo (S.)
Plaistow (E.)
Plymouth (E.)
Pooltiel (S.)
Portrush (N.I.)
Pwllheli (W.)
Quiraing (S.)
Ramsgate (E.)
Redditch (E.)
Rhayader (W.)
Richmond (E.)
Ringwood (E.)
Rochdale (E.)
Rothbury (E.)
Rothesay (S.)
St. Albans (E.)
St. Fergus (S.)
St. Helens (E.)
Saltburn (E.)
Sandgate (E.)
Sandwich (E.)

Sedbergh (E.)
Shanklin (E.)
Shelford (E.)
Shipston (E.)
Sidmouth (E.)
Skegnes (E.)
Skerries (W.)
Skifness (W.)
Sleaford (E.)
Southend (E.)
Spalding (E.)
Stafford (E.)
Stamford (E.)
Stanhope (E.)
Stanwell (E.)
Stirling (S.)
Stockton (E.)
Strabane (N.I.)
Stratton (E.)
Strichen (S.)
Surbiton (E.)
Swaffham (E.)
Talgarth (W.)
Talisker (S.)
Tamworth (E.)
Taransay (S.)
Thetford (E.)
Thornaby (E.)
Tiverton (E.)
Traquair (S.)
Tredegar (W.)
Tregaron (W.)
Trillick (N.I.)
Tunstall (E.)
Uckfield (E.)
Ullapool (S.)
Uxbridge (E.)
Wallasey (E.)
Wallsend (E.)
Wanstead (E.)
Westbury (E.)
Wetheral (E.)
Wetherby (E.)
Weymouth (E.)
Whithorn (S.)
Woodford (E.)
Woodside (S.)
Woolwich (E.)
Worthing (E.)
Yarmouth (E.)

9

Aberaeron (W.)
Aberdovey (W.)
Aberfeldy (S.)
Aberffraw (W.)
Aberfoyle (S.)

Aldeburgh (E.)
Aldershot (E.)
Allendale (E.)
Alresford (E.)
Ambleside (E.)
Ardrossan (S.)
Ashbourne (E.)
Ashburton (E.)
Avonmouth (E.)
Aylesbury (E.)
Ballintra (N.I.)
Ballymena (N.I.)
Banbridge (N.I.)
Beaumaris (W.)
Berridale (S.)
Bettyhill (S.)
Blackburn (E.)
Blacklarg (S.)
Blackpool (E.)
Blandford (E.)
Blisworth (E.)
Bracadale (S.)
Bracknell (E.)
Braeriach (S.)
Briantree (E.)
Brentford (E.)
Brentwood (E.)
Brighouse (E.)
Broadford (S.)
Broughton (E.)
Broughton (S.)
Buckhaven (S)
Bushmills (N.I.)
Cairntoul (S.)
Callander (S.)
Cambridge (E.)
Carstairs (S.)
Carnarvon (W.)
Carnforth (E.)
Castleton (E.)
Chesilton (E.)
Chingford (E.)
Clitheroe (E.)
Coleraine (N.I.)
Congleton (E.)
Cookstown (N.I.)
Cranborne (E.)
Cranbrook (E.)
Crewkerne (E.)
Criccieth (W.)
Cricklade (E.)
Cuckfield (E.)
Dartmouth (E.)
Devonport (E.)
Doncaster (E.)
Donington (E.)
Droitwich (E.)
Dronfield (E.)
Dumbarton (S.)

Dungannon (N.I.)
Dungeness (E.)
Dunstable (E.)
Edinburgh (S.)
Ellesmere (E.)
Faversham (E.)
Ferintosh (S.)
Festiniog (W.)
Fishguard (W.)
Fleetwood (E.)
Fochabers (S.)
Gateshead (E.)
Godalming (E.)
Gravesend (E .)
Greenwich (E.)
Grinstead (E.)
Guildford (E.)
Harrogate (E.)
Haslemere (E.)
Haverhill (E.)
Hawkhurst (E.)
Holmfirth (S.)
Ilchester (E.)
Immingham (E.)
Inchkeith (S.)
Inveraray (S.)
Inverness (S.)
Johnstone (S.)
Kettering (E.)
Kildrummy (S.)
King's Lynn (E.)
Kingswear (E.)
Kingussie (S.)
Kircubbin (N.I.)
Kirkcaldy (S.)
Lambourne (E.)
Lancaster (E.)
Leadhills (S.)
Leicester (E.)
Lichfield (E.)
Liverpool (E.)
Llanberis (W.)
Llandudno (W.)
Lochgelly (S.)
Lochinvar (S.)
Lochnagar (S.)
Lockerbie (S.)
Logierait (S.)
Longridge (E.)
Lowestoft (E.)
Lyme Regis (E.)
Lymington (E.)
Maidstone (E.)
Mansfield (E.)
Mauchline (S.)
Middleton (E.)
Milngavie (S.)
Moneymore (N.I.)
Newcastle (E.)

Newcastle (N.I.)
Newmarket (E.)
New Radnor (W.)
New Romney (E.)
Northwich (E.)
Otterburn (E.)
Pembridge (E.)
Penistone (E.)
Penkridge (E.)
Penyghent (E.)
Peterhead (S.)
Pickering (E.)
Pitlochry (S.)
Pontypool (E.)
Portadown (N.I.)
Port Ellen (S.)
Porthcawl (W.)
Portmadoc (W.)
Prestwick (S.)
Rasharkin (N.I.)
Riccarton (S.)
Rochester (E.)
Rostrevor (N.I.)
Rotherham (E.)
Rothiemay (S.)
St. Andrews (S.)
St. Austell (E.)
St. Fillans (S.)
Salisbury (E.)
Saltcoats (S.)
Saltfleet (E.)
Sevenoaks (E.)
Sheerness (E.)
Sheffield (E.)
Sherborne (E.)
Shieldaig (S.)
Slamannan (S.)
Smethwick (E.)
Southgate (E.)
Southport (E.)
Southwell (E.)
Southwold (E.)
Starcross (E.)
Stevenage (E.)
Stewarton (S.)
Stockport (E.)
Stokesley (E.)
Stourport (E.)
Stranraer (S.)
Stratford (E.)
Strathdon (S.)
Strontian (S.)
Tarporley (E.)
Tavistock (E.)
Tenterden (E.)
Thornhill (S.)
Tobermore (N.I.)
Tobermory (S.)
Todmorden (E.)

Tomintoul (S.)
Tonbridge (E.)
Tovermore (N.I.)
Towcester (E.)
Tynemouth (E.)
Ulverston (E.)
Upminster (E.)
Uppingham (E.)
Uttoxeter (E.)
Wainfleet (E.)
Wakefield (E.)
Warkworth (E.)
Welshpool (W.)
Weybridge (E.)
Whernside (E.)
Wimbledon (E.)
Wincanton (E.)
Wokingham (E.)
Woodstock (E.)
Worcester (E.)
Wymondham (E.)

10

Abbotsford (S.)
Accrington (E.)
Achnasheen (S.)
Aldborough (E.)
Altrincham (E.)
Anstruther (S.)
Applecross (S.)
Ardrishaig (S.)
Auchinleck (S.)
Ballantrae (S.)
Ballyclare (N.I.)
Ballymoney (N.I.)
Ballyroney (N.I.)
Barnstaple (E.)
Beaminster (E.)
Bedlington (E.)
Bellingham (E.)
Billericay (E.)
Birkenhead (E.)
Birmingham (E.)
Blackadder (S.)
Bridgnorth (E.)
Bridgwater (E.)
Bromsgrove (E.)
Broxbourne (E.)
Buckingham (E.)
Cader Idris (W.)
Caernarvon (W.)
Canterbury (E.)
Carmarthen (W.)
Carnoustie (S.)
Carshalton (E.)
Carsphairn (S.)
Castlederg (N.I.)
Castletown (S.)

Chelmsford (E.)
Cheltenham (E.)
Chichester (E.)
Chippenham (E.)
Chulmleigh (E.)
Coatbridge (S.)
Coggeshall (E.)
Colchester (E.)
Coldingham (S.)
Coldstream (S.)
Crickhowel (W.)
Cullompton (E.)
Cushendall (N.I.)
Dalbeattie (S.)
Darlington (E.)
Donaghadee (N.I.)
Dorchester (E.)
Drumlithie (S.)
Dukinfield (E.)
Eastbourne (E.)
East Linton (S.)
Eccleshall (E.)
Farningham (E.)
Ffestiniog (W.)
Folkestone (E.)
Freshwater (E.)
Galashiels (S.)
Gillingham (E.)
Glengariff (N.I.)
Glenrothes (S.)
Gloucester (E.)
Halesworth (E.)
Hartlepool (E.)
Haslingdon (E.)
Heathfield (E.)
Horncastle (E.)
Hornchurch (E.)
Hungerford (E.)
Hunstanton (E.)
Huntingdon (E.)
Ilfracombe (E.)
Johnshaven (S.)
Kenilworth (E.)
Kilcreggan (S.)
Killenaule (S.)
Kilmainham (S.)
Kilmalcolm (S.)
Kilmarnock (S.)
Kilwinning (S.)
Kincardine (S.)
Kingsbarns (S.)
Kingsclere (E.)
Kirkmaiden (S.)
Kirkoswald (E.)
Kirkoswald (S.)
Kirriemuir (S.)
Launceston (E.)
Leamington (E.)
Lennoxtown (S.)

Leominster (E.)
Lesmahagow (S.)
Linlithgow (S.)
Littleport (E.)
Livingston (S.)
Llandovery (W.)
Llanfyllin (W.)
Llangadock (W.)
Llangollen (W.)
Llanidloes (W.)
Maidenhead (E.)
Malmesbury (E.)
Manchester (E.)
Markethill (N.I.)
Mexborough (E.)
Micheldean (E.)
Middlewich (E.)
Mildenhall (E.)
Milnathort (S.)
Montgomery (W.)
Motherwell (S.)
Nailsworth (E.)
Nottingham (E.)
Okehampton (E.)
Orfordness (E.)
Pangbourne (E.)
Patrington (E.)
Peacehaven (E.)
Pittenweem (S.)
Plinlimmon (W.)
Pontefract (E.)
Portaferry (N.I.)
Porth Nigel (W.)
Portishead (E.)
Portobello (S.)
Portsmouth (E.)
Potter's Bar (E.)
Presteigne (W.)
Ravenglass (E.)
Rockingham (E.)
Ronaldsay (S.)
Rutherglen (S.)
Saintfield (N.I.)
St. Leonards (E.)
Saxmundham (E.)
Shepperton (E.)
Sheringham (E.)
Shrewsbury (E.)
Stalbridge (E.)
Stonehaven (S.)
Stonehouse (S.)
Stoneykirk (S.)
Stowmarket (E.)
Strangford (N.I.)
Strathaven (S.)
Strathearn (S.)
Strathmore (S.)
Sunderland (E.)
Tanderagee (N.I.)

Teddington (E.)
Teignmouth (E.)
Tewkesbury (E.)
Thamesmead (E.)
Torrington (E.)
Trowbridge (E.)
Tweedmouth (S.)
Twickenham (E.)
Warminster (E.)
Warrington (E.)
Washington (E.)
Wednesbury (E.)
Wellington (E.)
West Calder (S.)
Westward Ho! (E.)
Whitchurch (E.)
Whithaven (E.)
Whitstable (E.)
Whittlesey (E.)
Willenhall (E.)
Wilsontown (S.)
Winchelsea (E.)
Winchester (E.)
Windermere (E.)
Windlesham (E.)
Wirksworth (E.)
Withernsea (E.)
Wolsingham (E.)
Woodbridge (E.)
Workington (E.)

11

Aberchirder (S.)
Abergavenny (E.)
Aberystwyth (W.)
Ballycastle (N.I.)
Ballygawley (N.I.)
Balquhidder (S.)
Bannockburn (S.)
Basingstoke (E.)
Berkhamsted (E.)
Blairgowrie (S.)
Bognor Regis (E.)
Bournemouth (E.)
Braich-y-Pwll (W.)
Bridlington (E.)
Buntingford (E.)
Campbeltown (S.)
Carrickmore (N.I.)
Charlestown (S.)
Cleethorpes (E.)
Cockermouth (E.)
Crossmaglen (N.I.)
Cumbernauld (S.)
Downpatrick (N.I.)
Draperstown (N.I.)
Drummelzier (S.)

Dunfermline (S.)
East Retford (E.)
Ecclefechan (S.)
Enniskillen (N.I.)
Fettercairn (S.)
Fort William (S.)
Fraserburgh (S.)
Glastonbury (E.)
Great Marlow (E.)
Guisborough (E.)
Haltwhistle (E.)
Hampton Wick (E.)
Hatherleigh (E.)
Helensburgh (S.)
High Wycombe (E.)
Ingatestone (E.)
Invergordon (S.)
Kirkmichael (S.)
Leytonstone (E.)
Littlestone (E.)
Llantrisant (W.)
Londonderry (N.I.)
Lossiemouth (S.)
Lostwithiel (S.)
Ludgershall (E.)
Lutterworth (E.)
Mablethorpe (E.)
Machynlleth (W.)
Magherafelt (N.I.)
Manningtree (E.)
Market Rasen (E.)
Marlborough (E.)
Maxwelltown (S.)
Much Wenlock (E.)
Musselburgh (S.)
New Brighton (E.)
Newton Abbot (E.)
Northampton (E.)
Oystermouth (W.)
Petersfield (E.)
Pocklington (E.)
Port Glasgow (S.)
Portglenone (N.I.)
Port Patrick (S.)
Prestonpans (S.)
Pultneytown (S.)
Randalstown (N.I.)
Rathfriland (N.I.)

Rawtenstall (E.)
St. Margaret's (E.)
Scarborough (E.)
Shaftesbury (E.)
Southampton (E.)
South Molton (E.)
Stalybridge (E.)
Stourbridge (E.)
Strathblane (S.)
Tattershall (E.)
Wallingford (E.)
Walthamstow (E.)
Westminster (E.)
Whitechurch (E.)
Woodhall Spa (E.)

12

Attleborough (E.)
Auchterarder (S.)
Ballachulish (S.)
Bexhill-on-Sea (E.)
Castle Dawson (N.I.)
Castle Rising (E.)
Castlewellan (N.I.)
Chesterfield (E.)
Christchurch (E.)
East Kilbride (S.)
Five Mile Town (N.I.)
Fort Augustus (S.)
Gainborough (E.)
Garelochhead (S.)
Great Grimsby (E.)
Great Malvern (E.)
Hillsborough (N.I.)
Huddersfield (E.)
Ingleborough (E.)
Inishtrahull (N.I.)
Innerleithen (S.)
Lawrencekirk (S.)
Llandilofawr (W.)
Long Stratton (E.)
Loughborough (E.)
Macclesfield (E.)
Milton Keynes (E.)
Morecambe Bay (E.)
North Berwick (S.)

North Shields (E.)
North Walsham (E.)
Peterborough (E.)
Portmahomack (S.)
Shoeburyness (E.)
Shottesbrook (E.)
South Shields (E.)
Stewartstown (N.I.)
Stoke-on-Trent (E.)
Strathpeffer (S.)
Tillicoultry (S.)

13

Auchtermuchty (S.)
Barnard Castle (E.)
Bishop's Castle (E.)
Boroughbridge (E.)
Brightlingsea (E.)
Brookeborough (N.I.)
Burton-on-Trent (E.)
Bury St. Edmunds (E.)
Carrickfergus (N.I.)
Castle Douglas (S.)
Chipping Ongar (E.)
Cockburnspath (S.)
Dalmellington (S.)
Derrygonnelly (N.I.)
Finchampstead (E.)
Godmanchester (E.)
Great Yarmouth (E.)
Haverfordwest (W.)
Higham Ferrers (E.)
Inverkeithing (S.)
Inverkeithnie (S.)
Kidderminster (E.)
Kirkby Stephen (E.)
Kirkcudbright (S.)
Kirkintilloch (S.)
Knaresborough (E.)
Littlehampton (E.)
Lytham St. Annes (E.)
Market Deeping (E.)
Market Drayton (E.)
Melcombe Regis (E.)
Melton Mowbray (E.)
Merthyr Tydfil (W.)

Middlesbrough (E.)
Newton Stewart (S.)
Northallerton (E.)
Rothiemurchus (S.)
Saffron Walden (E.)
Shepton Mallet (E.)
Wolverhampton (E.)

14

Berwick-on-Tweed (E.)
Bishop Auckland (E.)
Bishops Waltham (E.)
Chipping Barnet (E.)
Chipping Norton (E.)
Hemel Hempstead (E.)
Kirkby Lonsdale (E.)
Market Bosworth (E.)
Mortimer's Cross (E.)
Newtown Stewart (N.I.)
Stockton-on-Tees (E.)
Stony Stratford (E.)
Sutton Courtney (E.)
Tunbridge Wells (E.)
Wellingborough (E.)
West Hartlepool (E.)
Wootton Basset (E.)

15

Ashton-under-Lyne (E.)
Barrow-in-Furness (E.)
Burnham-on-Crouch (E.)
Castle Donington (E.)
Leighton Buzzard (E.)
Newcastle-on-Tyne (E.)
St. Leonards-on-Sea (E.)
Stratford-on-Avon (E.)
Sutton Coldfield (E.)
Weston-super-Mare (E.)

16

Bishop's Stortford (E.)
Welwyn Garden City (E.)

Towns and cities: United States

4

Gary
Lima
Reno
Troy
York
Waco

5

Akron
Boise
Bronx
Butte
Flint
Miami
Omaha
Ozark
Salem
Selma
Tulsa
Utica

6

Albany
Austin
Bangor
Biloxi
Boston
Camden
Canton
Dallas
Dayton
Denver
Duluth
El Paso
Eugene
Fresno
Lowell
Mobile
Nassau
Newark
Oxnard
Peoria
St. Paul
Tacoma
Toledo
Topeka
Tucson
Urbana

7

Abilene
Anaheim
Atlanta
Boulder
Brooklyn
Buffalo
Chicago
Concord
Detroit
Hampton
Hoboken
Houston
Jackson
Lincoln
Madison
Memphis
Modesto
New York
Norfolk
Oakland
Orlando
Phoenix
Raleigh
Reading
Roanoke
St. Louis
Saginaw
San Jose
Seattle
Spokane
Wichita
Yonkers

8

Berkeley
Columbus
Dearborn
Green Bay
Hannibal
Hartford
Honolulu
Lakeland
Las Vegas
New Haven
Oak Ridge
Palo Alto
Pasadena
Portland
Richmond
San Diego
Santa Ana
Saratoga
Savannah
Stamford
Stockton
Syracuse
Wheeling

9

Anchorage
Annapolls
Arlington
Baltimore
Bethlehem
Cambridge
Champaign
Charlotte
Cleveland
Des Moines
Fairbanks
Fort Wayne
Fort Worth
Galveston
Hollywood
Johnstown
Kalamazoo
Lancaster
Lexington
Long Beach
Manhattan
Milwaukee
Nashville
New London
Northeast
Princeton
Riverside
Rochester
Tombstone
Waterbury
Worcester
Ypsilanti

10

Atomic City
Baton Rouge
Birmingham
Charleston
Cincinnati
Evansville
Greensboro
Greenville
Harrisburg
Huntsville
Jersey City
Kansas City
Little Rock
Long Branch
Los Angeles
Louisville
Miami Beach
Montgomery
New Bedford
New Orleans
Pittsburgh
Providence
Sacramento
Saint Louis
San Antonio
Washington
Youngstown

11

Albuquerque
Cedar Rapids
Chattanooga
Grand Rapids
Minneapolis
Newport News
Palm Springs
Schenectady
Springfield

12 AND OVER

Atlantic City (12)
Beverly Hills (12)
Colorado Springs (15)
Corpus Christi (13)
Fayetteville (12)
Fort Lauderdale (14)
Independence (12)
Indianapolis (12)
Jacksonville (12)
New Brunswick (12)
Niagara Falls (12)
Oklahoma City (12)
Philadelphia (12)
Poughkeepsie (12)
St. Petersburg (12)
Salt Lake City (12)
San Francisco (12)
Santa Barbara (12)

Towns and cities: rest of the world

3 AND 4

Agra (Ind.)
Aix (Fr.)
Albi (Fr.)
Ava (Burma)
Baku (Azer.)
Bâle (Swit.)
Bari (It.)
Bray (Ire.)
Brno (Cze.)
Caen (Fr.)
Cali (Colombia)
Cobh (Ire.)
Cork (Ire.)
Fez (Moroc.)
Gaza (Isr.)
Gera (Ger.)
Giza (Egypt)
Homs (Syria and Libya)
Hue (Viet.)
Kano (Nig.)
Kiel (Ger.)
Kiev (Ukr.)
Kobe (Jap.)
Köln (Ger.)
Lamu (Kenya)
Laon (Fr.)
Lodz (Pol.)
Luta (China)
Lvov (Ukr.)
Lyon (Fr.)
Metz (Fr.)
Nice (Fr.)
Omsk (Rus.)
Oran (Alg.)
Pécs (Hung.)
Pisa (It.)
Riga (Latvia)
Sian (China)
Suez (Egypt)
Suhl (Ger.)
Tour (Fr.)
Troy (Asia M.)
Tyre (Lebanon)
Ufa (Rus.)
Vigo (Sp.)

5

Ajmer (Ind.)
Alwar (Ind.)
Arles (Fr.)
Arras (Fr.)

Aswan (Egypt)
Balla (Ire.)
Basel
Basle } (Swit.)
Basra (Iraq)
Boyle (Ire.)
Beira (Moz.)
Brest (Fr. and Belo.)
Cadiz (Sp.)
Clare (Ire.)
Cuzco (Peru)
Delhi (Ind.)
Dijon (Fr.)
Essen (Ger.)
Galle (Sri)
Genoa (It.)
Ghent (Belg.)
Gorky (Rus.)
Hague (Neth.)
Haifa (Isr.)
Halle (Ger.)
Herat (Afghan.)
Izmir (Turk.)
Jaffa (Isr.)
Jidda (Saudi)
Kandy (Sri)
Kazan (Rus.)
Kells (Ire.)
Kotah (Ind.)
Kyoto (Jap.)
Liège (Belg.)
Lille (Fr.)
Lyons (Fr.)
Mainz (Ger.)
Malmö (Swed.)
Mecca (Saudi)
Memel (Lith.)
Milan (It.)
Minsk (Belo.)
Mosul (Iraq)
Namur (Belg.)
Nancy (Fr.)
Nîmes (Fr.)
Orange (Fr.)
Osaka (Jap.)
Ostia (It.)
Padua (It.)
Parma (It.)
Patna (Ind.)
Perth (Austral.)
Pinsk (Belo.)
Poona (Ind.)
Posen (Pol.)
Pskov (Rus.)
Pusan (S. Korea)

Rabat (Moroc.)
Reims (Fr.)
Rieti (It.)
Rouen (Fr.)
Sidon (Lebanon)
Siena (It.)
Simla (Ind.)
Sligo (Ire.)
Trent (It.)
Trier (Ger.)
Turin (It.)
Varna (Bulg.)
Vilna (Lith.)
Wuhan (China)
Yalta (Ukr.)
Ypres (Belg.)

6

Aachen (Ger.)
Abadan (Iran)
Aleppo (Syria)
Amiens (Fr.)
Anshan (China)
Arklow (Ire.)
Arnhem (Neth.)
Bantry (Ire.)
Baroda (Ind.)
Berber (Sudan)
Bergen (Nor.)
Bhopal (Ind.)
Bilbao (Sp.)
Bombay (Ind.)
Bochum (Ger.)
Bremen (Ger.)
Bruges (Belg.)
Calais (Fr.)
Canton (China)
Carlow (Ire.)
Cashel (Ire.)
Cassel (Ger.)
Dairen (China)
Danang (Viet.)
Danzig (Pol.)
Darwin (Austral.)
Dieppe (Fr.)
Dinant (Belg.)
Durban (S.A.)
Erfurt (Ger.)
Fushun (China)
Galway (Ire.)
Gdansk (Pol.)
Geneva (Swit.)
Harbin (China)

Hobart (Austral.)
Howrah (Ind.)
Ibadan (Nig.)
Imphal (Ind.)
Indore (Ind.)
Jaipur (Ind.)
Jhansi (Ind.)
Juarez (Mex.)
Kanpur (Ind.)
Kassel (Ger.)
Kaunas (Lith.)
Kohima (Ind.)
Krakow (Pol.)
Lahore (Pak.)
Leiden (Neth.)
Le Mans (Fr.)
Leyden (Neth.)
Lobito (Angola)
Lübeck (Ger.)
Lublin (Pol.)
Madras (Ind.)
Manila (Philip.)
Medina (Saudi)
Meerut (Ind.)
Mukden (China)
Munich (W. Ger.)
Mysore (Ind.)
Nagoya (Jap.)
Nagpur (Ind.)
Nantes (Fr.)
Napier (N.Z.)
Naples (It.)
Nelson (N.Z.)
Odessa (Ukr.)
Oporto (Port.)
Ostend (Belg.)
Puebla (Mex.)
Quebec (Can.)
Quetta (Pak.)
Rampur (Ind.)
Recife (Braz.)
Reggio (It.)
Regina (Can.)
Rheims (Fr.)
Rostov (Rus.)
Seville (Sp.)
Shiraz (Iran)
Smyrna (Turk.)
Soweto (S.A.)
Sparta (Gr.)
St. Malo (Fr.)
Sydney (Austral.)
Tabriz (Iran)
Thebes (Gr. and Egypt)
Tiflis (Geo.)

Tobruk (Libya)
Toulon (Fr.)
Trèves (Ger.)
Tsinan (China)
Venice (It.)
Verdun (Fr.)
Verona (It.)
Zagreb (Croatia)
Zurich (Swit.)

7

Ajaccio (Fr.)
Alençon (Fr.)
Alma-Ata (Kaz.)
Antwerp (Belg.)
Athlone (Ire.)
Avignon (Fr.)
Babylon (Asia)
Badajoz (Sp.)
Bandung (Indo.)
Bayonne (Fr.)
Benares (Ind.)
Blarney (Ire.)
Bologna (It.)
Breslau (Pol.)
Calgary (Can.)
Clonmel (Ire.)
Coblenz (Ger.)
Cologne (Ger.)
Cordoba (Sp. and Arg.)
Corinth (Gr.)
Cottbus (Ger.)
Donetsk (Ukr.)
Dongola (Sudan)
Dresden (Ger.)
Dundalk (Ire.)
Dunedin (N.Z.)
Dunkirk (Fr.)
Erzerum (Turk.)
Granada (Sp.)
Gwalior (Ind.)
Halifax (Can.)
Hamburg (Ger.)
Hanover (Ger.)
Homburg (Ger.)
Irkutsk (Rus.)
Isfahan (Iran)
Jericho (Asia)
Jodhpur (Ind.)
Kalinin (Rus.)
Karachi (Pak.)
Kharkov (Ukr.)
Kildare (Ire.)
Koblenz (Ger.)
Kunming (China)
Lanchow (China)
La Plata (Arg.)

Le Havre (Fr.)
Leipzig (Ger.)
Lemberg (Ukr.)
Lourdes (Fr.)
Lucerne (Swit.)
Lucknow (Ind.)
Malines (Belg.)
Mansura (Egypt)
Mashhad (Iran)
Memphis (Egypt)
Messina (It.)
Mombasa (Kenya)
München (Ger.)
Mycenae (Gr.)
Nanking (China)
Nicosia (Cyprus)
Orléans (Fr.)
Palermo (It.)
Palmyra (Syria)
Piraeus (Gr.)
Pompeii (It.)
Potsdam (Ger.)
Ravenna (It.)
Rostock (Ger.)
St. John's (Can.)
Salerno (It.)
San Remo (It.)
Sapporo (Jap.)
Tallinn (Est.)
Tangier (Moroc.)
Tbilisi (Geo.)
Taiyuan (China)
Tel Aviv (Isr.)
Toronto (Can.)
Trieste (It.)
Uppsala (Swed.)
Utrecht (Neth.)
Vatican (It.)
Vilnius (Lith.)
Wexford (Ire.)
Wicklow (Ire.)
Yakutsk (Rus.)
Yerevan (Arm.)
Youghal (Ire.)

8

Acapulco (Mex.)
Adelaide (Austral.)
Agartala (Ind.)
Alicante (Sp.)
Amritsar (Ind.)
Auckland (N.Z.)
Augsburg (Ger.)
Besançon (Fr.)
Bordeaux (Fr.)
Boulogne (Fr.)
Brisbane (Austral.)

Bulawayo (Rhodesia)
Calcutta (Ind.)
Carthage (N. Af.)
Cawnpore (Ind.)
Clontarf (Ire.)
Dortmund (Ger.)
Drogheda (Ire.)
Edmonton (Can.)
Florence (It.)
Grenoble (Fr.)
Göteborg (Swed.)
Haiphong (Viet.)
Hamilton (Can.)
Hannover (Ger.)
Ismailia (Egypt)
Istanbul (Turk.)
Jamalpur (Ind.)
Kandahar (Afghan.)
Kilkenny (Ire.)
Kingston (Can.)
Lausanne (Swit.)
Limerick (Ire.)
Listowel (Ire.)
Mafeking (S.A.)
Mandalay (Burma)
Mannheim (Ger.)
Maynouth (Ire.)
Montreal (Can.)
Nagasaki (Jap.)
Novgorod (Rus.)
Nürnberg (Ger.)
Omdurman (Sudan)
Pamplona (Sp.)
Pehawar (Pak.)
Port Said (Egypt)
Przemysl (Pol.)
Rathdrum (Ire.)
Salonika (Gr.)
Salzburg (Aust.)
Sao Paulo (Braz.)
Sarajevo (Yug.)
Schwerin (Ger.)
Shanghai (China)
Shenyang (China)
Shillong (Ind.)
Soissons (Fr.)
Smolensk (Rus.)
Srinagar (Ind.)
Surabaja (Indo.)
Syracuse (It.)
Tangiers (Moroc.)
Tashkent (Uzbek.)
The Hague (Neth.)
Tientsin (China)
Timbuktu (Mali)
Toulouse (Fr.)
Valencia (Sp.)
Varanasi (Ind.)
Victoria (Can.)

Winnipeg (Can.)
Yokohama (Jap.)
Zanzibar (Tanz.)
Zaragoza (Sp.)

9

Abbeville (Fr.)
Agrigento (It.)
Ahmedabad (Ind.)
Allahabad (Ind.)
Astrakhan (Rus.)
Bangalore (Ind.)
Barcelona (Sp.)
Beersheba (Isr.)
Brunswick (Ger.)
Byzantium (Turk.)
Cartagena (Sp. and
   Colombia)
Changchun (China)
Cherbourg (Fr.)
Cherkessk (Rus.)
Chungking (China)
Connemara (Ire.)
Darmstadt (Ger.)
Dordrecht (Neth.)
Eindhoven (Neth.)
Frankfurt (Ger.)
Gibraltar (Eur.)
Hiroshima (Jap.)
Hyderabad (Ind. and Pak.)
Innsbruck (Aust.)
Karaganda (Kaz.)
Killarney (Ire.)
Kimberley (S.A.)
Krivoi Rog (Ukr.)
Kuibyshev (Rus.)
Ladysmith (S.A.)
Las Palmas (Sp.)
Leningrad (Rus.)
Ljubljana (Slov.)
Magdeburg (Ger.)
Maracaibo (Venez.)
Marrakech ⎫
Marrakesh ⎭ (Moroc.)
Marseille (Fr.)
Melbourne (Austral.)
Monterrey (Mex.)
Newcastle (Austral.)
Nuremberg (Ger.)
Panmunjon (Korea)
Roscommon (Ire.)
Rotterdam (Neth.)
Samarkand (Uzbek.)
Santander (Sp.)
Saragossa (Sp.)
Stuttgart (Ger.)
Tipperary (Ire.)

Trondheim (Nor.)
Vancouver (Can.)
Volgograd (Rus.)
Waterford (Ire.)
Wiesbaden (Ger.)
Wuppertal (Ger.)

10

Alexandria (Egypt)
Baden Baden (Ger.)
Bad Homburg (Ger.)
Bratislava (Cze.)
Casablanca (Moroc.)
Chandigarh (Ind.)
Chittagong (Bangla.)
Darjeeling (Ind.)

Düsseldorf (Ger.)
Gothenburg (Swed.)
Heidelberg (Ger.)
Jamshedpur (Ind.)
Königsberg (Rus.)
Lubumbashi (Zaïre)
Marseilles (Fr.)
Montélimar (Fr.)
Port Arthur (China)
Sevastopol (Ukr.)
Shillelagh (Ire.)
Simonstown (S.A.)
Stalingrad (Rus.)
Strasbourg (Fr.)
Sverdlovsk (Rus.)
Trivandrum (Ind.)
Valparaiso (Chile)
Versailles (Fr.)

11

Armentières (Fr.)
Bahia Blanca (Arg.)
Ballymurphy (Ire.)
Bhubaneswar (Ind.)
Fredericton (Can.)
Grahamstown (S.A.)
Guadalajara (Mex.)
Helsingborg (Swed.)
Kaliningrad (Rus.)
Novosibirsk (Rus.)
Saarbrücken (Ger.)
Sharpeville (S.A.)
Vladivostok (Rus.)

12

Bloemfontein (S.A.)
Christchurch (N.Z.)
Johannesburg (S.A.)
Niagara Falls (Can.)
Rio de Janeiro (Braz.)
San Sebastian (Sp.)
St. Petersburg (Rus.)

13 AND OVER

Aix-la-Chapelle (Ger.) (13)
Belo Horizonte (Braz.) (13)
Charlottetown (Can.) (13)
Clermont-Ferrand (Fr.) (15)
Constantinople (Turk.) (14)
Dnepropetrovsk (Ukr.) (14)
Karl-Marx-Stadt (Ger.) (13)
Pietermaritzburg (S.A.) (16)
Port Elizabeth (S.A.) (13)

Waterfalls, the largest

Churchill (9) *Can.*
Gavarnie (8) *Fr.*
Giessbach (9) *Swit.*
Guaira (6) *Braz.*
Hamilton (8) *Can.*
Krimmler (8) *Aust.*

Multnomah (9) *U.S.A.*
Niagara (7) *Can.-U.S.A.*
Ribbon (6) *U.S.A.*
Roraima (7) *Guyana*
Salto Angel (10) *Venez.*
Sete Quedas (10) *Braz.*

Stanley (7) *Zaïre*
Sutherland (10) *N.Z.*
Trümmelbach (11) *Swit.*
Vettisfos (9) *Nor.*
Victoria (8) *Zambia, Zimbabwe*
Yosemite, Upper (13) *U.S.A.*

Weather

3 AND 4

bise
bora
calm
cold
cool
damp
dark
dry
dull
east
fog
föhn
gale
gust
hail
haze
hazy
heat

hot
icy
mild
mist
rain
smog
snow
sun
tide
veer
warm
west
wet
wind

5

buran
cirri

cloud
dusty
eurus
flood
foehn
foggy
frost
gusty
light
misty
muggy
north
rainy
sleet
snowy
south
storm
sunny
windy

6

arctic
auster
bright
chilly
cirrus
clouds
cloudy
colder
deluge
floods
freeze
frosty
hot day
lowery
meteor
mizzle
mizzly
nimbus

normal
samiel
shower
simoom
simoon
solano
squall
starry
stormy
sultry
torrid
trades
vortex
warmer
wet day
winter
wintry
zephyr

7

backing
blowing
climate
clouded
cold day
coldish
cumulus
cyclone
drizzle
drought
dry-bulb
fogbank
freshen
fresher
freshet
gregale
hailing
hottish

icy-cold
meltemi
mistral
monsoon
muggish
pampero
rainbow
raining
set fair
showery
sirocco
snowing
squally
stratus
summery
sunspot
tempest
thunder
tornado
typhoon
veering
warm day
warmish
wintery

8

autumnal
blizzard
cold snap
cyclonic
dead-calm
doldrums
downpour
easterly
east wind
eddy wind
fireball
freezing
heatwave
hot night
hurlwind
landwind
levanter
libeccio
lowering
meteoric
nubilous
overcast
rainfall

rainless
scirocco
snowfall
sunlight
thundery
tropical
westerly
west wind
wet night
windless

9

cold night
drift wind
drizzling
dry season
hailstorm
hard frost
harmattan
hoarfrost
hurricane
lightning
moonlight
northeast
northerly
northwest
north wind
nor'-wester
raincloud
sea breeze
snow-storm
southeast
southerly
southwest
south wind
sou'-wester
starlight
tidal wave
trade wind
unclouded
unsettled
warm night
whirlwind
zephyrous

10

arctic cold

black frost
changeable
depression
euroclydon
freshening
frostbound
hot climate
hot weather
land breeze
March winds
monsoonish
pouring-wet
Scotch mist
storm-cloud
waterspout
wet weather
white frost

11

anticyclone
cats and dogs
cold climate
cold weather
dull weather
etesian wind
foul weather
hard weather
lowering sky
mackerel sky
meteoroloy
mild weather
rain or shine
rainy season
stiff breeze
storm signal
summer cloud
temperature
tempestuous
thunderbolt
thunderclap
warm weather
wind backing
wind veering

12

anticyclonic
April showers

atmospherics
cirrocumulus
cirrostratus
currocumulus
currostratus
easterly wind
equinoctials
freezing rain
mackerel gale
shooting star
storm brewing
thundercloud
thunderstorm
tropical heat
tropical rain
weather glass
westerly wind
windy weather

13 AND 14

aurora borealis (14)
autumn weather (13)
cumulostratus (13)
frosty weather (13)
meteorological (14)
moonlight night (14)
northeast wind (13)
northerly wind (13)
northwest wind (13)
sheet lightning (14)
southeast wind (13)
southerly wind (13)
southwest wind (13)
starlight night (14)
summer weather (13)
thunder-shower (13)
torrential rain (14)
weather report (13)
weather prophet (14)
wintry weather (13)

15

forked lightning
meteoric showers
prevailing winds
summer lightning
tropical climate

LAW AND GOVERNMENT
Legal terms

2

J.P.
K.C.
Q.C.

3 AND 4

abet
act
aka
bail
bar
bars
case
dock
D.P.P.
fair
fee
fine
gaol
I.O.U.
jury
law
lien
m'lud
oath
plea
quit
rape
rent
riot
rob
seal
silk
stay
sue
suit
tort
use
will
writ

5

alias
alibi
alien
arson
award
bench
cause
clerk

costs
court
crime
false
forge
fraud
guilt
in rem
judge
juror
legal
libel
mulct
order
penal
plead
poach
police
prize
proof
quash
right
rules
steal
trial
trust
usher
usury
valid

6

access
action
affirm
appeal
arrest
attorn
bailee
bigamy
breach
camera
charge
commit
deceit
de jure
disbar
duress
elegit
equity
escrow
estate
felony
fiscal

forger
guilty
Hilary
incest
injury
insult
junior
legacy
malice
master
motion
murder
pardon
parole
piracy
police
prison
puisne
remand
repeal
set-off
surety
surtax

7

accused
alimony
assault
assizes
bailiff
battery
bequest
borstal
bribery
capital
case law
caution
circuit
codicil
consent
control
convict
coroner
counsel
cruelty
custody
damages
de facto
defence
divorce
ex parte
faculty
forgery

garnish
hanging
harming
hearsay
illegal
impeach
inquest
justice
land tax
larceny
lawless
lawsuit
licence
neglect
non suit
offence
penalty
perjury
poll tax
precept
probate
proving
querent
release
reserve
Riot Act
robbery
servant
service
sheriff
sine die
slander
statute
summary
summons
suspect
tel-quel
treason
trustee
verdict
warrant
witness

8

absolute
abstract
act of god
act of law
advocate
advowson
attorney
barratry
birching

bottomry
brawling
burglary
canon law
chancery
civil law
coercion
contract
covenant
criminal
deed poll
disorder
distress
drafting
entailed
estoppel
eviction
evidence
executor
felo de se
fidelity
forensic
guardian
homicide
in camera
indecent
judgment
judicial
law agent
law lords
legal aid
licensee
litigant
majority
mandamus
murderer
novation
nuisance
perjuror
petition
pleading
preamble
prisoner
receiver
recorder
reprieve
Salic law
sedition
sentence
Shops Act
stealing
subpoena
sui juris
testator
trespass

tribunal
Truck Act
true bill
unlawful
validity

9

abduction
accessory
acquittal
ademption
agreement
allotment
annulment
attainder
barrister
blackmail
bona fides
cestui que
champerty
code of law
collusion
common law
copyright
defendant
de son tort
deviation
discharge
dismissal
distraint
embracery
endowment
equitable
execution
executory
extortion
fee simple
feoffment
Gaming Act
good faith
grand jury
guarantee
guarantor
high court
income tax
indemnity
innocence
intestacy
intestate
judiciary
land court
licensing
litigious

131

loitering
mala fides
mandatory
murderous
not guilty
not proven
Old Bailey
plaintiff
precatory
precedent
privilege
probation
procedure
refresher
registrar
remission
restraint
servitude
solicitor
statutory
summing-up
surrender
testament
testimony

10

alienation
appearance
assessment
assignment
attachment
attornment
bankruptcy
common pleas
common riot
confession
connivance
conspiracy
corruption
decree nisi
deed of gift
defamation
disclaimer
enticement
estate duty
executrix
eye witness
finance act
forfeiture
fraudulent
gaming acts
government
gun licence
hard labour
high treason
illegality
impediment

in chambers
indictment
injunction
inter vivos
judicature
King's Bench
land tenure
law sitting
Law Society
legitimacy
limitation
liquor laws
litigation
magistrate
misconduct
misprision
negligence
next friend
parliament
Poor Law Act
post mortem
prize court
procurator
prosecutor
respondent
revocation
separation
settlement
trespasser
ultra vires

11

advancement
affiliation
appointment
arbitration
arrangement
assize court
assciation
attestation
civil wrongs
composition
concealment
condonation
congé d'élire
county court
criminal law
death duties
debtors' acts
deportation
dissolution
disturbance
enabling act
enforcement
engrossment
examination
extenuating

extradition
fair comment
fieri facias
foreclosure
impeachment
infanticide
issue of writ
king's pardon
maintenance
market overt
mayor's court
obstruction
prerogative
prosecution
Queen's Bench
regulations
requisition
restitution
root of title
royal assent
sheriff's act
stamp duties
stipendiary
subornation
suicide pact
third degree
trespassing
Vagrancy Act
vesting deed

12

adjudication
bona vacantia
case of thorns
causa proxima
caution money
caveat emptor
charter party
Companies Act
compensation
constabulary
conveyancing
co-respondent
crime and tort
cross-examine
crown witness
death penalty
disaffection
embezzlement
encroachment
express trust
ferae naturae
grand assizes
guardianship
Habeas Corpus
imprisonment
infringement

inherent vice
interpleader
intimidation
joint tenancy
king's proctor
land transfer
Lord Advocate
lord of appeal
manslaughter
mensa et thoro
misbehaviour
misdemeanour
misdirection
oral evidence
pendente lite
prescription
privy council
prostitution
Queen's Pardon
ratification
royal charter
royal warrant
sheriff clerk
supreme court
taxing master
testamentary

13

administrator
age of marriage
ancient lights
apportionment
appropriation
burden of proof
charging order
common assault
consideration
court of appeal
Court of Arches
criminal libel
damage feasant
ejection order
ejusdem generis
Ground Game Act
hereditaments
housebreaking
illegal action
interlocutory
judge advocate
justification
law of property
letters patent
lord president
nolle prosequi
parliamentary
petty sessions
public trustee

quantum meruit
recognisances
right of appeal
search warrant
simple larceny
statute barred
treasure trove
trial by combat
trial by ordeal
Witchcraft Act

14

act of indemnity
administration
Admiralty Court
choses in action
common nuisance
common sergeant
companies court
concealed fraud
conjugal rights
county judgment
court of justice
criminal appeal
default summons
false pretences
identification
identity parade
local authority
lord chancellor
naturalization
oyer and terminer
penal servitude
Queen's evidence
Queen's pleasure
second division
special licence
wrongful arrest

15

act of bankruptcy
act of parliament
Act of Settlement
attorney-general
autrefois acquit
benefit of clergy
charitable trust
commercial court
commisary court
compound a felony
compound larceny
consistory court
contempt of court
emergency powers
latent ambiguity

local government   official secrets
marital coercion   power of attorney
marriage licence   quarter sessions

Parliamentary and political

2
M.P.
P.M.
U.N.

3
act
bar
C.B.I.
C.I.A.
E.E.C.
gag
I.R.A.
K.G.B.
law
opt
P.L.O.
red
sit
tax
T.U.C.

4
ayes
bill
coup
Dail
D.O.R.A.
Duma
gain
left
lord
mace
N.A.T.O.
Nazi
noes
oath
pact
pass
peer
poll
rump
seat
Tory
veto

'vide
vote
vuli
Whig
whip
writ

5
agent
amend
boule
bylaw
chair
clerk
count
draft
edict
elect
enact
forum
house
junta
legal
lobby
Nazis
order
paper
party
Provo
purge
rally
right
S.E.A.T.O.
sit-in
valid
voter

6
assent
backer
ballot
budget
caucus
clause
colony
commie

Cortes
decree
divide
enosis
Fabian
Führer
govern
heckle
Labour
leader
Maoism
member
motion
nation
picket
policy
putsch
quorum
recess
record
reform
report
ruling
satrap
secede
senate
sirkar
speech
strike
summon
swaraj
tariff
teller
tyrant

7
adjourn
Al Fatah
anarchy
barrack
borough
boycott
cabinet
canvass
censure
chamber
closure
cold war

Comecon
Commons
commune
council
deficit
détente
dissent
elector
embargo
fascism
fascist
federal
finance
gallery
Hansard
heckler
hot line
Knesset
lock out
liberal
mandate
Marxism
neutral
new left
opening
outvote
pairing
passage
politic
poor law
premier
primary
prolong
radical
reading
recount
re-elect
re-enact
Riksdag
senator
session
speaker
statute
toryism
tribune
tyranny
vacancy
Zionism
Zionist

8
apartheid
assembly
autarchy
autocrat
Black rod
blockade
caudillo
chairman
Chiltern
  (Hundreds)
commissar
commoner
Congress
democrat
dictator
dissolve
division
dominion
ecclesia
election
elective
feminism
free vote
Gerousia
home rule
hustings
left-wing
majority
minister
ministry
minority
national
official
oligarch
politics
prorogue
republic
rollback
schedule
Sobranye
Storting
suffrage
Tanaiste
Treasury
triumvir
unionism
unionist
whiggery
woolsack

9
amendment
anarchism
autocracy
ballot-box
Barebone's
bicameral
Bundestag
coalition
Cominform
Comintern
committee
communism
communist
democracy
deterrent
Eduskunta
exchequer
first lord
legislate
oligarchy
ombudsman
politburo
poujadist
president
red guards
Reichstag
right-wing
sanctions
secretary
shire-moot
show trial
socialism
socialist
Stalinism
Taoiseach
terrorism

10
aristrocrat
block grant
by-election
capitalism
chancellor
collective
conference
devolution

government
guillotine
invalidate
monarchism
Monday Club
opposition
parliament
Plaid Cymru
plebiscite
psephology
radicalism
referendum
republican
resolution
revolution
scrutineer
sitting-day
Third Reich
Third World
trade union
Trotskyism
unicameral
Warsaw Pact
White House
white paper

11

adjournment
aristocracy
back-bencher
ballot-paper
bye-election

casting vote
coexistence
congressman
constituent
containment
co-operative
demarcation
dissolution
divine right
enfranchise
finance bill
imperialist
independent
legislation
legislative
legislature
McCarthyism
nationalist
package deal
party leader
prerogative
private bill
reactionary
revisionism
statute book
suffragette
syndicalism
syndicalist
Tammany Hall
Witenagemot
yeoman-usher

12

commissioner
Common Market
Commonwealth
conservatism
Conservative
constituency
constitution
dictatorship
division lobby
domino theory
federal union
House of Lords
house of peers
invalidation
lord advocate
lord chairman
privy council
reading clerk
snap division
ways and means
welfare state

13

demonstration
deputy-speaker
disengagement
free trade area
home secretary
international
lord president

lord privy seal
prime minister
shadow cabinet
single chamber
trade unionist
United Nations
vote of censure

14

constitutional
deputy chairman
deputy premier
deputy sergeant
gerrymandering
rord chancellor
representative
sergeant-at-arms
social democrat

15

attorney-general
cabinet minister
clerk of the house
general election
Marxist-Leninist
minister of state
people's republic
personality cult
totalitarianism

LITERATURE AND THE ARTS
Art

2 AND 3	**4**				
		icon	bloom	glaze	print
		ikon	blush	glory	putto
air	airy	limn	board	gloss	rebus
art	arts	line	brush	grave	salon
bur	base	lipo	burin	hatch	scene
del.	body	mass	cameo	inert	sculp
exc.	burr	nude	chalk	japan	secco
fec.	bust	pinx.	couch	lay-in	shade
hue	chic	pose	delin.	lumia	Stijl
inc.	dada	size	draft	magot	study
inv.	daub	tone	easel	model	stump
key	draw	wash	ember	mount	tondo
mat	etch		Fauve	mural	torso
oil	flat		fecit	nabis	trace
op	form	**5**	frame	paint	vertu
pop	gild		genre	pietà	virtu
sit	halo	batik	gesso	prime	

6

action
artist
ashcan
cachet
canvas
colour
crayon
cubism
depict
design
doctor
ectype
emblem
embos
enamel
engild
flambé
fresco
fylfot
gothic
ground
incavo
kitcat
kit-kat
limner
mastic
medium
mobile
mosaic
niello
nimbus
object
ormolu
ox-gall
pastel
patina
pencil
pinxit
plaque
plaster
purism
reflex
relief
rhythm
rococo
school
sculpt.
shadow
shippo
sitter
sketch
statue
studio
uncial

7

abbozzo
academy
acrylic
atelier
amorino
archaic
aureole
baroque
Bauhaus
bottega
bachiru
biscuit
camaieu
cartoon
carving
cissing
classic
collage
contour
Dadaism
daubing
De Stijl
diagram
diptych
draught
drawing
etching
excudit
faience
Fauvism
felt tip
gilding
glazing
gouache
graphic
hot tone
impaint
impasto
lacquer
lino-cut
lunette
montage
mordant
orphism
outline
painter
palette
picture
pigment
plastic
profile
realism
relievo
remodel
replica
reredos
rococco

scumble
sfumato
shading
sketchy
stabile
stencil
stipple
support
surlace
tableau
tempera
texture
tracery
T-square
varnish
vehicle
woodcut

8

abstract
academic
acid bath
acrolith
anaglyph
aquatint
armature
arriccio
artistic
blue four
charcoal
concours
cool tone
diaglyph
drypoint
engraver
figurine
fixative
freehand
frottage
Futurism
gargoyle
graffiti
grouping
hatching
half-tone
handling
idealism
intaglio
intonaco
luminist
majolica
makimono
monotype
mounting
negative
oil paint
ornament

painting
panorama
pastiche
penumbra
plein air
portrait
repoussé
romantic
seascape
seicento
statuary
symmetry
tachisme
tapestry
tectonic
tesserae
throwing
trecento
triglyph
triptych
vignette
warm tone

9

aggregate
alla prima
anti-cerne
appliqué
aquarelle
aquatinta
arabesque
asymmetry
ball-point
bas-relief
blockbook
bric-à-brac
cartridge
cartouche
cloisonné
colourist
crow quill
damascene
damaskeen
dichroism
distemper
emblemata
embossing
encaustic
engraving
facsimi1e
geometric
gradation
grisaille
grotesque
highlight
hot colour
indelible

indian ink
intimiste
japanning
landscape
lay figure
lithotint
mahlstick
mannerism
marquetry
maulstick
mezzotint
miniature
modelling
neo-gothic
oil colour
oleograph
painterly
phototype
polyptych
primitive
ready made
recession
sculpture
scumbling
serigraph
statuette
still-life
stippling
strapwork
stretcher
Symbolist
tailpiece
tattooing
tenebrism
Totentanz
Vorticism
woodblock
xylograph

10

accidental
achromatic
altogether
anaglyphic
anaglyptic
Art Nouveau
atmosphere
automatism
avant-garde
background
biomorphic
body colour
caricature
cartellino
cerography
classicism
cool colour

cornucopia
dead colour
embossment
embroidery
fitch brush
flat colour
foreground
full-length
hair pencil
half-length
India paper
Jugendstil
kinetic art
lithograph
mezzotinto
monochrome
naturalism
night piece
organic art
paint brush
pen and wash
pencilling
photograph
pietra dura
plasticity
portcrayon
Raphaelism
Raphaelite
Romanesque
serigraphy
silhouette
silk screen
Surrealism
synthesism
terracotta
turpentine

warm colour
xylography

11

academician
alto-relievo
aquatinting
battle piece
calligraphy
chiaroscuro
chinoiserie
chromograph
cinquecento
colour print
composition
concrete art
connoisseur
draughtsman
eclecticism
electrotype
engravement
foreshorten
found object
french chalk
ground plane
heliochrome
heliochromy
iconography
illusionism
imprimatura
life drawing
lithography
marqueterie
masterpiece

neo-romantic
oil painting
pavement art
perspective
photography
pointillism
portraiture
poster paint
primitivism
renaissance
restoration
scenography
stained glass
stereochromy
tessellation
tracing linen
tracing paper
watercolour

12

alkyd colours
bird's eye view
clare-obscure
illustration
palette knife
scraper board

13

balck and white
complementary
daguerreotype
decorative art

etching needle
expressionism
glass painting
Impressionism
Neo-Classicism
neoplasticism
Pre-Raphaelite
primary colour
social realism
tactile values
underpainting

14 AND OVER

action painting (14)
cabinet picture (14)
chromatography (14)
constructivism (14)
conversation piece (17)
draughtsmanship (15)
foreshortening (14)
Neo-Impressionism (16)
Neo-Romanticism (14)
pavement artist (14)
picture gallery (14)
plaster of paris (14)
portrait painter (15)
Post-Impressionism (17)
representational (16)
socialist realism (16)
steel engraving (14)
vanishing point (14)

Artists, architects, sculptors, cartoonists, etc.

3 AND 4				
	Dick	Gabo	Holl	Lely	Reni
	Dine	Gere	Home	Lion	Rich
Adam	Dix	Gill	Hone	Low	Rohe
Arp	Dodd	Gogh	Hook	Maes	Rosa
Bell	Doré	Good	Hunt	Marc	Ross
Bird	Dou	Gore	Jack	May	Ryn
Bone	Dufy	Gow	John	Miró	Sant
Both	Dyce	Goya	Kane	Mola	Shaw
Burn	Dyck	Gris	Kerr	Nash	Sime
Caro	Egg	Gros	King	Neer	Sims
Cima	Etty	Guys	Klee	Opie	Spee
Cole	Eves	Hals	Lam	Owen	Swan
Cox	Eyck	Hand	Lamb	Poy	Todd
Cuyp	Faed	Hart	Lane	Puy	Toft
Dadd	Fehr	Hemy	Lear	Pyne	Tuke
Dali	Ford	Herp	Lee	Reid	Wade

Wain
Ward
Watt
Webb
West
Wood
Wren

5

Aalto
Abbey
Adams
Allan
Allen
Amiet
Appel
Bacon
Baily
Balla
Banks
Barry
Barye
Bates
Beale
Bezzi
Blake
Boehm
Bosch
Bough
Brett
Brock
Brown
Bundy
Burra
Carra
Clark
Clint
Cohen
Cooke
Corot
Cross
Cossa
Costa
Cotes
Craig
Crane
Credi
Crome
Danby
David
Davie
Davis
Degas
Devis
Dixon
Drury
Durer
Ensor

Ernst
Foley
Freud
Frink
Frith
Furse
Gaddi
Gaudí
Gaunt
Gibbs
Giles
Gotch
Goyen
Grant
Grosz
Haden
Haghe
Hayes
Innes
Johns
Jones
Keene
Kelly
Klein
Klimt
Lance
Leech
Leger
Lemon
Le Vau
Lewis
Lippi
Lotto
Lowry
Lucas
Manet
Maris
Mason
Mauve
Moira
Monet
Moore
Munch
Nebot
Nervi
Nicol
Noble
Nolde
North
Orpen
Palma
Pater
Payne
Penny
Piper
Plaas
Platt
Ponte
Ponti

Poole
Prout
Pugin
Redon
Rodin
Rooke
Rossi
Sands
Scott
Segna
Short
Sleap
Small
Smith
Soane
Soest
Speed
Staël
Stark
Steen
Steer
Stone
Stott
Studd
Tobey
Tonks
Unwin
Uwins
Velde
Vicky
Vonet
Watts
Wells
White
Wiens
Woods
Wyatt
Wyeth
Wylie
Yeats
Zoppo

6

Abbott
Albers
Allori
Archer
Arnold
Ashton
Barker
Barton
Baskin
Behnes
Benson
Benton
Berman
Bettes

Bewick
Birley
Bodley
Boxall
Braque
Briggs
Brough
Brunel
Buchel
Burnet
Burton
Butler
Calder
Callow
Campin
Carter
Casson
Claude
Clouet
Colton
Conder
Cooper
Copley
Corbet
Cotman
Cowper
Cozens
Currie
Dahmen
Dawson
Derain
De Wint
Dobson
Draper
Duccio
Dunbar
Elwell
Erlach
Ferber
Fildes
Fisher
Forbes
Foster
Fraser
Fuller
Fuseli
Geddes
Gellée
Gérard
Gibson
Gilman
Ginner
Giotto
Girtin
Glover
Gordon
Graham
Greuze
Guardi

Gulich
Hacker
Harral
Haydon
Heckel
Hilton
Holmes
Howard
Hudson
Hughes
Hunter
Ingres
Jagger
Joseph
Kaprow
Kettle
Keyser
Knight
Laroon
Laszlo
Lavery
Lawson
Leader
Lebrun
Ledoux
Legros
Le Nain
Leslie
Linton
Mabuse
McEvoy
Manson
Marini
Martin
Massys
Mesdac
Millet
Monaco
Morley
Morone
Morris
Müller
Murray
Newton
Nisbet
Noland
Oliver
Olsson
O'Neill
Palmer
Panini
Parker
Parton
Paxton
Pegram
Penley
Perret
Pettie
Piombo

Pisano
Potter
Ramsay
Renoir
Ribera
Ridley
Rivera
Rivers
Robbia
Robert
Romano
Romney
Rothko
Rubens
Ruskin
Sadler
Sandby
Sandys
Seddon
Serres
Seurat
Sisley
Smirke
Smythe
Spence
Stokes
Storck
Storey
Strang
Strube
Stuart
Stubbs
Tadema
Tanguy
Tayler
Taylor
Thomas
Titian
Turner
Vacher
Van Ryn
Varley
Vernet
Walker
Waller
Wallis
Walton
Wardle
Warhol
Watson
Weekes
Weenix
Weyden
Wilkie
Wilson
Windus
Wright
Wyllie
Yeames

7

Alberti
Aretino
Baldung
Barlach
Bassano
Bateman
Beechey
Belcher
Bellini
Bennett
Berchem
Bernini
Bomberg
Bonnard
Boucher
Bramley
Bridell
Brouwer
Calvert
Cameron
Campion
Cellini
Cézanne
Chagall
Chardin
Charles
Cheston
Chirico
Christo
Cimabue
Clausen
Cockram
Collier
Collins
Connard
Corinth
Cortona
Courbet
Cranach
Cundell
Dalziel
Daniell
Daumier
Da Vinci
De Hooch
De Lazlo
Dicksee
Dighton
Douglas
Downman
Duchamp
Edridge
Edwards
El Greco
Emanuel
Epstein
Flaxman

Fouquet
Fox-Pitt
Francia
Gabriel
Garstin
Gauguin
Gertler
Gibbons
Gilbert
Gillray
Goodall
Goodwin
Greaves
Gregory
Gropius
Guarini
Guevara
Guthrie
Harding
Hartung
Hayward
Herbert
Herring
Hobbema
Hockney
Hofland
Hogarth
Hokusai
Holbein
Holland
Holroyd
Hoppner
Hopwood
Horsley
Housman
Indiana
Israels
Jackson
Jaggers
Johnson
Kneller
Knights
Kooning
Lambert
Lancret
Lanteri
Lessore
Linnell
Llander
Lucidel
Macbeth
Maccoll
Maclise
Maillol
Mansart
Maratti
Martini
Matisse
Memlinc

Merritt
Meunier
Michaux
Millais
Morandi
Morisot
Morland
Morrice
Murillo
Nasmith
Nattier
Neumann
Orcagna
Orchard
Osborne
Pacchia
Parrish
Parsons
Pasmore
Peacock
Peruzzi
Phidias
Philips
Phillip
Phil May
Philpot
Picabia
Picasso
Pickard
Pinwell
Pomeroy
Poussin
Poynter
Prinsep
Rackham
Raeburn
Raphael
Riviere
Roberts
Rouault
Roussel
Russell
Sargent
Schetky
Schiele
Shannon
Sickert
Siddall
Simpson
Smetham
Solomon
Spencer
Stanley
Stevens
Teniers
Tenniel
Thirtle
Thomson
Tiepolo

Uccello
Ugolino
Utrillo
Van Dyck
Van Eyck
Van Gogh
Vermeer
Watteau
Webster
Westall
Whiting
Woolner
Wynants
Zoffany

8

Allinson
Angelico
Armitage
Armstead
Aumonier
Beaumont
Beckmann
Beerbohm
Boccioni
Boffrand
Boughton
Brabazon
Bramante
Brancusi
Brangwyn
Brearley
Brooking
Brueghel
Calderon
Callcott
Calthorp
Carracci
Chambers
Chantrey
Crawhall
Creswick
Daubigny
De Keyser
De Laszlo
Delaunay
Del Prete
Deverell
Dietrich
Dressler
Dubuffet
Eastlake
Fielding
Fontaine
Frampton
Garofalo
Ghiberti

Giovanni
Gottlieb
Hartwell
Hepworth
Herkomer
Highmore
Hilliard
Hodgkins
Holloway
Houghton
Ibbetson
Inchbold
Jacobsen
Jan Steen
John Opie
Johnston
Jordaens
Kaufmann
Kirchner
Kokoshka
Kollwitz
Lambardo
Landseer
Lawrence
Leighton
Leonardo
Logsdail
Macallum
Macquoid
Magritte
Maitland
Mantegna
Marshall
Masaccio
Melville
Mondrian
Montalba
Montegna
Muirhead
Mulready
Munnings
Naviasky
Nevinson
Niemeyer
Palladio
Paolozzi
Paul Nash
Perugino
Phillips
Pissarro
Pontormo
Redgrave
Reynolds
Richmond
Ricketts
Robinson
Rossetti
Rousseau
Rugendas

Rushbury
Saarinen
Sassetta
Scamozzi
Schinkel
Segonzac
Severini
Simmonds
Solimena
Stanhope
Stothard
Stringer
Sullivan
Terbosch
Tinguely
Topolski
Vanbrugh
Van Goyen
Van Steen
Vasarely
Verbeeck
Veronese
Vlaminck
Waterlow
Wheatley
Whistler
Willcock
Williams
Woodward
Zakharov
Zurbarán

9

Ackermann
Alexander
Appleyard
Aston Webb
Bakhinzen
Beardsley
Biederman
Bonington
Botticini
Branwhite
Caldecot
Canaletto
Carpaccio
Collinson
Constable
Correggio
Delacroix
d'Erlanger
Donaldson
Donatello

Farington
Feininger
Fragonard
Franz Hals
Friedrich
Gastineau
Géricault
Giorgione
Griffiths
Grünewald
Guido Reni
Halswelle
Hatherell
Hawksmoor
Henderson
Honthorst
Hurlstone
Jawlensky
Kandinsky
Kemp-Welch
Kokoschka
Lancaster
Lanfranco
La Thangue
Lee-Hankey
Lightfoot
Llewellyn
Louis Wain
MacGregor
MacKennal
McLachlan
McWhirter
Martineau
Maundrell
Mazzolino
Mestrovic
Mondriaan
Nicholson
Nollekens
Northcote
Pisanello
Rembrandt
Salisbury
Sansovino
Schalcken
Singleton
Stanfield
Steenwyck
Stevenson
Strudwick
Thornhill
Velasquez
Verrochio
Waterford
Whitcombe

10

Alma-Tadema
Archipenko
Botticelli
Breenbergh
Brockhurst
Burne-Jones
Caravaggio
Cattermole
Cruikshank
Del Pacchia
di Giovanni
Fiddes-Watt
Friedenson
Fulleylove
Giacometti
Glendening
Holman-Hunt
Jan van Eyck
Kennington
La Fresnaye
Lethbridge
Liebermann
Lorenzetti
Mackintosh
Meissonier
Michelozzo
Modigliani
Onslow Ford
Orchardson
Peppercorn
Pollaiuolo
Praxiteles
Richardson
Rowlandson
Saint-Aubin
Sanmicheli
Shackleton
Simon Vonet
Somerville
Sutherland
Swynnerton
Tintoretto
Van der Goes
Van der Meer
Van de Velde
Waterhouse
Winstanley

11

Apollodorus
Copley Heath

Della Robbia
Farquharson
Fra Angelico
Ghirlandaio
Hondecoeter
Le Corbusier
Lloyd Wright
Margaritone
Pickersgill
Poelenburgh
Polycleitus
Polykleitos
Rippingille
San Severino
Somerscales
Thornycroft
Van der Plaas
Van Ruisdael

12 AND OVER

Brunelleschi (12)
de Hondecoeter (13)
Della Francesca (14)
de Loutherbourg (14)
Fantin-Latour (12)
Ford Madox Brown (14)
Gainsborough (12)
Gaudier-Brzeska (14)
Grandma Moes (12)
Haynes-Williams (14)
Heath Robinson (13)
Huchtenburgh (12)
Hughes-Stanton (13)
Leonardo da Vinci (15)
Lichtenstein (12)
Loutherbourg (12)
Michelangelo (12)
Muirhead-Bone (12)
Puvis de Chavannes (16)
Rauschenberg (12)
Rembrandt van Ryn (15)
Sassoferrato (12)
Sidney Cooper (12)
Spencer Pryse (12)
Toulouse-Lautrec (15)
Van der Weyden (12)
Van Huchtenburgh (15)
Van Ochtervelt (13)
Winterhalter (12)
Witherington (12)

Authors, poets, dramatists, etc.

3 AND 4

Amis
Ayer
Ball
Baum
Bede
Bell
Benn
Boll
Bolt
Buck
Cary
Coke
Cole
Dane
Day
Dell
Duse
Eden
Eyre
Ford
Fox
Fry
Fyfe
Gay
Gide
Glyn
Gray
Grey
Hall
Hart
Hay
Hine
Home
Hood
Hook
Hope
Hugo
Hume
Hunt
Hyne
Inge
Joad
Kant
King
Knox
Kyd
Lamb
Lang
Lear
Lee
Levi
Livy
Loos

Loti
Lyly
Lynd
Mais
Mann
Marx
Mill
More
Muir
Nash
Ovid
Owen
Poe
Pope
Pugh
Read
Reid
Rowe
Ruck
Sade
Sala
Shaw
Sims
Snow
Tate
Vane
Vega
Ward
West
Wood
Wren
Zola

5

Acton
Adams
Aesop
Agate
Aiken
Albee
Arden
Arlen
Auden
Ayres
Bacon
Barry
Barth
Bates
Behan
Betti
Beyle
Blake
Bloom

Blunt
Bowen
Bruce
Burke
Burns
Byron
Cable
Caine
Camus
Capek
Carew
Clare
Colum
Corvo
Couch
Croce
Dante
Dario
Defoe
Diver
Donne
Doyle
Dumas
Eliot
Ellis
Evans
Field
Freud
Frost
Gibbs
Glyot
Gogol
Gorki
Gosse
Gower
Grimm
Hardy
Harte
Hegel
Heine
Henry
Henty
Hesse
Homer
Hulme
Ibsen
Innes
Irwin
James
Jeans
Jones
Joyce
Kafka
Keats
Keith

Keyte
Lever
Lewis
Locke
Lodge
Logue
Lorca
Lucan
Lucas
Mason
Milne
Moore
Murry
Noyes
Odets
O'Dowd
Ogden
O'Hara
Orczy
Orton
Otway
Ouida
Paine
Pater
Peake
Peele
Pepys
Plato
Pliny
Pound
Praed
Prior
Raine
Reade
Ridge
Rilke
Rolfe
Sagan
Scott
Shute
Smart
Smith
Spark
Stark
Staël
Stein
Stern
Stowe
Swift
Synge
Taine
Tasso
Twain
Tynan
Udall

Varro
Verne
Vidal
Walsh
Waugh
Wells
Wilde
Woolf
Wyatt
Yates
Yeats
Yonge
Young
Zweig

6

Adcock
Aldiss
Anstey
Aragon
Archer
Arnold
Asimov
Austen
Bailey
Balzac
Barham
Barrie
Belloc
Bellow
Benson
Besant
Binyon
Borrow
Brecht
Bridie
Briggs
Brontë
Brooke
Brophy
Browne
Bryant
Buchan
Bunyan
Burgin
Burney
Burton
Butler
Caesar
Capote
Chekov
Church
Cicero

Clarke
Clough
Conrad
Cooper
Coward
Cowley
Cowper
Crabbe
Cronin
Curzon
Darwin
Daudet
Davies
Dekker
Dennis
Dobson
Dryden
Dunbar
Duncan
Empson
Ennius
Ervine
Euclid
Evelyn
Farnol
Fichte
France
Frazer
Freund
Froude
George
Gibbon
Godwin
Goethe
Gordon
Graeme
Graham
Graves
Greene
Hallam
Hamsun
Harris
Hawkes
Haynes
Hemans
Henley
Hesiod
Hobbes
Holmes
Holtby
Horace
Howard
Howitt
Hughes
Huxley

Ian Hay	Sapper	Carlyle	Hopkins	Sarasin	Catullus
Ibañez	Sappho	Carroll	Housman	Saroyan	Cervantes
Irving	Sardou	Chapman	Howells	Sassoon	Chambers
Jacobs	Sartre	Chaucer	Hueffer	Service	Christie
Jepson	Savage	Chekhov	Ionesco	Shelley	Congreve
Jerome	Sayers	Cheyney	Jimenez	Simenon	Conquest
Jonson	Scribe	Claudel	Johnson	Simonov	Cornford
Jowett	Sedley	Clayton	Juvenal	Sitwell	Crichton
Junius	Seneca	Clemens	Kinross	Skelton	Crockett
Keller	Sidney	Cobbett	Kipling	Southey	Crompton
Landor	Sladen	Colette	Leacock	Spencer	Cummings
Lao-Tse	Squire	Collier	Lehmann	Spender	Davidson
Larkin	Steele	Collins	Le Queux	Spenser	Day Lewis
Lawson	Sterne	Corelli	Lessing	Spinoza	De la Mare
Le Sage	Tagore	Craigie	Lindsay	Stevens	De Musset
London	Taylor	Crashaw	Macleod	Strauss	Disraeli
Lowell	Temple	Deeping	McKenna	Surtees	Donleavy
Ludwig	Thomas	Delaney	Malraux	Tacitus	Drummond
Lytton	Thorne	Dickens	Manzoni	Terence	Du Bellay
Mailer	Thrale	Diderot	Marryat	Thomson	Faulkner
Malory	Valery	Dodgson	Marlowe	Thoreau	Fielding
Mannin	Villon	Doughty	Marquez	Tolkien	Flaubert
Martyn	Virgil	Douglas	Marston	Tolstoy	Fletcher
Miller	Waller	Drabble	Martial	Ustinov	Fontaine
Milton	Walton	Drayton	Marvell	Vachell	Forester
Morgan	Watson	Dreiser	Maugham	Vaughan	Goncourt
Mörike	Wesker	Dunsany	Mauriac	Walkley	Goodyear
Morris	Weyman	Durrell	Maurois	Wallace	Grierson
Munthe	Wilson	Emerson	Maurras	Walpole	Guedalla
Murray	Wotton	Erasmus	Mazzini	Webster	Hamilton
Musset	Wilcox	Erskine	Mencken	Whitman	Heinlein
Necker		Flecker	Mérimée	Wickham	Hoffmann
Nerval		Forster	Meynell	Withers	Ibbetson
Nesbit	**7**	Foscolo	Moffatt	Zetland	Johnston
Newman		Frankau	Molière		Kavanagh
O'Brien	Abelard	Freeman	Montagu		Kingsley
O'Casey	Addison	Galileo	Murdoch	**8**	Kingston
Ogilvy	Alfieri	Gallico	Nabokov		Knoblock
O. Henry	Anouilh	Garnett	Newbolt	Albanesi	Koestler
O'Neill	Aquinas	Gaskell	Nichols	Alington	Laforgue
Onions	Ariosto	Gautier	Ogilvie	Andersen	Lagerlöf
Orwell	Baldwin	Gilbert	Osborne	Anderson	Langland
Parker	Beddoes	Gissing	Patmore	Andreyev	Lawrence
Pascal	Beeding	Glossop	Peacock	Apuleius	Leibnitz
Pepler	Belasco	Golding	Plautus	Atherton	Lonsdale
Petöfi	Bennett	Goldoni	Plummer	Aumonier	Leopardi
Pindar	Bentham	Gregory	Pushkin	Barbusse	Lovelace
Pinter	Bentley	Haeckel	Ransome	Beaumont	Ludovici
Pinero	Berchet	Haggard	Rastell	Beerbohm	Macaulay
Powell	Bergson	Hakluyt	Richter	Bensusan	MacNeice
Proust	Berners	Hartley	Rimbaud	Berkeley	Mallarmé
Racine	Birrell	Hassall	Rolland	Berryman	Melville
Rhodes	Blunden	Hazlitt	Romains	Betjeman	Menander
Riding	Boswell	Herbert	Ronsard	Bjornson	Meredith
Rohmer	Bridges	Herrick	Rostand	Bradbury	Merriman
Rowley	Burgess	Hewlett	Rushdie	Browning	Michelet
Runyon	Caedmon	Heywood	Rushkin	Bushnell	Mirabeau
Ruskin	Camoens	Hichens	Russell	Calderon	Mitchell
Sandys	Campion	Hocking	Sadleir	Campbell	Mortimer

Palgrave
Pattison
Perelman
Perrault
Petrarch
Plutarch
Ponsonby
Quennell
Rabelais
Rattigan
Reynolds
Rossetti
Rousseau
Sabatini
Salinger
Sandburg
Schiller
Shadwell
Sheridan
Sidgwick
Sillitoe
Sinclair
Smollett
Stendhal
Stephens
Strachey
Sturgess
Suckling
Taffrail
Tennyson
Thompson
Thurston
Tibullus
Tourneur
Traherne
Trollope
Turgenev
Vanbrugh
Verlaine
Voltaire
Vonnegut
Wheatley
Whittier
Williams
Zane Grey
Zangwill

9

Adam Smith
Addinsell
Aeschylus
Ainsworth
Aldington
Alec Waugh
Anita Loos
Antoninus
Aristotle

Bartimeus
Ben Jonson
Berta Ruck
Blackmore
Blackwood
Boccaccio
Bottomley
Bret Harte
Burroughs
Cervantes
Corneille
Churchill
Coleridge
D'Annunzio
David Hume
De la Roche
De Quincey
Descartes
Dickenson
Dos Passos
Dudintsev
Du Maurier
Eddington
Edgeworth
Ehrenburg
Euripides
Froissart
Giraudoux
Goldsmith
Goncharov
Gutenberg
Guy Thorne
Hall Caine
Hauptmann
Hawthorne
Heidegger
Hemingway
Herodotus
Heyerdahl
Hölderlin
Isherwood
Kaye-Smith
La Bruyère
La Fontaine
Lamartine
Leigh Hunt
Lermontov
Linklater
Lomonosov
Lord Byron
Lucretius
MacCarthy
Mackenzie
Macrobius
Madariaga
Mansfield
Mark Twain
Masefield
Massinger

Middleton
Mitchison
Montaigne
Nietzsche
Oppenheim
Pasternak
Pemberton
Pett Ridge
Priestley
Radcliffe
Robertson
Rochester
Ruby Ayres
Sackville
Sax Rohmer
Schreiner
Shenstone
Sholokhov
Sophocles
Spielmann
Stacpoole
Steinbeck
Stevenson
Suetonius
Swinburne
Thackeray
Tomlinson
Trevelyan
Turgeniev
Van Druton
Wodehouse
Wycherley

10

Ballantyne
Barrington
Baudelaire
Birmingham
Brett Young
Chatterton
Chesterton
Conan Doyle
don Marquis
Dostoevsky
Drinkwater
Dürrenmatt
Elinor Glyn
Emil Ludwig
Fitzgerald
Galsworthy
Hungerford
Hutchinson
Jack London
Jane Austen
John Buchan
Jules Verne
Longfellow

Lope de Vega
Lord Lytton
Maupassant
Mayakovsky
Mcgonagall
Mickiewicz
Mrs. Gaskell
Muriel Hine
Noel Coward
Oscar Wilde
Pierre Loti
Pirandello
Propertius
Pryce-Jones
Quintilian
Richardson
Ronaldshay
Saintsbury
Saint-Simon
Sean O'Casey
Strindberg
Tarkington
Thucydides
Victor Hugo
Williamson
Wordsworth

11

Abercrombie
Apollinaire
Demosthenes
Dostoievski
Garcia Lorca
Grillparzer
Kierkegaard
Maeterlinck
Montesquieu
Montherlant
Omar Khayyam
Ravenscroft
Sainte-Beuve
Shakespeare
Tocqueville
Watts-Dunton
Yevtushenko

12

Aristophanes
Beaumarchais
Bulwer Lytton
Chesterfield
De Selincourt
Fiona Macleod
Hans Andersen
Hergesheimer

Macchiavelli
Quiller-Couch
Rider Haggard
Robbe-Grillet
Rose Macaulay
Solzhenitsyn
Storm Jameson
Wittgenstein
Wyndham Lewis

13

Andrew Marvell

Arnold Bennett
Baroness Orczy
Cecil Day Lewis
Cosmo Hamilton
Edgar Allan Poe
Ford Madox Ford
Hilaire Belloc
Jeffrey Farnol
Jerome K. Jerome
Ohlenschlager
Rouget de Lisle
Sackville-West
Sinclair Lewis
Stacy Aumonier

14

Agatha Christie
Compton-Burnett
Eden Philpotts
Lecomte de Lisle
Marcus Aurelius
Middleton Murry
Rafael Sabatini
Rudyard Kipling

Upton Sinclair
Wilkie Collins

Warwick Deeping

15

Beverley Nichols
Booth Tarkington
Granville Barker
La Rochefoucauld
Millington Synge
Pierre de Ronsard
Somerset Maugham
Valerius Flaccus
Washington Irving (16)

Building and architecture

2 AND 3

bar
bay
hip
hut
inn
mew
pa
pub
spa
sty
won

4

apse
arch
area
bank
barn
bema
byre
café
cage
cell
cyma
club
cowl
crib
dado
dais
dike
dome
door
exit
fane

flag
flat
flue
fort
gaol
gate
grot
haha
hall
jail
jamb
keep
khan
kiln
kirk
lath
lift
lock
loft
mart
maze
mews
mill
mint
moat
mole
nave
nook
oast
ogee
oven
pale
pane
pave
pier
pile
plan
post

quay
rail
ramp
rink
roof
room
ruin
sash
seat
shed
shop
sill
sink
site
slat
stay
step
stoa
stud
tige
tile
tomb
town
trap
vane
vill
vyse
wair
wall
wing
wood
xyst
yard
yate

5

abbey
abode
aisle
alley
ambry
annex
attic
aulic
bayed
block
booth
bower
brace
brest
brick
build
built
cabin
choir
coign
compo
court
crypt
dairy
depot
domed
Doric
drain
eaves
entry
erect
fence
flats
floor
forum
gable

glass
glaze
grate
grout
gully
harem
hotel
house
hovel
hydro
igloo
ionic
jetty
joint
joist
jutty
kiosk
kraal
latch
ledge
lobbv
lodge
manse
mitre
newel
niche
order
oriel
paned
panel
patio
plank
pound
putty
quoin
raiIs
ranch
range

scape
serai
sewer
shaft
shelf
shell
slate
slatt
socle
solar
spire
stack
stage
stair
stake
stall
stand
steps
stile
stone
store
stove
strut
study
suite
tabby
thorp
tiled
torii
tourn
tower
trone
truss
Tudor
vault
villa
wharf
works

6

abacus
access
adytum
alcove
alette
annexe
arbour
arcade
ashlar
ashler
asylum
atrium
aviary
bakery
batten
belfry
bourse
bricks
canopy
casino
castle
cellar
cement
châlet
chapel
chevet
chunam
church
cilery
cimbia
cinema
cintre
circus
closet
coffer
coigne
column
coping
corbel
corona
coving
crèche
cupola
dagoba
débris
design
dogana
donjon
dralns
dug-out
ecurie
estate
exedra
façade
fascia
fillet
finial

fresco
friary
fylfot
gablet
garage
garret
gazebo
girder
glazed
godown
Gothic
grange
grille
grotto
gutter
hangar
hearth
hog-pen
hog-sty
hostel
impost
inwall
Ionian
kennel
ladder
lanary
larder
lean-to
lierne
linhay
lintel
locker
lock-up
loggia
log-hut
louver
louvre
lyceum
mantel
market
mihrab
mitred
morgue
mortar
mosaic
mosque
mud hut
museum
mutule
niched
Norman
office
outlet
pagoda
palace
paling
pantry
parget
paving

perron
pharos
piazza
pigsty
pillar
pinery
plinth
poling
portal
priory
prison
purlin
putlog
quarry
rabbet
rafter
rancho
recess
refuge
rococo
ropery
rosery
rubble
rustic
saloon
saw-pit
school
scroll
shanty
smiddy
smithy
soffit
spence
square
stable
stairs
staith
stores
stucco
studio
subway
tarsia
tavern
temple
tender
thatch
thorpe
tilery
tiling
timber
tolsey
torsel
trench
trough
turret
unroof
untile
veneer
vestry

vihara
vinery
vintry
vivary
volute
wattle
wicket
wigwam
window
xystos
zaccho
zareba
zenana

7

academy
acroter
air duct
air flue
alcazar
almonry
ambitus
ancones
annulet
anticum
arcaded
archway
armoury
atelier
balcony
ballium
baroque
bastion
bedroom
bossage
boudoir
brewery
builder
butlery
butment
buttery
cabinet
cafenet
canteen
capitol
cassino
castlet
ceiling
chamber
chancel
chantry
château
chevron
chimney
choltry
cistern
cob-wall

college
compost
conduit
convent
cornice
cortile
cottage
crocket
cubicle
culvert
curtain
deanery
demesne
domical
dooring
doorway
doucine
dovecot
dungeon
edifice
embassy
entasis
eustyle
factory
farmery
fernery
fixture
fluting
foundry
fullery
gallery
gateway
granary
grapery
grating
groined
grounds
hay loft
herbary
hip roof
hogcote
hospice
hot-wall
hydrant
impasto
jib door
joinery
juffers
kennels
keyho]e
kitchen
knocker
kremlin
landing
lantern
lattice
laundry
lazaret
library

lunette	shutter	buttress	fireclay	plashing
mansard	slating	caliduct	fish weir	platform
mansion	spicery	capstone	flagging	plumbing
masonry	stadium	caryatid	flashing	pointing
megaron	staging	casement	flatting	pothouse
mill dam	station	causeway	flooring	propylon
minaret	steeple	cavation	freehold	refinery
minster	storied	cenotaph	fretwork	registry
moellon	surgery	cesspool	frontage	rockwork
mud wall	systyle	chaptrel	fusarole	rood loft
mullion	tambour	chatelet	gargoyle	roof tree
munnion	tannery	cincture	geodesic	ropewalk
nailery	taproom	cloister	grillage	sacristy
narthex	tegular	clubroom	grouting	sail-loft
nogging	terrace	cockloft	handrail	sale room
nunnery	theatre	coliseum	hen house	scaffold
nursery	tie-beam	comptoir	hoarding	seminary
obelisk	tracery	concrete	hoistway	seraglio
oratory	tracing	contract	home farm	showroom
ossuary	transom	corn loft	hospital	skirting
out-gate	trellis	corridor	hostelry	skylight
paddock	turncap	cow house	hothouse	slop-shop
pantile	unbuilt	cradling	ice house	smeltery
parapet	unpaved	crescent	intrados	snuggery
parlour	untiled	cromlech	jalousie	soil pipe
passage	vachery	cross-tie	keystone	solarium
pension	varnish	cupboard	kingpost	spanroof
pentice	vaulted	curb roof	kingwood	stabling
pentile	veranda	cutchery	lathwork	stuccoed
piggery	viaduct	darkroom	lavatory	sudatory
pillbox	village	dead wall	legation	sun-proof
plaster	voluted	decorate	lichgate	taphouse
portico		detached	lift well	tectonic
postern		doghouse	log cabin	tenement
pugging	**8**	domicile	loghouse	terrninus
pug mill		door case	lychgate	toll-gate
pyramid	abat-jour	door nail	madhouse	townhall
quarrel	abattoir	doorpost	magazine	transept
railing	abat-voix	doorsill	memorial	trapdoor
rebuild	abutment	doorstep	mill pond	triglyph
rectory	acanthus	dovecote	monolith	tympanum
re-edify	air-drain	dovetail	monument	underpin
reeding	airtight	dowel pin	mortuary	upstairs
rejoint	anteroom	drainage	moulding	vicarage
repairs	apophyge	draughty	newsroom	wainscot
reredos	approach	dry store	openwork	wardroom
rockery	aquarium	dry stove	orangery	waxworks
roofing	arboured	dust hole	outhouse	well hole
rostrum	atheneum	dwelling	overhang	well room
rotunda	backdoor	elevator	palisade	windmill
sanctum	backroom	emporium	panelled	windowed
sawmill	ballroom	entrance	pantheon	woodwork
seabank	baluster	entresol	pavement	workroom
seawall	banister	epistyle	pavilion	workshop
section	basement	erection	pedestal	ziggurat
shebeen	basilica	espalier	pediment	
shelter	bathroom	estimate	pentroof	
shelves	building	excavate	pilaster	
shingle	bungalow	fanlight	pinnacle	

9

acropolis
acroteria
aerodrome
alarm bell
alignment
almshouse
apartment
arabesque
arch-brick
architect
archivolt
archstone
aerostyle
art school
ashlaring
athenaeum
bakehouse
bay window
bede house
bell gable
bell tower
belvedere
bivaulted
boathouse
bow window
brick clay
brick kiln
brick dust
campanile
cartouche
cathedral
ceilinged
cellarage
centering
chop house
claustral
clay slate
clay stone
cloakroom
clubhouse
coalhouse
cocoonery
coffer dam
colonnade
colosseum
construct
consulate
cooperage
copestone
courtyard
cross-beam
crown-post
day school
decastyle
distemper
doorplate
doorstead

doorstone
dormitory
dowelling
drain trap
dripstone
dust stove
earthbank
elevation
embrasure
episenium
eremitage
escalator
esplanade
estaminet
excavator
farmhouse
ferestral
firebrick
fireplace
fir-framed
fishgarth
flagstone
flashings
floriated
framework
frontdoor
frontroom
garreting
gatehouse
gravel pit
grotesque
guardroom
guestroom
guildhall
gullyhole
gymnasium
headstone
hermitage
hexastyle
homestall
homestead
hypocaust
hypostyle
infirmary
interaxal
interaxis
ironworks
jettyhead
jut-window
kalsomine
kerbstone
Kitchener
labyrinth
lazaretto
leasehold
letterbox
lift-shaft
linenfold
Lob's pound

mausoleum
metalling
mezzanine
modillion
monastery
music hall
music room
octastyle
octostyle
orphanage
oubliette
outer door
outer gate
palladian
pargeting
parquetry
parsonage
parthenon
partition
party-wall
pay office
penthouse
peristyle
pillarbox
playhouse
pleasance
pontifice
poorhouse
pressroom
prize ring
promenade
quicklime
race-stand
rail-fence
rainproof
raintight
refectory
rendering
reservoir
residence
residency
rest-house
ring-fence
sallyport
scagliola
scantling
scrimshaw
sectional
spareroom
staircase
stillroom
stinktrap
stockroom
stonewall
stonework
storeroom
stretcher
structure
stylobate

swinecote
synagogue
tablature
tenements
threshold
tile-drain
tollbooth
tollhouse
tower-room
townhouse
treillage
triforium
turf-house
turnstile
undermine
underprop
undrained
vestibule
wallpaper
wall-plate
warehouse
wastepipe
watertank
whitewash
windproof
windtight
winevault
wiregauze
workhouse

10

à la grecque
antechapel
antetemple
araeostyle
arc-boutant
architrave
archivault
backstairs
ball-flower
balustered
balustrade
bargeboard
bedchamber
bell-turret
brick-built
brick earth
cantilever
catafalque
chapellany
chimney cap
chimney pot
clerestory
clock tower
coachhouse
coalcellar
common room

conversion
Corinthian
court house
covered way
crenulated
cripplings
cross-aisle
crown glass
culver-tail
damp-course
decoration
decorative
depository
dining hall
dining room
dispensary
distillery
ditriglyph
dome-shaped
doorhandle
doricorder
double-hung
double lock
dowel joint
drawbridge
dryingroom
Dutch tiles
earth house
embankment
enrockment
engine-room
excavation
facia panel
fir-wrought
first floor
fives court
flint glass
flock paper
forcing-pit
foundation
garden city
glass-house
grandstand
Greek cross
greenhouse
grotto-work
ground-plan
ground-sill
guardhouse
habitation
hipped roof
hippodrome
hunting box
hypaethral
intramural
Ionic order
Ionic style
jerry-built
laboratory

lady chapel
lancet arch
Latin cross
lazar-house
lighthouse
lumber-room
maisonette
manor house
market town
monopteros
necropolis
Norman arch
overmantel
panopticon
persiennes
plastering
plate glass
portcullis
post office
power-house
propylaeum
proscenium
pycnostyle
quadrangle
repointing
repository
robing-room
rock-temple
Romanesque
roof garden
rose garden
rose window
roundhouse
roundtower
rubblework
sanatorium
sanitarium
settlement
skew bridge
skyscraper
slaked lime
smokestack
space frame
state house
stillatory
storehouse
streetdoor
structural
tetrastyle
tiring-room
Tudor style
undercroft
university
unoccupied
untenanted
varnishing
ventilator
vestry room
watch-house

watch-tower
water-tower
way-station
white-limed
wicket gate
window sash
windscreen
wine-cellar

11

antechamber
barge-course
caravansary
castellated
cementation
cementatory
chain-bridge
columbarium
compartment
concert hall
contabulate
coping stone
corbel steps
cornerstone
counterfort
curtail step
distempered
door knocker
dovetailing
drawing room
dress circle
entablature
entablement
finger plate
florid style
foundations
frieze-panel
glass-mosaic
ground-floor
hearthstone
lattice work
load-bearing
louvre-board
luffer board
machicoulis
mantelpiece
manufactory
market-cross
morning room
observatory
oeil-de-boeuf
office block
oriel window
out-building
picture rail
plasterwork
postern gate

postscenium
public house
purpose-built
reading room
reconstruct
renaissance
reservatory
residential
Roman cement
rustication
sarcophagus
scaffolding
shooting box
staddle roof
stringboard
sub-contract
summer house
superstruct
tessellated
tiled hearth
trelliswork
Turkish bath
Tuscan order
undercoated
unfurnished
uninhabited
ventilation
wainscoting
war memorial
water supply
weathercock
whitewashed
window frame
window glass
window ledge
wire grating
wooden house
wrought iron

12

amphitheatre
araeosystyle
archbuttress
architecture
assembly room
auction rooms
building site
caravanserai
chapel of ease
chimneypiece
chimneyshaft
cockle stairs
conservatory
construction
constructure
country house
covered court

culver-tailed
dormer window
draught-proof
dressing-room
entrance hall
floor timbers
folding doors
garden suburb
geodesic dome
guest chamber
half-timbered
Ionian column
kitchen range
labour-saving
lake dwelling
lightning-rod
lock-up garage
louvre window
machicolated
mansion house
meeting house
mission house
outer gateway
pantechnicon
parquet floor
penitentiary
power station
purbeck stone
retiring-room
spiral stairs
sub-struction
sub-structure
subterranean

sweating room
three-ply wood
tower bastion
town planning
tracing cloth
tracing linen
tracing paper
unmodernized
unornamental
unornamented
untenantable
unventilated
urban renewal
valance board
venetian door
wainscotting
weatherproof
winter garden

13

amphiprostyle
ancient lights
architectonic
architectural
assembly rooms
back staircase
breakfast room
butler's pantry
chimney corner
compass window
contabulation

coursing joint
Dutch clinkers
dwelling house
dwelling place
encaustic tile
entrance lobby
establishment
ferro-concrete
Grecian temple
lattice window
machicolation
martello tower
master builder
Norman doorway
portland stone
satellite town
skirting board
specification
sub-contractor
sweating house
transom window
triumphal arch
uninhabitable
vaulting shaft
venetian blind
vinyl emulsion
wattle and daub

14

architectonics
catherine wheel

central heating
drying cupboard
filling station
flying buttress
lath and plaster
mezzanine floor
office building
picture gallery
portland cement
powder magazine
reconstruction
superstructure
threshing floor
venetian window
wayside station
whispering dome

15

air conditioning
dampproof course
discharging arch
electric heating
feather boarding
foundation stone
hydraulic cement
pleasure gardens
pleasure grounds
refreshment room
spiral staircase
vitruvian scroll
weather boarding
withdrawing room

Characters in literature

Some characters from **Ben Jonson, Charlotte Brontë, Lord Byron, Chaucer,** and **Congreve**
List of works from which the following characters are taken, with reference numbers.

Ben Jonson

Ref. No.	Title	
1. Alchemist, The	(12 letters)	
2. Bartholomew Fayre	(16 ,,)	
3. Cynthia's Revels	(14 ,,)	
4. Devil is an Ass, The	(15 ,,)	
5. Epicoene	(8 ,,)	
6. Every Man in his Humour	(19 ,,)	
7. Every Man out of his Humour	(22 ,,)	
8. Magnetick Lady, The	(16 ,,)	
9. New Inn, The	(9 ,,)	
10. Poetaster, The	(12 ,,)	
11. Sad Shepherd, The	(14 ,,)	
12. Sejanus	(7 ,,)	
13. Volpone	(7 ,,)	
14. (Various)		

Lord Byron

Ref. No.	Title	
15. Don Juan	(7 letters)	
16. (Various)		
Charlotte Brontë		
17. Jane Eyre	(8 letters)	
18. Professor, The	(12 ,,)	
19. Shirley	(7 ,,)	
20. Villette	(8 ,,)	
Chaucer (Geoffrey)		
21. Canterbury Tales	(15 letters)	
Congreve (William)		
22. Double Dealer, The	(15 letters)	
23. Love for Love	(11 ,,)	
24. Mourning Bride, The	(16 ,,)	
25. Old Bachelor, The	(14 ,,)	
26. Way of the World, The	(16 ,,)	

Note: The numbers in brackets indicate *the works* in which the characters appear.

3 AND 4

Alp (16)
Anah (16)
Azo (16)
Baba (15)
Beck (20)
Busy (2)
Cash (6)
Cave (19)
Cob (6)
Cos (3)
Daw (5)
Dent (17)
Dudu (15)
Echo (3)
Ella (21)
Eyre (17)
Face (l)
Fly (9)
Gale (19)
Hall (19)
Hogg (19)
Home (20)
Hugo (16)
Inez (15)
Lara (16)
Lucy (25)
May (21)
Nero (12)
Otho (16)
Paul (18, 20)
Prue (23)
Pug (4)
Raby (15)
Rud (17)
Seyd (16)
Wasp (l)
Whit (2)
Zara (24)

Froth (22)
Gabor (16)
Hedon (3)
Jenny (23)
Julia (10)
Kaled (16)
Laura (16)
Leila (15, 16)
Lloyd (17)
Lolah (15)
Lorel (11)
Lovel (9)
Lupus (10)
Manly (4)
Mason (17)
Minos (10)
Mitis (7)
Moore (19)
Moria (3)
Morus (3)
Mosca (13)
Neuha (16)
Osman (24)
Poole (17)
Pryor (19)
Roger (21)
Rufus (12)
Scott (19)
Selim (16)
Shift (7)
Snowe (20)
Steno (16)
Surly (l)
Tipto (9)
Topas (21)
Varro (12)
Ulric (16)
Waspe (2)
Whipp (19)
Yorke (19)

Earine (11)
Emilia (21)
Ferret (9)
Foible (9)
Formal (6)
Gallus (10)
Giaour (The) (16)
Gelaia (3)
Graham (20)
Haidee (15)
Harold (16)
Hassan (16)
Horace (10)
Jaques (14)
Jeremy (23)
Kitely (6)
Lambro (15)
Legend (23)
Luscus (10)
Malone (19)
Mammon (l)
Marina (16)
Marino (16)
Maxime (21)
Medora (16)
Morose (5)
Myrrha (16)
Opsius (12)
Overdo (2)
Pliant (l)
Plyant (22)
Polish (8)
Reuter (18)
Setter (25)
Silvia (25)
Simkin (21)
St. John (Mr.) (17)
Subtle (l)
Symkin (21)
Tartar (dog) (19)
Tattle (23)
Temple (17)
Thopas (21)
Virgil (10)
Walter (21)
Werner (16)
Wittol (25)

Beleses (16)
Belinda (25)
Belmour (25)
Bertram (16)
Bobadil (6)
Boultby (19)
Bretton (20)
Buckram (23)
Buffone (7)
Clement (6)
Corvino (13)
Cutting (2)
Cynthia (3, 22)
Don José (15)
Don Juan (15)
Dorigen (21)
Drugger (14)
Emanuel (20)
Eudenus (12)
Eugenie (5)
Ezzelin (16)
Fainall (26)
Fairfax (17)
Faliero (16)
Foscari (16)
Fungoso (6, 7)
Gamelyn (21)
Giaffir (16)
Gulnare (16)
Harriet (20)
Hartley (19)
Hunsden (18)
John Daw (5)
Katinka (15)
Keeldar (19)
Knockem (2)
Kno'well (6)
Leonora (16)
MacTurk (19)
Marwood (26)
Matthew (6)
Mercury (3)
Mincing (26)
Minotti (16)
Mrs. Gale (19)
Mrs. Hogg (19)
Mrs. Reed (17)
Nunnely (19)
Olimpia (16)
Ovidius (10)
Palamon (21)
Placebo (21)
Plautia (10)
Regulus (12)
Samiasa (16)
Scandal (23)
Sejanus (12)
Sharper (25)
Sordido (7)

5

Abbot (17)
Aesop (10)
Alken (11)
Arete (3)
Asper (7)
Beppo (16)
Betty (25)
Brisk (7, 22)
Burns (17)
Celia (13)
Chloe (10)
Cotta (12)
Cupid (3)
Donne (19)
Frail (23)

6

Albius (10)
Alison (21)
Arcite (21)
Arnold (16)
Asotus (3)
Bessie (17)
Caesar (10)
Canace (21)
Common (1)
Conrad (16)
Crites (3)
Damian (21)
Dapper (l)
Deliro (7)
Drusus (12)

7

Abolson (21)
Almeria (24)
Anaides (3)
Apicata (12)
Arbaces (16)
Astarte 16)
Azaziel (16)
Baillie (21)

149

Stephen (6)
Sympson (19)
Theseus (21)
Tiburce (21)
Torquil (16)
Troilus (21)
Volpone (13)
Zuleika (16)

8

Abdallah (16)
Amorphus (3)
Angelica (23)
Araminta (25)
Argurion (3)
Caligula (12)
Camballo (21)
Careless (22)
Cordalus (7)
Custance (21)
Cytheris (10)
Donegild (21)
Edgworth (2)
Epicoene (5)
Griselda (21)
Gulbeyaz (15)
Helstone (19)
Hesperus (3)
Jane Eyre (17)
Joe Scott (19)
John Gale (19)
John Reed (17)
Laetitia (25)
Latiaris (12)
Loradano (16)
Mary Cave (19)
Maskwell (22)
Mecaenas (10)
Melibeus (21)
Mirabell (26)
Miss Prue (23)
Montano (6)
Mooncalf (2)
Mrs. Frail (23)
Mrs. Poole (17)
Mrs. Pryor (19)
Mrs. Whipp (19)
Mrs. Yorke (19)
Murcraft (4)
Nicholas (21)
Parisina (16)
Pedrillo (15)
Petulant (26)
Prudence (21)
Quarlous (2)
Seacombe (18)
Sir Topas (21)

Suwarrow (15)
Sweeting (19)
Tiberius (12)
Trapland (23)
Tynedale (18)
Vainlove (25)
Valerian (21)
Waitwell (26)
Wishfort (26)
Witwould (26)

9

Angiolina (16)
Arviragus (21)
Ben Legend (23)
Brainworm (6)
Cambuscon (21)
Christian (16)
Clerimont (5)
Corbaccio (13)
Crispinus (14)
Cyril Hall (19)
Demetrius (10)
Dol Common (l)
Donna Inez (15)
Doricourt (26)
Downright (6)
Dr. Boultby (19)
Eglantine (21)
Eliza Reed (17)
Fitz-Fulke (15)
Foresight (25)
Francesca (16)
Goodstock (9)
Heartwell (25)
Hermegyld (21)
Josephine (16)
Lady Froth (22)
Littlewit (2)
Loadstone (8)
Lord Froth (22)
Lucy Snowe (20)
Macilente (7)
Marchmont (20)
Mark Yorke (19)
Meercraft (4)
Mellefont (22)
Millamont (26)
Miss Abbot (17)
Morphides (3)
Mrs. Polish (8)
Noll Bluff (25)
Oliver Cob (6)
Phantaste (3)
Philantia (3)
Pinchbeck (15)
Pomponius (12)

Prosaites (3)
Rochester (17)
Rose Yorke (19)
Scatcherd (17)
Seremenes (16)
Sir Thopas (21)
Steighton (18)
Terentius (12)
The Giaour (16)
Touchwood (22)
Valentine (23)
Walravens (20)

10

Adam Overdo (2)
Aholibamah (16)
Aurora Raby (15)
Ballendino (14)
Crimsworth (18)
Don Alfonso (15)
Donna Julia (15)
Fondlewife (25)
Helen Burns (17)
Hiram Yorke (19)
Lady Plyant (22)
Lord Conrad (15)
Louis Moore (19)
Madame Beck (20)
Miss Temple (17)
Mrs. Bretton (20)
Mrs. Fainall (26)
Mrs. Fairfax (17)
Mrs. Marwood (26)
Paul Plyant (22)
Propertius (10)
Rev. Mr. Donne (19)
Sanguinius (12)
Sir Ezzelin (16)
Sir John Daw (5)
Thomas Cash (6)
Wife of Bath (The) (21)

11

Abel Drugger (14)
Barraclough (19)
Bertha Mason (17)
Captain Whit (2)
Colonel Dent (17)
Fitzdottrel (4)
Gerard Moore (19)
Jessie Yorke (19)
Lady Adeline (15)
Leatherhead (2)
Martin Yorke (19)
Michel Steno (16)

Mike Hartley (19)
Ned Careless (22)
Nightingale (2)
Paulina Home (20)
Robert Moore (19)
Roger Formal (6)
Simon Simkin (21)
Stralenheim (16)
Tom Quarlous (2)
Tribulation (1)

12

Asinius Lupus (10)
Brocklehurst (17)
Captain Bluff (25)
Carlo Buffone (7)
Harold Childe (16)
Harry Baillie (21)
John Seacombe (18)
Joseph Wittol (25)
Lady Wishfort (26)
Lord Tynedale (18)
Margaret Hall (19)
Matthew Yorke (19)
Monsieur Paul (18, 20)
Poore Persoun (The)
  (21)
Rev. Cyril Hall (19)
Richard Mason (17)
Sardanapalus (16)
St. John Rivers (17)
Symond Symkyn (21)

13

Dr. John Bretton (20)
Edward Belmour (25)
Edward Kno'well (6)
Epicure Mammon (l)
Georgiana Reed (17)
Hortense Moore (19)
Hugh of Lincoln (21)
Humphrey Waspe (2)
James Helstone (19)
James Loredano (16)
John Littlewit (2)
Lady Loadstone (8)
Lady Pinchbeck (15)
Lady Touchwood (22)
Lord Touchwood (22)
Magnetick Lady (The)
  (8)
Marino Faliero (16)
Master Stephen (6)
Miss Marchmont (20)
Miss Scatcherd (17)

Mrs. Crimsworth (18)
Philip Nunnely (19)
Rev. Mr. Sweeting (19)
Sir Paul Plyant (22)

14

Augustus Caesar (10)
Augustus Malone (19)
Captain Bobadil (6)
Captain Keeldar (19)
Edward Mirabell (22)
Francis Foscari (16)
Justice Clement (6)

Rev. Peter Malone (19)
Shirley Keeldar (19)
Wilful Witwould (26)

15

Anthony Witwould (26)
Clerk of Oxenford (21)

Ezekiel Edgworth (2)
Fastidious Brisk (7)
George Downright (6)
Hon. John Seacombe (18)
Madame Eglantine (21)
Sir Joseph Wittol (25)

Some characters from **Charles Dickens**
Lists of works from which the following characters are taken, with reference numbers.

Ben Jonson		
Ref. No.	Title	
1. Barnaby Rudge	(12 letters)	
2. Battle of Life, The	(15 ,,)	
3. Bleak House	(10 ,,)	
4. Chimes, The	(9 ,,)	
5. Christmas Carol, A	(15 ,,)	
6. Cricket on the Hear, The	(21 ,,)	
7. David Copperfield	(16 ,,)	
8. Dombey and Son	(12 ,,)	
9. Edwin Drood	(10 ,,)	
10. Great Expectations	(17 ,,)	
11. Hard Times	(9 ,,)	
12. Haunted Man, The	(13 ,,)	
13. Little Dorrit	(12 ,,)	

Lord Byron		
Ref. No.	Title	
14. Martin Chuzzlewit	(16 letters)	
15. Master Hurnphrey's Clock	(20 ,,)	
16. Mudfog Papers, The	(15 ,,)	
17. Nicholas Nickleby	(16 ,,)	
18. Old Curiosity Shop, The	(19 ,,)	
19. Oliver Twist	(11 ,,)	
20. Our Mutual Friend	(15 ,,)	
21. Pickwick, or The Pickwick Papers	(8 or 17 ,,)	
22. Sketches by Boz	(13 ,,)	
23. Tale of Two Cities, A	(16 ,,)	

Note: The numbers in brackets indicate *the works* in which the characters appear.

2 – 4

Aged (The) (10)
Bell (16)
Bet (19)
Bray (17)
Bung (22)
Cobb (1)
Cute (4)
Dick (19)
Fang (19)
Fern (4)
Fips (14)
Fogg (21)
Gamp (14)
Gay (8)
Grip (bird) (1)
Grub (21)
Hawk (17)
Heep (7)
Hugh (1)
Jane (22)
Jip (dog) (7)

Jo (3)
Joe (21)
Jupe (11)
Kit (18)
Knag (17)
Mary (21)
Meg (4)
Mell (7)
Muff (16)
'Nemo' (3)
Peel (21)
Pell (21)
Peps (8)
'Pip' (10)
Pott (21)
Prig (14)
Pyke (17)
Riah (20)
Rosa (3)
Rugg (13)
Slug (16)
Slum (18)
Tigg (14)

Tim (5)
Tox (8)
Veck (4)
Wade (13)
Wegg (20)

5

Agnes (7)
Alice (15)
Bates (19)
Betsy (19)
Bevan (14)
Biddy (10)
Bloss (22)
Boxer (6)
Brass (18)
Brick (14)
Brown (8, 22)
'Caddy' (3)
Casby (13)
Chick (8)
Choke (14)

Clare (3)
Crupp (7)
Daisy (1)
Diver (14)
Drood (9)
Dumps (22)
Emily (7)
Evans (22)
Fagin (19)
Filer (4)
Fixem (22)
Flite (3)
Giles (19)
Gills (8)
Gowan (13)
Grace (2)
Green (22)
Gride (17)
Grove (18)
Guppy (3)
Gwynn (21)
Hardy (22)
Hicks (22)

Janet (7)
Jerry (18)
Jones (2)
Kenge (3)
Krook (3)
Lobbs (21)
Lorry (23)
Lupin (14)
Maggy (13)
Marks (15)
Miggs (1)
Mills (7)
Minns (22)
Molly (10)
Monks (19)
Mould (14)
Nancy (19)
Neddy (21)
Noggs (17)
Perch (8)
Pinch (14)
Pluck (17)
Price (17)

Pross (23)
Quale (3)
Quilp (18)
Rudge (1)
Sarah (22)
Scott (18)
Sikes (19)
Slyme (14)
Smart (21)
Smike (17)
Sophy (7)
Squod (3)
Stagg (1)
Tibbs (22)
Toots (8)
Tozer (8)
Trabb (10)
Trent (18)
Trott (22)
Tuggs (22)
Twist (19)
Venus (20)
Wosky (22)

6

Alfred (2)
Babley (7)
Badger (3)
Bagman (The) (21)
Bailey (14)
Bamber (21)
Bantam (21)
Barker (22)
Barkis (7)
Barley (10)
Barney (19)
Barton (22)
Beadle (13)
Bedwin (19)
Benton (15)
Bertha (6)
Bitzer (11)
Boffin (20)
Bowley (4)
Briggs (8, 22)
Bucket (3)
Budden (22)
Budger (21)
Bumble (19)
Bumple (22)
Bunsby (8)
Butler (22)
Buzfuz (21)
Calton (22)
Carker (8)
Carton (23)
'Cherub' (The) (20)
Codlin (18)
Cooper (22)
Corney (19)
Cousin (8)
Craggs (2)
Cuttle (8)
Dadson (22)
Danton (22)
Darnay (23)
Dartle (7)
Denham (12)
Dennis (1)
Dodson (21)
Dombey (8)
Dorrit (13)
Dounce (22)
Dowler (21)
Dr. Peps (8)
Durden (3)
Edkins (22)
Endell (7)
Etella (10)

'Fat Boy' (The) (21)
Feeder (8)
Folair (17)
George (3)
Gordon (l)
Graham (14)
Grueby (1)
Guster (3)
Harmon (20)
Harri (14, 18, 22)
Hawdon (3)
Helves (22)
Hexham (20)
Higden (20)
Hilton (22)
Hobler (22)
Hubble (10)
Hunter (21, 22)
Hutley (21)
Jarley (18)
Jasper (9)
Jingle (21)
Johnny (20)
Lammle (20)
Lumbey (17)
Magnus (21)
Marion (2)
Marley (5)
Martha (22)
Marton (18)
Maylie (19)
Merdle (13)
Milvey (20)
Mivins (21)
Moddle (14)
Morfin (8)
Mullet (14)
Muzzle (21)
Nathan (22)
Nipper (8)
Noakes (22)
Orlick (10)
Pancks (13)
Parker (22)
Pegler (11)
Peploe (22)
Perker (21)
Phunky (21)
Pipkin (21)
Pirrip (10)
Pocket (10)
Pogram (14)
Potter (22)
Purday (22)
Rachel (11)
Raddle (21)
Redlaw (12)
Rigaud (13)

Rogers (22)
Sapsea (9)
Sawyer (21)
Sleary (11)
Sloppy (20)
Strong (7)
Stubbs (22)
Tapley (14)
Timgon (22)
Toodle (8)
Tottle (22)
Tupman (21)
Tupple (22)
Varden (1)
Walker (22)
Warden (2)
Wardle (21)
Waters (22)
Weller (21)
Wilfer (20)
Willet (1)
Wilson (22)
Winkle (21)

7

Barbara (18)
Bardell (21)
Bazzard (9)
Blimber (8)
Blotton (21)
Bobster (17)
Boldwig (21)
Britain (2)
Brooker (17)
Browdie (17)
Bullamy (14)
'Charley' (3)
Chester (1)
Chillip (7)
Chivery (13)
Chuffey (14)
Cleaver (20)
Clenham (11)
Crackit (19)
Creakle (7)
Crewler (7)
Dawking (19)
Dedlock (3)
Defarge (23)
Drummle (10)
Dr. Wosky (22)
Edmunds (21)
Evenson (22)
Fleming (19)
Gargery (10)
Garland (18)
Gazingi (17)

General (13)
Granger (8)
Gridley (3)
Grimwig (19)
Grinder (18)
Groffin (21)
Heyling (21)
Hopkins (21)
Jackman (24)
Jackson (21)
Jaggers (10)
Jeddler (2)
Jellyby (3)
Jiniwin (18)
Jinkins (21)
Jobling (3, 14)
Jorkins (7)
Kenwigs (17)
Larkins (7, 22)
Lewsome (14)
Loggins (22)
Macklin (22)
Manette (23)
Manners (22)
Meagles (13)
Mowcher (7)
Mrs. Heep (7)
Mrs. Pott (21)
Nadgeth (14)
Neckett (3)
Newcome (2)
Nubbles (18)
Nupkins (21)
O'Bleary (22)
Overton (22)
Pawkins (14)
Peecher (20)
Pipchin (8)
Plummer (6)
Podsnap (20)
Redburn (15)
Richard (4)
Sampson (20)
Scadder (14)
Scrooge (5)
Simpson (22)
Skewton (8)
Slammer (21)
Slowboy (6)
Slunkey (21)
Smangle (21)
Smauker (21)
Snagsby (3)
Snawley (17)
Snubbin (21)
Snuffin (17)
Sparsit (11)
Spenlow (7)
Squeers (17)

Stryver (23)
Swidger (12)
Taunton (22)
'The Aged' (10)
'Tiny Tim' (5)
Tippins (20)
Todgers (14)
Tom Cobb (l)
Tomkins (22)
Trotter (21)
Trundle (21)
Wackles (18)
Wemmuck (10)
Whimple (10)
Whisker (pony) (18)
Wickham (8)
Wilkins (22)
Wobbler (13)

8

Ada Clare (3)
Alphonse (17)
Aunt Jane (22)
Bachelor (The) (18)
Bagstock (7)
Barnacle (13)
Beckwith (12)
Beverley (22)
Blathers (19)
Brandley (10)
Bravassa (17)
Brittles (19)
Brownlow (19)
Bull's Eye (dog) (19)
Carstone (3)
Chadband (3)
Chitling (19)
Claypole (19)
Cleriker (10)
Cluppins (21)
Cratchit (5)
Crummles (17)
Crumpton (22)
Cruncher (23)
Crushton (21)
Dingwall (22)
Diogenes (dog) (8)
Dr. Lumbey (17)
Dr. Strong (7)
Evrémond (23)
Fielding (6)
Finching (13)
Fladdock (14)
Flammell (22)

Fledgeby (20)
Gashford (1)
Haredale (l)
Harleigh (22)
Havisham (10)
Hortense (3)
Humphrey (15)
Jarndyce (3)
Jem Grove (18)
Jennings (22)
La Creevy (17)
Langford (12)
Ledbrain (16)
Ledbrook (17)
Lenville (17)
Littimer (7)
Lobskini (22)
Losberne (19)
Magwitch (10)
Micawber (7)
Miss Knag (17)
Miss Wade (13)
Mrs. Bloss (22)
Mrs. Crupp (7)
Mrs. Gowan (13)
Mrs. Lupin (14)
Mrs. Perch (8)
Mrs. Rudge (1)
Mrs. Tibbs (22)
Nicholas (22)
Nickleby (17)
Old Lobbs (21)
Peggotty (7)
Petowker (17)
Pickwick (21)
Plornish (13)
Robinson (22)
Skettles (8)
Skiffins (10)
Skimpole (3)
Slinkton (10)
Smithers (22)
Snitchey (2)
Sparkins (22)
Sparkler (13)
Stiggins (21)
Tetterby (12)
Toby Veck (4)
Tom Pinch (14)
Tom Scott (18)
Tom Smart (21)
Traddles (7)
Trotwood (7)
Uncle Tom (22)
Westlock (14)
Whiffers (21)
Will Fern (4)
Woolford (22)

9

Amy Dorrit (13)
Belvawney (17)
Betsy Prig (14)
Bill Sikes (19)
Blackpool (11)
Bob Sawyer (21)
Bounderby (11)
Boythorne (3)
Charlotte (19)
Cherryble (17)
Chickweed (19)
'Cleopatra' (8)
Compeyson (10)
Dr. Blimber (8)
Dr. Jeddler (2)
Dr. Jobling (14)
Dr. Slammer (21)
Fleetwood (22)
Gattleton (22)
Gradrind (11)
Gregsbury (17)
Grewgious (9)
Harthouse (11)
Headstone (20)
Jem Hutley (21)
Joe Willet (l)
Leo Hunter (21)
Lightwood (20)
Lillyvick (17)
'Lord Peter' (22)
Malderton (22)
Mantalini (17)
Maplesone (22)
Markleham (7)
Miss Flite (3)
Miss Gwynn (21)
Miss Miggs (l)
Miss Mills (7)
Miss Pross (23)
Mrs. Bedwin (19)
Mrs. Briggs (22)
Mrs. Budger (21)
Mrs. Corney (19)
Mrs. Craggs (2)
Mrs. Dadson (22)
Mrs. Dowler (21)
Mrs. Harris (14)
Mrs. Hubble (10)
Mrs. Hunter (21)
Mrs. Jarley (18)
Mrs. Lammle (20)
Mrs. Maylie (19)
Mrs. Merdle (13)
Mrs. Milvey (20)
Mrs. Parker (22)
Mrs. Pegler (11)
Mrs. Peploe (22)

Mrs. Raddle (21)
Mrs. Stubbs (22)
Mrs. Varden (1)
Mrs. Wilfer (20)
Murdstone (7)
Ned Dennis (l)
Nell Trent (18)
Old Orlick (10)
Pardiggle (3)
Pecksniff (14)
Phil Squod (3)
Potterson (20)
Riderhood (20)
Ruth Pinch (14)
Sam Weller (21)
Sarah Gamp (14)
Silas Wegg (20)
Sludberry (22)
Smallweed (3)
Smorltork (21)
Snodgrass (21)
Spruggins (22)
Swiveller (18)
Tackleton (6)
Tappertit (l)
'The Bagman' (21)
'The Cherub' (20)
'The Fat Boy' (21)
Tom Codlin (18)
Towlinson (8)
Uncle Bill (22)
Uriah Heep (7)
Veneering (20)
Verisopht (17)
Walter Gay (8)
Wickfield (7)
Will Marks (15)
Wisbottle (22)
Witherden (18)
Woodcourt (3)
Wrayburne (20)

10

Alice Brown (8)
Aunt Martha (2)
Ayresleigh (21)
Betsy Clark (22)
Bill Barker (22)
Bill Barley (10)
Billsmethi (22)
Bitherston (8)
Chevy Slyme (14)
Chuzzlewit (14)
'Cymon' Tuggs (22)
Dame Durden (3)
Doctor Peps (8)
Edwin Drood (9)

Emma Porter (22)
Flintwinch (13)
Heathfield (2)
Henry Gowan (13)
'Honest John' (22)
Jack Bamber (21)
Jack Bunsby (8)
Jem Larkins (22)
Job Trotter (21)
Joe Gargery (10)
John Carker (8)
John Dounce (22)
John Grueby (8)
John Harman (20)
John Willet (l)
'Kit' Nubbles (18)
Kittlebell (22)
Knight Bell (16)
Little Dick (19)
Little Paul (8)
MacStinger (8)
Mark Tapley (14)
Mary Graham (14)
Miss Benton (15)
Mrs. Bardell (21)
Mrs. Clenham (13)
Mrs. Crewler (7)
Mrs. Gargery (10)
Mrs. Garland (18)
Mrs. General (13)
Mrs. Grudden (17)
Mrs. Jellyby (3)
Mrs. Jiniwin (18)
Mrs. Kenwigs (17)
Mrs. Macklin (22)
Mrs. Meagles (13)
Mrs. Nubbles (18)
Mrs. Parsons (22)
Mrs. Pipchin (8)
Mrs. Skewton (8)
Mrs. Sparsit (11)
Mrs. Squeers (17)
Mrs. Swidger (12)
Mrs. Taunton (22)
Mrs. Todgers (14)
Mrs. Wackles (18)
Mrs. Whimple (10)
Mrs. Wickham (8)
Paul Dombey (8)
Rosa Dartle (7)
Rose Maylie (19)
Rouncewell (3)
Sally Brass (18)
Sempronius (22)
Signor Jupe (11)
Simon Tuggs (22)
Sliderskew (17)
Smallweed (3)
Sowerberry (19)

Stareleigh (21)
Steerforth (7)
Tattycoram (13)
Tony Weller (21)
Turveydrop (3)
Williamson (22)
Wititterly (17)

11

Abel Garland (18)
Arthur Gride (17)
Balderstone (22)
Bella Wilfer (20)
Betsey Quilp (18)
Betty Higden (20)
Bob Cratchit (5)
Cecilia Jupe (11)
Copperfield (7)
Daniel Quilp (18)
Doctor Wosky (22)
Dolge Orlick (10)
Dora Spenlow (7)
Edith Dombey (8)
Emily Wardle (21)
Emma Peecher (20)
Fanny Dombey (8)
Fanny Dorrit (13)
Frank Milvie (20)
Gabriel Grub (21)
'Game Chicken' (The) (8)
Ham Peggotty (7)
Harry Maylie (19)
Jack Hopkins (21)
Jack Redburn (15)
Jacob Barton (22)
James Carker (8)
Jarvis Lorry (23)
Jemima Evans (22)
Jesse Hexham (20)
John Browdie (17)
John Chivery (7)
John Dawkins (19)
John Edmunds (21)
John Evenson (22)
John Jobling (14)
John Podsnap (20)
John Smauker (21)
John Wemmock (10)
Joseph Tuggs (22)
Lady Dedlock (3)
Lady Tippins (20)
Linkinwater (17)
Little Emily (7)
Louisa Chick (8)
Lucretia Tox (8)
Misses Brown (22)

Miss Gazingi (17)
Miss Larkins (7)
Miss Mowcher (7)
Monflathers (18)
Mrs. Brandley (10)
Mrs. Clupping (21)
Mrs. Crummles (17)
Mrs. Dingwall (22)
Mrs. Fielding (6)
Mrs. Finching (13)
Mrs. Gummidge (7)
Mrs. Micawber (7)
Mrs. Nickleby (17)
Mrs. Plornish (13)
Mrs. Sparkler (13)
Mrs. Tetterby (12)
Newman Noggs (17)
Oliver Twist (19)
Perrybingle (6)
Percy Noakes (22)
Peter Magnus (21)
Polly Toodle (8)
Pumblechook (10)
Robin Toodle (8)
Slackbridge (11)
Snevellicci (17)
Solomon Peel (21)
Solomon Pell (21)
Susan Nipper (8)
Susan Weller (21)
Sweedlepipe (14)
'The Bachelor' (18)
Tim Cratchit (5)
Toby Crackit (19)
Tom Chitling (19)
Tony Jobling (3)
Tracy Tupman (21)
Tulkinhorn (3)
Uncle George (22)
Uncle Robert (22)

12

Abel Magwitch (10)
Agnes Fleming (19)
Alderman Cute (4)
Alfred Jingle (21)
Alfred Lammle (20)
Amelia Martin (22)
'Artful Dodger' (The) (19)
Aunt Margaret (22)
Barnaby Rudge (1)
Bayham Badger (3)
Bully Stryver (23)
Charles Tuggs (22)
Charley Bates (19)
Colonel Diver (14)

Doctor Lumbey (17)
Doctor Strong (7)
Dr. Parker Peps (8)
Edith Granger (8)
Edward Cuttle (8)
Edward Dorrit (13)
Elijah Pogram (14)
Emily Taunton (22)
Emma Haredale (1)
Emma Micawber (7)
Esther Hawdon (3)
Fanny Cleaver (20)
Fanny Squeers (17)
Feenix Cousin (8)
George Gordon (1)
Grace Jeddler (2)
Honeythunder (9)
Horace Hunter (22)
Joe, the 'Fat Boy' (21)
John Jarndyce (3)
John Westlock (14)
Julia Manners (22)
Kate Nickleby (17)
Koeldwethout (17)
Little Dorrit (13)
Lizzie Hexham (20)
Lord Barnacle (13)
Lucie Manette (23)
Madeline Bray (17)
Major Pawkins (14)
Martha Endell (7)
Mary Fielding (6)
Matilda Price (17)
Milly Swidger (12)
Miss Bravassa (17)
Miss Havisham (10)
Miss La Creevy (17)
Miss Ledbrook (17)
Miss Skiffins (10)
Miss Willises (22)
Miss Woolford (22)
Montague Tigg (14)
Mrs. Gradgrind (11)
Mrs. Maplesone (22)
Mrs. Markleham (7)
Mrs. Pardiggle (3)
Mrs. Veneering (20)
Mulberry Hawk (17)
Noah Claypole (19)
'Peepy' Jellyby (3)
Phillip Pirrip (10)
Phillip Redlaw (12)
Sampson Brass (18)
Samuel Briggs (22)
Samuel Weller (21)
Solomon Daisy (1)
Solomon Gills (8)
Sophy Crewler (7)
Stoney Briggs (8)

Sydney Carton (23)
Thomas Sapsea (9)
Tilly Slowboy (6)
Tite Barnacle (13)
Tom Gradgrind (11)
Tom Malderton (22)
William Guppy (3)
William Sikes (19)

13

Alfred Tomkins (22)
Anabella Allen (21)
Arthur Clenham (13)
Augustus Minns (22)
Belinda Pocket (10)
Belinda Waters (22)
Benjamin Stagg (1)
Bertha Plummer (6)
'Bob the Grinder' (8)
Brook-Dingwall (22)
Captain Bunsby (8)
Captain Cuttle (8)
Captain Dowler (21)
Captain George (3)
Captain Hawdon (3)
Captain Purday (22)
Captain Waters (22)
Charles Darnay (23)
Charles Timson (22)
Charley Hexham (23)
Clara Peggotty (7)
Dick Swiveller (18)
Doctor Blimber (8)
Doctor Jeddler (2)
Doctor Jobling (14)
Doctor Manette (23)
Dodson and Fogg (21)
Dr. John Jobling (14)
Edward Chester (1)
Edward Plummer (6)
Emily Peggotty (7)
Emily Smithers (22)
Ernest Defarge (23)
Flora Finching (13)
Gabriel Varden (1)
George Heyling (21)
George Nupkins (21)
George Sampson (20)
Geore Swidger (12)
Harriet Beadle (13)
Harriet Carker (8)
Herbert Pocket (10)
Jane Murdstone (7)
Jerry Cruncher (23)
Joseph Overton (22)
Lavinia Wilfer (20)
Lord Verisopht (17)

Madame Defarge (23)
Maria Crumpton (22)
Marion Jeddler (2)
Mary Ann Raddle (21)
Matthew Pocket (10)
Mealy Potatoes (7)
Michael Bumple (22)
Michael Warden (2)
Minnie Meagles (13)
Miss Belvawney (17)
Miss Lillerton (22)
Miss Potterson (20)
Misses Kenwigs (The) (17)
Misses Wackles (The) (18)
Mistress Alice (15)
Mrs. Macstinger (8)
Mrs. Rouncewell (3)
Mrs. Sowerberry (19)
Mrs. Williamson (22)
Peg Sliderskew (17)
Philip Swidger (12)
Professor Muff (16)
Rachael Wardle (21)
Ralph Nickleby (17)
Richard Babley (7)
Sally Tetterby (12)
Samuel Slumkey (21)
Samuel Wilkins (22)
Septimus Hicks (22)
Seth Pecksniff (14)
Thomas Groffin (21)
Tumley Snuffim (17)
Watkins Tottle (22)
William Barker (22)
William Dorrit (13)

14

Abbcy Potterson (20)
Agnes Wickfield (7)
Alexander Trott (22)
Allen Woodcourt (3)
Amelia Crumpton (22)
Anthony Jedder (2)
Augustus Cooper (22)
Augustus Moddle (14)
Barnet Skettles (8)
Bentley Drummle (10)
Betsey Cluppins (21)
Betsey Trotwood (7)
Captain Boldwig (21)

Caroline Wilson (22)
Cecilia Bobster (17)
'Charlotta' Tuggs (22)
Chickenstalker (4)
Daniel Peggotty (7)
'Dot' Peerybingle (6)
Edward Sparkler (13)
Edwin Cherryble (17)
Florence Dombey (8)
Francis Spenlow (7)
Frank Cheeryble (17)
Frederick Trent (18)
General Scadder (14)
Harold Skimpole (3)
Hiram Grewgious (9)
Honoria Dedlock (3)
Isabella Wardle (21)
Jefferson Brick (14)
Johnny Tetterby (12)
Lavinia Spenlow (7)
Master Humphery (15)
Mercy Pecksniff (14)
'Merry' Pecksniff (14)
Monsieur Rigaud (13)
Mrs. Betty Higden (20)
Mrs. Copperfield (7)
Mrs. Peerybingle (6)
Mrs. Polly Toodle (8)
Mrs. Snevellicci (17)
Nicodemus Dumps (22)
Octavius Budden (22)
Reginald Wilfer (20)
Reuben Haredale (1)
Rev. Frank Milvey (20)
Roger Riderhood (20)
Samuel Pickwick (21)
Serjeant Buzfuz (21)
Signor Lobskini (22)
Simon Tappertit (1)
Sir John Chester (1)
Sophia Tetterby (12)
'The Game Chicken' (8)
Therese Defarge (23)
Thomas Traddles (7)
Tim Linkinwater (17)
William Swidger (12)

15

Alexander Briggs (22)
Alexander Budden (22)

Alfred Mantalini (17)
Benjamin Britain (2)
Caroline Jellyby (3)
'Cherry' Pecksniff (14)
Clarissa Spenlow (7)
Clemency Newcome (2)
Conkey Chickweed (19)
Cornelia Blimber (8)
'Dolphus Tetterby (12)
Dora Copperfield (7)
Ebenezer Scrooge (5)
Edward Murdstone (7)
Estella Havisham (10)
Eugene Wrayburne (20)
Ferdinand Barnacle (13)
Frederick Dorrit (13)
General Fladdock (14)
Georgina Podsnap (20)
Godfrey Nickleby (17)
Henrietta Boffin (20)
Henry Wititterly (17)
Hon. Elijah Pogram (14)
Horatio Sparkins (22)
'Horatio St. Julien' (22)
James Steerforth (7)
John Peerybingle (6)
Jonas Chuzzlewit (14)
Josephine Sleary (11)
Josiah Rounderby (11)
Julia Wititterly (17)
Lavinia Dingwall (22)
Louisa Gradgrind (11)
MacChoakumchild (11)
Madame Mantalini (17)
Mary Peerybingle (6)
Miss Snevellicci (17)
Monsieur Defarge (23)
Mrs. Joseph Porter (22)
Nathaniel Pipkin (21)
Nathaniel Winkle (21)
Nicodemus Boffin (20)
Ninetta Crummles (17)
Paul Sweedlepipe (14)
Professor Mullet (14)
Richard Carstone (3)
Serjeant Snubbin (21)
Sir Joseph Bowley (4)
Sir Mulberry Hawk (17)
Smallweed Family (3)
Teresa Malderton (22)
'The Artful Dodger' (17)

Some characters from **Dryden, George Eliot, Fielding,** and **Goldsmi**th.
List of works from which the following characters are taken, with reference numbers.

Dryden

Ref. No.	Title	
1. Absalom and Achitophel		(20 letters)
2. (Various)		

George Eliot

11. Adam Bede		(8 letters)
12. Clerical Life, Scenes from	(12 or 22	„)
13. Daniel Deronda	(13	„)
14. Felix Holt	(9	„)
15. Middlemarch	(11	„)
16. Mill on the Floss, The	(17	„)
17. Romola	(6	„)
18. Silas Marner	(11	„)
19. Spanish Gipsy, The	(15	„)

Fielding (Henry)

Ref. No.	Title	
3. Amelia		(6 letters)
4. Jonathan Wild		(12 „)
5. Joseph Andrews		(13 „)
6. Mock Doctor, The		(13 „)
7. Pasquin		(7 „)
8. Tom Jones		(8 „)
9. Tom Thumb		(8 „)
10. (Various)		

Goldsmith (Oliver)

20. Citizen of the World, The		(20 letters)
21. Good-Natured Man, The		(17 „)
22. She Stoops to Conquer		(18 „)
23. Vicar of Wakefield, The		(19 „)
24. (Various)		

Note: The numbers in brackets indicate *the works* in which the characters appear.

2 – 4

Agag (1)
Amri (1)
Arod (1)
Bath (3)
Bede (11)
Cass (18)
Cei (17)
Cora (1)
Dane (18)
Doeg (1)
Holt (14)
Iras (2)
Juan (19)
Juno (dog) (11)
Lisa (17)
Lyon (14)
Maso (11)
Moss (16)
Og (1)
Omri (1)
Rann (11)
Rock (20)
Saul (1)
Snap (4)
Tibs (20)
Wild (4)
Wyld (4)

5

Adams (5)

Amiel (l)
Balak (l)
Bardo (17)
Booby (5)
Booth (3)
Burge (11)
Caleb (l)
Calvo (17)
David (1)
Deane (16)
Dorax (2)
Edwin (24)
Eppic (18)
Fanny (5)
Garth (15)
Glegg (16)
Gomaz (2)
Guest (16)
Jakin (16
Jonas (1)
Jones (8)
Kezia (16)
Lofty (21)
Macey (18)
Moody (2)
Nadab (l)
Nello (17)
Place (7)
Sagan (1)
Sheva (1)
Tessa (17)
Tibbs (20)
Vincy (16)
Wakem (16)

Whang (20)
Zadoc (1)
Zarca (19)
Zelis (20)
Zimri (1)

6

Abdael (1)
Adriel (1)
Alexas (2)
Amelia (3)
Antony (2)
Arnold (23)
Badger (10)
Barton (12)
Bennet (3)
Blaize (24)
Blifil (8)
Brooke (15)
Casson (11)
Crispe (23)
Dobson (16)
Dr. Rock (20)
Elvira (2)
Emilia (2)
Garnet (21)
Gilfil (12)
Hingpo (20)
Honour (8)
Irwine (11)
Jarvis (21)
Jasper (6)

Jerwyn (14)
La Ruse (4)
Marlow (22)
Marner (18)
Massey (11)
Melema (17)
Michal (1)
Morris (11)
Olivia (21)
Phaleg (1)
Pounce (5)
Poyser (11)
Pullet (16)
Quaver (10)
Romola (17)
Shimel (1)
Skeggo (23)
Sorrel (11)
Square (8)
Squint (20)
Supple (8)
Waters (8)
Wilmot (23)

7

Absalom (1)
Andrews (5)
Annabel (1)
Artemis (2)
Aurelia (2)
Bagshot (4)
Beatrix (2)

Bellamy (2)
Benaiah (1)
Blister (10)
Bridget (8)
Brigida (17)
Buzzard (3)
Camillo (2)
Chettam (15)
Celadin (2)
Cennini (17)
Croaker (21)
Davilow (13)
Debarry (14)
Deronda (13)
Diggory (22)
Dominic (2)
Fedalma (19)
Glasher (13)
Gregory (6)
Grizzle (9)
Honoria (2)
Jim Salt (11)
Leonora (2)
Lumpkin (22)
Lydate (15)
Mariana (10)
Maximin (2)
Meyrick (13)
Mrs. Bede (11
Neville (22)
Phaedra (2)
Spanker (23)
Spindle (24)
Squeeze (20)

Edward Casaubon (15)
Frederick Vincy (15)
George Primrose (23)
Harold Transome (14)
Jenny Tinderbox (20)
Kate Hardcastle (22)
Maggie Tulliver (16)
Maximus Debarry (14)
Miss Hardcastle (22)

Mrs. Cadwallader (15)
Mrs. Fitzpatrick (8)
Olivia Primrose (23)
Sophia Primrose (23)

15

Augustus Debarry (14)

Leontine Croaker (21)
Mrs. Lydia Glasher (13)
Olivia Woodville (21)
Parson Trulliber (5)
Sir James Chettam (15)
Squire Thornhill (23)
Thomas Heartfree (4)

Some characters from **Thomas Hardy**
List of works from which the following characters are taken, with reference numbers.

Ref. No.	Title		Ref. No.	Title	
1.	A Laodicean	(10 letters)	9.	The Mayor of Casterbridge	(22 letters)
2.	A Pair of Blue Eyes	(15 „)	10.	The Return of the Native	(20 „)
3.	Desperate Remedies	(17 „)	11.	The Trumpet Major	(15 „)
4.	Far From the Madding Crowd	(22 „)	12.	The Woodlands	(12 „)
5.	Jude the Obscure	(14 „)	13.	Time's Laughing Stocks	(19 „)
6.	Life's Little Cronies	(18 „)	14.	Wessex Poems	(11 „)
7.	Tess of the D'Urbervilles	(21 „)	15.	Wessex Tales	(11 „)
8.	The Hand of Ethelberta	(19 „)			

Note: The numbers in brackets indicate *the works* in which the characters appear.

4 – 6

Anna (6)
David (11)
Dr. Bath (9)
Hannah (13)
Laura (13)
Marion (7)
Meggs (14)
Michel (14)
Molly (11)
Sophy (6)
Unity (2)

7

Aguette (13)
Amos Fry (13)
Ann Dewy (13)
Barbree (14)
Bob Dewy (13)
Cawtree (12)
Charlie (10)
Cockton (1)
Dr. Chant (7)
Dr. Jones (12)
Haymoss (13)

Jim Caro (13)
Knowles (1)
Leverre (13)
Michael (13)
Mr. Cecil (13)
Mr. Hewby (2)
Rev. Glin (2)
Vilbert (5)

8

Boldwood (9)
Buzzford (9)
Cain Ball (4)
Car Darch (7)
Dick Dewy (13)
Dr. Breeve (8)
Fancy Day (13)
Humphrey (10)
Izz Huett (7)
Maitland (14)
Matt Grey (15)
Mr. Grower (9)
Mr. Lester (6)
Mrs. Edlin (5)
Mrs. Hurst (4)
Rev. P. Cope (6)

Uncle Joe (5)

9

Amos Graye (3)
Arice Caro (13)
Bannister (11)
Battersby (14)
Bessy Dewy (13)
Elijah New (15)
Henry Fray (4)
Jan Coggan (4)
Jane Smith (2)
Jim Clarke (15)
Jimmy Dewy (13)
Jim Owlett (15)
Jim Weedle (6)
John Biles (6)
John Green (15)
John Power (1)
John Smith (2)
John South (12)
Laban Tall (4)
Mark Clark (4)
Mr. Bollens (3)
Mr. Harnham (6)
Mr. Wilkins (1)

Mrs. Brooks (7)
Mrs. Martin (13)
Mrs. Morris (3)
Owen Graye (3)
Rev. Walker (6)
Sam Hobson (6)
Sarah Hall (15)
Stanidge (9)
Susan Dewy (13)
Tony Kytes (6)

10

Abner Power (1)
Angel Clare (7)
Anne Seaway (3)
Beck Knibbs (7)
Bob Loveday (11)
Captain Vye (10)
Chalkfield (10)
Dr Charlson (15)
Emily Darth (6)
Fanny Robin (4)
Felix Clare (7)
Fred Shiner (13)
Gabriel Oak (4)
Helena Hall (15)

Henry Giles (6)
Jack Dollop (7)
Jack Winter (6)
James Clare (7)
J. Appleseed (7)
John Chiles (6)
John Upjohn (12)
Jude Fawley (5)
Lucy Savile (15)
Marty South (12)
Mercy Chant (7)
Milly Birds (1)
Mr. Cartlett (5)
Mrs. Dollery (12)
Mrs. Goodman (1)
Mrs. Palmley (6)
Nancy Darch (7)
Olive Pawle (6)
Olly Dowden (10)
Patty Beads (13)
Paula Power (1)
Philip Hall (15)
Reuben Dewy (13)
Rev. Melrose (15)
Rev. Twycolt (6)
Rhoda Brook (7) (15)
Sammy Blore (13)
Thomas Leaf (13)
Tim Tankens (14)

11

Abel Whittle (9)
Alfred Neigh (8)
Andrew Jones (15)
Anne Garland (11)
Charles Raye (6)
Charles Dewy (13)
Diggory Venn (10)
Dr. J. St. Cleeve (13)
Elias Spinks (13)
Esther Beach (11)
Eustacia Vye (10)
Faith Julian (8)
Farmer Groby (7)
Farmer Lodge (15)
Giles Martin (13)
Henry Knight (12)
Jacob Noakes (11)
Jane Vallens (6)
Jasper Clift (6)
Job Mitchell (11)
Julia Aspent (6)
Lucy Melbury (12)
Martha Sarah (15)
Matthew Moon (4)
Michael Mail (13)
Mr. Gradfield (3)

Mrs. Rolliver (7)
Nancy Weedle (6)
Nat Callcome (13)
Ned Hipcroft (6)
Oliver Giles (15)
Rev. A. Maybold (13)
Rev. Woodwell (1)
Robert Penny (13)
Robert Trewe (15)
Simon Burden (11)
Tabitha Lark (13)
Unity Sallet (6)
Wat Ollamore (6)
Wilf Latimer (15)
William Dare (1)
William Dewy (13)
William Worm (2)

12

Abraham Brown (3)
Alfred Somers (13)
Ann Arice Caro (13)
Anthony Green (13)
Arabella Donn (5)
Betty Privett (6)
Charles Downe (15)
Conjurer Fall (7) (9)
Damon Wildere (10)
Dr. E. Fitzpiers (12)
Edith Harnham (6)
Emily Hanning (6)
Felix Jethway (2)
Fred Beancock (12)
George Barnet (15)
Grace Melbury (12)
Henri Leverre (13)
James Comfort (11)
Jonathan Kale (7)
Levi Everdene (4)
Mary Ann Money (4)
Miss Bicknell (2)
Miss Fontover (5)
Mother Cuxsom (9)
Mrs. M. Pine-Avon (13)
Phyllis Grove (6)
Retty Priddle (7)
Rev. M. St. Cleeve (13)
Richard Crick (7)
Robert Dowdle (6)
Solomon Selby (6)
Sue Bridehead (5)
Susan Nonsuch (10)
Thomas Ballam (15)
Timothy Tanfs (12)
Tina Matthews (6)
Win. Marchmill (15)

13

Aeneas Manston (3)
Albert Fellmer (6)
Andrew Satchel (6)
Captain Flower (8)
Captain T. Hardy (11)
Charles Darton (15)
Clyn Yeobright (10)
Cuthbert Clare (7)
Cytherea Graye (3)
Dan Chickerell (8)
Donald Farfree (9)
Elizabeth Leat (3)
Ella Marchmill (15)
Eunice Manston (3)
Farmer Jollice (6)
George Melbury (12)
Gertrude Lodge (15)
Grammer Oliver (12)
James Everdene (4)
James Hardcome (6)
Johnny Nonsuch (10)
Joseph Lickpan (2)
Hezekiah Biles (13)
Humphrey Gould (6)
Isaac Pierston (13)
Lady Petherwin (8)
Lizzy Newberry (15)
Lord Luxellian (2)
Louisa Menlove (8)
Martha Garland (11)
Miller Loveday (11)
Milly Richards (6)
Mrs. Goodenough (9)
Netty Sargeant (6)
Parson Thirdly (4)
Robert Creedle (12)
Robert Lickpan (2)
Robert Loveday (11)
Sergeant Brett (11)
Stephen F. Smith (2)
Steve Hardcome (6)
Susan Henchard (9)
Rev. Torkingham (13)
Trumpeter Buck (11)

14

Adelaide Hinton (3)
Arabella Fawley (5)
Billy Smallbury (4)
Caroline Aspent (6)
Christina Crick (7)
Cuningham Haze (1)
Drusilla Fawley (5)
Felice Charmond (12)
Festus Derriman (11)

George Somerset (1)
Grandfer Cantle (10)
Hannah Jolliver (6)
Harriet Palmley (6)
Jacob Smallbury (4)
Jean Bernadotte (14)
Joanna Jolliffe (6)
Joanna Phippard (6)
Joey Chickerell (8)
John Springrove (3)
Joseph Chinnery (3)
Lady E. Luxellian (2)
Liddy Smallbury (4)
Lieutenant Mild (1)
Lord Mountclere (8)
Lucetta Le Sueur (9)
Marion Bencombe (13)
Matilda Johnson (11)
Mayor Camperton (1)
Parson Tringham (7)
Philip Hookhorn (6)
Rev. John Raunham (3)
Rosa Halborough (6)
Timothy Fairway (10)
Timothy Summers (15)
William Privett (6)

15

Alec D'Urberville (7)
Arthur Kingsmore (2)
Captain de Stancy (1)
Charlotte Moulin (8)
Christian Cantle (10)
Edgar Mountclere (8)
Eustace Ladywell (8)
General Angcrean (14)
George Crookhill (6)
Gertrude Jethway (2)
Hayomont Goumont (14)
Joan Durbeyfield (7)
Jocelyn Pierston (13)
John Durbeyfield (7)
Joseph Poorgrass (4)
Lady Constantine (13)
Martin Cannister (2)
Michael Henchard (9)
Randolph Twycolt (6)
Rev. Billy Toogood (6)
Richard Crickett (3)
Sergeant Stanner (11)
Sir B. Constantine (13)
Sir P. D'Urberville (7)
Swithin St. Cleeve (13)
Tess Durbeyfield (7)
Tranter Sweatley (14)
William Boldwood (4)
William Tremlett (11)

16

Benjamin Derriman (11)
Captain Aldclyfte (3)
Captain S. Jolliffe (6)
Christopher Bless (6)
Christopher Coney (9)
Edward Springrove (3)
Elfride Swancourt (2)
Frances Frankland (6)
George Gillingham (5)
Grandfather James (13)
Hongomont Goumont (6)
John Winterbourne (12)
Joshua Halborough (6)
Leonora Frankland (6)
Little Father Time (5)
Lord and Lady Baxby (6)
Marshal Macdonald (14)
Mr. and Mrs. Belmaine (8)
Richard Stockdale (15)
Selina Halborough (6)

17

Bathsheba Everdene (4)
Charlotte de Stancy (1)
Christopher Julian (8)
Corporal Tullridge (11)
Cuthbert Helmsdale (13)
Cytherea Aldclyfte (3)
Eliza L. Durbeyfield (7)
Giles Winterbourne (12)
J. Stoke D'Urberville (7)
Miss Ruth Stockwool (13)
Mr. and Mrs. Doncastle (8)
Myrtyle Chickerell (8)
Picotee Chickerell (8)
Richard Phillstson (5)
Sir Ralph Petherwin (8)
Thomasin Yeobright (10)

18 AND 19

Anthony Cripplestran (11)
Bishop of Melchester (13)
Cornelia Chickerell (8)
Cornelius Halborough (6)
Elizabeth Endorfield (13)
Ethelberta Petherwin (8)
Geoffrey and Jane Day (13)
Georgina Chickerell (8)
Jones Saddle-Sergeant (11)
Mr. and Mrs. Chickerell (8)
Mrs. Charlotte Troyton (2)
Sergeant Francis Troy (4)
Sir William de Stancy (1)

20 – 25

Elizabeth Jane Henchard (9)
George and Jim Jolliffe (6)
Gwendoline Chickerell (8)
Rev. Christopher Swancourt (2)
Sir Cyril and Lady Blandsbury (8)

Some characters from **Jane Austen, Charles Kingsley, Kipling,** and **Longfellow**
List of works from which the following characters are taken, with reference numbers.

Jane Austen

Ref. No.		Title	
1. Emma			(4 letters)
2. Lady Susan			(9 „)
3. Mansfield Park			(13 „)
4. Northanger Abbey			(15 „)
5. Persuasion			(10 „)
6. Pride and Prejudice			(17 „)
7. Sense and Sensibility			(19 „)
8. Watsons, The			(10 „)

Charles Kingsley

16. Alton Locke		(10 letters)
17. Hereward the Wake		(15 „)
18. Two Years Ago		(11 „)
19. Westward Ho!		(10 „)
20. Yeast		(5 „)
21. (Various)		

Rudyard Kipling

Ref. No.		Title	
9. Captains Courageous			(18 letters)
10. Day's Work, The			(11 „)
11. Life's Handicap			(13 „)
12. Naulahka, The			(11 „)
13. Soldiers Three			(13 „)
14. Stalky and Co			(11 „)
15. (Various)			

Longfellow

22. Evangeline		(10 letters)
23. Golden Legend, The		(15 „)
24. Hiawatha		(8 „)
25. Hyperion		(8 „)
26. Kavanagh		(8 „)
27. Miles Standish		(13 „)
28. (Various)		

Note: The numbers in brackets indicate *the works* in which the characters appear.

3 – 5

	Bukta (10)	Elton (l)	Hogan (13, 14)	Mason (14)	Penn (9)
	Cary (19)	Emma (l)	Hurst (6)	Maxim (12)	Platt (9)
Alden (27)	Chinn (10)	Estes (12)	Kamal (15)	Mowis (22)	Price (3)
Algar (17)	Croft (5)	Fawne (10)	Kim (15)	M'Turk (14)	Prout (14)
Allen (4)	Darcy (6)	Felix (23)	King (14)	Nixon (14)	Scott (10)
Basil (22)	Doone (13)	Four (14)	Leigh (19)	Nolan (12)	Shadd (13)
Bates (1)	Drake (19)	'Foxy' (14)	Lewis (12, 21)	O'Hara (13, 15)	Shott (15)
Brady (9)	Elsie (23)	Grant (3)	Locke (16)	Osseo (24)	Slane (13)

Smith (4, 20)
Sneyd (3)
Titus (23)
Troop (9)
Tulke (14)
Uriel (23)
Ward (3)
White (14)
Yates (3)
Yeo (19)
Zouch (19)

6

Alfgar (17)
Ansell (14)
Arnoul (17)
Beetle (14)
Bennet (6)
Blayne (13)
Blazes (13)
Briggs (18)
Burton (21)
Carson (14)
Cheyne (9)
Clewer (14)
Conrad (21)
Coulan (13)
Dabney (14)
Elliot (5)
Elsley (18)
Folsom (10)
Gadsby (13, 15)
Gallio (13)
Godiva (17)
Godwin (17)
Harper (10)
Harvey (18)
Howard (8)
Hunter (8)
Hurree (15)
Jasoda (13)
Kinzey (9)
Lilian (16)
Maffin (13)
Mahbub (15)
Mannel (9)
Martin (1, 2, 9, 14)
Martyn (10)
McPhee (10)
Mellot (18)
Morton (7)
Mowgli (15)
Mutrie (12)
Norris (3)
O'Brien (8)
Palmer (7)
Raynes (10)

Sefton (14)
Stalky (14)
Steele (7)
Swayne (14)
Tarvin (12)
Thorpe (4)
Tilney (4)
Verney (17)
Vernon (2)
Watson (8)
Weston (1)
Willis (18)
Wilton (10)
Winter (19)

7

Baldwin (17)
Berkley (25)
Bertram (3)
Bingley (6)
Brandon (7)
Campian (19)
Collins (6)
Corkran (14)
Curtiss (13)
De Sussa (13)
Dr. Grant (3)
Edwards (8)
Fairfax (1)
Ferrars (7)
Fleming (25)
Gilbert (28)
Gillett (14)
Hartopp (14)
Headley (18)
Heckler (12)
Holdock (10)
Huneefa (15)
Hypatia (21)
Johnson (2)
Learoyd (11, 13)
Leblanc (22)
Leofric (17)
Lilinau (22)
Lucifer (23)
Mackage (21)
Mackesy (13)
Manders (14)
Mildred (15)
Morland (4)
Mullins (13)
Nokomis (24)
Osborne (8)
Oxenham (19)
Oweenee (24)
Parsons (19)
Pelagia (21)

Perowne (14)
Pycroft (15)
Raleigh (19)
Rattray (14)
Salters (9)
Sheriff (12)
Simmons (13)
Vaughan (26)
Vaurien (20)
Wardrop (10)
Wenonah (24)

8

Aben-Ezra (21)
Basselin (28)
Bingleys (The) (6)
Campbell (14, 18)
Crawford (3)
Dan Troop (9)
Dashwood (7)
De Bourgh (6)
De Courcy (2)
Dick Four (14)
Dumachus (23)
Fastrada (23)
Felician (22)
Filomena (28)
Gardiner (6)
Gottlieb (23)
Grenvile (19)
Harrison (14)
Hereward (17)
Hiawatha (24)
Hyperion (25)
Jan Chinn (10)
Jennings (7)
Jervoise (13)
Kavanagh (26)
Lady Bath (19)
Limmason (11)
Long Jack (9)
Lvnedale (16)
M'Cartney (10)
McRimmon (10)
Miss Carr (8)
Mrs. Allen (4)
Mrs. Blake (8)
Mrs. Estes (12)
Mrs. Hurst (6)
Mrs. Leigh (19)
Mrs. Price (3)
Mrs. Sneyd (3)
Mulvaney (13)
Musgrave (8)
Newbroom (20)
Ortheris (13)
Passmore (19)

Preciosa (28)
Salterne (19)
Schaefer (9)
Standish (27)
Stettson (14)
Threegan (13)
Thurnall (18)
Tom Platt (9)
Torfrida (17)
Treboaze (18)
Tregarva (20)
Vavasour (18)
Waltheof (1)
Will Cary (19)

9

Andromeda (21)
Armsworth (18)
Ashburton (25)
Azacanora (19)
Carmathan (12)
Churchill (1, 26)
Collinson (14)
Creighton (15)
Dave Lewis (12)
Deercourt (13)
Elizabeth (21)
Finlayson (15)
Hitchcock (10)
John Alden (27)
John Chinn (10, 15)
Knightley (l)
Lavinton (20)
Lightfoot (17)
MacDonald (9)
Mahbab Ali (15)
Maria Ward (3)
McAndrews (15)
Middleton (7)
Minnehaha (24)
Miss Bates (1)
Miss Sneyd (3)
Mrs. Cheyne (9)
Mrs. Harvey (18)
Mrs. McPhee (10)
Mrs. Mutrie (12)
Mrs. Norris (3)
Mrs. Palmer (7)
Mrs. Purvis (8)
Mrs. Vernon (2)
Mrs. Watson (8)
Mrs. Weston (1)
Nick Brady (9)
Priscilla (27)
Rushworth (3)
Sam Watson (8)
Stangrave (18)

161

The Mugger (15)
Tim Coulan (13)
Victorian (28)
Vieuxbois (20)
Wentworth (5)
Woodhouse (1)

10

Alton Locke (16)
Arnyas Leigh (19)
Anne Elliot (5)
Dinah Shadd (13)
Dirkovitch (11)
Disko Troop (9)
Dr. Thurnall (18)
Earl Godwin (17)
Emma Watson (8)
Evangeline (22)
Fanny Price (3)
Findlayson (10)
Godwinsson (17)
Jane Bennet (6)
John Briggs (18)
John Thorpe (4)
King Ranald (17)
Lady Godiva (17)
Lady Vernon (2)
Lajeunesse (22)
Lucy Steele (7)
Mainwaring (2)
Miss Kinzey (9)
Miss Martin (10)
Miss M'Kenna (13)
Miss Morton (7)
Mrs. De Sussa (13)
Mrs. Edwards (8)
Mrs. Holdock (10)
Mrs. Johnson (2)
Mrs. Mullins (13)
Prometheus (28)
Strickland (11)
Teshoo Lama (15)
Tom Bertram (3)
Villamarti (15)
Willoughby (7)

11

Alfred Chinn (10)
Barraclough (11)
Bracebridge (2)
Count of Lara (28)

Count Robert (17)
Dundas Fawne (10)
Earl Leofric (17)
Fanny Norris (3)
Frances Ward (3)
Harry Verney (20)
Henry Tilney (4)
Hinchcliffe (15)
James Burton (21)
Jane Fairfax (l)
Jerry Blazes (13)
John Gillett (14)
John Learoyd (11)
John Oxenham (19)
Kate Sheriff (12)
Lady Bertram (3)
Lady Osborne (8)
Lionel Chinn (10)
Lord Osborne (8)
Lucy Ferrars (7)
Lurgan Sahib (15)
Lydia Bennet (6)
Mary Edwards (8)
Megissogwon (24)
Mudjekeewis (24)
Mrs. Dashwood (7)
Mrs. Gardiner (6)
Mrs. Jennings (7)
Paul Fleming (25)
René Leblanc (22)
Rev. Mr. Howard (8)
Rev. Mr. Norris (3)
Shawondasee (24)
Susan Vernon (2)
Thomas Leigh (19)
Tom Musgrave (8)
Tom Thurnall (18)

12

Abbot Leofric (17)
Admiral Croft (5)
Brimblecombe (19)
Brugglesmith (10)
Captain Leigh (19)
Colonel Nolan (12)
Dick Grenvile (19)
Earl of Mercia (17)
Earl of Wessex (17)
Eustace Leigh (19)
Frank Headey (18)
Harriet Smith (4)
Harvey Cheyne (9)
Jack Thurnall (18)

Jasper Purvis (8)
John Dashwood (7)
Julia Bertram (3)
Lady de Bourgh (6)
Lady de Courcy (2)
Lady Grenvile (19)
Lord Lynedale (16)
Lucy Passmore (19)
Maria Bertram (3)
Mary Crawford (3)
Miss Bingleys (The) (6)
Miss Newbroom (20)
Miss Standish (27)
Mrs. Rushworth (3)
Paul Tregarva (20)
Pau-Puk-Keewis (24)
Robert Martin (1)
Robert Watson (8)
Rose Salterne (19)
Salvation Yeo (19)
Samuel Burton (21)
Sandy Mackage (16)
Uncle Salters (9)
William Price (3)

13

Admiral Winter (19)
Ali Baba Mahbub (15)
Alicia Johnson (2)
Bellefontaine (22)
Captain Gadsby (13, 15)
Captain Hunter (8)
Captain Maffin (13)
Captain O'Brien (8)
Captain Willis (18)
Colonel Dabney (14)
Corporal Slane (13)
Edmund Bertram (3)
Edward Ferrars (7)
Eleanor Tilney (4)
Emma Deercourt (13)
Emma Woodhouse (1)
Fanny Dashwood (7)
Father Campian (19)
Father Parsons (19)
Henry Crawford (3)
Henry Dashwood (7)
Humphrey Chinn (10)
John Middleton (7)
Julia Crawford (3)
Lady Middleton (7)
Lancelot Smith (20)
Little Mildred (15)

Lord Vieuxbois (20)
Major Campbell (18)
Mark Armsworth (18)
Mary Armsworth (18)
Mary Ashburton (25)
Miles Standish (27)
Raymond Martin (14)
Robert Ferrars (7)
Simon Salterne (19)
Thomas Bertram (3)
William Martin (10)

14

Captain Raleigh (19)
Cecilia Vaughan (26)
Colonel Brandon (7)
Earl Godwinsson (17)
Edward Thurnall (18)
Elinor Dashwood (7)
Emanuel Pycroft (15)
Father Felicien (22)
Frank Churchill (l)
Isabella Thorpe (4)
Miss Mainwaring (2)
Nicholas Tarvin (12)
Oliver Basselin (28)
Penelope Watson (8)
Rev. John Gillett (14)
Robert of Sicily (28)
Sir James Martin (2)
Thomas Thurnall (18)
Walter of Varila (21)

15

Amos Barraclough (11)
Catherine Vernon (2)
Elizabeth Bennet (6)
Elizabeth Watson (8)
Hereward the Wake (17)
Humphrey Gilbert (28)
Lady Susan Vernon (2)
Martin Lightfoot (17)
Private Mulvaney (13)
Private Ortheris (13)
Raphael Aben-Ezra (21)
Richard Grenvile (19)
Sergeant Mullins (13)
Sir Francis Drake (19)
Squire Lavington (20)
Valentia Headley (18)

Some characters from **Meredith, Milton** and **Thomas Moore**
List of works from which the following characters are taken, with reference numbers.

George Meredith

Ref. No.	Title	
1. Beauchamp's Career	(16 letters)	
2. Egoist, The	(9 „)	
3. Evan Harrington	(14 „)	
4. Harry Richmond	(13 „)	
5. Rhoda Fleming	(12 „)	
6. Richard Feverel	(14 „)	
7. One of our Conquerors	(18 „)	
8. Sandra Belloni	(13 „)	
9. Vittoria	(8 „)	
10. (Various)		

John Milton

Ref. No.	Title	
11. Comus	(5 letters)	
12. Paradise Lost	(12 „)	
13. Paradise Regained	(16 „)	
14. (Various)		

Thomas Moore

15. Lalla Rookh	(10 „)

Note: The numbers in brackets indicate *the works* in which the characters appear.

3 – 5

Alvan (10)
Azim (15)
Beppo (9)
Berry (6)
Camph (10)
Chloe (10)
Chump (8)
Comus (11)
Corte (9)
Dagon (12)
Dale (2)
Diana (10)
Drew (l)
Forey (6)
Forth (3)
Goren (3)
Hafed (15)
Hinda (15)
Kilne (3)
Kirby (10)
Moody (5)
Mount (6)
Ople (10)
Pole (8)
Powys (9)
Rizzo (9)
Selim (15)
Uriel (12)

6

Abdiel (12)
Aliris (15)
Arioch (12)

Austin (1)
Azazel (12)
Azazil (12)
Barmby (7)
Barnes (3)
Belial (12)
Benson (6)
Blaize (6)
Boulby (5)
Burman (7)
Busshe (2)
Callet (7)
Corney (2)
Dacier (10)
Dalila (14)
Daphne (13)
Denham (1)
Durham (2)
Eccles (5)
Eglett (10)
Farina (10)
Gammon (5)
Graves (7)
Harley (6)
Kionis (4)
Laxley (3)
Lespel (1)
Lovell (5)
Lowton (3)
Manoah (14)
Nereus (11)
Noorka (10)
Oggler (1)
Oxford (2)
Pompey (13)
Radnor (7)
Raikes (3)

Romara (9)
Samfit (5)
Scipio (13)
Sedley (9)
Semele (13)
Strike (3)
Summer (8)
Syrinx (13)
Tethys (11)
Tinman (10)
Turbot (1)
Uploft (3)
Waring (5)
Zelica (15)

7

Ammiani (9)
Amymone (13)
Antiopa (13)
Asmadai (12)
Bagarag (10)
Barrett (8)
Beamish (10)
Belloni (8)
Beltham (4)
Billing (5)
Calisto (13)
Clymene (13)
Cougham (1)
Culling (l)
De Craye (2)
Durance (7)
Farrell (10)
Feverel (6)
Fleming (5)

Gambier (8, 9)
Gosstre (8)
Grossby (3)
Hackbut (5)
Halkett (1)
Harapha (14)
Jocelyn (3)
Killick (1)
Latters (5)
Lycidas (14)
Lydiard (l)
Mohanna (15)
Namouna (15)
Ottilia (4)
Parsley (3)
Pelleas 13)
Pempton (7)
Peridon (7)
Perkins (3)
Piavens (9)
Pierson (9)
Raphael (12)
Romfrey (1)
Sabrina (11)
Saracco (9)
Sedgett (5)
Shagpat (10)
Skepsey (7)
Sowerby (7)
Thyrsis (14)
Tuckham (1)
Warwick (10)
Weyburn (10)
Wicklow (5)
Zophiel (12)

8

Al Hassan (15)
Bakewell (6)
Blancove (5)
Blandish (6)
Braintop (8)
Crossjay (2)
De Saldar (3)
Dr. Corney (2)
Dunstane (10)
Fenellan (7)
Feramorz (15)
Ithuriel (12)
Lancelot (13)
Miss Dale (2)
Mortimer (6)
Mrs. Berry (6)
Mrs. Chump (8)
Mrs. Forey (6)
Mrs. Mount (6)
Patterne (2)
Pericles (8, 10)
Redworth (10)
Richmond (4)
Shrapnel (1)
Thompson (6)
Ugo Corte (9)
Vittoria (9)
Whitford (2)
Woodseer (10)

9

Adela Pole (8)
Armstrong (5)

Balderini (9)
Baskelett (1)
Beauchamp (1)
Beelzebub (12)
Blathenoy (7)
Cogglesby (3)
de Pyrmont (9)
Fadladeen (15)
Fleetwood (10)
Ilchester (4)
Jenkinson (2)
Lady Camph (10)
Maccabeus (13)
Middleton (2)
Mrs. Boulby (5)
Mrs. Burman (7)
Mrs. Harley (6)
Mrs. Lovell (5)
Mrs. Samfit (5)
Mrs. Sedley (9)
Nourmahal (15)
Pellemore (13)
Todhunter (6)
Tom Blaize (6)
Wentworth (6)

10

Adramelech (12)
Barrington (3)
Barto Rizzo (9)
Danisburgh (10)
de Croisnel (1)
Desborough (6)
Dr. Shrapnel (l)
Harrington (3)
Lady Busshe (2)
Lady Eglett (10)
Lalla Rookh (15)
Lord Laxley (3)
Lord Ormont (10)
Mark Tinman (10)
Miss Denham (1)
Mrs. Culling (1)
Mrs. Fleming (6)
Mrs. Lydiard (1)
Mrs. Wicklow (5)
Von Rüdiger (10)

11

Beau Beamish (10)
Blackington (7)
Dr. Middleton (2)
General Ople (10)
Jenny Denham (1)
Lady Feverel (6)
Lady Gosstre (8)
Lady Jocelyn (3)
Lady Romfrey (1)
Lenkenstein (9)
Lord Romfrey (1)
Major Waring (5)
Mountfalcon (6)
Mountstuart (2)
Mrs. Mortimer (6)
Percy Dacier (10)
Percy Waring (5)
Quidascarpi (9)
Ralph Morton (6)
Rose Jocelyn (3)
Roy Richmond (4)
Tom Bakewell (6)
Tripehallow (1)
Weisspriess (9)
Wilfrid Pole (8)

12

Adrian Harley (6)
Arabella Pole (8)
Carlo Ammiani (9)
Colonel Corte (9)
Cornelia Pole (8)
Count Ammiani (9)
Countess Lena (9)
Diana Warwick (10)
Duchess Susan (10)
Emma Dunstane (10)
Farmer Blaize (6)
George Lowton (3)
George Uploft (3)
Harry Jocelyn (3)
Harry Latters (5)
Lady Blandish (6)
Lady Patterne (2)
Laetitia Dale (2)
Laura Piavens (9)
Luigi Saracco (9)

Madame Callet (7)
Master Gammon (5)
Merthyr Powys (9)
Mrs. Beauchamp (1)
Mrs. Blathenoy (7)
Mrs. Cogglesby (3)
Mrs. Jenkinson (2)
Mrs. Wentworth (6)
Nataly Radnor (7)
Robert Eccles (5)
Runningbrook (8)
Squire Uploft (3)
Tom Cogglesby (3)
Victor Radnor (7)
William Moody (5)

13

Aminta Farrell (10)
Austin Feverel (6)
Captain Oxford (2)
Colney Durance (7)
Dahlia Fleming (5)
Daniel Skepsey (7)
Drummond Forth (3)
Dudley Sowerby (7)
Emilia Belloni (8)
Farmer Fleming (5)
Gower Woodseer (10)
Grancey Lespel (1)
Harapha of Gath (14)
Harry Richmond (4)
Horace De Craye (2)
John Todhunter (6)
Justice Harley (6)
Lawyer Perkins (3)
Luciano Romara (9)
'Mel' Harrington (3)
Mrs. Doria Forey (6)
Mrs. Harrington (3)
Sandra Belloni (8)
Shibli Bagarag (10)
Squire Beltham (4)
Timothy Turbot (1)

14

Anthony Hackbut (5)
Butcher Billing (5)

Captain Gambier (8, 9)
Caroline Strike (3)
Cecilia Halkett (l)
Clara Middleton (2)
Colonel De Craye (2)
Colonel Halkett (1)
Doctor Shrapnel (1)
Edward Blancove (5)
Evan Harrington (3)
Everard Romfrey (1)
Hippias Feverel (6)
Janet Ilchester (4)
Jonathan Eccles (5)
Lord Danisburgh (10)
Lucy Desborough (6)
Major de Pyrmont (9)
Margaret Lovell (5)
Matthew Weyburn (10)
Mrs. Mountstuart (2)
Nevil Beauchamp (1)
Richard Feverel (6)
Ripton Thompson (6)
Septimus Barmby (7)
Simeon Fenellan (7)
Thomas Redworth (10)
Vernon Whitford (2)
William Fleming (5)

15

Algernon Feverel (6)
Anna Lenkenstein (9)
Antonio Pericles (10)
Austin Wentworth (6)
Captain Fenellan (7)
Charlotte Eglett (10)
Countess Ammiani (9)
Dartrey Fenellan (7)
Earl of Fleetwood (10)
Lady Blackington (7)
Lena Lenkenstein (9)
Lord Mountfalcon (6)
Noorna fin Noorka (10)
Princess Ottilia (4)
Priscilla Graves (7)
Renée de Croisnel (1)
Robert Armstrong (5)
Rosamund Culling (1)
Samson Agonistes (14)
Sir George Lowton (3)

Some characters from **Sir Walter Scott**
List of works from which the following characters are taken, with reference numbers.

Ref. No.	Title		Ref. No.	Title	
1.	Abbot, The	(8 letters)	20.	Lay of the Last Minstrel, The	(23 letters)
2.	Anne of Geierstein	(16 „)	21.	Legend of Montrose, The	(19 „)
3.	Antiquary, The	(12 „)	22.	Marmion	(7 „)
4.	Aunt Margaret's Mirror	(19 „)	23.	Monastery, The	(12 „)
5.	Betrothed, The	(12 „)	24.	Old Mortality	(12 „)
6.	Black Dwarf, The	(13 „)	25.	Peveril of the Peak	(16 „)
7.	Bridal of Triermain, The	(20 „)	26.	Pirate, The	(9 „)
8.	Bride of Lammermoor, The	(20 „)	27.	Quentin Durward	(14 „)
9.	Castle Dangerous	(15 „)	28.	Redgauntlet	(11 „)
10.	Count Robert of Paris	(18 „)	29.	Rob Roy	(6 letters)
11.	Fair Maid Of Perth, The	(18 letters)	30.	Rokeby	(6 „)
12.	Fortunes of Nigel, The	(18 „)	31.	St. Ronan's Well	(12 „)
13.	Guy Mannering	(12 „)	32.	Surgeon's Daughter, The	(19 „)
14.	Heart of Midlothian, The	(20 „)	33.	Talisman, The	(11 „)
15.	Highland Widow, The	(16 „)	34.	Tapestried Chamber, The	(20 „)
16.	Ivanhoe	(7 „)	35.	Two Drovers, The	(13 „)
17.	Kenilworth	(10 „)	36.	Waverley	(8 „)
18.	Lady of the Lake, The	(16 „)	37.	Woodstock	(9 „)
19.	Laird's Jock, The	(13 letters)			

Note: The numbers in brackets indicate *the works* in which the characters appear.

3 AND 4

Adie (23)
Anna (Princess) (10)
Anne (Princess) (27)
Bean (36)
Beg (11)
Dods (31)
Eva (11)
Faa (13)
Gow (11)
Gray (8, 32)
Lee (37)
Lyle (21)
René (King) (2)
Tuck (16)
Weir (28)

5

Abney (37)
Allan (13)
Allen (24)
André (27)
Aston (37)
Aymer (16)
Bevis (horse) (22)
Binks (31)
Blair (11)
Block (2)

Blood (25)
Boeuf (16)
Brand (18)
Brown (29)
Caxon (3)
Clegg (25)
Croye (Countess) (27)
Deans (14)
Edgar (8)
Edith (Lady) (16)
Eppie (31)
Evans (25)
Ewart (28)
Glass (14)
Hadgi (33)
Hakim (33)
Hamet (16)
Harry (11)
Howie (36)
Irene (33)
Isaac (16)
Jabos (13)
Luira (dog) (18)
Mengs (2)
Nixon (28)
Norna (26)
North (Lord) (25)
Olave (26)
Penny (13)
Ralph (25)
Smith (17)

Timms (35)
Tinto (8, 31)
Troil (26)
Urgan (18)
Vanda (5)
Wamba (16)
Wilsa (12)

6

Airlie (Earl of) (21)
Alasco (17)
Alison (17)
Amelot (5)
Amoury (33)
Andrew (13)
Anselm (11)
Arnold (16)
Ashton (8)
Avenel (Lady of) (23)
Aylmer (37)
Badger (17)
Bailie (13)
Baliol (15)
Bayard (horse) (18)
Benjie (28)
Bennet (23)
Bertha (10)
Bibbet (37)
Blount (17)

Blower (31)
Bowyer (17)
Brakel (25)
Browne (34)
Bulmer (31)
Butler (14)
Caspar (2)
Cedric (16)
Copley (17)
Damien (16)
de Lacy (5)
de Vaux (7)
Elliot (6)
Empson (25)
Faggot (28)
Foster (17)
Foxley (28)
Geddes (28)
Glover (11)
Graeme (1)
Gyneth (7)
Halcro (26)
Hamako (33)
Happer (23)
Hastie (28)
Hector (21)
Hudson (25)
Inglis (24)
Jarvie (29)
Jin Vin (12)
Jobson (29)

Judith (12)
Lesley (27)
Louise (11)
Lumley (24)
MacIan (11)
Martha (10)
Martin (28)
Mattie (29)
Mervyn (13)
Mornay (27)
Morris (29)
Morton (Earl of) (1, 23, 24)
Norman (8)
Quitam (29)
Ramsay (12)
Red-Cap (12)
Robert (Count) (10)
Rob Roy (29)
Rowena (16)
Seyton (1)
Sharpe (24)
Stubbs (14)
Tacket (23)
Talbot (36)
Tormot (11)
Tyrrel (31)
Ulrica (10, 16)
Ursula (9)
Varney (17)
Vernon (29)
Vipont (16)
Warden (23)
Watley (25)
Wilson (14)
Winnie (8)

7

Abdalla (16)
Ackland (37)
Aikwood (3)
Aldrick (25)
Ambrose (1, 16, 28)
Anthony (9, 31)
Arnheim (2)
Baldwin (Count) (10, 16)
Balfour (24)
Barston (25)
Beaujeu (12, 36)
Berkely (Lady) (9)
Bertram (13)
Berwine (5)
Bidmore (Lord) (31)
Bletson (37)
Bridget (1)
Brydone (23)
Calista (33)

Cargill (31)
Corsand (13)
Crosbie (28)
de Boeuf (16)
de Bracy (16)
Dinmont (13)
Dorothy (11)
Douglas (18)
Dubourg (29)
Durward (27)
El Hadgi (33)
El Hakim (33)
Elspeth (3, 13)
Eustace (16, 23)
Feltham (12)
Fenella (25)
Fleming (1, 9, 14)
Francis (11, 27)
Glossin (13)
Godfrey (23)
Gosling (17)
Gourlay (8)
Grahame (24)
Guthrie (27)
Hartley (32)
Hayston (8)
Herries (Lord) (1)
Hesketh (35)
Hillary (32)
Hinchup (14)
Ivanhoe (16)
Joliffe (37)
Kennedy (13)
Kenneth (Sir) (33)
Langley (6)
Latimer (28)
Leopold (33)
MacEagh (21)
MacIvor (36)
MacTurk (31)
Malachi (28)
Margery (5)
Marmion (22)
Matilda (30)
Maxwell (12, 24, 28)
Meg Dods (31)
Mertoun (26)
Mowbray (31)
Neville (3)
Nosebag (36)
Oldbuck (3)
Pacolet (26)
Peebles (28)
Peveril (25)
Ramorny (11)
Rattray (12)
Rebecca (16)
Redmond (30)
Robsart (17)

Ruthven (Lord) (1)
Saladin (33)
Sampson (13)
Scholey (26)
Sellock (25)
Shafton (23, 29)
Staples (17)
Stephen (16)
Taffril (3)
Tancred (10)
Tomkins (37)
Torquil (11)
Tresham (29)
Trotter (31)
Vanwelt (5)
Vincent (12)
Wakeman (25)
Waldeck (3)
Wayland (17)
Wenlock (5)
Wilfrid (29)

8

Alberick (5, 33)
Alice Lee (37)
Anderson (31)
Argentin (2)
Baldrick (5)
Berenger (5)
Bohemond (Prince) (10)
Boniface (1, 23)
Bullseg (36)
Burleigh (Lord) (21)
Campbell (14,15, 21, 28)
Cantrips (28)
Carleton (25)
Christie (12, 23)
Clifford (33, 37)
Colkitto (21)
Conachar (11)
Dalgarno (Lord) (12)
Dalgetty (21)
Damiotti (4)
Debbitch (25)
de Multon (33)
Dennison (24)
de Wilton (22)
Engelred (16)
Evandale (Lord) (24)
Fairford (28)
Falconer (4, 36)
Fitzurse (Lord) (16)
Flammock (5)
Forester (4)
Geraldin (Lord) (3)
Guenevra (33)
Headrigg (24)

Henry Gow (11)
Henry Lee (37)
Hereward (10)
Hermione (12)
Ingelram (23)
Jamieson (32)
Jellicot (37)
King René (2)
Lapraick (28)
l'Hermite (2, 27)
Locksley (16)
Macaulay (21)
Macready (29)
Margaret (Ladye) (20)
Melville (1)
Menteith (Earl of) (21)
Meredith (28)
Misbegot (3)
Mrs. Allan (13)
Mrs. Glass (14)
Musgrave (20)
Nicholas (23)
Olifaunt (12)
O'Todshaw (13)
Pauletti (Lady) (12)
Pleydell (13)
Porteous (14)
Protocol (13)
Quodling (25)
Rentowel (36)
Ringwood (12)
Scriever (36)
Spitfire (37)
Staunton (14)
Steenson (28)
Swanston (28)
Texartis (10)
Trapbois (12)
Turnbull (28)
Waltheof (11)
Waverley (36)
Wetheral (16)
Wildfire (14)
Wildrake (37)
Woodcock (1)
Wycliffe (30)

9

Agelastes (10)
Arbert Lee (37)
Aldovrand (5)
Alice Bean (36)
Alice Gray (8)
Annot Lyle (21)
Armstrong (6, 12, 19)
Bellenden (24)
Bickerton (14)

Biederman (2)
Bimbister (26)
Bindloose (31)
Blackless (33)
Brengwain (5)
Cadwallon (5)
Chiffinch (25)
Christian (25)
Cleveland (Duchess of) (25, 26)
Clippurse (36)
Constance (22)
Cranstoun (20)
Cresswell (25)
de la Marck (27)
de Moncada (32)
de Valence (9)
Dick Tinto (8, 31)
Elshender (6)
Friar Tuck (16)
Galbraith (29)
Gellatley (36)
Guendolen (7)
Howleglas (1)
Inglewood (29)
Jack Jabos (13)
Jock Penny (13)
John Mengs (2)
Johnstone (13)
Josceline (33)
Lady Binks (31)
Ladv Edith (16)
Lochinvar (22)
Lord North (25)
MacAlpine (29)
MacGregor (29)
MacIntyre (3)
MacTavish (15)
Major Weir (28)
Malvoisin (16)
Mannering (13)
Maugrabin (27)
Mayflower (37)
Merrilies (13)
Middlemas (32)
Mortcloke (13)
Mrs. Aylmer (37)
Mrs. Baliol (15)
Mrs. Blower (31)
Mumblazen (17)
Ochiltree (3)
Poundtext (24)
Ratcliffe (6)
Rewcastle (6)
Risingham (30)
Sturmthal (2)
Thoulouse (10)
Touchwood (31)
Turnpenny (28)

Twigtythe (36)
Wackbairn (14)
Wakefield (35)
Woodville (34)
Yellowley (26)
Zimmerman (2)

10

Alice Brand (18)
Amy Robsart (16)
Anne Bulmer (23)
Athelstane (16)
Aunt Judith (12)
Beaumanoir (16)
Bingo Binks (Sir) (31)
Blind Harry (11)
Blinkinsop (28)
Bridgeward (1, 23)
Colonel Lee (37)
Cranbourne (25)
Croftangry (11)
Dame Martin (28)
Davie Deans (14)
Desborough (37)
Donald Bean (36)
Dr. Damiotti (4)
Dryfesdale (1)
Earnscliff (6)
Effie Deans (14)
Enguerraud (33)
Flockheart (36)
Gabriel Faa (13)
Geierstein (2)
Gideon Gray (32)
Glee-Maiden (The) (11)
Grinderson (3)
Hammerlein (27)
Hatteraick (13)
Holdenough (37)
Howlaglass (25)
Hugo de Lacy (5)
Humgudgeon (37)
Huntingdon (Earl of) (33)
Ian Vanwelt (6)
Jacob Aston (37)
Jacob Caxon (3)
Jamie Howie (36)
Jenny Caxon (3)
Jerningham (25)
Lucy Ashton (8)
Meiklewham (31)
Mrs. Crosbie (28)
Mrs. Nosebag (36)
Murdochson (14)
Nanty Ewart (28)
Ned Shafton (29)
Old Dorothy (11)

Old Elspeth (3)
Penfeather (31)
Phillipson (2)
Quackleben (31)
Ravenswood (8)
Rough Ralph (25)
Saddletree (14)
Scambister (26)
Sir Kenneth (33)
Stanchells (29)
Sweepclean (3)
Theodorick (33)
Tibb Tacket (23)
Tom Hillary (32)
Toschach Beg (11)
Tressilian (17)
Whitecraft (25)
Will Badger (17)

11

Abel Sampson (13)
Adam Hartley (32)
Annie Winnie (8)
Auld Elspeth (13)
Balderstone (8)
Bet Jamieson (32)
Blandeville (36)
Bradwardine (36)
Brenda Troil (26)
Bridgenorth (25)
Chamberlain (25)
Claud Halcro (26)
Claverhouse (8)
Count Robert (10)
Craigdallie (11)
Craigengelt (8)
Dame Hinchup (14)
Dame Margery (5)
David Ramsay (12)
de Crevecour (27)
Diana Vernon (29)
Donnerhugel (2)
Dumbiedikes (14)
Fairbrother (14)
Fairservice (29)
Father Blair (11)
Frank Tyrrel (31)
Giles Bailie (13)
Glendinning (1)
Goldiebirds (3)
Graneangowl (21)
Henry Morton (24)
Henry Warden (23)
Isaac of York (16)
James Sharp (13)
Jeanie Deans (14)
John Balfour (24)

John Grahame (24)
John Guthrie (27)
John Mowbray (31)
John Ramorny (11)
Lady Berkely (9)
Lady Fleming (1)
Lord Bidmore (31)
Lord Herries (1)
Lord Ruthven (l)
Lucy Bertram (13)
MacMurrough (36)
Magnus Troil (26)
Martin Block (2)
Mary Fleming (1)
Montreville (32)
Mrs. Cantrips (28)
Mucklewrath (24)
Mysie Happer (23)
Nicol Jarvie (29)
Pate Maxwell (28)
Plantagenet (33)
Princess Ann (27)
Ralph Morton (24)
Redgauntlet (28)
Robln Hastie (28)
Roderick Dhu (18)
Rougedragon (28)
Silas Morton (24)
Simon Glover (11)
Sir Henry Lee (37)
Smotherwell (11)
Tam O'Todshaw (13)
Thomas Blood (25)
Tomahourich (35)
Walkingshaw (28)
Wild Wenlock (5)

12

Adam Woodcock (1)
Adrian Brakel (25)
Ailie Dinmont (13)
Andrew Wilson (14)
Arthur Mervyn (13)
Balmawhapple (36)
Baron Arnheim (2)
Basil Mertoun (26)
Bittlebrains (Lord) (8)
Black Feltham (12)
Blattergrowl (3)
Buonaventura (28)
Captain Brown (13)
Cholmondeley (25)
Cisly Sellock (25)
Clara Mowbray (31)
Clement Blair (11)
Colonel Blood (25)
Count Baldwin (10)

167

Damian de Lacy (5)
Dougal Cratur (The) (29)
Dr. Gideon Gray (32)
Dr. Quackleben (31)
Eachin MacIan (11)
Earl of Airlie (21)
Earl of Morton (23)
Earl of Oxford (2)
Ellen Douglas (18)
Flora MacIvor (36)
Frank Hayston (8)
Frank Kennedy (13)
Giles Gosling (17)
Glendinnings (The) (23)
Gowkthrapple (36)
Guy Mannering (13)
Hector MacIan (11)
Henry Bertram (13)
Hobbie Elliot (6)
Jock Scriever (36)
John Christie (12)
John Porteous (14)
Joseph Jobson (29)
Joshua Geddes (28)
Knockwinnock (3)
Lady Forester (39)
Lady Pauletti (12)
Lady of Avenel (23)
Little Benjie (28)
Lord Burleigh (21)
Lord Dalgarno (12)
Lord Evandale (24)
Lord Fitzurse (16)
Lord Geraldin (3)
Major Neville (3)
Malagrowther (12)
Martin Tacket (23)
Mary Campbell (14)
Master Bibbet (37)
Master Bowyer (17)
Meg Merrilies (13)
Mother Red-Cap (12)
Mrs. Bickerton (14)
Mucklebackit (3)
Nelly Trotter (31)
Old Alice Gray (8)
Old Mortality (24)
Osbaldistone (29)
Pate Macready (29)
Peter Peebles (28)
Princess Anna (10)
Ralph Hesketh (35)
Ralph Latimer (28)
Randal de Lacy (5)
Reuben Butler (14)
Roland de Vaux (7)
Roland Graeme (1)
Rose Flammock (5)
Sir Josceline (33)

Sister Ursula (9)
Squire Foxley (28)
Thomas Copley (17)
Tom Turnpenny (28)
Vanbust Brown (13)
Wayland Smith (17)
Wild Spitfire (37)
William Evans (25)
Witherington (32)

13

Abbot Boniface (23)
Abbot Ingleram (23)
Adam Zimmerman (2)
Ailsie Gourlay (8)
Allan Fairford (28)
Allan Macaulay (21)
Angus Macaulay (21)
Anthony Foster (17)
Baillie Jarvie (29)
Brother Bennet (23)
Caltain Lumley (24)
Christal Nixon (28)
Colonel Ashton (8)
Colonel Morton (24)
Colonel Talbot (36)
Cornet Grahame (24)
Corporal Timms (36)
Dandie Dinmont (13)
Darsie Latimer (28)
de Grantmesnil (16)
Dousterswivel (3)
Edie Ochiltree (3)
Eppie Anderson (31)
Father Ambrose (1)
Father Eustace (23)
Fergus MacIvor (36)
Fleecebumpkin (35)
General Browne (34)
George Wakeman (25)
Goody Jellicot (37)
Hector MacTurk (31)
Holdfast Clegg (25)
Jenkin Vincent (12)
Jenny Dennison (24)
John Armstrong (19)
John Bindloose (31)
John of Moidart (21)
John Rewcastle (6)
Jonathan Brown (29)
Joseph Tomkins (37)
Joshua Bletson (37)
Josiah Cargill (31)
Julian Peveril (25)
Kate Chiffinch (25)
Kettledrummle (24)
Lady Bellenden (24)

Ladye Margaret (20)
Lord Woodville (34)
Ludovic Lesley (27)
MacAnaleister (29)
Madge Wildfire (14)
Major Falconer (4)
Martin Waldeck (3)
Matthew Foxley (28)
Meg Murdochson (14)
Mother Bridget (1)
Nelly Christle (12)
Nigel Olifaunt (12)
O'Neale Redmond (30)
Peter Protocol (13)
Ralph de Wilton (22)
Ranald MacEagh (21)
Richard Walley (25)
Ringan Aikwood (3)
Robert of Paris (Count) (10)
Roger Wildrake (37)
Sir Bingo Binks (31)
Sir Hugo de Lacy (5)
Sir Jacob Aston (37)
Stephen Butler (14)
Thomas Ackland (36)
William Ashton (8)

14

Adonbec el Hakim (33)
Augusta Bidmore (31)
Baldwin de Oyley (16)
Blondel de Nesle (33)
Brother Ambrose (16)
Captain Hillary (32)
Captain MacTurk (31)
Clement Dubourg (29)
Colonel Grahame (24)
Corporal Inglis (24)
Cuddie Headrigg (24)
Dame Whitecraft (25)
Davie Gellatley (36)
de Bois Guilbert (16)
Dirk Hatteraick (13)
Dominie Sampson (13)
Duncan Campbell (21)
Earl of Menteith (21)
Earl of Seaforth (21)
Edith Bellenden (24)
Edward Waverley (36)
Elspeth Brydone (23)
Eric Scambister (26)
Father Boniface (1)
Father Waltheof (11)
Geoffrey Hudson (25)
George Staunton (14)
Gilbert Glossin (13)

Grace Armstrong (6)
Harry Wakefield (35)
Heatherblutter (36)
Helen MacGregor (29)
Henry Cranstoun (20)
Jabesh Rentowel (36)
Jemima Forester (4)
Jessie Cantrips (28)
John Phillipson (2)
John Whitecraft (25)
Julia Mannering (13)
Lady Penfeather (31)
Maggie Steenson (28)
Major Bellenden (24)
Major Galbraith (29)
Malcolm Fleming (9)
Margaret Blower (31)
Margaret Ramsay (12)
Maria MacIntyre (3)
Martha Trapbois (12)
Nicholas Blount (17)
Nicholas Faggot (28)
Paulus Pleydell (13)
Peter Proudtext (24)
Phili Forester (4)
Piercie Shafton (23)
Prince Bohemond (10)
Quentin Durward (27)
Richard Grahame (24)
Robert Melville (1)
Runnion Rattray (12)
Sir Gibbs Amoury (33)
Sir John Ramorny (11)
Thomas de Multon (33)
Thomas Turnbull (28)
Wilkin Flammack (5)
William Crosbie (28)
William Maxwell (24)
Willie Steenson (28)
Zamet Maugrabin (27)
Zarah Christian (25)
Zilia de Moncada (32)

15

Abdallah el Hadgi (33)
Adam Craigdallie (11)
Adie of Aikenshaw (23)
Albert Malvoisin (16)
Archie Armstrong (12)
Arnold Biederman (2)
Augustus Bidmore (31)
Balfour of Burley (24)
Brother Nicholas (23)
Captain Campbell (15)
Captain Carleton (25)
Captain Porteous (14)
Captain Waverley (36)

Catherine Glover (11)
Catherine Seyton (1)
Claus Hammerlein (27)
Countess of Croye (27)
Count Geierstein (2)
Deborah Debbitch (25)
Duncan Galbraith (29)
Edgar Ravenswood (8)
Edward Christian (25)
Ephraim Macbriar (24)
Erminia Pauletti (12)
Eveline Berenger (5)
Father Howleglas (1)
Flibbertigibbet (17)
General Campbell (28)
Geraldin Neville (3)
Hamish MacGregor (29)
Hamish MacTavish (15)
Hector MacIntyre (3)
Hector of the Mist (21)
Hubert Ratcliffe (6)

Jeanie MacAlpine (29)
Joceline Joliffe (37)
Jonathan Oldbuck (3)
Lady Mary Fleming (1)
Lady Plantagenet (14)
Lady Rougedragon (28)
Lawrence Scholey (26)
Lawrence Staples (17)
Lawyer Clippurse (36)
Madame Cresswell (25)
Madge Murdochson (14)
Magdalene Graeme (1)
Malcolm Misbegot (3)
Miss Walkingshaw (28)
Monsieur Dubourg (29)
Mordaunt Mertoun (26)
Murdoch Campbell (21)
Peter Bridgeward (1, 23)
Philip Malvoisin (16)
Phoebe Mayflower (37)
Raymond Berenger (5)

Richard Musgrave (20)
Richard Waverley (36)
Robert MacGregor (29)
Rob-Roy MacGregor (29)
Rose Bradwardine (36)
Simon of Hackburn (6)
Sir Damian de Lacy (5)
Sir Randal de Lacy (5)
Sir Thomas Copley (17)
Squire Inglewood (29)
Stephen Wetheral (16)
The Dougal Cratur (29)
Thomas Chiffinch (25)
Torquil of the Oak (11)
Tristan l'Hermite (2, 27)
Valentine Bulmer (31)
Wandering Willie (28)
Widow Flockheart (36)
Wilfrid Wycliffe (30)
Willie Johnson (13)

Characters from Shakespeare
List of plays from which the following characters are taken, with reference numbers.

Ref. No.	Title		Ref. No.	Title	
1.	All's Well that Ends Well	(20 letters)	20.	Love's Labour's Lost	(16 letters)
2.	Antony and Cleopatra	(18 „)	21.	Macbeth	(7 „)
3.	As You Like It	(11 „)	22.	Measure for Measure	(17 „)
4.	Comedy of Errors, A	(15 „)	23.	Merchant of Venice, The	(19 „)
5.	Coriolanus	(10 „)	24.	Merry Wives of Windsor	(19 „)
6.	Cymbeline	(9 „)	25.	Midsummer Night's Dream, A	(21 „)
7.	Hamlet (Prince of Denmark)	(6 „)	26.	Much Ado About Nothing	(19 „)
8.	Julius Caesar	(12 „)	27.	Othello, The Moor of Venice	(7 „)
9.	King Henry IV, Part 1	(7 or 11 „)	28.	Pericles, Prince of Tyre	(8 „)
10.	King Henry IV, Part 2	(7 or 11 „)	29.	Romeo and Juliet	(14 „)
11.	King Henry V	(6 or 10 „)	30.	Taming of the Shrew, The	(19 „)
12.	King Henry VI, Part 1	(7 or 11 „)	31.	Tempest, The	(10 „)
13.	King Henry VI, Part 2	(7 or 11 „)	32.	Timon of Athens	(13 „)
14.	King Henry VI, Part 3	(7 or 11 „)	33.	Titus Andronicus	(15 „)
15.	King Henry VIII	(9 or 13 „)	34.	Troilus and Cressida	(18 „)
16.	King John	(8 „)	35.	Twelfth Night; or, What You Will	(12 „)
17.	King Lear	(8 „)	36.	Two Gentlemen of Verona	(20 „)
18.	King Richard II	(9 or 13 „)	37.	Winter's Tale, The	(14 „)
19.	King Richard III	(10 or 14 „)			

Note: The numbers in brackets indicate *the plays* in which the characters appear.

(A.-B. of) = Archbishop of.   (B. of) = Bishop of.   (Card.) = Cardinal.   (C. of) = Count of.
(C'ess of) = Countess of.   (D. of) = Duke of.   (D'ess of) = Duchess of.   (E. of) = Earl of.
(K. of) = King of.   (M. of) = Marquis of.   (P. of) = Prince of.   (P'ess of) = Princess of.
(Q. of) = Queen of.

3 *AND* 4

Adam (3)
Ajax (34)

Anne (Lady) (19)
Bona (14)
Cade (13)
Cato (8)

Davy (10)
Dick (13)
Dion (37)
Dull (20)

Eros (2)
Fang (10)
Ford (24)
Ford (Mrs.) (24)

Grey (11)
Grey (Lady) (14)
Grey (Lord) (19)
Hero (26)

Hume (13)
Iago (27)
Iden (13)
Iris (31)
Jamy (11)
John (10)
John (Don) (26)
John (K.) (16)
Juno (31)
Kent (E. of) (17)
Lear (K.) (17)
Lion (25)
Luce (4)
Lucy (12)
Moth (20, 25)
Nym (11, 24)
Page (24)
Page (Mrs.) (24)
Peto (9, 10)
Puck (25)
Ross (Lord) (18)
Ross (21)
Say (Lord) (13)
Snug (25)
Time (37)
Vaux (13, 15)
Wart (10)
York (A.-B. of)
   (9, 10, 19)
York (D'ess of)
   (18, 19)
York (D. of)
   (11, 18, 19)

5

Aaron (33)
Abram (29)
Alice (11)
Angus (21)
Ariel (31)
Bagot (18)
Bates (11)
Belch (35)
Bigot (16)
Biron (20)
Blunt (9, 10)
Boult (28)
Boyet (20)
Bushy (18)
Butts (15)
Caius (6, 24)
Casca (8)
Celia (3)
Ceres (31)
Cinna (8)
Cleon (28)
Clown (22, 35)

Corin (3)
Court (11)
Curan (17)
Curio (35)
Denny (15)
Diana (1, 28)
Edgar (17)
Egeus (25)
Elbow (22)
Essex (E. of) (16)
Evans (24)
Flute (25)
Froth (22)
Ghost (7)
Gobbo (23)
Gower (10, 11, 28)
Green (18)
Helen (6, 34)
Henry (19)
Henry (K.) (9, 10, 11,
   12, 13, 15)
Henry (P.) (16)
Julia (36)
Lafeu (1)
Louis (Dauphin)
   (11, 16)
Louis (K.) (14)
Louis (Lord) (19)
Lucio (22)
March (E. of) (9)
Maria (20)
Melun (16)
Menas (2)
Milan (D. of) (36)
Mopsa (37)
Osric (7)
Paris (29, 34)
Pedro (Don) (26)
Percy (9, 10, 18)
Percy (Lady) (9)
Peter (13, 22)
Phebe (3)
Philo (2)
Pinch (4)
Poins (9, 10)
Priam (34)
Queen (6)
Regan (17)
Robin (24)
Romeo (29)
Rugby (24)
Sands (Lord) (15)
Snare (10)
Snout (25)
Speed (36)
Timon (32)
Tubal (23)
Varro (8)
Viola (35)

Wales (P. of)
   (9, 10, 19)

6

Adrian (31)
Aegeon (4)
Aeneas (34)
Albany (D. of) (17)
Alexas (2)
Alonso (31)
Amiens (3)
Angelo (4, 22)
Antony (2)
Armado (20)
Arthur (16)
Audrey (3)
Banquo (21)
Basset (12)
Bianca (27, 30)
Blanch (16)
Blount (19)
Bottom (25)
Brutus (5, 8)
Bullen (15)
Cadwal (6)
Caesar (2)
Caphis (32)
Cassio (27)
Chiron (33)
Cicero (8)
Clitus (8)
Cloten (22)
Cobweb (25)
Curtis (30)
Dennis (3)
Dorcas (37)
Dorset (M. of) (19)
Dromio (4)
Dumain (20)
Duncan (K.) (21)
Edmund (14, 17)
Edward (13)
Edward (K.) (19)
Edward (P. of Wales)
   (14, 19)
Elinor (16)
Emilia (27, 37)
Exeter (D. of)
   (11, 14)
Fabian (35)
Feeble (10)
Fenton (24)
France (K. of)
   (1, 17)
France (P'ess of)
   (20)
Gallus (2)

George (13, 14, 19)
Grumio (30)
Gurney (16)
Hamlet (7)
Hecate (21)
Hector (34)
Helena (1, 25)
Henry V (K.) (11)
Hermia (25)
Horner (13)
Imogen (6)
Isabel (11)
Jaques (3)
Juliet (22, 29)
Launce (36)
Le Beau (3)
Lennox (21)
Lovell (15)
Lucius (8, 32, 33)
Marina (28)
Morgan (6)
Morton (10, 19)
Mouldy (10)
Mr. Ford (24)
Mr. Page (24)
Mutius (33)
Nestor (34)
Oberon (25)
Oliver (3)
Olivia (35)
Orsino (35)
Oswald (17)
Oxford (D. of) (14)
Oxford (E. of) (19)
Pedant (30)
Philip (K.) (16)
Pierce (18)
Pistol (10, 11, 24)
Portia (8, 23)
Quince (25)
Rivers (Earl) (19)
Rivers (Lord) (14)
Rogero (37)
Rumour (10)
Scales (Lord) (13)
Scarus (2)
Scroop (9, 10, 18)
Scroop (Lord) (11)
Seyton (21)
Shadow (10)
Silius (2)
Silvia (36)
Simple (24)
Siward (21)
Strato (8)
Surrey (D. of) (18)
Surrey (E. of) (15, 19)
Talbot (12)
Talbot (Lord) (12)

Tamora (33)
Taurus (2)
Thaisa 28)
Thisbe (25)
Thomas(22)
Thurio (36)
Tranio (30)
Tybalt (29)
Tyrrel (19)
Ursula (26)
Venice (D. of) (23, 27)
Verges (26)
Vernon (9, 12)
Wolsey (Lord) (15)

7

Adriana (4)
Aemilia (4)
Agrippa (2)
Alarbus(33)
Alencon (D. of) (12)
Antenor (34)
Antonio (23, 26, 31, 35, 36)
Arragon (P. of) (23)
Aumerle (D. of) (18)
Bedford (D. of) (11, 12)
Berkley (Earl) (18)
Bertram (1)
Bourbon (D. of) (11)
Brandon (15)
Calchas (34)
Caliban (31)
Camillo (37)
Capulet (29)
Capulet (Lady) (29)
Cassius (8)
Catesby (19)
Cerimon (28)
Charles (3)
Charles (Dauphin) (11)
Charles (K.) (11)
Claudio (22, 26)
Conrade (26)
Costard (20)
Cranmer (A.-B.) (15)
Dauphin, The (12, 16)
Dionyza (28)
Don John (26)
Douglas (E. of) (9)
Eleanor (13)
Escalus (22, 29)
Escanes (28)
Flavius (8, 32)
Fleance 21)
Gloster (D'ess of) (18)
Gloster (D. of) (11 ,14, 19)

Gloster (E. of) (12)
Gloster (P. of) (10)
Goneril (17)
Gonzalo (31)
Gregory (29)
Helenus (34)
Henry IV (K.) (9, 10)
Henry VI (K.) (12, 13, 14)
Herbert (19)
Horatio (7)
Hostess (30)
Hotspur (9, 10)
Iachimo (6)
Jessica (23)
Laertes (7)
Lavinia (33)
Leonato (26)
Leonine (28)
Leontes (37)
Lepidus (2)
Lincoln (B. of) (15)
Lord Say (13)
Lorenzo (23)
Lucetta (36)
Luciana (4)
Macbeth (21)
Macbeth (Lady) (21)
Macduff (21)
Macduff (Lady) (21)
Malcolm (21)
Marcius (5)
Mardian (2)
Mariana (1, 22)
Martext (3)
Martius (33)
Mercade (20)
Messala (8)
Michael (13)
Michael (Sir) (9, 10)
Miranda (31)
Montano (27)
Morocco (P. of) (23)
Mowbray (18)
Mowbray (Lord) (10)
Mrs. Ford (24)
Mrs. Page (24)
Nerissa (23)
Norfolk (D. of) (14, 15, 18, 19)
Octavia (2)
Ophelia (7)
Orlando (3)
Orleans (D. of) (11)
Othello (27)
Paulina (37)
Perdita (37)
Phrynia (32)
Pisanio (6)

Proteus (36)
Publius (8, 33)
Pucelle (12)
Pyramus (25)
Quickly (Mrs.) (9, 10, 11, 24)
Quintus (33)
Richard (13, 14, 19)
Richard (K.) (18, 19)
Salanio (23)
Salerio (23)
Sampson (29)
Setebos (31)
Shallow (10, 24)
Shylock (23)
Silence (10)
Silvius (3)
Simpcox (13)
Slender (24)
Solinus (4)
Stanley (13, 14)
Stanley (Lord) (19)
Suffolk (D. of) (13, 15)
Suffolk (E. of) (12)
Theseus (25)
Thryeus (2)
Titania (25)
Travers (10)
Troilus (34)
Ulysses (34)
Urswick (19)
Valeria (5)
Varrius (2, 22)
Vaughan (19)
Velutus (5)
Warwick (E. of) (10, 11, 12, 13, 14)
William (3)

8

Abhorson (22)
Achilles (34)
Aemilius (33)
Aufidius (5)
Auvergne (C'ess of) (12)
Baptista (30)
Bardolph (9, 10, 11, 24)
Bardolph (Lord) (10)
Bassanio (23)
Beatrice (26)
Beaufort (12)
Beaufort (Card.) (13)
Belarius (6)
Benedick (26)
Benvolio (29)
Bernardo (7)
Borachio (26)

Bouchier (Card.) (19)
Bullcalf (10)
Burgundy (D. of) (11, 12, 17)
Campeius (Card.) (15)
Canidius (2)
Capucius (15)
Charmian (2)
Clarence (D. of) (10, 19)
Claudius (8)
Claudius (K.) (7)
Clifford (13)
Clifford (Lord) (13, 14)
Colville (10)
Cominius (5)
Cordelia (17)
Cornwall (D. of) (17)
Cressida (34)
Cromwell (15)
Dercetas (2)
Diomedes (2, 34)
Dogberry (26)
Don Pedro (26)
Edward VI (K.) (19)
Eglamour (36)
Falstaff (9, 10, 24)
Fastolfe (12)
Florence (D. of) (1)
Florizel (37)
Fluellen (11)
Gadshill (9)
Gardiner (15)
Gargrave (13)
Gertrude (Q.) (7)
Gratiano (23, 27)
Griffith (15)
Harcourt (10)
Hastings (Lord) (10, 14, 19)
Herrnione (37)
Hunphrey (10, 13)
Isabella (22)
Jack Cade (13)
Jourdain (13)
King John (16)
King Lear (17)
Lady Anne (19)
Lady Grey (14)
Lawrence (29)
Leonardo (23)
Leonatus (6)
Ligarius (8)
Lodovico (27)
Lord Grey (19)
Lord Ross (18)
Lucentio (30)
Lucilius (8, 32)
Lucullus (32)
Lysander (25)

171

Malvolio (35)
Margaret (12, 13, 19, 26)
Margaret (Q.) (14)
Marullus (8)
Mecaenas (2)
Menelaus (34)
Menteith (21)
Mercutio (29)
Montague (29)
Montague (Lady) (29)
Montague (M. of) (14)
Mortimer (9, 12, 14)
Mortimer (Lady) (9)
Mountjoy (11)
Old Gobo (23)
Overdone (Mrs.) (22)
Pandarus (34)
Pandulph (Card.) (16)
Panthino (36)
Parolles (1)
Patience (15)
Pembroke (E. of) (14, 16)
Pericles (28)
Philario (6)
Philemon (28)
Philotus (32)
Pindarus (8)
Polonius (7)
Polydore (6)
Prospero (31)
Rambures (11)
Ratcliff (19)
Reignier (12)
Reynaldo (7)
Richmond (E. of) (19)
Roderigo (27)
Rosalind (3)
Rosaline (20)
Rotheram (19)
Salarino (23)
Seleucus (2)
Somerset (D. of) (13,14)
Stafford (13)
Stafford (Lord) (14)
Stephano (23, 31)
Thaliard (28)
Timandra (32)
Titinius (8)
Trinculo (31)
Vicentio (22)
Violenta (l)
Virgilia (5)
Volumnia (5)
Whitmore (13)
Williams (11)

9

Agamemnon (34)

Aguecheek (35)
Alexander (34)
Antigonus (37)
Antiochus (28)
Apemantus (32)
Archibald (9, 10)
Arviragus (6)
Autolycus (37)
Balthazar (4, 23, 26, 29)
Bassianus (33)
Biondello (30)
Brabantio (27)
Caithness (21)
Cambridge (E. of) (11)
Cassandra (34)
Chatillon (16)
Cleomenes (37)
Cleopatra (2)
Constance (16)
Cornelius (6, 7)
Cymbeline (6)
Dardanius (8)
Deiphobus (34)
Demetrius (2, 25, 33)
Desdemona (27)
Dolabella (2)
Donalbain (21)
Elizabeth (19)
Enobarbus (2)
Erpingham (11)
Ferdinand (31)
Ferdinand (K.) (20)
Fitz-Peter (16)
Fitzwater (Lord) (18)
Flaminius (32)
Francisca (22)
Francisco (7, 31)
Frederick (3)
Friar John (29)
Glansdale (12)
Glendower (9)
Grandpree (11)
Guiderius (6)
Guildford (15)
Helicanus (28)
Henry VIII (K.) (15)
Hippolyta (25)
Hortensio (30)
Katharina (30)
Katharine (15, 20)
Katharine (P'ess) (11)
Lady Percy (9)
Lancaster (D. of) (18)
Lancaster (P. of) (9, 10)
Longsword (16)
Lord Lovel (19)
Lord Sands (15)
Lychorida (28)
Macmorris (11)

Mamillius (37)
Marcellus (7)
Mareshall (16)
Moonshine (25)
Nathaniel (20)
Patroclus (34)
Petruchio (30)
Polixenes (37)
Richard II (K.) (18)
Rousillon (C. of) (1)
Rousillon (C'ess of) (1)
Salisbury (E.of) (11, 12, 13, 16, 18)
Sebastian (31, 35)
Servilius (32)
Simonides (28)
Southwell (13)
Tearsheet (10)
Thersites (34)
Trebonius (8)
Valentine (35, 36)
Ventidius (2, 32)
Vincentio (30)
Voltimand (7)
Volumnius (8)
Woodville (12)
Worcester (E. of) (9, 10)
Young Cato (8)

10

Alcibiades (32)
Andromache (34)
Andronicus (33)
Anne Bullen (15)
Antipholus (4)
Archidamus (37)
Barnardine (22)
Brakenbury (19)
Buckingham (D. of) (13, 15, 19)
Calphurnia (8)
Canterbury (A.-B. of) (11, 15, 19)
Coriolanus (5)
Duke of York (11, 18, 19)
Earl of Kent (17)
Earl Rivers (19)
Euphronius (2)
Fortinbras (7)
Henry Percy (9, 10, 18)
Holofernes (20)
Hortensius (32)
Jaquenetta (20)
John Talbot (12)
King Henry V (10)
Longaville (20)
Lord Rivers (14)

Lord Scales (13)
Lord Scroop (11)
Lord Talbot (12)
Lysimachus (28)
Marc Antony (2)
Margarelon (34)
Menecrates (2)
Montgomery (14)
Mrs. Quickly (9, 10, 11, 24)
Prince John (10)
Proculeius (2)
Richard II (K.) (19)
Saturninus (33)
Sempronius (32)
Sir Michael (9, 10)
Somerville (14)
Starveling (25)
Touchstone (3)
Willoughby (Lord) (18)
Winchester (B. of) (15)

11

Abergavenny (Lord) (15)
Artimidorus (8)
Bishop of Ely (11, 19)
Bolingbroke (13, 18)
Dame Quickly (9, 10)
Doctor Butts (15)
Doctor Caius (24)
Duke of Milan (36)
Earl Berkley (18)
Earl of Essex (16)
Earl of March (9, 14)
James Gurney (16)
John of Gaunt (18)
King Henry IV (9, 10)
King Henry VI (12, 13, 14)
Lady Capulet (29)
Lady Macbeth (21)
Lady Macduff (21)
Lord Mowbray (10)
Lord Stanley (19)
Mrs. Anne Page (24)
Mrs. Overdone (22)
Mustardseed (25)
Peasblossom (25)
Philostrate (25)
Plantagenet (12, 13, 14)
Prince Henry (16)
Robert Bigot (16)
Rosencrantz (7)
Westminster (A.-B. of) (18)
William Page (24)
Young Siward (21)

12

Decius Brutus (8)
Duke of Albany (17)
Duke of Exeter (11, 14)
Duke of Oxford (14)
Duke of Surrey (18)
Duke of Venice (23, 27)
Earl of Oxford (19)
Earl of Surrey (15, 19)
Falconbridge (16)
Falconbridge (Lady) (16)
Guildenstern (7)
Julius Caesar (8)
Junius Brutus (5)
King of France (1, 17)
Lady Montague (29)
Lady Mortimer (9)
Lord Bardolph (10)
Lord Clifford (13, 14)
Lord Hastings (10, 14, 19)
Lord Stafford (14)
Marcus Brutus (8)
Popilius Lena (8)
Sir Hugh Evans (24)
Sir Nathaniel (20)
Sir Toby Belch (35)
Thomas Horner (13)
Three Witches (21)
Titus Lartius (5)
Westmoreland (E. of) (9, 10, 11, 14)
Young Marcius (5)

13

Alexander Iden (13)
Doll Tearsheet (10)
Duchess of York (18, 19)
Duke of Alencon (12)
Duke of Aumerle (18)
Duke of Bedford (11, 12)
Duke of Bourbon (11)
Duke of Gloster (11, 14, 19)
Duke of Norfolk (14, 15, 18, 19)

Duke of Orleans (11)
Duke of Suffolk (13, 15)
Earl of Douglas (9)
Earl of Gloster (17)
Earl of Suffolk (12)
Earl of Warwick (10, 11, 12, 13, 14)
Friar Lawrence (29)
Hubert. de Burgh (16)
Joan la Pucelle (12)
King Henry VIII (15)
King Richard II (18)
Lord Fitzwater (18)
Owen Glendower (9)
Prince of Wales (10, 19)
Queen Margaret (14)
Sir Thomas Grey (11)
Young Clifford (13)

14

Cardinal Wolsey (15)
Christopher Sly (30)
Duke of Burgundy (11, 12, 17)
Duke of Clarence (10, 19)
Duke of Cornwall (17)
Duke of Florence (1)
Duke of Somerset (13, 14)
Earl of Pembroke (14, 16)
Earl of Richmond (19)
Edmund Mortimer (9, 12)
Hostess Quickly (9, 10)
Justice Shallow (10)
King Richard III (19)
Launcelot Gobbo (23)
Lord Willoughby (18)
Marcus Antonius (8)
Metellus Cimber (8)
Northumberland (E. of) (9, 10, 14, 18)
Northumberland (Lady) (10)
Octavius Caesar (2, 8)
Peter of Pomfret (16)
Pompeius Sextus (2)
Prince Humphrey (10)

Queen Elizabeth (19)
Queen Katharine (15)
Sextus Pompeius (2)
Sir James Blount (19)
Sir James Tyrrel (19)
Sir John Stanley (13)
Sir Walter Blunt (9, 10)
Sir William Lucy (12)
Smith the Weaver (13)
Tullus Aufidius (5)
Walter Whilmore (13)

15

Aemilius Lepidus (8)
Bishop of Lincoln (15)
Dromio of Ephesus (4)
Duke of Lancaster (18)
Earl of Cambridge (11)
Earl of Salisbury (11, 12, 13, 16, 18)
Earl of Worccster (9, 10)
Edmund of Langley (18)
Lord Abergavenny (15)
Margery Jourdain (13)
Marquis of Dorset (19)
Menenius Agrippa (5)
Prince of Arragon (23)
Prince of Morocco (23)
Robin Goodfellow (25)
Sicinius Volutus (5)
Sir Anthony Denny (16)
Sir Hugh Mortimer (14)
Sir John Falstaff (9, 10, 24)
Sir John Fastolfe (12)
Sir John Mortimer (14)
Sir Nicholas Vaux (15)
Sir Thomas Lovell (15)
Titus Andronicus (33)

Some characters from **Shelley, Sheridan** and **Smollett**
List of works from which the following characters are taken, with reference numbers.

Percy Bysshe Shelley

Ref. No.	Title	
1.	Cenci, The	(8 letters)
2.	Prometheus Unbound	(17 „)
3.	Swellfoot the Tyrant	(18 „)
4.	(Various)	

Richard Bringley Sheridan

5.	Critic, The	(9 letters)
6.	Duenna, The	(9 „)
7.	Pizarro	(7 „)
8.	Rivals, The	(9 „)

Ref. No.	Title	
9.	School for Scandal, The	(19 letters)
10.	St. Patrick's Day	(13 „)
11.	Trip to Scarborough, A	(18 „)

Tobias Smollett

12.	Count Fathom	(11 letters)
13.	Humphry Clinker	(14 „)
14.	Peregrine Pickle	(15 „)
15.	Roderick Random	(14 „)
16.	Sir Launcelot Greaves	(19 „)

Note: The numbers in brackets indicate *the works* in which the characters appear.

3 AND 4

Asia (2)
Cora (7)
Crab (15)
Fag (8)
Ione (2)
Ivy (13)
Joey (15)
Lory (11)
Loyd (13)
Lucy (8)
Mab (4)
Puff (5)
Quin (13)
Rosy (10)
Trip (9)

5

Acres (8)
Cenci (1)
Clara (6)
Crowe (16)
Dakry (3)
Daood (4)
David (8)
Flint (10)
Frail (14)
Gawky (15)
Gomez (7)
Gwynn (13)
Jones (13)
Julia (8)
Lewis (13)
Lopez (6)
Maria (9)
Moses (3, 9)
Oakum (15)
Ocean (2)

Orano (7)
Pipes (14)
Probe (11)
Rifle (15)
Rolla (7)
Scrag (14)
Snake (9)
Sneer (5)
Strap (15)

6

Alonzo (7)
Amanda (11)
Andrea (1)
Apollo (2)
Banter (15)
Barton (13)
Bumper (9)
Clumsy (11)
Cythna (4)
Dangle (5)
Darnel (16)
Dr. Rosy (10)
Duenna (The) (6)
Elvira (7)
Emilia (14)
Fathom (12)
Ferret (16)
Gobble (16)
Hassan (4)
Hatton (5)
Hoyden (11)
Ianthe (4)
Jermyn (13)
Julian (4)
Louisa (6)
Mahmud (4)
Mammon (3)
Martin (13)

Marzio (l)
Morgan (15)
Murphy (13)
Norton (13)
Oregan (15)
Orsino (1)
Pallet (14)
Pickle (14)
Random (15)
Rattle (15)
Rowley (9)
Simper (15)
Teazle (9)
Thomas (8)
Townly (11)
Vandal (15)
Weazel 15)
Willis (13)
Zuluga (7)

7

Adonais (4)
Alastor (4)
Almagro (7)
Ataliba (7)
Baynard (13)
Bowling (15)
Bramble (13)
Bulford (13)
Buzzard (13)
Camillo (1)
Candour (9)
Celinda (12)
Clinker (13)
Coupler (11)
Cringer (15)
Davilla (7)
Dick Ivy (13)
Dr. Lewis (13)

Fashion (11)
Freeman (15)
Giacomo (1)
Gonzalo (7)
Greaves (16)
Griskin (13)
Gwyllim (13)
Hopkins (5)
Jackson (15)
Jenkins (13)
Macully (13)
Maddalo (4)
Melford (13)
Mendoza (6)
Mercury (2)
Milfart (13)
Mrs. Loyd (13)
O'Connor (10)
Olimpio (1)
Panthea (2)
Pizarro (7)
Raleigh (5)
Rattlin (15)
Savella (1)
Silenus (4)
Snapper (15)
Solomon (3)
Sparkle (15)
Surface (9)
Taurina (3)
Thicket (15)
Trounce (10)
Ulysses (4)
Wagtail (15)
Whiffle (15)

8

Absolute (8)
Backbite (9)

Bernardo (1)
Besselia (16)
Bob Acres (8)
Burleigh (5)
Campbell (13)
Careless (9)
Crabshaw (16)
Crabtree (9, 14)
Crampley (15)
Cropdale (13)
Dallison (13)
Dennison (13)
Hatchway (14)
Hercules (2)
Languish (8)
Las Casas (7)
Lauretta (10)
La Varole (11)
Lavement (15)
Loveless (11)
Malaprop (8)
Marmozet (15)
Melville (8)
Mendlegs (11)
Molopoyn (15)
Mrs. Gawky (15)
Mrs. Gwynn (13)
Mrs. Jones (13)
Narcissa (15)
O'Donnell (15)
Orozembo (7)
O'Trigger (8)
Phillips (13)
Plagiary (5)
Purganax (3)
Queen Mab (4)
Rosalind (4)
Staytape (15)
St. Irvyne (4)
Straddle (15)
Swillpot (15)

Thompson (15)
Tom Pipes (14)
Trunnion (14)
Valverde (7)
Williams (15)

9

Ahasuerus (4)
Berinthia (11)
Credulous (10)
Don Carlos (6)
Don Jerome (6)
Dr. Wagtail (15)
Faulkland (8)
Ferdinand (6)
Gauntlett (14)
Hugh Strap (15)
Lady Frail (14)
Lismahago (13)
Mackshane (15)
Mary Jones (13)
Mrs. Dangle (5)
Mrs. Jermyn (13)
Mrs. Norton (13)
Mrs. Weazel (15)
Mrs. Willis (13)
Quiverwit (15)
Sneerwell (9)
Strutwell (15)
Swellfoot (3)
The Duenna (6)
Tilburing (5)
Zephaniah (3)

10

Constancia (4)
Count Cenci (1)
Demogorgon (2)

Doctor Rosy (10)
Don Antonio (6)
Donna Clara (6)
Father Paul (6)
Foppinton (11)
Helen Gwynn (13)
John Thomas (13)
Lady Teazle (9)
Lord Rattle (15)
Miss Hoyden (11)
Mitchelson (13)
Mrs. Bramble (13)
Mrs. Candour (9)
Mrs. Gwyllim (13)
Mrs. Jenkins (13)
Mrs. Snapper (15)
Prometheus (2)
Ritornello (5)
Rory Random (15)
Tom Bowling (15)
Tom Fashion (11)

11

Cadwallader (14)
Count Fathom (12)
Donna Louisa (6)
Dr. Mackshane (15)
Harry Bumper (9)
Iona Taurina (3)
Jack Rattlin (15)
Lady Bulford (13)
Lady Griskin (13)
Letty Willis (13)
Miss Snapper (15)
Miss Sparkle (15)
Miss Withers (15)
Mrs. Lavement (15)
Mrs. Malaprop (8)
Peter Teazle (9)
Saint Ervyne (4)

Squire Gawky (15)
Tim Cropdale (13)

12

Captain Crowe (16)
Captain Oakum (15)
Count Maddalo (4)
Don Ferdinand (6)
Ensign Murphy (13)
Gosling Scrag (14)
Isaac Mendoza (6)
Lord Burleigh (5)
Lord Straddle (15)
Lord Swillpot (15)
Lydia Melford (13)
Master Rowley (9)
Miss Williams (15)
Mrs. Credulous (10)
Mrs. Mary Jones (13)
Whiskerandos (5)
Witch of Atlas (4)

13

Aurelia Darnel (16)
Captain Oregan (15)
Captain Weazel (15)
Colonel Townly (11)
Corporal Flint (10)
Earl Strutwell (15)
Father Francis (6)
Joseph Surface (9)
Julia Melville (8)
Justice Gobble (16)
Lady Sneerwell (9)
Launcelot Crab (15)
Lord Quiverwit (15)
Lydia Languish (8)
Mrs. Helen Gwynn (13)

Oliver Surface (9)

14

Captain Whiffle (15)
Charles Surface (9)
Clumsy Tunbelly (11)
Dougal Campbell (13)
Francesco Cenci (l)
Hawser Trunnion (14)
Humphry Clinker (13)
Justice Buzzard (13)
Laetitia Willis (13)
Lord Foppington (11)
Lucius O'Trigger (8)
Matthew Bramble (13)
Roderick Random (15)
Sir Harry Bumper (9)
Sir John Sparkle (15)
Sir Peter Teazle (9)
Squire Dallison (13)
Sunders Macully (13)
Tabitha Bramble (13)
Watkin Phillips (13)

15

Anthony Absolute (8)
Captain Absolute (8)
Cardinal Camillo (1)
Charles Dennison (13)
Earl of Leicester (5)
Emilia Gauntlett (14)
Father Augustine (6)
Ferdinand Fathom (12)
Peregrine Pickle (14)
Serjeant Trounce (10)
Timothy Crabshaw (16)
Tyrant Swellfoot (3)
Winifred Jenkins (13)

Some characters from **Southey, Spenser** and **Tennyson**
List of works from which the following characters are taken, with reference numbers.

Robert Southey

Ref. No.	Title	
1.	Curse of Kehama, The	(16 letters)
2.	Madoc	(5 „)
3.	Roderick, the Last of the Goths	(8 „)
4.	Thalaba the Destroyer	(19 „)
5.	(Various)	

Edmund Spenser

Ref. No.	Title	
6.	Colin Clout's Come Home Again	(24 letters)
7.	Faerie Queene, The	(15 „)
8.	Shephearde's Calender, The	(22 „)
9.	(Various)	

Lord Tennyson

10.	Enoch Arden	(10 letters)
11.	Idylls of the King	(15 „)
12.	(Various)	

Note: The numbers in brackets indicate *the works* in which the characters appear.

3 AND 4

Alma (7)
Ate (7)
Atin (7)
Azla (1)
Azub (3)
Baly (1)
Cid (The) (5)
Dony (7)
Dora (12)
Dove (5)
Ebba (3)
Enid (11)
Flur (11)
Hoel (2)
Ida (12)
Lee (10)
Lot (11)
Lucy (7)
Mary (5)
Maud (12)
Ray (10)
Rose (12)
Una (7)

5

Alice (12)
Amias (7)
Anton (11)
Arden (10)
Aswad (4)
Balan (11)
Balin (11)
Belge (7)
Bleys (11)
Brute (7)
Celia (7)
Clare (12)

Cleon (7)
Clout (6)
Cuddy (8)
David (King) (2)
Dolon (7)
Doorm (11)
Edyrn (11)
Error (7)
Eudon (3)
Furor (7)
Guyon (7)
Indra (1)
Isolt (11)
Isond (11)
Laila (4)
Madoc (2)
Moath (4)
Odoar (3)
Orpas (3)
Pedro (3)
Phaon (7)
Talus (7)
Torre (11)
Tyler (5)
Urban (3)
Urien (2)
Willy (8)
Yamen (1)
Yniol (11)
Ysolt (11)

6

Abessa (7)
Action (6)
Adicia (7)
Alcyon (9)
Amavia (7)
Amidas (7)
Amoret (7)
Astery (9)

Aullay (l)
Aylmer (12)
Briana (7)
Burbon (7)
Cavall (dog) (11)
Coatel (2)
Diggon (8)
Donica (5)
Dubrie (11)
Duessa (7)
Elaine (11)
Elissa (7)
Favila (3)
Gareth (11)
Gawain (11)
Glauce (7)
Godiva (12)
Godmer (7)
Guisla (3)
Guizor (7)
Harold (12)
Igerna (11)
Ignaro (7)
Iseult (11)
Isolde (11)
Jasper (5)
Julian (3)
Kehama (1)
Khawla (4)
Lilian (12)
Llaian (2)
Magued (3)
Mammon (7)
Medina (7)
Merlin (11)
Modred (11)
Moorna (5)
Munera (7)
Newman (5)
Oenone (12)
Oneiza (4)
Orelio (horse) (3)

Oriana (12)
Orraca (Queen) (5)
Paeana (7)
Pelago (3)
Quiara (5)
Romano (3)
Ronald (12)
Senena (2)
Serena (7)
Sergis (7)
Shedad (4)
Terpin (7)
The Cid (5)
Thenot (8)
Theron (dog) (3)
Timias (7)
Turpin (7)
Vivian (12)
Vivien (11)
Witiza (3)
Yeruti (5)
Ygerne (11)
Yseult (11)
Zeinab (4)

7

Acrasia (7)
Adeline (12)
Aemelia (7)
Aladine (7)
Aloadin (4)
Amphion (12)
Aragnol (9)
Argante (7)
Artegal (7)
Arvalan (1)
Aveugle (7)
Cambina (7)
Casyapa (1)
Corydon (7)

Cynetha (2)
Dagonet (11)
Diamond (7)
Egilona (3)
Ereenia (1)
Ettarre (11)
Everard (12)
Favinia (3)
Fidessa (7)
Galahad (11)
Geraint (11)
Gorlois (11)
Ibrahim (3)
Igrayne (11)
Lavaine (11)
Lincoya (2)
Lynette (11)
Lyonors (11)
Maimuna (4)
Maleger (7)
Malinal (2)
Mariana (12)
Marinel (7)
Melibee (7)
Mohareb (4)
Monnema (5)
Mordure (7)
Morrell (8)
Padalon (1)
Penlake (5)
Perissa (7)
Philtra (7)
Pollear (l)
Rudiger (5)
Rusilla (3)
Samient (7)
Sansfoy (7)
Sansjoy (7)
Sansloy (7)
Sir Owen (5)
Thalaba (4)
Ulysses (12)

8

Abdaldar (4)
Adosinda (3)
Alcahman (3)
Alphonso (3)
Amalahta (2)
Annie Lee (10)
Arthegal (7)
Bevidere (11)
Blandina (7)
Bracidas (7)
Busirane (7)
Calepine (7)
Calidore (7)
Claribel (7-12)
Clarinda (7)
Erillyab (21)
Eurytion (7)
Ferraugh (7)
Florimel (7)
Florinda (3)
Fradubio (7)
Gaudiosa (3)
Gauvaine (11)
Geryoneo (7)
Gloriana (7)
Harpalus (6)
Helinore (7)
Hobbinol (8)
Hodeirak (4)
Hudibras (7)
Jane Grey (12)
Ladurlad (1)
Lancelot (11)
Lucifera (7)
Maccabee (3)
Madeline (12)
Malbecco (7)
Margaret (12)
Mercilla (7)
Meridies (11)
Muscarol (9)
Nealling (1)
Numacian (3)
Occasion (7)
Oliphant (7)
Oroglio (7)
Palinode (8)
Phaedria (7)

Placidas (7)
Pollente (7)
Pyrocles (7)
Radigond (7)
Roderick (King) (3)
Rosalind (8)
Sanglier (7)
Satyrane (7)
Sir Anton (11)
Sir Guyon (7)
Sir Torre (11)
Sisibert (3)
Siverian (3)
Spumador (7)
St. Dubrie (11)
Thomalin (8)
Triamond (7)
Trompart (7)
Wat Tyler (5)

9

Abdalazis (3)
Abulcacem (3)
Amaryllis (6)
Anguisant (11)
Archimage (7)
Archimago (7)
Astrophel (8)
Belphoebe (7)
Bladamour (7)
Brigadore (7)
Britomart (7)
Cadwallon (2)
Charyllis (6)
Corfiambo (7)
Cymochles (7)
Dame Celia (7)
Espriella (5)
Eumnestes (7)
Fourdelis (7)
Grantorto (7)
Grenville (12)
Guinevere (11)
Gwenhidwy (11)
Hermesind (3)
King David (2)
Lady Clare (12)
Llewellyn (2)

Lorrimite (l)
Malecasta (7)
Malengrin (7)
Mirabella (7)
Philip Ray (10)
Philotine (7)
Pithyrian (5)
Portamour (7)
Priscilla (7)
Rosalinda (9)
Ruddymane (7)
Scudamore (7)
Sir Sergis (7)
Sir Terpin (7)
Tezozomoe (2)
The Soldan (7)

10

Blandamour (7)
Bruncheval (7)
Colin Clout (6)
Count Eudon (3)
Count Pedro (3)
Cradlemont (11)
Doctor Dove (5)
Enoch Arden (10)
Kirkrapine (7)
Lady Godiva (12)
Lord Ronald (12)
Marriataby (1)
Pastorella (7)
Sanglamore (7)
Sir Dagonet (11)
Sir Galahad (11)
Sir Geraint (11)
Sir Lavaine (11)
Sir Paridel (7)
Sir Pelleas (11)
Theodofred (3)
Vere de Vere (12)
Waterproof (12)

11

Britomaris (7)
Count Julian (3)
Davie Diggon (8)

Lady Lyonors (11)
Queen Orraca (5)
Saint Dubrie (11)
Sir Bedivere (11)
Sir Calepine (7)
Sir Calidore (7)
Sir Claribel (7)
Sir Ferraugh (7)
Sir Hudibras (7)
Sir Lancelot (11)
Sir Persaunt (11)
Sir Satyrane (7)
Sir Trevisan (7)
Sir Tristram (11)
Yuhidthiton (2)

12

Blatant Beast (The) (7)
Braggadochio (7)
Dame Helinore (7)
King Roderick (3)
Lady Gaudiosa (3)
Lady Jane Grey (12)
Oliver Newman (5)
Prince Pelayo (3)
Sir Percivale (11)
Sir Perimones (11)
Sir Pertolope (11)
Sir Scudamore (7)

13 AND OVER

Chindasuintho (3)
Emma Plantagenet (2)
Father Maccabee (3)
Lady of Shalott (12)
Marian Margaret (6)
Red-Cross Knight (7)
Richard Penlake (5)
Saint Gualberto (5)
Sir Aylmer Aylmer (12)
Sir Richard Grenville (12)
Sir Shan Sanglier (7)
Sir Walter Vivian (12)
Squire of Dames, The (7)
Will Waterproof (12)

Some characters from **Thackeray**
List of works from which the following characters are taken, with reference numbers.

Ref. No.	Title		Ref. No.	Title	
1.	Adventures of Philip, The	(21 letters)	10.	Major Gahagan, The	
2.	Barry Lyndon	(11 ,,)		Adventures of	(27 letters)
3.	Book of Snobs, The	(14 ,,)	11.	Newcomes, The	(11 ,,)
4.	Catherine	(9 ,,)	12.	Pendennis	(9 ,,)
5.	Denis Duval	(10 ,,)	13.	Rebecca and Rowena	(16 ,,)
6.	Fatal Boots, The	(13 ,,)	14.	Shabby Genteel Story, A	(19 ,,)
7.	Great Hoggarty Diamond, The	(23 ,,)	15.	Vanity Fair	(10 ,,)
8.	Henry Esmond	(11 ,,)	16.	Virginians, The	(13 ,,)
9.	Lovel the Widower	(15 ,,)	17.	Wolves and the Lamb, The	(19 ,,)

Note: The numbers in brackets indicate *the works* in which the characters appear.

3 AND 4

Bell (12)
Bond (1)
Bows (12)
Bull (3)
'Cat' (4)
Craw (6)
Cuff (15)
Drum (7)
Gann (14)
Gray (3)
Grig (3)
Hall (4)
Holt (8)
Huff (2)
Hunt (1)
Kew (11)
Laws (16)
Legg (3)
Levy (5)
Maw (3)
Moss (15)
Nabb (6)
Page (5, 17)
Pash (7)
Pump (3)
Quin (2)
Ruck (7)
Runt (1, 2)
Sago (3)
Tagg (3)
Tidd (7)
Veal (15)
Ward (16)
Wing (5)
Wirt (3)
Wood (4)

5

Amory (12)
Arbin (5)
Baker (9)
Barry (2)
Bates (6)
Becky (14, 15)
Bevil (5)
Biggs (10)
Bluck (15)
Boots (9)
Bowls (15)
Brady (2)
Brock (4)
Bulbo (15)
'Carry' (14)
Chuff (3)
Clap (15)
Clink (15)
Clump (15)
Crabb (14)
Crump (3)
Daisy (mare) (2)
Denis (5)
Dobbs (4)
Dr. Maw (3)
Duffy (19)
Dumps (3)
Duval (5)
Fagan (2)
Fitch (14)
Flint (5)
Foker (12, 16)
Freny (2)
Gates (7)
Gorer (dog) (15)
Gumbo (16)
Hagan (16)
Hayes (4)
Hicks (3)
Higgs (15)
Hobbs (4)
Hugby (3)
Jowls (2)
Ketch (4)
Kicks (6)
Lovel (9)
Macan (10)
Macer (3)
March (Lord) (16)
Mohun (8)
O'Dowd (3, 15)
Piper (9)
Pippi (2)
Ponto (3)
Prior (9, 17)
Query (7)
Rudge (5)
Sambo (15)
Score (4)
Screw (2)
Sharp (15)
Smith (7)
Straw (7)
Tiggs (3)
Tizzy (3)
Toole (2)
Trial (1, 16)
Tufto (3)
Walls (1)
Wamba (13)
Wolfe (16)

6

Bagwig (Lord) (2, 3)
Barker (5)
Barlow (17)
Bayham (12)
Baynes (1)
Beales (5)
Bidois (5)
Billee (12)
Binnie (11)
Blades (3)
Briggs (15)
Brough (7)
Bungay (12)
Caffin (5)
Cedric (13)
Corbet (8)
Crutty (6)
Curbyn (2)
Dobbin (15)
Dobble (6)
Doolan (12)
Dr. Huff (2)
Dr. Wing (5)
Esmond (8, 16)
Famish (3)
Fermin (1)
Fizgig (7)
Franks (16)
Glowry (12)
Gobble (4)
Gretch (4)
Holkar (10)
Hooker (5)
Howard (5)
Howell (17)
Jowler (10)
Jowler (dog) (6)
Kiljoy (2)
Lyndon (2)
Martha (5)
Measom (5)
Moffat (4)
Morgan (2, 12)
Morris (16)
Murphy (2)
O'Dwyer (2)
Parrot (5)
Perron (10)
Philip (1)
Pincot (9)
Punter (2)
Puppet (7)
Rawson (2)
Redcap (4)
Ridley (1)
Rowena (13)
Rummer (12)
Scales (5)
Sedley (15)
Sheeny (10)
Smirke (12)
Snobky (3)
Spavin (3, 12)
Splint (2)
Steele (8)
Steyne (15)
St. John (Mr.) (8)
Strong (12)
Stubbs (6)
Swigby (14)
Tatham (12)
Temple (3)
Thrupp (10)
Tusher (8)
Waggle (3)
Waters (6)
Wenham (15)
Weston (5)
Wiggle (3)

7

Barnard (5)
Bavieca (horse) (13)
Bedford (9)
Boswell (2)
Brandon (1, 14)
Brisket (6)
Brownie (dog) (1)
Buckram (3)

Bulcher (10)
Bullock (4, 15)
Bunting (6)
Cassidy (1)
Clopper (6)
Cramley (3)
Crawley (15)
Danvers (16)
Dolphin (9)
Dr. Bates (6)
Dr. Dobbs (4)
Dr. Piper (9)
Fantail (4)
Gahagan (10)
Glogger (10)
Gregson (5)
Hawbuck (3)
Hookham (5)
Hoskins (7)
Huckles (9)
Humbold (16)
Ivanhoe (13)
Jawkins (3)
Jim Ward (7)
Johnson (2, 16)
Lambert (16)
Macarty (14)
Mrs. Gann (14)
Mrs. Kirk (15)
Mrs. Laws (16)
Mrs. Pash (7)
Mrs. Sago (3)
Mrs. Todd (15)
Mugford (1)
Mulcahy (7)
Newcome (11)
Osborne (15)
Parkins (12)
Pearson (5)
Pcnfold (1)
Perreau (5)
Pincott (12)
Pinhorn (9)
Portman (12)
Preston (7)
Purcell (2)
Rebecca (13, 15)
Rebecca (mare) (12)
Saladin (14)
Sampson (8, 16)
Sargent (9)
Scraper (3)
Shandon (12)
Sicklop (4)
Slumley (9)
Sniffle (3)
Snobley (3)
Snorter (6)
Sowerby (l)

Spiggot (3)
Stuffe (10)
Swinney (7)
Thunder (2)
Tickler (2)
Tiggins (7)
Tiptoff (7)
Touchit (17)
Trippet (4)
Twysden (1)
Wapshot (12)
Woolsey (1)
Worksop (8)

8

Abednego (7)
Billings (4)
Bill Tidd (7)
Bob Tizzy (3)
Braddock (16)
Bulkeley (9, 17)
Cinqbars (14)
Clarisse (5)
Clodpole (4)
Cockspur (3)
Costigan (12)
Delamere (9)
Dempster (16)
Drencher (9)
Dr. Fermin (1)
Dr. Tusher (8)
Dr. Waters (6)
Dubobwig (6)
Fakenham (2)
Franklin (16)
Goldmore (3)
Golloper (3)
Hawkshaw (8)
Highmore (7)
Hoggarty (7)
Honeyman (9, 11)
Horrocks (15)
Jellicoe (5)
Lady Drum (7)
Lady Sark (8)
Lavender (2)
Lockwood (8, 16)
Lord Lake (10)
Lorrimer (3)
Lovelace (3)
Macheath (5)
MacManus (7)
Macmurdo (15)
Malowney (6)
Manasseh (6)
Marchand (10)
Milliken (17)

Miss Bell (12)
Miss Runt (14)
Miss Wirt (3,15)
Mountain (16)
Mrs. Amory (12)
Mrs. Barry (2)
Mrs. Brady (2)
Mrs. Chuff (3)
Mrs. Crabb (14)
Mrs. Dobbs (4)
Mrs. Duval (5)
Mrs. Foker (16)
Mrs. Hayes (4)
Mrs. Lovel (9)
Mrs. Macan (10)
Mrs. O'Dowd (15)
Mrs. Ponto (3)
Mrs. Prior (9, 17)
Mrs. Rowdy (15)
Mrs. Score (4)
M'Whirter (7)
Napoleon (10)
Plugwell (9)
Ribstone (12)
Ringwood (1)
Sherrick (9)
Smithers (7)
Sullivan (2)
Talmadge (16)
Titmarsh (7)
Tom Walls (1)
Trestles (5)
Tufthunt (14)
Westbury (8)
Woolcomb (1)

9

Altamount (12)
Augustine (14)
Batchelor (9)
Bell Brady (2)
Bellenden (9)
Bernstein (16)
Bloundell (12)
Bob Stokes (7)
Bob Stubbs (6)
Broadbent (16)
Catherine (4)
Charlotte (1)
Clavering (12)
de la Motte (5)
de Saverne (5)
Dinwiddie (16)
Doctor Maw (3)
Dr. Barnard (5)
Dr. Johnson (2, 16)
Dr. Portman (12)

Dr. Snorter (6)
Dr. Squills (15)
Farintosh (11)
Firebrace (16)
Flowerdew (15)
Geoghegan (16)
Goldsmith (2)
Jack Ketch (4)
James Gann (14)
Joe Swigby (14)
John Hayes (4)
'Jos' Sedley (15)
Lady Barker (9)
Lady Fanny (16)
Lady Maria (16)
Laura Bell (12)
Lightfoot (12)
Lilywhite (10)
Lord Mohun (8)
Macdragon (3)
Mackenzie (11)
Marrowfat (3)
Mary Smith (7)
Miss Brett (12)
Miss Prior (17)
Miss Pybus (12)
Miss Rudge (5)
Montholen (10)
Mrs. Barker (5)
Mrs. Baynes (1)
Mrs. Bonner (12)
Mrs. Brough (7)
Mrs. Fermin (1)
Mrs. Firkin (15)
Mrs. Glowry (15)
Mrs. Gretel (4)
Mrs. Haller (12)
Mrs. Jowler (10)
Mrs. Rummer (12)
Mrs. Scales (5)
Mrs. Sedley (15)
Mrs. Stokes (7)
Mrs. Tinker (15)
Mrs. Tusher (8)
Mrs. Weston (5)
Nora Brady (2)
Pendennis (1, 12)
Pinkerton (15)
Pontypool (12)
Rev. Mr. Holt (8)
Rev. Mr. Runt (2)
Rev. Mr. Veal (15)
Robin Hood (13)
Rory Barry (2)
Roundhand (7)
Sheepskin (8)
Swishtail (6, 15)
Tom Caffin (5)
Tom Esmond (8)

Tom Measom (5)
Tom Parrot (5)
Whitfield (16)

10

Agnes Duval (5)
Athelstane (13)
Becky Sharp (15)
Biddy Brady (2)
Bonnington (9, 17)
Bullingdon (2)
Castlewood (8, 16)
Cissy Lovel (9)
Coplestone (8)
Denis Duval (5)
Dick Steel (8)
Doctor Wing (5)
Eliza Kicks (6)
Fitzboodle (9)
Fred Bayham (12)
Goodenough (1)
Gus Hoskins (7)
Harry Barry (2)
Harry Foker (12)
Henry Foker (12)
Jack Morris (16)
James Wolfe (16)
John Brough (7)
John Howell (17)
Kicklebury (17)
Killblazes (7)
King George (16)
Lady Lyndon (2)
Lady Rowena (13)
Lord Bagwig (2)
Lord Steyne (15)
Mackanulty (10)
Maid Marian (13)
Major Macan (10)
Major Macer (3)
Major O'Dowd (15)
Major Ponto (3)
Mary Barlow (17)
Mary Waters (6)
Miss Clancy (2)
Miss Hunkle (12)
Miss Kiljoy (2)
Miss Pierce (12)
Miss Snobky (2)
Miss Swarby (15)
Mrs. Barnard (5)
Mrs. Brandon (1)
Mrs. Bulcher (10)
Mrs. Lambert (16)
Mrs. Macarty (14)
Mrs. Mugford (1)
Mrs. Penfold (1)

Mrs. Twysden (1)
Mrs. Wapshot (12)
Mrs. Woolsey (1)
Mrs. Worksop (8)
Mysie Brad (2)
Nan Fantail (4)
Peter Brock (4)
Peter Denis (5)
Peter Hobbs (4)
Phil Murphy (2)
Pocahontas (16)
Poly Anthus (3)
Pump Temple (3)
Rev. Mr. Crisp (15)
Rev. Mr. Jowls (2)
Sextonbury (3)
Silverkoop (4)
Solomonson (6)
Sukey Rude (5)
'The Captain' (1)
Tom Hookham (5)
Tom Humbold (16)
Tom Sniffle (3)
Tom Wheeler (7)
Tufton Hunt (1)
Ulick Brady (2)
Warrington (12, 16)
Washington (16)
Will Esmond (16)

11

'Andrea' Fitch (14)
Andrew Fitch (14)
Baron de Barr (6)
Barry Lyndon (2)
Biddlecombe (9)
Black George (horse) (2)
Bryan Lyndon (2)
Bute Crawley (15)
Captain Bull (3)
Captain Craw (6)
Captain Grig (3)
Captain Legg (3)
Captain Page (17)
Captain Quin (2)
Captain Wood (4)
Chowder Loll (10)
Claude Duval (5)
Collingwood (15)
Countess Ida (2)
Dick Bedford (9)
Dick Bunting (6)
Doctor Dobb (4)
Doctor Piper (9)
Dr. Swishtail (6, 15)
Earl of March (16)
Edward Bevil (5)

Eliza Stubbs (6)
Emily Blades (3)
Ensign Hicks (10)
Essex Temple (3)
Fotheringay (12)
General Lake (10)
General Sago (3)
Harry Esmond (8)
Henry Esmond (8)
Jack Spiggot (3)
James Binnie (11)
Julia Jowler (10)
Juliana Gann (14)
King Richard (13)
Lady Crawley (15)
Lady Hawbuck (3)
Lady Scraper (3)
Lady Tiptoff (7)
Lord Buckram (3)
Lucy Hawbuck (3)
Major Thrupp (10)
Mary Pinhorn (9)
Miss Clopper (6)
Miss Crawley (15)
Miss Saltire (15)
Miss Sowerby (1)
Miss Swindle (15)
Montanville (9)
Montfitchet (1)
Mrs. Hoggarty (7)
Mrs. Hollyock (15)
Mrs. Jellicoe (5)
Mrs. Manasseh (6)
Mrs. Mountain (16)
Mrs. Titmarsh (7)
Peggy O'Dwyer (2)
Pitt Crawley (15)
Pompey Hicks (3)
Popham Lovel (9)
Prince Bulbo (15)
Raymond Gray (7)
Robert Gates (7)
Roger Hooker (5)
Roger Lyndon (2)
Samuel Arbin (5)
Simon de Bary (2)
Stiffelkind (6)
Susan Stubbs (6)
Theo Lambert (16)
Thistlewood (12)
Thomas Flint (5)
Tom Tufhunt (14)
Van Den Bosch (16)

12

Agnes Twysden (1)
Alderman Pash (7)

Amelia Sedley (15)
Bella Macarty (14)
Betsy Brisket (6)
Blanche Amory (12)
Captain Baker (9)
Captain Biggs (10)
Captain Denis (5)
Captain Duffy (10)
Captain Fagan (2)
Captain Freny (2)
Captain Prior (9)
Caroline Gann (14)
Cecilia Lovel (9)
Chesterfield (16)
Clive Newcome (11)
Colonel Wolfe (16)
Count Gahagan (10)
Donnerwetter (14)
Dr. Goodenough (1)
Dr. von Glauber (15)
Emily Scraper (3)
Ensign Dobble (6)
Ensign Famish (3)
Ethel Newcome (11)
General Tufto (3)
General Wolfe (16)
George Fermin (l)
George Weston (5)
Helena Flower (2)
Hetty Lambert (16)
Honoria Brady (2)
Jack Costigan (12)
Jack Lockwood (8)
John Jorrocks (15)
Joseph la Rose (4)
Joseph Sedley (15)
Joseph Weston (5)
Lady de Mogyns (3)
Lady Golloper (3)
Lady Ribstone (12)
Linda Macarty (14)
Little Billee (12)
Little Sister (The) (1)
Lord Cinqbars (14)
Lord Ringwood (1)
Major Danvers (16)
Major Gahagan (10)
Mary Malowney (6)
Michael Brady (2)
Mick Hoggarty (7)
Miss Delamere (9)
Miss Tingwood (1)
Morgan Doolan (12)
Mrs. Lightfoot (12)
Mrs. Newbright (15)
Mrs. Pendennis (12)
Philip Fermin (1)
Prince Arthur (13)
Prince Victor (2)

Rachel Esmond (16)
Rebecca Sharp (15)
Redmond Barry (2)
Reginald Cuff (15)
Selina Stokes (7)
Thomas Stubbs (6)
Ulysses Brady (2)

13

Barnes Newcome (11)
Beatrix Esmond (8)
Belinda Brough (7)
Bryan Hawkshaw (8)
Captain Dobble (6)
Captain Fizgig (7)
Captain Franks (16)
Captain Punter (2)
Captain Steele (5)
Captain Strong (12)
Captain Waters (6)
Carrickfergus (14)
Catherine Hall (4)
Charles Lyndon (2)
Clarence Baker (9)
Colonel Dobbin (15)
Colonel Esmond (8)
Colonel Jowler (10)
Comte de Florac (11)
Cornet Gahagan (10)
Corporal Brock (4)
Corporal Clink (15)
Countess of Kew (11)
Count of Chalus (13)
Doctor Barnard (5)
Doctor Johnson (16)
Earl of Tiptoff (7)
Emily Costigan (12)
Ensign Macarty (14)
Fanny Mountain (15)
Francis Esmond (8)
General Baynes (1)
George Osborne (15)
Goody Billings (4)
Hester Lambert (16)
Hon. Poly Anthus (3)
Jack Firebrace (16)
Joseph Addison (8)
Kitty Lorrimer (3)
Lady Clavering (12)
Lady Pontypool (12)
Letty Lovelace (3)
Lord Firebrace (8)
Lydia den Bosch (16)
Martha Crawley (15)
Martin Lambert (16)
Matilda Briggs (15)
Miss Bellenden (9)

Miss Bonnyface (2)
Miss Pinkerton (15)
Mrs. Blenkinsop (15)
Mrs. Bonnington (9)
Mrs. Goodenough (1)
Mrs. Silverkoop (4)
Parson Sampson (8, 16)
Philip Purcell (2)
Rawdon Crawley (15)
Robert Swinney (7)
Rosa Mackenzie (11)
Sir Peter Denis (5)
Snobley Snobky (3)
Talbot Twysden (1)
Thomas Bullock (4)
Thomas Gregson (5)
Thomas Trippet (4)
Tobias Tickler (2)
Violet Crawley (15)
William Dobbin (15)

14

Agnes de Saverne (5)
Arabella Briggs (15)
Belinda Bulcher (10)
Betty Flannigan (15)
Blanche Twysden (1)
Captain Clopper (6)
Captain Osborne (15)
Captain Pearson (5)
Captain Shandon (15)
Captain Thunder (2)
Captain Touchit (17)
Catherine Hayes (4)
Colonel Cramley (3)
Colonel Lambert (16)
Colonel Newcome (11)
Colonel Snobley (3)
Cornelius Barry (2)
Corporal Steele (8)
Count de Saverne (5)
Dora Warrington (16)
Earl of Ringwood (l)
Elizabeth Prior (9)
Ensign Macshame (4)
Frederick Lovel (9)
General Bulcher (10)
General Tinkler (10)
George Milliken (17)
Godfrey Gahagan (10)
Gregory Gahagan (10)
Helen Pendennis (12)
Horace Milliken (17)
Lady Castlewood (8, 16)
Lady Fanny Rakes (7)
Lady Huntingdon (13)
Lady Kicklebury (17)

Lady Warrington (16)
Laura Pendennis (12)
Lord Bullingdon (2)
Lord Castlewood (8, 16)
Lord Sextonbury (3)
Magdalen Crutty (6)
Major Pendennis (12)
Michael Cassidy (1)
Mlle Augustine (14)
Mrs. Biddlecombe (9)
Mrs. Blackbrooks (15)
Mrs. Juliana Gann (14)
Mrs. Montfitchet (1)
Princess Olivia (2)
Rev. Bute Crawley (15)
Rev. Mr. Flowerdew (15)
Richard Bedford (9)
Samuel Titmarsh (7)
Sir Pitt Crawley (15)
Sir Popham Baker (9)
Thomas Billings (4)
Thomas Clodpole (4)
von Galgenstein (4)
Wilfred Ivanhoe (13)

15

Arthur Pendennis (1, 12)
Captain Costigan (12)
Captain Macheath (5)
Captain Macmurdo (15)
Captain Westbury (8)
Captain Woolcomb (1)
Charles Honeyman (11)
Charlotte Baynes (1)
Dr. Tobias Tickler (2)
Flora Warrington (16)
General Braddock (16)
George Marrowfat (3)
Harry Warrington (16)
Henry Warrington (16)
Isabella Macarty (14)
Jemima Pinkerton (15)
Lady Jane Crawley (15)
Lady Jane Preston (7)
Marquis of Bagwig (3)
Marquis of Steyne (15)
Misses Pinkerton (The) (15)
Miss Fotheringay (12)
Miss Montanville (9)
Mrs. Cecilia Lovel (9)
Queen Berengaria (13)
Ringwood Twysden (1)
Rosalind Macarty (14)
Sir George Esmond (8)
Sir John Hawkshaw (8)

Some characters from **Anthony Trollope**
List of works from which the following characters are taken, with reference numbers.

Ref. No.	Title		Ref. No.	Title	
1. Alice Dugdale	(12 letters)		10. Lady of Launay, The	(15 letters)	
2. American Senator, The	(18	„)	11. Last Chronicle of Barset, The	(24	„)
3. Barchester Towers	(16	„)	12. La Vendée	(8	„)
4. Dr. Thorne	(8	„)	13. Ralph the Heir	(12	„)
5. Editor's Tales, An	(14	„)	14. Small House at Allington, The	(24	„)
6. Eustace Diamonds, The	(18	„)	15. Tales of all Countries	(19	„)
7. Framley Parsonage	(16	„)	16. Telegraph Girl, The	(16	„)
8. Frau Frohmann	(12	„)	17. Three Clerks, The	(14	„)
9. Is He Popenjoy?	(12	„)	18. Warden, The	(9	„)

Note: The numbers in brackets indicate *the works* in which the characters appear.

3 *AND* 4

Bean (2)
Bell (18)
Bold (3, 7, 18)
Bolt (9)
Boom (17)
Bull (8)
Cann (6)
Cox (13)
Dale (11, 14)
Dove (6)
Dunn (11)
Erle (6)
Fawn (6)
Gazy (18)
Grey (6)
Hall (16)
Hoff (8)
Jack (horse) (2)
Knox (9)
Love (14)
Lund (15)
Nogo (17)
Pie (3, 4)
Pile (13)
Pole (7)
Ring (15)
Toff (9)
Trow (15)
Watt (5)

5

Anton (8)
Baker (4)
Boyce (11, 14)
Brown (6,15,16, 17)
Brush (17)
Bunce (18)
Carey (13)

Crump (11, 14)
Dandy (horse) (6, 7)
Davis (17)
Denot (12)
Dobbs (14)
Donne (5)
Eames (11, 14)
Fooks (13)
Foret (12)
Fritz (15)
Gager (6)
Glump (13)
Green (2, 4, 9,11, 16)
Grice (2)
Handy (18)
Hearn (14)
Heine (15)
Hiram (18)
Janet (4)
Jones (7, 9, 15,17)
Joram (13)
Knowl (10)
Krapp (8)
Lebas (12)
Lupex (14)
Mason (11)
Miles (10)
Moggs (13)
Moody (18)
M'Ruen (17)
Muntz (8)
Nobbs (2)
Oriel (4, 11)
Penge (2)
Plume (12)
Pratt (11, 14)
Price (9)
Pryor (10)
Regan (5)
Ribbs (2)
Robin (7)
Romer (4)

Runce (2)
Sally (16)
Scott (17)
Sharp (5)
Slope (3)
Smlth (5, 9, 15)
Snape (9, 17)
Stein (12)
Stemm (13)
Tozer (7, 11)
Tudor (17)
Tweed (1)
Upton (15)
Vigil (17)
Wheal (17)

6

Apjohn (4)
Arabin (3, 7, 9, 14)
Athill (4)
Aunt Ju (9)
Austen (7)
Battle (9)
Bawwah (13)
Baxter (11)
Bergen (15)
Bonner (13)
Boodle (6)
Botsey (2)
Brumby (5)
Buffle (11, 14)
Bunfit (6)
'Caudle' (14)
Clarke (4)
Cobard (8)
Cobble (1)
Conner (14)
Cooper (2)
Croft (11, 14)
Currie (2)

D'Elbee (12)
Draper (11)
Dr. Bold (18)
Duplay (12)
Fiasco (14)
Finney (18)
Finnie (3, 4)
Fisher (14)
Flurry (11)
Garrow (15)
Giblet (9)
Glemax (2)
Goarly (2)
Gowran (6)
Graham (16)
Greene (15)
Griggs (6)
Grimes (5)
Gwynne (3)
Hallam (5)
Harter (6)
Holmes (15)
Hoppet (2)
Jemima (7)
Jemima (mare) (2)
Jerome (12)
Joseph (15)
Launay (10)
Lupton (7, 11)
Mewmew (3)
Moffat (4)
Molloy (5)
Morgan (6)
Morris (6, 11, 13)
Morton (2, 15)
'Mrs. Val' (17)
Murray (16)
Nappie (6)
Neefit (13)
Neroni (3)
Newton (13)
Nickem (2)

Norman (17)
Nupper (2)
O'Brien (15)
Onslow (15)
Pabsby (13)
Pepper (13)
Precis (17)
Puffle (5)
Sawyer (9)
Scruby (9)
Seppel (8)
Sludge (11)
Smiler (6)
Soames (11)
Spicer (13)
Spruce (14)
Staple (3)
Stiles (3)
Stokes (9)
Temple (11)
Tendel (8)
Tewett (6)
Thorne (3, 4, 7,11)
Towers (3, 7, 18)
Trauss (8)
Ushant (2)
Waddle (13)
Walker (7, 9, 11, 13, 15)
Wallop (13)
Weston (15)
Wilson (6, 16)

7

Adolphe (13)
Bangles (11)
Barrère (12)
Bateson (4)
Baumann (9)
Berrier (12)
Bonteen (6)
Boullin (12)
Buggins (7)
Burnaby (13)
Cashett (9)
Century (4)
Chapeau (12)
Chilton (6)
Cloysey (15)
Cobbold (2)
Coelebs (9)
Collins (5)
Conolin (8)
Couthon (12)
Cradell (11, 14)
Crawley (7, 11)
Crosbie (11, 14)
Crumbie (13)

Crumple (18)
De Baron (9)
Debedin (12)
de Guest (11, 14)
de Salop (17)
Dingles (14)
Dugdale (l)
Eardham (13)
Easyman (7)
Emilius (6)
Eustace (6)
Gazebee (4, 11, 14)
Germain (9)
Glossop (2)
Goesler (6)
Gotobed (2)
Grantly (3, 4, 7, 11, 18)
Gregory (10)
Gresham (4, 6, 7)
Gresley (5)
Gruffen (14)
Gushing (4)
Hampton (2)
Harng (3, 7,11, 14, 18)
Hoffman (2)
Hoggett (11)
Hopkin (2,11, 14)
Jobbles (17)
Johnson (18)
Judkins (15)
Kissing (11, 14)
'Kit' Dale (14)
Masters (2)
M'Buffer (17)
Mealyer (14)
Mildmay (9)
Minusex (17)
Monsell (7)
Mrs. Bold (3)
Mrs. Dale (11, 14)
Mrs. Gamp (mare) (7)
Mrs. Grey (6)
Mrs. Pole (7)
Mrs. Toff (9)
Mutters (18)
Pawkins (14)
Plomacy (3)
Podgens (7)
Poojean (13)
Porlock (4, 14)
Poulter (15)
Protest (9)
Proudie (3, 4, 7, 11)
Pumpkin (17)
Purefoy (2)
Puttock (2)
Roanoke (6)
Robarts (7, 11)
Rufford (2)

Scalpen (3)
Scrobby (2)
Scuttle (11)
Simkins (1)
Skulpit (18)
Snapper (11)
Sowerby (7)
Spooner (13)
Spriggs (18)
Starbod (17)
Surtees (2)
Talboys (15)
Tankard (2)
Tempest (11)
Thumble (11)
Tickler (7)
Toogood (11)
Trefoil (2, 3)
Trigger (13)
Tuppett (2)
Umbleby (4)
Wanless (1)
Wilkins (11)

8

Abel Ring (15)
Allchops (17)
Anticant (18)
Aunt Jane (6)
Bell Dale (14)
Benjamin (6)
Brabazon (9)
Brownlow (13)
Bumpwell (3)
Caneback (2)
Chadwick (3, 7, 11, 18)
Champion (11)
Charette (12)
Chiltern (6)
Coldfoot (6)
De Courcy (4, 11, 14)
de Laroch (12)
Dr. Crofts (11, 14)
Dr. Gwynne (3)
Dr. Nupper (2)
Dr. Thorne (3, 4, 7, 11)
Drummond (2)
Dumbello (7, 11, 14)
Fanfaron (14)
Filgrave (11)
Fleabody (9)
Fletcher (11)
Fleurist (12)
Frohmann (8)
Frummage (14)
Geraghty (17)
Groschut (9)

Gumption (7)
Hittaway (6)
Horsball (13)
Houghton (9)
Isa Heine (15)
John Bold (3, 18)
Jolliffe (14)
Lady Dale (14)
Lady Fawn (6)
Lily Dale (11, 14)
Lovelace (9)
Macallum (6)
Mary Bold (3, 18)
Mary Jane (5)
Meredith (7)
Morrison (10)
Mrs. Boyce (11, 14)
Mrs. Crump (14)
Mrs. Davis (17)
Mrs. Eames (14)
Mrs. Green (16)
Mrs. Hearn (14)
Mrs. Knowl (10)
Mrs. Lupex (14)
Mrs. Miles (10)
Mrs. Pryor (10)
Mrs. Ribbs (2)
Mrs. Roper (14)
Mrs. Scott (17)
Mrs. Smith (7)
Mrs. Tudor (17)
Mrs. Tweed (1)
Mrs. Upton (15)
Mrs. Vigil (17)
Nine Fawn (6)
'Old Nosey' (17)
Palliser (6, 14)
Pat Regan (5)
Phillips (3)
Popenjoy (9)
Pountner (9)
Richards (3, 17)
Robinson (15, 17)
Rossiter (1)
Runciman (2)
Santerre (12)
Siph Dunn (11)
Stanhope (3, 18)
Stringer (11)
Tallowax (9)
Thompson (7, 11)
Tom Tozer (7)
Truepeny (13)
Uncle Bat (17)
Uppinall (17)
Winthrop (11)
Woodward (17)
Youngall (17)

9

Aaron Trow (15)
Abel Handy (18)
Applejohn (7)
Arkwright (15)
Beelzebub (colt) (3)
Billy Cann (6)
Boanerges (7)
Bonchamps (12)
Bourbotte (12)
Broughton (15)
Burmeston (1)
Carbuncle (6)
Carstairs (6)
Chouardin (12)
Coverdale (15)
Crabstick (6)
Culpepper (7)
Cuttwater (17)
Dalrymple (11)
Dan Morris (11)
Danny Lund (15)
de Lescure (12)
Demalines (11)
Diana Fawn (6)
Donnessan (12)
Dr. Century (4)
Dr. Easyman (7)
Dr. Gresley (5)
Dr. Gruffen (14)
Dr. Robarts (7)
Dr. Tempest (11)
Dr. Trefoil (3)
Dr. Whiston (18)
Dunstable (4, 7, 11)
Effingham (6)
Fanny Dale (14)
Fillgrave (4)
Godolphin (2)
Golightly (17)
Greenacre (3)
Grey Moody (18)
Greystock (6)
Haphazard (18)
Hardlines (17)
Hartletop (7, 11, 14)
Herr Weiss (8)
Jean Stein (12)
Joe Hoppet (2)
John Eames (11, 14)
John Hiram (18)
John Runce (2)
John Smith (15)
Karl Muntz (8)
Lady Sarah (9)
Le Smyrger (15)
Lookaloft (3)
Lydia Fawn (6)

Mackenzie (5)
Mackinnon (15)
Manylodes (17)
Mary Eames (14)
Miss Moggs (13)
Mistletoe (2)
Mrs. Arabin (7, 11)
Mrs. Baxter (11)
Mrs. Brumby (5)
Mrs. Connor (14)
Mrs. Croft (11)
Mrs. Draper (11)
Mrs. Finnie (3)
Mrs. Garrow (15)
Mrs. Goarly (2)
Mrs. Greene (15)
Mrs. Grimes (5)
Mrs. Molloy (5)
Mrs. Morris (11)
Mrs. Morton (2)
Mrs. Neefit (13)
Mrs. Pabsby (13)
Mrs. Thorne (4, 7, 11)
Mrs. Walker (11)
Ned Botsey (2)
Neverbend (17)
'Onty' Moggs (13)
Partridge (11)
Polperrow (13)
Prettyman (11)
Quiverful (3, 7, 11, 18)
Reddypalm (4)
Rerechild (3, 4)
Roodiland (13)
Scatcherd (4)
Schlessen (8)
St. Quinten (5)
Stubbings (2)
Suse Krapp (8)
Tom Austen (7)
Tom Staple (3)
Tom Towers (3, 7, 18)
Twentyman (2)
Undershot (17)
Underwood (13)
'Undy' Scott (17)
Van Siever (11)
Westerman (12)
Widow Bold (7)

10

Agnes Heine (15)
Alec Murray (16)
Amelis Fawn (6)
Andy Gowran (6)
Annot Stein (12)
Bessy Pryor (10)

Bideawhile (4)
Brotherton (9)
Butterwell (11, 14)
Camperdown (6)
Captain Val (17)
Carruthers (6)
Cartwright (8)
Clantanham (3)
Dean Arabin (11)
Dr. Anticant (18)
Dr. Bumpwell (3)
Dr. Filgrave (11)
Dr. Fleabody (9)
Dr. Pountner (9)
Fothergill (4, 7, 11)
Frank Miles (10)
Fred Pepper (13)
Goodenough (18)
Gus Eardham (13)
Gus Mildmay (9)
Harry Baker (4)
Harry Jones (9)
Hatto Heine (15)
Henry Baker (4)
Herr Bawwah (13)
Herr Trauss (8)
Holdenough (9)
Ida Talboys (15)
Jack Hallam (5)
Jacky Joram (13)
Jacob Brush (17)
Jem Scuttle (11)
Joe Mutters (18)
Joe Skulpit (18)
John Austen (7)
John Grimes (5)
John Morton (2)
Johnny Bell (18)
Johnny Bold (3, 18)
John Walker (11)
Lady Lufton (7, 11)
Lady Tewett (6)
Lady Ushant (2)
Lilian Dale (14)
Linlithgow (6)
Lord Giblet (9)
Lord Lufton (7, 11)
Lucy Graham (16)
Lucy Morris (6)
MacFarlane (6)
Mackintosh (6)
Mainwaring (2)
Mark Antony (horse) (3)
Mary Bonner (13)
Mary Thorne (4)
Mary Walker (9, 11)
Miss Bergen (15)
Miss Holmes (15)

Miss Launay (10)
Miss Spruce (14)
Miss Thorne (3, 4)
Mrs. Bateson (4)
Mrs. Bonteen (6)
Mrs. Cradell (11)
Mrs. Crawley (11)
Mrs. Dugdale (1)
Mrs. Grantly (3, 4, 7, 11, 18)
Mrs. Gresham (7)
Mrs. Gresley (5)
Mrs. Hopkins (2)
Mrs. Masters (2)
Mrs. Podgers (7)
Mrs. Proudie (3, 4, 7, 11)
Mrs. Robarts (7, 11)
Mrs. Talboys (15)
Mrs. Tickler (7)
Mrs. Umbleby (4)
Musselboro (11)
Nina Cobard (8)
Oldeschole (17)
Omicron Pie (3, 4)
Peter Stein (12)
Rev. Mr. Slope (3)
Scatterall (17)
Sir Jib Boom (17)
Spiveycomb (13)
Thomas Dove (6)
'Turtle' Dove (6)
Twistleton (14)
Uncle Hatto (15)
Walter Watt (5)
Westmacott (13)

11

Abraham Hall (16)
Alaric Tudor (17)
Amelia Roper (14)
Augusta Fawn (6)
Bella Holmes (15)
Bernard Dale (11, 14)
Bertram Dale (11)
Bessy Garrow (15)
Bobby Sludge (11)
Caleb Morton (15)
Captain Dale (11, 14)
Cathelineau (12)
Cecilia Fawn (6)
Clutterbuck (11)
Colonel Dale (14)
Dan Stringer (11)
Dick Hampton (2)
Dr. Fillgrave (4)
Eleanor Bold (3)
Ernest Heine (15)
Farmer Price (9)

Fitzmaurice (6)
Fowler Pratt (11, 14)
Frank Garrow (15)
Gitemthruet (17)
Green Walker (7)
Harold Smith (7)
Harry Garrow (15)
Harry Norman (17)
Henry Norman (17)
Henry Thorne (4)
Jabesh M'Ruen (17)
Jack De Baron (9)
Jane Crawley (11)
Jane Robarts (7)
Jaquêtanape (17)
John Eustace (6)
Johnny Eames (11, 14)
John Poulter (15)
John Roberts (7)
Julia Weston (15)
Kate Masters (2)
Lady Chilton (6)
Lady de Guest (14)
Lady Eardham (13)
Lady Eustace (6)
Lady Germain (9)
Lady Protest (9)
Lady Purefoy (2)
Lady Trefoil (2)
Lady Wanless (1)
Legge Wilson (6)
Lord Chilton (6)
Lord de Guest (14)
Lord Germain (9)
Lord Porlock (4, 14)
Lord Ruffold (2)
Lord Trefoil (2)
Lucy Robarts (7, 11)
Madame Heine (15)
Major Fiasco (14)
Major Garrow (15)
Mark Robarts (7)
Mary Gresley (5)
Mary Masters (2)
Miss Bateson (4)
Miss Collins (5)
Miss De Groat (2)
Miss Gushing (4)
Miss Mealyer (14)
Miss Proudie (3)
Miss Roanoke (6)
Miss Spooner (13)
Miss Trefoil (3)
Miss Wanless (1)
Mountfencer (9)
Mrs. Allchops (17)
Mrs. Brownlow (13)
Mrs. de Courcy (14)
Mrs. Frummage (14)

Mrs. Hittaway (6)
Mrs. Houghton (9)
Mrs. Phillips (3)
Mrs. Richards (3 ,17)
Mrs. Robinson (15)
Mrs. Rossiter (1)
Mrs. Stanhope (3)
Mrs. Woodward (17)
Paulo Neroni (3)
Philip Miles (10)
Polly Neefit (13)
Polly Puffle (5)
'Posy' Grantly (11)
Ralph Newton (13)
Rev. Mr. Arabin (7, 14)
Rev. Mr. Clarke (4)
Rev. Mr. Temple (11)
Robespierre (12)
Sophy Greene (15)
Sophy Wilson (16)
Supplehouse (7)
Tony Tuppett (2)
William Gazy (18)
Winterbones (4)
Woolsworthy (15)

12

Adolphe Denot (12)
Alice Dugdale (1)
Andrew Gowran (6)
Aunt Penelope (15)
Baron Crumbie (13)
Chaffonbrass (17)
Charles Tudor (17)
Dean Lovelace (9)
Doctor Thorne (3, 4, 11)
Dolly Masters (12)
Duke of Omnium (4, 6, 11)
Edith Wanless (1)
Elias Gotobed (2)
Fanny Gresley (5)
Fanny Monsell (7)
Fanny Robarts (7)
Farmer Walker (13)
Father Gerome (12)
Frank Gresham (4, 7)
Frau Frohmann (8)
Frederic Fawn (6)
George Morris (13)
George Scruby (9)
George Walker (11)
Giles Hoggett (11)
Grace Crawley (7, 11)
Henry Grantly (11, 18)
John Chadwick (11)
John De Courcy (14)

John Robinson (15)
John Rossiter (1)
Judge Crumbie (13)
Julia de Guest (11)
Lady Brabazon (9)
Lady De Courcy (3, 4, 11, 14)
Lady Dumbello (14)
Lady Meredith (7)
Lady Palliser (9)
Lord De Courcy (3, 4)
Lord Drummond (2)
Lord Dumbello (7,11, 14)
Lord Gossling (9)
Lord Popenjoy (9)
Major Grantly (11)
Mary Lovelace (9)
Miss Macnulty (6)
Miss Manasseh (17)
Miss Tallowax (9)
Monica Thorne (3, 4, 11)
Mrs. Arkwright (15)
Mrs. Broughton (11)
Mrs. Carbuncle (6)
Mrs. Crinoline (17)
Mrs. Greystock (6)
Mrs. Lookaloft (3)
Mrs. Mackinnon (15)
Mrs. Opie Green (4)
Mrs. Quiverful (3, 7)
Mrs. St. Quinten (5)
Mrs. Van Siever (11)
Nearthewinde (4)
Netta Proudie (3)
Obadiah Slope (3)
Patmore Green (9)
Patrick Regan (5)
Peter Berrier (12)
Philip Launay (10)
Rev. Evan Jones (7)
Rev. Mr. Crawley (7)
Rev. Mr. Gregory (10)
Rev. Mr. Robarts (11)
Rev. Mr. Surtees (2)
Richard Carey (13)
Samuel Nickem (2)
Sir Simon Bolt (9)
'Soapy' Grantly (18)
Sophy Gresham (4)
Squire Newton (13)
Susan Grantly (11)
Susan Harding (18)
Uncle Gregory (13)
Yates Umbleby (4)

13

Amelia Gregory (10)
Anne Prettyman (11)

Apollo Crosbie (14)
Babette Seppel (8)
Bishop Grantly (3, 18)
Bishop Proudie (4, 7, 11)
Blanch Robarts (7)
Captain Boodle (6)
Captain Glomax (2)
Charles O'Brien (15)
Charles Puffle (5)
Clara Hittaway (6)
Dean Greystock (6)
de Montmorenci (5)
Eleanor Duplay (12)
Farmer Cloysey (15)
Father Conolin (8)
General Bonner (13)
Georgiana Fawn (6)
Gerald Robarts (7)
Godfrey Holmes (15)
Gregory Newton (13)
Griffenbottom (13)
Helena Gresham (4)
Henry Lovelace (9)
Herbert Onslow (15)
Herr Schlessen (8)
Hetta Houghton (9)
Janet Rossiter (1)
John Broughton (15)
Jonathan Brown (5)
Joseph Cradell (14)
Josephine Bull (8)
Josiah Crawley (11)
Kate Coverdale (15)
Katie Woodward (17)
Lady Demalines (11)
Lady Fanny Dale (14)
Lady Hartletop (7, 11, 14)
Lady Penwether (2)
Lady Scatcherd (4)
Lady Underwood (13)
Linda Woodward (17)
Lord Boanerges (7)
Lord Hartletop (11)
Lord Mistletoe (2)
Lord Polperrow (13)
Macasser Jones (17)
Madame Goesler (6)
Major Caneback (2)
Major Rossiter (1)
Mary Jane Wheal (17)
Mathew Spriggs (18)
Michael Molloy (5)
Miss Dunstable (4, 7)
Miss Godolphin (2)
Miss Le Smyrger (15)
Miss Partridge (11)
Mrs. Clantanham (3)
Mrs. Goodenough (18)
Mrs. Mainwaring (2)

Norah Geraghty (17)
Olivia Proudie (3)
Patience Oriel (4)
Peter Frohmann (8)
Rev. Caleb Oriel (4)
Samuel Grantly (18)
Sarah Thompson (7)
Selina Gresham (4)
Signora Neroni (3)
Sir Omicron Pie (3, 4)
Sophia Wanless (1)
Vesey Stanhope (18)
Wilfred Thorne (3)

14

Alphabet Precis (17)
Amalia Frohmann (8)
Augusta Protest (3)
Bertie Stanhope (3)
Captain De Baron (9)
Churchill Smith (5)
Clara Van Siever (11)
Clary Underwood (13)
Countess of Care (9)
Dick Scatterall (17)
Eleanor Harding (18)
Emily Dunstable (5)
Erle Barrington (6)
Fanny Arkwright (15)
Fidus Neverbend (17)
Francis Gresham (4)
Frank Greystock (6)
Fraulein Tendel (8)
Fritz Schlessen (8)
General Talboys (15)
Gilbert de Salop (17)

Gregory Masters (2)
Grizzel Grantly (18)
Harry Arkwright (15)
Harry Stubbings (2)
Henry Arkwright (15)
Isabella Holmes (15)
Jacques Chapeau (12)
Lady Brotherton (9)
Lady Linlithgow (6)
Lady Margaretta (14)
Larry Twentyman (2)
Lord Brotherton (9)
Lord Carruthers (6)
Lucinda Roanoke (16)
Lydia St. Quinten (5)
Mary Anne Neefit (13)
Maryanne Ruffle (5)
Matilda Johnson (18)
Mrs. Harold Smith (7)
Parson Rossiter (1)
Parry Coverdale (15)
Parry Underwood (13)
Reginald Morton (2)
Rev. Arthur Donne (5)
Rev. Mark Robarts (7)
Senator Gotobed (2)
Sir John Purefoy (2)
Sir Lamda Mewmew (3)
Valentine Scott (17)
Verax Corkscrew (17)

15

Adelaide De Baron (9)
Adolphus Crosbie (11, 14)
Anastasia Bergen (15)
Arabella Trefoil (2)

Archibald Currie (2)
Augusta De Courcy (4)
Baroness Baumann (9)
Beatrice Gresham (4)
Canon Holdenough (9)
Christopher Dale (14)
Conrad Mackinnon (15)
Conway Dalrymple (11)
Dr. Vesey Stanhope (3, 18)
Elizabeth Garrow (15)
Farmer Greenacre (3)
Florinda Grantly (18)
Griselda Grantly (7, 11)
Hon. John De Courcy (4, 14)
Jacintha Pigtail (17)
Jonathan Crumple (18)
Jonathan Oldbuck (15)
Julius Mackenzie (5)
Lady Mountfencer (9)
Lieutenant Smith (9)
Lizzie Greystock (6)
Lord Mountfencer (9)
Madame de Lescure (12)
Maior Mackintosh (6)
Malchen Frohmann (8)
Martha Dunstable (7)
Mortimer Gazebee (11, 14)
Mrs. Patmore Green (9)
Oliva Q. Fleabody (9)
Onesiphorus Dunn (11)
Orlando Hittaway (6)
Rev. Caleb Thumble (11)
Rev. Mr. Mainwaring (2)
Septimus Harding (11, 18)
Serjeant Burnaby (13)
Sir George Walker (15)
Sir Raffle Buffle (11)
Violet Effingham (6)

Composers

3 – 5				Sor	6
Arne	Brian	Field	Lalo	Sousa	
Auric	Bruch	Finck	Lehar	Spohr	Ansell
Bach	Bush	Friml	Liszt	Suk	Arnold
Balfe	Byrd	Gatty	Lully	Suppé	Barber
Bart	Cage	Gaul	Marks	Tosti	Bartok
Bax	Carse	Gluck	Nono	Verdi	Berlin
Berg	Cowen	Grieg	Orff	Weber	Bishop
Berio	Cui	Haydn	Parry	Weill	Boulez
Bizet	Dufay	Henze	Ravel	Wiren	Brahms
Bliss	Dukas	Holst	Reger	Wolf	Bridge
Bloch	Durby	Ibert	Rosse	Ysaye	Busoni
Boyce	Elgar	Ives	Satie		Chopin
	Falla	Jones	Shaw		Clarke
	Fauré	Kern	Smyth		

Coates
Coward
Czerny
Delius
Demuth
Duparc
Dussek
Dvořák
Enesco
Foster
Foulds
Franck
German
Gillet
Glinka
Gounod
Handel
Hummel
Isolde
Kodály
Lassus
Liadov
Mahler
Morley
Mozart
Norton
Parker
Philip
Piston
Pleyel
Porter
Quantz
Rameau
Ronald
Schütz
Searle
Seiber
Stuart
Tallis
Taylor
Viotti
Wagner
Waller
Walton
Webern
Wesley

7

Albeniz
Arriaga
Bantock
Bazzini
Bellini
Bennett
Berlioz
Blacher
Borodin

Britten
Cleaver
Copland
Corelli
Debussy
Delibes
Dowland
Dunhill
Frankel
Fricker
Galuppi
Gibbons
Godfrey
Hermann
Ireland
Janáček
Joachim
Ketelby
Lambert
Litolff
Lutyens
Martinů
Menotti
Milhaud
Nicolai
Nielsen
Novello
Poulenc
Puccini
Purcell
Quilter
Rodgers
Rossini
Roussel
Smetana
Stainer
Stamitz
Strauss
Tartini
Tavener
Tippett
Torelli
Vivaldi
Warlock
Weelkes

8

Albinoni
Ancliffe
Berkeley
Boughton
Brockman
Bruckner
Chabrier
Cimarosa
Couperin
Dohnanyi

Fletcher
Gabrieli
Gershwin
Glazunov
Grainger
Granados
Holbrook
Honegger
Kreisler
Marcello
Mascagni
Massenet
Messager
Messiaen
Monckton
Paganini
Palmgren
Panufnik
Petrassi
Pizzetti
Raybould
Respighi
Schnabel
Schubert
Schumann
Scriabin
Sibelius
Stanford
Sullivan
Svendsen
Telemann
Tosselli
Victoria
Vittoria
Wagenaar

9 AND 10

Addinsell (9)
Balakirev (9)
Beethoven (9)
Bernstein (9)
Boccherini (10)
Boieldieu (9)
Buxtehude (9)
Cherubini (9)
Cole Porter (10)
Donizetti (9)
Hindemith (9)
Kabalevsky (10)
Locatelli (9)
Macdowell (9)
Manfredini (10)
Meyerbeer (9)
Miaskovsky (10)
Monteverdi (10)
Mussorgsky (10)
Offenbach (9)

Pachelbel (9)
Paisiello (9)
Palestrina (10)
Pergolesi (9)
Ponchielli (10)
Prokofiev (9)
Rawsthorne (10)
Rodriguez (9)
Rubinstein (10)
Saint Saëns (10)
Scarlatti (9)
Schoenberg (10)
Schönberg (9)
Skalkottas (10)
Stravinsky (10)
Vieuxtemps (10)
Villa-Lobos (10)
Waldteufel (10)

11

Dimitriesen
Dittersdorf
Frescolbaldi
Humperdinck
Leoncavallo
Mendelssohn
Moussorgsky
Rachmaninov
Stockhausen
Tailleferre
Tchaikovsky
Wolf-Ferrari

12 AND OVER

Coleridge Taylor (15)
Dallapiccola (12)
Josquin des Prés (14)
Khachaturian (12)
Maxwell Davies (13)
Lennox Berkeley (14)
Rachmaninoff (12)
Racine Fricker (13)
Rimsky Korsakov (14)
Richard Strauss (14)
Shostakovich (12)
Sterndale Bennett (16)
Tschaikovsky (12)
Vaughan Williams (15)

Music, musical instruments and terms

1 – 3

air
alt
bar
bis
bow
cue
do
doh
duo
f
fa
fah
ff
gu
gue
hum
jig
key
kit
la
lah
lay
mi
p
Piu
pop
pp.
rag
ray
re
run
sax
si
soh
sol
tie
ut
va
vox
zel

4

alla
alto
arco
aria
ayre
band
bard
base
bass
beat
bell
brio
clef
coda
drum
duet
echo
fife
fine
flat
fret
glee
gong
harp
high
hold
horn
hymn
jazz
kent
koto
lead
Lied
lilt
lute
lyre
mass
mode
mood
mort
mute
neum
node
note
oboe
opus
part
peal
pean
pipe
poco
port
reed
reel
rest
root
sang
sign
sing
slur
solo
song
stop
tace
time
toll
tone
trio
tuba
tune
turr
vamp
vina
viol
vivo
voce
vola
wind
wood

5

acuta
adapt
album
arsis
assai
atone
banjo
basso
basta
baton
bebop
bells
blare
blues
bones
brass
breve
bugle
canon
canto
carol
cello
cento
chant
cheng
chime
choir
chord
clang
clank
corno
croma
crook
croon
crowd
crwth
dance
dirge
ditty
dolce
drone
duple
elegy
étude
flute
forte
fugal
fugue
galop
gamba
gamut
gigue
grace
grave
knell
kyrie
largo
lento
lyric
major
march
metre
mezzo
minim
minor
molto
mosso
motet
motif
naker
nebel
neume
nodal
nonet
notes
octet
opera
organ
paean
pause
pavan
pedal
piano
pieno
piper
pitch
polka
primo
quill
rebec
reeds
regal
resin
rondo
round
sanko
sansa
scale
scena
score
segno
segue
senza
shake
shalm
sharp
shawn
sitar
sixth
slide
snare
soave
sol-fa
sound
stave
strad
strum
suite
swell
swing
tabor
tacet
tardo
tempo
tenor
theme
third
thrum
tonic
tonus
tosto
triad
trill
trite
trope
tuner
tutti
twang
valse
vibes
viola
vocal
voice
volee
volta

6

volti
waits
waltz
wrest
yodel
zinke

accent
adagio
anthem
arioso
atabal
atonal
attune
aubade
ballad
ballet
beemol
bolero
bridge
bugler
cadent
cantor
catgut
chaunt
chimes
choral
choric
chorus
citole
contra
corona
cornet
crooks
cymbal
da capo
damper
design
diesis
ditone
divoto
drones
duetto
dulcet
eighth
encore
euphon
fading
fiddle
figure
finale
fluter

follia
fugato
gallop
giusto
graces
ground
guitar
hammer
intone
Ionian
jingle
kettle
legato
Lieder
litany
lutist
lydian
lyrist
manual
medley
melody
minuet
monody
motive
nobile
oboist
octave
off-key
pavane
phrase
plagal
player
presto
quaver
rattan
rattle
rebeck
record
revert
rhythm
rounds
rubato
sacbut
sancho
scales
sennet
septet
serial
sestet
sextet
shanty
shofar
singer
sonata
spinet

stanza	bassoon	gavotte	saxhorn	**8**	dulcimer	nocturne
string	bazooka	gittern	scherzo		eleventh	notation
subito	bellows	gravita	schisma	absonant	energico	notturno
tabour	bitonal	gravity	sciolto	absonous	ensemble	obligato
tabret	bravura	G-string	scoring	addition	entr'acte	operatic
tam-tam	cadence	harmony	secondo	alto-clef	euphonic	operetta
tenuto	cadency	harpist	septole	antiphon	euphonon	oratorio
tercet	cadenza	hautboy	serpent	arch-lute	exercise	organist
tierce	calando	juke-box	settina	arpeggio	falsetto	ostinato
timbal	calypso	karaoke	settino	autoharp	fandango	overture
timbre	cantata	keynote	seventh	bagpipes	fantasia	pan-pipes
tirade	canzona	locrian	shophar	baritone	fantasie	part-song
tom-tom	canzone	lullaby	singing	barytone	flautist	pastoral
treble	caprice	maestro	sistrum	bassetto	folk-song	phantasy
trigon	celesta	marimba	sithara	bass-drum	forzando	phrasing
tucket	'cellist	mazurka	skiffle	bass-horn	galement	Phrygian
tune up	cembalo	measure	slurred	bass note	galliard	pianette
tuning	chamade	mediant	soloist	bass oboe	gemshorn	plectrum
tymbal	chanson	melisma	soprano	bass-viol	grazioso	post horn
tzetze	chanter	melodic	sordine	beat-time	guimbard	psaltery
unison	chikara	mistune	sordono	bell harp	half-note	quantity
up-beat	chorale	musette	sospiro	berceuse	harmonic	recorder
vamper	cithara	musical	spinnet	canticle	harp lute	reed pipe
veloce	cithern	natural	stopped	canzonet	hawk-bell	register
ventil	clapper	ocarina	stretto	carillon	high note	resonant
vielle	clarion	octette	strophe	castanet	hornpipe	response
violin	clavier	offbeat	sub-bass	castrato	infinito	rhapsody
vivace	con brio	organum	subject	cavatina	interval	rigadoon
volata	concert	pandora	syncope	chaconne	intonate	saraband
volume	conduct	pan-pipe	taborer	cheville	isotonic	semitone
warble	cornett	phonica	taboret	clappers	Jew's-harp	septette
zambra	counter	pianino	tambour	clarinet	jongleur	sequence
zincke	cremona	pianist	tambura	clarsach	keyboard	serenade
zither	crooner	pianola	theorbo	clavecin	key-bugle	serenata
	crotalo	pibroch	tibicen	claviary	knackers	sestetto
	cymbals	piccolo	timbrel	composer	lentando	sextette
7	czardas	piffero	timpani	composto	libretto	sforzato
	descant	pomposo	timpano	con amore	ligature	shamisen
aeolian	descend	posaune	tipping	con anima	lutanist	side drum
acolist	descent	prelude	toccata	concerto	lutenist	smorzato
agitato	diagram	ragtime	tone-row	confusco	madrigal	sonatina
allegro	dichord	quartet	tremolo	conjusto	maestoso	songster
alt-horn	discord	quintet	triplet	continuo	major key	spiccato
amoroso	distune	recital	trumpet	couranto	martenot	spinette
andante	dittied	refrain	tubicen	cromorna	melodeon	staccato
angelot	drummer	reprise	tuneful	crotchet	melodics	sticcado
animato	epicede	requiem	ukelele	deep-tone	melodist	subtonic
apotome	euphony	rescore	upright	demi-tone	melodize	symmetry
apotomy	eutonia	ripieno	up-tempo	diapason	minor key	symphony
arghool	fagotto	romance	vespers	diatonic	minstrel	syntonic
arietta	fanfare	rondeau	vibrato	diminish	mirliton	tabourer
ariette	fermata	rondino	vihuela	ding-dong	miserere	tabouret
ars nova	fiddler	rosalia	violist	distance	moderato	tamboura
attuned	fistula	roulade	violone	doloroso	modulate	tell-tale
bagpipe	flatten	sackbut	warbler	dominant	monotone	tenoroon
ballade	flutina	sambuca	whistle	down beat	monotony	terzetto
bandore	flutist	sambuke	zithern	drumbeat	movement	threnody
baryton	fuguist	samisen	zuffolo	drum-head	musicale	timoroso
bassist	furioso	sarangi		duettist	musician	tonalist

tonality
tone down
tone poem
trap-drum
tremando
triangle
trichord
trombone
tympanon
tympanum
vigoroso
virginal
virtuosi
virtuoso
vocalion
vocalist
voce colo
warbling
wood-wind
zambomba

9

accordion
acoustics
all-breve
allemande
alto-viola
andamento
andantino
antiphony
arabesque
archilute
atonality
bagatelle
balalaika
banjoline
barcarole
bass-flute
bird-organ
bombardon
bow-string
brass-band
brillante
bugle-horn
cacophony
cantabile
capriccio
castanets
celestina
charivari
chromatic
clarionet
claviharp
coach-horn
conductor
consonate
contralto

cornopean
crescendo
cymbalist
dead-march
death-bell
decachord
deep-toned
dissonant
dithyramb
drone-pipe
drumstick
dulcitone
elbow-pipe
elevation
euphonism
euphonium
euphonize
extempore
fiddle-bow
flageolet
flute-stop
folk-music
furibondo
gallopade
generator
glissando
grace-note
gradation
grandioso
Gregorian
guitarist
half-shift
hand organ
harmonica
harmonics
harmonium
harmonize
hexachord
high-pitch
high-toned
homophony
imbroglio
immusical
impromptu
improvise
in harmony
interlude
intonation
inversion
irregular
jazz music
lagrimoso
languente
larghetto
leger-line
leitmotif
mandoline
mandolute
melodious

metronome
mezzo-voce
modulator
monochord
monophony
monotonic
mouth harp
music-book
nose-flute
obbligato
octachord
orchestra
part music
pastorale
phonetics
pianolist
pitch-pipe
pizzicato
plainsong
polonaise
polychord
polyphony
polytonal
pricksong
quadrille
quailpipe
quartette
quintette
recording
reed organ
rehearsal
resonance
rhythmics
ricercare
roundelay
saxophone
semibreve
semitonic
septimole
seraphine
sforzando
siciliana
siciliano
signature
slow march
snare-drum
soft pedal
solfeggio
sollecito
sopranist
sostenuto
sotto-voce
sound-post
spiritosa
spiritual
strascino
succentor
symphonic
syncopate

tablature
tabourine
tail-piece
tambourin
tenor bass
tenor clef
tenor horn
tenor tuba
tenor viol
tessitura
theorbist
time-table
timpanist
trillando
trumpeter
tubophone
tympanist
union-pipe
unmusical
untunable
variation
viola alto
violinist
voluntary
vox humana
whistling
xylophone

10

accidental
adaptation
affettuoso
allegretto
appoggiato
attunement
background
bandmaster
barcarolle
base-spring
basset-horn
bassoonist
binotonous
bull fiddle
cantillate
canzonetta
chiroplast
chitlarone
chorus girl
clarichord
clavichord
colorature
concertina
con-spirito
continuato
contrabass
cor anglais
cornettist

dance-music
demiditone
diastaltic
diminuendo
discordant
disharmony
dissonance
dissonancy
dolcemente
double bass
double time
dulcet-tone
embouchure
enharmonic
Eolian harp
Eolian lyre
euphonicon
euphonious
extraneous
flügelhorn
folk-singer
fortissimo
French harp
French horn
gramophone
grand piano
grand opera
ground bass
harmonicon
harp-string
homophonic
hurdy-gurdy
incidental
instrument
intermezzo
intonation
kettle-drum
lentamente
light opera
major chord
major scale
minor chord
minor scale
minstrelsy
mixolydian
modulation
monotonous
mouth-organ
mouth-piece
musica viva
musicology
opera buffa
opera music
ophicleide
orchestral
orpheoreon
pentachord
percussion
pianissimo

pianoforte
polyphonic
prima donna
recitative
recitativo
ritardando
ritornello
semiquaver
sourdeline
sousaphone
staphyline
Stradivari
Strathspey
strepitoso
string-band
stringendo
submediant
supertonic
suspension
symphonion
symphonist
syncopated
syncopator
tamboureen
tambourine
tarantella
tersanetus
tetrachord
tin whistle
tonic chord
tonic major
tonic minor
tonic-sol-fa
triple-time
trombonist
troubador
tuning fork
twelve-tone
undulation
variamento
vibraphone
vistomente
vocal music
zumpé piano

11

accelerando
Aeolian harp
Aeolian lyre
alla capella
alto-ripieno
arrangement
ballad opera
barrel-organ
bene-placito
broken chord
canned music

capriccioso
church music
clairschach
clarion note
composition
concertante
contra-basso
contrapunto
contra-tenor
counterpart
decrescendo
demi-cadence
diatessaron
discordance
discordancy
equisonance
extemporize
fiddlestick
figured-bass
finger-board
first violin
graphophone
Guido's scale
harmoniphon
harmonizing
harpsichord
high-pitched
hunting-horn
hydraulicon
incantation
madrigalist
mandolinist
minnesinger
music-master
natural note
nickelodeon
opera bouffe
orchestrate
passing-bell
passing-note
piano player
piano-violin
polyphonism
polyphonist
prestissimo
progression
quarter note

quarter-tone
rallentando
rock and roll
sacred music
saxophonist
senza rigore
solmization
string music
subsemitone
symphonious
syncopation
transposing
tridiapason
unaccordant
viola d'amore
viol da gamba
violoncello
vivacissimo
voce-di-petto
voce-di-testa
volti-subito

12

accordionist
acoustic bass
allegrissimo
appassionata
appoggiatura
assai-allegro
augmentation
bass baritone
boogie-woogie
cembal d'ambre
chamber music
chromaticism
clarinettist
clavicembalo
comedy ballet
concert grand
concert-pitch
contrapuntal
cottage piano
counterpoint
counter-tenor
divertimento

double-octave
extravaganza
false cadence
fiddle-string
funeral march
glockenspiel
inharmonious
instrumental
marcatissimo
mezzo-relievo
mezzo-soprano
military band
musicologist
opéra comique
orchestrator
organ-grinder
organ recital
pandean-pipes
passion music
penny whistle
philharmonic
philomusical
polytonality
pralltriller
repercussion
sesquialtera
sounding-post
spheremelody
Stradivarius
thorough-bass
tuning-hammer
ukulele-banjo
viola da gamba
vocalization

13

accompaniment
bagpipe player
choral singing
conservatoire
cornet-à-piston
disharmonious
harmonic chord
musical comedy
music festival

operatic music
orchestration
ranz-des-vaches
sacred concert
sol-fa notation
staff notation
string octette
string quartet
superdominant
swanee whistle
terpsichorean
tetradiapason
transposition
violoncellist

14 AND OVER

Ambrosian chant (14)
banjo-mandoline (14)
brass instrument(s) (15, 16)
chromatic scale (14)
demisemiquaver (14)
direct interval (14)
double-tongueing (15)
electric guitar (14)
electronic music (15)
fife-and-drum band (15)
flute-flageolet (14)
Gregorian chant (14)
Highland bagpipe (15)
instrumentalist (15)
instrumentation (15)
Lowland bagpipe (14)
mandoline player (15)
musical director (15)
musical festival (15)
musique concrète (15)
regimental band (14)
string quartette (15)
symphony concert (15)
tmtinnabulary (14)
tintinnabulate (14)
tintinnabulation (16)
triple-tongueing (15)
wind instrument(s) (14, 15)

Poetry, prose and grammar

2 AND 3

do
ego
lay
ms.

nõ
nõh
ode
pun
tag
wit

4

agon
bard
case
coda

copy
dual
duan
Edda
epic
epos

foot
form
gest
glee
hymn
iamb

idyl
mime
mood
myth
noun
past

pean
play
plot
poem
poet
quip
rime
root
rule
rune
saga
scan
song
tone
verb
weak
word

5

affix
blurb
canto
caret
carol
casal
codex
colon
comma
dirge
ditty
drama
elegy
elide
epode
essay
fable
farce
folio
geste
gloss
haiku
humor
ictus
idiom
idyll
Iliad
image
index
infix
irony
lyric
maxim
metre
motif
novel
paean
poesy

prose
psalm
quote
rhyme
rondo
runic
scald
scene
shift
slang
stich
style
sylva
tense
theme
tilde
triad
Vedas
verse
vowel

6

accent
active
adonic
adverb
Aeneid
alcaic
annals
anthem
aorist
aptote
ballad
bathos
chanty
chorus
clause
cliché
climax
comedy
crisis
critic
dactyl
dative
define
derive
digram
dipody
ending
epodic
epopee
finite
future
gender
genius
gerund
gnomic

govern
heroic
hiatus
homily
hubris
humour
hybris
hymnal
hyphen
iambic
iambus
jargon
kabuki
lacuna
legend
lyrist
macron
mantra
memoir
monody
neuter
number
object
parody
pathos
period
person
phrase
pidgin
plural
poetic
poetry
prefix
review
rhythm
riddle
rondle
satire
simile
sketch
slogan
sonnet
stanza
stress
strong
suffix
symbol
syntax
thesis
umlaut
verbal
zeugrna

7

adjunct
anagram
analogy

analyse
anapest
antonym
apocope
apology
article
ballade
berhyme
bucolic
cadence
caesura
cantata
cedilla
chanson
choreus
collate
content
context
couplet
decline
descant
diction
digraph
distich
eclogue
edition
elegiac
elision
epicene
epigram
epistle
epitaph
fantasy
fiction
Georgic
harmony
Homeric
homonym
idyllic
imagery
inflect
introit
journal
lampoon
leonine
lexicon
litotes
lyrical
meiosis
mimesis
nemesis
novella
Odyssey
paradox
parsing
passive
peanism
perfect
persona

phoneme
poetics
polemic
present
pronoun
prosaic
prosody
proverb
psalter
refrain
regular
requiem
Sapphic
sarcasm
scaldic
semiped
servile
setting
sextain
spondee
stichic
strophe
subject
syncope
synonym
systole
tiercet
tragedy
trilogy
triolet
triplet
trochee
villain
virelay
Vulgate
war song
western

8

ablative
absolute
acrostic
allusion
alphabet
amoebean
analysis
anapaest
anaphora
anti-hero
antiphon
apodosis
archaism
assonant
asterisk
bacchius
balladry
caesural

canticle
chiasmus
choliamb
choriamb
clerihew
contrast
critique
dactylic
definite
dieresis
dialogue
discrete
doggerel
dramatic
ellipsis
enclitic
epic poem
epigraph
epilogue
epitrite
euphuism
feminine
folktale
footnote
full-stop
generate
genitive
glossary
guttural
horation
language
laureate
libretto
limerick
logogram
lyricism
madrigal
metaphor
metrical
mispoint
mock epic
morpheme
negative
nonsense
optative
Ossianic
oxymoron
paradigm
particle
partsong
pastoral
personal
phonetic
Pindaric
poetical
positive
prologue
quantity
quatrain

relative
rhapsody
rhetoric
romantic
scanning
scansion
scenario
sentence
singular
solecism
stanzaic
suspense
swan song
syntaxis
systolic
temporal
threnody
thriller
tribrach
trimeter
triptote
unpoetic
versicle
vignette
vocative
whodunit
word play

9

accidence
adjective
ampersand
anapestic
Anglicism
anonymous
anthology
antispast
apocopate
archetype
Asclepiad
assonance
biography
birthsong
broadside
burlesque
cacophony
catharsis
classical
conjugate
consonant
criticism
decastich
diaeresis
dipthong
dithyramb
ditrochee
elegiacal

enclitics
etymology
euphemism
facsimile
flashback
formative
free verse
Gallicism
gerundive
grammatic
hemistich
hendiadys
hexameter
hexastich
hypallage
hyperbole
idiomatic
imperfect
inflexion
inversion
irregular
leitmotiv
lyric poem
masculine
metaplasm
minor poet
monometer
monorhyme
nonostich
neologism
objective
parataxis
partitive
past tense
phillipic
philology
Pindarism
platitude
poetaster
pot boiler
potential
preterite
pricksong
principal
privative
prose poem
prosodian
prosodist
quartette
quotation
recension
reddition
reflexive
roundelay

sea chanty
semantics
semicolon
semivowel
soliloquy
syllepsis
symbolism
symposium
symptosis
synalepha
syntactic
telestich
terza rima
trisagion
Virgilian

10

accusative
amphibrach
amphimacer
anapaestic
anarthrous
anastrophe
anastrophy
antagonist
antepenult
anticlimax
antiphonal
antiphonic
apostrophe
apposition
atmosphere
avant-garde
bestseller
blank verse
bowdlerize
caricature
choliambic
choriambic
choriambus
circumflex
colloquial
comparison
declension
definition
definitive
derivation
derivative
dissonance
dolichorus
epenthesis
epenthetic

generative
government
grammarian
hexametric
hyperbaton
hyphenated
imperative
impersonal
indefinite
infinitive
inflection
intonation
involution
linguistic
manuscript
metathesis
mock heroic
morphology
neuter verb
nom de plume
nominative
ottava rima
palindrome
paraphrase
participle
passion play
pentameter
Petrarchan
picaresque
plagiarism
pluperfect
pronominal
provection
reciprocal
short story
similitude
spoonerism
subjective
synaeresis
tetracolon
tetrameter
tetrastich
transitive
unpoetical
vernacular

11

alexandrine
amphibology
anacoluthon
antispastic
antiphrasis

antistrophe
aposiopesis
association
ballad style
bibliomancy
catastrophe
chansonette
comic relief
comparative
concordance
conjunction
conjunctive
constituent
declination
descriptive
disjunctive
dissyllabic
dissyllable
dithyrambic
dithyrambus
future tense
ghost writer
grammatical
hemistichal
heteroclite
hudibrastic
linguistics
lyric poetry
miracle play
oblique case
parenthesis
portmanteau
preposition
proposition
punctuation
regular verb
reiterative
subjunctive
subordinate
substantive
superlative
suppression
syntactical
tragicomedy
trimetrical

12

alliteration
alliterative
alphabetical
anteposition
antibacchius

antimetrical
antiphonical
antiphrastic
antistrophic
archilochian
bibliography
deponent verb
dissyllabify
distributive
epigrammatic
episodically
epithalamium
etymological
grammaticism
grammaticize
heteroclitic
hexametrical
indeclinable
intransitive
metaphorical
minnesingers
nursery rhyme
onomatopoeia
perfect tense
poet laureate
postposition
prescriptive
present tense
prothalamium

13 AND OVER

antepenultimate (15)
definite article (15)
epigrammatical (14)
frequentative (13)
future perfect (13)
historic present (15)
hysteron proteron (16)
indicative mood (14)
interrogative (13)
inverted commas (14)
irregular verb (13)
lyrical poetry (13)
objective case (13)
personification (15)
poetic licence (13)
positive degree (14)
possessive case (14)
science fiction (14)
split infinitive (15)
transformation (14)
ungrammatical (13)

Theatre, opera, ballet, cinema, television and radio

2 AND 3

act
arc
bit
bow
box
cue
dub
fan
gag
ham
hit
mug
nō
pan
pit
rag
rep
run
set
tag
TV
wig

4

bill
book
boom
busk
cast
clap
clip
crew
dais
diva
duet
Emmy
epic
exit
film
flop
foil
gala
gods
grid
hero
idol
joke
lead
line
live
mask
mike
mime
mute
part
play
prop
role
rush
shot
show
skit
solo
spot
star
take
team
turn
wing

5

actor
ad lib
agent
angel
apron
aside
baton
break
clown
comic
debut
decor
drama
dry up
enact
exode
extra
farce
flies
focus
foyer
heavy
hokum
house
lines
mimer
mimic
movie
on cue
opera
Oscar
piece
props
radio
revue
scene
stage
stall
stunt
telly
usher
wings

6

acting
action
appear
backer
ballet
barker
big top
boards
buskin
camera
chorus
cinema
circle
circus
claque
comedy
critic
dancer
direct
dubbed
effect
encore
finale
flyman
kabuki
lights
make-up
masque
method
motley
movies
mummer
nautch
number
on tour
one act
parody
patron
patter
player
podium
prompt
puppet
recite
repeat
ring up
rushes
satire
screen
script
season
serial
series
singer
sitcom
sketch
speech
stalls
stooge
studio
talent
talkie
ticket
tights
timing
tinsel
troupe
TV show
viewer
walk-on
warm-up
writer

7

acrobat
actress
all-star
amateur
balcony
benefit
bit part
booking
buffoon
callboy
cabaret
cartoon
casting
catcall
catwalk
channel
charade
chorine
circuit
clapper
close-up
commère
company
compère
concert
console
costume
curtain
dancing
danseur
deadpan
dress up
drive in
dubbing
fan club
farceur
fantasy
feature
film set
gallery
heroine
ingenue
juggler
leg show
leotard
long run
matinée
mimicry
mummery
musical
mystery
new wave
on stage
overact
pageant
perform
phone-in
Pierrot
players
playing
playlet
pop star
portray
prelude
present
preview
produce
program
recital
reciter
re-enact
resting
revival
rostrum
scenery
show biz
showman
sponsor
stadium
stagery
staging
stand-in
stardom
starlet
support
tableau
talkies
theatre
the gods
tragedy
trailer
trilogy
trouper
tumbler
upstage
variety
vehicle
viewing
western

8

applause
artistry
audience
audition
backdrop
bioscope
burletta
carnival
chat show
Cinerama
clapping
clowning
coliseum
comedian
conjurer
coryphée
costumer
coulisse
danseuse
dialogue
director
disguise
dramatic
dumb show
duologue
entr'acte
entrance
epilogue
exit line
farceuse
fauteuil
festival
figurant
film crew
film star
film unit
filmgoer
first act
funny man
ham actor
interval
juggling
libretto
live show
location
magician
male lead
morality
newsreel
offstage
operatic
operetta
overture
parterre
pastoral
peep show
pictures
pit stall
platform
playbill
playgoer
première
producer
prologue
prompter
protasis
quiz show
rehearse
ring down
scenario
set piece
showbill
side show
smash hit
stagebox
star turn
straight
stripper
subtitle
telecast
Thespian
third act
tragical

travesty
typecast
wardrobe
wigmaker

9

animation
announcer
arabesque
backcloth
backstage
ballerina
bandstand
barnstorm
bit player
box office
broadcast
burlesque
cameraman
character
chorus boy
cinematic
clip joint
cloakroom
Columbine
conjuring
costumier
coulisses
criticism
cyclorama
discovery
double act
down stage
dramatics
dramatist
dramatize
drop scene
entertain
entrechat
exhibiter
figurante
film actor
film extra
filmstrip
first lead
flashback
floorshow
folkdance
full house
gala night
guest star
Harlequin
impromptu
interlude
limelight
love scene
low comedy

major role
melodrama
minor role
monodrama
monologue
movie-goer
movie star
music hall
night club
orchestra
panel game
pantaloon
pantomime
pas de deux
performer
photoplay
Pierrette
pirouette
pit-stalls
play-actor
playhouse
portrayal
programme
prompt-box
publicity
punch-line
quartette
rehearsal
repertory
represent
second act
slapstick
soap opera
soliloquy
soubrette
spectacle
spectator
spotlight
stage door
stagehand
stage left
stage-name
stage play
take a part
tap dancer
the boards
title role
tragedian
usherette
wisecrack

10

afterpiece
appearance
auditorium
chorus girl
clapper-boy

comedienne
comedietta
comic opera
commercial
continuity
coryphaeus
crowd scene
denouement
disc jockey
drama group
dramaturge
dramaturgy
fantoccini
film house
filmscript
first night
footlights
get the bird
high comedy
hippodrome
histrionic
horror film
horse opera
impresario
intermezzo
in the round
in the wings
junior lead
leading man
legitimate
librettist
marionette
masquerade
microphone
movie actor
music drama
newscaster
on location
opera buffa
opera house
performing
play-acting
playwright
prima donna
production
prompt-book
properties
proscenium
Pulcinella
puppet-show
rave notice
rave review
recitation
repertoire
repetiteur
ringmaster
screenplay
silent film
sound track

stagecraft
stage fever
stage right
star player
striptease
substitute
sword-dance
tap dancing
tear-jerker
television
theatre box
theatrical
torchdance
travelogue
understudy
variety act
vaudeville
walk-on part
wide screen

11

accompanist
all-star cast
art director
balletomane
barnstormer
black comedy
broadcaster
cap and bells
Cinemascope
circus-rider
cliff-hanger
comedy drama
comic relief
commentator
concert hall
credit title
cutting room
dance troupe
documentary
drama critic
drama school
dramatic art
dress circle
electrician
entertainer
equilibrist
exeunt omnes
feature film
film theatre
fire curtain
folkdancing
funambulist
greasepaint
Greek chorus
histrionics
illusionist

impersonate
kitchen-sink
leading lady
legerdemain
light comedy
matinée idol
method actor
miracle play
opera bouffe
opera singer
pantomimist
Passion play
performance
picture show
problem play
protagonist
psychodrama
Punchinello
scene change
set designer
set the scene
showmanship
show-stopper
sound effect
spectacular
stage design
stage effect
stage fright
stage player
stage school
stage-struck
star billing
star quality
star-studded
talent scout
technicolor
terpsichore
thaumaturgy
theatregoer
theatre land
theatricals
Thespian art
tragedienne
tragicomedy
trick-riding
unrehearsed
upper circle
variety show
ventriloquy
word-perfect

12

academy award
actor-manager
amphitheatre
ballet-dancer
balletomania

choreography
cinema studio
clapperboard
concert party
credit titles
dramaturgist
dressing-room
exotic dancer
extravaganza
film director
film festival
film producer
first-nighter
Grand Guignol
harlequinade
impersonator
introduction
juvenile lead
make-up artist
melodramatic
method acting
minstrel show
modern ballet
morality play
name in lights

natural break
opera glasses
orchestra pit
principal boy
Punch and Judy
puppet-player
scene-painter
scene-shifter
scene-stealer
screenwriter
scriptwriter
show business
silver screen
song and dance
sound effects
stage manager
stage whisper
starring role
steal the show
stock company
straight part
top of the bill

13

ballet dancing
burlesque show
cinematograph
contortionist
curtain-raiser
dance festival
emergency exit
entertainment
musical comedy
projectionist
Russian ballet
safety curtain
sleight-of-hand
sound engineer
studio manager
thaumaturgics
theatre school
ventriloquist

14 AND 15

acrobatic troupe (15)
ballet-mistress (14)
classical ballet (15)
continuity girl (14)
dancing academy (14
domestic comedy (14)
dramatic critic (14)
dramatic society (15)
prima ballerina (14)
property master (14)
school of acting (14)
school of dancing (15)
shooting script (14)
situation comedy (15)
slide projector (14)
smoking concert (14)
sound-projector (14)
stage carpenter (14)
stage properties (15)
strolling player (15)
tableaux-vivants (16)
talking pictures (15)
tightrope-walker (15)
touring company (14)
variety theatre (14)

MEASUREMENT
Coins and currency

2 AND 3

as
bit
bob
cob
dam
ecu
far
fin
lac
lat
leu
lev
mag
mil
mna
oof
ore
pie
red
ree
rei
sen
sho
sol
sou
tin
won
yen
zac
zuz

4

anna
baht
beka
biga
buck
cash
cent
chip
daum
dawm
dime
doit
duro
geld
joey
kick
kran
kyat
lakh
lira
lire
loot
mail
mark
merk
mina
mite
note
obol
para
peag
peak
peso
pice
quid
rand
real
rial
riel
ryal
tael
taka
unik
yuan
zack

5

agora
angel
asper
aurei
belga
betso
boole
brass
bread
chiao
colon
conto
copec
crore
crown
daric
dinar
dough
ducat
eagle
franc
grand
groat
haler
koban
kopek
krona
krone
liard
libra
litas
livre
locho
lolly
louis
lucre
medio
mohar
mohur
moola
noble
obang
ochre
oncer
paolo
pence
pengo
penny
plack
pound
ready
rhino
ruble
rupee
sceat
scudi
scudo
semis
soldi
soldo
stica
styca
sucre
sugar
sycee
tical
ticcy
tizzy
toman
uncia
unite
zloty

6

amania
aureus
balboa
baubee
bawbee
bezant
bodole
boodle
condor
copang
copeck
change
copper
couter
deaner
décime
denier
dirhem
doblon
dollar
escudo
florin
forint
fuorte
gourde
guinea
gulden
heller
kobang
kopeck

lepton
markka
nickel
obolus
pagoda
pagode
peseta
rosser
rouble
rupiah
sceatt
sequin
shekel
souran
stater
stiver
talari
talent
tanner
tester
teston
thaler
tickey
tizzie
tomaun
valuta
zechin

7

angelot
bolivar
carolus
centava
centavo
centime
cordoba
crusado
denarii
drachma
guilder
jacobus
lempira
manilla
milreis
moidore
ngusang

pfennig
piastre
pistole
quarter
ringgit
sextans
stooter
testoon
testril
thrymsa
unicorn

8

ambrosin
denarius
didrachm
doubloon
ducatoon
farthing
florence
groschen
half anna
half mark
imperial
johannes
kreutzer
louis d'or
maravedi
megabuck
napoleon
new pence
new penny
picayune
portague
quadrans
quetzale
sesterce
shilling
sixpence
stotinka

9

boliviano
cuartillo

didrachma
dupondius
gold broad
gold noble
gold penny
half ackey
half angel
half broad
half crown
half groat
halfpenny
lilang-eni
pistareen
rixdollar
rose-noble
schilling
sestertii
sovereign
spur royal
two mohars
two mohurs
yellow boy

10

broad piece
crown piece
double pice
easterling
emalangeni
first brass
gold stater
half florin
half guinea
half laurel
quadrussis
sestertium
silverling
stour-royal
threepence
threepenny
tripondius
venezolano

11

Briton crown
double crown
double eagle
george noble
guinea piece
half guilder
half thistle
silver penny
spade guinea
tetradrachm
twelvepenny
two guilders

12 AND 13

antoninianus (12)
double sequin (12)
half farthing (12)
half rose-noble (13)
half sovereign (13)
mill sixpence (12)
quarter angel (12)
quarter dollar (13)
quarter florin (13)
quarter laurel (13)
quarter noble (12)
shinplaster (12)
silver-stater (12)
sixpenny piece (13)
tribute penny (12)
twenty dollars (13)
twopenny piece (13)
two-pound piece (13)

14 AND OVER

barbadoes penny (14)
five-guinea piece (15)
five-pound piece (14)
Hong Kong dollar (14)
quarter guilder (14)
three farthings (14)
threepenny piece (16)
twenty shillings (15)
two-guilder piece (15)
two-guinea piece (14)

Time (including specific dates, periods, seasons, annual festivals, etc.)

(H.) = Hindu. (I.) = Islam. (J.) = Jewish months (variously spelt). (R.) = Roman.

2 – 4

Ab (J.)
Abib (J.)
A.D.
Adar (J.)
aeon
age
ages
ago
A.M.
B.C.
B.S.T.
date
dawn
day
Elul (J.)
eon
era
ever
fast
G.M.T.
Holi (H.)
hour
Ides (R.)
Iyar (J.)
July
June
last
late
Lent
May
morn
noon
now
N.S.
oft
once
O.S.
P.M.
slow
soon
span
term
then
tick
time
utas
week
when
Xmas
year
yore

Yuga (H.)
Yule

5

adays
after
again
alway
April
bells
clock
cycle
daily
dated
early
epact
epoch
Fasti (R.)
feast
first
flash
horal
jiffy
Kalpa (H.)
later
March
month
never
night
Nisan (J.)
nones
of old
often
quick
reign
Sivan (J.)
spell
Tebet (J.)
teens
times
Tisri (J.)
to-day
trice
until
watch
while

6

always
annual

August
autumn
before
betime
brumal
Cisleu
curfew
decade
Diwali (H.)
Easter
faster
feriae
ferial
Friday
future
heyday
hourly
hiemal
Julian
Kislev (J.)
Lammas
lately
latest
Lenaea
May day
memory
mensal
midday
minute
modern
moment
Monday
morrow
o'clock
off-day
pay-day
period
record
rhythm
season
second
seldom
Shebat (J.)
slower
slowly
spring
summer
Sunday
sunset
Tammuz (J.)
Tebeth (J.)
termly
timely
timous

Tishri (J.)
ultimo
Veadar (J.)
Veader (J.)
vernal
vesper
weekly
whilom
whilst
winter
yearly

7

almanac
already
ancient
anights
antique
bedtime
betimes
by and by
Calends (R.)
century
chiliad
Chisleu (J.)
dawning
daytime
diurnal
dog days
earlier
epochal
equinox
estival
eternal
etesian
evening
fast day
fête day
half-day
harvest
Heshvan (J.)
high day
hock-day
holiday
holy day
instant
interim
January
jubilee
lady day
lay-days
lustrum

mail day
mid-Lent
midweek
monthly
morning
new moon
nightly
noonday
October
post-day
proximo
quartan
quarter
quicker
quickly
quintan
Ramadan (I.)
regency
rent day
sabbath
slowest
sundial
sundown
sunrise
tea time
tertian
Thammuz (J.)
timeful
time gun
timeous
tonight
triduan
Tuesday
undated
wartime
weekday
weekend
whilere
workday
Xmas day
yestern

8

aestival
annually
antecede
antedate
anterior
biennial
bimensal
birthday
biweekly

calendar
carnival
chiliasm
chiliast
day by day
daybreak
dead-slow
December
Dionysia
domesday
doomsday
duration
earliest
eggtimer
estivate
eternity
eventide
every day
February
festival
forenoon
formerly
futurist
futurity
gangweek
Georgian
gloaming
half-past
half-term
half-time
half-year
hibernal
high noon
Hock-tide
Hogmanay
holidays
holy week
interval
kalendar
latterly
leap year
Lord's day
mealtime
menology
midnight
minutely
natal day
new style
noontide
noon-time
November
nowadays
nundinal
oft-times

old style
Olympics
overtime
past time
periodic
postpone
punctual
quickest
Ramadhan (I.)
right now
Saturday
seasonal
seed time
semester
se'nnight
sidereal
slow time
sometime
speedily
Stone Age
Thurday
time ball
time bill
timeless
tomorrow
twilight
untimely
up to date
vacation
whenever
Yuletide
zero hour

9

Adar Shani (J.)
aforetime
after ages
afternoon
afterward
All Hallow
anciently
antedated
antelucan
antiquity
bimonthly
Boxing Day
Candlemas
centenary
Christmas
civil year
close time
continual
decennary
decennial
diurnally
diuturnal
Easter Day

Edwardian
Ember days
Ember fast
Ember tide
Ember week
eternally
feast days
fortnight
fruit time
Gregorian
Halloween
hard times
hereafter
hodiernal
honeymoon
hourglass
immediate
indiction
instantly
lean years
Low Sunday
lunar year
lunch time
market day
Martinmas
matutinal
menstrual
midsummer
midwinter
nightfall
night-time
nightward
novitiate
octennial
overnight
past times
peace time
postponed
premature
presently
quarterly
quick time
quotidian
recurrent
return day
right away
September
sexennial
sometimes
speech day
sunrising
Thermidor
ticket day
timepiece
timetable
triennial
trimester
Victorian
Wednesday

whole time
yesterday
yestereve

10

aftertimes
afterwards
All Hallows
antecedent
antemosaic
anteriorly
anticipate
beforehand
before time
behind time
biennially
bimestrial
centennial
chiliastic
chronogram
continuous
days of yore
dinner time
diuturnity
Easter term
Ember weeks
estivation
Father Time
fence month
Good Friday
half-yearly
hebdomadal
Hilary term
isochronal
lunar cycle
lunar month
Lupercalia
Michaelmas
Middle Ages
millennium
natalitial
occasional
oftentimes
olden times
Palm Sunday
quarter day
Quirinalia
record time
Saturnalia
seasonable
septennial
sexagesima
Shrovetide
solar month
sowing-time
spring time
summer term

summertime
sunsetting
synchronal
Theban year
thereafter
tiffin time
time enough
timekeeper
time server
time signal
triverbial
twelfth day
unpunctual
vespertine
watch night
wedding day
Whit Sunday
winter time
working day

11

All Fools' Day
All Souls' Day
anniverary
antecedence
antemundane
antenuptial
antepaschal
anteriority
Anthesteria
bacchanalia
Bank Holiday
behindtimes
bicentenary
Black Monday
Chalk Sunday
chronograph
chronometer
closing time
continually
cosmic clock
discount day
Elizabethan
everlasting
fashionable
fortnightly
half holiday
harvest home
harvest time
hebdomadary
holiday time
immediately
interregnum
isochronism
isochronous
jubilee year
Judgment Day

leisure time
millenarian
New Year's Day
New Year's Eve
Passion Week
prehistoric
prematurely
present time
pudding time
punctuality
quadrennial
quartz clock
Rosh Hashonah (J.)
seeding time
settling day
synchronism
synchronize
synchronous
thenceforth
time bargain
Tudor period
twelvemonth
ultramodern
Whitsuntide
yesternight

12

afterthought
All Saints' Day
antediluvial
antediluvian
antemeridian
anticipation
Ash Wednesday
betrothal day
bicentennial
carbon dating
Christmas Day
Christmas Eve
continuously
duodecennial
early closing
Easter Sunday
Embering days
emergent year
hebdomatical
luncheon time
Midsummer Day
Midsummer Eve
occasionally
old-fashioned
platonic year
Plough Monday
post-diluvial
post-diluvian
post-meridian
postponement

postprandial	*13*	Gregorian year	*14* AND *15*
quadragesima		holiday season	
quinquennial	All Hallowmass	lunisolar year	behind the times (14)
red-letter day	All Hallowtide	Michaelmas Day	biological clock (15)
Rogation days	April Fools' Day	once upon a time	day in and day out (14)
Rogation week	breakfast time	Shrove Tuesday	early closing day (15)
sidereal year	calendar month	silver wedding	early Victorian (14)
standard time	Childermas day	thenceforward	Maundy Thursday (14)
synchronized	Christmastide	Trinity Sunday	Michaelmas term (14)
tercentenary	Christmastime	Valentine's Day	prehistoric age(s)
time contract	Edwardian days		(14–15)
tricentenary	everlastingly		sabbatical year (14)
tropical year	golden jubilee		synchronization (15)
twelfth night	golden wedding		synodical month (14)
			Walpurgis night (14)

Weights and measures

(A.) = Argentina	(G.) = Greece	(Malay.) = Malaysia	(S.A.) = South Africa
(B.) = Brazil	(H.) = Hebrew	(min.) = mining	(SI) = Système
(b.) = bread	(Hon.) = Honduras	(Mor.) = Morocco	International:
(C.) = Canada	(I.) = India	(N.) = Norway	metric system
(c.) = coal	(Ice.) = Iceland	(O.) = Oriental	(T.) = Turkey
(Ch.) = China	(Indo.) = Indonesia	(pap.) = paper	(Thai.) = Thailand
(E.) Egypt	(Ire.) = Ireland	(print.) = printing	(U.S.) = United States
(elec.) = electricity	(It.) = Italy	(R.) = Russia	(v.) = various
(Eth.) = Ethiopia	(J.) = Japan	(Rom.) = Roman	commodities
(F.) = France	(liq.) = liquids	(S.) = Spain	(w.) = wool
(f.) = fish	(M.) = Malta	(s.) = silk or cotton	(w.y.) = worsted yarn

Note: Words with no references against them are British weights or measures not necessarily confined to particular commodities. Many of the units listed are no longer in use.

1 – 3	erg	nit	tan (Ch.)	case (v.)	hand (horses)
	fen (Ch.)	niu (Thai.)	to (J.)	cask (liq.)	hank (w.y.)
aam	fou	ohm (elec.)	tod (w.)	ch'ih (Ch.)	hath (I.)
A4 (pap.)	g. (SI)	oka (E.)	tog	chop (Ch.)	heml (E.)
amp (elec.)	hin (H.)	oke (T.)	ton	comb	hide
are (SI)	kat (E.)	os	tot	cord	hour
as (Rom.)	keg	oz.	tun (liq.)	coss (I.)	inch
A.S.A.	ken (J.)	pic (E.)	vat (liq.)	cran (f.)	keel (c.)
aum (S.A.)	kg.	pin	wah (Thai.)	darg	kela (E.)
B.S.I.	kin (J. and Ch.)	piu (It.)	wey (w.)	demy (pap.)	kilo (SI)
B.T.U.	km.	pot (pap.)		drah (Mor.)	knot
cab (H.)	kor (H.)	pnd		dram	koku (J.)
cho (J.)	lac (I.)	rad	*4*	drop	koss (I.)
cor (H.)	Ib.	rai (Thai.)		drum (v.)	kwan (J.)
cm. (SI)	lea (s.)	rem	acre	dyne	lakh (I.)
cwt.	li (Ch.)	ri (J.)	area	epha (H.)	last (f., w.)
day	log (H.)	rio	bale (v.)	feet	link
D.I.N.	m.	rod	bath (H.)	foot	load (min.)
dwt.	mho (elec.)	sen (Thai.)	bind (f.)	funt (R.)	maze (f.)
el	mil	sho (J.)	boll	gill	mile
em (print.)	mow (Ch.)	SI	butt (liq.)	gram (SI)	mina (H.)
en (print.)	mu	sun (J.)	cade (f.)	half	moio

mudd	**5**	maund (I.)	arpent	pottle (liq.)	quantar (E.)
muid (S.A.)		mease	arroba (A. and B.)	quarto (pap.)	quantum
nail	almud (T.)	meter (SI)	arshin (T.)	rotolo (M.)	quartan
natr (Eth.)	anker (S.A.)	metre (SI)	assize	sajene (R.)	quarter
oket (Eth.)	ardeb (E.)	minim (liq.)	bandle (Ire.)	schene (E.)	quinary
omer (H.)	bahar (I.)	month	barrel (v.)	second	quintal
onza (A.)	barge (c.)	neper	batman (T.)	shekel (H.)	röntgen
paal	baril (G.)	obole	bundle (v.)	shtoff (R.)	rottolo
pace	barre (I.)	ocque (G.)	bushel	staten (G.)	sarplar (w.)
pack	bekah (H.)	okieh (E.)	calory	suttle	scruple
pail (lard)	bidon (liq.)	ounce	candie	talent (G.)	seamile
pair	bigha (I.)	pally (I.)	cantar (E. and T.)	thrave (Ice.)	spindle (s.)
palm	brace	pearl	casing (pap.)	thread (s.)	stadium (G.)
peck	cable	perch	cental (C. and U.S.)	tierce (liq.)	stature
phon	candy (I.)	pecul	cental (B. and G.)	visham (I.)	stremma (G.)
phot	caneh	picul (Ch.)	chatak (I.)	weight	ternary
pike (G.)	canna	piede (M.)	chopin (liq.)	yojana	ternion
pint	carat	plumb	cottah (I.)		tonnage
pipe (liq.)	catty (Ch.)	point (print.)	cuarta (A.)	**7**	virgate
pole	cawny (I.)	poise	decare		
polt	chain	pound	denier	acreage	**8**
pood (R.)	chang	proof	djerib (T.)	boiling	
post (pap.)	cheki	pugil	double	braccio	alqueire (B.)
pund (N.)	chien	purse (T.)	drachm	caldron (c.)	angstrom
raik (I.)	cloff	qirat (E.)	endaze (T.)	calorie	caroteel (O.)
ream (pap.)	clove	quart	fanega (S.)	Celsius	centiare
reed (H.)	coomb	quire (pap.)	fathom	centner	centibar
reel (s.)	count (w.y.)	quota	feddan (E.)	century	chaldron (c.)
rood	crore (I.)	royal (pap.)	firkin	chalder	chaudron (c.)
rope	crown (pap.)	sajen (R.)	firlot	chittak (I.)	chetvert (R.)
rotl (E.)	cubic	shaku (J.)	fother	coulomb (elec.)	cubic ton
sack (c. w.)	cubit	sheet (pap.)	gallon (liq.)	dangali (I.)	decagram
sawk	cusec	shock (U.S.)	gramme (SI)	deciare	decigram
seah	cycle	sicca (I.)	kantar (Eth.)	decibel	distance
seam	danda (I.)	skein (s.)	kelvin	diopter	division
seer (I.)	ephah (H.)	stere (SI)	kentle	drachma (G.)	elephant (pap.)
sone	farad	stone	league	ellwand	foolscap (pap.)
span	fermi	stoup (liq.)	libbra (M.)	furlong	footrule
step	galon (A.)	terce (liq.)	megohm (elec.)	gilbert	freezing
tael (Ch.)	gauge	tesla	metric	gravity	graviton
tare	gerah (H.)	therm	micron (SI)	half-aum (S.A.)	half hour
tola (I.)	grain	tithe	minute	half-ton	half inch
torr	gross	toise (F.)	modius	hectare (SI)	half mile
tret	henry	token (pap.)	moiety	koonkee (I.)	hogshead (liq.)
troy	hertz (elec.)	tonne	morgen (S.A.)	leaguer (S.A.)	imperial (pap.)
ts'un (Ch.)	homer (H.)	trone	newton	maximum	infinity
unit	joule	truss	noggin	measure	kassabah (E .)
vara (Hon.)	kaneh	tsubo (J.)	obolus (G.)	megaerg	kilodyne
volt (elec.)	katti	ungul (I.)	octant	megaton	kilogram
warp (f.)	kileh (T.)	vedro (R.)	octave	mileage	kilowatt (elec.)
watt (elec.)	leash	verst (R.)	octavo	millier	kincatty (Ch.)
week	legua (A.)	weber	oxgang	minimum	metrical
wrap (w.y.)	liang (Ch.)	yojan (I.)	parsec	minimus	mutchkin (liq.)
yard	libra (B.)		pascal	modicum	parasang (Iran)
year	ligne	**6**	pocket (hops)	outsize	plateful
	lippy			pailful	puncheon (liq.)
	litre (SI)	ampère (elec.)		poundal	quadrant
	livre (F. and G.)	aroura (E. and G.)		per cent.	roentgen
	masha (I.)				

quantity
quartern (b.)
serplath
ship-load (c.)
short ton (C. and U.S.)
spoonful
toll dish
tonelada (A.)
yardland
yardwand
zolotnik (R.)

9

altimetry
amplitude
areometry
bisegment
cubic foot
cubic inch
cubic yard
cuartilla (A.)
decalitre (SI)
decametre (SI)
decilitre (SI)
decimetre (SI)
decistere (F.)
dekalitre (SI)
dekametre (Sl)
dimension
foot-pound
half ounce
half pound
hectogram (Sl)
isometric
kilocycle
kilohertz (elec.)
kilolitre (SI)
kilometre (SI)
large sack (c.)
light year
long dozen
megacycle
megahertz (elec.)
metric ton
milestone

milligram (SI)
nanometre (SI)
net weight
quadruple
quarterly
quintuple
sea league
three-fold
yardstick

10

barleycorn
barrel-bulk
centesimal
centigrade
centilitre (SI)
centimetre (SI)
centistere (F.)
cubic metre (SI)
dead-weight
decagramme (SI)
decigramme (SI)
dessiatine (R.)
dessyatine (R.)
double-demy (pap.)
double-post (pap.)
dry measure
eighth-part
Fahrenheit
fifty-fifty
fluid ounce
hectolitre (SI)
hectometre (SI)
kilogramme (SI)
lunar month
microfarad (elec.)
millesimal
millilitre (SI)
millimetre (SI)
millionary
quadrantal (Rom.)
square foot
square inch
square mile
square yard

super-royal (pap.)
tripartite
tron weight
troy weight

11

avoirdupois
baker's dozen
centigramme (SI)
day's journey
double-crown (pap.)
double-royal (pap.)
equibalance
equidistant
fluid drachm
half and half
hand-breadth
heavyweight
hectogramme (SI)
imperial-cap (pap.)
long hundred
  (eggs and f.)
long measure
milligramme (SI)
pennyweight
shipping ton
short weight
square metre (SI)
tape-measure
thermal unit
thermometer
trone weight
two-foot rule
wlne measure
yard measure

12

angström unit
areometrical
auncel weight
bantam-weight
boiling point
cable's length

cubic measure
eleventh part
equidistance
great hundred
hair's breadth
half-quartern
measured mile
metric system
printer's ream (pap.)
quantitative
quartern loaf (b.)
Réaumur scale
water measure

13

calendar month
decimal system
feather-weight
freezing point
hundredweight
hypermetrical
inside measure
linear measure
medicine glass
square measure
three-foot rule

14

cubic decimetre (SI)
double-foolscap (pap.)
double-imperial (pap.)
outside measure
zenith distance

15

centigrade scale
cubic centimetre (SI)
square decimetre (SI)

NATURAL HISTORY (I) LIVING CREATURES
Animals

2 AND 3						
	bat	cub	dso	gib	kob	orc
	bok	cur	dzo	gnu	ky	ox
ai	cat	dam	elk	goa	man	pad
ape	cob	doe	ewe	hog	mog	pig
ass	cow	dog	fox	kid	nag	ram

rat	joey	titi	fitch	rasse	angola	galago
Rex	jomo	topi	fossa	ratel	angora	garran
roe	kine	unau	gayal	royal	argali	garron
sai	koba	urus	genet	sable	aswail	gavial
seg	kudu	urva	goral	saiga	aye-aye	gelada
sow	lamb	vari	grice	sajou	baboon	gerbil
tat	lion	vole	grise	sasin	badger	gibbon
teg	lynx	wolf	gyall	screw	bandar	ginnet
tit	maki	yale	harpy	serow	bandog	gopher
tod	mara	zati	hinny	sheep	barrow	goslet
tup	mare	zebu	horse	shoat	bawsin	grison
ure	mice	zobo	hound	shott	bawson	grivet
wat	mico	zuna	hutia	shrew	bayard	guemal
yak	mink		hyena	simia	beagle	guenon
zho	moco	**5**	hyrax	skunk	beaver	hacker
zo	mohr		indri	sloth	beeves	halfer
	moke	addax	inuus	sorel	bobcat	hangul
	mole	aguti	izard	sorex	boomer	heifer
4	mule	alces	jocko	spade	bovine	hircus
	mona	ammon	jumbo	spado	bronco	hogget
alce	musk	ariel	kaama	spitz	brumby	howler
anoa	napu	arnee	kalan	staig	burhel	hybrid
Arab	neat	baloo	kevel	steed	cabrie	impala
atoc	nout	beast	koala	steer	cabrit	inyala
atok	nowt	bhyle	kulan	stirk	castor	jackal
axis	oont	bidet	kyloe	stoat	catalo	jaguar
baln	oryx	biped	lemur	swine	cattle	jennet
barb	oxen	bison	llama	tabby	cayman	jerboa
bear	paca	bitch	loris	talpa	cayuse	Jersey
boar	paco	bongo	magot	tapir	cervus	jument
buck	pala	brach	major	tatou	chacma	kalong
bull	pard	brock	manis	taxel	chetah	kelpie
cain	peba	bruin	manul	tayra	coaita	keltie
calf	pika	bunny	maral	tiger	cocker	kennet
cavy	poka	burro	meles	tigon	colugo	kitten
colt	pony	camel	mhorr	tucan	cosset	koodoo
cony	prad	caple	moose	urial	cougar	kyloes
coon	pudu	capra	morse	urson	coyote	langur
dant	puma	capul	mount	ursus	craber	lapdog
dauw	quey	chiru	mouse	vison	cuscus	lechwe
deer	rane	civet	nagor	vixen	dassie	lionel
dieb	reem	coati	nandu	waler	desman	malkin
dogy	roan	coney	nyala	whale	dickey	malmag
dood	runt	coypu	okapi	whelp	dik-dik	mammal
douc	rusa	crone	oribi	yapok	dobbin	margay
euro	saki	cuddy	otary	zebra	dogape	marmot
eyra	seal	daman	otter	zerda	dog fox	marten
fawn	seeg	dhole	ounce	zibet	donkey	mataco
foal	shou	dingo	panda	zizel	dragon	mawkin
gaur	skug	dipus	pekan	zoril	dzeren	merino
girl	sore	dogie	phoca	zorra	dzeron	messin
goat	stag	drill	pinto	zorro	entire	monkey
gyal	stot	dsomo	pongo		ermine	morkin
hack	stud	eland	potto		farrow	musk ox
hare	suni	equus	poyou	**6**	fennec	musmon
hart	tahr	fauna	punch		ferret	mustac
hind	tait	felis	puppy	agouti	fisher	nahoor
ibex	tegg	filly	quoll	aliped	foussa	nilgai
jade	tehr		ranny	alpaca	fox bat	nilgau

ocelot	tomcat	chincha	macacus	sapajou	anteater	kolinsky
onager	tupala	clumber	macaque	sapling	antelope	lamantin
oorial	tusker	colobus	madoqua	sassaby	babirusa	lamentin
ourebi	urchin	courser	mammoth	sciurus	Bactrian	landrace
ovibos	vermin	dasypod	manatee	scorpio	bathorse	macropus
padnag	vervet	dasypus	mangaby	sea-bear	behemoth	mammalia
pallah	vicuna	dasyure	Manx cat	sea-calf	black fox	mandrill
panter	walrus	dinmont	maracan	sea-lion	black rat	mangabey
poodle	wapiti	dolphin	marikin	serpent	bontebok	mantiger
porker	warine	draft-ox	mariput	sheltie	brant fox	marmoset
possum	weanel	eanling	markhor	siamang	brown rat	mastodon
pownie	weasel	Echidna	marmose	Siamese	bull-calf	meriones
pugdog	weeper	echimyd	megamys	silenus	bushbaby	maverick
pygarg	wether	echinus	meerkat	soliped	bushbuck	milch-cow
python	wivern	epizoan	minever	sondeli	cachalot	mongoose
quagga	wombat	epizoon	miniver	sounder	cacholot	moufflon
quokka	wow-wow	ermelin	mole-rat	souslik	capuchin	musk deer
rabbit	wyvern	fatling	mongrel	spaniel	capucine	musquash
racoon	yapock	finback	monture	spanker	capybara	noctilio
red fox		fitchet	morling	spitter	carcajou	ouistiti
reebok		fitchew	mormops	stembok	cariacou	packmule
renard	**7**	foumart	moschus	sumpter	cavebear	palebuck
rhebok		fur seal	mouflon	sunbear	cavicorn	pangolin
rhesus	acouchy	galla ox	muglamb	tadpole	chimaera	physeter
ridgil	ant-bear	gazelle	muntjak	tamanoa	chipmuck	platypus
roarer	assapan	gelding	musiman	tamarin	chipmunk	polliwig
rodent	aurochs	gemsbok	musk rat	tarsier	civet-cat	pollywog
ronion	banting	genette	mustang	tatouay	coachdog	polo pony
rouncy	bearcat	gerenuk	mustela	terrier	colocola	porkling
sagoin	bettong	giraffe	mycetes	testudo	cotswold	porpoise
saguin	bighorn	glutton	mycetis	thiller	creodont	red panda
sambar	blesbok	gorilla	mylodon	tigress	cricetus	reedbuck
sambur	blue cat	grampus	narwhal	toxodon	cunjevoi	reindeer
sarlac	bonasus	griffin	nasalis	trotter	demi-wolf	riverhog
sarlyk	boshbop	griffon	noctule	twinter	dinosaur	Rodentia
sea-ape	Bovidae	grizzly	nylghau	unicorn	dormouse	ruminant
sea cow	brawner	guanaco	opossum	urocyon	duckbill	schimmel
serval	brocket	hackney	palfrey	urodele	duckmole	sea-otter
setter	broncho	halfape	panther	vampire	earthhog	serotine
shammy	bubalis	hamster	pardale	vansire	Echippus	sewelled
sheass	buffalo	harrier	peccary	vicuana	elephant	sewer-rat
shelty	bulchin	huanaco	polecat	viverra	entellus	shorling
sorrel	bulldog	hystrix	potoroo	voengra	filander	sika deer
sphinx	bullock	jacchus	prancer	wallaby	foxhound	sirenian
sponge	burmese	jackass	pricket	wart-hog	galloway	springer
suslik	bushcat	jumbuck	primate	wheeler	gin-horse	squirrel
taguan	bush pig	karagan	procyon	wild ass	grysbock	staggard
tajacu	caracal	keitloa	pterope	wild cat	Guernsey	stallion
talbot	caribou	kidling	raccoon	wild dog	hairseal	steambok
taurec	cattalo	klipdas	red deer	wistiti	hartbeer	stinkard
tapeti	cervine	lagomys	reed rat	wolf-dog	hedgehog	suilline
tarand	cetacea	lambkin	rietbok	zamouse	hedgepig	suricate
tarpan	chamois	lemming	roe buck	zorille	hoggerel	surmulot
taurec	charger	leopard	rock doe		hog steer	tabby-cat
taurus	cheetah	leveret	roe deer		hylobate	talapoin
teledu	cheslip	libbard	rorqual	**8**	indigene	teguexin
tenrec	cheviot	linsang	sagouin		kangaroo	terrapin
thamin	chikari	lioness	saimiri	aardvark	kinkajou	tetrapod
theave	chimera	lurcher	sambhur	aardwolf	kiwikiwi	tiger cat

tortoise
treefrog
twinling
ungulata
viscacha
wallaroo
wanderoo
war-horse
warrigal
water-hog
water-rat
weanling
wild boar
wild goat
yeanling
yearling

9

adelopode
alligator
amphioxus
amphipoda
Angola cat
annellata
anthobian
arctic fox
armadillo
babacoote
babyrussa
bandicoot
barbastel
batrachia
bay-duiker
bezantler
binturong
black bear
black buck
blue whale
brood-mare
brown bear
buckhound
canpagnol
carnivore
carpincho
cart-horse
catamount
chameleon
chickadee
chickaree
coalmouse
colemouse
commensal
dachshund
deermouse
delundung
dicotyles
didelphys

dinoceras
draught-ox
dray-horse
dromedary
dziggetai
eared seal
flying fox
glyptodon
greyhound
grimalkin
ground-hog
gruntling
guineapig
honey-bear
ichneumon
lagomorph
leviathan
livestock
malt-horse
marsupial
megalonyx
monoceros
monotreme
mousedeer
orang-utan
pachyderm
pack-horse
pademelon
padymelon
percheron
petaurist
phalanger
pipistrel
polar bear
porcupine
post-horse
predacean
prong-buck
prong-horn
quadruman
quadruped
racehorse
razorbuck
rearmouse
reermouse
reremouse
retriever
rosmarine
shearling
shoreling
shorthorn
shrew-mole
silver fox
sitatunga
southdown
spatangus
springbok
steerling
steinbock

stonebuck
stud-horse
tchneuman
thylacine
todlowrie
tragelaph
tree hyrax
tree shrew
trematode
trematoid
waterbuck
watermole
watervole
white bear
wild horse
wolverene
wolverine
woodchuck
woodshock
youngling
zoophagon

10

amorphozoa
amphibials
angora goat
angwantibo
animalcule
anthropoid
articulata
babiroussa
barasingha
Barbary ape
birch mouse
bloodhound
bottlenose
buckjumper
camelopard
cardophagi
catarrhine
chevrotain
chimpanzee
chinchilla
chiroptera
chittagong
chousingha
clydesdale
coach-horse
coatimondi
cockatrice
cottontail
dachshound
Diphyodont
dolichotis
draft-horse
fallow deer
fieldmouse

fistulidae
giant panda
halmaturus
hartebeest
hippogriff
hippogryff
housemouse
human-being
Kodiak bear
Malay tapir
marsupials
monotremes
muscardine
musk beaver
natterjack
paddymelon
pantheress
paradoxure
Persian cat
pichiciago
pilot whale
pine marten
prairie dog
pygmy shrew
quadricorn
quadrumana
raccoon dog
rhinoceros
right whale
river horse
rock badger
rock rabbit
ruminantia
saki monkey
scavernick
sea-leopard
sea-unicorn
shrew-mouse
sperm whale
springhaas
starveling
Thecodonts
vampire bat
wildebeest

11

American elk
anoplothere
barbastelle
black cattle
blood-sucker
branchireme
brown hyena
bullterrier
chlamyphore
digitigrade
douroucouli

entomophaga
fistulidans
flying lemur
flying mouse
fox squirrel
globigerina
Grevy's zebra
grizzly-bear
horned-horse
insectivora
jumping deer
kangaroo rat
killer whale
Megatherium
mountain cat
orang-outang
pipistrelle
praire wolf
Pterodactyl
red kangaroo
red squirrel
rock wallaby
sea elephant
sleuthhound
snow leopard
tragelaphus
vespertilio
wildebeeste
wishtonwish
woolly lemur

12

anthropoglot
Barbary sheep
Bengal monkey
catamountain
chlamyphorus
chrysochlore
draught-horse
elephant seal
ferae-naturae
flittermouse
grey squirrel
harvest mouse
hippopotamus
horseshoe bat
klipspringer
Megalosaurus
mountain hare
mountain lion
pachydermata
Paleotherium
pouched mouse
rhesus monkey
rock squirrel
scheltopusik
Shetland pony

Simmenthaler
spider monkey
spotted hyena
striped hyena
tree kangaroo
water opossum
water spaniel
woolly monkey

13

Abyssinian cat
Anoplotherium
Australian cat
Bactrian camel
bearded lizard
carriage horse

Chapman's zebra
Cheirotherium
chinchilla cat
European bison
galeopithecus
golden hamster
hermaphrodite
Indian buffalo
laughing hyena
mountain zebra
Parry's wallaby
polyprotodont
ring-tail coati
sable antelope
semnopithecus
shorthorn bull
solidungulate
spiny anteater

Tasmanian wolf
tree porcupine

14

Australian bear
bridled wallaby
Burchell's zebra
crab-eating seal
dormouse-possum
flying squirrel
ground squirrel
Indian elephant
Indian pangolin
Isabelline bear
laughing hyaena
marmoset monkey

Patagonian cavy
snoeshoe rabbit
Tasmanian devil

15

African elephant
American buffalo
Barber Leicester
Bennett's wallaby
flying phalanger
rabbit bandicoot
sabretooth tiger
Tasmanian possum
Thomson's gazelle

Birds

2 AND 3

auk
cob
daw
emu
fop
fum
hen
jay
ka
kae
kea
kia
mew
moa
owl
pen
pie
poe
ree
roc
ruc
tit
tui

4

alca
anas
arco
aves
barb

baya
bird
bubo
chat
cock
coot
crax
crow
dodo
dove
duck
dupe
erne
eyas
fowl
fung
gawk
gier
guan
gull
hawk
hern
huia
huma
ibis
iunx
kaka
kite
kiwi
knot
koel
kora
kuku
lark

loom
loon
lory
mina
myna
naff
nene
nias
nyas
otis
pauw
pavo
pern
pica
piet
poll
pope
pout
rail
rhea
rixy
roch
rock
rook
ruff
rukh
runt
rype
shag
skua
smee
smew
sora
sord

sore
spot
swan
taha
teal
tern
tody
wavy
wren
xema
yaup
yite
yunx
zati

5

agami
ajuru
amsel
amzel
ardea
ariel
biddy
bongo
booby
bowet
brant
bucco
capon
chick
chirm
claik

colin
crake
crane
creak
daker
didus
diver
drake
dunny
eagle
egret
eider
finch
galah
ganza
geese
glede
goose
goura
grebe
gripe
harpy
heron
hobby
jager
junco
larus
lowan
lyrie
macaw
madge
maneh
mavis
merle

minah
miner
monal
murre
mynah
nandu
noddy
ornis
ortyx
ousel
ouzel
owlet
pewet
pewit
picus
pipit
pitta
poaka
poult
purre
quail
radge
raven
reeve
robin
rodge
sacre
saker
sally
sasia
saury
scape
scarf
scaup

scops
scray
senex
serin
shama
sitta
skite
snipe
solan
soree
spink
squab
stare
stilt
stint
stork
strix
swift
tarin
terek
topau
topet
twite
umbre
urubu
veery
virgo
wader
wagel
whaup
wonga

6

aiglet
aigret
alcedo
alcyon
ancona
argala
avocet
avoset
bantam
barbet
bonxie
bowess
brolga
buffel
bulbul
cagmag
canary
chewet
chough
chukar
citril
condor
corbie
corvus
coucal
cuckoo
culver
curlew
cushat
cygnet
cygnus
darter
dipper
drongo
ducker
dunlin
eaglet
einack
elanet
falcon
fulmar
galeen
gambet
gander
gannet
garrot
gentoo
godurt
godwit
gooney
gorhen
goslet
grakle
grouse
hacket
hagden
hammer

hareld
hoazin
hoopoe
hoopoo
howlet
jabiru
jacana
jaeger
jerkin
kakapo
kiddow
lanner
leipoa
linnet
loriot
magpie
marrot
martin
menura
merlin
merops
merula
missel
monaul
mopoke
mot-mot
musket
nandow
nestor
oriole
osprey
oxbird
parrot
paster
pavone
peahen
pecker
peewit
pernis
petrel
pigeon
plover
poulet
pouter
powter
puffin
pullet
pygarg
queest
quelea
racama
ratite
redcap
reeler
roberd
roller
rotche
ruddoc
runner

scamel
scobby
scoter
sea-bar
sea-cob
sea-mew
sea-pie
shrike
shrite
sicsac
simurg
siskin
smeath
strich
strick
sultan
tarsel
tercel
thrush
tirwit
tomtit
toucan
towhee
tringa
trogon
turaco
turbit
Turdus
turkey
turner
turtle
waggel
weaver
wigeon
willet
witwal
woosel
yaffle
ynambu
zivola
zoozoo

7

apteryx
attagas
attagen
awl-bird
babbler
barn owl
bee-bird
bittern
blue-cap
bluetit
buceros
bull-bat
bummalo
bunting

buphaga
bustard
buzzard
cackler
caponet
cariama
carvist
cat-bird
cheeper
chewink
chicken
ciconia
coaltit
cobswan
colibri
columba
corella
cotinga
courlan
courser
cow-bird
creeper
cropper
Cuculus
dorhawk
dorking
dottrel
doucher
dovekie
dovelet
dum-bird
dunnock
egg-bird
emu-wren
fantail
fen duck
fern owl
fig-bird
fin-foot
flusher
gadwall
gavilan
gobbler
gorcock
gorcrow
goshawk
gosling
grackle
grallae
greyhen
greylag
griffin
haggard
halcyon
harfang
harrier
hawk owl
hen-harm
hickway

hoatzin
horn owl
ice-bird
impeyan
jacamar
jackass
jackdaw
jacksaw
jacobin
jashawk
jedcock
kamichi
kestrel
killdee
kinglet
lagopus
lapwing
lavrock
Leghorn
lentner
lich-owl
limpkin
lorilet
mallard
manakin
manikin
marabou
maracan
martlet
megamys
migrant
modwall
moorhen
motacil
moth-owl
mudlark
muggent
ortolan
oscines
ostrich
oven-tit
pandion
partlet
peacock
peafowl
pelican
penguin
percher
peterel
phaeton
phoenix
pinnock
pintado
pintail
pochard
poe-bird
poultry
puttock
quabird

quetzel
raddock
rantock
redhead
redpoll
redwing
robinet
rooster
rosella
rotchie
ruddock
sakeret
sawbill
scammel
scooper
sea-crow
sea-duck
sea-fowl
seagull
sea-hawk
senegal
seriema
serinus
shirley
simargh
sirgang
skimmer
skylark
snow-owl
spadger
sparrow
squacco
staniel
stannel
stanyel
stumpie
sturnus
sunbird
swallow
swimmer
tadorna
tanager
tarrock
tattler
tiercel
tinamou
tinamus
titlark
titling
titmice
touraco
tree tit
trochil
tumbler
turakoo
vulture
vulturn
wagtail
wapacut

warbler
waxbill
waxwing
weebill
whooper
widgeon
wimbrel
witlock
witwall
wood owl
wrybill
wryneck
yeldrin

8

aasvogel
accentor
adjutant
aigrette
alcatras
amadavat
arapunga
avadavit
barnacle
beam-bird
becafico
bee-eater
bell-bird
blackcap
bluebird
blue-wren
boat-bill
boat-tail
bobolink
bob-white
bockelet
bockeret
brancher
brevipen
bush chat
bush lark
calandra
calangay
caneroma
caracara
cardinal
cargoose
cheewink
clot-bird
cockatoo
cockerel
coquimbo
corn bird
curassow
cursores
cutwater
dabchick

daker-hen
dandy-hen
didapper
dinornis
dipchick
dorr-hawk
dotterel
duck-hawk
duckling
dun-diver
eagle-owl
estridge
fauvette
fig-eater
finnikin
firetail
fish-hawk
flamingo
gairfowl
gamecock
gang-gang
garefowl
garganey
great tit
greenlet
grey teal
grosbeak
guachero
hackbolt
hamburgh
hawkfinch
hazel-hen
hemipode
hernshaw
hickwall
hornbill
hula-bird
keskidee
killdeer
kingbird
landrail
langshan
lanneret
laverock
lorikeet
love-bird
lyrebird
mandarin
marabout
marsh tit
megapode
mina bird
mire crow
mire drum
moorcock
moorfowl
moorgame
morillon
musk duck

mute swan
mynabird
nestling
nightjar
notornis
nuthatch
oldsquaw
paitrick
parakeet
paroquet
peachick
petchary
percolin
pheasant
plungeon
podargus
popinjay
prunella
puff-bird
redshank
redstart
ricebird
ring dove
ring-tail
rock dove
sagecock
sandpeep
screamer
scrub-tit
sea-eagle
shelduck
shoebill
shoveler
sittella
skuagull
snowbird
snowy owl
songbird
songlark
songster
starling
struthio
swamphen
tanagers
tantalus
tawny owl
terntero
thrasher
thresher
throstle
titmouse
tomnoddy
tragopan
tuke-nose
umbrette
waterhen
wheatear
whimbrel
whinchat

whip-bird
whistler
white-ear
white-eye
wildfowl
woodchat
woodcock
wood duck
woodlark
xanthura
yeldring
yeldrock
yoldring
zopilote

9

aepyornis
accipiter
albatross
andorinha
ant-thrush
autophagi
baltimore
bean goose
beccafico
beefeater
bell-minah
bergander
birgander
blackbird
black cock
black duck
black swan
blacktail
black tern
blue crane
bottletit
bower-bird
brambling
broadbill
brown hawk
bullfinch
buzzardet
campanero
cassowary
cereopsis
chaffinch
chatterer
chevalier
chickling
church owl
cockatiel
columbine
cormorant
corncrake
crossbill
currawong

dandy-cock
deinornis
dowitcher
eagle-hawk
eider duck
field-duck
fieldfare
field wren
fig parrot
figpecker
firecrest
francolin
French pie
friar-bird
fringilla
frogmouth
gallinazo
gallinule
gerfalcon
gier-eagle
glaucopis
goldcrest
golden-eye
goldfinch
goldspink
goosander
grassbird
grass wren
great skua
grenadier
grey heron
grossbeak
guillemot
guinea-hen
gyrfalcon
hammerkop
heathbird
heathcock
heronshaw
horned owl
Jenny-wren
jerfalcon
kittiwake
lint-white
log-runner
lorrikeet
macartney
mallemuck
mango bird
marshbird
merganser
merulidan
miresnipe
mollymauk
mouse-hawk
mud-sucker
muscicapa
natatores
night hawk

ossifrage
paradisea
paraquito
pardalote
parrakeet
parroquet
partridge
passerine
peregrine
phalarope
pied-goose
pinefinch
ptarmigan
quachilto
razorbill
redbreast
red grouse
rhynchops
rifle-bird
ring-ousel
rosefinch
rossignol
salangale
sandpiper
scratcher
scrub-bird
scrub-fowl
scrub-wren
seaparrot
shearbill
sheldrake
shitepoke
shoveller
shrike-tit
silver-eye
skunk-bird
snake-bird
snow goose
sooty tern
soareagle
sore eagle
spinebill
spoonbill
stick-bird
stilt-bird
stock-dove
stonechat
stone-hawk
storm-bird
strigidae
swamp-hawk
swine-pipe
talegalla
tetraonid
thickhead
thornbill
tiercelet
trochilus
trumpeter

turnstone
waterbird
waterfowl
water-rail
wedgebill
wheat-bird
whiteface
whitetail
widow-bird
wild goose
willow tit
windhover
woodspite
wyandotte

10

aberdevine
ant-catcher
Arctic skua
Arctic tern
bell-magpie
bird of prey
blight-bird
blue-bonnet
blue-breast
blue-throat
boobook owl
brent goose
budgerigar
budgerygah
burrow-duck
butter-bird
butterbump
canary bird
canvas-back
chiffchaff
coddy-moddy
cow-bunting
crested tit
crow-shrike
demoiselle
didunculus
dishwasher
dollar bird
dusky minah
dusky robin
ember goose
eurylaimus
eyas-musket
fallochat
fledgeling
flycatcher
fratercula
goatmilker
goatsucker
goldhammer
gooneybird

grassfinch
greenfinch
greenshank
grey falcon
grey parrot
grey plover
ground dove
ground lark
ground robin
guinea-fowl
gymnocitta
harpy eagle
hen-harrier
honeyeater
honey-guide
hooded crow
jungle-fowl
kingfisher
king parrot
kookaburra
love-parrot
magpie-lark
mallee-fowl
maned-goose
meadow-lark
mutton-bird
night heron
night raven
noisy-minah
nutcracker
parson-bird
peewee-lark
petty-chaps
prairie hen
pratincole
ramphastos
regent-bird
rock parrot
rock pigeon
sagegrouse
salpinctes
sanderling
sandgrouse
sandmartin
sassorolla
screech-owl
sea-swallow
shearwater
silver-gull
solan goose
song shrike
song thrush
summer-duck
tailor-bird
talegallus
tanagridae
tit-warbler
tree-runner
tropic-bird

turkey-cock
turtle dove
water-ousel
wattle-bird
weasel-coat
weaver-bird
whidah-bird
white brant
white egret
white stork
whydah-bird
willow wren
wonga-wonga
woodgrouse
woodpecker
wood-pigeon
wood-shrike
yaffingale
yellow-bird
yellowlegs
zebra finch

11

apostle-bird
banded stilt
barn swallow
black falcon
black martin
bonebreaker
bristle-bird
brush-turkey
bush-creeper
butcher-bird
Canada goose
carrion crow
cattle egret
chanticleer
cochinchina
cock-sparrow
conirostres
corn bunting
Dorking fowl
dragoon-bird
fairy martin
fallow finch
flock pigeon
frigate-bird
fruit-pigeon
gallows-bird
gnat-snapper
golden eagle
grallatores
grey wagtail
harrier-hawk
herring gull
hooded robin
house martin

humming-bird
insectivora
kestrel-hawk
king penguin
king vulture
lammergeier
leatherhead
leptodactyl
lily-trotter
magpie-goose
meadow-pipit
mocking-bird
mulga parrot
Muscovy duck
nightingale
Pacific gull
plain-turkey
powerful-fowl
procellaria
pterodactyl
punchinello
quail-thrush
querguedule
rainbow-bird
reed bunting
reed sparrow
reed warbler
rhamphastos
rock warbler
scarlet ibis
scissor-bill
sea-pheasant
shell-parrot
shrike-robin
singing-bird
snow-bunting
snow-ortolan
soldier-bird
song sparrow
sparrowhawk
stone curlew
stone plover
storm petrel
tree-creeper
tree sparrow
tree swallow
wall-creeper
whitethroat
whooper swan
wood-swallow
wood warbler
yellow robin

12

Adele penguin
adjutant bird
bronze pigeon

burrowing-owl
capercaillie
capercailzie
cardinal-bird
collared dove
crested grebe
cuckoo-shrike
curvirostral
dentirostres
falcon-gentle
fairy penguin
fissirostres
golden oriole
golden plover
grass warbler
ground thrush
harvestgoose
hedge sparrow
honey-buzzard
house sparrow
marsh harrier
marsh warbler
missel-thrush
mistel-thrush
mourning-dove
musophagidae
nutmeg-pigeon
painted quail
pallid-cuckoo
peaceful dove
pink cockatoo
razor-grinder
red-head finch
sage-thrasher
sedge warbler
serpent eater
shrike-thrush
stone-chatter
stone's-mickle
stormy petrel
stubble-goose
stubble-quail
swamp-harrier
tachydromian
tenuirosters
tiger-bittern
turbit-pigeon
turner-pigeon
water-wagtail
wattle turkey
whip-poor-will
white goshawk
yellowhammer

13

Baltimore bird
barnacle goose

black cockatoo
carrier pigeon
coachwhip-bird
crested pigeon
fantail pigeon
long-tailed tit
mistletoe-bird
musk parrakeet
owlet-nightjar
oystercatcher
plain-wanderer
recurviroster
red-wattle bird

rosella parrot
secretary bird
shining parrot
spider-catcher
stink-pheasant
swallow-shrike
tumbler-pigeon
turkey-buzzard
turkey vulture
white cockatoo
willow warbler
yellow bunting
yellow wagtail

14

babbling thrush
bird of paradise
canvas-back duck
diamond sparrow
double-bar finch
golden pheasant
horned screamer
king-lory parrot
Manx shearwater
mountain thrush
nankeen kestrel

prairie-chicken
rhinoceros-bird
robin-redbreast
silver pheasant
spotted harrier
tawny frogmouth
welcome swallow
whistling eagle

Dogs

3 AND 4

chow
cur
lyam
lym
minx
peke
pom
pug
pup
rach
rug
skye
tike
tyke

5

bitch
boxer
brach
cairn
corgi
dhole
dingo
hound
husky
laika
pi-dog
pooch
puppy
spitz
whelp

6

afghan
bandog
barbet
basset
beagle
borzoi
bowwow
canine
cocker
collie
Eskimo
gun-dog
jowler
lap-dog
limmer
pariah
poodle
pug-dog
pye-dog
pyrame
ranger
ratter
saluki
setter
shough
talbot
toy dog

7

basenji
beardie
bird-dog
bulldog
clumber

deer-dog
dry-foot
griffon
harrier
lion-dog
lurcher
mastiff
mongrel
pointer
samoyed
spaniel
starter
tarrier
terrier
tumbler
whippet
wolf-dog

8

Airedale
Alsatian
Blenheim
chow-chow
coach-dog
demi-wolf
Derby dog
Doberman
elkhound
field-dog
foxhound
hound-dog
house dog
keeshond
Labrador
malemute
papillon
Pekinese

St. Hubert
samoyede
sealyham
sheepdog
spitz dog
springer
turnspit
watchdog
water-dog

9

badger dog
boarhound
buckhound
chihuahua
dachshund
Dalmatian
deerhound
Eskimo dog
Great Dane
greyhound
harehound
Kerry blue
limehound
Llewellyn
Molossian
Pekingese
police dog
red setter
retriever
St. Bernard
Schnauzer
staghound
wolfhound
yellow dog

10

Bedlington
bloodhound
Clydesdale
dachshound
elterwater
fox terrier
Iceland dog
Maltese dog
otter hound
Pomeranian
prairie dog
Rottweiler
schipperke
Welsh corgi
Welsh hound

11

Afghan hound
basset hound
Bruxelloise
bull mastiff
bull terrier
carriage dog
Irish setter
Kerry beagle
King Charles
Skye terrier
wishtarwish

12

Belvoir hound
Cairn terrier
Dandy Dinmont

	13	*14* AND *1 5*	Highland terrier (15)
gazelle hound			Irish wolfhound (14)
German collie	Alpine spaniel	Aberdeen terrier (15)	Japanese spaniel (15)
Gordon setter	border terrier	Airedale terrier (15)	Lakeland terrier (15)
Irish spaniel	Boston terrier	American pitbull (15)	Norfolk spaniel (14)
Irish terrier	cocker spaniel	blue Gascon hound (15)	Norfolk springer (15)
Newfoundland	Dandie Dinmont	Brussels griffon (15)	Porcelaine hound (15)
Saint Bernard	English setter	clumber spaniel (14)	Pyrenean mastiff (15)
Saintongeois	French bulldog	Cuban bloodhound (15)	Scottish terrier (15)
shepherd's dog	Scotch terrier	Egyptian bassett (15)	Siberian wolf-dog (15)
water spaniel	southern hound	English springer (15)	springer spaniel (15)
Welsh terrier	Sussex spaniel	German shepherd (14)	Thibetan mastiff (15)
		golden retriever (15)	Tibetan mastiff (14)

Fish, etc.

2 – 4	hag	sei	elops	salmo	alevin	ganoid
	hake	shad	elver	sargo	allice	gardon
amia	huck	snig	fleck	saury	anabas	ginkin
bass	huso	sole	fusus	scrod	angler	goramy
bib	id	tai	gadus	scurf	barbel	gurami
blay	ide	tau	gibel	sepia	beakie	grilse
bley	jack	tope	gummy	sewin	belone	groper
bret	kelt	tuna	guppy	shark	beluga	gunnel
brit	keta	tusk	hilsa	skate	blenny	gurnet
burt	ling	woof	julis	smelt	blower	hermit
cale	lipp	zant	laker	smolt	bonito	hilsah
carp	lob		loach	smout	bounce	hussar
chad	lox		loche	smowt	bowfin	isopod
char	lomp	*5*	maray	snook	braise	jerkin
chub	luce		minim	solen	buckie	keltie
chum	mako	ablen	moray	sprag	burbot	kipper
clam	masu	ablet	morse	sprat	caplin	launce
cod	moki	allis	mugil	sprod	caranx	loligo
coho	mort	angel	muray	squid	cepola	maigre
crab	newt	apode	murry	sudak	cheven	margot
cusk	opah	banny	mysis	sweep	chevin	meagre
dab	orca	beroe	myxon	tench	clupea	medusa
dace	orfe	binny	nacre	toado	cockle	megrim
dar	parr	blain	nurse	togue	comber	milter
dare	peal	bleak	perai	torsk	conger	minnow
dart	pike	bleck	perca	troll	conner	morgay
dorn	pope	bogue	perch	trout	cultch	mud-eel
dory	pout	boops	phoca	tunny	cuttle	mullet
eel	quab	bream	piper	twait	dagoba	mussel
eft	raun	brill	pogge	umber	dentex	narwal
elva	ray	charr	porgy	whelk	diodon	nereid
esox	roe	cisco	poulp	whiff	doctor	otaria
fash	rudd	cobia	powan	witch	Dorado	oyster
file	ruff	cohoe	prawn		dugong	partan
fin	sapo	cuddy	reeve		dun-cow	pholas
gar	sar	cudle	roach		ellops	plaice
ged	scad	danio	roker	*6*	espada	pollan
goby	scar	doree	ruffe		finnan	porgie
grig	scup	dorse	saith	alburn	gadoid	poulpe

puffer	ulican	fin-back	pollard	**8**	hair-tail
puller	urchin	fin-fish	pollock		halicore
quahog	vendis	finnock	polypus	acalepha	hand-fish
redcap	wapper	garfish	pomfret	albacore	horn-beak
red-cod	weever	garpike	quinnet	albicore	horn-fish
red-eye	whaler	garvock	rat-tail	ammodyte	jentling
remora	winkle	girrock	red-fish	anableps	John Dory
robalo	wirrah	gladius	reef-eel	anguilla	jugulars
rochet	wrasse	goldney	ripsack	arapaima	kelp-fish
romero	zander	gourami	rock-cod	arapunga	king crab
roughy	zeidae	gournet	ronchil	argonaut	king-fish
ruffin	zingel	grampus	ronquil	asterias	lady-fish
runner		grouper	rorqual	band-fish	lancelet
sabalo		grundel	rotifer	barnacle	land crab
sadina	**7**	grunter	sand-eel	bill fish	lump-fish
saithe		gudgeon	sardine	blue fish	lung-fish
salmon	abalone	gurnard	sawfish	boarfish	mackerel
samlet	acaleph	gwiniad	scallop	buckling	malarmat
sander	actinia	gwyniad	schelly	bullhead	melanure
sardel	ale-wife	haddock	scomber	cachalot	menhaden
sargus	anchovy	hagbolt	sculpin	cackerel	monkfish
sauger	asterid	haireel	sea-bass	calamory	moon-fish
saurel	batfish	halibut	sea-bear	cetacean	moray eel
saynay	bergylt	herling	sea-calf	chimaera	mormyrus
scampi	bloater	herring	sea-fish	coalfish	nannygai
scarus	blue-cap	homelyn	sea-hare	corkwing	numbfish
scurff	blue-eye	houting	sea-lion	corystes	ophidion
sea-ape	bocking	jewfish	sea-pike	crawfish	pennydog
sea-bat	bonetta	keeling	sea-slug	crayfish	phinnock
sea-cat	box-fish	lampern	sea-wolf	dapedium	physalia
sea-cow	brassie	lamprey	shadine	dapedius	physeter
sea-dog	bubbler	latchet	sillock	dealfish	pickerel
sea-eel	bummalo	lobster	silurus	dragonet	pigmy-eel
sea-egg	calamar	long-tom	skegger	drum-fish	pilchard
sea-fox	capelin	mahseer	smerlin	eagle-ray	pipe-fish
sea-hog	cat-fish	manatee	snapper	earshell	piraruck
sea-owl	catodon	manchet	sock-eye	errantes	polyneme
sea-pad	cetacea	merling	spawner	eulachon	Poor John
sea-pig	chimera	monodon	sphyrna	exocetus	porpoise
sephen	cichlid	moon-eye	squalus	file-fish	raft-fish
shanny	cidaris	morwong	sterlet	fin-scale	redbelly
shiner	cod-fish	mud-fish	stripey	fire-fish	red perch
shrimp	codling	muraena	sun-fish	flagtail	rhizopod
snacol	copepod	murexes	thwaite	flatfish	rock-bass
soosoo	cow-fish	murices	tiddler	flathead	rock-cale
sparid	crabite	narwhal	top-knot	flounder	rock-fish
sucker	croaker	nautili	torgoch	forktail	rockling
tailor	crucian	oar-fish	torpedo	fox-shark	roncador
tarpon	crusien	octopod	tub-fish	frog-fish	sail-fish
tarpum	cyprine	octopus	ulichon	gillaroo	salt-fish
tautog	dog-fish	old-wife	umbrine	gilt-head	sand-fish
tawtog	dolphin	osseter	vendace	glass-eel	sardelle
teredo	drummer	pandore	whiting	goatfish	saw-shark
tiburo	dun-fish	pegasus	worm-eel	goldfish	scopelus
tomcord	echinus	pen-fish	xippias	graining	sea-acorn
trygon	eel-fare	piddock		grayling	sea-devil
turbit	eel-pout	pig-fish		green eel	sea-horse
turbot	escolar	pointer		grub-fish	sea-lemon
twaite	fiddler	pollack		gymnotus	sea-louse

212

sea-perch
sea robin
sea snipe
shore-eel
siskiwit
skipjack
snake-eel
sparling
spelding
speldrin
speldron
spirling
springer
spurling
starfish
sting-ray
sturgeon
sun-bream
surf-fish
tarwhine
teraglin
testacea
thornbut
thrasher
thresher
toad-fish
trevally
troutlet
tusk-fish
water-fox
weed-fish
wolf-fish
zoophyte

9

acalephae
acipenser
angel-fish
Argentine
ascidians
asteroida
barracuda
blackfish
black sole
blue nurse
blue shark
blue sprat
bony bream
brandling
bulltrout
bummaloti
calamarys
ceratodus
chaetodon
cling-fish
cole-perch
conger eel

coral fish
coryphene
cover-clip
crampfish
crustacea
devil fish
dimyarian
dolphinet
echinidan
engraulis
finny-scad
fire-flair
fish-louse
fish-royal
fortesque
frost-fish
globe-fish
goldsinny
golomynka
grenadier
grey nurse
hard-belly
hardyhead
hippodame
houndfish
hybodonts
jaculator
jellyfish
John Dorée
jollytail
kingstone
lampshell
mango fish
menominee
murray cod
ostracian
pilot fish
porbeagle
pyllopodo
razor fish
red mullet
river crab
roundhead
sand-lance
saury-pike
schnapper
sea-mullet
sea-needle
sea-nettle
sea-spirit
sea-urchin
sheat-fish
silver-eel
spear-fish
stargazer
stingaree
sting-fish
stink-fish
stockfish

stomapoda
suctorian
surmullet
sweetlips
swordfish
thorn-back
threadfin
tiffenbat
tittlebat
troutling
trumpeter
trunk fish
tunny fish
whitebait
whitefish
wobbegong

10

acornshell
amblyopsis
amphytrite
angel-shark
angler fish
archerfish
banstickle
barracoota
barracouta
basket fish
black bream
black whale
blind shark
blue groper
blue puller
bottle-fish
bottle-nose
brown trout
butterfly
canolefish
cestracion
clouded eel
clypeaster
cock-paddle
coelacanth
cowanyoung
ctenoidans
cuttlefish
demoiselle
dragon-fish
echinoderm
fiddle-fish
fingerling
fistularia
flute-mouth
flying fish
ganoidians
garter fish
ghost-shark

giant toado
goblin-fish
great skate
grey mullet
groundling
hammerfish
hammerhead
hermit crab
holothuria
horseleech
knight-fish
loggerhead
lumpsucker
maskanonge
maskinonge
mirror dory
morris pike
Moses perch
parrot-fish
pearl perch
periwinkle
pigmy perch
purplefish
pycnodonts
rapier fish
red gurnard
red morwong
red rockcod
ribbon-fish
ribbon worm
robbercrab
rudder-fish
Samsonfish
sand-hopper
sand-mullet
sandy sprat
scopelidae
sea-garfish
sea-leopard
sea poacher
sea-unicorn
silver dory
silverfish
silverside
square-tail
squeteague
sturionian
sucker-fish
tailor-fish
tassel-fish
tiger shark
tongue-sole
triple-tail
turret-fish
velvet-fish
weaver-fish
whale-shark
white shark
yellow-tail

zebra shark

11

balance-fish
banded toado
bellows-fish
black-angler
blue-pointer
bridled goby
brineshrimp
brown-groper
brown-puller
calling-crab
carpet-shark
carp-gudgeon
chanda perch
chondrostei
common skate
common toado
crested goby
cycloidians
electric eel
electric ray
finner-whale
five-fingers
flying squid
golden perch
green turtle
gurnet perch
herring-cale
hippocampus
holothurian
jackass-fish
javelin-fish
Jumping-Joey
kingsnapper
leatherskin
leopard-fish
lepidosiren
little tunny
man-o'-war fish
Moorish idol
orange perch
papersailor
peacock-fish
peacock-sole
pearl mussel
pearl oyster
pennant-fish
prickleback
pterichthys
rainbow-fish
red bullseye
red fire-fish
rock-whiting
salmon-trout
sand-whiting

school-shark
scleroderms
sea-cucumber
sea-elephant
sea-hedgehog
sea-scorpion
serpentfish
silver-belly
silver perch
silver toado
smooth toado
soldier-crab
soldier-fish
starry toado
stickleback
stonelifter
suckingfish
surgeon-fish
swallow-fish
tallegalane
trumpet-fish
wheelanimal
whistle-fish
wolf-herring

12

basking shark
black drummer
black rock-cod
blue trevally
coachwhip ray
cucumber-fish
dipterygians
dusky morwong
fan-tailed ray
fatherlasher
fighting-fish
forehead-fish
gargoyle-fish
giant herring
gray tusk-fish
oyster-blenny
painted saury
piked dog-fish
plectognathi
Plesiosaurus
rainbow-trout
rat-tailed ray
river garfish
rock flathead
scarlet bream
seaporcupine
sentinel crab
silver mullet
smooth angler
Stout Long-Tom

213

13

allports perch
banded-pigfish
barred-garfish
Barred Long-Tom
black king-fish
black-trevally
branchiostoma
climbing perch
dactylopterus
dusky flathead
entomostracan
findon-haddock
finnan-haddock
flying gurnard
giant boar-fish
horse-mackerel
leafy seahorse
leatherjacket
long-finned eel
magpie-morwong
marbled angler
mountain-trout
ox-eyed herring

paper nautilus
porcupine-fish
Red-Indian fish
salmon catfish
salt-water fish
sandpaper-fish
scarlet angler
Sergeant Baker
silver batfish
silver drummer
snub-nosed dart
southern tunny
spiny flathead
spiny seahorse
striped angler
thresher-shark
tiger-flathead

14

banded sea-perch
black stingaree
branchiostegan
brown-sweetlips
butterfly-bream

enaliosaurians
estuary cat-fish
Greenland-shark
Greenland-whale
king barracouta
king parrot-fish
little numbfish
Macquarie perch
many-banded sole
marine annelida
one-finned shark
painted gurnard
purple sea-perch
red gurnet-perch
river blackfish
short-finned eel
shovel-nosed ray
Slender Long-Tom
smooth flathead
spotted whiting
striped catfish
striped gudgeon
striped sea-pike
white horse-fish

15

acanthopterygii
Australian perch
Australian smelt
beaked coral-fish
bottle-nose shark
common stingaree
crusted flounder
crusted weed-fish
edriophthalmata
frigate mackerel
hairback herring
little cling-fish
little conger eel
long-finned perch
marbled flathead
painted dragonet
short sucker-fish
small-headed sole
smooth stingaree
spangled grunter
Spanish mackerel
spotted cat-shark
spotted eagle-ray
spotted pipe-fish
white-spotted ray

Fossils, shells, etc.
(f.s.) = fossil shell (s.) = shell

4 AND 5

amber
auger
baler
chama (s.)
chank (s.)
conch (s.)
cone (s.)
donax (s.)
drill (s.)
galea
gaper (s.)
murex (s.)
nacre
ormer
peuce
razor (s.)
snail (s.)
tooth (s.)
tulip (s.)
Venus (s.)
whelk (s.)

6

bonnet (s.)
buckie (s.)
chiton (s.)
cockle (s.)
cowrie
crinoid
fornix (s.)
helmet (s.)
jingle (s.)
limpet (s.)
macoma (s.)
matrix
mussel (s.)
natica (s.)
nerite (s.)
Ogygia
olenus
oyster (s.)
quahog (s.)
seaear
tellin (s.)
triton (s.)
trivea (s.)

turban (s.)
volute (s.)
winkle (s.)

7

abalone (s.)
artemis (s.)
astarte (s.)
Babylon
crabite
crinoid
discoid (s.)
fungite
muscite
neptune (s.)
ovulite
piddock (s.)
scallop (s.)
zoolite

8

ammonite (f.s.)
argonaut (s.)
ark shell (s.)
balanite
buccinum (s.)
capstone
ceratite
choanite
cololite
conchite (f.s.)
dendrite
dog whelk (s.)
ear shell (s.)
echinite
epiornis
escallop (s.)
favosite
fig shell (s.)
galerite
janthina (s.)
mangelia (s.)
muricite
mytilite

nautilus (s.)
penshell (s.)
phyllite
ram's horn (f.s.)
retinite
scaphite (f.s.)
seashell
sea snail
solenite (f.s.)
strombus (s.)
testacel (s.)
topshell (s.)
trochite
tunshell (s.)
volulite (f.s.)
volutite (f.s.)

9

aepiornis
alasmodon (s.)
alcyonite
belemnite
buccinite (f.s.)

cancerite
carpolite
clam shell (s.)
comb shell (s.)
cone shell (s.)
Conularia
copralite
corallite
crow stone
dicynodon
encrinite
fan mussel (s.)
file shell (s.)
foot shell (s.)
frog shell (s.)
giant clam (s.)
harp shell (s.)
hippurite
horn shell (s.)
lima shell (s.)
lithocarp
lithophyl
marsupite
miliolite (f.s.)
moon shell ⎱ (s.)
moon snail ⎰
muscalite (f.s.)
nautilite
nummulite
ostracite (f.s.)
palmacite
patellite (f.s.)
polymorphe (s.)
reliquiae
rock-borer (s.)
serpulite (f.s.)
slip shell (s.)

star shell (s.)
stone lily
strombite (f.s.)
tellinite (f.s.)
trilobite
turbinite (f.s.)
turrilite (f.s.)
tusk shell (s.)

10

agate shell
batrachite
canoe shell (s.)
confervite
dendrolite
entomolite
entrochite
euomphalus (f.s.)
gyrogonite
odontolite
palmacites
periwinkle (s.)
razor shell (s.)
screw shell (s.)
snake stone (f.s.)
tiger shell (s.)
tubiporite
ulodendron
wentletrap (s.)
wing oyster (s.)
xanthidium

11

asterialite
asterolepis
basket shell (s.)
carpet shell (s.)
cetotolites
cheirolepis
dinotherium
fairy stones
finger shell (s.)
finger stone
furrowshell (s.)
gongiatites (f.s.)
helmet shell (s.)
ichthyolite
madreporite
margin shell
milleporite
mohair shell (s.)
needle shell ⎱ (s.)
needle whelk ⎰
ornitholite
oyster drill (s.)
rhyncholite
sting winkle (s.)
strobolites
sunset shell (s.)
tiger cowrie (s.)
trough shell (s.)
turtle shell (s.)

12

amphibiolite
brocade shell (s.)

Chinama's hat (s.)
cornu-ammonis (f.s.)
deinotherium
figured stone
holoptychis
Hungarian cap (s.)
lantern shell (s.)
macrotherium
megalichthys
pandora shell (s.)
pelican's foot (s.)
pentacrinite
saddle oyster (s.)
serpentstone
slipper shell (s.)
spindle shell (s.)
sundial shell (s.)
trumpet shell (s.)
zamiostrobus

13 AND 14

bothrodendron (13)
carboniferous (13)
conchyliaceous (f.s.) (14)
dolichosaurus (13)
lepidodendron (13)
lithoglyphite (13)
nacreous shells (s.) (14)
necklace shell (s.) (13)
palaeontology (13)
porphyry shell (s.) (13)
staircase shell (s.) (14)
syringodendron (14)
woodcock shell (s.) (13)

Insects, etc.

3 AND 4

ant
bee
bot
boud
bug
cleg
cob
dart
dor
flea
fly
frit
gnat

goat
grig
grub
lema
lice
mawk
mida
mite
moth
nit
pium
pug
pupa
puss
puxi

slug
sow
tant
tau
tick
wasp
worm
zimb

5

acera
aphid
aphis

atlas
borer
brize
cimex
comma
culex
drake
drone
egger
emmet
eruca
fluke
imago
julus
larva

limax
louse
midge
musca
ox-fly
pulex
satyr
sauba
snail
splex
tinea
vespa

6

acarid
acarus
ant cow
aphids
aptera
ash-fly
bedbug
bee fly
beetle
blatta
botfly
breese
breeze

burnet
buzzer
caddis
chafer
chegre
chigoe
chigre
chinch
cicada
cicala
cimbex
cimiss
coccus
cocoon
crabro

cynips
dayfly
diurna
dog-bee
dog-fly
dorfly
earwig
elater
epeira
eupoda
evania
gadfly
hop-fly
hopper
hornet
jigger
lappet
larvae
locust
maggot
mantis
maybug
may-fly
midget
motuca
mutuca
mygale
saw-fly
scarab
sow-bug
sphinx
spider
squill
termes
Thecla
Thrips
tipula
tsetse
veneer
weevil
woubit

7

acerans
agrilus
annelid
antenna
ant-hill
ant-lion
aphides
athalia
bean fly
beehive
bee moth
blowfly
boat fly
bruchus

bull-bee
bull fly
carabus
cestoid
cheslip
coronet
crambus
cricket
culicid
cyclica
daphnia
deer-fly
diopsis
diptera
duck-ant
epeirid
epizoon
fig gnat
firefly
fish fly
frogfly
fulgora
gallfly
globard
grayfly
gum moth
hexapod
hine-bee
horn-bug
hornfly
June bug
katydid
lady-cow
lampfly
lobworm
lugworm
lycaena
mawworm
microbe
papilio
path fly
pismire
puceron
pug moth
rose-bug
rotifer
salamis
sand fly
sawback
shad fly
skipper
snowfly
stylops
termite
tin-worm
tortrix
Vanessa
wasp-fly
wax-moth

wood-ant

8

acaridan
adder-fly
antennae
arachnid
attercop
black ant
black-fly
bookworm
braconid
bullhead
calandra
calandre
calomela
case-moth
case-worm
cerambyx
chelifer
cocktail
Colorado
corn-moth
crane-fly
dog-louse
drake-fly
drone-bee
drone-fly
dybiscus
ephemera
erotylus
erycinia
ettercap
flatworm
flesh-fly
fossores
fruit-fly
gall-gnat
gall-wasp
gammarus
glow worm
goat-moth
green-fly
hawk-moth
honey-bee
horse-bot
horse-fly
house-fly
Isoptera
itchmite
lace-lerp
ladybird
leaf-moth
lecanium
longhorn
mealy-bug
milleped

mosquito
mucivora
multiped
myriapod
natantes
night-fly
nocturna
parasite
paropsis
pedipalp
phyllium
pupipara
puss moth
queen ant
queen-bee
rotifera
sand-flea
sand-wasp
scolytus
scorpion
shipworm
sparkler
stone-fly
tapeworm
tenebrio
tetrapod
tung-tung
water-bug
water-fly
wheat-fly
whirlwig
white ant
white fly
wireworm
woodlice
wood-mite
wood-moth

9

Amazon act
anopheles
aphid pest
arachnida
book louse
breezefly
brimstone
bumble-bee
burrel-fly
butterfly
buzzardet
caddis fly
canker-fly
cedar-moth
centipede
cheesefly
chrysalis
churrworm

cicindela
clavicorn
cochineal
cockroach
coffeebug
coleopter
corn-aphis
corn borer
crab-louse
cynipides
dermestes
dipterans
dorbeetle
dragon-fly
driver-ant
dumbledor
earthworm
eggar-moth
egger-moth
eumenidae
fig-psylla
flying-ant
forest-fly
forficula
gall-midge
ghost-moth
grain-moth
hemiptera
hornet fly
humble-bee
ichneumon
lac-insect
leaf-louse
longicorn
membracid
millipede
orange-bug
orange-tip
pine-aphis
plant-lice
pyralidae
rug-weevil
sheep-lice
sheep-tick
spider-fly
squash-bug
sugar-mite
tanystoma
tarantula
tarentula
thysamura
tiger moth
tree-louse
tsetse-fly
tumblebug
turnip-fly
warble-fly
water-flea
wax-insect

wax-worker
wheat-moth
whirlygig
wood-borer
wood-louse
worker ant
worker bee
xylophaga

10

acacia-moth
arthropods
bark-weevil
bird-spider
blister-fly
bluebotte
boll-weevil
bombardier
burnet moth
cabbage-fly
caddicefly
cankerworm
carpet moth
cheese-mite
chrysomela
coccinella
cockchafer
coleoptera
corn-beetle
corn-weevil
death's-head
death-watch
digger wasp
dolphin-fly
dorr-beetle
drosophila
drumbledor
dumbledore
dung beetle
dynastidan
entomolite
ephemerans
fan-cricket
fen-cricket
flea-beetle
fritillary
frog-hopper
goat-chafer
greendrake
hairstreak
harvest bu;g
harvest man
hessian-fly
horse-emmet
jigger flea
lantern-fly
lappet moth

leaf-insect
leaf-roller
looper-moth
musk beetle
neuroptera
orthoptera
palnerworm
phylloxera
pine-weevil
plant-louse
red admiral
ribbonworm
rice-weevil
ring-barker
rosechafer
saltigrade
sand-hopper
scaraebeus
seed-weevil
sheep-louse
silver-fish
soldier ant
Spanish fly
stag beetle
star-psylla
stone-flies
timber-moth
turnipflea
twig-psylla
veneer moth
voetganger
vorticella
wheatmidge
willow-moth
winter-moth
wolf-spider
xylophagan

11

ametabolian
apple-sucker
arachnidans
auger beetle

balm-cricket
beehawk moth
black beetle
bloodsucker
cabbage moth
cantharides
capharis bug
caterpillar
chalcia wasp
clothes moth
codling moth
coprophagan
cryptophago
drinker moth
Emperor moth
entomophaga
Ephemeridae
flour weevil
gallinipper
grain beetle
grasshopper
green-bottle
horse-marten
Hymenoptera
leaf-bag moth
Lepidoptera
mole-cricket
painted lady
pine-girdler
scolopendra
scorpion-fly
snout-beetle
sponge-flies
stick-insect
subulicorns
swallow-tail
terebrantia
tetrapteran
thysanurans
tiger-beetle
timber-borer
Trichoptera
tussock-moth
vine-fretter
water beetle

water-skater
wattle moths
wheel-animal
wood-fretter

12

bent-wing moth
book-scorpion
buzzard-clock
cabbage white
carpenter ant
carpenter bee
cecropia moth
cinnabar moth
clerid-beetle
diadem spider
dimerosomata
flower-beetle
ground beetle
horned-clerid
horse-stinger
milk-white ant
money-spinner
pinhole-borer
nightcrawler
red-cedar moth
Rhynchophera
saprophagans
scarab beetle
sexton beetle
spring beetle
spruce sawfly
sycamore-moth
walking-stick
water-boatman
wattle-psylla
white admiral

13

black-lecanium
blister beetle

carpenter's bee
daddy-long-legs
diamond beetle
fig-leaf beetle
giant wood-moth
goliath-beetle
green wood-moth
ichneumon-wasp
jumping-spider
leather-jacket
lime-tree borer
mangold beetle
praying mantis
purple emperor
shot-hole borer
slender-weevil
tailed-emperor

14

bag-shelter moth
bimia-longicorn
cabbage-root fly
Colorado beetle
death's-head moth
elephant-beetle
fig-branch borer
Hercules beetle
ichneumon flies
ironbark saw-fly

15

furniture beetle
seedling-gum-moth
serricorn beetle
striped hawk-moth
thickset-chalcid
wheel-animalcule
yellow-longicorn

Marine growths, etc.

4 – 6

algae (5)
astrea (6)
coral (5)
dulse (5)
fungia (6)
kelp (4)
laver (5)

limpet (6)
mussel (6)
naiads (6)
polyp (5)
sponge (6)
tang (4)
tangle (6)
varec (5)
ware (4)

wrack (5)

7 AND 8

actinia (7)
agar agar (8)
alcyonic (8)
astraea (7)

badioga (7)
barnacle (8)
blubber (7)
calycle (7)
eschara (7)
fungite (7)
gulf weed (8)
polypary (8)
polypus (7)

porifera (8)
red algae (8)
red coral (8)
sea moss (7)
seaweed (7)
seawrack (8)
tubipore (8)
zoophyte (8)

9

alcyoneae
alcyonite
bathybius
blue algae
ecardines
Irish moss
madrepore

millepore		animal flower (12)
nullipore	*10 AND OVER*	bladder kelp (11)
pink coral	abrotanoid (10)	bladderwrack (12)
sea nettle	acorn barnacle (13)	brown algae (10)
zoophytes	alva marina (10)	coral zoophytes (14)

goose barnacle (13) milliporite (11)
lithodendron (12) sea anemone (10)
lithogenous (11) tubiporite (10)
lithophyte (10) ulotrichales (12)
marine plants (12) utricularia (11)

Molluscs

3 – 5

bulla
chank
clam
clio
ensis
fusus
gaper
helix
murex
mya
sepia
slug
snail
solen
spat
squid
unio
venus
whelk

6

buckie
chiton

cockle
cuttle
dodman
dolium
isopod
limpet
loligo
mantle
mussel
naiads
nerite
ostrea
oyster
pecten
quahog
sea ear
teredo
triton
voluta
winkle

7

acerans
actaeon
aplysia

ascidia
balanus
bivalve
diceras
eschera
etheria
glaucus
mollusc
mytilus
nauplii
octopod
octopus
patella
piddock
polyzoa
purpura
quahaug
scallop
scollop
sea hare
spirula
spondyl
taccata
tellina
toheroa

8

anodonta
argonaut
blue-nose
buccinum
decapoda
Limnaeid
mollusca
nautilus
ostracea
pagurian
pedireme
sea lemon
spirifer
strombus
teredine
tridacna
tunicary

9

acephalan
clausilia
dentalium
dolabella

ecardines
gastropod
giant clam
hodmandod
lithodome
ostracian
pondsnail
pteropods
scaphopod
shellfish

10

amphineura
amphitrite
brachiopod
cephalopod
conchifera
cuttlefish
date-mussel
haliotidae
heteropoda
periwinkle
razorshell
stone borer
stone eater

11

dragon shell
fasciolaria
gasteropoda
pearl oyster
river oyster
siphonifers
terebratula
trachelipod

12 AND OVER

boring mussel (12)
cyclobranchiata (15)
entomostomata (13)
lamellibranch (13)
pelican's foot (12)
spindleshell (12)
tectibranchiata (15)

Reptiles and amphibians

3 – 5

aboma
adder
agama
anole
anura
apod
asp
aspic
boa
bom
cobra
draco

eft
elaps
emys
evet
frog
gecko
guana
hydra
jiboa
kaa
krait
kufi
mamba
naga

naia
naia
newt
olm
pama
pipa
rana
seps
skink
snake
toad
varan
viper
waral

worm

6

agamid
anolis
caiman
cayman
daboia
dipsas
dragon
gavial
hassar

hydrus
iguana
karait
lizard
moloch
mugger
python
Sauria
taipan
triton
turtle
uraeus
vipera
worral

worrel

7

axolotl
chelone
coluber
gharial
ghavial
hicatee
labarri
lacerta
langaha

monitor
ophidia
paddock
rattler
saurian
scincus
serpent
snapper
tadpole
testudo
tuatara
urodela
varanus
zonurus

8

acontias
amphibia
anaconda
asp viper
basilisk
bull frog
cat snake
cerastes
chelonia
Congo eel
dinosaur
dragonet
fox snake
hatteria
hiccatee
horn toad
jararaca
keelback
lachesis
matamata
menopome
moccasin
pit viper
platanna
rat snake
red snake
ringhals
sand fish
sand toad
sea snake
slow-worm
terrapin
tortoise
tree frog
typhlops

9

alligator
batrachia
blind-worm
blue krait
boomslang
chameleon
chelonian
corn snake
crocodile
dart snake
eyed skink
galliwasp
giant frog
giant toad
green toad
hamadryad
horned asp
king cobra
king snake
marsh frog
Ophidians
pine snake
Pterosaur
puff adder
ring snake
terrapeen
tree snake
water newt
white snake
wolf snake

10

amphibians
black mamba
black snake
bushmaster
clawed frog

cockatrice
copperhead
coral snake
Cotylosaur
dabb lizard
death adder
dendrophis
Diplodocus
edible frog
eyed lizard
false viper
fer-de-lance
glass snake
grass snake
green mamba
green racer
green snake
hellbender
homorelaps
horned frog
Mosasaurus
natterjack
night adder
Plesiosaur
river snake
rock python
salamander
sand lizard
sea serpent
sidewinder
smooth newt
tic polonga
tiger snake
wall lizard
water pilot
water snake

11

banded krait
black cayman
carpet viper
cottonmouth
crested newt
flying snake
Gaboon viper
gartersnake
gila monster
green lizard
green turtle
horned viper
Ichthyosaur
Indian cobra
lace monitor
leopard frog
midwife toad
Ophiosaurus
Pterodactyl
rattlesnake
royal python
smooth snake
Stegosaurus
Surinam toad
thorn lizard
thorny devil
Triceratops
water lizard
water python

12

Brontosaurus
chained snake
chicken snake
flying lizard
green tree boa
herpetofauna

horned iguana
horned lizard
Hylaesaurus
Komodo dragon
leopard snake
pond tortoise

13 AND OVER

aquatic lizard (13)
boa constrictor (14)
brown tree snake (14)
coach-whip snake (14)
cobra de capello (14)
Dolichosaurus (13)
egg-eating snakes (15)
fire salamander (14)
four-lined snake (14)
frilled lizard (13)
giant tortoise (13)
golden tree frog (14)
golden tree snake (15)
green pit viper (13)
green tree frog (13)
Himalayan viper (14)
horn-nosed viper (14)
Ichthyosaurus (13)
long-nosed viper (14)
Nile crocodile (13)
painted terrapin (15)
rat-tailed snake (14)
Russell's viper (13)
saw-scaled viper (14)
schaapsticker (13)
snake-eyed skink (14)
snapping turtle (14)
spade-foot toad (13)
spotted lizard (13)
Tyrannosaurus (13)
water moccasin (13)

NATURAL HISTORY (2) PLANTS
Cereals, etc.

3 AND 4

bere
bigg
bran
corn
dari
dohl
dura
far
gram

malt
meal
oats
oca
poar
rice
rye
sago
tef
teff
zea

5

bajra
bajri
brank
durra
durum
emmer
ervum
fundi
grain

grama
grist
grout
maize
mummy
paddy
panic
pulse
rivet
spelt
straw

typha
wheat

6 AND 7

barley (6)
casava (6)
corncob (7)
darnel (6)
dhurra (6)

farina (6)
groats (6)
hominy (6)
mealie (6)
meslin (6)
millet (6)
muesli (6)
nocake (6)
raggee (6)
rokeage (7)
shorts (6)

sorghum (7)
taploca (7)
zea mays (7)

8 AND 9

arrowroot (9)
buckwheat (9)
espiotte (8)
garavance (9)

mangcorn (8)	semolina (8)		Indian corn (10)	spring wheat (11)
middlings (9)	sweet corn (9)		Indian millet (12)	summer wheat (11)
pearl rice (9)		***10 AND OVER***	mountain rice (12)	turkey wheat (11)
pot barley (9)		barleycorn (10)	pearl barley (11)	winter barley (11)
seed corn (8)		barleymeal (10)	pearl millet (11)	winter wheat (11)
seed grain (9)		German millet (12)	Scotch barley (12)	
		Guinea corn (10)		

Flowers

3 AND 4

aloe
arum
balm
flag
geum
iris
ixia
lei
lily
lote
may
musk
pink
rabi
rose
sego
weld
whin
wold

oxlip
padma
pagle
pansy
peony
petal
phlox
poker
poppy
sepal
stock
tansy
thyme
tulip
viola
yucca
yulan

5

agave
aspic
aster
avens
blite
briar
broom
canna
daisy
erica
faham
flora
gilia
gorse
gowan
henna
lilac
linum
lotus
lupin
orris
ox-eye

6

acacia
acaena
acorus
alisma
alpine
alsike
arnica
azalea
balsam
bellis
bennet
borage
cactus
camass
cistus
clover
coleus
cosmea
cosmos
crants
crocus
dahlia
datura
fennel
iberis
kochia

lupine
madder
mallow
malope
mimosa
myrtle
nerine
nuphar
opulus
orchid
orchis
oxalis
paeony
paigle
reseda
rocket
rosula
salvia
scilla
sesame
silene
sundew
thrift
torana
tulipa
violet
wattle
zinnia

7

aconite
alonsoa
aloysia
alyssum
anchusa
anemone
begonia
blawort
blewert
blossom
bouquet
bugloss
campion
candock
catmint

chaplet
chelone
chicory
clarkia
cowslip
cup rose
cytisus
day lily
deutzia
dittany
dog rose
festoon
freesia
fuchsia
gazania
genista
gentian
gerbera
godetia
heather
honesty
hyacine
jacinth
jasmine
jessamy
jonquil
kingcup
lantana
linaria
lobelia
lupinus
marybud
may-lily
melissa
milfoil
mimulus
nelumbo
nemesia
nigella
nosegay
opuntia
papaver
petunia
picotee
primula
rambler
rampion

sea-pink
seringa
spiraea
statice
succory
syringa
tagetes
tea rose
thistle
tritoma
ursinia
verbena
vervain
witloof

8

abutilon
acanthus
achillia
ageratum
amaranth
angelica
arum lily
asphodel
aubretia
auricula
bartonia
bearsear
bedstraw
bignonia
bluebell
buddleia
calamint
camellia
capsicum
catchfly
cattleya
clematis
cockspur
cyclamen
daffodil
dianthus
dicentra
dropwort
erigeron

feverfew
foxglove
gardenia
geranium
gillyvor
girasole
gladiola
gladiole
glaucium
gloriosa
gloxinia
harebell
haresear
helenium
hepatica
hibiscus
hottonia
hyacinth
japonica
laburnum
larkspur
lavatera
lavender
lent-lily
magnolia
marigold
martagon
moss rose
musk rose
myosotis
nenuphar
noisette
nymphaea
oleander
phacetia
phormium
plumbago
pond lily
primrose
rock-rose
scabious
skull-cap
snowdrop
stapelia
starwort
sweetpea
tigridia

toad-flax
tuberose
turnsole
valerian
veronica
viscaria
wild rose
wisteria
woodbind
woodbine
xanthium

9

Aaron's-rod
achimines
amaryllis
anagallis
aquilegia
buttercup
calendula
campanula
candytuft
carnation
carthamus
celandine
cherry pie
China rose
cineraria
clove pink
cockscomb
colt's foot
columbine
composite
coreopsis
corn-poppy
dandelion
digitalis
dog violet
dove's foot
edelweiss
eglantine
forsythia
gessamine
gladiolus
golden rod

hellebore
hollyhock
hydrangea
jessamine
kniphofia
lotus lily
mayflower
meadowrne
monkshood
moon daisy
narcissus
nemophila
oenothera
pimpernel
polygonum
pyrethrum
remontant
rudbeckia
saxifrage
speedwell
spikenard
sunflower
tiger lily
twayblade
verbascum
water flag
waterlily
wolf's-bane

10

agapanthus
amaranthus
aspidistra
belladonna
bell flower
caffre lilly
calliopsis

China aster
chionodoxa
cinquefoil
coquelicot
cornflower
corn violet
crane's-bill
crow flower
damask rose
delphinium
Easter lily
fritillary
gaillardia
gelder rose
goatsbeard
golden drop
gypsophila
heart's-ease
helianthus
heliophila
heliotrope
immortelle
lady's-mock
limnanthes
marguerite
mayblossom
mignonette
nasturtium
nightshade
orange lily
ox-eye-daisy
penny-royal
pentstemon
periwinkle
poinsettia
polianthus
potentilla
ranunculus
snapdragon

sweet briar
thalictrum
wallflower
white poppy
wind flower

11

antirrhinum
blood flower
cabbage rose
calandrinia
calceolaria
cheiranthus
convallaria
convolvulus
cotoneaster
everlasting
featherstar
fig marigold
forget-me-not
gillyflower
globeflower
greendragon
guelder rose
helichrysum
honey-flower
honeysuckle
kidney-vetch
lady's mantle
London pride
loosestrife
love-in-a-mist
meadowsweet
Nancy pretty
pelargonium
pepper elder
poppy mallow

ragged robin
rambler rose
red-hot poker
schizanthus
sea lavender
spear flower
sweet rocket
sweet sultan
tiger flower
wild flowers
wood anemone
xeranthemum

12

apple blossom
autumn crocus
boraginaceae
bougainvilia
cuckoo-flower
heather bells
horn-of-plenty
Iceland poppy
Jacob's ladder
lady's slipper
none-so-pretty
old man's-beard
orange flower
pasque flower
pheasant's ego
rhododendron
salpiglossis
shirley poppy
snow in summer
Solomon's seal
sweet william
tradescantia
virgin's bower

13

alpine flowers
blanket flower
bleeding heart
bougainvillea
Bristol flower
cherry blossom
Christmas rose
chrysanthemum
creeping jenny
crown imperial
eschscholtzia
grape-hyacinth
huntsman's horn
marsh marigold
orange blossom
passion flower
sweet calabash
traveller's joy
trumpet flower
water hyacinth

14 AND 15

Canterbury bell (14)
cardinal flower (14)
Christmas flower (15)
lily of the valley (15)
lords and ladies (14)
love-in-idleness (14)
Michaelmas daisy (15)
shepherd's purse (14)
star of Bethlehem (15)

Fruit

3 AND 4

akee
bito
Cox
crab
date
fig
gage
gean
haw
hep
hip

kaki
kiwi
lime
mare
mast
musa
nut
ogen
pear
pepo
plum
pome
rasp

skeg
sloe
ugli
uva

5

abhal
agava
agave
akena
anana
apple

arnot
betel
cubeb
drupe
eleot
grape
grout
guava
lemon
lichi
mango
melon
merry

morel
morus
naras
olive
papaw
peach
pecan
prune
regma
ribes
rubus
whort
whurt

6

achene
almond
ananas
banana
beurré
biffin
cedrat
cherry
citron
citrus
cobnut

colmar
damson
drupel
durian
egriot
elk nut
ginger
groser
lichee
longan
loquat
lychee
mammee

medlar
muscat
narras
nelies
nutmeg
orange
papaya
pawpaw
peanut
pignut
pippin
pomelo
punica
quince
raisin
rennet
russet
samara
walnut
zapote

7

apricot
avocado
bilimbi
buckeye
bullace
capulin
cassava
catawba
cedrate
cheston
coconut
codling
corinth
costard
currant
deal-nut
dessert
dog-wood
etaerio
filbert
genipap
golding
hautboy
hog-plum
karatas
kumquat
litchee
mahaleb
malmsey
mayduke
mineola
morello

naartje
pompion
pumpkin
quashey
rhubarb
rizzart
rosehip
satsuma
soursop
sultana
tangelo
wilding
winesap

8

allspice
bayberry
beechnut
bergamot
betelnut
bilberry
breadnut
buckmast
burgamot
calabash
cat's-head
chestnut
citrange
coquilla
cream-nut
date-plum
dogberry
earthnut
earthpea
fenberry
fig-apple
fox grape
hastings
hazelnut
honeydew
ivory nut
japonica
jonathan
mandarin
may apple
minneola
mulberry
muscadel
muscatel
musk pear
oleaster
pearmain
plantain
prunello

quandong
queening
rambutan
shaddock
spondias
sweeting
tamarind
Valencia
whitsour
windfall

9

alkekengi
apple-john
aubergine
beechmast
blueberry
brazilnut
buck's horn
butternut
cantaloup
canteloup
carmelite
cherimoya
chokepear
corozo nut
crab-apple
cranberry
damascene
drupaceae
elvas plum
greengage
groundnut
haanepoot
hindberry
king apple
love apple
melocoton
mirabelle
monkey nut
muscadine
musk-apple
musk-melon
nectarine
nonpareil
ortanique
oxycoccus
persimmon
pineapple
pistachio
rambootan
rambostan
raspberry
star apple

tamarinds
tangerine
victorine
Worcester

10

adam's apple
bird cherry
blackberry
blackheart
breadfruit
cantaloupe
charentais
clementine
clingstone
corozo nuts
cream-fruit
damask plum
dried fruit
elderberry
florentine
gooseberry
granadilla
grapefruit
Indian date
loganberry
Madeira nut
mangosteen
marking nut
melocotoon
orange musk
pome-citron
pompelmous
queen apple
redcurrant
redstreak
sorbapple
stone fruit
strawberry
waterlemon
watermelon
wild cherry
winter pear

11

anchovy pear
bitter apple
blood orange
boysenberry
candleberry
China orange
chokecherry

coquilla nut
French berry
granny smith
huckleberry
hurtleberry
Jaffa orange
leathercoat
monkey bread
myrtle berry
navel orange
pomegranate
pompelmoose
quarrington
russet apple
scuppernong
winter apple

12

bitter almond
blackcurrant
chaumontelle
Chester grape
chocolate nut
cochineal fig
cooking apple
custard apple
mammeesapote
passionfruit
pistachio nut
serviceberry
Victoria plum
white currant
whortleberry
winter cherry
winter citron

13 AND OVER

alliator pear (13)
Barbados cherry (14)
Blenheim orange (14)
Cape gooseberry (14)
Catherine pear (13)
conference pear (14)
cornelian cherry (16)
golden delicious (15)
mandarin orange (14)
morello cherry (13)
preserved fruit (14)
Seville orange (13)

Herbs and spices

3 – 5

anise
balm
basil
bay
chive
cive
clary
cress
cumin
dill
grass
mace
mint
myrrh
rape
rue
sage
senna
tansy
thyme
woad

6

bennet
betony
borage
capers
chilli

chives
cloves
endive
fennel
galega
garlic
ginger
hyssop
isatis
lovage
lunary
nutmeg
orpine
savory
sesame
simple
sorrel

7

aconite
burdock
caraway
catmint
cayenne
chervil
chicory
comfrey
dittany
frasera
gentian

henbane
juniper
lettuce
milfoil
mustard
oregano
panicum
paprika
parsley
pot herb
rampion
saffron
spignel
succory
vanilla

8

agrimony
angelica
camomile
cinnamon
hog's-bean
lavender
lungwort
marigold
marjoram
mouse ear
origanum
plantain
purslane

reedmace
rosemary
samphire
spicknel
tarragon
turmeric
waybread
wormwood

9

baneberry
bear's foot
chickweed
coriander
coronopus
eyebright
fenugreek
finocchio
goose foot
groundsel
hellebore
horehound
liquorice
sea fennel
sweet herb
tormentil

10

cassumunar
hyoscyamus
lemon thyme
motherwort
penny royal
peppermint
watercress
willow herb

11

dog's cabbage
dragon's head
hedge hyssop
horseradish
pot marigold
pot marjoram
sweet rocket
swine's cress
winter green

12 AND OVER

adder's tongue (12)
Florence fennel (14)
medicinal herb (14)
mournful widow (13)
mustard and cress (15)
southernwood (12)
summer savory (12)
sweet marjoram (13)
thoroughwort (12)
winter savory (12)

Plants

3

box
cos
ers
hay
hop
ivy
nep
oat
oca
pea
pia
poa
rue
rye

seg
tea
tef
tod
yam
zea

4

aira
akee
alfa
aloe
anil
arum

balm
bean
beet
bent
bigg
bulb
cane
coca
coco
coix
cole
corn
crab
dari
dill
diss

dock
doob
dorn
ecad
fern
flag
flax
gale
gama
geum
goss
hemp
herb
holm
ilex
iris

iute
kail
kale
kali
kans
leek
ling
mint
moss
musa
musk
nard
peat
pipi
race
rami

rape
reed
rhea
rice
root
rusa
rush
ruta
sage
sago
sida
sium
sloe
sola
spud
star

tara
tare
taro
teff
thea
tree
tule
tutu
ulex
vine
wald
weed
weld
whin
woad
wold

wort

5

agave
ajuga
algae
alpia
anise
apium
arnut
aspic
aster
avena
bhang

brake
brank
briar
broom
bugle
cacao
calla
canna
cicer
clary
clote
clove
couch
cress
cumin
cycad
daisy
dicot
dryas
durra
dwale
erica
eruca
ficus
fitch
fungi
furze
glaux
goman
gorse
gourd
grama
grass
grias
henna
holly
hosta
kunai
ledum
liana
liane
lotus
loufa
lupin
madia
maize
medic
melic
morel
moril
mucor
mudar
musci
napal
olive
orach
orpin
orris
oryza

oshac
osier
oxlip
paddy
palas
palea
panic
poker
radix
reate
rheum
roosa
rubia
rubus
runch
savin
savoy
scrog
sedge
shrub
sison
solah
starr
stipa
stole
sumac
swede
tacca
tamus
tansy
thorn
thyme
trapa
tucum
urena
vetch
vicia
vinca
viola
vitis
wahoo
wapon
wheat
whort
withy
wrack
yerba
yucca
yupon
zamia

6

acorus
alisma
amomum
aninga
annual

arabis
arbute
azalea
bamboo
barley
batata
bejuco
bennet
betony
biblus
borage
bryony
burnet
cactal
cactus
caltha
cassia
catnip
cicely
cicuta
cissus
cistus
clover
cockle
conium
conyza
cosmos
cowage
croton
cynara
daphne
darnel
dodder
eddoes
elaeis
endive
eringo
eryngo
exogen
fathen
fennel
ferula
fescue
filago
fimble
fiorin
frutex
fungus
funkia
fustet
galium
garlic
garrya
gervan
gnetum
gromil
guills
henbit
hervea

hyssop
iberis
indigo
jawari
jujube
juncus
kalmia
kiekie
kousso
lichen
locust
lolium
loofah
lupine
luzula
madder
maguey
mallow
manioc
marram
matico
milium
millet
mimosa
myrica
myrtle
nardoo
nerium
nettle
nubbin
oilnut
orache
orchid
orchis
origan
osmund
oxalis
paigle
pampas
peanut
peplis
pepper
phleum
potato
privet
protea
quinoa
quitch
radish
raggee
rattan
redtop
reseda
rocket
ruscus
sabine
savine
savory
scilla

secale
sesame
sesban
seseli
smilax
sorrel
spurge
squash
squill
stolon
styrax
sumach
sundew
teasel
teazel
thrift
tutsan
urtica
viscum
wicker
yamboo
yarrow

7

absinth
aconite
alcanna
alhenna
all-good
all-heal
althaea
aquatic
arabine
arbutus
awlwort
azarole
barilla
bartram
begonia
bistort
bogbean
bracken
bramble
bugloss
bugwort
bulbule
bulrush
burdock
bur-reed
calamus
calypso
campion
cannach
caraway
carduus
cassada
cassado

cassava
catmint
chicory
clarkia
clivers
clot-bur
columba
comfrey
cowbane
cowhage
cow-itch
cowslip
cow-weed
creeper
cudbear
cudweed
cup moss
cytisus
dionaea
dittany
dogbane
dog's rue
ear-wort
ehretia
elatine
epacris
esparto
eugenia
euryale
euterpe
felwort
festuca
ficaria
figwort
fitweed
foggage
foxtail
frogbit
fumaria
funaria
genista
gentian
gerbera
ginseng
gladwyn
gunnera
gutwort
hardock
heather
hemlock
henbane
herbage
honesty
hop-bind
hop-bine
hop-vine
humulus
ipomaea
jasmine

Jew's ear	truffle	cleavers	glyceria	roccella
jonquil	turpeth	clematis	goutweed	rock-rose
juniper	uncaria	clubmoss	goutwort	rosebush
karatas	vanilla	clubrush	gratiola	rosemary
kedlack	verbena	cocculus	gromwell	rye grass
lobelia	vervain	cockspur	hagtaper	sainfoin
lucerne	vetiver	cockweed	harebell	saltwort
lychnis	waratah	coleseed	hare's ear	scammony
madwort	wcorara	cornflag	hartwort	seedling
mahonica	zalacca	cornrose	hawkweed	sengreen
matweed	zanonia	costmary	hawthorn	septfoil
melilot	zedoary	cowberry	hibiscus	shamrock
monocot	zizania	cowgrass	hockherb	simaruba
munjeet		cow-wheat	ice plant	skull-cap
mustard		crithmum	isnardia	smallage
nonsuch	*8*	crow silk	knapweed	soapwort
opuntia		cunjevoli	lacebark	sourdock
panicum	acanthus	damewort	laceleaf	sow bread
papyrus	adiantum	danewort	larkspur	stapelia
pareira	agrimony	dewberry	lavender	starwort
parella	air plant	diandria	lungwort	strobile
parelle	amaranth	dog briar	lustwort	sun-plant
parsley	amphigen	dog grass	male fern	sweetsop
primula	angelica	dog's bane	mandrake	tamarack
pumpion	anthemis	dolichos	mangrove	tamarisk
pumpkin	asphodel	downweed	marjoram	tara fern
quamash	banewort	dropwort	matfelon	tarragon
quassia	barberry	duckmeat	mat grass	tea plant
ragwort	barometz	duckweed	may bloom	tentwort
rambler	bearbind	dumb-cane	mezereon	tickweed
rampion	bear's ear	earth nut	milkweed	toad-flax
rhatany	bellwort	earth-pea	monocarp	tree-fern
rhubarb	berberis	echinops	moonseed	tremella
robinia	berberry	eggplant	moonwort	triticum
ruderal	bignonia	eglatere	mulewort	tuberose
saffron	bilberry	eleusine	mushroom	turk's cap
saligot	bindweed	epiphyte	myosotis	turmeric
salsify	bogberry	erigeron	nonesuch	turnsole
salsola	bogwhort	erisimum	nut grass	valerian
sanicle	boxthorn	euonymus	oenanthe	veratrum
sarcina	brassica	feverfew	oleander	veronica
saw-wort	bullweed	finochio	oleaster	viburnum
sencion	bullwort	fireweed	orchanet	victoria
senecio	calamint	flaxweed	paspalum	wait-a-bit
seringa	camomile	fleabane	peat moss	wall-moss
solanum	cannabis	fleawort	phormium	wall-wort
sonchus	capsicum	flixweed	pilewort	wartwort
soybean	carraway	foalfoot	pink root	water-poa
spiraea	cassweed	foxglove	plantlet	wild oats
sporule	catchfly	fragaria	plantule	wild rose
statice	cat's tail	fumitory	plumbago	wind seed
syringa	centaury	fussball	polygala	wistaria
tagetes	cerealia	galangal	pond weed	with-wine
talipot	cetraria	garcinia	prunella	woodbine
taliput	charlock	gillenia	puffball	woodroof
tannier	chayroot	girasole	purslane	woodruff
thistle	choyroot	gloxinia	putchock	woodsage
tobacco	cinchona	glumales	red algae	woodwart
trefoil	cinnamon	glumella	rib grass	wormwood

4

wrightia
xanthium
zingiber

9

abrotanum
aerophyte
alpargata
amaryllis
ampelosis
arbor-vine
arracacha
arsesmart
artemisia
artichoke
asclepias
balsamine
basil weed
bean caper
bearberry
bent grass
bird's foot
bloodroot
bloodwort
blue algae
briar-root
brooklime
brookmint
brookweed
broomcorn
broomrape
burstwort
butterbur
candytuft
canebrake
caprifole
cardamine
cariopsis
carrageen
caryopsis
celandine
cetrarine
chamomile
chaparral
chaya root
cherry-bay
chickweed
china root
choke-weed
cineraria
club-grass
coal plant
cockscomb
cock's head
colchicum
colocynth
colt's foot

columbine
commensal
coniferae
coral wort
coriander
corn poppy
corn salad
cotyledon
cramp-bark
crataegus
crowberry
cuckoo bud
culver key
cyclamine
decagynia
decandria
desert rod
didynamia
digitalis
digitaria
dittander
dockcress
doob grass
duck's foot
duck's meat
dulcamara
dyer's weed
eglantine
elaeagnus
equisetum
euphorbia
euphrasia
evergreen
evolvulus
eyebright
fenugreek
fever root
feverwort
forsythia
gamagrass
gelanthus
germander
glasswort
golden cup
golden rod
goose corn
goosefoot
grapewort
grasspoly
greenweed
ground ivy
groundnut
groundsel
hair grass
hellebore
hoarhound
holly fern
honeywort
horehound

horsefoot
horsetail
hypericum
Indian fig
jessamine
Job's tears
kite's foot
knee holly
knot grass
lady's muck
lark's heel
laserwort
liquorice
liverwort
meadow rue
milk vetch
mistletoe
monk's hood
moschatel
mousetail
nelumbium
nepenthes
nicotiana
patchouli
pellitory
penstemon
pilularia
pimpernel
planticle
poison ivy
poison oak
pyracanth
pyrethrum
rafflesia
red clover
red pepper
rocambole
rockcress
rosmarine
safflower
saintfoin
saxifrage
smartweed
snakeroot
snakeweed
snowberry
soap plant
socotrine
spearmint
spearwort
speedwell
spikenard
spirogyra
spoonwort
stellaria
stonecrop
sugarbeet
sugar cane
sun spurge

sweet flag
sweet john
sweet root
sweet rush
sweet wood
sweet wort
taraxacum
thallogen
theobroma
thorn-bush
toadstool
tonka bean
toothwort
tormentil
trifolium
twayblade
umbilicus
villarsia
wakerobin
wall cress
waterlath
waterwort
wax myrtle
whitecrop
widow wail
wincopipe
wolf's bane
wolf's claw
wormgrass
woundwort
xanthosia

10

Adam-and-Eve
adam's apple
adder grass
agrostemma
alabastrus
alexanders
amaranthus
angiosperm
arbor vitae
asarabacca
beccabunga
belladonna
bitterwort
brome grass
brown algae
butterbush
butterweed
butterwood
butterwort
candelilla
cascarilla
cassumunar
cellulares
cinquefoil

cloudberry
corn cockle
corn rocket
cotton rose
cottonweed
couch grass
cow parsley
crake berry
crotalaria
cuckoopint
devil's club
diadelphia
dog's fennel
dog's poison
dog's tongue
dracontium
elacampane
elaeococca
entophytes
eriocaulon
eriophoron
escallonia
eupatorium
fimble-hemp
friar's cowl
fritillary
furrow weed
gaultheria
globe daisy
globularia
goatsbeard
goldenhair
goldy locks
goose grass
granadilla
grass-wrack
gymnosperm
heartsease
helianthus
hemp neetle
herb robert
herds grass
honey stalk
Indian corn
Indian reed
Indian shot
Jew's mallow
kidney-wort
king's spear
knapbottle
lycopodium
maidenhair
manila hemp
may blossom
mock orange
mock privet
muscardine
nasturtium
nightshade

nipplewort
panic grass
passiflora
pennyroyal
pentstemon
peppermint
pepperwort
periwinkle
poker plant
potentilla
pyracantha
race ginger
ranunculus
rest harrow
rhein berry
rhinanthus
rose acacia
rose mallow
salicornia
saprophyte
sarracenia
setterwort
shave grass
silver weed
sneezewort
sow thistle
Spanish nut
speargrass
spleenwort
stavesacre
stitchwort
stonebreak
stork's bill
sweet briar
sweet brier
swine bread
swinegrass
swordgrass
throatwort
tiger's foot
touch-me-not
tragacanth
tropaeolum
Venus's comb
wall pepper
water plant
way thistle
whitethorn
wild indigo
willow herb
willow weed
witch hazel
wolf's peach
wood sorrel
yellow-root
yellow-wort

11

bear's breech
bishop's weed
blackbonnet
bottle gourd
brank ursine
calceolaria
calcyanthus
canary grass
chanterelle
coffee plant
contrayerva
convolvulus
corn parsley
cotton grass
cotton plant
crest marine
cuckoo's meat
dame's violet
dog's cabbage
dog's mercury
dracunculus
dragon's head
Dragon's wort
Dutch clover
erythronium
everlasting
fescue grass
fig marigold
finger grass
fuller's weed
gentianella
giant cactus
giant fennel
greendragon
guelder rose
hart's tongue
holy thistle
honeysuckle
humble plant
Iceland moss
Indian berry
Indian cress
indigo plant
ipecacuanha
kidney vetch
latticeleaf
laurustinus
London pride
marram grass
marsh mallow
meadow-sweet
milk thistle
millet grass
moon trefoil
moving plant
myoporaceae
oyster plant

pedicedaris
pelargonium
pepper grass
poison sumac
prickly pear
red-hot poker
ribbon grass
ripple grass
scurvy grass
sempervivum
serpentaria
snail clover
snail flower
sparrow wort
spergularia
stagger bush
star thistle
sulphur-wort
swallow-wort
sweet cicely
sweet cistus
sweet potato
swine's cress
thorough wax
tinkar's root
tonquin bean
tussac grass
twitch grass
viper's grass
water radish
water violet
welwitschia
white clover
white darnel
winter berry
winter bloom
winter cress
wintergreen
wood anemone
xanthoxylum
zygophyllum

12

adderstongue
adderstoupie
aerial plants
bladderwrack
buffalo grass
Christ's thorn
coloquintida
compass plant
corn marigold
cow's lungwort
custard apple
deadly carrot
dragon's blood
echinocactus

erythroxylon
feather grass
fennel flower
fool's parsley
German millet
globe thistle
hempagrimony
hound's tongue
Indian millet
Indian turnip
mangel wurzel
marsileaceae
melon thistle
palma christi
pickerel weed
pitcher plant
quaking grass
reindeer moss
rhododendron
sarsaparilla
snail trefoil
Solomon's seal
southern wood
Spanish broom
Spanish grass
sparrow-grass
spear thistle
strangleweed
swine thistle
telentospore
timothy grass
tobacco plant
torch thistle
Venus flytrap
Venus's sumack
vinegar plant
virgin's bower

water parsnip
water pitcher
water soldier
white campion
whitlow grass
whortleberry
wild williams
winter cherry
xanthorrhiza
yellow rattle

13

chrysanthémum
crown imperial
dog's-tail grass
elephant grass
elephant's foot
eschscholtzia
flowering fern
flowering rush
globe amaranth
golden thistle
Indian tobacco
meadow saffron
raspberry bush
Scotch thistle
spike lavender
summer cypress
sweet marjoram
traveller's joy
Venus's fly trap
vervain mallow
viper's bugloss
wall pennywort
water calamint

water crowfoot
water hyacinth
wayfaring tree

14

blackberry bush
blue couch grass
carline thistle
distaff thistle
fuller's thistle
giant groundsel
golden lungwort
golden mouse-ear
gooseberry bush
lords and ladies
mountain sorrel
prince's feather
sensitive plant
shepherd's pouch
shepherd's purse
shepherd's staff
snake's-head iris
Spanish bayonet
starch hyacinth
treacle mustard
wood nightshade

15

golden saxifrage
Italian rye grass
shepherd's needle
Venus's navelwort
virginia creeper
woody nightshade

Trees, shrubs, etc.

2 AND 3

asa
ash
bay
bel
bo
box
elm
fig
fir
gum
haw
hip
hop

ita
ivy
may
nut
oak
sal
sap
tea
ti
tod
yew

4

acer
akee
aloe
amla
arar
arum
atap
bael
balm
bark
bass
bead
beam

bhel
bito
bixa
bole
cork
dali
dari
date
deal
dhak
doob
holm
huon
hura
ilex

jaca
kina
kiri
lana
leaf
lime
lote
milk
mowa
nipa
ombu
palm
pear
pine
pipe

plum	glory	yucca	laurel	**7**	margosa
pole	grass	yulan	lignum		mastich
rata	grove	zamia	linden	ailanto	moriche
rimu	guava		locust	ambatch	moringa
roan	hazel		macoya	amboyna	nut pine
root	henna	**6**	mallee	aniseed	oakling
rose	holly		manuka	Arbutus	oak tree
shea	iroko	abroma	mastic	ash tree	oil palm
sloe	jambu	acacia	medlar	avocado	orchard
sorb	judas	alerce	mimosa	banksia	platane
teak	karri	almond	miriti	bay tree	pollard
teil	kauri	aralia	myrtle	blossom	quercus
toon	kokra	arbute	nargil	blue gum	quillai
twig	kunai	arolla	nettle	boxwood	red pine
ulex	larch	balata	obeche	bubinga	redwood
upas	lemon	balsam	orange	buckeye	saksaul
vine	lilac	bamboo	papaya	bursera	sandbox
	macaw	banana	pawpaw	cabbage	sanders
	mahwa	banyan	pepper	camphor	sapling
5	mango	baobab	pinery	cam-wood	sapwood
	maple	bog-oak	poplar	canella	Sequoia
abele	mulga	bombax	privet	catalpa	seringa
Abies	myall	bo-tree	quince	champac	service
acorn	ngaio	bottle	redbud	coconut	shallon
afara	nyssa	branch	red fir	conifer	shittah
agave	oaken	brazil	red gum	coquito	shittim
agila	olive	buriti	ricker	corylus	silk oak
alder	osier	busket	rubber	cowtree	snow-gum
almug	palas	butter	sallal	cypress	sour-sop
amber	palay	button	sallow	daddock	spindle
anise	papaw	carapa	sapota	dammara	sundari
anona	peach	carica	sappan	determa	tanghin
apple	pecan	cashew	saxaul	dogwood	teatree
arbor	picea	catkin	she-oak	dottard	varnish
areca	pinon	caudex	sissoo	duramen	wallaba
Argan	pipal	cedrat	sorrel	elk-wood	wax palm
aspen	plane	cembra	souari	elm tree	wax tree
assai	plank	cerris	spruce	emblica	wych-elm
balsa	quina	cerrus	sumach	enterpe	
Banga	roble	cherry	sylvan	fan palm	
beech	roots	citron	tallow	fig tree	**8**
belah	rowan	coffee	tamanu	fir cone	
birch	salal	cornel	tewart	fir tree	agalloch
bunya	salix	daphne	timber	foliage	agalwood
butea	sally	deodar	titoki	genipap	alburnum
cacao	saman	elaeis	tooart	gum tree	algaroba
carob	sapan	emblic	tupelo	hemlock	allspice
cedar	smoke	fustet	veneer	hickory	arbuscle
china	sumac	fustic	vinery	hog palm	ash grove
clove	taxus	gatten	walnut	holm oak	bass wood
copse	thorn	ginkgo	wampee	jasmine	beam tree
coral	tilia	gomuti	wattle	jugians	beachnut
durio	tingi	gomuto	wicken	juniper	benjamin
dwarf	trunk	illipe	willow	king gum	black gum
ebony	tsuga	jarool	yampon	kumquat	box elder
elder	tuart	jarrah		lentisk	bud-scale
fagus	tulip	kittul		logwood	calabash
fruit	ulmus	kumbuk		lumbang	castanea
glade	walan	kunari		madrono	chestnut

229

cinchona
coco-palm
coco-tree
cork tree
coolabah
crab-tree
date palm
date plum
doom-palm
eucalypt
fraxinus
gardenia
giant gum
Groogroo
guaiacum
hardbeam
hawthorn
holly-oak
hornbeam
ironbark
ironwood
jack tree
jack wood
kingwood
laburnum
lacebark
lima wood
long jack
magnolia
mahogany
mangrove
manna-ash
mezereon
milk tree
mulberry
musk wood
mustaiba
oiticica
oleaster
palmetto
palm tree
pandanus
pear tree
pichurim
pinaster
pine cone
pine tree
pistacia
pockwood
quillaia
raintree
red cedar
red maple
rosemary
rosewood
royal oak
sago palm
sandarac
sapindus

scrub-oak
searwood
seedling
silky oak
sugar gum
swamp oak
sweet-bay
sweet gum
sycamore
tamarind
tamarisk
taxodium
toon-wood
tungtree
white ash
white fir
white gum
white oak
wistaria
witch-elm

9

adansonia
ailanthus
algarroba
aloes wood
alpine fir
angophora
araucaria
balsam fir
blackwood
brown pine
buckthorn
butternut
calambour
caliatour
caliature
china tree
chincapin
courbaril
crab apple
Cupressus
deciduous
erythrine
evergreen
forest oak
fruit tree
grapevine
greenwood
ground ash
ground oak
hackberry
ivory palm
jacaranda
Judas tree
kokrawood
lance wood

lentiscus
maracauba
mustahiba
paper bark
persimmon
pistachio
plane tree
quickbeam
rowan tree
sandarach
sapan wood
sapodilla
saskatoon
sassafras
satinwood
Scotch elm
Scotch fir
screw-pine
scrogbush
shade tree
shell-bark
silver fir
sloethorn
snake-wood
sour-gourd
spicewood
stone pine
suradanni
terebinth
thorn tree
tigerwood
toothache
touch-wood
tulip tree
whitebeam
white pine
whitewood
woodlayer
yacca wood
zebra wood

10

agollochum
almond tree
artocarpus
balaustine
blackthorn
blue spruce
brazilwood
breadfruit
bunji-bunji
bunya-bunya
burra-murra
butter tree
coastal-tea
coccomilia
coniferous

cotton tree
cottonwood
Douglas fir
eucalyptus
fiddle wood
flindersia
flooded gum
garlic-pear
green-heart
hackmatack
holly berry
Indian date
japati palm
kunai grass
letter wood
lilly-pilly
manchineel
mangosteen
orange-ball
orange wood
palisander
paper birch
pine needle
prickly ash
quercitron
redsanders
sandalwood
sand-cherry
sand-myrtle
Scotch pine
silk-cotton
silver-bell
sneeze-wood
Spanish fir
strawberry
sugar-maple
swamp maple
tall wattle
thyine wood
weeping ash
white cedar
white thorn
wild cherry
witch hazel
woolly butt
yellow-wood

11

Algerian fir
bean trefoil
black walnut
black wattle
black willow
bottle-brush
cedar wattle
chrysobalan
coconut palm

cootamundra
copper beech
cypress pine
elaeocarpus
eriodendron
golden chain
golden mohur
hoary poplar
honey locust
Japan laurel
leper-wattle
lignum vitae
mountain ash
pandanaceae
phoenix-palm
pomegranate
quicken tree
red-iron bark
red mahogany
sideroxylon
silver birch
stringybark
white poplar

white spruce
white willow

12

almond willow
benjamin-tree
betel-nut palm
caryophyllus
crow's-foot elm
cucumber tree
custard apple
flowering ash
golden wattle
horse-chestnut
monkey-puzzle
Norway spruce
silver-wattle
Spanish cedar
tree of heaven
umbrella palm
virgin's-bower
weeping birch

wellingtonia
white cypress
winter cherry
xylobalsamum

13 AND OVER

bird's-eye maple (13)
campeachy wood (13)
Cedar of Lebanon (14)
Christmas tree (13)
cornus florida (13)
dog-wood wattle (13)
galactodendron (14)
horse-chestnut (13)
Japanese cedar (13)
partridge wood (13)
Spanish chestnut (15)
sunshine wattle (14)
toxicodendron (13)
trembling poplar (15)
weeping willow (13)

Vegetables

3 AND *4*

bean
beet
cole
corn
faba
kale
leek
lima
neep
oca
okra
pea(s)
sage
soy(a)
spud
urd
yam

5

caper
chard
chick
chili
chive

cibol
colza
cress
fitch
gourd
maize
navew
onion
orach
pease
pulse
savoy
swede

6

carrot
celery
daucus
endive
fennel
garlic
girkin
greens
lentil
marrow
murphy

nettle
orache
porret
potato
pratie
radish
sprout
squash
tomato
turnip

7

batatas
cabbage
cardoon
chicory
frijole
gherkin
haricot
hotspur
lactuca
lettuce
mustard
parsley
parsnip
pea bean

peppers
pimento
pompion
pumpkin
salsify
seakale
shallot
skirret
spinach
sprouts
zanonia

8

allspice
beetrave
beetroot
borecole
broccoli
capsicum
celeriac
chickpea
colewort
cucumber
eggplant
eschalot
hastings

kohlrabi
lima bean
mirepoix
mushroom
plantain
scallion
smallage
soyabean
tickbean
zucchini

9

artichoke
asparagus
aubergine
broad bean
calabrese
courgette
curly kale
dandelion
green peas
horsebean
mangetout
marrowfat
red pepper
split peas

sweetcorn
turban-top
turnip top

10

adzuki bean
beet radish
cos lettuce
cow parsnip
French bean
kidney bean
King Edward
red cabbage
runner bean
scorzonera
turnip tops
watercress
Welsh onion

11

cauliflower
French beans
green pepper
haricot bean
horseradish
ratatouille
scarlet bean
spinach beet
sweet potato
water radish
water rocket

12

bamboo shoots
chat potatoes
corn on the cob
giant shallot

savoy cabbage
Spanish onion
spring onions
spring greens
white cabbage

13 AND OVER

broccoli sprouts (15)
Brussels sprouts (15)
globe artichoke (14)
horse cucumber (13)
ladies' fingers (13)
marrowfat peas (13)
purple broccoli (14)
scarlet runner (13)
spring cabbage (13)
tankard turnip (13)
vegetable marrow (15)

PEOPLES AND LANGUAGES
African tribes

3

Ewe
Fon
Ibo
Ijo
Iru
Suk
Tiv
Vai
Yao

4

Agni
Baga
Bena
Bete
Bini
Bisa
Bubi
Fang
Fula
Guro
Haya
Hehe
Hima
Hutu
Lala
Lozi
Mali

Meru
Nama
Nupe
Nyao
Teso
Yako
Zulu

5

Afars
Anuak
Bamum
Bantu
Bassa
Baule
Bemba
Chewa
Chopi
Dinka
Dogon
Galla
Ganda
Gissi
Grebo
Hausa
Iraqu
Kamba
Lulua
Lunda
Masai

Mende
Mossi
Nandi
Ngoni
Nguni
Nguru
Pygmy
Riffs
Rundi
Shona
Sotho
Swazi
Tonga
Tussi
Tutsi
Venda
Xhosa

6

Angoni
Bakota
Balega
Basuto
Bateke
Bayaka
Chagga
Fulani
Herero
Ibibio
Kikuyu
Kpwesi

Lumbwa
Luvale
Murozi
Ngwato
Rolong
Sambaa
Senufo
Somali
Sukuma
Thonga
Tlokwa
Tsonga
Tswana
Tuareg
Veddah
Warega
Yoruba

7

Ashanti
Baganda
Bakweii
Bambara
Bangala
Bapende
Barotse
Barundi
Basonge
Batonka
Batutsi
Berbers

Bunduka
Bushmen
Dagomba
Griquas
Mashona
Namaqua
Nilotes
Samburu
Shillak
Songhai
Turkana
Watutsi

8

Bergdama
Bushongo
Kipsigis
Mamprusi
Mandingo
Matabele
Tallensi

9 AND OVER

Bangarwanda (11)
Bathlaping (10)
Hottentots (10)
Karamojong (10)
Kgalagedi (9)
Lunda-Bajokwe (12

American Indian peoples

3 AND 4

Cree
Crow
Fox
Hopi
Hupa
Iowa
Maya
Moki
Pima
Sauk
Ute
Yuma
Zuni

5

Aztec
Blood
Caddo
Campa
Creek
Haida
Huron
Incas
Kansa
Kiowa
Lipan
Miami
Moqui
Nahua
Omaha
Osage
Sioux
Teton
Wappo
Yaqui
Yuchi
Yunca

6

Abnaki
Apache
Aymara
Aztecs
Biloxi
Caribs
Cayuga
Cocopa
Dakota
Dogrib
Kichai
Mandan
Micmac
Mixtec
Mohave
Mohawk
Navaho
Nootka
Ojibwa
Oneida
Ostiak
Ottawa
Paiute
Pawnee
Pequot
Pericu
Piegan
Pueblo
Quakaw
Salish
Santee
Sarcee
Seneca
Toltec
Warrau

7

Abenaki

Amerind
Arapaho
Araucan
Arikara
Catawba
Chilcal
Chinook
Choctaw
Hidatsa
Mapuche
Mohegan
Mohican
Natchez
Ojibway
Orejone
Quechua
Serrano
Shawnee
Stonies
Tlingit
Tonkawa
Wichita
Wyandot

8

Aguaruna
Cherokee
Cheyenne
Comanche
Delaware
Illinois
Iroquois
Kickapoo
Kootenay
Kwakiutl
Menomini
Muskogee
Nez Percé
Onondaga
Powhatan

Quichuan
Seminole
Shoshoni
Shushwap

9

Algonkian
Algonquin
Apalachee
Ashochimi
Blackfeet
Chickasaw
Chipewyan
Chippeway
Flatheads
Karankawa
Menominee
Penobscot
Tuscarora
Winnebago

10

Araucanian
Assiniboin
Athabascan
Bella Coola
Leni-Lenapé
Minnetaree
Montagnais
Shoshonean

11 AND 12

Narraganset (11)
Pasamaquoddy (12)
Root-diggers (11)
Susquehanna (11)

Languages, nationalities and races

2 AND 3

Edo
Ewe
Fon
Fur

Ga
Gur
Hun
Ibo
Ido
Ila

Jew
Kru
Kui
Kwa
Lao
Luo

Mon
Shi
Tiv
Twi
Vai
Wa

Wu
Yao

4

Akan
Ambo
Arab
Avar

Bali	5	Lomwe	Berber	Pushto
Beja		Malay	Bokmal	Pushtu
Bini	Acoli	Mande	Brahui	Rajput
Bodo	Aleut	Maori	Breton	Romaic
Boer	Aryan	Masai	Briton	Romany
Celt	Asian	Mossi	Bulgar	Rwanda
Chad	Attic	Munda	Celtic	Ryukyu
Copt	Bantu	Nandi	Chokwe	Sabine
Dane	Bassa	Naron	Coptic	Samoan
Efik	Batak	Negro	Creole	Sérère
Erse	Bemba	Ngala	Cymric	Sindhi
Fang	Benga	Nguni	Danish	Slavic
Finn	Berta	Nkore	Dorian	Slovak
Garo	Bhili	Norse	Eskimo	Somali
Gaul	Bulom	Nyong	Fijian	Soviet
Ge'ez	Bussi	Nyoro	French	Sukuma
Gogo	Carib	Oriya	Fulani	Syriac
Gond	Chaga	Oscan	Gaelic	Syrian
Grig	Chopi	Punic	Gallic	Telegu
Igbo	Croat	Roman	Gascon	Teuton
Kelt	Cuban	Ronga	German	Theban
Kurd	Cymry	Rundi	Gothic	Thonga
Lala	Czech	Sango	Hebrew	Tongan
Lapp	Dayak	Saudi	Herero	Trojan
Lari	Dinka	Saxon	Ibibio	Tsonga
Lett	Doric	Scots	Indian	Tswana
Loma	Dutch	Shilh	Inupik	Tuareg
Lozi	Dyold	Shona	Ionian	Tungus
Luba	Dyula	Sinic	Italic	Turkic
Mano	Fante	Sotho	Jewess	Tuscan
Manx	Frank	Swazi	Jewish	Viking
Moor	Galla	Swede	Judaic	Votyak
Moxu	Ganda	Swiss	Kabyle	Yankee
Naga	Gbari	Tamil	Kaffir	Yemeni
Nuba	Gipsy	Temne	Kanuri	Yoruba
Nuer	Gondi	Tigré	Kikuyu	Zenaga
Nupe	Greek	Tonga	Korean	
Pali	Gypsy	Uzbeg	Kpelle	
Pedi	Hadza	Venda	Kpessi	7
Pict	Hausa	Welsh	Kurukh	
Pole	Hindi	Wolof	Libyan	Acadian
Russ	Idoma	Xhosa	Luvale	African
Scot	Indic	Yupik	Manchu	Amharic
Sena	Ionic	Zande	Mongol	Angolan
Serb	Iraqi		Navaho	Arabian
Shan	Irish		Ndonga	Aramaic
Sikh	Kadai	6	Nepali	Aramean
Slav	Kafir		Ngbaka	Armoric
Sobo	Kamla	Acholi	Ngombe	Asiatic
Susu	Karen	Aeolic	Norman	Avestan
Teso	Kazak	Afghan	Nsenga	Bagirmi
Thai	Khasi	Altaic	Nubian	Balanta
Tswa	Khmer	Arabic	Nyanja	Balochi
Turk	Kissi	Arawak	Ostman	Bambara
Urdu	Kongo	Argive	Papuan	Bedouin
Wend	Lamba	Aymara	Parian	Belgian
Zend	Lango	Baltic	Parsee	Bengali
Zulu	Latin	Baoule	Patois	Bisayan
	Lenge	Basque	Polish	British

234

Burmese
Bushmen
Catalan
Chechen
Chilean
Chinese
Cornish
Cypriot
Dagomba
Dalicad
Dialect
English
Finnish
Fleming
Flemish
Frisian
Gambian
Gaulish
Guarani
Haitian
Hamitic
Hebraic
Hessian
Hittite
Iberian
Ilocano
Iranian
Israeli
Italian
Karanga
Khoisan
Kirghiz
Kurdish
Kuwaiti
Laotian
Laotien
Lappish
Latvian
Lingala
Lombard
Lugbara
Maduran
Malinke
Maltese
Mandyak
Manxman
Marathi
Mexican
Moorish
Mordvin
Morisco
Mozareb
Mulatto
Nahuatl
Nauruan
Ndebele
Negress
Ngbandi
Nilotic

Nynorsk
Ottoman
Pahlavi
Palaung
Persian
Prakrit
Punjabi
Quechua
Romance
Romansh
Russian
Rwandan
Samiote
Samoyed
Sandawe
Santali
Semitic
Serbian
Shilluk
Siamese
Slovene
Songhai
Spanish
Spartan
Swahili
Swedish
Tagalog
Tibetan
Tigrina
Turkish
Ugandan
Umbrian
Umbundu
Venetic
Walloon
Yiddish
Zairese
Zambian

8

Abderite
Akkadian
Albanian
Algerian
American
Andorran
Antiguan
Armenian
Assamese
Assyrian
Austrian
Balinese
Bavarian
Bermudan
Bohemian
Bolivian
Cambrian

Canadian
Chaldaic
Chaldean
Chamorro
Cherokee
Corsican
Cushitic
Cyrenaic
Delphian
Dutchman
Egyptian
Estonian
Ethiopic
Etruscan
Eurasian
Frankish
Gallican
Georgian
Germanic
Ghanaian
Gujarati
Gujariti
Guyanese
Hawaiian
Hellenic
Helvetic
Honduran
Illyrian
Irishman
Japanese
Javanese
Kashmiri
Kimbundu
Kingwana
Kuki-Chin
Kukuruku
Kwanyama
Lebanese
Liberian
Makassar
Malagasy
Malawian
Mandarin
Mandingo
Mandinka
Memphian
Moroccan
Moru-Madi
Negritos
Nepalese
Nigerian
Nuba-Fula
Nyamwesi
Octoroon
Old Norse
Old Saxon
Parthian
Pelasgic
Peruvian

Phrygian
Prussian
Romanian
Romansch
Rumanian
Sanskrit
Scotsman
Scottish
Sicilian
Slavonic
Spaniard
Sudanese
Sumerian
Teutonic
Tunisian
Turanian
Turkomen
Vandalic
Visigoth
Welshman

9

Abkhasian
Afrikaans
Afrikaner
Anatolian
Armorican
Barbadian
Bengalese
Brazilian
Bulgarian
Byzantian
Byzantine
Cambodian
Cantonese
Caucasian
Ceylonese
Chari-Nile
Cheremiss
Cimmerian
Colombian
Congolese
Dravidian
Esperanto
Esquimaux
Ethiopian
Frenchman
Hanseatic
Hibernian
Hottentot
Hungarian
Icelander
Icelandic
Israelite
Jordanian
Kabardian
Kannarese

Low German
Malayalam
Malaysian
Mauritian
Mongolian
Negrillos
Nepaulese
Norwegian
Ostrogoth
Pakistani
Provencal
Red Indian
Rhodesian
Roumanian
Samaritan
Sardinian
Sere Mundu
Sinhalese
Sri Lankan
Sundanese
Taiwanese
Tanzanian
Tocharian
Ukrainian
Ulotrichi
Uruguayan

10

Abyssinian
Afrikander
Algonquian
Anglo-Saxon
Australian
Autochthon
Babylonian
Circassian
Costa Rican
Ecuadorian
Englishman
Finno-Ugric
Florentine
Guatemalan
High German
Hindustani
Indonesian
Israelitic
Lithuanian
Melanesian
Mingrelian
Monegasque
Neapolitan
Nicaraguan
Nicobarese
Niger-Congo

Panamanian
Paraguayan
Patagonian
Philippine
Philistine
Phoenician
Polynesian
Pomeranian
Portuguese
Rajasthani
Senegalese
Serbo-Croat
Singhalese
Venezuelan
Vernacular
Vietnamese

11

Afro-Asiatic
Argentinian
Azerbaijani
Bangladeshi
Greenlander
Indo-Hittite
Indo-Iranian
Mauretanian

Palestinian
Scots Gaelic
Sino-Tibetan
Trinidadian

12

Basic English
Byelorussian
Indo-European
King's English
Moru-Mangbetu
mother tongue
New Zealander
Plattdeutsch
Scandinavian
Tibeto-Burman

13

Pidgin English
Queen's English
Rhaeto-Romanic
Serbo-Croatian

RELIGION AND MYTHOLOGY
Biblical characters

3

Asa
Eve
God
Ham
Job
Lot

4

Abel
Adam
Agag
Ahab
Amos
Baal
Boaz
Cain
Esau
Jael
Jehu
Joab

John
Jude
Leah
Levi
Luke
Magi (The)
Mark
Mary
Moab
Noah
Paul
Ruth
Saul
Shem

5

Aaron
Annas
Caleb
David
Demas
Devil (The)

Elihu
Enoch
Herod
Hiram
Hosea
Isaac
Jacob
James
Jesse
Jesus
Joash
Jonah
Judas
Laban
Linus
Lydia
Micah
Moses
Nahum
Naomi
Peter
Satan
Sihon
Silas

Simon
Titus
Uriah
Uriel
Zadok

6

Abijah
Andrew
Balaam
Christ
Daniel
Darius
Dorcas
Elijah
Elisha
Esther
Festus
Gehazi
Gideon
Haggai
Isaiah

Jahweh
Jairus
Joseph
Joshua
Judith
Kohath
Miriam
Naaman
Naboth
Nathan
Philip
Pilate
Rachel
Reuben
Samson
Samuel
Simeon
Sisera
Thomas
Uzziah
Yahweh

7

Abraham
Absalom
Ananias
Azariah
Clement
Delilah
Eleazar
Ephraim
Ezekiel
Gabriel
Japheth
Jehovah
Jezebel
Joiakim
Lazarus
Lucifer
Malachi
Matthew
Meshach
Michael
Obadiah
Pharaoh

Raphael
Shallum
Solomon
Stephen
Timothy
Zebulon

8

Abednego
Barnabas
Benjamin
Caiaphas
Gamaliel
Habakkuk
Hezekiah
Issachar

Jeremiah
Jeroboam
Jonathan
Maccabee
Matthias
Mordecai
Nehemiah
Philemon
Rehoboam
Sapphira
Shadrach
Zedekiah

9

Abimelech
Ahasuerus

Bathsheba
Jehoiakim
Nathanael
Nicodemus
Thaddaeus
Zacchaeus
Zachariah
Zacharias
Zechariah
Zephaniah

10

Bartimaeus
Belshazzar
Holofernes
Methuselah

Theophilus

11

Bartholomew
Jehoshaphat
Melchizedek
Sennacherib

13 AND 14

Mary Magdalene (13)
John the Baptist (14)
Nebuchadnezzar (14)
Pontius Pilate (13)

Mythology

2 AND 3

Aah
Aea
Ahi
Ali
Amt
Ana
Anu
Aon
As
Ate
Bel
Bes
Con
Cos
Dis
Ea
elf
Eos
Eru
fay
Fum
Ge
Gog
Heh
Hel
Ida
Ino
Io
Ira
Lar
Ler
Lif

Mab
Min
Neo
Nix
Nox
Nut
On
Ops
Pan
Pax
Ra
Ran
Roe
Set
Shu
Sol
Sua
Tiw
Tyr
Ule
Uma
Ve

4

Abae
Abas
Abia
Abii
Acis
Agni
Ajax
Amam

Amen
Amor
Amsi
Amsu
Anit
Ankh
Annu
Anpu
Apia
Apis
Area
Ares
Argo
Asia
Askr
Aten
Atys
Auge
Baal
Bakh
Bast
Beda
Beli
Bias
Bilé
Bran
Buto
Ceyx
Chac
Chin
Clio
Core
Danu
Deva

Dice
Dido
Dino
Donu
Duse
Dwyn
Echo
Eden
Elli
Enna
Enyo
Eris
Eros
Esus
Fama
Faun
Frig
Fury
Gaea
gods
gram
Gwyn
Gyes
Hapi
Hebe
Heno
Hera
hero
Hest
Idas
Ikto
Ilia
Ilus
Iole

Iris
Irus
Isis
Issa
Itys
Iynx
jinn
Jove
Juno
Kali
kama
Lear
Leda
Leto
Llyr
Lofn
Loki
Maat
Maia
Mara
Mark
Mars
Math
Medb
Moly
Mors
muse
Myth
Nabu
Naga
Nebu
Nick
Nike
Nila

Nubu
Nudd
Odin
ogre
Pasi
Peri
Pero
pixy
Ptah
Puck
Rahu
Raji
Rama
Rhea
Roma
saga
Selk
Shai
Sita
Siva
Soma
Styx
Susa
tabu
Tadg
Thia
Thor
Tros
Troy
Tupa
Tyro
Upis
Vata
Vayu

Wasi	Bennu	Fates	Laius	Pluto
Xulu	Beroe	Fauna	Lamia	Poeas
Yama	Bitol	Fides	Lamus	Priam
Yggr	Biton	Flora	lares	Pwyll
Ymir	Bogie	Freya	Lethe	Remus
Yoga	Borvo	Freyr	Liber	Rimac
Yuga	Bragi	Friga	Linus	Rudra
yule	Butis	Fulla	Lludd	Sakra
Zeus	Byrsa	Gades	Lotis	Salus
Zume	Cacus	Galar	Lugus	santa
	Cales	Galli	Lycus	satyr
	Canis	Garme	Macar	Sesha

5

	Capra	genii	Macha	Sibyl
	Capys	Getae	Maera	Sinis
Abila	Carna	ghoul	Magog	Sinon
Acron	Ceres	giant	Manes	Siren
Actor	Chaos	Gihil	Maron	Skuld
Aedon	Cilix	gnome	Mazda	Sulis
Aegir	Circe	Gorge	Medea	Supay
Aegis	Coeus	Grail	Medon	sylph
Aegle	Creon	Gwyar	Melia	Syren
Aello	Crete	Gyges	Metis	taboo
Aenea	Cupid	Gymir	Midas	Tages
Aesir	Cyane	Hades	Mimas	Talos
Aeson	Dagda	Harpy	Mimir	Tanen
Aesop	Dagon	Helen	Minos	tarot
Aetna	Damon	Helle	Mitra	Ta-urt
Agave	Danaẽ	Herse	Moira	Theia
Ahura	Dares	Homer	Molus	Thoas
Alope	Delos	Honor	Momus	Thoth
Amata	demon	Horae	Monan	Thule
Ammon	Deuce	Horta	Mothi	Thyia
Amset	Deuse	Horus	Mullo	Titan
Anava	devas	houri	Muses	Tohil
angel	Diana	Hydra	naiad	Tonan
Anher	Dione	Hylas	Nanda	Troll
Anhur	Dirce	Hymen	Nandi	Uazit
Anius	djinn	Hymir	Nemon	Uller
Antea	Dolon	Iamus	Niobe	Urien
Anxor	Donar	Iapyx	Nisus	Urthr
Anxur	Doris	Iason	Nixie	Ushas
Apepi	Dryad	Ichor	Norna	Vanir
Arawn	Durga	Idmon	norns	Venti
Arete	dwarf	Idyia	Nymph	Venus
Argos	Dyaus	Ilama	Orcus	Vesta
Argus	Dylan	Ilium	Oread	Woden
Ariel	Edoni	Indra	Orion	Wotan
Arimi	Egypt	Ionia	Paean	Xquiq
Arion	elfin	Iphis	Pales	Zamna
Armes	elves	Irene	Panes	Zelia
Artio	embla	Istar	Paris	Zetes
Ashur	Enlil	Iulus	Pavan	
Asius	Epeus	Ixion	Perse	
Atlas	Epona	Janus	Phaon	

6

Attis	Erato	Jason	Phyto	
Aulis	Estas	Jorth	Picus	Abaris
Bacis	Evius	Kaboi	pigmy	Abdera
Barce	faery	Kabul	pisky	Abeona
Belus	fairy	Ladon	pixie	Abydos

Acamus	Bendis	Eostre	Icarus	Niskai
Achaei	Benshi	Eponae	Ilaira	Nomius
Achaia	Bestla	Erebus	Iliona	Nornas
Actaea	Bitias	Erinys	Inferi	nymphs
Admeta	Boreas	Euneus	Iolaus	Oberon
Adonis	Brahma	Europa	Iphias	Oeneus
Aeacus	Byblis	Evadne	Ishtar	Oenone
Aeetes	Byblus	Evenus	Iseult	Oeonus
Aegeus	Cabiri	Faerie	Isolde	Ogmios
Aegina	Cadmus	Faunus	Ismene	ogress
Aegypt	Calais	Febris	Italus	Ogyges
Aeneas	Canens	Fenrir	Ithaca	Ogygia
Aeneid	Cardea	Fenris	Ithunn	Oileus
Aeolus	Caryae	fetish	Itonia	Olenus
Aerope	Castor	Fidius	Kobold	Ophion
Aethra	Caurus	Fimila	Kraken	oracle
Africa	Celeus	Fjalar	Kvasia	Ormuzd
Agenor	Charis	Foliot	Latona	orphic
Aglaia	Charon	Fornax	Lilith	Orthia
Agrius	cherub	Frigga	Lucina	Orthus
Alecto	Chione	Furies	Lycaon	Osiris
Aletes	Chiron	Furnia	Lyceus	Palici
Aleuas	Chryse	Galeus	Maenad	Pallas
Aloeus	Clotho	Ganesh	Mamers	Pallos
Althea	Clytie	Gemini	Mammon	Panope
Amazon	Codrus	Genius	Marica	Paphus
Amen-Ra	Comana	Geryon	Medusa	Parcae
Ampyse	Consus	Ghanna	Megara	Peleus
Amycus	Cratos	Glance	Memnon	Pelias
Amydon	Creios	Goblin	Mentor	Pelion
Anapus	Creusa	Gorgon	Merlin	Pelops
Andros	Crissa	Graces	Merman	Peneus
Angont	Crocus	Graeae	Merops	Perdix
Antium	Cronus	Haemon	Mestra	Peryda
Anubis	Cybele	Haemus	Mictla	Phenix
Anukit	Cycnus	Hafgan	Milcom	Pheres
Aphaca	Cyrene	Hamhit	Miming	Phoebe
Apollo	Damona	Haokah	Mintha	Pholus
Aquilo	Danaus	Hather	Minyas	Phylas
Araxes	Daphne	Hecale	Mithra	Pirene
Arctos	Daulis	Hecate	Moccos	Pistor
Arthur	Daunus	Hector	Moirae	Plutus
Asgard	Delius	Hecuba	Moloch	Polias
Asopus	Delphi	Helice	Mopsus	Pollux
Athena	Dictys	Helios	Munnin	Pomona
Athene	Dipsas	Hellen	Mygdon	Prithi
Athens	Dirona	Hermes	Mythic	Prithu
Atreus	Dodona	Hesiod	naiads	Pronax
Augeas	Dragon	Hestia	Narada	Psyche
Aurora	Dryads	Heyoka	Natose	Pulaha
Avatar	Dryope	Hroptr	Nectar	Pushan
Avalon	Dumuzi	Huginn	Neleus	Pyrrha
Baalim	Durinn	Hyades	Nereid	Python
Bacabs	Echion	Hygeia	Nereus	Rhenea
Balder	Egeria	Hyllus	Nergal	Rhesus
Balius	Egesta	Ianthe	Nessus	Rhodes
Battus	Elatus	Iarbas	Nestor	Rhodos
Baucis	Elymus	Iasion	Ninlil	Rumina
Befana	Empusa	Iasius	Nireus	Safekh

Samana	Xelhua	Arachne	Cocytus
Sancus	Xolotl	Arcadia	Copreus
Sappho	Xuthus	Arestor	Coronis
Saturn	Yaksha	Ariadne	Creteus
Satyrs	Zancle	Arsinoë	Curetes
Scylla	Zethus	Artemis	Cyaneae
Scyros	zombie	Asathor	Cyclops
sea-god		Astarte	Cythera
Selene		Asteria	Dactyls
Semele	**7**	Astraea	Daphnis
Semnai		Ataguju	Delphus
Sestus	Abderus	Athamas	Demeter
Sethon	Acarnam	Atropos	demi-god
Sibyls	Acastus	Autonoë	Diomede
Sigeum	Acerbas	Auxesia	Dwynwen
Simois	Acestes	Avatars	Echemus
Sirens	Achaeus	Avernus	Echidna
Sirona	Achates	Bacchae	Ehecatl
Somnus	Acheron	Bacchus	Electra
Sothis	Acoetes	banshee	Elicius
Sphinx	Actaeon	banshie	Elpenor
spirit	Admetus	Belenos	Elysian
sprite	Aegaeon	Bellona	Elysium
Sthanu	Aegiale	Beltane	Epaphus
Syrinx	Aenaria	Bifrost	Epigoni
Talaus	Aepytus	bogyman	Erigone
Tammuz	Aesacus	Bochica	Erinyes
Tarvos	Aetolus	Bona Dea	erl-king
Tellus	Agamede	Brahman	Eumaeus
Tereus	Agyieus	Branwen	Eumelus
Tethys	Ahriman	Brauron	Eunomia
Teucer	Alastor	Briseis	Euryale
Thalia	Alcides	Bromius	Eurybia
Theano	Alcmene	Brontes	Euterpe
Themis	Alcyone	brownie	Evander
Thetis	Alpheus	Busiris	evil eye
Thisbe	Aluberi	Caeneus	Exadius
Thunor	Amathus	Calchas	Februus
Thyone	Amazons	Calypso	Feronia
Tiamat	Ampelus	Camelot	Formiae
Titans	Amphion	Camenae	Fortuna
Tityus	Ampycus	Camilla	Fylgjur
Tlaloc	Amymone	Canopus	Galatea
Tmolus	Amyntor	Capella	Galleus
Triton	Anaburn	Caranus	Gargara
Typhon	Anagnia	Carneus	Gelanor
Ulixes	Anaphae	Cecrops	Glaucus
Umbria	Anaurus	Celaeno	Gnossos
Undine	Ancaeus	centaur	Goibniu
Urania	Angitia	Cepheus	Gordius
Uranus	Anigrus	Cercyon	Gorgons
Utgard	Antaeus	Cessair	Grannus
Utopia	Antenor	Chelone	Gremlin
Vacuna	Anteros	Chimera	griffin
Valkyr	Anthene	Chloris	Grimnir
Varuna	Antiope	Chryses	Gryphon
Vishnu	Antissa	Cinyras	Gungnir
Vulcan	Aphetae	Cleobis	Halesus
Xangti	Aphytos	Clymene	Hamoneu

hanuman	Morrigu	Qabanil	Yolcuat
Harpies	Musaeus	Racumon	Zagreus
Helenus	Myrddin	Renenet	Zipacna
Helicone	Nemesis	Rhamnus	
Hesione	Nephele	Rhoecus	
Hilaira	Neptune	Rhoetus	*8*
Hor-Amen	Nereids	Rig-Veda	
Hun-Ahpu	Nokomis	Robigus	Abantias
Hunbatz	Nycteus	Romulus	Absyrtus
Hurakan	Nysaeus	Rubicon	Academus
Hydriad	Oceanus	Rukmini	Achelons
Hygeian	Ocyrhoe	Samblin	Achilles
Hylaeus	Oeagrus	Scandea	Acidalia
Iacchus	Oedipus	Scaptia	Aconteus
Ialemus	Ogygian	Scheria	Acontius
Iapetus	Old Nick	Scythia	Acrisius
Icarius	Olympia	Segesta	Adrastia
Idalium	Olympus	Selleis	Adrastus
Idothea	Omphale	Serapis	Aeacides
Iguvium	Onniont	Setebos	Aegimius
Inarime	oracles	Sicinus	Aegyptus
incubus	Orestes	Silenus	Acneades
Inferno	Ormenus	Skirnir	Agamedes
Iobates	Orphean	Soranus	Aganippe
Ioskeha	Orpheus	Spright	Aglauros
Ismenos	Ortygia	sprites	Alberich
Itzamna	Pandion	Stentor	Albiorix
Iztal Ix	Pandora	Stimula	Alcathoe
Iztat Ix	Parvati	sylphid	Alcestis
Jocasta	Pegasus	Talarea	Alcimede
Jupiter	Penates	Telamon	Alcinous
Juturna	Perseis	Telemus	Alcmaeon
Krishna	Perseus	Temenus	Amaethon
Laeradh	Petasus	Thaumas	Amalthea
Laertes	Phegeus	Theonoe	Ambrosia
Laocoon	Phemius	Theseus	Anacreon
Laodice	Phineus	Thialfi	Anatarho
Larunda	Phoebus	Titania	Anchiale
Latinus	Phoenix	Triopas	Anchises
Lavinia	Phorcus	Tristan	Anemotis
Leander	Phrixus	Troilus	Angharad
Lemures	Phyllis	Ulysses	Antemnae
Lorelei	Pierian	unicorn	Anthedon
Lothurr	Pleiads	Unktahe	Anthemus
Lynceus	Pleione	vampire	Anthylla
Macaria	Plouton	Veionis	Anticlea
Machaon	Pluvius	Venilia	Antigone
Maenads	Polites	vestals	Antiphus
Maponos	Priapus	Vintios	Apaturia
Megaera	Procles	Virbius	Apidonus
Menippe	Procris	Vitharr	Apollyon
Mercury	Proetus	Walkyrs	Appareus
mermaid	Proteus	Wayland	Arcesius
Metylto	Pryderi	Wieland	Arethusa
Michabo	Purusha	wood god	Argonaut
Midgard	Pylades	Xanthus	Arianrod
Minerva	Pyramus	Xibalba	Ascanius
Mithras	Pyrrhus	Xmucane	Asterion
Mordred	Pythias	Yakshas	Astraeus

Astyanax	Elivager	Megareus	Rakshasa
Ataensic	Endymion	Melampus	Rhodopis
Atalanta	Enigorio	Meleager	Rosmerta
Atlantis	Entellus	Menelaus	Rubezahl
Avernian	Enyalius	Merodach	Sahadeva
basilisk	Epicaste	Minotaur	Sarawati
Bebryces	Epidanus	Morpheus	Sarpedon
Bedivere	Eriphyle	Mulciber	Schedius
Belisama	Eteocles	Myrtilus	Sciathus
bogeyman	Eteoclus	Narayana	Seriphos
Bolthorn	Eumolpus	Nausicaa	Silvanus
Branchus	Euphemus	Nephthys	Sipontum
Bubastis	Euryabus	Niflheim	Sisyphus
Bylazora	Euryclea	Nin-Lilla	Sparsana
Caduceus	Eurydice	Oceanids	Srikanta
Caeculus	Eurynome	Odysseus	succubus
Calliope	Faesulae	Oenomaus	Summanus
Callisto	Farbauti	Olympian	Talassio
Camaxtli	Favonius	Orithyia	talisman
Camazotz	folklore	Othrerir	Tantalus
Capaneus	Fornjotr	Pacarina	Tartarus
Carmenta	Ganymede	Palaemon	Tecmessa
Castalia	Gigantes	Pandarus	Telephus
Celaenae	Gilgames	Panopeus	Terminus
centaurs	good folk	Panthous	Thamyri
Centeotl	Govannon	paradise	Thanatos
Cephalus	Gucumatz	Parjanya	Theogony
Cerberus	Halcyone	Pasiphaë	Thyestes
Cercopes	Harmonia	Pasithea	Tiresias
Chalybes	Haroeris	Pelasgus	Tithonus
Chantico	Heliadae	Penelope	Tonatiuh
Charites	Heracles	Pentheus	Tristram
Chimaera	Hercules	Pephredo	Ucalegon
Chryseis	Hermione	Percival	Valhalla
Cimmerii	Hersilia	Periphas	Valkyrie
Cipactli	Hesperus	Pessinus	Vasudeva
Cocidius	Hyperion	Phaethon	Vesuvius
Coroebus	Iardanes	Philemon	Victoria
Cretheus	Ilithyia	Phintias	Virginia
Crommyon	Illatici	Phlegyas	Visvampa
Cyclades	Iphicles	Phoronis	Wakinyan
Cylopes	Jarnsaxa	Picumnus	water god
Cyllarus	Jurupari	Pierides	Waukkeon
Cynosura	Keridwen	Pilumnus	werewolf
Cytherea	Kukulcan	Pisander	Xpiyacoc
Daedalus	Labdacus	Pittheus	Yadapati
Damascus	Lachesis	Pleiades	Zalmoxis
Damastes	Lampetie	Podarces	Zephyrus
Damocles	Lancelot	Polyxena	
Dardanus	Laodamas	Porthaon	
Deianira	Laodamia	Poseidon	**9**
Dervones	Laomedon	Prithivi	
Dionysos	Lapithae	Proximae	Acherusia
Dionysus	Libertas	Psamathe	Achilleum
Dioscuri	Libitina	Pulastya	Acmonides
Dodonian	Lupercus	Quiateot	Adsullata
Doybayba	Maeander	Quirinal	Aegialeus
Draupnir	Mama Nono	Quirinus	Aegisthus
El Dorado	Marpessa	Ragnarok	Aethiopia

Agamemnon
Agathyrsi
Akha-Kanet
Alcathous
Alcyoneus
Amalivaca
Ambrosial
Amphrysus
Anaxarete
Andraemon
Androclus
Androgeus
Andromeda
Antandrus
Antevorta
Aphrodite
Areithous
Areopagus
Argonauts
Aristaeus
Ascalabus
Asclepius
Ashtoreth
Assoracus
Autolycus
Automeden
Aventinus
Bacchante
Bosphorus
Brunhilde
Bucentaur
Byzantium
Cassandra
Cerberean
Chalcodon
Charybdis
Chthonius
Clitumnus
Coatlicue
Cockaigne
Concordia
Cytherean
Davy Jones
Deiphobus
Demophoon
Dervonnae
Deucalion
Diancecht
Diespiter
Dionysius
Domdaniel
Enceladus
Epidaurus
Eumenides
Euphorbus
Eurybates
Eurypylus
Eurysaces
Excalibur

Fabia Gens
Fairyland
fairy tale
Faustulus
Ferentina
Feretrius
Fjawrgynn
Friar Tuck
Gagurathe
Gargaphin
Ghisdubar
Guinivere
Hamadryad
Harmakhis
Heimdallr
Hippolyte
hobgoblin
Holy Grail
Hypsipyle
Idacanzas
Idomeneus
Indigetes
Iphigenia
Iphimedia
Ixiomides
Jotunheim
Lyonesse
Melanthus
Melisande
Melpomene
Menoeceus
Menoetius
Metaneira
Missibizi
Mnemosyne
Mnestheus
Nanahuatl
Narcissus
Noncomala
Nyctimene
Oceanides
Orgiastic
Palamedes
Pandareos
Pandrosos
Parnassus
Patroclus
Pelopidae
Periander
Philammon
Philomela
Phoroneus
Pirithous
Polydamas
Polydorus
Polynices
Polyphron
Portumnus
Postvorta

Pudicitia
Pygmalion
Quahootze
Rakshasas
Rediculus
Rigasamos
Robin Hood
Sagittary
Salmoneus
Samavurti
Saturnius
Scamander
Scyllaeum
Sibylline
Siegfried
Sthenelus
Strophius
Taranucus
Tawiscara
Telchines
Telegonus
Thersites
Thymoetes
Tisamenus
Tisiphone
Toutiorix
Uxellimus
Valkyrean
Valkyries
Vasishtha
Vertumnus
Walpurgis
white lady
wood nymph
Xbakiyalo
Xbalanque
Yggdrasil
Zacynthus
Zerynthus

10

Abantiades
Achillides
Aetholides
Ahsonnutli
Ahura Mazda
Ambisagrus
Amisodarus
Amnisiades
Amphiaraus
Amphictyon
Amphitrite
Amphitryon
Andromache
Antilochus
Antitaurus
Arcesilaus

Archemoros
Berecyntia
Bussumarus
Callirrhoe
Cassiopeia
changeling
Cihuacoatl
cockatrice
compitalia
cornucopia
Corybantes
Cyparissus
Delphinium
Eileithyia
Eldhrimnir
Emathiades
Epimenides
Epimetheus
Erechtheum
Erechtheus
Erymanthus
Euphrosyne
fisher king
Galinthias
Gwenhwyvar
Hamadryads
Heliopolis
Hephaestus
Hesperides
Hippocrene
Hippodamia
Hippogriff
Hippolytus
Hippomedon
Hippothous
Horbehutet
Jabberwock
Juggernaut
Kaneakeluh
King Arthur
leprechaun
Lifthrasir
little folk
Maid Marian
Mama Quilla
Melanippus
Melanthius
Menestheus
mundane egg
Nausithous
Necessitas
Nilmadhava
Onocentaur
Pachacamac
Palladinus
Pallantias
Parnassian
Persephone
Phlegethon

243

Phosphorus
Pigwidgeon
Plisthenes
Polydectes
Polydeuces
Polyhymnia
Polymestor
Polyphemus
Porphyrion
Prajapatis
Procrustes
Prometheus
Proserpina
Qebhsennuf
Rhea Silvia
Round Table
Sakambhari
Samothrace
Santa Claus
Saptajihiva
sea serpent
Strophades
Talthybíus
Telemachus
Tlepolemus
Trophonius
Utgardloki
Visvakarma
Visvamitra
Vrihaspati
Vukub-Cakix
Wonderland
Yajneswara
Yoganindra

11

Aesculapius
Alaghom Naom
Alalcomenae
Amphilochus
Anna Perenna
Antaeopolis
Anthesteria
Aphrodisias
Apocatequil
Arimaspians
Atius Tirawa
Awonawilona
Bellerophon
Britomartis
Canopic jars
Cueravaperi
Dam Gal Nunna
Eileithyias
Enigohatgea
Erysichton
Eurysthenes
Ginnungagap
Gladsheimir
Harpocrates
Heracleidae
mythologist
mythologize
Nantosvelta
Neoptolemus
Pandora's box
Penthesilea
Philoctetes
Polyphontes
Protesilaus
Savitripati
Scamandrius

12

Acca Larentia
Achaemenides
Acroceraunia
Agathodaemon
Aius Locutius
Ancus Martius
Bandersnatch
Belatucadrus
Chrysothemis
Clytemnestra
Erichthonius
Gigantomachy
Golden Fleece
Hippocentaur
Hyperboreans
Hypermnestra
Jormundgandr
Kittanitowit
Mount Olympus
mythographer
mythological
Pallas Athene
Purushattama
Quetzalcoatl
Rhadamanthus
Tezcatlipoca

Sraddhadeva
Symplegades
Terpsichore
Thrasymedes
Triptolemus
troglodytes
Ultima Thule
Vishnamvara

Theoclymenus
Trismegistus
Wandering Jew
white goddess
Xochiquetzal
Yohualticitl
Yudhishthira

13 AND OVER

Achilleus Dromos (15)
Apochquiahuayan (15)
Apple of Discord (14)
Augean stables (13)
Calydonian Hunt (14)
Colonus Hippius (14)
Damocles' sword (13)
Elysian Fields (13)
Father Christmas (15)
Halirrhathius (13)
Hermaphroditus (14)
Huitzilopochtli (15)
Itsikamahidis (13)
Jupiter Elicius (14)
Jupiter Pluvius (14)
Laestrygonians (14)
Llew Llaw Gyffes (14)
Mayan Mythology (14)
Never Never Land (14)
Oonawieh Unggi (13)
Phoebus Apollo (13)
Quetzalcohuatl (14)
Tloque Nahuaque (14)
Tonacatecutli (13)
Tuatha de Danann (14)
Walpurgis night (14)
Yoalli Ehecatl (13)

Religion, ecclesiastical terms, etc.

2 – 4

abbé	Copt	guni	Jew	pica	Siva
alb	cowl	hadj	joss	pie	soul
alms	curé	hajj	ka'ba	pome	Sufi
amen	dana	hell	lama	pope	text
apse	dean	holy	lay	pray	Toc H
ark	Ebor	host	Lent	pyx	Veda
ave	Eden	hymn	mass	R.I.P.	veil
Baal	Eve	icon	monk	rite	vow
bier	evil	idol	nave	rood	Xmas
bon	ewer	I.H.S.	N. or M.	rupa	yang
chan	fane	Imam	nun	sect	yin
cope	fast	I.N.R.I.	obit	see	yoga
	font	jah	pall	sext	Zen
	God	Jain	pew	sin	Zion

5

abbey
abbot
abdal
agape
aisle
Allah
altar
amice
angel
Arian
banns
beads
Bible
bigot
bless
bodhi
burse
canon
carol
chant
chela
choir
credo
creed
cross
curia
Dagon
deify
deism
deist
deity
demon
devil
dirge
dogma
double
druid
elder
ephod
exeat
faith
fakir
friar
glory
godly
grace
Grail
guild
hades
hafiz
Hindu
image
imaum
Islam
Kaaba
karma
Koran

laity
lauds
logos
manse
matin
mitre
morse
myrrh
pagan
papal
pasch
paten
piety
pious
prior
psalm
purim
rabbi
relic
saint
Sarum
Satan
selah
stole
Sudra
Sunna
sutra
synod
taboo
terce
Torah
tract
vedic
vicar
vigil
zazen

6

abbacy
abbess
adamic
Advent
adytum
anoint
anthem
ashram
aumbry
banner
beadle
Belial
bikkhu
bikshu
bishop
Brahma
Buddha
burial
cantor

censer
chapel
cherub
chrism
Christ
church
cierge
clergy
cleric
corban
culdee
cruets
curacy
curate
deacon
decani
dervis
devout
dharma
divine
donary
dossal
dunker
Easter
Elohim
Exodus
ferial
flamen
friary
gloria
Gospel
hallow
heaven
Hebrew
Hegira
heresy
hermit
homily
housel
hymnal
I-ching
intone
Jesuit
Jewess
Jewish
Judaic
keblah
latria
lavabo
lector
legate
Levite
litany
living
mantra
martyr
matins
missal
Mormon

mosaic
Moslem
mosque
mullah
Muslim
mystic
novice
nuncio
oblate
octave
ordain
orders
orison
pagoda
painim
palmer
papacy
papism
papist
parish
Parsee
parson
pastor
popery
prayer
preach
priest
primus
priory
proper
psalms
pulpit
purana
Quaker
rector
repent
ritual
rochet
rosary
rubric
sacred
Saddhu
sangha
santon
schism
scribe
seraph
sermon
server
Shaker
shaman
Shiite
Shinto
shrine
shrive
sinful
sinner
solemn
Sofism

spirit
Sunday
suttee
Talmud
tantra
te deum
temple
theism
trance
triune
tunker
verger
vestry
virgin
Vishnu
votive
Wahabi

7

Aaronic
Abaddon
abelian
acolyte
acolyth
Adamite
advowee
Alcoran
Alkoran
alms-bag
ampulla
angelic
angelus
animism
apostle
Arahant
atheism
atheist
baptism
baptist
baptize
beatify
Beghard
Beguard
Beguine
bigotry
biretta
Brahman
Brahmin
calvary
cassock
chalice
chancel
chaplet
chapter
charity
chrisom
Cluniac

collect	lamaism	saviour	Buddhism
confirm	Lateran	sedilia	Buddhist
convent	lectern	service	cantoris
convert	lection	Shaster	capuchin
croslet	liturgy	Shastra	cardinal
crozier	Lollard	Sivaite	carmelin
crusade	low mass	soutane	catacomb
dataria	madonna	steeple	canonize
deanery	maniple	stipend	cathedral
decanal	mattins	sub-dean	Catholic
deified	messiah	Sunnite	cemetery
dervise	mid-Lent	synodal	cenobite
dervish	minaret	tantric	cenotaph
devilet	minster	tempter	chasuble
diocese	miracle	tonsure	cherubim
diptych	mission	trinity	chimere
diviner	muezzin	tunicle	chrismal
docetae	mystics	unblest	christen
Elohist	narthex	unction	ciborium
epistle	nirvana	unfrock	cincture
Essenes	nocturn	Vatican	clerical
eternal	numbers	Vedanta	compline
evangel	nunnery	vespers	conclave
exegete	oratory	Vulgate	confalon
faculty	ordinal	worship	corporal
fasting	orphrey	Xmas day	covenant
frontal	Our Lady		creation
Galilee	penance		credence
gaudete	peshito	**8**	crucifer
Gehenna	pietist		crucifix
Genesis	pilgrim	ablution	dalmatic
gentile	piscina	aceldama	deaconry
glorify	pontiff	acephali	deifical
gnostic	popedom	advowson	demoness
goddess	prayers	agnostic	devilish
godhead	prebend	agnus dei	devilkin
godhood	prelate	alleluia	devotion
godless	prester	almighty	diaconal
godlike	primacy	altarage	dies irae
godling	primate	anathema	diocesan
godship	profane	anchoret	disciple
gradine	prophet	Anglican	ditheism
gradual	psalter	anointed	ditheist
gremial	puritan	antiphon	divinity
hassock	Quakery	antipope	divinize
heathen	Ramadan	antistes	doctrine
heretic	rebirth	apostasy	Donatism
hexapla	rectory	apostate	donatist
holy day	requiem	apparels	doxology
hosanna	reredos	Arianism	druidess
impiety	retable	Arminian	druidism
incense	retreat	atheneum	ebionite
infidel	Sabbath	ave maria	elements
introit	sacring	beatific	Ember Day
Jainism	sainted	benifice	enthrone
Jehovah	saintly	bénitier	epiphany
Judaism	sanctum	biblical	episcopy
Judaize	Saracen	brethren	epistler
Lady Day	satanic	breviary	Erastian

Essenism
Eternity
ethereal
Eusebian
evensong
evermore
evildoer
exegesis
exegetic
exorcist
faithful
feretory
foot-pace
frontlet
futurist
God's acre
Hail Mary
heavenly
hell fire
hierarch
high mass
hinayana
holy name
homilies
holy rood
Holy Week
Huguenot
hymn book
idolater
idolatry
immortal
indevout
infernal
Jesuitic
Jesuitry
Judaizer
lay-clerk
libation
literate
lord's day
Lutheran
lych-gate
mass-book
mahayana
minister
ministry
minorite
miserere
modalist
Mohammed
monachal
monastic
moravian
nativity
navicula
Nazarene
nethinim
novatian
obituary

oblation
offering
ordinary
orthodox
paganism
pantheon
papistry
pardoner
Passover
pharisee
pontifex
preacher
predella
priestly
prioress
prophecy
prophesy
Proverbs
psalmist
psalmody
Puseyism
Puseyite
quietism
quietist
Ramadhan
recollet
redeemer
religion
response
reverend
reverent
rogation
Romanism
Romanist
Romanize
sacristy
Sadducee
sanctify
sanctity
satanism
sequence
seraphim
sidesman
skullcap
Sunnites
superior
surplice
swastika
tenebrae
thurible
thurifer
transept
trimurti
triptych
unbelief
unbishop
unchurch
venerate
versicle

vestment
viaticum
vicarage
zoolatry

9

ablutions
alleluiah
allelujah
All Hallow
All Saints
alms bason
altar tomb
anchorite
anointing
antipapal
apocrypha
apostolic
archangel
archfiend
archiarcy
Ascension
athenaeum
atonement
Ayatollah
baptismal
beatitude
Beelzebub
beneficed
bishopric
bismillah
black mass
blasphemy
Calvinism
Candlemas
Carmelite
catechism
cathedral
celestial
cere-cloth
Christian
Christmas
churching
clergyman
co-eternal
communion
confessor
Cordelier
cremation
Dalai Lama
dalmatica
damnation
deaconess
dedicated
desecrate
diaconate
dissenter

dissident
dominical
eagle-wood
Easter day
Easter eve
Ember Days
Ember Fast
Ember Tide
episcopal
epistoler
eucharist
eutychian
evangelic
gospeller
Gregorian
Halloween
hierarchy
hierogram
hierorlogy
high mass
holy ghost
holy water
incumbent
induction
interdict
interment
Islamitic
Jansenism
Jansenist
Jesuitism
joss-stick
Lammas Day
lay reader
Lazarists
Lazarites
Levitical
Leviticus
Low Church
Low Sunday
Mahomedan
Maronites
martyrdom
Methodism
Methodist
moderator
monachism
monastery
Mormonism
mundatory
Mussulman
Nestorian
obeisance
offertory
orthodoxy
ostensory
pantheism
pantheist
paraclete
Parseeism

247

patriarch
Pentecost
pharisaic
plainsong
prayer mat
prayer rug
preaching
precentor
presbyter
priestess
proselyte
prothesis
purgatory
pyrolatry
Quakerism
quasimodo
quicunque
reading-in
reconvert
red rubric
reliquary
religieux
religious
repentant
responses
reverence
ritualism
ritualist
rural dean
sabbatism
sabianism
sacrament
sacrifice
sacrilege
sacristan
salvation
sanctuary
Scripture
semi-Arian
sepulchre
shamanism
solemnity
solemnize
spiritual
sub-beadle
subdeacon
subrector
succentor
suffragan
suffrages
sutteeism
synagogue
synergism
synodical
teleology
Testament
theatines
theocracy
theomachy

theomancy
theopathy
theophany
theosophy
Theravada
tritheism
Vaishnava
Vajrayana
venerable
vestments
Waldenses

10

Abelonians
absolution
abstinence
aladinists
Albigenses
alkoranist
All Hallows
altar bread
altar cloth
altar cross
altar light
altar piece
altar steps
altar table
Anabaptism
Anabaptist
anointment
antichrist
apocalypse
apostolate
apotheosis
archbishop
archdeacon
archflamen
archimagus
archpriest
armageddon
assumption
Athanasian
baptistery
benedicite
Bernardine
Bethlemite
bible class
biblically
black friar
Brahminism
Buddhistic
Carthusian
catechumen
Celestines
ceremonial
cherubical
chronicles

church army
churchgoer
church work
churchyard
Cistercian
confessant
confession
conformist
consecrate
consistory
cosmolatry
devotional
ditheistic
divination
Dominicans
doxologize
dragonnade
Eastertide
ecumenical
Ember Weeks
episcopacy
episcopate
epistolary
evangelism
evangelist
evangelize
free chapel
Free Church
Genevanism
gnosticism
Good Friday
gospel side
gymnosophy
halleluiah
hallelujah
hallowmass
heathenism
heaven-born
heliolater
heliolatry
heptateuch
hierocracy
High Church
high priest
holy orders
holy spirit
hylotheism
hyperdulia
iconoclasm
iconoclast
iconolater
iconolatry
idolatress
impanation
indulgence
infallible
invocation
irreligion
irreverent

juggernaut
lady chapel
lay brother
lectionary
magnificat
mariolatry
meditation
ministrant
missionary
Mohammedan
monotheism
monotheist
monstrance
omnipotent
ophiolatry
ordination
Palm Sunday
Pentateuch
pentecost
pharisaism
pilgrimage
prayer book
prayer flag
prebendary
presbytery
priesthood
prophetess
Protestant
puritanism
rectorship
redemption
repentance
reproaches
revelation
rock temple
rood screen
sacerdotal
sacrosanct
sanctified
sanctifier
schismatic
scriptural
septuagint
sepulchral
Sexagesima
Shrovetide
subdeanery
syncretism
tabernacle
temptation
39 articles
Tridentine
unanointed
unbaptized
unbeliever
uncanonize
unclerical
unorthodox
veneration

visitation
white friar
Whit Sunday
worshipper
Zend-Avesta

11

acephalites
agnosticism
All Souls' Day
altar screen
antepaschal
antependium
antiphonary
apotheosize
archdiocese
arches court
Arminianism
aspersorium
baldeochino
Benedictine
benediction
benedictory
bibliolatry
bibliomancy
black rubric
blasphemous
Bodhisattva
Catabaptist
Catholicism
chalice veil
celebration
chrismation
chrismatory
Christendom
christening
church house
commination
communicant
consecrator
convocation
crematorium
crucifixion
deification
desecration
devotionist
divine light
doxological
ecclesiarch
episcopalia
epistle-side
Erastianism
eschatology
eternal life
evangelical
evening hymn
everlasting

exhortation
fire-worship
freethinker
Geneva Bible
genuflection
hagiography
Hare Krishna
hierarchism
hierography
humeral veil
immortality
incarnation
inquisition
intercessor
irreligious
irreverence
Karmathians
Latin Church
Lord's supper
Lutheranism
miracle play
mission room
Mohammedism
Nicene Creed
œcumenical
parishioner
passing bell
passionists
passion play
Passion Week
paternoster
patron saint
Pedobaptism
pharisaical
Plymouthism
pontificate
pontifician
prayer wheel
priestcraft
procession
proselytism
proselytize
protomartyr
purificator
Reformation
religionary
religionism
religionist
religiosity
reservation
ritualistic
Roman Church
sacramental
sacring-bell
Sadduceeism
sarcophagus
scientology
Socinianism
theosophist

trinitarian
unbeneficed
uncanonical
undedicated
unorthodoxy
unrighteous
Wesleyanism
Whitsuntide
Zoroastrian

12

All Saints' Day
annunciation
altar frontal
archdeaconry
Ascension Day
Ash Wednesday
Augustinians
Bible Society
chapel of ease
choir service
Christianity
Christmas Day
Christmas Eve
church living
church parade
churchwarden
confessional
confirmation
Confucianism
congregation
consecration
consistorial
devil worship
discipleship
disciplinant
disestablish
dispensation
ditheistical
Easter Sunday
Ecclesiastes
ecclesiastic
ecclesiology
enthronement
episcopalian
evangelicism
exomologesis
frankincense
hot gospeller
image worship
intercession
interdiction
Low Churchman
metropolitan
mission house
New Testament
nunc dimittis

obedientiary
Old Testament
omnipresent
postillation
Presbyterian
purification
Quadragesima
reconsecrate
reconversion
red letter day
religionless
residentiary
Resurrection
Rogation Days
Rogation Week
Salvationist
sanctus bell
spiritualism
Sunday school
superfrontal
thanksiving
Unitarianism
universalism
unscriptural
vicar general

13

All Hallowmass
All Hallows Eve
All Hallowtide
Anglican music
Anglo-Catholic
antichristian
antiepiscopal
Apostles' Creed
archarchitect
archbishopric
archdeaconate
baptismal shell
beatification
bidding prayer
burial service
burnt offering
canonical hour
ceremoniarius
Christianlike
church service
confessionary
convocational
Corpus Christi
credence table
devotionalist
Eastern Church
excommunicate
glorification
High Churchman
holy innocents

incense burner
lord spiritual
miracle worker
mission church
Mohammedanism
Nonconformist
paschal candle
pastoral staff
pectoral cross
prayer-meeting
Protestantism
Quinquagesima
Roman Catholic
reincarnation
Sacerdotalism
Salvation Army
sanctuary-lamp
scripturalist
Shrove Tuesday
Swedenborgian
Tractarianism
Trinity Sunday
unconsecrated
unevangelical
way of the cross

14

antiscriptural
black letter day
burnt sacrifice
church assembly
communion table
crutched friars
Easter offering
ecclesiastical
Ecclesiasticus
ecclesiologist
evangelicalism
evangelization
extreme unction
fire-worshipper
fundamentalism
Gregorian chant
high priesthood
Maundy Thursday
Orthodox Church
Oxford Movement
psilanthropism
psilanthropist
reconsecration
redemptionists
Reformed Church

Rogation Sunday
sacramentarian
sanctification
sign of the cross
transmigration
trine immersion
Trinitarianism
vicar apostolic

15

antievangelical
antiministerial
antitrinitarian
Athanasian Creed
cardinal virtues
Episcopalianism
excommunication
harvest festival
infernal regions
Jehovah's Witness
metropolitanate
Mothering Sunday
Presbyterianism
suffragan bishop
transfiguration

Saints

Note.—The numbers of letters mentioned do not include "St" or "Saint", for which allowances should be made when necessary.

3 AND 4
Abb
Ann
Anne
Bee
Bede
Bega
Chad
Cyr
Ebba
Eloi
Gall
Jean
Joan
John
Jude
Just
Loe
Luce
Lucy
Luke
Mark

Mary
Paul
Roch
Zeno

5
Agnes
Aidan
Alban
Amand
André
Asaph
Barbe
Basil
Bavon
Bride
Bruno
Clair
Clara
David
Denis

Elias
Genny
Giles
Hilda
James
Kilda
Louis
Lucia
Marie
Olave
Paola
Peter

6
Albert
Andrea
Andrew
Anselm
Ansgar
Bertin
Brieuc

Claire
Cosmas
Fabian
Fergus
Gallus
George
Helena
Heiler
Hilary
Hubert
Jerome
Joseph
Ludger
Magnus
Martha
Martin
Maurus
Michel
Monica
Philip
Pierre
Thomas
Ursane

Ursula
Valery
Xavier

7
Ambrose
Anschar
Anthony
Austell
Barbara
Bernard
Bridget
Cecilia
Charles
Clement
Crispin
Dominic
Dorothy
Dunstan
Elsinus
Emidius

Etienne	**8**	**9**	Christopher (11)
Eustace			Ethelburga (10)
Francis	Aloysius	Apollonia	Eustochium (10)
Germain	Augustus	Augustine	Gallo Abbato (11)
Gregory	Barnabas	Catherine	Gaudentius (10)
Isodore	Benedict	Christina	Hippolytus (10)
Joachim	Bernhard	Demetrius	Jeanne d'Arc (10)
Leonard	Cuthbert	Eanswythe	Mercuriale (10)
Matthew	Damianus	Elizabeth	Peter Martyr (11)
Maurice	Denevick	Exuperius	Philip Neri (10)
Michael	Donatian	Fredewith	Scholastica (11)
Nazaire	Eusebius	Hyacinthe	Symphorien (10)
Nicolas	Ignatius	Joan of Arc	Zaccharias (10)
Pancras	Lawrence	Mamertius	
Patrick	Longinus	Sebastian	
Raphael	Margaret	Servatius	**12** AND OVER
Raymond	Nicholas	Sylvester	
Romuald	Paulinus	Valentine	Anthony of Padua (14)
Saviour	Placidus	Walpurgis	Bridget of Sweden (15)
Stephen	Polycarp		James the Great (13)
Swithin	Vericona		James the Less (12)
Swithun	Walpurga	**10** AND **11**	John the Baptist (14)
Vincent	Waltheof		Louis of Toulouse (15)
William	Winifred	Apollinaris (11)	Mary Magdalene (13)
	Zenobius	Athanasius (10)	Nicholas of Bari (14)
		Bartholomew (11)	Nicholas of Myra (14)
		Bernardino (10)	Simon Stylites (13)
		Benhardino (11)	Thomas Aquinas (13)
		Bonaventura (11)	Vincent Ferrer (13)

SCIENCE AND TECHNOLOGY
Agriculture

3	kex	**4**	cote	lamb	quey
	kid		crop	lime	rabi
awn	kip	akee	culm	loam	rake
bin	lea	aril	curb	lyme	rape
cob	moo	avel	drey	malm	resp
cod	mow	bale	dung	mare	rime
cow	pig	barn	farm	marl	root
cub	pip	bawn	foal	meal	roup
dig	ram	beam	gait	milk	runn
ear	ret	beef	galt	neat	rust
erf	rye	bent	gape	neep	ryot
ewe	sow	bere	harl	nide	sand
far	ted	bigg	haum	nout	scab
feu	teg	boon	herd	nowt	seed
gid	tup	bran	hind	oast	sere
hay	vag	bull	hink	oats	shaw
hep	vat	byre	holt	odal	silo
hip	zea	calf	hops	paco	skep
hoe		cart	hull	peat	skug
hog		clay	husk	pest	slob
ket		corn	kine	pone	sock

soil	halfa	binder	piglet	docking
soya	hards	bosket	pigsty	drought
span	haugh	bottle	plough	droving
stot	haulm	butter	podzol	eanling
teff	hedge	carney	polder	erosion
toft	hilum	cattle	porker	farming
tope	hoove	cereal	potato	fee-tail
tore	horse	clover	punner	foaling
udal	humus	colter	raggee	foldage
vale	kulak	corral	rancho	foot rot
vega	lande	cowman	realty	forcing
weed	llano	cratch	reaper	fox trap
wold	lobby	cutter	roller	gadsman
yean	maize	digger	runrig	granger
zebu	mower	disbud	sheave	grazing
	mummy	dobbin	silage	hallier
	ovine	drover	socage	harvest
5	plant	earing	sowans	hay cart
	ranch	eatage	sowing	hay rick
ammon	rumen	écurie	spruit	hedging
aphid	sewel	enspan	stable	herding
araba	sheep	fallow	steppe	hogcote
baler	sheth	farina	stover	hop pole
beans	shoat	farmer	tanist	hunkers
bhyle	shuck	fodder	tomand	implant
biddy	spelt	forage	travis	infield
borax	spuds	furrow	trough	innings
bosky	staig	gargol	turnip	kidling
bothy	stall	garran	turves	lamb-ale
braxy	stead	gaucho	warble	lambing
briza	stich	gimmer	weevil	laniary
calve	stipa	gluten		layland
carse	stock	grains		leasowe
cavie	straw	grange	**7**	lucerne
chaff	swill	harrow		maizena
churn	tilth	heifer	acidity	marlite
clevy	tiver	hogget	aerator	milk can
closh	tuber	hogsty	alfalfa	milking
couch	veldt	hopper	amidine	misyoke
croft	vimen	huller	anthrax	morling
crone	vives	incult	avenage	multure
crops	vomer	inning	binding	murrain
dairy	wagon	inspan	boscage	novalia
ditch	wheat	intine	budding	nursery
drill	withe	jument	bulchin	pabular
drove	withy	linhay	bullock	paddock
durra	worms	llanos	buttery	panicum
ergot	yield	malkin	cabbage	pannage
ervum		manger	calving	pasture
farcy		manure	combine	peonage
fruit	**6**	mealie	compost	piggery
fungi		merino	copland	pinetum
gavel	angora	milium	cornage	pinfold
gebur	animal	millet	coulter	polders
glume	arable	milsey	cowherd	popcorn
grain	arista	mowing	cowshed	poultry
grass	barley	nubbin	demesne	prairie
graze	basset	padnag	digging	praties
guano	beeves	pampas	dipping	predial

	8	dairy-farm	husbandman
provine		dairymaid	irrigation
pruning	agronomy	disc drill	mould-board
pulping	branding	fertility	plantation
pummace	breeding	fungicide	rounding-up
radicel	clipping	gathering	self-binder
raking	cropping	grassland	transplant
rancher	ditching	harrowing	weed killer
reaping	drainage	harvester	wheatfield
rearing	elevator	haymaking	
retting	ensilage	hop-picker	
rhizome	farmyard	horserake	**11**
rokeage	forestry	husbandry	
rundale	gleaning	implement	agriculture
rustler	grafting	incubator	cake crusher
ryotwar	hayfield	livestock	chaff cutter
sickled	haymaker	pasturage	chicken farm
slanket	haystack	penthouse	crude plough
spancel	haywagon	phosphate	cultivation
stacker	hopfield	pig trough	fertilizing
station	kohlrabi	ploughing	germination
stooker	landgirl	rice field	insecticide
stubble	loosebox	screening	motor plough
stuckle	milkcart	separator	pastureland
subsoil	pedigree	shorthorn	poultry farm
swinery	pig-swill	sugar beet	reclamation
tantony	plougher	sugar cane	stock-taking
tascall	rootcrop	swineherd	water-trough
tax cart	rotation	thrashing	weed control
threave	shearing	threshing	
thwaite	sheep-dip	trenching	
tillage	vineyard	winnowing	**12**
tilling	watering		
tractor	wireworm		agricultural
trammel		**10**	feeding-stock
trekker			fermentation
trotter	**9**	agronomist	horticulture
udaller		battery hen	insemination
vaquero	agrimotor	cattle cake	market garden
vitular	agroville	cultivator	smallholding
wagoner	allotment	fertilizer	swathe turner
windrow	cornfield	harvesting	turnip cutter
yardman			

Astronomy
(a.) = asteroid. (c.) = constellation. (c.p.) = constellation (popular name).
(g.) = group of stars. (p.) = planet. (s.) = noted star. (sa.) = large satellite.

2 – 4	Crow (c.p.)	Juno	Moon
	Crux (c.)	Leo (c.)	Net (c.p.)
Apus (c.)	Cup (c.p.)	limb	Node
Ara (c.)	Eros	Lion (c.p.)	nova
Argo (c.)	Grus (c.)	Lynx (c.) (c.p.)	orb
belt	halo	Lyra (c.)	Pavo (c.)
Bull (c.p.)	Hare (c.p.)	Lyre (c.p.)	pole
coma	Hebe	Mars (p.)	Ram (c.p.)
Crab (c.p.)	Io	Mira (s.)	Rhea (sa.)

Sol
Star
Sun
Swan (c.p.)
Vega (s.)
Wolf (c.p.)

5

Algol (s.)
Altar (c.p.)
Ariel (sa.)
Aries (c.)
Arrow (c.p.)
Ceres
Cetus (c.)
Clock (c.p.)
comet
Crane (c.p.)
Deneb (s.)
Digit
Dione (sa.)
Draco (c.)
Eagle (c.p.)
Earth (p.)
epact
epoch
error
flare
giant
Hamal (s.)
Hyads (g.)
Hydra (c.)
Indus (c.)
label
Lepus (c.)
Libra (c.)
lunar
Lupus (c.)
Mensa (c.)
Mimas (sa.)
Musca (c.)
nadir
Norma (c.)
orbit
Orion (c.)
phase
Pluto (p.)
Regel (s.)
Rigel (s.)
solar
space
Spica (s.)
stars
Titan (sa.)
Tucan (c.p.)
Twins (c.p.)
umbra

Venus (p.)
Vesta (a.)
Virgo (c.)

6

albedo
Altair (s.)
Antlia (c.)
apogee
Apollo
Aquila (c.)
Archer (c.p.)
astral
Auriga (c.)
aurora
binary
Boötes (c.)
Bolide
Caelum (c.)
Cancer (c.)
Castor (s.)
colure
Corona
Corvus (c.)
crater
Crater (c.)
Cygnus (c.)
Deimos (sa.)
Dipper
domify
Dorado (c.)
Dragon (c.p.)
Europa (sa.)
Fishes (c.p.)
Fornax (c.)
galaxy
Gemini (c.)
gnomon
Hyades (g.)
Hydrus (c.)
Icarus (a.)
Indian (c.p.)
Leonid
Lizard (c.p.)
lunary
meteor
moonet
nebula
Oberon (sa.)
Octans (c.)
Octant (c.p.)
octile
Pallas (a.)
parsec
Persei (g.)
Phobos (sa.)
Phoebe (sa.)

Pictor (c.)
Pisces (c.)
planet
Plough (g.)
Pollux (s.)
pulsar
quasar
Radius
Saturn (p.)
Scales (c.p.)
Sirius (s.)
sphere
Square (c.p.)
sun-dog
syzygy
Taurus (c.)
Tethys (sa.)
Triton (sa.)
Tucana (c.)
Uranus (p.)
vector
vertex
Viking
Virgin (c.p.)
Volans (c.)
zenith
zodiac

7

Airpump (c.p.)
Alphard (s.)
Antares (s.)
apogean
auroral
azimuth
big-bang
Canopus (s.)
Capella (s.)
Centaur (c.p.)
Cepheid
Cepheus (c.) (c.p.)
cluster
Columba (c.)
cometic
Dog Star (s.)
Dolphin (c.p.)
eclipse
equator
equinox
furnace (c.p.)
gibbous
Giraffe (c.p.)
Iapetus (sa.)
Jupiter (p.)
Lacerta (c.)
Mariner
Mercury (p.)

metonic
mock sun
nebulae
nebular
Neptune (p.)
new moon
Peacock (c.p.)
Pegasus (c.)
perigee
Perseus (c.)
Phoenix (c.) (c.p.)
Pleiads (g.)
Polaris (s.)
Procyon (s.)
Proxima (s.)
radiant
Regulus (s.)
Sagitta (c.)
Scorpio (c.)
Sea goat (c.p.)
Serpens (c.)
Serpent (c.p.)
Sextans (c.)
Sextant (c.p.)
sextile
spectra
sputnik
stellar
sunspot
Titania (sa.)
transit
Umbriel (sa.)
Unicorn (c.p .)

8

Achernar (s.)
aerolite
aerolith
almagest
Alpherat (s.)
altitude
aphelion
Aquarius (c.)
Arcturus (s.)
asterism
asteroid
Callisto (sa.)
canicula
Circinus (c.)
cometary
Denebola (s.)
draconic
ecliptic
epicycle
Equuleus (c.)
Eridanus (c.)
evection

Explorer
fireball
free fall
full moon
Ganymede (sa.)
Great Dog (c.p.)
Hercules (c.) (c.p.)
Hesperus
Hyperion (a.)
latitude
Leo Minor (c.)
Loadstar (s.)
Lodestar (s.)
meridian
meteoric
Milky Way
nutation
occulted
parallax
parhelia
penumbra
perigean
Pleiades (g.)
Pole Star (s.)
quadrant
quadrate
quartile
quintile
red giant
red shift
Scorpion (c.p.)
Sculptor (c.)
Ship Argo (c.p.)
sidereal
solstice
spectrum
spheroid
starless
stellary
sublunar
systemic
tetragon
Triangle (c.p.)
universe
Van Allen
Vanguard
variable
zodiacal

9

aerolitic
Aldebaran (s.)
Andromeda (c.) (c.p.)
arc-en-ciel
ascendant
ascension
astrology

astronomy
azimuthal
black hole
canicular
celestial
Centaurus (c.)
Chamaelon (c.)
Chameleon (c.p.)
Compasses (c.p.)
cosmogeny
cosmology
Curtation
Delphinus (c.)
draconian
elevation
Enceladus (sa.)
ephemeris
epicyclic
firmament
Fomalhaut (s.)
Great Bear (c.p.)
hour angle
light-year
Little Dog (c.p.)
longitude
lunisolar
magnitude
meteorite
meteoroid
meteorous
Minuteman
Monoceros (c.)
Nubeculae
Noah's Dove (c.p.)
novilunar
Ophiuchus (c.)
parhelian
planetary
planetoid
planetule
Ploughman (c.p.)
Ptolemaic
reflector
refractor
Reticulum (c.)
satellite
solar wind
star-gazer
starlight
sublunary
supernova
Sword-fish (c.p.)
synodical
telescope
Telescope (c.p.)
trioctile
uranology
Ursa Major (c.)
Ursa Minor (c.)

Via Lactea
Vulpecula (c.)

10

aberration
altazimuth
apparition
asteroidal
astrologer
astrometer
astronomer
astronomic
Atlantides (g.)
atmosphere
Betelgeuse (s.)
brightness
Canis Major (c.)
Canis Minor (c.)
Cassiopeia (c.) (c.p.)
Charioteer (c.p.)
cometarium
Copernican
cosmic rays
Crab nebula
depression
discoverer
dispositor
double star
earthshine
elongation
exaltation
extra-solar
Flying Fish (c.p.)
Greyhounds (c.p.)
hour circle
Little Bear (c.p.)
Little Lion (c.p.)
lunar cycle
lunar month
lunar probe
Microscope (c.p.)
North Star
opposition
outer space
perihelion
Piscis Aust. (c.)
precession
prominence
quadrature
refraction
retrograde
rudolphine
Sea Monster (c.p.)
siderolite
star-gazing
supergiant
terminator

trajectory
Triangulum (c.)
uranoscopy
Watersnake (c.p.)
white dwarf

11

astrography
astronomize
blazing star
Capricornus (c.)
conjunction
declination
Evening Star (p.)
falling star
giant planet
Hunter Orion (c.p.)
last quarter
Little Horse (c.p.)
metemptosis
meteorolite
minor planet
Morning Star (p.)
neutron star
occultation
photosphere
observatory
planetarium
Sagittarius (c.)
solar system
Southern Fly (c.p.)
spectrology
Telescopium (c.)
terrestrial
uranography
Water-bearer (c.p.)
Winged Horse (c.p.)

12

astronautics
astronomical
astrophysics
Charles's Wain (g.)
chromosphere
doppler shift
eccentricity
first quarter
Flying-dragon (c.p.)
Halley's comet
Horologium (c.)
intermundane
interstellar
lunar eclipse
lunar rainbow
Microscopium (c.)

Saturn's rings
shooting star
sidereal time
solar eclipse
Southern Fish (c.p.)
spectroscope
spiral galaxy
uranographic
Van Allen Belt
variable star

13

Alpha Centauri (s.)
Berenice's Hair (c.p.)
Canes Venatici (c.)
Coma Berenices (c.)
constellation
Crux Australis (c.)
meteorography
Northern Crown (c.p.)

Painter's Easel (c.p.)
River Eridanus (c.p.)
Serpent-bearer (c.p.)
sidereal clock
Southern Cross (c.p.)
Southern Crown (c.p.)
zodiacal light

14

annular eclipse
Aurora Borealis
Bird of Paradise (c.p.)
Camelopardalis (c.)
Corona Borealis (c.)
interplanetary
Musca Australis (c.)
radio astronomy
radio telescope
right ascension
Sculptor's Tools (c.p.)

summer solstice
transit of Venus
vertical circle
winter solstice
Wolf-Rayet star
zenith distance

15 AND 16

Alphonsine tables (16)
armillary sphere (15)
astronomical unit (16)
Aurora Australis (15)
celestial sphere (15)
Corona Australis (c.) (15)
Fraunhofer lines (15)
Magellanic Clouds (16)
meteoric showers (15)
Piscis Australis (c.) (15)
Sculptor's Chisel (c.) (15)

Biology, botany, and zoology

2 AND 3

ADH
ADP
ATP
bud
CNS
cud
DNA
ear
egg
ER
eye
FAD
fin
gel
gum
gut
IAA
jaw
lip
NAD
ova
pod
rib
RNA
rod
sap
sex

4

anal
anus
apex
axon
bark
bile
bird
body
bone
bulb
burr
cell
claw
cone
cork
corm
cyst
food
foot
gall
gene
germ
gill
haem
hair
hand
head
hoof

host
iris
leaf
lens
life
limb
lung
milk
NADH
NADP
neck
node
ovum
palp
pith
pome
pore
root
salt
seed
skin
stem
tail
urea
vein
wilt
wing
wood
yolk

5

actin
aorta
aster
auxin
berry
birth
blood
bract
brain
calyx
chyle
chyme
cilia
class
cline
clone
codon
colon
cutin
cycad
cycle
death
digit
drupe
druse
fauna
femur
fibre

flora
fruit
genus
gland
gonad
graft
heart
hilum
humus
hymen
ileum
imago
larva
latex
liver
lymph
molar
mouth
mucus
NADPH
nasal
nasty
nerve
order
organ
ovara
ovary
ovule
penis
petal

phage	caudal	pelvis	cardiac	plastid
plant	chitin	phloem	carotid	plumule
pubic	climax	phylum	cell sap	protein
pubis	cloaca	pistil	chaetae	pyloric
pupil	coccyx	plasma	chalaza	radicle
ramus	cocoon	pollen	chiasma	rhachis
resin	coelum	purine	chorion	rhizoid
scale	cornea	radius	cochlea	rhizome
semen	cortex	rectum	conifer	root cap
sense	dermis	retina	corolla	species
sepal	dormin	runner	cranial	spindle
shell	embryo	sacrum	cranium	sternum
shoot	enamel	sexual	creeper	stomach
sinus	energy	spinal	cristae	stomata
skull	enzyme	spleen	culture	suberin
smell	facial	stamen	cuticle	synapse
sperm	faeces	stigma	cutting	syngamy
spine	family	stolon	diploid	systole
spore	fibril	sucker	dormant	tapetum
stoma	fibrin	tactic	ecdysis	tap root
style	fibula	tannin	ecology	teleost
sweat	floral	telome	elastin	tetanus
taste	flower	tendon	enteron	thallus
testa	foetus	tenson	epiboly	thyroid
thigh	forest	testis	epigeal	trachea
tibla	floral	thorax	gastric	triceps
touch	fusion	tissue	genital	trophic
trunk	gamete	tongue	gizzard	tropism
tuber	gemmae	turgor	glottis	urethra
urine	genome	ureter	habitat	vacuole
vagus	girdle	uterus	haploid	viscera
villi	growth	vagina	hearing	vitamin
virus	gullet	vessel	hepatic	zoology
whorl	hybrid	vision	histone	
wrist	hyphae	zygote	hormone	
xylem	joints		humerus	
	labial		incisor	**8**
	labium	**7**	insulin	abductor
6	labrum		isogamy	abscisin
	lamina	abdomen	jcjunum	acoelous
achene	larynx	adenine	keratin	acrosome
aerobe	leaves	adipore	lacteal	adductor
albino	lignin	adrenal	linkage	aeration
allele	mammal	aerobic	mammary	alkaloid
amnion	mantle	albumen	medulla	allogamy
animal	marrow	anatomy	meiosis	alveolus
annual	mucous	annulus	mitosis	amoeboid
anther	muscle	antenna	myotome	anaerobe
artery	mutant	antigen	nectary	antibody
atrium	nastic	asexual	nostril	apospory
biceps	nectar	atavism	nucleus	appendix
biotic	neural	auricle	oogonia	auditory
botany	neuron	biology	organic	autogamy
branch	oocyte	biotope	osmosis	bacteria
bulbil	oogamy	bipolar	oviduct	biennial
caecum	palate	bladder	petiole	bile duct
canine	pappus	bronchi	pharynx	biomorph
carpal	pectin	cambium	pigment	bisexual
carpel	pelvic	capsule	pinnate	blastula

257

brachial
carapace
carotene
cellular
cell wall
cerebral
cerebrum
chordate
clavicle
cleavage
clitoris
coenzyme
collagen
cytology
dendrite
duodenum
ectoderm
efferent
egestion
endoderm
feedback
flagella
flatworm
follicle
ganglion
genetics
genitals
genotype
germ cell
holdfast
holozoic
homodont
hypogeal
inner ear
lamellae
lenticel
life span
ligament
mast cell
maxillae
membrane
meristem
mesoderm
midbrain
moulting
movement
muscular
mutation
mycelium
nerve net
nucellus
ontogeny
pancreas
papillae
parasite
pectoral
perianth
pericarp
perineum

placenta
plankton
polarity
polysome
pregnant
prop root
protozoa
receptor
ribosome
root hair
ruminant
sclereid
seedling
skeleton
spiracle
symbiont
syncarpy
taxonomy
tegument
tentacle
thalamus
tracheid
tympanum
vascular
vertebra
virology
zoospore

9

adrenalin
allantois
amino acid
anabolism
anaerobic
anisogamy
antennule
appendage
arteriole
autonomic
basal body
branchial
branching
capillary
carnivore
cartilage
cellulase
cellulose
centriole
chiasmata
chromatid
chromatin
chrysalis
commensal
community
corpuscle
cotyledon
cytoplasm

Darwinism
diaphragm
digestion
dominance
dura mater
dysploidy
ecosystem
ectoplasm
endocrine
endoplasm
endostyle
epidermis
eukaryote
evolution
excretion
excretory
exodermis
fertilize
forebrain
germinate
gestation
guttation
gynaecium
haemocoel
halophyte
herbivore
hindbrain
histology
homospory
hypocotyl
ingestion
inhibitor
internode
intestine
life cycle
life forms
megaspore
micropyle
middle ear
migration
mutagenic
nephridia
nerve cell
notochord
nucleolus
olfactory
oogenesis
operculum
optic lobe
organelle
organogeny
oxidation
pacemaker
perennial
pericycle
phagocyte
phellogen
phenotype
phylogeny

pituitary
proboscis
pulmonary
recessive
reflex arc
reticulum
retractor
sclerotic
sebaceous
secretion
secretory
selection
sieve cell
sieve tube
sporangia
Sporogony
sterility
stone cell
substrate
succulent
symbiosis
tricuspid
umbilical
unisexual
ventricle
xerophyte

10

acoelomate
actomyosin
alimentary
androecium
antheridia
anticlinal
aortic arch
apical cell
archegonia
autecology
biological
blastocoel
blastocyst
blastoderm
blastomere
blastopore
bronchiole
catabolism
centromere
centrosome
cerebellum
chemotaxis
chromomere
chromosome
coleoptile
copulation
dehiscence
dermatogen
entomology

epididymis
epiglottis
epithelium
fibrinogen
generation
geotropism
glomerulus
grey matter
guard cells
hemocyanin
hemoglobin
herbaceous
hereditary
heterodont
homocercal
homozygous
hygrophyte
hypophysis
incubation
inhibition
integument
interferon
Krebs cycle
Lamarckism
leaf sheath
leucoplast
locomotion
lymphocyte
mesenteron
metabolism
monoecious
morphology
mother cell
mycorrhiza
negentropy
nerve fibre
neural tube
nitrifying
nucleotide
oesophagus
omnivorous
osteoblast
osteoclast
parasitism
parenchyma
pathogenic
periosteum
phelloderm
photonasty
phototaxis
physiology
pineal body
polyploidy
population
prokaryote
prothallus
protoplasm
pyramidine

saprophyte
sarcolemma
schizogony
sieve plate
splanchnic
sporophyte
strophiole
subspecies
succession
synecology
vegetation
vegetative
vertebrate
viviparity

11

aestivation
allelomorph
antibiotics
archenteron
autotrophic
autotropism
carbon cycle
carboxylase
carnivorous
chlorophyll
chloroplast
collenchyma
competition
conjugation
deamination
dessication
endothelium
environment
erythrocyte
exoskeleton
facultative
gall bladder
gametophyte
genetic code
germination
Golgi bodies
haemocyanin
haemoglobin
heterospory
hibernation
homeostatic
homeostatis
infundibulum
inheritance
loop of Henle
monoculture
muscle fibre
nematoblast
nucleic acid

orientation
parturition
pericardium
pinocytosis
plasmolysis
polar bodies
pollination
polypeptide
pseudopodia
respiration
somatic cell
spermatozoa
sub-cellular
tapetal cell
thermotaxis
triploblast
white matter
zooplankton

12

all-or-nothing
archesporium
back-crossing
bacteriology
biochemistry
buccal cavity
central canal
chondroblast
denitrifying
diploblastic
distribution
ectoparasite
endoparasite
endoskeleton
fermentation
flexor muscle
gastrulation
heliotropism
heterocercal
heterogamete
heterozygous
hypothalamus
invagination
invertebrate
mammary gland
medullary ray
microbiology
mitochondria
myelin sheath
nerve impulse
palaeobotany
phospholipid
phototropism
red blood cell
reductionism

reproduction
sclerenchyma
smooth muscle
spermatozoid
telolecithal

13

accommodation
bacteriophage
bicuspid valve
binary fission
cephalization
chemoreceptor
decomposition
dental formula
erector muscle
extracellular
Fallopian tube
fertilization
hermaphrodite
homoiothermic
insectivorous
intracellular
marine biology
mitochondrion
morphogenesis
multinucleate
ovoviviparity
palisade cells
parthenocarpy
photoreceptor
phytoplankton
plasmodesmata
proprioceptor
striped muscle
thermotropism
thigmotropism
translocation
transpiration

14 AND 15

Brunner's glands (14)
chemosynthesis (14)
extensor muscle (14)
Haversian canal (14)
multiple fission (15)
osmoregulation (14)
oxyhaemoglobin (14)
parthenogenesis (15)
photoperiodism (14)
photosynthesis (14)
poikilothermic (14)
polysaccharide (14)
vascular bundle (14)

Chemistry and metallurgy

2 AND 3

azo
DDT
DNA
E.M.F.
fat
gas
ion
mu
oil
ore
pH
pKa
PVC
RNA
sol
TCP
tin
TNT

4

acid
acyl
alum
aryl
atom
base
bond
cell
clay
coal
coke
enol
gold
iron
keto
lead
lime
meta
mica
mole
mond
neon
rust
salt
slag
soda
spin
zinc

5

aldol
alkyl
alloy
amide
amine
amino
anion
anode
arene
argon
azote
basic
beryl
borax
boron
brass
chalk
ester
ether
ethyl
freon
glass
group
imine
invar
ionic
lipid
lysol
metal
model
molal
molar
monad
muntz
niton
nitre
nylon
oxide
ozone
phase
radon
redox
resin
roast
salol
smelt
solid
steel
sugar
vinyl
wootz
xenon

6

acetal
acetic
acetyl
acidic
adduct
aerate
alkali
alkane
alkene
alkyne
amatol
ammine
atomic
aufbau
barium
baryta
biuret
bleach
borane
borate
bronze
buffer
butane
carbon
casein
cation
cerium
chrome
cobalt
copper
cresol
curium
dipole
dry ice
energy
enzyme
erbium
ethane
ferric
galena
gangue
gypsum
halide
helium
indium
iodate
iodide
iodine
iodite
iodize
ionium
isomer

ketone
ligand
liquid
litmus
methyl
nickel
octane
olefin
osmium
oxygen
period
pewter
phenol
phenyl
potash
proton
quartz
raceme
radium
redman
reduce
refine
retort
ribose
rutile
silica
silver
sinter
sodium
solder
solute
starch
sterol
sulfur
tannin
teepol
teflon
thymol

7

acetate
acetone
acidity
aerosol
alchemy
alcohol
alumina
amalgam
ammonal
ammonia
analyse
aniline

anodize
antacid
arsenic
aspirin
bauxite
benzene
bismuth
bonding
bromate
bromide
bromine
cadmium
caesium
calcium
calomel
camphor
carbide
cathode
chemist
chloric
cocaine
codeine
cyanate
cyanide
diamond
dioxide
ebonite
element
entropy
ferment
fermium
ferrate
ferrous
formate
gallium
gelatin
glucose
hafnium
halogen
holmium
hydrate
hydride
iridium
isotope
krypton
lithium
menthol
mercury
methane
mineral
monomer
naptha
neutral
neutron

niobium
nitrate
nitride
nitrite
nucleon
orbital
organic
osmosis
osmotic
oxidant
oxidize
oxyacid
pentane
peptide
perspex
pig iron
plastic
polymer
propane
protein
pyrites
quantum
quinine
reagent
redlead
rhenium
rhodium
silicon
soda-ash
soluble
solvent
spectra
spelter
sucrose
sulfate
sulfide
sulfite
sulphur
terbium
terpene
thorium
thulium
titrate
toluene
tritium
uranium
valence
valency
veronal
vitamin
vitriol
wolfram
yttrium

8

actinide
actinium

aldehyde
alkaline
aluminum
ammonium
analysis
antimony
aromatic
asbestos
astatine
atropine
Bakelite
Bessemer
caffeine
carbolic
carbonic
carbonyl
cast iron
catalyst
charcoal
chemical
chlorate
chloride
chlorine
chromate
chromite
chromium
cinchona
cinnabar
corundum
covalent
cryolite
cyanogen
diatomic
diborane
didymium
disilane
dissolve
electron
europium
emission
enthalpy
ethylene
firedamp
fluoride
fluorine
formalin
francium
fructose
glucinum
glycerol
graphite
gunmetal
half-life
haloform
hematite
hydrated
hydrogen
hydroxyl
ideal gas

inert gas
iodoform
kerosene
kinetics
litharge
lone pair
lutecium
lutetium
magnesia
manganin
marsh gas
masurium
methanol
molecule
morphine
nichrome
nicotine
nitrogen
nobelium
noble gas
non-metal
oxyanion
paraffin
particle
periodic
peroxide
phosgene
platinum
plumbago
polonium
pot metal
reactant
reaction
refining
rock salt
rubidium
samarium
saturate
scandium
selenium
silicane
silicate
solution
spectrum
suboxide
sulphate
sulphide
sulphite
tantalum
test tube
thallium
titanium
tungsten
unit cell
unstable
vanadium
water gas

9

acetylene
acylation
alchemist
alcoholic
aliphatic
allotropy
aluminate
aluminium
americium
amino acid
anhydrous
anti-knock
apparatus
aqua regia
bell metal
berkelium
beryllium
blacklead
brimstone
carbonate
carbonium
catalysis
cellolose
cellulose
chemistry
chokedamp
colombium
corrosion
deuterium
diazonium
digitalin
duralumin
galvanize
germanium
guncotton
gunpowder
haematite
histamine
homolysis
hydration
hydroxide
indicator
inorganic
insoluble
isomerism
lanthanum
limestone
limewater
magnesium
magnetite
manganese
metalloid
millerite
molecular
monatomic
neodymium
neptunium

nitration
nitronium
oxidation
palladium
permalloy
petroleum
phosphate
phosphide
plutonium
polar bond
polyester
polythene
polyvinyl
potassium
quicklime
rare gases
reductant
reduction
ruthenium
resonance
saltpetre
semi-metal
solvation
stability
strontium
sulphuric
synthesis
synthetic
tellurium
titration
verdigris
vulcanite
whitelead
ytterbium
zirconium

exothermic
flotation
formic acid
free energy
gadolinium
heavy water
hydrolysis
isocyanide
laboratory
lactic acid
lanthanide
latent heat
lawrencium
mass number
metallurgy
mischmetal
molybdenum
Muntz metal
natural gas
neutralize
nitric acid
nucleotide
oxalic acid
phosphorus
polyatomic
polymerize
promethium
rare earths
saccharide
solubility
technetium
transition
whitemetal
zinc blende
zwitterion

hydrocyanic
hydroxonium
ipecacuanha
laughing gas
litmus paper
mendelevium
Muntz's metal
naphthalene
non-metallic
nucleophile
paraldehyde
phosphorous
pitchblende
polystyrene
precipitate
prussic acid
quicksilver
radioactive
ribonucleic
sal ammoniac
Schiff's base
sublimation
substituent
tautomerism
transuranic
wrought iron

Prince's metal
protactinium
rate constant
Rochellesalt
sulphonamide
tartaric acid
zone refining

13

Bessemer steel
carbon dioxide
chain reaction
chromium steel
giant molecule
lattice energy
molecular mass
paramagnetism
periodic table
petrochemical
precipitation
protoactinium
radioactivity
reaction order
recrystallize
semiconductor
sulphuric acid
trisaccharide

12

acetaldehyde
alkali metals
alkyl halides
atomic number
atomic weight
benzaldehyde
blast furnace
carbohydrate
carbonic acld
chlorination
condensation
covalent bond
deliquescent
diamagnetism
disaccharide
displacement
dissociation
distillation
electrolysis
electrophile
fermentation
formaldehyde
German silver
Haber process
halogenation
hydrochloric
hydrogen bond
permanganate
praseodymium

14 AND OVER

Born-Haber cycle (14)
Britannia metal (14)
carbon monoxide (14)
carboxylic acid (14)
Chile saltpetre (14)
decarbonization (15)
deoxyribonucleic (16)
electrochemical (15)
esterification (14)
ferro-manganese (14)
Grignard reagent (15)
monosaccharide (14)
organo-metallic (14)
oxidizing agent (14)
phosphor bronze (14)
photosynthesis (14)
polysaccharide (14)
reaction profile (15)
saponification (14)
trinitrotoluene (15)

10

acetic acid
alkalinity
allotropes
amphoteric
analytical
bimetallic
bond energy
bond length
carnallite
catenation
caoutchouc
chalybeate
chemically
chloroform
constantin
dative bond
double bond
dysprosium
electronic
enantiomer

11

acetylation
benzoic acid
bicarbonate
californium
carborundum
cassiterite
cholesterol
crystallize
cyclohexane
dehydration
einsteinium
electrolyte
elimination
endothermic
equilibrium
free radical
German steel
glauber salt
ground state
hydrocarbon

Computers

1 AND 2
AI
C
IT
PC
WP

3
ADA
alt
APL
APT
BOS
bug
CAD
CAM
CPU
DOS
DTP
end
esc
fax
key
pad
PIN
PSU
RAM
ROM
RSI
tab
VDU
VDT
WPM
zap

4
boot
byte
chip
code
copy
data
disc
disk
down
drag
dump
edit
exit
feed

file
font
hack
home
icon
ikon
LISP
load
LOGO
loop
menu
MIDI
move
peek
poll
port
quit
save
scan
sort
type
unit
WIMP

5
ALGOL
ASCII
BASIC
COBOL
COMAL
CORAL
crash
debug
drive
enter
field
FORTH
fount
input
key in
log in
log on
macro
micro
modem
mouse
queue
reset
slave
store
virus

6
AZERTY
back up
binary
boot up
cursor
decode
delete
escape
folder
format
hacker
hopper
indent
laptop
memory
on-line
ouput
PASCAL
PILOT
PROLOG
QUERTY
reboot
return
screen
server
sign on
SNOBOL
window

7
booting
circuit
command
corrupt
default
density
emulate
execute
FORTRAN
hot zone
imaging
kilobit
monitor
network
pointer
polling
printer
program
readout
recover
scanner

sort key
storage
toolkit

8
arrow key
capacity
caps lock
cold boot
databank
database
document
emulator
facsimile
function
hard disc
hard disk
hardware
joystick
keyboard
key punch
kilobyte
megabyte
password
printout
real time
recovery
scramble
shift key
shut down
software
space bar
spooling
terminal
typeface
warm boot
word wrap

9
alternate
backspace
character
cycle time
directory
disc drive
disk drive
dot matrix
half space
hard error
interface

jumbo chip
mail-merge
mainframe
microchip
overwrite
paper tray
processor
range left
scrambler
shift key
soft error
throughput
word break

10
de-scramble
floppy disc
floppy disk
numeric pad
peripheral
processing
programmer
range right
repeat key
spellcheck
stand alone
system disc
system disk
wraparound

11
circuit card
cut and paste
diagnostics
display mode
display unit
function key
input device
machine code
numberic pad
programmer
silicon chip
spreadsheet
unformatted

12
addition time
circuit board
dumb terminal

home computer
housekeeping
integer BASIC
laser printer
machine cycle
output device
response time
serial access
user friendly

13

alphabetic pad
compatibility
display screen
double density
justified text
microcomputer
postprocessor
query language
remote station
word processor

14

author language
computer dating
data protection
microprocessor
remote terminal
systems analyst
word processing

15

double-sided disk
machine language
natural language
systems analysis

16

assembly language
compiler language

computer engineer
computer language
computer literacy
computer-literate
computer operator
control character
low-level language
personal computer

17

assembler language
dedicated computer
desk top publishing
high-level language
satellite computer
satellite terminal
synthetic language

Dyes, paints and colours

3

bay
dun
hue
jet
lac
red
tan
vat

4

acid
anil
ashy
bice
bise
blue
buff
cyan
dark
deep
drab
ebon
ecru
fast
fawn

food
gilt
gold
gray
grey
gris
hoar
jade
kohl
lake
navy
pale
pink
puce
roan
room
rose
ruby
rust
sage
weld
wine
woad
wold

5

amber

argal
argol
ashen
azoic
azure
azurn
basic
beige
black
brown
camel
chica
coral
cream
diazo
ebony
flame
grain
green
gules
hazel
henna
hoary
ivory
jetty
khaki
lemon
liard
light

lilac
livid
lovat
mauve
murex
ocher
ochre
ochry
olive
orpin
paint
perse
raven
roset
rouge
ruddy
sable
sandy
sepia
snowy
sooty
stain
swart
taupe
tawny
ulmin
umber
white

6

ambery
anotta
anotto
archil
auburn
aureat
aurora
azured
bablah
bistre
bluish
cerise
cherry
chrome
claret
cobalt
copper
damask
direct
enamel
fallow
flaxen
fulvid
fustic
ginger
golden
greeny

indigo
isabel
kamalla
kamilla
kermes
lac dye
litmus
madder
mallow
marone
maroon
minium
modena
morone
murrey
orange
pastel
purple
raddle
reddle
reseda
roucou
rubian
rubied
rubric
ruddle
rufous
russet
sallow
sanded
sienna
silver
sorrel
spotty
Tyrian
umbery
vermil
violet
virent
yellow

7

alizare
alkanet
almagra
annotta
annotto
apricot
arnotto
aureate
barwood
bezetta
biscuit
camboge
camwood
carmine
carroty

cassius
catechu
cerulin
cesious
chermes
citrine
coupler
cramesy
crimson
cudbear
cyanine
darkish
dracina
dracine
emerald
filemot
flavine
fulvous
fuscous
gamboge
gentian
grayish
greyish
grizzle
grizzly
hazelly
ingrain
logwood
magenta
mahaleb
minious
mordant
mottled
munjeet
mustard
nacarat
nankeen
nattier
natural
neutral
old gold
olivine
piebald
pigment
pinkish
plunket
reddish
red lead
rubican
ruby red
russety
saffron
scarlet
silvern
silvery
sinopia
sinopis
sky blue
solvent

spotted
stammel
streaky
striped
sulphur
swarthy
verdant
vermiel
watchet
whiting
whitish
xanthic
zaphara

8

alizarin
amaranth
amethyst
ashy pale
bloncket
blood red
brownish
caesious
cardinal
carotene
cerulean
chay-root
chestnut
chromule
cinnabar
croceate
croceous
disperse
glaucous
greenish
gridelin
grizzled
icterine
iron grey
jet black
lavender
litharge
luteolin
mazarine
navy blue
nut brown
oak stain
ochreous
off-white
palomino
pea green
philamot
purplish
rose hued
rose pink
rubrical
saffrony

sanguine
sap green
sapphire
saxe blue
sea green
speckled
streaked
titanium
turmeric
verditer
viridian
xanthine
xanthium

9

alizarine
argentine
aubergine
azure tint
bloodshot
bone black
brilliant
carnation
chaya root
chocolate
coal black
cochineal
colcothar
colour box
columbine
coralline
curcumine
developer
double dye
draconine
duck green
dun colour
Dutch pink
dyer's weed
dye stuffs
encrimson
envermeil
erythrean
euchloric
foliomort
Indian red
jade green
kalsomine
lampblack
leaf-green
lily white
lime green
myrobalan
oil colour
oxidation
pigmental
prasinous

puniceous
purpureal
purpurine
quercetin
royal blue
rufescent
safflower
sallowish
santaline
sapan wood
sap colour
sarcoline
Saxon blue
sky colour
silver grey
snow white
steel blue
turkey red
turquoise
verdigris
verditure
vermilion
vinaceous
virescent
white-lead
willowish
yellowish
zinc-white

10

alutaceous
apple green
aquamarine
atramental
aurigerous
Berlin blue
body colour
Brazil wood
Braziletto
burnt umber
carthamine
cobalt-blue
coquelicot
coromandel
double-dyed
endochrome
erubescent
flavescent
florentine
French navy
giallolina
grass green
heliotrope
indigo blue
indigotine
ivory white
morbidezza

mosaic gold
ochraceous
olivaceous
olive green
petrol blue
powder blue
puce colour
quercitrin
roan colour
rose colour
ruby colour
salmon pink
smaragdine
snowy white
spadiceous
Spanish red
stone ochre
strawberry
swartiness
terra-cotta
terre verte
violaceous
whity-brown

11

aerial tints
anthocyanin
ash-coloured
atramentous
bombycinous
bottle green
burnt orange
burnt sienna
chlorophyll
chrome green
cineritious
cinnamon red
crimson lake
dun-coloured
ferruginous
feuillemort
fiesta pink
flame colour
flesh colour
fluorescent
incarnadine
king's yellow
lateritious
lemon yellow
liver colour
mandarining
neutral tint
orange tawny
peach colour
peacock blue
stone colour
straw colour

terra sienna
ultramarine
Venetian red
viridescent
water colour
yellow ochre

12

airforce blue
Avignon berry
cherry colour
chrome colour
claret colour
chrome yellow
copper colour
dragon's blood
Egyptian blue
electric blue
emerald green
ferruginated
feuillemorte
golden yellow
grain colours
Indian madder
Indian yellow
Lincoln green
midnight blue
Naples yellow
Persian berry
pillar-box red
Prussian blue
rose-coloured
sapphire blue
Spanish black
Spanish brown
Spanish white
thenard's blue
Tyrian purple

13

Adrianople red
auripigmentum
cadmium yellow
chestnut brown
couleur de rose
cream-coloured
fibre-reactive
flame-coloured
flesh-coloured
peach-coloured
rainbow-tinted
Scheele's green
straw-coloured
trout-coloured
versicoloured
yellow colours

14 – 15

atramentaceous (14)
Brunswick black (14)
Brunswick green (14)
chocolate colour (15)
copper-coloured (14)
divers-coloured (14)
Frankfort black (14)
highly coloured (14)
quercitron bark (14)

Engineering
See also **Instruments** and **Tools and simple machines**

2 AND 3

ace
amp
B.H.P.
bit
cam
cog
dam
E.M.F.
erg
fan
fit
gab
hob
H.P.
hub
I.H.P.
ion
key
lag
nut
ohm
oil
ram
rig
R.P.M.
sag
tap
tew
tie
U.H.F.
V.H.F.

cowl
flaw
flux
fuel
fuse
gear
gibs
glue
hasp
hook
hose
jack
kiln
lens
lift
link
lock
loom
main
mill
mine
nail
nave
oily
pawl
pile
pipe
plan
plug
pump
rack
rail
reel
road
rope
rung
rust
shop
skid
slag
slue
stay
stop
stud
suck
sump
tamp

tank
test
tire
tool
tram
tube
turn
tyre
unit
vane
vent
void
volt
weir
weld
wire
work
worm

5

alloy
anode
binac
blast
braze
cable
chair
chase
civil
clamp
cleat
compo
crane
crank
crate
deuce
dowel
drill
drive
elbow
emery
felly
flawy
flows

flume
flush
force
gauge
girder
grace
H-beam
helix
hinge
hoist
ingot
input
jantu
jenny
jewel
joint
joist
keyed
laser
level
lever
lewis
maser
miner
model
motor
mould
oakum
oiler
pedal
pivot
plant
power
press
pylon
quern
radar
radio
ratch
relay
resin
rigid
rivet
rough
rusty
screw
shaft

short
shunt
slack
slide
sling
smelt
spoke
spool
spout
stamp
steam
still
strap
strut
stulm
swage
swape
taper
tewel
tommy
tools
tooth
T-rail
train
valve
video
waste
wedge
wharf
wheel
willy
wiper
works
X-rays

4

arch
axle
beam
belt
bolt
burr
byte
cast
coak
cone

6

analog
aerial
anneal
axunge
barrel
bit-end
blower
bobbin

boiler	siding	caisson	pig iron	voltaic
bridge	sleeve	casting	pinhole	welding
buffer	sluice	cathode	pontoon	wet dock
burner	smiddy	chafery	program	wringer
camber	smithy	chamfer	pug mill	wrought
clutch	socket	chimney	rag bolt	
coppin	solder	cistern	railway	
cotter	spigot	clacker	ratchet	**8**
couple	static	column	reactor	
cradle	stoker	conduit	refract	acentric
cut-out	strain	cutting	rejoint	air brake
damper	stress	derrick	riveter	air valve
derail	strike	digital	road bed	annealed
duplex	sucker	drawbar	roadway	aqueduct
dynamo	switch	drawing	sawmill	axletree
energy	swivel	dry dock	scissel	balancer
engine	system	dry pile	seabank	ball cock
fitter	tackle	dynamic	seawall	bevelled
flange	taglia	exciter	shackle	bridging
flashe	tappet	exhaust	shuttle	caliduct
funnel	temper	eyebolt	sleeper	camshaft
geyser	tender	factory	smelter	cam wheel
gutter	thrust	ferrule	soup pan	cassette
hinged	tie-bar	firebox	spindle	castings
hooter	tie-rod	fitting	stamper	cast iron
ingate	tinned	forging	stand-by	catenary
intake	toggle	founder	statics	chainlet
jigger	torque	foundry	stopper	chauffer
kibble	tripod	fulcrum	succula	cog wheel
lacing	trolly	furnace	suction	compound
ladder	tubing	fuse box	sump-pit	computer
lamina	tunnel	gas trap	support	concrete
latten	tuyere	gearing	syringe	corn mill
magnet	uncoil	gimbals	tamping	coupling
milled	vacuum	gudgeon	telefer	cradling
mining	washer	hydrant	templet	cryotron
moment	welded	inertia	tension	cylinder
monkey	welder	jointer	test bay	Davy lamp
nipple	windle	journal	testing	dead lift
nozzle		lagging	thimble	declutch
oil can		lockage	tie-beam	draw gear
oil gas	**7**	lock-nut	tilting	draw link
output		machine	tinfoil	edge rail
petrol	adapter	magneto	tin mine	electric
pinion	air duct	manhole	tinning	elevator
piston	airfoil	mill cog	torsion	engineer
pulley	air pipe	mill dam	tracing	enginery
punkah	air pump	milling	tramcar	eolipile
rarefy	air tube	monitor	tramway	fan blast
repair	air trap	moulded	treadle	feed pipe
retard	artisan	moulder	trendle	feed pump
rigger	autocar	mud hole	trolley	fireclay
rocket	autovac	mud sill	turbine	fireplug
roller	battery	nuclear	turning	flywheel
rotary	bearing	Ohm's law	unrivet	fracture
rundle	belting	oil fuel	unscrew	friction
sagger	booster	oil lamp	ventage	fuse clip
saw pit	bracket	oil pump	viaduct	galvanic
sheave	cab tyre	pattern	voltage	gas gauge

268

gas mains
gas works
gland nut
governor
gradient
hardware
hot blast
hot press
ignition
injecter
injector
ink stone
insulate
ironwork
irrigate
Jacquard
joint box
junk ring
klystron
laminate
land roll
leverage
limekiln
linch pin
linotype
lock gate
lock sill
lock weir
loop line
machinal
magnetic
main line
mechanic
mill pond
mill race
momentum
monorail
monotype
moulding
movement
mud valve
oilstone
oil store
oil stove
operator
ozonizer
pendulum
penstock
pile shoe
platform
polarity
pressure
puddling
pump gear
pump hood
purchase
radiator
rag wheel
rail road

recharge
refinery
register
repairer
repolish
rheostat
rigidity
ring bolt
rotatory
shearing
silk mill
skew arch
smeltery
smelting
soft iron
software
spinnery
split pin
stamping
standard
starling
stone pit
stopcock
strength
stuffing
tail race
tapering
telotype
tempered
template
terminal
textbook
throttle
tidegate
tide mill
tile kiln
time ball
tinplate
tractile
traction
tractive
train oil
tram rail
tramroad
turbojet
turnpike
tympanum
unclutch
uncoiled
unsolder
velocity
water gas
windmill
wind pump
wire-draw
wireless
wood mill
workable
workshop

wormgear

9

acoustics
air engine
air filter
air vessel
amplifier
artificer
baseplate
bevel gear
brakedrum
brakepipe
brick kiln
blue light
blueprint
cast steel
chain belt
chain pump
clockwork
condenser
conductor
cotter pin
craftsman
crosshead
cyclotron
datum-line
dead level
diaphragm
disc brake
disk brake
dynamical
earthwork
eccentric
electrify
electrize
electrode
equirotal
escalator
female die
fire brick
fish joint
fishplate
floodgate
fog signal
foot valve
force pump
framework
funicular
galvanism
galvanist
galvanize
gas engine
gas fitter
gas geyser
gas holder
gasometer

gas retort
gearwheel
horse mill
hydraulic
hydrostat
idle wheel
induction
inductive
inertness
injection
insertion
insulated
insulator
ironsmith
ironworks
jet engine
knife edge
laminated
lewis bolt
Leyden jar
limelight
lubricant
lubricate
machinery
machinist
magnetist
magnetize
male screw
man engine
master key
mechanics
mechanism
mechanist
mechanize
mild steel
millstone
mine shaft
mud sluice
nodal line
nose piece
off-spring
oil engine
oil geyser
perforate
petrol can
piston rod
pneumatic
polarizer
porous pot
power loom
programme
propeller
prototype
pump break
pump spear
pump stock
radiation
rectifier
reflector

regulator
repairing
reparable
reservoir
resultant
rheomotor
rheophore
road metal
roughcast
sandpaper
scapement
shop board
shunt coil
sliderule
smack mill
soapworks
soldering
spring box
spur wheel
stanchion
steam pipe
stiffener
stock lock
stoke hole
structure
superheat
telephone
tempering
tin lining
tin mining
train road
transform
trunk line
tunnel pit
turntable
twin cable
unscrewed
vibration
voltatype
vulcanite
vulcanize
waste weir
watermark
water tank
well drain
wheelrace
whip graft
white heat
winepress
wire gauze
wire wheel
worm wheel
X-ray plant

10

accelerate
air machine

alarm gauge
alternator
anelectric
automation
automobile
bevel wheel
broad gauge
cantilever
caseharden
centigrade
clack valve
coach screw
combustion
crankshaft
crown wheel
dead weight
derailment
dielectric
discharger
disc wheels
dish wheels
diving bell
donkey pump
drawbridge
earth plate
economizer
efficiency
electrical
electronic
embankment
emery cloth
emery paper
emery wheel
engine room
escapement
fire escape
flange rail
fluid drive
footbridge
fuse holder
galvanized
gas turbine
glass paper
goods train
goods truck
grid system
gudgeon pin
guillotine
hair spring
heart wheel
hogger pump
horsepower
hydrophore
Indian fire
inertitude
inflexible
instrument
insulating
insulation

iron heater
irrigation
isodynamic
laboratory
lamination
leaf bridge
lewis joint
lock paddle
locomotive
lubricator
macadamize
magnetizer
male thread
mechanical
nodal point
paper cable
pentaspast
percolator
petrol tank
piledriver
pneumatics
powder mill
powerhouse
power-plant
programmer
pulverizer
pump-handle
recondense
refraction
rejointing
resistance
revolution
rubber-wire
safety-lamp
scoop-wheel
self-acting
skew bridge
smokestack
soap boiler
socket pipe
socket pole
solid state
spokeshave
stationary
steam gauge
stiffening
streamline
structural
swing wheel
swivel hook
telegraphy
telescopic
television
telpherage
temper heat
thermopile
thermostat
toll bridge
torque tube

transients
transistor
tunnelling
unclutched
unpatented
unsoldered
voltaic arc
voltaplast
water crane
water power
watertight
water tower
waterwheel
waterwings
waterworks
wave motion
well-boring
windtunnel
wiped joint

11

accelerator
accumulator
aerodynamics
air fountain
anelectrode
atomic clock
bell founder
bell foundry
block system
Bramah press
brush wheels
cable laying
candlepower
carburetter
carburettor
compression
computation
contrivance
coupling box
coupling pin
damask steel
diamagnetic
driving band
driving belt
dynamometer
edge railway
electrician
electricity
electric jar
electrolyze
electrolyte
electronics
endless belt
enginneering
exhaust pipe
female screw

frame bridge
gas governor
graving dock
gutta percha
helical gear
incinerator
inking table
iron filings
iron founder
iron foundry
laminations
latten-brass
lock chamber
low pressure
lubrication
machine-tool
maintenance
manilla rope
manufactory
mechanician
mini-computer
mono-railway
narrow gauge
oil purifier
oil strainer
perforation
piledriving
pilot engine
power factor
rack-railway
rarefaction
reconstruct
retardation
revolutions
rolling mill
rubber cable
safety valve
searchlight
service pipe
skeleton key
socket joint
steam boiler
steam engine
steam hammer
stuffing box
suction pipe
suction pump
summit level
superheater
swing bridge
switchboard
synchronism
synchronize
synchrotron
tappet valve
toggle joint
transformer
transmitter
trundle head

tube railway
underground
uninsulated
voltaic pile
vulcanizing
warping bank
water cement
water engine
water furrow
water hammer
water supply
welding heat
wind furnace
wire drawing
wire grading
workmanship
wrought iron

12

acceleration
anti-friction
arterial road
artesian well
assembly line
balance wheel
belt fastener
blast furnace
block machine
block signals
canalization
chain reactor
coaxial cable
counterpoise
danger signal
diamagnetism
diesel engine
differential
disc coupling
disintegrate
donkey engine
double acting
driving shaft
driving wheel
dry-core cable
eccentric rod
eduction pipe
electric bulb
electric fire
electric fuse
electric iron
electric wire
electrolysis
electromotor
endless screw
engine driver
exhaust valve
female thread

flexible wire
floating dock
flying bridge
flying pinion
founder's dust
founder's sand
gas condenser
gas container
gas regulator
hanging valve
high pressure
hydraulic ram
hydrodynamic
inking roller
installation
jewel bearing
lubrifaction
machine tools
magnetomotor
make-and-break
manilla paper
marine boiler
marine engine
master spring
negative pole
non-conductor
nuclear power
oxy-acetylene
palification
paratonnerre
pattern maker
petrol engine
petrol filter
plummer block
polarization
pressure pump
pyro-electric
radiator muff
ratchet wheel
Réaumur scale
rolling press
rolling stock
service cable
short circuit
shunt winding
single acting
sleeve button
slitting mill
solar battery
specific heat
spinning mill
stamping mill
steam heating
steam turbine
steam whistle
suction valve
synchronized
terminal post
thermocouple

toothed wheel
transmission
unmechanical
unmechanized
vibratiuncle
water battery
water turbine
wheel-and-axle
wheel cutting
working model

13

buffing spring
civil engineer
compound-wound
contrate wheel
control theory
Cornish boiler
Cornish engine
counterweight
direct current
draught engine
drummond light
eccentric gear
electric cable
electric clock
electric fluid
electric light
electric motor
electric stove
electrifiable
electrization
electromagnet
engine-turning
expansion gear
ferrumination
flexible cable
floodlighting
fluid flywheel
friction balls
friction cones
inflexibility
injection cock
insulated wire
kinetic energy
lifting bridge
liquid starter
lubrification
magnetic fluid
magnetization
movement maker
non-conducting
overshot wheel
pneumatic tyre
pontoon bridge
pressure gauge
printing press

rack-and-pinion
roller bearing
series winding
shock absorber
snifting valve
standard gauge
telegraph line
telegraph pole
telegraph wire
telephone line
telephone wire
thermo-current
throttle valve
thrust bearing
water drainage
wave mechanics
whirling table
X-ray apparatus

14

analog computer
blowing machine
contra rotation
diesel-electric
discharge valve
discharging rod
disintegration
eccentric strap
eccentric wheel
electric cooker
electric cut-out
electric kettle
electrodynamic
electrostatics

electrothermic
explosive rivet
floating bridge
friction clutch
friction wheels
galvanized iron
hydraulic-press
insulated cable
lubricating oil
magnetic needle
multi-core cable
nuclear reactor
petrol strainer
plaster of paris
pneumatic drill
portable engine
reconstructlon
resino-electric
resultant force
shellac-varnish
shunt regulator
thermo-electric
three-core cable
traction engine
universal joint
vitreo electric
voltaic battery
washing machine
wave telegraphy

15 AND 16

brake horsepower
block signalling
Centigrade scale

concentric cable
digital computer
electric battery
electric circuit
electric current
electric machine
electrification
electrochemical
electrodynamics
electrokinetics
electromagnetic
electronegative
electronic brain
electropositive
expansion engine
Fahrenheit scale
friction rollers
galvanic battery
hydraulic cement
insulating paper
irrigation canal
linotype machine
machine language
magnetic battery
magneto-electric
ohmic resistance
perpetual motion
pressure machine
railway engineer
smelting furnace
specific gravity
spigot-and-socket
synchrocyclotron (16)
tensile strength
water-tube boiler

Instruments
See also **Engineering** and **Tools and simple machines**

2

p.c.

4 – 6

abacus
agate
camera
clock
dial
dynamo
filter
flange

fleam
flume
funnel
gasket
gauge
grid
lancet
laptop
laser
lens
lever
maser
megger
meter
nozzle

octant
octile
orrery
pole
probe
relay
rule
ruler
scale
square
style
tester
tool
trocar
toner

tube
U-tube
valve

7

aerator
ammeter
aneroid
balance
bearing
bellows
binocle
caltrop

compass
counter
divider
doubler
pH meter
quadrat
scriber
sextant
snubber
sundial
T-square
turbine
vernier
wet-bulb

8

analyser
biograph
bioscope
boot-jack
boot-last
boot-tree
calipers
computer
detector
diagraph
gasmeter
horologe
iriscope
manostat
odometer
ohm-meter
otoscope
quadrant
receiver
recorder
rheostat
solenoid
spy glass
udometer
waywiser
wireless
zootrope

9

acoumeter
aeolipile
aerometer
altimeter
altometer
ambulator
antimeter
apparatus
arcograph
areometer
astrolabe
atmometer
auriscalp
auxometer
backstaff
barograph
barometer
baroscope
clepsydra
compasses
condenser
cornmeter
cosmolabe
dynameter
dynometer
eidograph

engiscope
eriometer
excitator
flow meter
gasometer
garoscope
generator
graduator
gyroscope
heliostat
hodometer
holometer
hour glass
litholabe
lithotome
logometer
lucimeter
magnifier
manometer
marigraph
megaphone
megascope
metronome
microtome
microtron
nilometer
oleometer
optigraph
optometer
pedometer
periscope
polygraph
polyscope
pyrometer
pyroscope
rain gauge
rectifier
retractor
rheometer
rheoscope
rheotrope
rotameter
saccarium
scarifier
set-square
shot gauge
slide rule
sonometer
steelyard
tasimeter
taximeter
telegraph
telephone
telescope
televisor
tellurion
tide gauge
trebuchet
voltmeter

wattmeter
wind gauge
zoeotrope

10

acetimeter
acidimeter
altazimuth
anemograph
anemometer
anemoscope
angioscope
anglemeter
astrometer
astroscope
audiometer
audiophone
balling-gun
binoculars
calculator
calorifier
chiroplast
clinometer
collimator
cometarium
cross-staff
cryophorus
cyanometer
cyclograph
declinator
drosometer
duplicator
ear-trumpet
elaeometer
elaiometer
endiometer
field glass
goniometer
gravimeter
heliograph
heliometer
helioscope
heliotrope
hydrometer
hydrophore
hydroscope
hyetograph
hyetometer
hygrometer
hygroscope
lactometer
lactoscope
litrameter
macrometer
metrograph
micrometer
microphone

microscope
multimeter
multiplier
night glass
nitrometer
noctograph
ombrometer
operameter
ozonometer
pantagraph
pantograph
pantometer
pelvimeter
pentagraph
phonograph
phonoscope
photometer
photophone
piezometer
plane-table
planimeter
pleximeter
pole-finder
protractor
pulsimeter
radiometer
respirator
spirometer
steam-gauge
tachometer
teinoscope
theodolite
thermostat
transistor
tribometer
tuning-fork
typewriter
viscometer
voltameter
water-clock
water-gauge
water-meter
water-poise

11

actinograph
actinometer
aleurometer
alkalimeter
atmidometer
beam compass
calorimotor
cardiograph
chlorometer
chronograph
chronometer
chronoscope

clog almanac
comptometer
conchometer
cosmosphere
craniometer
dendrometer
depth-finder
diagnometer
dynamometer
eccaleobion
eclipsareon
elatrometer
graphometer
indigometer
locatograph
magnetophon
odontograph
optical lens
plantascope
pluviameter
pluviometer
poking stick
polarimeter
polariscope
polemoscope
pseudoscope
range-finder
salinometer
seismograph
seismometer
seismoscope
sideroscope
sliding-rule
spherograph
spherometer
stereometer
stereoscope
stethometer
stethoscope
teleprinter
thaumatrope
thermometer
thermoscope
torsiograph
transformer
transmitter
zymosimeter

12

aethrioscope
alcoholmeter

arithmometer
assay balance
averruncator
blanchimeter
bow compasses
burning glass
camera lucida
centrolinead
chondrometer
control valve
declinometer
ductilimeter
electrepeter
electrometer
electrophone
electroscope
ellipsograph
elliptograph
endosmometer
enorthotrope
evaporometer
field glasses
galactometer
galvanometer
galvanoscope
harmonometer
inclinometer
kaleidoscope
laryngoscope
machine ruler
magnetograph
magnetometer
measuregraph
microcoustic
night glasses
opera glasses
oscillograph
otacousticon
perambulator
psychrometer
reading glass
scarificator
sliding scale
spectrometer
spectroscope
speed-counter
sphygmometer
thermocouple
tuning hammer
weather glass
zenith sector

13

alcoholimeter
alcoholometer
bubble chamber
burning mirrow
camera obscura
chromatometer
diaphanometer
dipleidoscope
dipping needle
electric meter
electrophorus
esthesiometer
Geiger counter
parallel ruler
pneumatometer
potentiometer
pressure gauge
probe scissors
pyrheliometer
reflectometer
refractometer
saccharometer
sidereal clock
spring balance
sympiesometer
watt-hour meter

14

aesthesiometer
air thermometer
circumferentor
desk calculator
diffractometer
dinactinometer
geothermometer
hydrobarometer
interferometer
manifold writer
ophthalmoscope
radio telescope
sonic altimeter
wire micrometer

15

chemical balance
digital computer
magnifying glass
mariner's compass
solar microscope

Mathematics

2 AND 3

add
arc
cos
csc
Ln
log
p.c.
pi
set
tan

4

area
axes
axis
base
cone
cube
edge
face
line
loci
math
mean
plus
ring
root
sine
term
unit
zero

5

acute
angle
chord
conic
cosec
cotan
cubic
curve
equal
focal
focus
force
graph
group
index
lemma

limit
locus
maths
minus
plane
point
power
probe
proof
radii
range
ratio
slope
solid

6

centre
choice
circle
conics
conoid
convex
cosine
cuboid
degree
divide
domain
equals
factor
height
matrix
maxima
median
minima
minute
modulo
moment
motion
normal
number
oblate
oblong
obtuse
period
radial
radian
radius
random
scalar
secant
sector
series
sphere

square
subset
vector
vertex
volume

7

algebra
average
cissoid
complex
concave
conical
cycloid
decagon
divisor
ellipse
evolute
hexagon
indices
inverse
mapping
maximum
minimum
modulus
nonzero
numeral
oblique
octagon
percent
polygon
produce
prolate
problem
pyramid
rhombic
rhombus
scalene
section
segment
subtend
surface
tangent
theorem
trapeze
unitary

8

abscissa
addition
analysis

binomial
bisector
calculus
centroid
circular
codomain
constant
converse
cosecant
cube root
cuboidal
cylinder
diagonal
diameter
dihedral
distance
division
elliptic
equation
friction
frustrum
function
geometer
geometry
gradient
helicoid
heptagon
identity
infinity
integers
integral
involute
matrices
meridian
momentum
multiply
negative
new maths
operator
ordinate
osculate
parabola
parallel
pentagon
positive
quadrant
quartile
quotient
rational
rhomboid
rotation
sequence
spheroid
subtract
symmetry

triangle
trigonal
variable
velocity

9

amplitude
asymptote
Cartesian
chi-square
corollary
cotangent
directrix
dodecagon
ellipsoid
expansion
factorize
frequency
geometric
half-angle
hexagonal
hyperbola
identical
imaginary
increment
induction
inflexion
intersect
isosceles
logarithm
Napierian
numerator
numerical
octagonal
parabolic
parameter
perimeter
polygonal
polyhedra
primitive
quadratic
rectangle
remainder
resultant
spherical
trapezium
trapezoid

10

arithmetic

concentric
continuity
decahedron
derivative
dimensions
eigenvalue
epicycloid
equivalent
expression
hyperbolic
hypotenuse
hypothesis
irrational
kinematics
multiplier
octahedron
orthogonal
osculation
paraboloid
percentage
polyhedral
polyhedron
polynomial
proportion
regression
right angle
semi-circle
square root
statistics
stochastic
tangential
unit vector

11

approximate
associative

coefficient
combination
commutative
coordinates
denominator
determinant
eigenvector
equiangular
equilateral
equilibrium
exponential
geometrical
hyperboloid
icosahedron
integration
isomorphism
orthocentre
permutation
probability
progression
real numbers
rectangular
rectilinear
right-angled
subtraction
symmetrical
tetrahedron
translation

12

acceleration
conic section
differential
dodecahedron
eccentricity
harmonic mean

intersection
least squares
number theory
semicircular
straight line
substitution
trigonometry

13

approximation
circumference
geometric mean
linear algebra
parallelogram
perpendicular
plane geometry
power function
quadrilateral
right bisector
solid geometry

14 AND 15

arithmetic mean (14)
binomial theorem (15)
complex numbers (14)
convexo-concave (14)
differentiation (15)
multiplication (14)
natural numbers (14)
rational numbers (15)
transformation (14)

Medicine

2 AND 3		4				
	lip		clot	gena	mole
	LSD		cold	germ	nail
ana	ME	ache	corn	gore	neck
arm	MS	acne	cure	gout	nose
ear	pox	ACTH	cyst	hand	otic
ECT	pus	ague	damp	head	ovum
ENT	rib	AIDS	derm	heal	pain
eye	tic	back	diet	heel	pang
fit	toe	bile	disk	iris	pill
flu	VD	bleb	dope	knee	rale
hip	wen	boil	dose	lame	rash
HIV		bone	drug	limb	rete
ill		burn	face	lint	scab
jaw		chin	falx	lobe	scar
leg		clap	foot	lung	shin

sick	leech	uvula	idiocy	tongue
skin	liver	virus	infect	tonsil
sore	lymph	wound	infirm	torpor
stye	M and B	wrist	insane	trance
swab	mania	X-rays	iodine	tremor
tolu	mouth		iritis	trepan
ulna	mucus		kidney	troche
vein	mumps	**6**	larynx	tumour
ward	myopy		lesion	typhus
wart	navel	ailing	lotion	unwell
weal	nerve	angina	lunacy	uterus
womb	nurse	anemia	maimed	vagina
X-ray	opium	antrum	malady	vomica
yaws	ovary	apepsy	maniac	
	ozena	armpit	matron	
	palsy	artery	matter	**7**
5	penis	asthma	megrim	
	phial	ataxia	morula	abdomen
achor	piles	aurist	muscle	abscess
acute	plica	axilla	myopia	acidity
agony	polio	bellon	opiate	aconite
algid	probe	biceps	oxygen	adenoid
algor	pulse	bruise	pelvis	adipose
aloes	reins	bulimy	pepsin	ailment
ancon	rheum	bunion	perone	albumen
angst	rigor	cancer	phenol	aliment
ankle	salts	canker	phenyl	allergy
aorta	salve	caries	physic	alopecy
ataxy	scald	clinic	pimple	amnesia
aural	scalp	coccyx	plague	anaemia
belly	scurf	cornea	pleura	anatomy
blend	semen	coryza	poison	anconal
blood	senna	deflux	potion	anodyne
botch	serum	dengue	powder	antacid
bowel	sinus	doctor	quinsy	anthrax
brain	skull	dorsal	radium	antigen
cheek	sleep	dosage	ranula	apepsia
chest	sling	dropsy	remedy	aphasia
chill	spasm	earlap	renule	arsenic
chyle	sperm	eczema	retina	aseptic
cilia	spine	elixir	saliva	aspirin
colio	sprue	emetic	scurvy	atrophy
colon	stoma	fester	sepsis	autopsy
copos	stone	fibula	spleen	bandage
cough	stool	finger	splint	bilious
cramp	stupe	flexor	sprain	blister
croup	swoon	foment	stitch	boracic
dress	tabes	gargle	stupor	bromide
drops	teeth	gather	tablet	bubonic
elbow	thigh	goitre	tannin	calomel
ether	thumb	gravel	tartar	cardiac
faint	tibia	gripes	temple	cascara
femur	tonic	grippe	tendon	catarrh
fever	torso	growth	tetany	caustic
gland	toxin	gullet	thorax	cautery
heart	truss	healer	throat	chafing
ileac	ulcer	health	thrush	chloral
joint	unfit	heroin	thymol	choking
lance	urine	herpes	tissue	cholera

chronic
cocaine
cranium
cupping
curable
culture
cuticle
deltoid
dentist
dietary
dieting
disease
dissect
draught
dresser
dysopsy
earache
eardrum
empyema
endemic
enteric
erosion
eupepsy
fasting
femoral
fistula
forceps
forearm
formula
gastric
glottis
gumboil
harelip
healing
healthy
heparin
hormone
humerus
hygiene
illness
insulin
invalid
knuckle
leprosy
leprous
linctus
lockjaw
lozenge
lumbago
luminal
lunatic
malaria
massage
measles
medical
menthol
microbe
mixture
morphia

myalgia
nervous
nostrum
occiput
oculist
operate
organic
ossicle
otalgia
palsied
panacea
patella
patient
pharynx
pillbox
pink-eye
planury
plaster
polypus
pustule
pyretic
quinine
recover
rickets
roseola
scabies
scalpel
seasick
sick-bay
stamina
starved
sterile
sternum
stertor
stomach
stunned
styptic
sunburn
surgeon
surgery
symptom
syncope
syringe
tetanus
therapy
thyroid
toxemia
trachea
triceps
tympana
typhoid
vaccine
variola
veronal
vertigo
vitamin
wet-pack
whitlow
wry-neck

8

abortion
abrasion
acidity
acidosis
adenoids
adhesion
albumina
amputate
aneurysm
antibody
antidote
apoplexy
appendix
Asian flu
asphyxia
atropine
backache
bacteria
baldness
beri beri
blue pill
botulism
caffeine
cataract
club foot
collapse
compress
creosote
cyanche
cystitis
dandruff
deafness
debility
deceased
deformed
delirious
delirium
delivery
demented
dementia
diabetes
diagnose
diseased
dressing
drop-foot
dropsied
dyslexia
emulsion
epidemic
epilepsy
excision
eyedrops
fainting
feverish
first aid
flat feet
forehead

formalin
fracture
freckles
fumigate
ganglion
gangrene
glaucoma
hay fever
headache
heat spot
hiccough
hip joint
hospital
hygienic
hypnotic
hysteria
impetigo
incision
infected
inflamed
insanity
iodoform
irritant
jaundice
lameness
laudanum
laxative
lethargy
ligament
ligature
liniment
magnesia
malarial
mal-de-mer
medicine
melanoma
membrane
mescalin
migraine
morphine
narcosis
narcotic
neuritis
neurotic
ointment
otoscope
overdose
paranoia
paranoic
paranoid
paroxysm
pastille
phthisis
pleurisy
poisoned
poultice
progeria
ptomaine
pulmonic

recovery
Red Cross
remedial
rest cure
revivify
ringworm
sanitary
schizoid
sciatica
sedative
shingles
shoulder
sickness
sickroom
smallpox
sneezing
specific
surgical
swelling
syphilis
tapeworm
terminal
tincture
underfed
uric acid
varicose
vertebra
vomiting
wheezing
windpipe

9

adrenalin
alleviate
allopathy
ambulance
analgesic
antalkali
antitoxin
arthritis
asthmatic
bedridden
blindness
Caesarean
carbuncle
cartilage
castor oil
catalepsy
cauterize
chilblain
cirrhosis
cold cream
contagion
contusion
cortisone
curvature
deformity

delirious
dentistry
deodorant
diagnosis
diaphragm
diathermy
dietetics
dietetist
dietician
digestion
digestive
disinfect
dislocate
dissector
doctoring
dropsical
dysentery
dyspepsia
emaciated
emollient
epileptic
eye lotion
eyestrain
faintness
frost-bite
gastritis
gathering
germicide
giddiness
glycerine
hartshorn
healthful
heartburn
hepatitis
hunchback
hygienist
hypnotism
hypnotist
hysterics
impactation
infirmary
influenza
inoculate
invalided
isolation
isoniazid
leucaemia
leukaemia
liquorice
listerine
liver spot
long-sight
medicated
medicinal
menopause
monomania
nephritis
neuralgia
nightmare

nostalgia
novocaine
nux vomica
open-heart
operation
osteopath
paralysis
paralytic
phlebitis
physician
pneumonia
poisoning
poisonous
pregnancy
psychosis
psychotic
pulmonary
pulsation
pyorrhoea
radionics
rheumatic
rock-fever
sclerosis
silicosis
sinusitis
soporific
squinting
sterilize
stiff neck
stiffness
stimulant
stone dead
stone deaf
stretcher
sunstroke
toothache
treatment
umbilicus
underdose
unhealthy
vaccinate
vasectomy
water cure

10

albuminous
amputation
antibiotic
anti-poison
antiseptic
apoplectic
apothecary
aureomycin
blood count
brain fever
breastbone
bronchitis

chicken pox
chloroform
collar bone
concussion
congestion
contortion
convalesce
convulsion
cotton wool
depression
diphtheria
dipsomania
disability
dispensary
dispensing
dissecting
dissection
double bind
emaciation
enervation
epidemical
epiglottis
Epsom salts
erysipelas
eucalyptus
euthanasia
fibrositis
flatulence
fumigation
gingivitis
gonorrhoea
healthless
heat stroke
hemorrhage
homoeopath
hydropathy
hypodermic
incubation
indisposed
infectious
inhalation
insanitary
interferon
ionization
knock-kneed
laryngitis
lung cancer
medicament
meningitis
metabolism
nettle rash
ophthalmia
orthocaine
osteopathy
out-patient
oxygen tent
palllative
penicillin
pestilence

post mortem
psychiatry
quarantine
recuperate
relaxation
rheumatism
sanatorium
sanitarium
scarlatina
shell-shock
short sight
sickle-cell
specialist
spinal cord
stammering
starvation
stone blind
strengthen
strychnine
stuttering
tourniquet
tracheitis
transplant
unremedied
urethritis

11

acupuncture
albuminuria
aminobutene
anaesthetic
anti-pyretic
asthmatical
astigmatism
bandy-legged
barbiturate
biliousness
calabar bean
circulation
cod-liver oil
colour-blind
consumption
consumptive
corn plaster
dengue fever
disablement
dislocation
embrocation
epileptical
face-lifting
finger stall
fomentation
frostbitten
haemophilia
haemorrhage
homoeopathy
hydrophobia

hypothermia
inoculation
intercostal
intravenous
jungle fever
mustard bath
nursing home
palpitation
peritonitis
perspiration
prickly heat
psittacosis
radiography
restorative
sal volatile
seasickness
spina bifida
stethoscope
stomach-pump
suppuration
temperature
thalidomide
therapeutic
tonsillitis
tracheotomy
transfusion
trench fever
typhus fever
unconscious
vaccination
vivisection
yellow fever

12

alexipharmic
appendicitis
carbolic acid
chemotherapy
convalescent
cough lozenge
cough mixture
court plaster
day blindness
degeneration
disinfectant
disinfection
Dover's powder
enteric fever
friar's balsam
gastric fever
group therapy
growing pains
heart disease
hospital case
homoeopathic
hysterectomy
immunization

inflammation
menstruation
mesothelioma
neurasthenia
Politzer's bag
prescription
prophylactic
psychiatrist
radiotherapy
recuperation
recuperative
sarsaparilla
scarlet fever
sclerodermia
skin-grafting
spinal column
streptococci
streptomycin
subcutaneous
taka diastase
talcum powder
tartar emetic
tertian fever
thyroid gland
tuberculosis
typhoid fever
unremediable
zinc ointment

13

adipose tissue
anti-spasmodic
bubonic plague
contraception
convalescence
duodenal ulcer
dusting powder
elephantiasis
eucalyptus oil
fever hospital
gamma globulin
German measles
hydrocephalus
indisposition
ipecacuanha
lead poisoning
malarial fever
materia medica
medical school
medicine glass
mononucleosis
mortification
non-contagious
osteomyelitis
pharmacopoeia
poliomyelitis
pyretic saline

radioactivity
St. Vitus's-dance
schizophrenia
shooting pains
shoulder blade
smelling salts
social disease
sterilization
stretcher case
tranquillizer
varicose veins
whooping cough

14

Achilles tendon
angina pectoris
blood poisoning
Bright's disease
cascara segrada
conjunctivitis
corticosteroid
corticotrophin
floating kidney
Gregory's powder
hallucinations
hallucinogenic
housemaid's-knee
medical student
medicine bottle
mucous membrane
mustard plaster
night blindness
organic disease
pasteurization
patent medicine
plastic surgery
psychoanalysis
Seidlitz powder
smelling bottle

15

Addison's disease
adhesive plaster
alimentary canal
blackwater fever
counter-irritant
delirium tremens
endocrine glands
Eustachian tubes
linseed poultice
locomotor ataxia
manic depression
medicine dropper
radiation hazard
radium treatment

unconsciousness
water on the brain

Minerals (including metals, ores, precious stones, rocks, etc.)

3 AND 4

alum
bort
calx
cauk
clay
coal
gold
grit
iron
jade
jet
lead
lias
mawl
mica
onyx
opal
rock
ruby
sard
spar
talc
tin
tufa
wad
wadd
zinc

5

agate
albin
alloy
amber
argil
argon
baria
beryl
borax
boron
brass
chalk
chert
emery
erbia
flint
fluor
frass
invar
macle
magma
nitre
ochre
pitch
prase
shale
silex
slate
spalt
steel
topaz
tutty
yeode

6

albite
aplome
augite
barium
bargyta
basalt
blende
cerite
cherty
cobalt
copper
davina
dipyre
doggar
egeran
erbium
gabbro
galena
garnet
glance
gneiss
gypsum
humite
indium
iolite
jargon
jasper
kaolin
kunkur
marble
mesole
mundic
nappal
nickel
nosean
ophite
ormolu
pewter
pinite
plasma
potash
pumice
pyrite
pyrope
quartz
radium
rutile
schorl
silica
silver
sinter
sodium
speiss
sphene
thoria
tombac
xylite
yenite
zircon

7

adamant
alumina
alunite
amianth
anatase
apatite
aphrite
arsenic
asphalt
axilite
azurite
barytes
bauxite
biotime
biotite
bismuth
bitumen
bornite
breccia
cadmium
calcite
calcium
caliche
calomel
cat's-eye
cuprite
cyprine
desmine
diamond
diorite
edelite
emerald
epidote
epigene
erinite
euclase
fahlerz
fahlore
felsite
felspar
fuscite
gassoul
glucina
granite
greisen
helvine
hessite
hyalite
ice spar
iridium
jargoon
kainite
kyanite
lignite
lithium
macadam
mellite
mercury
nacrite
olivine
peridot
petzite
pycnite
pyrites
realgar
romeine
sahlite
sinoper
sinople
sulphur
syenite
talcite
thorite
thorium
thulite
tripoli
uranium
wolfram
wurgite
yttrium
zeolite
zeuxite
zincite
zoisite
zorgite
zurlite

8

achirite
adularia
acrolite
amethyst
andesite
antimony
aphanite
asbestos
blue John
austerite
boracite
bronzite
brookite
calamine
calc-spar
cast iron
chabasie
chlorite
chromite
chromium
cinnabar
corundum

cryolite
dendrite
diallage
diopside
dioptase
dolerite
dolomite
embolite
epsomite
essonite
feldspar
felstone
fireclay
fluorite
graphite
hematite
hyacinth
idocrase
ilmenite
jasponyx
konilite
laterite
lazulite
ligurite
limonite
lirocone
litharge
lomonite
magnesia
massicot
meionite
melanite
melilite
mesolite
mesotype
micanite
mimetene
monazite
napolite
nemalite
nephrite
obsidian
orpiment
pagodite
pea stone
petalite
platinum
plumbago
porphyry
prehnite
psammite
pyroxene
ragstone
reussite
rhyolite
rock cork
rock salt
rock soap
rock wood

sagenite
sanidine
sapphire
sardonyx
selenite
siberite
siderite
smaltine
sodalite
spinelle
steatite
stellite
stibnite
stilbite
thallium
tin stone
titanium
trachyte
trap-rock
triphane
tungsten
turmalin
vesuvian
voltzite
weissite
wood opal
wood rock
worthite
wurtzite
xanthite
xylonite
yanolite
zirconia

9

alabaster
allophane
almandine
aluminium
alum shale
alum slate
amianthus
amphibole
anamesite
anglesite
anhydrite
anomalite
anorthite
aphrisite
argentite
argillite
aromatite
arquifoux
asphaltum
austerite
baikalite
basaltine

boltonite
brick-clay
brown-coal
brown-spur
byssolite
carbonado
carbuncle
carnelian
carnalite
casholong
cat-silver
cerussite
ceylanite
chabasite
chabazite
chalybite
cobaltine
columbite
cornelian
corn stone
earth flax
elaeolite
elaterite
erythrine
erythrite
eudyalite
eukairite
firestone
fluorspar
galactite
gmelinite
granitite
granulite
graystone
graywacke
greensand
grenatite
greystone
greywacke
haematite
heavy spar
horn slate
hornstone
indianite
ironstone
ittnerite
johannite
killinite
latrobite
laumonite
lenzinite
limbilite
limestone
lodestone
magnesite
magnesium
magnetite
malachite
manganese

marcasite
margarite
marmatite
melaphyre
mellitite
meteorite
mica slate
mispickel
moonstone
moorstone
muscovite
nagyagite
natrolite
necrolite
necronite
needletin
nepheline
niccolite
noumeaite
omphacite
ozokerite
pargasite
pearl spar
pectolite
pegmatite
periclase
petroleum
phenacite
phonolite
physalite
pleonaste
plinthite
potassium
proustite
pyrophane
quartzite
raphilite
rhodonite
rhombspar
rubellite
sandstone
satin spar
scapolite
scheelite
scolecite
soapstone
spinthere
spodumene
streamtin
strontium
sylvanite
tantalite
tautalite
tellurium
torbanite
torrelite
tremolite
tridymite
turnerite

turquoise
uvarovite
veinstone
vulcanite
wavellite
wernerite
willemite
withamite
witherite
woodstone
wulfenite
xanthocon
zinc bloom
zirconite

10

actinolite
amianthoid
amygdaloid
anthracite
aquamarine
aventurine
azure stone
batrachite
bergmanite
beudantite
bismuthite
bloodstone
calaverite
cannel coal
carnallite
cervantite
chalcedony
chalybeate
chonikrite
chrysolite
clinkstone
constantan
cross-stone
diallogite
dyscrasite
eagle stone
false topaz
floatstone
gabbronite
garnierite
glauberite
glauconite
glottalite
greenstone
heterosite
heulandite
hornblende
hornsilver
hydrophane
hyperstene
indicolite

iridosmine
iron glance
karpholite
Kentish rag
kieselguhr
koupholite
lead glance
lepidolite
malacolite
meerschaum
melaconite
mica schist
mocho stone
molybdenum
monelmetal
nussierite
nuttallite
orthoclase
osmiridium
paranthine
phosphorus
picrosmine
polyhalite
pyrochlore
pyrolusite
rathoffite
redruthite
retinalite
rock butter
rose quartz
sapphirine
sardachate
saussurite
schalstein
serpentine
sismondine
smaragdite
sparry iron
sphalerite
stalactite
stalagmite
staurolite
stephanite
talc schist
thomsonite
topazolite
tourmaline
vanadinite
villarsite
websterite
zinc blende

11

alexandrite
amblygonite
amphibolite
amphiboloid

Babbit metal
black silver
brewsterite
cassiterite
chlorophane
chondrodite
chromic iron
chrysoberyl
cobalt bloom
crichtonite
crocidolite
dendrachate
diving stone
epistilbite
ferrachrome
figure stone
franklinite
hypersthene
Iceland spar
iron pyrites
lapis lazuli
libethenite
milky quartz
molybdenite
Muller glass
muschel kalk
napoleonite
needlestone
octahedrite
phillipsite
pitchblende
polymignite
psilomelane
pyrallolite
pyrargyrite
pyrosmalite
rock crystal
sillimanite
smithsonite
smoky quartz
sordavalite
sphaerulite
tetradymite
thumerstone
titanic iron
yttrocerite

12

aerosiderate
artvedsonite
chalcopyrite
cobalt glance
copper glance
forest marble
fuller's earth
greyweathers
jeffersonite

kupfernickel
mineral black
mineral green
mineral resin
montmartrite
mountain cork
mountain flax
mountain milk
mountain soap
murchisonite
oriental ruby
puddingstone
pyrargillite
pyromorphite
quartz schist
silver glance
somervillite
Spanish chalk
specular iron
speisscobalt
sprig crystal
strontianite
tetrahedrite
woolastonite

13

agaric mineral
anthophyllite
chlorophaeite
cinnamon stone
cleavelandite
copper pyrites
emerald copper
kerosene shale
needle zeolite

14 AND 15

antimony glance
arkose sandstone
bituminous coal
britannia metal
brown haematite
Cairngorm stone
chlorite schist
elastic bitumen
graphic granite
hydromica schist
mountain leather
quartz porphyry

Physics

2 AND 3

a.c.
bar
bel
e.m.f.
erg
gas
lux
mev
ohm
rpm
UHF
VHF

4

atom
cell
dyne
flux
foci
halo
heat
kaon
lens
mach
mass
muon
node
pile
pion
pole
rays
spin
tube
volt
watt
wave
work
X-ray

5

anode
curie
cycle
diode
earth
farad
field
fluid
focus

force
image
joule
laser
lever
light
lumen
maser
meson
motor
phase
pitch
power
prism
radar
radio
shell
solid
sonic
sound
speed
valve
weber

6

ampere
atomic
baryon
camera
charge
corona
dipole
energy
fusion
impact
isobar
kelvin
lepton
liquid
magnet
moment
motion
newton
optics
period
photon
plasma
proton
quanta
torque
triode
vacuum
vector

weight

7

ammeter
aneroid
battery
beta ray
calorie
candela
cathode
Celsius
circuit
coulomb
crystal
current
damping
decibel
density
dry cell
elastic
element
entropy
fission
gaseous
gravity
hyperon
impulse
inertia
machine
maxwell
neutron
nuclear
nucleon
nucleus
nuclide
optical
orbital
pi-meson
quantum
reactor
röntgen
spectra
statics
thermal
torsion
voltage
voltaic

8

adhesion
aerofoil

antinode
beat note
betatron
brownian
cohesion
duo-diode
dynamics
electric
electron
emission
free fall
friction
graviton
half-life
infra-red
isogonic
kilowatt
kinetics
klystron
magnetic
magneton
molecule
momentum
negative
negatron
neutrino
overtone
particle
pendulum
polaroid
positive
positron
pressure
rest mass
roentgen
solenoid
spectrum
subshell
velocity

9

acoustics
adiabatic
amplifier
amplitude
antimeson
barometer
black body
bolometer
capacitor
coherence
condenser
conductor

cyclotron
electrode
frequency
gamma rays
generator
gyroscope
harmonics
impedance
induction
insulator
isoclinic
Leyden jar
magnetism
magnetron
manometer
mechanics
plutonium
potential
radiation
radio wave
real image
rectifier
resonance
spark coil
vibration
viscosity
voltmeter

10

aberration
absorption
achromatic
antilepton
antimatter
antiproton
atomic bomb
atomic mass
ballistics
binoculars
cathode ray
Centigrade
conduction
convection
cosmic rays
dielectric
dispersion
electrical
Fahrenheit
heavy water
horsepower
inductance
ionization
kinematics

latent heat
microscope
omega meson
oscillator
precession
reflection
refraction
relativity
resistance
ripple tank
scattering
shunt-wound
supersonic
thermionic
thermopile
transistor
vacuum tube
wavelength

11

accelerator
band spectra
capacitance
capillarity
centrifugal
centripetal
compression
conductance
declination
diffraction
electricity
falling body
focal length
gravitation
hypercharge
newton-metre
oscillation
positronium
radioactive
resistivity
restitution
series-wound

solar energy
spectrogram
statcoulomb
synchrotron
temperature
transformer
transuranic

12

acceleration
angstrom unit
antiparticle
atomic number
atomic weight
beta particle
centre of mass
cloud chamber
conductivity
critical mass
diamagnetism
eccentricity
electrolysis
electroscope
interference
kilowatt-hour
oscilloscope
permittivity
polarization
specific heat
spectrograph
wave equation

13

alpha particle
bubble chamber
chain reaction
critical angle
discharge tube
elastic impact
electric field

electric motor
electric power
electromagnet
electromotive
electron shell
electrostatic
geiger counter
gravitational
induction coil
kinetic energy
magnetic field
magnetic poles
paramagnetism
photoelectric
quantum number
quantum theory
radioactivity
rectification
scintillation
semiconductor
standing waves
thermal capacity
transmutation

14 AND OVER

centre of gravity (15)
electric current (15)
electric energy (14)
electrification (15)
electromagnetic (15)
electrostatics (14)
ferromagnetism (14)
nuclear reactor (14)
Planck's constant (15)
potential energy (15)
specific gravity (15)
terminal velocity (16)
thermodynamics (14)
thermoelectric (14)
Wheatstone bridge (16)

Poisons

4 AND 5
acids
agene
bane
coca
drug
dwale

ergot
fungi
lysol
nitre
opium
toxin
upas
venom

6
alkali
brucia
cicuta
curare
heroin
iodine

ourali
phenol

7
aconite
alcohol

ammonia
aniline
arsenic
atropia
atropin
bromine
brucina
brucine

cadmium
calomel
caustic
chloral
coal gas
cocaine
gamboge
henbane
hyoscin
hypoxia
markuri
veronal
violine
vitriol
woorali
woorara
woralli
wourali

8

antidote
antimony
atropina
atropine
botulism
chlorine
chromium
ergotine
morphine
nicotine
oenanthe

paraquat
pearl ash
phosgene
ptomaine
ratsbane
selenium
soap lees
sulfonal
veratrum

9

amanitine
antiarine
baneberry
beryllium
chromates
colchicum
colocynth
croton oil
echidnine
grapewort
hellebore
herbicide
lead ethyl
mercurial
monkshood
nux vomica
potassium
rat poison
spit venom
strychnia

toadstool
white lead
wolf's bane
zinc ethyl

10

antiseptic
aqua fortis
belladonna
chloroform
cyanic acid
mustard gas
nightshade
nitric acid
oxalic acid
phosphorus
picric acid
salmonella
snake venom
strychnine
thorn apple
weed-killer

11

blue vitriol
boracic acid
caustic soda
dog's mercury
insecticide

lead acetate
luna caustic
prussic acid
snake poison
sugar of lead

12

barbiturates
bitter almond
carbonic acid
fool's parsley
pharmacolite
water hemlock
white arsenic

13 AND OVER

allantotoxicum (14)
carbonate of lead (15)
carbonic oxide (13)
carbon monoxide (14)
caustic alkali (13)
caustic potash (13)
deadly nightshade (16)
hydrocyanic acid (15)
irritant poisons (15)
meadow saffron (13)
narcotic poisons (15)
sulphuric acid (13)
yellow arsenic (13)

Sciences

5 AND **6**

augury (6)
botany (6)
conics (6)
logic (5)
optics (6)

7

algebra
anatomy
biology
cookery
ecology
farming
finance
geodesy

geogony
geology
gunnery
history
hygiene
myology
orology
otology
pandect
phonics
physics
poetics
science
statics
surgery
tanning
trivium
weaving
zoology

zootomy

8

aerology
agronomy
analysis
atmology
barology
bio-assay
biometry
breeding
bryology
calculus
commerce
cytology
dairying
dosology

dynamics
ethology
etiology
eugenics
forestry
genetics
geometry
glyptics
horology
kinetics
medicine
mycology
nosology
ontology
penology
pharmacy
politics
pomology
posology

rheology
rhetoric
sinology
sitology
spherics
taxonomy
tidology
tocology
topology
typology
virology
zymology

9

acoustics
aerometry
aetiology
agriology
aitology
allopathy
altimetry
anemology
annealing
areometry
astronomy
barometry
biometrics
bleaching
cartology
chemistry
chiropody
chorology
cosmology
dentistry
dietetics
diplomacy
economics
embalming
emetology
engraving
ethnology
gardening
geography
gnomonics
harmonics
histology
horometry
husbandry
hydrology
hygrology
hymnology
ichnology
lithology
mammalogy
mechanics
micrology
neurology

ophiology
orography
osteology
otography
pathology
petrology
philology
phonetics
phonology
phytogeny
phytology
phytotomy
radiology
sitiology
sociology
surveying
taxidermy
telephony
uranology
zoography

10

actinology
aerography
aesthetics
apiculture
archaeology
arithmetic
ballistics
bathymetry
biophysics
cardiology
catoptrics
cell biology
chromatics
clinometry
conchology
craniology
demography
dendrology
docimology
Egyptology
embryology
energetics
entomology
entomotomy
enzymology
eudiometry
game theory
gastrology
geophysics
homeopathy
hydraulics
hydrometry
hydropathy
hygrometry
hypsometry

immunology
kinematics
lexicology
metallurgy
microscopy
morphology
nematology
nephrology
nosography
obstetrics
odontology
oneirology
organology
osteopathy
pedagogics
pediatrics
phlebology
photometry
phrenology
physiology
planimetry
pneumatics
potamology
psychiatry
psychology
relativity
seismology
selenology
semeiology
somatology
spasmology
spermology
splenology
splenotomy
statistics
technology
telegraphy
teratology
topography
toxicology
trepanning
typography

11

aeronautics
aerostatics
agriculture
anemography
arachnology
archaeology
arteriology
arteriotomy
campanology
carcinology
cartography
chondrology
chronometry

climatology
cosmography
craniometry
criminology
cupellation
cybernetics
dermatology
dermography
desmography
diacoustics
electricity
electronics
engineering
entozoology
ethnography
foundations
games theory
geomedicine
gynaecology
haematology
heliography
homoeopathy
hydrography
hyetography
ichthyology
ichthyotomy
lichenology
linguistics
mathematics
methodology
micrography
myodynamics
neurography
ornithology
osteography
paleography
petrography
photography
phytography
probability
prophylaxis
pteridology
radiography
sericulture
skeletology
spectrology
stereometry
stereoscopy
stethoscopy
stratigraphy
thanatology
uranography
ventilation
watch-making

12

aerodynamics
amphibiology

anthropology
architecture
astrophysics
atomic theory
auscultation
biochemistry
biogeography
brachygraphy
chronography
cometography
cytogenetics
econometrics
electropathy
epidemiology
epirrheology
floriculture
geochemistry
horticulture
hydrostatics
lexicography
lymphography
microbiology
nephrography
neuroanatomy
neurobiology
number theory
oceanography
orthalmology
organography
ornithoscopy
palaeography
pharmacology
physiography
pisciculture
pneumatology
protozoology
real analysis
seismography
silviculture
spectroscopy
spermatology

stratigraphy
sylviculture
syndesmology
synosteology
trigonometry
zoophytology

13

anthropometry
arboriculture
arteriography
bioenergetics
cephalography
chondrography
chrematistics
climatography
combinatorics
crustaceology
endocrinology
geochronology
geomorphology
helminthology
hydrodynamics
hydrokinetics
ichthyography
land measuring
land surveying
lichenography
linear algebra
marine biology
matrix algebra
meteorography
palaeontology
pharmaceutics
psychophysics
psychotherapy
quantum theory
saccharometry
sedimentology

splanchnology
stoichiometry
wave mechanics
zoophysiology

14

architectonics
bioclimatology
chromatography
cinematography
electrobiology
electrostatics
fluid mechanics
hippopathology
hydrophytology
macroeconomics
microeconomics
natural history
natural science
parapsychology
photogrammetry
phytopathology
psychonosology
radiochemistry
symptomatology
syndesmography
thermodynamics

15

computer science
crystallography
electrodynamics
electrokinetics
material science
neurophysiology
psychopathology
thermochemistry

Tools and simple machines
See also **Engineering** and **Instruments**

3
adz
awl
axe
bit
die
dog
fan
gad
gin
hod
hoe
jig
loy
saw
zax

4
adze
bill
bore
brog
burr
cart
celt
crab
file
fork
frow
gage
hink
hook
jack
last
loom
mall
maul
mule
nail
peel
pick
pike
plow
rake
rasp
rule
sock
spud
tool
trug
vice
whim

5

anvil
auger
basil
beele
bench
besom
betty
bevel
blade
borer
brace
burin
chuck
churn
clamp
clams
clasp
cleat
cramp
crane
croom
croze
cupel
dolly
drill
flail
flang
forge
gauge
gavel
gouge
hoist
incus
jacks
jemmy
jimmy
knife
lathe
level
lever
mower
parer
peavy
plane
plumb
preen
prise
prong
punch
quern
quoin
ratch
razor
sarse
screw
sieve
spade

spike
spile
spill
swage
temse
tommy
tongs
tromp
trone
wedge
winch

6

barrow
beetle
bender
blower
bodkin
borcer
bow-saw
brayer
broach
burton
chaser
chisel
colter
crevet
cruset
dibber
dibble
doffer
dredge
driver
fanner
faucet
ferret
folder
gimlet
graver
hackle
hammer
harrow
jagger
jigger
jig saw
ladder
laptop
lister
mallet
mortar
muller
oliver
pallet
pencil
pestle
pitsaw
planer

pliers
plough
pontee
pooler
rammer
rasper
reaper
riddle
ripsaw
rubber
sander
saw-set
screen
scythe
segger
shears
shovel
sickle
sifter
skewer
sledge
slicer
square
stadda
stiddy
stithy
strike
tackle
tenter
trepan
trowel
tubber
turrel
wimble
wrench

7

bandsaw
boaster
bradawl
capstan
catling
cautery
chamfer
chip-axe
chopper
cleaver
couloir
coulter
crampon
crisper
crowbar
cuvette
derrick
diamond
dog-belt
drudger
fistuca

forceps
fretsaw
fruggin
gradine
grainer
grapnel
grub axe
hacksaw
handsaw
hatchel
hatchet
hay fork
jointer
mandrel
mattock
nippers
nut hook
pickaxe
piercer
pincers
plummet
pole axe
pounder
pricker
salt-pan
scalpel
scauper
scraper
screwer
scriber
seed lop
spaddle
spanner
spittle
sprayer
strocal
tenoner
thimble
trestle
triblet
T-square
twibill
twister
whip-saw
whittle
woolder

8

bark mill
bar shear
beakiron
bench peg
bill hook
bistoury
bloomary
blowlamp
blowpipe

boathook
bowdrill
bull nose
butteris
calender
calipers
canthook
centre bit
chopness
crow mill
crucible
die stock
dowel bit
drill bow
edge tool
filatory
fire kiln
flame gun
flax comb
gavelock
gee cramp
glass pot
handloom
handmill
hand vice
hay knife
horse hoe
lapstone
lead mill
mitre box
molegrip
muck rake
nut screw
oilstone
paint pad
panel saw
picklock
pinchers
plumb bob
polisher
power saw
prong-hoe
puncheon
reap hook
saw wrest
scissors
scuffler
shoehorn
slate axe
stiletto
strickle
tenon saw
throstle
tooth key
tweezers
twist bit
watercan
water ram
weed hook

windlass
windmill

turnscrew
watermill

cigar cutter
countersink
crazing mill
crisping pin
crosscut saw
drill barrow

drill grubber
driving shaft
driving wheel
emery grinder
flour dresser
glass furnace

9

baseplate
belt punch
bench hook
bolt auger
boot crimp
canker bit
cannipers
can opener
centrebit
compasses
corkscrew
cotton gin
cramp iron
curry comb
cutter bar
dog clutch
draw knife
draw-plate
excavator
eyeleteer
fillister
fining pot
fork chuck
gas pliers
hammer axe
handbrace
handscrew
handspike
holing axe
hummeller
implement
jackknife
jackplane
jackscrew
lace frame
lawnmower
nail punch
nut wrench
pitch fork
plane iron
planisher
plumbline
plumbrule
screwjack
scribe awl
shearlegs
sheep hook
steelyard
sugar mill
tin opener
try square
turf spade
turn bench

10

bush harrow
churn staff
claspknife
clawhammer
cold chisel
crane's bill
cultivator
dray plough
drift bolts
drillpress
drillstock
emery wheel
fire engine
fire escape
firing iron
grindstone
instrument
masonry bit
masticator
mitre block
motor mower
mould board
nail drawer
paintbrush
perforator
pipe wrench
safety lamp
screw press
sleek stone
snowplough
spokeshave
steam press
stepladder
tenterhook
thumbscrew
thumbstall
tilt hammer
trip hammer
turf cutter
turnbuckle
watercrane
watergauge
waterlevel
wheel brace

11

breast drill
chaff cutter
chain blocks
chain wrench
cheese press

drill harrow
drill plough
fanning mill
grubbing hoe
helvehammer
jagging iron
machine tool
monkey block
paint roller
ploughshare
pointed awl
pruning hook
rabbet plane
reaping-hook
sawing stool
screwdriver
single-edged
skim coulter
snatch block
spirit level
squaring rod
steam hammer
stone hammer
straw cutter
strike block
stubble rake
sward cutter
swingplough
tapemeasure
turfing iron
two-foot rule
warping hook
warping post
weeding fork
weeding hook
weeding rhim
wheelbarrow

12

barking irons
belt adjuster
brace-and-bits
branding iron
breastplough
caulking tool
counter gauge
cradle scythe
cramping iron
crimping iron
crisping iron
curling tongs

hat stretcher
hydraulic ram
mandrel lathe
marline spike
monkey wrench
pruning knife
pulley blocks
running block
scribing iron
sledge hammer
sliding bevel
socket chisel
stone breaker
straightedge
straightener
swingle knife
touch needles
trench plough
turfing spade
turning lathe
water bellows
weeding tongs

13

butcher's broom
chopping block
chopping knife
cylinder press
electric drill
grappling-iron
hydraulic jack
mowing machine
packing needle
scribing block
sewing machine
soldering bolt
soldering iron
sowing machine
spinning jenny
spinning wheel
stocking frame
subsoil plough
three-foot rule
two-hole pliers
weeding chisel

14

blowing machine
carding machine

draining engine
draining plough
pneumatic drill
reaping machine
shepherd's crook
smoothing plane

swingling knife
three-metre rule
thrusting screw
weeding forceps

15

carpenter's bench
crimping machine
dredging machine
drilling machine

envelope machine
entrenching tool
pestle and mortar
pump screwdriver
weighing machine
whitworth thread

TRANSPORT
Aviation and space travel

3 AND *4*

ace
air
bank
bay
bump
buzz
car
crew
dive
dope
drag
fin
flap
fly
fuel
gap
gas
hull
jet
kite
knot
land
lane
leg
lift
loop
mach
mig
nose
prop
rev
rib
roll
slip
span
spar
spin
tail
taxi
trim
UFO
veer
wash

wind
wing
yaw
york
zoom

5

aloft
apron
bends
cabin
cargo
chock
chord
cleat
climb
craft
crash
crate
ditch
drift
flaps
flier
float
glide
jumbo
pitch
plane
prang
pylon
radar
range
rev up
rigid
slots
stall
strut
stunt
valve

6

aerial
airbus
airman
airway
basket
beacon
bomber
camber
canard
cruise
cut out
drogue
fabric
flight
floats
flying
gas-bag
glider
hangar
intake
launch
module
nose-up
octane
piston
ram jet
refuel
rocket
rudder
runway
wash-in
yawing

7

aileron
air base
aircrew
airdrop
air flow
air foil

air lane
airlift
airline
airport
air-raid
airship
aviator
ballast
balloon
banking
biplane
birdman
bale out
bomb bay
capsule
ceiling
cellule
charter
chassis
chopper
clipper
cockpit
compass
contact
co-pilot
cowling
descent
ejector
fairing
fighter
flyover
flypast
gliding
gondola
helibus
inflate
landing
lift-off
Mae West
nacelle
nose-cap
on board
pancake
payload
re-entry

ripcord
rolling
sponson
sputnik
tail fin
take-off
taxiing
Trident
Tristar
twin-jet
wingtip

8

aerodyne
aerofoil
aeronaut
aerostat
air brake
airborne
aircraft
airfield
air force
airframe
airliner
air route
air scoop
airscrew
airspace
airspeed
airstrip
airwoman
altitude
approach
anhedral
autogiro
aviation
aviatrix
ballonet
bomb-rack
buoyancy
Concorde
corridor
cruising
decalage
dihedral
drip-flap
elevator
envelope
flat spin
fuel pipe
fuselage
grounded
gyrostat
heliport
in flight
intercom

jet pilot
jet plane
joystick
moonshot
non-rigid
nose-cone
nosedive
nose down
pitching
pulse-jet
radiator
seaplane
sideslip
spaceman
squadron
stopover
streamer
subsonic
tail-boom
tail-skid
tail unit
terminal
throttle
triplane
turbojet
twin-tail
volplane
warplane
wind cone
windsock
wing-flap
Zeppelin

9

aerodrome
aeroplane
air intake
air pocket
airworthy
altimeter
amphibian
astrodome
astronaut
autopilot
backplate
cabin crew
caravelle
carlingue
cosmonaut
countdown
crash-land
crow's-foot
delta-wing
dirigible
doodlebug
empennage

fuel gauge
fuel intake
gyroplane
jet bomber
launch pad
launching
lift-wires
longerons
low-flying
monocoque
monoplane
navigator
overshoot
parachute
power dive
propeller
rudder bar
sailplane
satellite
semi-rigid
spacecrew
spaceship
spacesuit
spacewalk
stability
stratojet
sweepback
tailplane
test pilot
touch down
turboprop
twin-screw
wind gauge

10

aerobatics
aero-engine
aeronautic
aerostatic
air balloon
air control
air defence
air hostess
air service
air steward
air support
air traffic
anemometer
ballooning
balloonist
cantilever
cargo plane
Challenger
dive bomber
flight deck
flight path

flight plan
flying boat
ground crew
helicopter
hydroplane
jet fighter
landing run
mach number
outer space
oxygen mask
pilot plane
robot plane
rudder-post
slipstream
solo flight
spacecraft
space probe
splashdown
stabilizer
stewardess
supersonic
test flight
V-formation

11

aeronautics
aerostatics
afterburner
air terminal
air umbrella
blind flying
combat plane
ejector-seat
flying speed
free balloon
ground speed
heat barrier
heavy bomber
kite-balloon
laminar flow
landing deck
landing gear
leading-edge
loop the loop
moon landing
mooring-mast
ornithopter
parachutist
retro-rocket
retractable
sesquiplane
slotted wing
soft landing
space centre
space flight
space rocket
space travel

stabilizers
stunt flying
vapour trail
weather-vane

12

aerodynamics
airfreighter
air-sea rescue
arrester gear
beacon lights
belly landing
control tower
crash landing
ejection seat
fighter pilot
flying clrcus
flying saucer
gliding-angle
jet-propelled
landing light

landing speed
landing wires
launching pad
maiden flight
manned rocket
night fighter
pilot balloon
pressure suit
pursuit plane
radar scanner
radial-engine
sound barrier
space capsule
space station
space vehicle
trailing-edge

13 AND OVER

aircraft-carrier (15)
airworthiness (13)
control-column (13)
cruising speed (13)
decompression (15)
engine-mounting (14)
escape-velocity (14)
forced landing (13)
ground control (13)
heavier-than-air (14)
in-line-engines (13)
lighter-than-air (14)
looping the loop (14)
radio-location (13)
semi-retractable (15)
shock-absorber (13)
space traveller (14)
stalling-speed (13)
troop-transport (14)
undercarriage (13)
weightlessness (14)

Boats and ships
See also **Nautical terms**

3 AND 4

ark
bac
bark
boat
brig
buss
caic
cog
cot
dhow
dory
dow
duck
four
gig
grab
hoy
hulk
junk
keel
koff
pair
pram
proa
punt
raft

saic
scow
ship
snow
sub
T.B.D.
tub
tug
yawl

5

aviso
balsa
barca
barge
batel
boyer
canoe
caper
casco
coble
craft
crare
E-boat
eight
ferry

fifie
fleet
float
funny
kayak
ketch
kobil
liner
oiler
P-boat
praam
prahu
prove
Q-ship
razee
R-boat
saiok
scull
shell
skiff
sloop
smack
tramp
U-boat
umiak
whiff
xebec
yacht

6

argosy
banker
barque
bateau
bawley
bireme
bug-eye
caique
carvel
coggle
cooper
crayer
cutter
decker
dinghy
dogger
droger
dugout
galeas
galiot
galley
gay-you
hopper
hooker
kumpit
launch

lorcha
lugger
masula
oomiak
packet
pedalo
pirate
puffer
pulwar
puteli
PT boat
randan
saique
sampan
sealer
settee
slaver
tanker
tartan
tender
tosher
trader
trough
vessel
wafter
whaler
wherry

293

7

airboat
almadie
budgero
bumboat
caravel
carrack
carrier
catboat
clinker
clipper
coaster
cockler
collier
coracle
corsair
cruiser
currach
dredger
drifter
drogher
dromond
eel punt
felucca
flyboat
four-oar
frigate
galleon
galliot
gondola
gunboat
gunship
hog-boat
ice-boat
lighter
man-o'-war
minisub
mistico
monitor
mudscow
muletta
pair-oar
permagy
pinnace
piragua
pirogue
polacca
polacre
pontoon
rowboat
sea-sled
shallop
shoaler
spy boat
steamer
tartane
tonkong
tow boat

trawler
trireme
tugboat
warship

8

baghalak
bilander
car ferry
coalship
cockboat
corocole
corvette
dahabeah
dahabiya
derelict
eight-oar
fireboat
fireship
flagship
galleass
galliass
gallivat
hoogarts
hoveller
ice yacht
Indiaman
ironclad
johnboat
keelboat
lifeboat
longboat
mailboat
man-of-war
netlayer
sailboat
schooner
showboat
smuggler
steam-tug
tilt-boat
trimaran
waterbus
well-boat
woodskin

9

bomb-ketch
bucentaur
cable ship
canal boat
cargo boat
catamaran
container
crocodile

depot ship
destroyer
ferryboat
fire-float
freighter
frigatoon
funny-boat
guard boat
guard ship
herringer
horse-boat
houseboat
hydrofoil
jollyboat
lightship
minelayer
motorboat
oil tanker
outrigger
peter-boat
pilot boat
pilot ship
powerboat
privateer
prize ship
river boat
rotor ship
sand yacht
sheer-hulk
slave dhow
speedboat
steamboat
steamship
storeship
submarine
swampboat
transport
troopship
tunny-boat
two-decker
whaleboat
wheelboat

10

advice boat
barge-yacht
barkentine
battleship
bomb vessel
brigantine
cattleboat
chain-ferry
cockleboat
Deal lugger
flying boat
four-master
hovercraft

hydroplane
icebreaker
monkey-boat
motor yacht
narrowboat
nuclear sub
ocean liner
ore-carrier
packet-boat
paddleboat
patrol boat
picket boat
pirate-ship
quadrireme
repair-ship
rescue boat
rivercraft
rowing boat
royal barge
sloop-of-war
small craft
submarine
supply ship
survey ship
target ship
tea-clipper
turret ship
victualler
Viking ship
windjammer
watercraft

11

barquentine
capital ship
chasse-marée
cockleshell
dreadnought
fishing boat
galley foist
hydroglider
merchantman
minesweeper
motor launch
motor vessel
mystery ship
naval vessel
pilot cutter
prize vessel
quinquereme
racing shell
Rob-Roy canoe
sailing boat
sailing ship
sardine boat
slavetrader
steam launch

steam vessel
submersible
three-decker
three-master
torpedo boat
victual ship

12

cabin cruiser
coasting boat
coasting ship
despatch boat
East Indiaman
ferry steamer
fishing smack
heavy cruiser
landing barge
landing craft
light cruiser
merchant ship
motor drifter
motor trawler
pirate cutter

pleasure boat
police launch
pontoon crane
river gunboat
sailing barge
sailing craft
sculling boat
square-rigger
steam gondola
stern-wheeler
survey vessel
Thames bawley
training ship

13

battlecruiser
Bermuda cutter
Canadian canoe
container ship
double-sculler
four-oared boat
hovelling-boat
motor lifeboat

paddle-steamer
passenger-boat
passenger-ship
sailing vessel
ship-of-the-line
trading vessel

14 AND 15

aircraft-carrier (15)
cable-laying ship (15)
cable-repair ship (15)
coasting vessel (14)
despatch cutter (14)
eight-oared boat (14)
electric launch (14)
flotilla leader (14)
seaplane tender (14)
submarine chaser (15)
topsail schooner (15)
torpedo-gunboat (14)
Yorkshire coble (14)

Motoring

2 AND 3

A.A.
c.c.
air
cam
can
cap
car
cog
fan
fit
gas
G.T.
hub
h.p.
jam
jet
key
lap
lug
map
M.O.T.
nut
oil
pin
pit

R.A.C.
rev
rim
rod
run
ton
top

4

axle
belt
body
bolt
boot
boss
bulb
bush
clip
coil
dash
disc
door
drum
flat
fuse

gear
hood
hoot
horn
idle
jack
lane
lock
nail
park
pink
plug
pump
road
roll
rope
seat
skid
sump
tail
tank
test
tire
tour
tube
tyre
veer

wing

5

apron
brake
cable
chain
chart
choke
clamp
coupé
cover
crank
cut in
drive
float
frame
gauge
joint
knock
lay-by
level
lever
model
motor

on tow
pedal
rally
rev up
rivet
rotor
route
scale
screw
sedan
shaft
shift
spark
speed
spoke
squab
stall
start
ton up
tools
tread
U-turn
valve
wheel
wiper
works

6

adjust
big end
bonnet
bumper
bypass
camber
car tax
charge
clutch
cut out
dazzle
de-icer
de luxe
detour
dickey
divert
driver
dynamo
engine
fitter
flange
funnel
garage
gasket
grease
handle
hooter
hot rod
hubcap
idling
klaxon
lock-up
louvre
mascot
milage
mirror
octane
oilcan
one-way
petrol
pile up
pinion
piston
saloon
signal
spokes
spring
swerve
switch
tappet
timing
torque

7

air hose
airlock
axle-box
battery
bearing
blowout
bollard
build-up
bus lane
bus stop
carpark
carport
cat's eye
chassis
contact
control
cooling
dipping
drive-in
driving
exhaust
fanbelt
flyover
gearbox
give way
goggles
gudgeon
hardtop
highway
joyride
L driver
L plates
licence
linkage
locknut
log book
luggage
magneto
map-case
mileage
misfire
missing
mixture
muffler
no entry
non-skid
offside
oil-feed
parking
pillion
pinking
pull out
reverse
roadhog
roadmap
roadtax
rolling

run into
seizing
service
skidpan
spindle
springs
starter
test run
toolkit
top gear
touring
towrope
traffic
trailer
viaduct
warning
wingnut

8

air brake
air inlet
airtight
armature
arterial
Autobahn
backfire
back seat
bodywork
brakerod
camshaft
cat's eyes
clearway
coasting
converge
coupling
crankpin
cruising
cul-de-sac
cylinder
declutch
delivery
dipstick
driveway
fastback
fast lane
feed pipe
feed pump
flat tyre
flywheel
foglight
footpump
freezing
friction
fuelpipe
fuel tank
garaging
gasoline

gradient
guide-rod
handpump
ignition
inlet cam
knocking
manifold
missfire
motoring
motorist
motorway
mudguard
nearside
oil gauge
oncoming
open road
overhaul
overpass
overtake
overturn
pavement
prowl car
puncture
radiator
rattling
rear axle
rear lamp
ring road
roadside
road sign
road test
roofrack
rush hour
side road
sideslip
silencer
skidding
skid mark
slip road
slow down
slow lane
speeding
squad car
stock car
tail skid
tail gate
taxi rank
throttle
tire pump
two-speed
tyre pump

9

air filter
alignment
anti-glare
autoroute

back wheel
ball-valve
batteries
brakedrum
brakeshoe
breakdown
bus driver
cab driver
car driver
car polish
chain-link
chauffeur
clearance
coachwork
concourse
condenser
cotter pin
crank axle
crankcase
crossroad
cutting in
dashboard
dashlight
defroster
dipswitch
direction
dirt track
diversion
estate car
filler cap
footbrake
framework
free-wheel
front axle
front seat
fuel gauge
gear lever
generator
Grand Prix
grease-box
grease-gun
guarantee
handbrake
headlight
hit-and-run
indicator
inner tube
insurance
limousine
lubricate
motorbike
motorcade
motor show
nipple key
oil filter
overdrive
passenger
patrol car
petrol can

piston rod
point duty
police car
racing car
rear light
reflector
revving up
road sense
road works
saloon car
sidelight
spare tire
spare tyre
sports car
spotlight
switch off
tail-light
taximeter
third gear
tire lever
T-junction
tramlines
trunk road
two-seater
tyre lever
underpass
underseal
wheel base
wheel spin
white line

10

access road
adjustment
amber light
anti-dazzle
antifreeze
bevelwheel
bottom gear
box-spanner
brakeblock
brake light
brake pedal
broken down
car licence
coachbuilt
combustion
commutator
crankshaft
crossroads
dickey seat
dry battery
four-seater
front wheel
gear casing
gear change
green light

gudgeon pin
headlights
horsepower
inlet valve
insulation
lighting up
low-tension
lubricator
motorcycle
overtaking
petrol pump
petrol tank
piston ring
private car
radial tire
radial tyre
rear mirror
rev counter
right of way
roadworthy
roundabout
safety belt
signalling
spare wheel
speed limit
streamline
suspension
tachometer
third-party
three-speed
toll bridge
touring car
traffic cop
traffic jam
two-wheeler
upholstery
ventilator
wheelbrace
windscreen
wing mirror

11

accelerator
accessories
accumulator
blind corner
brake-lining
built-up area
carburetter
carburettor
carriageway
clutch pedal
compression
convertible
crash helmet
decarbonize
de-luxe model

distributor
driving test
exhaust pipe
exhaust port
feeler-gauge
front lights
highway code
ignition key
interrupter
lorry driver
lubrication
luggage rack
motor spirit
needle-valve
number plate
oil pressure
overhauling
overheating
over-revving
owner-driver
petrol gauge
pre-ignition
racing model
radiator cap
request stop
reverse gear
reverse turn
rotary valve
screen-wiper
self-starter
sliding roof
speedometer
sports model
streamlined
sunshine roof
synchromesh
tappet valve
thermometer
through road
ticking over
trafficator
vacuum brake
valve-timing
wheel wobble

12

acceleration
approach road
arterial road
ball-bearings
breakdown van
clutch-spring
coachbuilder
contact-screw
countershaft
cylinder head
diesel engine

differential
double-decker
driving-chain
driving-shaft
exhaust valve
float-chamber
freewheeling
fuel injection
gear changing
lock-up garage
miles per hour
motor scooter
motor vehicle
motorcyclist
parking light
parking meter
parking place
petrol filter
pillion rider
racing driver
ratchet-wheel
registration
repair outfit
road junction
running-board
single-decker
sparking plug
steering gear
transmission
two-speed gear
warning light

13

admission-pipe
breakdown gang
chain-adjuster
connecting rod
cooling system
driving mirror
fluid flywheel
hydraulic jack
induction pipe
inspection pit
licence-holder
pillion-riding
pressure-gauge
rack-and-pinion
roller-bearing
servo-assisted
shock absorber
shooting brake
speed merchant
starting motor
steering wheel
traffic signal

14

adjusting-screw
circuit-breaker
compression tap

contact-breaker
double-declutch
driving licence
exhaust-cam axle
filling station
friction-clutch
grease-injector
lighting-up time
lubricating oll
luggage-carrier
miles per gallon
propeller shaft
reclining seats
reversing lights
service station
starting handle
steering column
third-party risk
three-speed gear
universal joint

15

carriage-builder
dual carriageway
instrument panel
insurance policy
seating capacity
windscreen wiper

Nautical terms
See also **Boats and ships**

2 AND 3	hog	top	bunt	foam	hulk
	jaw	tow	buoy	fore	hull
A.B.	jib	way	calk	foul	jack
aft	lee	yaw	calm	frap	junk
A1	log		coak	furl	keel
bay	man		comb	gaff	knot
bow	nut	*4*	cott	gale	land
box	oar		crew	gang	last
cat	ply	ahoy	deck	gear	lead
cay	ram	alee	dive	girt	leak
C.I.F.	rig	back	dock	grog	line
con	R.M.	bale	down	hank	list
cox	R.N.	beam	dune	hard	load
ebb	rum	beat	east	haul	loof
fay	run	bend	eddy	haze	luff
fid	sag	bitt	fake	hazy	lute
F.O.B.	sea	boom	fend	head	mast
fog	set	bows	flag	helm	mess
guy	SOS	brig	floe	hold	mine
H.M.S.	tar	bunk	flow	hove	mist

mole	wing	douse	royal	burton	neaped
moor	yard	downs	sally	cablet	needle
navy	yarn	dowse	salve	canvas	offing
neap		draft	salvo	careen	on deck
oars		drift	sands	carina	outfit
peak	**5**	embay	screw	comber	paddle
pier		entry	sheer	convoy	patrol
poop	aback	fanal	sheet	course	pay off
port	abaft	flake	shelf	crotch	pay out
prow	abeam	fleet	shoal	cruise	pennon
punt	afore	float	shore	debark	Pharos
quay	afoul	fluke	siren	diving	pillow
raft	after	foggy	skeet	double	pintle
rail	ahead	gauge	sling	driver	piracy
rake	ahull	grave	sound	earing	pirate
rank	aloft	gusty	spars	embark	piston
rate	apeak	hands	spoom	engine	pooped
rear	aport	hatch	sprit	ensign	poppet
reef	atrip	haven	steer	escort	raider
ride	avast	hawse	stern	fathom	rating
roll	awash	hitch	storm	fender	ratlin
rope	beach	hoist	surge	fo'c'sle	reefed
rove	belay	horse	swell	for'ard	reefer
rung	belee	jetty	swing	fother	rigged
sail	below	jutty	thole	funnel	rigger
scud	berth	kedge	tidal	furled	rocket
seam	bibbs	kevel	trice	galley	rudder
ship	bight	lay-to	truck	gasket	sailor
sink	bilge	lay up	truss	gromet	saloon
skid	bilts	leach	waist	gunnel	salute
slip	bitts	leaky	watch	halser	salvor
slue	blirt	leech	weigh	hawser	sculls
spar	block	ligan	wharf	hounds	sealer
stay	board	liner	wheel	hove-to	seaman
stem	bosun	lobby	windy	inship	seaway
step	bower	lurch	woold	jetsam	sheets
surf	bowse	metal	wreck	jetson	shroud
swab	brace	misty		jigger	signal
swig	brail	naval		kedger	sinker
tack	bream	north	**6**	lading	sinnet
taut	briny	oakum		lateen	splice
tend	cabin	ocean	aboard	launch	squall
tide	cable	order	adrift	lay-off	square
tilt	cadet	orlop	afloat	leeway	stocks
toss	canal	panch	anchor	Lloyd's	stormy
trim	cargo	pitch	armada	locker	strake
trip	caulk	prick	ashore	manned	strand
vang	chain	prize	astern	marina	stream
veer	chart	prore	aweigh	marine	tackle
voya	check	radar	awning	marker	tender
waft	chock	radio	balker	maroon	thwart
wake	clamp	range	batten	marque	tiller
wapp	cleat	refit	beacon	masted	timber
warp	craft	rhumb	becket	mayday	toggle
wave	crank	right	billow	mid-sea	towage
wear	cuddy	roads	bonnet	mizzen	unbend
west	davit	ropes	bridge	moored	unbitt
whip	depth	route	bumkin	mutiny	uncoil
wind	diver	rower	bunker	nautic	undock

unfurl
unlade
unload
unmoor
unship
vessel
voyage

7

aground
athwart
backing
bale out
ballast
beached
bearing
beating
bilboes
blister
boarder
bobstay
bollard
boomkin
bowline
bow wave
boxhaul
bracing
breaker
bulwark
bunkage
buntine
bunting
buoyage
caboose
calking
can-buoy
capsize
capstan
captain
cast off
catfall
cathead
cat's-paw
channel
charter
claw off
coaling
coaming
cockpit
compass
conning
cordage
corsair
counter
cresset
cringle
cyclone

deadeye
deep-sea
degauss
dismast
dockage
dog-vane
dolphin
drabler
draught
dry-dock
dunnage
ease off
ebb-tide
embargo
eye-bolt
fairway
fishery
flotsam
flotson
fogbank
foghorn
foretop
forward
founder
freight
freshen
freshet
frogman
futtock
gangway
gimbals
go about
go below
grapnel
grating
graving
grommet
gudgeon
gun-deck
gunnage
gun-port
gun-room
gunwale
guy-rope
half pay
halyard
harbour
harpoon
haul off
head off
head sea
headway
heave to
horizon
iceberg
icefloe
inboard
inshore
Jack Tar

jib boom
jibstay
keelage
keelson
landing
laniard
lanyard
lashing
lastage
latches
leaking
lee-gage
lee side
lee tide
leeward
listing
loading
logbook
logline
logreel
lookout
luffing
lugsail
maintop
mariner
marines
marline
marling
matelot
mistral
monsoon
moorage
mooring
mudhook
oarsman
oceanic
offward
old salt
on board
outport
oversea
painter
pennant
pooping
port-bar
quayage
rafting
rations
ratline
reefing
reeming
ride out
rigging
rollers
rolling
rope-end
rostrum
rowlock
rundown

sailing
salvage
scupper
scuttle
seacard
seafolk
sea-lane
sea-legs
seamark
sea-ooze
sea-room
seasick
seaward
set sail
sextant
shallow
shelves
shipper
shipway
shrouds
sick-bay
sinking
skipper
skysail
slipway
spanker
spencer
squally
stand-by
steward
stopper
stowage
tacking
tackled
tackler
tactics
tempest
thimble
tonnage
top deck
top mast
topping
topsail
topside
tornado
torpedo
towline
towpath
towrope
transom
trysail
typhoon
unladen
unsling
unslung
veering
waftage
ward off
warping

wavelet
waveson
wet dock
whistle
wrecked
wrecker
yardarm

8

anchored
anteport
aplustre
approach
armament
at anchor
aweather
backstay
backwash
barbette
bargeman
barnacle
beam-ends
bearings
becalmed
berthage
berthing
binnacle
boat-deck
boathook
bolt-rope
bowsprit
broach to
bulkhead
bulwarks
buntline
castaway
caulking
claw away
club-haul
coasting
crossing
cruising
cutwater
dead slow
deadwood
deckhand
derelict
disembay
ditty-bag
ditty-box
dockyard
dogwatch
doldrums
doubling
downhaul
drifting
driftway

easterly	mainboom	sheer off	all aboard	house-flag
eastward	main deck	ship ahoy	alongside	houseline
even keel	mainmast	shipmate	amidships	hurricane
fife-rail	mainsail	shipment	anchorage	jack-block
flag-rank	mainstay	ship oars	anchoring	jack-staff
floating	mainyard	shipping	back-stays	jack-stays
flotilla	make sail	sounding	bargepole	kentledge
fogbound	maritime	spy-glass	barnacles	land ahead
foot-rope	martinet	squadron	beaconage	lobscouse
forefoot	masthead	standard	below deck	lower deck
foremast	mastless	stand off	bilge-keel	maelstrom
forepeak	messmate	staysail	bilge-pump	mainbrace
foresail	midships	steerage	blue peter	mainsheet
foreship	moorings	sternage	boardable	manoeuvre
forestay	moulinet	sternway	boat drill	midstream
forewind	mutineer	stowaway	broadside	minefield
free-port	mutinous	stranded	bunkering	minute-gun
gaffsail	nauscopy	streamer	captaincy	mizzentop
go aboard	nautical	stunsail	careenage	naumachia
go ashore	navigate	submerge	chartered	navicular
halliard	neap tide	tackling	chartroom	navigable
hard-alee	ordnance	tafferel	close haul	navigator
hatchway	outboard	taffrail	coastwise	neptunian
headfast	overrake	thole-pin	companion	northerly
head into	overseas	timoneer	corposant	northward
headwind	paravane	tranship	crossjack	north wind
helmless	periplus	traverse	crosstree	ocean lane
helmsman	picaroon	unbuoyed	crosswind	orlop deck
high seas	pierhead	uncoiled	crow's nest	outrigger
high tide	pilotage	underset	Davy Jones	overboard
hornpipe	plimsoll	under way	dead-water	parbuckle
hull-down	poop deck	unfurled	deck cargo	periscope
icebound	porthole	vanguard	demurrage	press-gang
icefield	portoise	wall-knot	departure	privateer
iron-sick	portside	wardroom	disanchor	prize-crew
jackstay	pratique	waterman	discharge	promenade
jettison	pumproom	water-rot	disembark	quicksand
jury mast	put about	waterway	doggerman	recharter
keelhaul	put to sea	waveworm	dogshores	reckoning
keel over	quarters	welldeck	dress ship	red ensign
land ahoy!	reef-knot	westerly	drift-sail	reef-point
landfall	re-embark	westward	driftwood	refitment
landmark	ride easy	west wind	Elmo's-fire	revictual
landsman	ride hard	windlass	false keel	rhumb-line
landward	roadster	wind-rode	firedrill	roadstead
land wind	sail-loft	wind-sail	floodmark	rockbound
larboard	sail-room	windward	flood-tide	royal mast
lead-line	sail-yard	woolding	flying jib	Royal Navy
leeboard	salvable	wreckage	foreshore	rum-runner
lee shore	salvager	yachting	foundered	sailcloth
lifebelt	sandbank		gangboard	seafaring
lifebuoy	scudding		gangplank	sea-letter
lifeline	seaborne	**9**	gather way	sea-robber
load-line	sea-chest		groundage	seaworthy
loblolly	seafarer	about-ship	half-hitch	semaphore
logboard	seagoing	admiralty	hard aport	sheething
long haul	sea-rover	affreight	high water	shipboard
low water	shallows	afterdeck	hoist sail	shipowner
magazine	shark-net	air-funnel	holystone	ship's crew

shipshape
shipwreck
shoreward
sick-berth
sidelight
sight land
southerly
southward
south wind
sou'wester
spindrift
spinnaker
spritsail
stanchion
starboard
stateroom
steersman
sternfast
sternmost
sternpost
stokehold
storm-beat
stormsail
stormstay
stretcher
tarpaulin
telescope
tide-table
tophamper
trade wind
twin-screw
two-decker
unballast
uncharted
unharbour
unlighted
unsounded
upper deck
water-line
water-sail
whirlwind
wind-bound
wring-bolt
yachtsman

10

A1 at Lloyd's
aboard ship
after-guard
after-hatch
after-sails
alongshore
anchorable
anchor buoy
anchor hold
astarboard
ballasting

batten down
Bermuda rig
bilgewater
blue ensign
bluejacket
breakwater
bootlegger
breastfast
bridge deck
cargo space
cast anchor
casting-net
catch a crab
chain-cable
chain-plate
charthouse
coal-bunker
cork-jacket
cross-piece
crosstrees
deadlights
degaussing
diving-bell
dockmaster
downstream
drop anchor
drop astern
embarkment
engine room
escutcheon
fathomless
fiddlehead
figurehead
fore-and-aft
forecastle
forge ahead
freightage
freshwater
frostbound
full-rigged
gaff rigged
harbourage
heavy-laden
high-and-dry
hollow-mast
jigger-mast
Jolly Roger
jury-rigged
jury rudder
landlocked
landlubber
lateen sail
lateen yard
lay a course
liberty-man
life-jacket
lighterage
lighthouse
lookout-man

loxodromic
manoeuvres
marine soap
marker buoy
martingale
middle deck
midshipman
mizzenmast
mizzensail
mizzenstay
navigating
navigation
night-watch
ocean-going
orthodromy
parcelling
pilothouse
pipe aboard
port of call
powder-room
prize-court
prize-money
quarantine
raking fire
reduce sail
rendezvous
reshipment
rope-ladder
round-house
rudderless
rudder post
Samson post
seamanlike
seamanship
ship-broker
shipmaster
shipwright
signalling
skyscraper
slack-water
spring-tide
square-sail
stanchions
stay-tackle
stern-board
stern-frame
sternsheet
submariner
supercargo
take in sail
tally-clerk
tidal basin
tidal river
tiller-rope
topgallant
unfathomed
unfordable
upperworks
water-borne

waterspout
watertight
wheel-house
wring-staff

11

abandon ship
beachcomber
belaying pin
captainship
centreboard
chafing-gear
close-hauled
compass card
compass rose
contact mine
debarkation
depth-charge
dismastment
diving bell
diving suit
dock charges
echo-sounder
embarcation
embarkation
escape hatch
foam-crested
fore-topmast
foul weather
gallows-tops
get under way
go alongside
graving-dock
ground-swell
harbour dues
harness-cask
hug the shore
innavigable
keelhauling
landing deck
lifeboatman
loblolly-boy
loxodromics
maintopmast
maintopsail
make headway
marine store
mess steward
middle watch
mizzen course
monkey-block
naval rating
orthodromic
overfreight
paddle wheel
port charges
port of entry

press-of-sail
quarterdeck
range-finder
reconnoitre
riding-light
sailing date
Samson's-post
searchlight
seasickness
sheet anchor
shipbreaker
ship's doctor
ship's papers
sliding-keel
snatch-block
sounding-rod
south-wester
spanking boom
spring a leak
standing off
station-bill
steerage-way
stern-chaser
sternsheets
storm signal
three-masted
thwartships
tidal waters
torpedo tube
unballasted
unchartered
under canvas
under-masted
unnavigable
unnavigated
unsheltered
unsoundable
waistcloths
waterlogged
weather-gage
weathermost
weather-roll
weather side
weigh anchor
white ensign

12

air-sea rescue
between-decks
bill of lading
breeches-buoy
cable's-length
canvas length
caulking iron
change course
collision-mat
companionway

conning tower
counter-brace
displacement
double-banked
double-braced
double-manned
equinoctials
fishing fleet
floating dock
futtock-plate
ground-tackle
hard-aweather
jack-o'-lantern
jacob's ladder
lateen-rigged
line of battle
longshoreman
magnetic mine
maiden voyage
man overboard
marine boiler
marine engine
marline-spike
measured mile
minesweeping
naval command
navigability
orthodromics
outmanoeuvre
outward-bound
Plimsoll line
Plimsoll mark
privateering
recommission
ride at anchor
ship-chandler
shipping line
ship's husband
slack in stays
square-rigged
starboard bow
stream anchor
studding sail
tourist class
training ship
transhipment
Trinity House
undercurrent
unfathomable
war-insurance
weatherboard
weatherbound
weather cloth
weatherglass
weatherproof
westerly wind
will-o'-the-wisp

13

affreightment
cat-o'-nine-tails
close quarters
compass signal
dead reckoning
deck passenger
fishing-tackle
floating light
grappling-iron
high-water mark
hurricane deck
life-preserver
mizzen rigging
naval dockyard
naval ordnance
navigableness
north-east wind
northerly wind
north-west wind
order-of-battle
re-embarkation
royal dockyard
ship-of-the-line
south-east wind
southerly wind
south-west wind
spilling-lines
starboard beam
starboard side
steering-wheel
weather report

14

circumnavigate
compass-bearing
disembarkation
futtock shrouds
hard-astarboard
letter-of-marque
Lloyd's Register
mushroom-anchor
naval architect
powder magazine
prevailing wind
running-rigging
schooner-rigged
screw-propeller
ship's-carpenter
swivel-rowlocks
topgallant mast

15

Admiralty Office
circumnavigable
command of the sea

companion ladder
marine insurance
mariner's compass
operation orders
victualling yard

Vehicles

2 – 4	*5*		*fourgon*	*Cadillac*
		hansom	fourgon	Cadillac
		hearse	growler	carriage
Audi	artic	itney	gyrocar	carriole
auto	bandy	Jaguar	hackery	carrycot
bier	bogey	jalopy	hackney	clarence
biga	bogie	Lancia	haywain	curricle
bike	brake	landau	helibus	cycle-car
BR	brett	limber	kibitka	dustcart
bus	buggy	litter	mail car	equipage
cab	caddy	Morris	mail-van	goods van
car	chair	oxcart	minibus	handcart
cart	coach	pochay	minicab	ice-yacht
DAF	coupé	pulkha	minicar	jetliner
dan	crate	saloon	omnibus	jump-seat
drag	cycle	sledge	pedrail	mail-cart
dray	dilly	sleigh	phaeton	milk-cart
duck	float	spider	pullman	motorbus
ekka	lorry	surrey	railcar	motorcar
Fiat	moped	tandem	railbus	old crock
fly	motor	tender	Renault	pushcart
Ford	plane	tri-car	scooter	quadriga
gig	pulka	troika	sidecar	rickshaw
GWR	Rover	waggon	Sputnik	roadster
heap	sedan	whisky	taxicab	rockaway
jeep	sulky		tilbury	runabout
jet	tonga		tipcart	sociable
limo	train	*7*	tonneau	stanhope
LMS	truck		tractor	steam-car
LNER	Volvo	amtrack	trailer	tarantas
loco	wagon	autobus	tramcar	toboggan
MG		autocar	trishaw	tricycle
mig		balloon	Triumph	Vauxhall
mini	*6*	bicycle	trolley	victoria
Opel		britzka	trundle	zeppelin
pram	Austin	Bugatti	tumbrel	
RY	banger	caboose	tumbril	
Saab	barrow	cacolet	turnout	*9*
Seat	Berlin	caravan	vis-á-vis	
skis	calash	caravel	voiture	aeroplane
sled	chaise	cariole		ambulance
SR	dodgem	caroche		amphibian
tank	dennet	chariot	*8*	applecart
taxi	doolie	chopper		bandwagon
tram	drosky	Citroën	barouche	bath-chair
trap	engine	Daimler	brakevan	boat-train
tube	fiacre	dogcart	britzska	bob-sleigh
van	gingle	droshky	brougham	box-wagon
wain	go-cart	flivver	cablecar	bubblecar

304

bulldozer
cabriolet
charabanc
Chevrolet
diligence
dining car
dodgem car
dormobile
guard's van
hansom cab
hatchback
ice skates
landaulet
land rover
limousine
mail-coach
mail-train
milkfloat
motorbike
motorcade
muletrain
palanquin
prison van
Rolls-Royce
saloon car
sand yacht
sportscar
streetcar
stretcher
wagonette
water-cart

10

automobile
Black Maria
boneshaker
chapel cart
conveyance
donkey-cart
fire-engine
four-in-hand
glass coach
goods train
goods truck
hackney cab
hand-barrow
hovercraft
invalid cab
jinricksha
knockabout
locomotive
motorcoach
motorcycle
motor lorry
post-chaise
pullman car
sedan chair
smoking car
snowplough
spacecraft
spring-cart
stagecoach
state coach
timwhiskey
tip-up lorry
touring car
tramway-car

trolley-bus
trolley-car
velocipede
waggonette
war chariot
wheelchair

11

armoured car
brewer's dray
bullock cart
caterpillar
delivery van
fire balloon
four-wheeler
goods waggon
gun-carriage
horse-litter
jaunting-car
landaulette
mail phaeton
sleeping car
state landau
steam engine
steamroller
three-in-hand
waggon train
wheelbarrow

12

baby carriage
coach-and-four

coach-and-pair
furniture-van
hackney-coach
invalid chair
luggage train
magic carpet
motor scooter
pantechnicon
perambulator
railway train
three-wheeler
watering-cart

13

ambulance cart
electric truck
governess cart
mourning-coach
penny-farthing
state carriage
steam-carriage
wheel-carriage

14 AND 15

ambulance wagon (14)
bathing-machine (14)
hackney carriage (15)
invalid carriage (15)
luggage trailer (14)
prairie-schooner (15)
railway carriage (15)
traction-engine (14)

IVRs (Vehicle Registration)

A	Austria	C	Cuba
ADN	Yemen	CDN	Canada
AND	Andorra	CH	Switzerland
AUS	Australia	CI	Ivory Coast
B	Belgium	CL	Sri Lanka
BDS	Barbados	CO	Columbia
BG	Bulgaria	CS	Czechoslovakia
BH	British Honduras	CY	Cyprus
BR	Brazil	D	Germany
BRN	Bahrain	DDR	E. Germany
BRU	Brunei	DK	Denmark
BS	Bahamas	DOM	Dominican Republic
BUR	Burma	DY	Dahomey

DZ	Algeria	PAK	Pakistan
E	Spain	PE	Peru
EAK	Kenya	PL	Philippines
EAT	Tanzania	PY	Paraguay
EAU	Uganda	R	Romania
EC	Ecuador	RA	Argentina
ET	Egypt	RC	Taiwan
F	France	RCA	Central African Republic
FJI	Fiji	RCB	Congo
FL	Liechtenstein	RCH	Chile
GB	Great Britain	RH	Haiti
GBA	Alderney	RI	Indonesia
GBG	Guernsey	RIM	Mauretania
GBJ	Jersey	RL	Lebanon
GBM	Isle of Man	RM	Madagascar
GBZ	Gibraltar	ROK	Korea
GCA	Guatemala	RSM	San Marino
GH	Ghana	RU	Burundi
GR	Greece	RWA	Rwanda
GUY	Guyana	S	Sweden
H	Hungary	SD	Swaziland
HKJ	Jordon	SGP	Singapore
I	Italy	SME	Surinam
IL	Israel	SN	Senegal
IND	India	SU	Soviet Union
IR	Iran	SWA	South West Africa
IRL	Ireland	SY	Seychelles
IRQ	Iraq	SYR	Syria
IS	Iceland	T	Thailand
J	Japan	TG	Togo
JA	Jamaica	TN	Tunisia
K	Kampuchea	TR	Turkey
KWT	Kuwait	TT	Trinidad and Tobago
L	Luxembourg	U	Uraguay
LAO	Laos	USA	U.S.A.
LAR	Libya	V	Vatican City
LB	Liberia	VN	Vietnam
LS	Lesotho	WAG	Gambia
M	Malta	WAL	Sierra Leone
MAL	Malaysia	WAN	Nigeria
MC	Monaco	WG	Granada, Windward Islands
MEX	Mexico	WL/WV	Windward Islands (St Lucia
MS	Mauritius		and St Vincent)
MV	Malawi	WS	Western Samoa
N	Norway	YU	Yugoslavia
NA	Netherlands Antilles	YV	Venezuela
NL	Netherlands	Z	Zambia
NZ	New Zealand	ZA	South Africa
P	Portugal	ZR	Zaire
PA	Panama	ZW	Zimbabwe

MISCELLANEOUS
Abbreviations

1 AND 2

A	ampere	C.J.	Chief Justice	G.C.	George Cross
A.A.	Automobile Association, Anti-aircraft, Alcoholics Anonymous	cl.	class, clause	G.I.	general issue (U.S.A.)
		cm.	centimetre		
		C.O.	commanding officer, Colonial Office	Gk.	Greek
				gm.	gram(s)
A.B.	ablebodied seaman	Co.	company, county	G.M.	George Medal, Grand Master
A.C.	alternating current	c/o	care of		
a/c	account	Cr.	creditor	G.P.	General Practitioner
A.D.	Anno Domini (In the year of our Lord)	C.U.	Cambridge University	G.R.	Georgius Rex (King George)
		d.	daughter, old penny, old pence, died	Gr.	Greek
A.F.	Admiral of the Fleet			gr.	grain(s), grammar, gross
A.G.	Adjutant-General	D.C.	direct current, District of Columbia (U.S.)		
a.m.	ante meridiem (before noon)			gs.	guineas
				Gt.	great
A1	First-class in Lloyd's Register	D.D.	Doctor of Divinity	h.	hour(s)
		DM	Deutschemark	H.C.	House of Commons
AS	Anglo-Saxon	do.	ditto	H.E.	high explosive, His (Her) Excellency
A.V.	Authorised Version	D.P.	displaced person		
Av.	avenue, average	D.R.	District Railway	H.F.	high frequency
b.	born, bowled	Dr.	drachm, drachma, doctor, debtor	hf.	half
B.A.	Bachelor of Arts			H.H.	His (Her) Highness
B.C.	Before Christ, British Columbia	D.V.	deo volente (God willing)	H.M.	His (Her) Majesty
				H.O.	Home Office
B.D.	Bachelor of Divinity	E.	east, Ecstasy	h.p.	high pressure, horsepower
b.l.	bill of lading	ea.	each		
B.M.	British Museum	E.C.	east-central	H.Q.	headquarters
B.P.	British Pharmacopœia	Ed.	editor	hr.	hour
		E.E.	electrical engineer, errors excepted	H.T.	high tension
b.p.	boiling point			HZ	Hertz
Bp.	Bishop	e.g.	exempli gratia (for example)	Ia.	Iowa
B.S.	Bachelor of Surgery, Bachelor of Science			id.	idem (the same)
		E.I.	East Indies	i.e.	id est (that is)
Bt.	Baronet	eq.	equal	in.	inch(es)
C.	centigrade, Conservative	E.R.	Elizabeth Regina (Queen), East Riding (Yorkshire)	Is.	island
				I.W.	Isle of Wight
c.	caught, chapter, cents, circa			J.	Joule, judge
		ex.	example, without, from	Jn.	junction
ca.	circa (around, about)			J.P.	Justice of the Peace
		F.	Fahrenheit	Jr.	junior
C.A.	chartered accountant	f.	feminine, francs, forte	K	kelvin
				K.C.	King's Counsel, Knight Commander
C.B.	Companion of the Bath, confined to barracks	F.A.	Football Association		
		F.C.	football club		
		ff.	fortissimo	kc	kilocycle
C.C.	cricket club, county council	F.M.	field-marshal, frequency modulation	K.G.	Knight of the Garter
				kg.	kilogram(s)
C.E.	Church of England, civil engineer			km.	kilometre(s)
		F.O.	Foreign Office	K.P.	Knight of St. Patrick
C.F.	Chaplain to the Forces	fo.	folio	Ks.	Kansas
		Fr.	French, Friday	K.T.	Knight of the Thistle
ch.	chapter	ft.	foot, feet	Kt.	knight
C.I.	Channel Islands	G.B.	Great Britain	L.	Latin, Liberal

307

l.	litre	O.C.	Officer Commanding		son, south
lb.	libra (pound)	O.E.	Old English, Old	S.A.	South Africa
L.C.	Lord Chancellor		Etonian(s)		
l.c.	lower case	O.M.	Order of Merit	s.c.	small capitals
	(printing)	Op.	opus (work)		(printing)
Ld.	limited, lord	o.p.	out of print	S.E.	south-east
L.F.	low frequency	Or.	Oregon	s.g.	specific gravity
L.P.	low pressure	O.S.	old style	S.J.	Society of Jesus
L.T.	low tension	O.T.	Old Testament	S.M.	Sergeant-Major
Lt.	Lieutenant, light	O.U.	Oxford University	sq.	square
M.	monsieur, member,	oz.	ounce(s)	sr.	senior
	thousand (mille)	P.	Prince, President	s.s.	same size, steamship
m.	metre(s), mile(s),	p.	page, penny, pence,	St.	Saint, street, stone
	masculine,		piano		(wt.), stumped
	married	P.C.	Police Constable,	S.W.	south-west
M.A.	Master of Arts		Privy Councillor	T.B.	torpedo-boat,
M.B.	Bachelor of Medicine	p.c.	per cent., post card		tuberculosis
M.C.	Master of Ceremonies,	p.d.	per diem, potential	T.D.	Territorial
	Military Cross		difference		Decoration
M.D.	Doctor of Medicine	pd.	paid	T.T.	teetotal
ME	Middle English	pf.	pianoforte	TV	television
	myalgic	pl.	plural, place	u.c.	upper case
	encephalomyelitis	P.M.	Prime Minister,		(printing)
mf.	Mezzoforte		Provost Marshal,	U.K.	United Kingdom
mg.	milligram		Past Master,	U.N.	United Nations
M.I.	mounted infantry		Postmaster	U.S.	United States
M.M.	Military Medal	p.m.	post meridiem, post	V	volt
MM.	Messieurs (Fr.)		mortem	v.	verb, versus
mm.	millimetre(s)	P.O.	post office, postal		(against)
M.O.	medical officer		order	Va.	Virginia
Mo.	Missouri, month	pp.	pages, pianissimo	V.C.	Victoria Cross
M.P.	Member of	p.p.	Per procuration (by	V.D.	Volunteer
	Parliament		proxy)		Decoration,
M.R.	Master of the Rolls	P.S.	postscript		Venereal
Mr.	mister	Pt.	part, port		Disease(s)
MS	manuscript	pt.	pint, point	v.g.	very good
MS	multiple sclerosis	q.	query, question	V.O.	Victorian Order
Mt.	mount	Q.C.	Queen's Counsel	V.R.	Victoria Regina
M.T.	mechanical	Q.M.	Quartermaster		(Queen)
	transport	qr.	quarter	W.	watt, west
N.	newton, north,	qt.	quart	W.C.	water closet, West
	nitrogen	q.v.	quod vide (which see)		Central
n.	neuter, noun	R.	Réaumur, Royal, Rex	W.D.	War Department
N.B.	North Britain, nota		(King), Regina	w.f.	wrong fount
	bene (note well)		(Queen), right,		(printing)
N.E.	north-east		rupee	W.O.	War Office, Warrant
N.F.	National Front	R.A.	Royal Academician,		Officer
No.	number (numero)		Royal Artillery	wt.	weight
N.P.	new paragraph	R.C.	Roman Catholic	yd.	yard
n.p.	new pence	Rd.	road	yr.	your
nr.	near	R.E.	Royal Engineers		
N.S.	New style, Nova	R.M.	Royal Mail, Royal		
	Scotia		Marines	**3**	
N.T.	New Testament	R.N.	Royal Navy		
N.W.	north-west	Rs.	Rupees	A.A.A.	Amateur Athletic
N.Y.	New York	R.U.	Rugby Union		Association,
N.Z.	New Zealand	ry.	railway		American
O.	Ohio, oxygen	S.	Saint, second,		Automobile
ob.	obiit (died)		singular, shilling,		Association

A.A.G.	Assistant Adjutant-General	cap.	capital		Service Cross
ABC	alphabet	C.B.E.	Commander of the British Empire (Order)	D.Sc.	Doctor of Science
Abp.	archbishop			D.S.M.	Distinguished Service Medal
A.C.A.	Associate of the Institute of Chartered Accountants	C.B.I.	Confederation of British Industry	D.S.O.	Distinguished Service Order
		C.I.A.	Central Intelligence Agency	dwt.	pennyweight
A.C.F.	Army Cadet Force	C.I.D.	Criminal Investigation Department	E.E.C.	European Economic Community
A.C.W.	Aircraftwoman			e.m.e.	electro-motive force
A.D.C.	aide-de-camp, amateur dramatic club	C.I.E.	Companion of the Indian Empire (Order)	E.N.E.	east-north-east
				E.S.E.	east-south-east
				Esq.	Esquire
adj.	adjective			Etc.	etcetera
Adm.	Admiral	c.i.f.	cost, insurance, freight	f.a.s.	free alongside ship
adv.	adverb			F.A.A.	Fleet Air Arm
A.E.U.	Amalgamated Engineering Union	C.I.O.	Congress of Industrial Organizations (U.S.)	F.B.A.	Fellow of the British Academy
				F.B.I.	Federal Bureau of Investigation
A.O.C.	Army Ordnance Corps	C.M.G.	Companion of St. Michael and St. George (Order)	F.C.A.	Fellow of the Institute of Chartered Accountants
A.O.D.	Army Ordnance Dept.				
A.O.F.	Ancient Order of Foresters	co.	company	F.C.S.	Fellow of the Chemical Society
		c.o.d.	cash on delivery		
A.P.M.	Assistant Provost Marshal	col.	Colonel, column		
		C.P.R.	Canadian Pacific Railway	Feb.	February
Apr.	April			fem.	feminine
A.R.A.	Associate of the Royal Academy	C.S.M.	Company Sergeant-Major	F.G.S.	Fellow of the Geological Society
Ark.	Arkansas	C.V.O.	Commander of the Victorian Order	F.I.A.	Fellow of the Institute of Actuaries
A.R.P.	Air Raid Precautions				
arr.	arrive(s, ed)	cwt.	hundredweight		
A.T.C.	Air Training Corps	D.A.G.	Deputy Adjutant-General	Fig.	figure
A.T.S.	Auxiliary Territorial Service			F.L.A.	Fellow of the Library Association
Aug.	August	D.B.E.	Dame Commander of the British Empire (Order)	f.o.b.	free on board
aux.	auxiliary			F.R.S.	Fellow of the Royal Society
ave.	avenue				
B.B.C.	British Broadcasting Corporation	D.C.L.	Doctor of Civil Law	fur.	furlong
		D.C.M.	Distinguished Conduct Medal	F.Z.S.	Fellow of the Zoological Society
B.C.L.	Bachelor of Civil Law	DDT	dichlorodiphenyl trichlorocethane		
bde.	brigade			gal.	gallon(s)
B.E.F.	British Expeditionary Force	Dec.	December	G.B.E.	Knight Grand Cross of the British Empire
		deg.	degree(s)		
		D.E.S.	Department of Education and Science		
b.h.p.	Brake horsepower			G.C.A.	Ground Control Approach (Aviation)
B.M.A.	British Medical Association	D.F.C.	Distinguished Flying Cross		
B.M.J.	British Medical Journal	D.F.M.	Distinguished Flying Medal	G.C.B.	Knight Grand Cross of the Bath
B.O.T.	Board of Trade	div.	Dividend	G.C.F.	greatest common factor
Bro.	brother	D.L.O.	Dead Letter Office		
B.Sc.	Bachelor of Science	D.N.A.	deoxyribonucleic acid	G.C.M.	greatest common measure
B.T.U.	British Thermal Unit(s)	D.O.E.	Department of the Environment		
				Gen.	General
B.V.M.	Blessed Virgin Mary	doz.	dozen	G.H.Q.	General Headquarters
B.W.G.	Birmingham Wire Gauge	D.S.C.	Distinguished		

Gib. *Gibraltar*

G.L.C. *Greater London Council*

G.M.T. *Greenwich mean time*

G.O.C. *General Officer Commanding*

G.O.M. *grand old man*

G.P.O. *General Post Office*

G.T.C. *Girl's Training Corps*

gym. *gymnasium*

H.A.C. *Hon. Artillery Company*

H.B.M. *His (Her) Britannic Majesty*

h.c.f. *highest common factor*

Heb. *Hebrew(s)*

H.I.H. *His (Her) Imperial Highness*

H.I.M. *His (Her) Imperial Majesty*

HIV *Human Immuno-deficiency Virus*

H.L.I. *Highland Light Infantry*

H.M.S. *His (Her) Majesty's ship or Service*

Hon. *honorary, Honourable*

H.R.H. *His (Her) Royal Highness*

hrs. *hours*

I.B.A. *Independent Broadcasting Authority*

I.C.S. *Indian Civil Service*

i.h.p. *indicated horsepower*

I.H.S. *Jesus, Saviour of men (Iesus Hominum Salvator)*

I.L.O. *International Labour Organization*

I.L.P. *Independent Labour Party*

Inc. *incorporated*

I.O.F. *Independent Order of Foresters*

I.O.U. *(acknowledgment of debt)*

I.O.W. *Isle of Wight*

I.R.A. *Irish Republican Army*

I.S.O. *Imperial Service Order*

I.T.V. *Independent Television*

I.U.D. *intra-uterine device*

Jan. *January*

Jas. *James*

Jos. *Joseph*

jun. *junior*

Kan. *Kansas*

K.B.E. *Knight Commander of the British Empire (Order)*

K.C.B. *Knight Commander of the Bath*

K.G.B. *Komitet Gosudarstvennoi Bezopasnosti (Committee of State Security)*

K.K.K. *Ku-Klux-Klan*

K.L.I. *King's Light Infantry*

Knt. *knight*

Lab. *Labour*

l.b.w. *leg before wicket*

L.C.C. *London County Council*

L.C.J. *Lord Chief Justice*

l.c.m. *lowest common multiple*

L.D.S. *Licentiate in Dental Surgery*

LL.B. *Bachelor of Laws*

LL.D. *Doctor of Laws*

loq. *loquitur (speaks)*

L.S.D. *lysergic acid diethylamide*

L.s.d. *Librae (pounds); solidi (shillings); denarii (pence)*

L.S.E. *London School of Economics*

Ltd. *Limited*

Maj. *Major*

Mar. *March*

M.B.E. *Member of the British Empire (Order)*

M.C.C. *Marylebone Cricket Club*

M.F.B. *Metropolitan Fire Brigade*

M.F.H. *Master of Foxhounds*

mil. *military*

min. *mineralogy*

Mme. *Madame*

M.O.D. *Ministry of Defence*

M.O.T. *Ministry of Transport*

m.p.h. *miles per hour*

M.Sc. *Master of Science*

MSS. *Manuscripts*

M.T.B. *motor-torpedo boat*

M.V.O. *Member of the Royal Victorian Order*

N.C.O. *non-commissioned officer*

neg. *negative*

N.F.S. *National Fire Service*

n.h.p. *nominal horsepower*

N.N.E. *north-north-east*

N.N.W. *north-north-west*

Nos. *numbers*

N.P.G. *National Portrait Gallery*

N.R.A. *National Rifle Association*

N.S.W. *New South Wales*

N.U.J. *National Union of Journalists*

N.U.M. *National Union of Mineworkers*

N.U.R. *National Union of Railwaymen*

N.U.S. *National Union of Seamen, National Union of Students*

N.U.T. *National Union of Teachers*

O.B.E. *Officer of the British Empire (Order)*

Obs. *obsolete*

Oct. *October*

Ont. *Ontario*

Ord. *order, ordinary, ordnance, ordained*

O.T.C. *Officers' Training Corps*

Pan. *Panama*

par. *paragraph, parish, parallel*

P.G.M. *Past Grand Master*

Ph. D. *Doctor of Philosophy*

P.L.O. *Palestine Liberation Organization*

P.M.G. *Postmaster-General*

pop. *population*

P.P.C. *Pour prendre congé (to take leave)*

P.R.A. *President of the Royal Academy*

P.R.O. *Public Relations Officer*

pro. *professional*

P.T.O. *please turn over*

P.V.C. *polyvinyl chloride*

P.W.D. *Public Works Department*

q.e.d.	*quod erat demonstrandum (which was to be demonstrated)*	S.P.G.	*Society for the Propagation of the Gospel*	A.R.C.M.	*Associate of the Royal College of Music*
q.e.f.	*quod erat faciendum (which was to be done)*	S.S.E.	*south-south-east*	asst.	*assistant*
		S.S.W.	*south-south-west*	B.A.O.R.	*British Army of the Rhine*
Q.M.G.	*Quartermaster-General*	Stg.	*sterling*	Bart.	*baronet*
		str.	*stroke (rowing)*	Beds.	*Bedfordshire*
Q.M.S.	*Quartermaster-Sergeant*	S.W.G.	*standard wire gauge*	Brit.	*British*
		T.B.D.	*torpedo-boat destroyer*	Bros.	*brothers*
Que.	*Quebec*	T.N.T.	*trinitrotoluene (explosive)*	B.Th.U.	*British Thermal Unit*
R.A.C.	*Royal Armoured Corps, Royal Automobile Club*	T.U.C.	*Trades Union Congress*	Capt.	*Captain*
				Cent.	*centigrade*
R.A.F.	*Royal Air Force*	typ.	*typography*	C.E.R.N.	*Conseil Européen pour la Recherche Nucléaire*
R.A.M.	*Royal Academy of Music*	U.D.A.	*Ulster Defence Association*		
R.B.A.	*Royal Society of British Artists*	U.D.I.	*unilateral declaration of independence*	C.E.T.S.	*Church of England Temperance Society*
R.C.M.	*Royal College of Music*	uhf	*ultra-high frequency*	C. of E.	*Church of England*
		ult.	*ultimo (last month)*	Coll.	*college*
R.C.P.	*Royal College of Physicians*	U.N.O.	*United Nations Organization*	Corp.	*Corporal, corporation*
R.C.S.	*Royal College of Surgeons*	U.S.A.	*United States of America*	C.U.A.C.	*Cambridge University Athletic Club*
ref.	*reference*	V.A.D.	*Voluntary Aid Detachment*		
Rev.	*Reverend*			C.U.B.C.	*Cambridge University Boat Club*
R.F.A.	*Royal Field Artillery*	Ven.	*The Venerable*		
R.G.A.	*Royal Garrison Artillery*	vhf	*very high frequency*	C.U.C.C.	*Cambridge University Cricket Club*
		Vet.	*veterinary surgeon*		
R.H.A.	*Royal Horse Artillery*	V.I.P.	*very important person*		
R.I.P.	*requiescat in pace (may he (or she) rest in peace)*	viz.	*videlicet (namely)*	D.A.A.G.	*Deputy Assistant Adjutant General*
		Vol.	*volunteer*	Dept.	*department*
R.M.A.	*Royal Military Academy*	vol.	*volume*	D.H.S.S.	*Department of Health and Social Security*
		W.M.S.	*Wesleyan Missionary Society*		
R.M.C.	*Royal Military College*	W.N.W.	*west-north-west*	D.Lit.	*Doctor of Literature*
R.M.S.	*Royal Mail steamer*	W.P.C.	*Woman Police Constable*	D.O.R.A.	*Defence of the Realm Act*
R.N.R.	*Royal Naval Reserve*	W.S.W.	*west-south-west*	E. & O.E.	*errors and omissions excepted*
R.S.M.	*Regimental Sergeant-Major*			Ebor.	*Eboracum (York)*
R.S.O.	*Railway Sorting Office*	**4**		E.C.S.C.	*European Coal and Steel Community*
R.T.C.	*Royal Tank Corps*	ACTH	*adrenocorticotrophin*	E.F.T.A.	*European Free Trade Association*
R.T.O.	*Railway Transport Officer*	actg.	*acting*		
		Adjt.	*adjutant*	elec.	*electrical, electricity*
R.U.C.	*Royal Ulster Constabulary*	advt.	*advertisement*	E.N.S.A.	*Entertainments National Service Association*
		AIDS	*Acquired Immune Deficiency Syndrome*		
R.Y.S.	*Royal Yacht Squadron*			Epis.	*Episcopal*
		anon.	*anonymous*	exam.	*examination*
S.C.C.	*Sea Cadet Corps*	A.Q.M.G.	*Assistant Quartermaster-General*	F.I.D.O.	*Fog Investigation Dispersal Operation*
Sec.	*secretary*				
sen.	*senior*				
seq.	*sequens (the following)*	A.R.A.M.	*Associate of the Royal Academy of Music*	F.R.A.M.	*Fellow of the Royal Academy of Music*
Soc.	*society*				

F.R.A.S.	Fellow of the Royal Astronomical Society	M.I.E.E.	Member of the Institution of Electrical Engineers	recd.	received
F.R.C.P.	Fellow of the Royal College of Physicians	M.I.M.E.	Member of the Institution of Mechanical Engineers	Regt.	regiment
F.R.C.S.	Fellow of the Royal College of Surgeons			R.E.M.E.	Royal Electrical and Mechanical Engineers
F.R.G.S.	Fellow of the Royal Geographical Society	Mlle.	Mademoiselle	R.I.B.A.	Royal Institute of British Architects
F.R.S.L.	Fellow of the Royal Society of Literature	M.R.C.P.	Member of the Royal College of Physicians	R.N.V.R.	Royal Naval Volunteer Reserve
G.A.T.T.	General Agreement on Tariffs and Trade	M.R.C.S.	Member of the Royal College of Surgeons	R.S.V.P.	Réspondez s'il vous plaît (please reply)
G.C.I.E.	Knight Grand Commander of the Indian Empire (Order)	Mus.B.	Bachelor of Music	R.W.G.M.	Right Worshipful Grand Master
		Mus.D.	Doctor of Music	Sept.	September
		Myth.	mythology	S.P.C.K.	Society for Promoting Christian Knowledge
		N.A.T.O.	North Atlantic Treaty Organization		
G.C.M.G.	Knight Grand Cross of St. Michael and St. George (Order)			sp. gr.	specific gravity
		N.E.D.C.	National Economic Development Commission	Supt.	superintendent
G.C.S.I.	Knight Grand Commander of the Star of India (Order)			Surg.	surgeon
				T.H.W.M.	Trinity High-water Mark
		O.E.C.D.	Organization for Economic Co-operation and Development	Toc H	Talbot House
G.C.V.O.	Knight Grand Cross of the Victorian Order			T.G.W.U.	Transport and General Workers' Union
geog.	geography	O.E.E.C.	Organization for European Economic Co-operation	W.A.A.F.	Women's Auxiliary Air Force
geom.	geometry			W. Cdr.	Wing Commander
gram.	grammar			W.J.A.C.	Women's Junior Air Corps
inst.	instant (in the present month), institution, Institute	O.H.M.S.	On His (Her) Majesty's Service	W.R.N.S.	Women's Royal Naval Service
		O.U.A.C.	Oxford University Athletic Club	Xmas.	Christmas
I. of W.	Isle of Wight	O.U.B.C.	Oxford University Boat Club	Y.M.C.A.	Young Men's Christian Association
K.C.I.E.	Knight Commander of the Indian Empire (Order)	O.U.C.C.	Oxford University Cricket Club		
		O.U.D.S.	Oxford University Dramatic Society	Y.W.C.A.	Young Women s Christian Association
K.C.M.G.	Knight Commander (of the Order of) St. Michael and St. George	P.A.Y.E.	pay as you earn	zool.	zoology
		pref.	preference		
K.C.V.O.	Knight Commander of the Royal Victorian Order	pres.	present		
		Prof.	professor		
		prox.	proximo (next month)	**5**	
L.R.A.M.	Licentiate of the Royal Academy of Music	R.A.M.C.	Royal Army Medical Corps	A.A.Q.M.G.	Acting Assistant Quartermaster-General
L.R.C.M.	Licentiate of the Royal College of Music	R.A.O.B.	Royal Antediluvian Order of Buffaloes	ad lib.	ad libitum (as much as desired)
		R.A.O.C.	Royal Army Ordnance Corps	Anzac.	Australian and New Zealand Army Corps
L.R.C.P.	Licentiate of the Royal College of Physicians	R.A.S.C.	Royal Army Service Corps		
masc.	masculine	R.A.V.C.	Royal Army Veterinary Corps	A.R.I.B.A.	Associate of the Royal Institute of British Architects
math.	mathematics				
mech.	mechanics	R.C.M.P.	Royal Canadian Mounted Police		
memo.	memorandum				

Assoc.	*associate, association*	N.A.A.F.I.	*Navy, Army and Air Force Institutes*	Lieut-Col. (8)	*Lieutenant-Colonel*
A.S.T.M.S.	*Association of Scientific Technical and Managerial Staffs*	N.S.P.C.C.	*National Society for the Prevention of Cruelty to Children*	Lieut.-Gen. (8)	*Lieutenant-General*
Bart's.	*St. Bartholomew's Hospital*	P. and O.	*Peninsular and Oriental*	Lieut.-Gov. (8)	*Lieutenant-Governor*
Corpn.	*corporation*	photo.	*photograph*	Lit. Hum. (6)	*Literæ Humaniores (classics)*
D.A.D.O.S.	*Deputy Assistant Director of Ordnance Services*	R.A.F.V.R.	*Royal Air Force Volunteer Reserve*	Maj.-Gen. (6)	*Major-General*
D.A.Q.M.G.	*Deputy Assistant Quartermaster-General*	Recce.	*reconnaissance*	Matric (6)	*matriculation*
		R.S.P.C.A.	*Royal Society for the Prevention of Cruelty to Animals*	Messrs. (6)	*Messieurs*
D.Litt.	*Doctor of Letters*	Rt. Hon.	*Right Honourable*	M. Inst. C.E. (7)	*Member of the Institution of Civil Engineers*
Elect.	*electrical, electricity*	Rt. Rev.	*Right Reverend*		
et seq.	*et sequens (and what follows)*	Salop.	*Shropshire*	nem. con. (6)	*nemine contradicente (none objecting)*
		S.E.A.T.O.	*South-east Asia Treaty Organization*		
ex div.	*without dividend*				
F.R.I.B.A.	*Fellow of the Royal Institute of British Architects*	Sergt.	*Sergeant*	Non-com. (6)	*non-commissioned officer*
		Suppl.	*supplement (al, ary)*		
		Treas.	*treasurer*		
Hants.	*Hampshire*	U.N.R.R.A.	*United Nations Relief and Rehabilitation Administration*	per pro (6)	*per procurationem (by proxy)*
ht. wkt.	*hit wicket*				
incog.	*incognito*			prelim. (6)	*preliminary*
Lieut.	*Lieutenant*			pro tem. (6)	*pro tempore (for the time being)*
Litt.D.	*Doctor of Letters*	Xtian	*Christian*		
L.R.C.V.S.	*Licentiate of the Royal College of Veterinary Surgeons*			prox. acc. (7)	*proxime accessit (a close second)*
Lt.-Col.	*Lieutenant-Colonel*			U.N.E.S.C.O. (6)	*United Nations Educational Scientific and Cultural Organization*
Lt.-Com.	*Lieutenant-Commander*	**6** AND OVER			
Lt.-Gen.	*Lieutenant-General*	Cantab. (6)	*of Cambridge*		
Lt.-Gov.	*Lieutenant-Governor*	Cantuar. (7)	*of Canterbury*	verb. sap. (7)	*verbum sapienti (a word to the wise)*
Mlles.	*Mesdemoiselles*	Col.-Sergt. (8)	*Colour-Sergeant*		
M.R.C.V.S.	*Member of the Royal College of Veterinary Surgeons*	Dunelm. (6)	*of Durham*		
		E. and O.E. (6)	*Errors and omissions excepted*		

Apostles

Andrew (6)	Jude (4)/Thaddeus (8)
Bartholomew (11)	Matthew (7)
James the Elder (13)	Peter (5)
James the Less (12)	Simon (5)
John (4)	Thomas (6)
Judas (5)	Philip (6)

Bibles

Authorised (10)
Bishop's (7)
Coverdale (9)
Cranmer (7)
Cromwell (8)
Donai (5)
Geneva (6)
Great (5)

Gutenberg (9)
Indian (6)
Itala (5)
Judas (5)
King James (9)
Kralitz (7)
Matthew (7)
Mazarin (7)

Printers' (8)
Revised (7)
Taverner (8)
Tyndale (7)
Vinegar (7)
Wyclif (6)

Books of the Apocrypha

Baruch (6)
Bel and the Dragon (15)
Ecclesiasticus (14)
Epistle of Jeremy (15)
Esdras (6)
Esther (6)

History of Susanna (16)
Judith (6)
Maccabees (9)
Song of the Three Holy Children (26)
The Prayer of Manasses (19)
The Wisdom of Solomon (18)

Chemical elements

Name	Symbol	Name	Symbol
ACTINIUM	Ac.	EUROPIUM	Eu.
ALUMINIUM	Al.	FLUORINE (gas)	F.
ANTIMONY	Sb.	GADOLINIUM	Gd.
ARGON (gas)	Ar.	GALLIUM	Ga.
ARSENIC	As.	GERMANIUM	Ge.
ASTATINE	At.	GLUCINUM	Gl.
BARIUM	Ba.	GOLD	Au.
BERYLLIUM	Be.	HAFNIUM	Hf.
BISMUTH	Bi.	HELIUM (gas)	He.
BORON	B.	HOLMIUM	Ho.
BROMINE	Br.	HYDROGEN	H.
CADMIUM	Cd.	ILLINIUM	Il.
CAESIUM	Cs.	INDIUM	In.
CALCIUM	Ca.	IODINE	I.
CARBON	C.	IRIDIUM	Ie.
CERIUM	Ce.	IRON	Fe.
CHLORINE (gas)	Cl.	KRYPTON (gas)	Kr.
CHROMIUM	Cr.	LANTHANIUM	La.
COBALT	Co.	LEAD	Pb.
COLUMBIUM	Cb.	LITHIUM	Li.
COPPER	Cu.	LUTECIUM	Lu.
DYPROSIUM	Dy.	MAGNESIUM	Mg.
ERBIUM	Er.	MANGANESE	Mn.

Name	Symbol	Name	Symbol
MASURIUM	Ma.	SCANDIUM	Sc.
MERCURY	Hg.	SELENIUM	Se.
MOLYBDENUM	Mo.	SILICON	Si.
NEODYMIUM	Nd.	SILVER	Ag.
NEON (gas)	Ne.	SODIUM	Na.
NEOYTTERBIUM	Yb.	STRONTIUM	Sr.
NEPTUNIUM	Np.	SULPHUR	S.
NEUTRON (gas)	Nu.	TANTALUM	Ta.
NICKEL	Ni.	TELLURIUM	Te.
NIOBIUM	Nb.	TERBIUM	Tb.
NITROGEN (gas)	N.	THALLIUM	Tl.
OSMIUM	Os.	THORIUM	Th.
OXYGEN (gas)	O.	THULIUM	Tm.
PALLADIUM	Pd.	TIN	Sn.
PHOSPHORUS	P.	TITANIUM	Ti.
PLATINUM	Pt.	TUNGSTEN	W.
PLUTONIUM	Pu.	URANIUM	U.
POTASSIUM	K.	VANADIUM	V.
PRASEODYMIUM	Pr.	WOLFRAM	W.
RADIUM	Ra.	XENON (gas)	Xe.
RHENIUM	Rn.	YTTERBIUM	Yb.
RHODIUM	Rh.	YTTRIUM	Y.
RUBIDIUM	Rb.	ZINC	Zn.
RUTHENIUM	Ru.	ZIRCONIUM	Zr.
SAMARIUM	Sm.		

Deserts

Arabian (7)
Atacama (7)
Australian (10)
Gobi (4)
Kalahari (8)
Kara Kum (7)

Mojave (6)
Patagonia (9)
Sahara (6)
Sonoran (7)
Takla Makan (10)
Thar (4)

French revolutionary calendar

Nivôse (6) *snow, Dec.*
Floréal (7) *blossom, April*
Ventôse (7) *wind, Feb.*
Brumaire (8) *fog, Oct.*
Fervidor (8) *heat, July*
Frimaire (8) *sleet, Nov.*
Germinal (8) *seed, March*

Messidor (8) *harvest, June*
Pluviôse (8) *rain, Jan.*
Prairial (8) *pasture, May*
Fructidor (9) *fruit, Aug.*
Thermidor (9) *heat, July*
Vendémiaire (11) *vintage, Sept.*

Fuels

Alcohol (7)
Anthracite (10)
Argol (5)
Astatki (7)
Benzine (7)
Benzol (6)
Benzole (7)
Calor gas (8)
Coal (4)
Coke (4)
Derv (4)

Diesel (6)
Electricity (11)
Ethyl (5)
Fluothane (9)
Gas (3)
Gascoal (7)
Gascoke (7)
Gasoline (8)
Halothane (9)
Hydrocarbon (11)
Kerosene (8)

Lignite (7)
Methane (7)
Naphtha (7)
Oil (3)
Paraffin (8)
Peat (4)
Petrol (6)
Petroleum (9)
Spirit (6)
Turf (4)
Wood (4)

Group terms

3 AND 4

band (of musicians)
bevy (of larks, quails, roes, or women)
box (of cigars)
brew (of beer)
case (of whisky or wine)
cast (of hawks)
cete (of badgers)
clan (people)
club (people)
crew (oarsmen or sailors)
crop (of farm produce)
down (of hares)
dule (of doves)
fall (of woodcock)
form (at schools)
four (card-players, oarsmen, or polo team)
gang (of elk, hooligans, labourers, slaves or thieves)
hand (at cards)
herd (of asses, buffalo, cattle, cranes, deer, giraffes, goats, or oxen)
host (of angels)
hunt (hounds and hunters)
husk (of hares)
knob (of pochards, teal, toads, or widgeon)
leap (of leopards)
lepe (of leopards)
lot (in auctioneering)
meet (of hounds and hunters)
mess (military and naval)
mute (of hounds)

nest (of machine-guns, mice, rabbits, or wasps)
nide (of pheasants)
nine (baseball team)
pace (of asses)
pack (of grouse, hounds, wolves, or cards)
pair (of oarsmen and various)
park (of guns or cars)
peal (of bells)
pile (of arms)
pod (of whiting or peas)
pony (betting; £25)
pool (various)
posy (of flowers)
rag (of colts)
rope (of onions or pearls)
rout (of wolves)
run (of poultry)
rush (of pochards)
sect (of religious people)
set (of various articles)
show (of agricultural products, dogs, horses, etc.)
side (of players)
six (of cub scouts, sportsmen)
sord (of mallards or wild-fowl)
stud (of horses and mares)
sute (of mallards or wild-fowl)
trio (of musicans)
team (of ducks, horses, oxen, or players)
tuft (of grass)
walk (of snipe)
wing (of plovers)
wisp (of snipe)
wood (trees)

yoke (of oxen)

5

batch (of bread and various)
bench (of bishops or magistrates)
blast (of hunters)
blush (of boys)
board (of directors)
brace (of ducks, partridges, etc.)
brood (of hens)
bunch (of flowers, grapes, teal, or widgeon)
caste (of bread)
charm (of goldfinches)
class (of children at schools)
clump (of trees)
copse (trees)
covey (of grouse, partridges, or other birds)
crowd (of people)
doylt (of tame swine)
draft (of police or soldiers)
drove (of cattle or kine)
eight (oarsmen)
field (hunters, race-horses, or runners)
fiver (money; £5)
fleet (of motor-cars or ships)
flock (of birds, pigeons, or sheep)
flush (at cards)
genus (of animals or plants)
grand (money; £1000 or $1000)

group (photographic and various)
guard (soldiers)
hoard (of gold, etc.)
horde (of savages)
leash (of bucks or hounds)
party (of people)
plump (of wildfowl)
posse (of police)
pride (of lions)
scrum (at rugby football)
sedge (of bitterns or herons)
sheaf (of corn)
shoal (of fish)
siege (of herons)
skein (of geese, silk, or wool)
skulk (of foxes)
sloth (of bears)
squad (of beaters or soldiers)
staff (of officials or servants)
stalk (of foresters)
stand (of arms)
state (of princes)
swarm (of bees and other insects)
table (of bridge or whist players)
tribe (of goats or people)
trick (at cards)
troop (of boy-scouts, brownies, cavalry, kangaroos, lions, or monkeys)
truss (of hay)
twins (people)
watch (of nightingales or sailors)

6

barren (of mules)
basket (of strawberries)
budget (of papers)
bundle (of asparagus, firewood, and various)
caucus (of politicians)
cellar (of wine)
clique (of people)
clutch (of eggs)
colony (of gulls or people)
covert (of coots)
desert (of lapwings)
double (in betting)
eleven (cricket and other teams)
faggot (of sticks)
family (of people or sardines)
flight (of aeroplanes, doves, dunlins, or pigeons)

gaggle (of geese)
galaxy (of beauties)
harras (of horses)
kennel (of dogs)
kindle (of kittens)
labour (of moles)
litter (of cubs, pigs, pups, or whelps)
melody (of harpers)
monkey (in betting; £500)
museum (of antiques, works of art, etc.)
muster (of peacocks or soldiers)
nation (of people)
outfit (of clothes or sails)
packet (of cigarettes)
parade (of soldiers)
punnet (of strawberries)
quorum (minimum number of people)
rayful (of knaves)
rubber (at cards)
school (of porpoises or whales)
sextet (of musicians)
sleuth (of bears)
spring (of teal)
stable (of horses)
string (of pearls or racehorses)
tenner (money; £10)
throng (of people)
trophy (of arms, etc.)
troupe (of actors, dancers, or minstrels)
twelve (lacrosse team)
vestry (parochial assembly)

7

battery (of guns)
bouquet (of flowers)
brigade (of troops)
clamour (of rooks)
clouder (of cats)
cluster (of grapes or stars)
company (of actors, capitalists, or widgeon)
council (advisers or local authorities)
dopping (of sheldrakes)
draught (of butlers)
fifteen (rugby football team)
gallery (of pictures)
library (of books or music)
nosegay (of flowers)
orchard (of fruit trees)
quartet (of musicians)
service (of china or crockery)

sounder (of boars or swine)
spinney (of trees)
thicket (of trees)
vintage (of wine)

8

assembly (of people)
audience (of people)
building (of rooks)
division (of troops)
flotilla (of boats)
jamboree (of boy-scouts)
paddling (of ducks)
partners (in business or games)
regiment (of soldiers)
richesse (of martens)
sequence (at cards)
squadron (of cavalry or ships)
triplets (people)

9

army corps (of troops)
badelynge (of ducks)
committee (people)
community (of people or saints)
cowardice (of curs)
gathering (of people and the clans)
morbidity (of majors)
orchestra (of musicians)
sachemdom (N. American Indians)
shrubbery (of shrubs)
subtiltie (of sergeants)
syndicate (of capitalists)

10

assemblage (of clergy and various)
buttonhole (of flowers)
chattering (of choughs)
collection (of stamps, works of art, etc.)
commission (committee of enquiry)
detachment (of police or soldiers)
exaltation (of larks)
exhibition (of commercial products, pictures, works of art, etc.)
observance (of hermits)
shrewdness (of apes)
simplicity (of subalterns)

11 AND OVER

confraternity (brotherhood, usually religious) (13)

congregation (of birds or worshippers) (12)

constellation (of stars) (13)

convocation (of clergy or university authorities) (11)

murmuration (of starlings) (11)

Hebrew alphabet

Aleph (5)
Beth (4)
Gimel (5)
Daleth (6)
He (2)
Vain (4)/Zayin (5)
Cheth (5)/Heth (4)

Teth (4)
Jod /Yod (3)
Caph/Kaph (4)
Lamed (5)
Mem (3)
Nun (3)
Samech (6)/Samekh (6)

Ain (3)/Ayin (4)
Pe (2)
Tzaddi (6)/Zade (4)
Koph (4)
Resh (4)
Schin (5)/Shin (4)
Tau (3)

Heraldry

2 – 4

arms
band
bar
bend
boar
coué
dawl
delf
enty
erne
fess
fret
garb
gore
gray
kite
lion
or
orle
pale
pall
paly
pean
pile
posé
rose
semé
vair

vert
label

5

alant
animé
armed
azure
badge
barry
baton
bendy
bouche
bowed
breys
cable
chief
crest
cross
eagle
erect
ermin
fesse
field
fusil
garbe
gorge
gules
gurge

gyron
label
motto
pheon
rebus
rompu
sable
scarp
torse
waved

6

aiglet
apaumy
argent
armory
at gaze
attire
baston
bazant
bendil
bevile
bezant
billet
blazon
border
buckle
canton

charge
checky
chequy
cleché
cotise
couché
coward
dexter
dragon
ermine
escrol
etoile
falcon
fillet
flanch
fleury
florid
fretty
fylfot
garter
ground
guttée
heater
herald
jessed
knight
manche
mascle
maunch
mullet

naiant
Norroy
pallet
rebate
rustre
sejant
shield
square
timbre
vairée
vested
voided
voider
volant
vorant
wivern
wyvern

7

adorsed
adossed
alberia
annulet
arrière
arrondi
attired
barruly
bearing

bendlet
bevilly
bordure
bottony
brisure
cadency
chapter
chevron
clarion
courant
croslet
dolphin
dormant
emblaze
embowed
embrued
enarmed
endorse
engoulé
engrail
ermelin
estoile
fretted
fructed
gardant
griffin
Ich Dien
leopard
lioncel
lozenge

lozengy	couchant	displayed	pursuivant
martlet	crescent	embattled	quartering
miniver	dancetty	enveloped	quatrefoil
nombril	emblazon	environed	quintefoil
passant	englante	erminites	rebatement
potence	enmanché	estoillee	surmounted
purpure	erminois	florettée	
quarter	escallop	hatchment	
raguled	gonfalon	lionceaux	**11** *AND OVER*
rampant	haurient	lioncelle	
roundel	heraldic	Lyon-Court	bend-sinister (12)
salient	insignia	regardant	bendy-sinister (13)
saltire	Lyon King	scutcheon	bicapitated (11)
sea-lion	mantling	spur-rowel	College of Arms (13)
sexfoil	naissant	supporter	counter-paled (12)
shafted	opinicus		counter-passant (14)
sinople	ordinary		countervair (11)
statant	renverse	**10**	cross-crosslet (13)
swallow	roundlet		cross-fleury (11)
torqued	sea-horse	barrybendi	cross-patencée (13)
torteau	sinister	barry-bendy	Earl Marshal (11)
trefoil	standard	bicorporal	emblazonment (12)
unicorn	tincture	blue mantle	engrailment (11)
	tressure	cinquefoil	escarbuncle (11)
		Clarenceux	escutcheoned (12)
		coat-of-arms	garde-visure (11)
8	**9**	cross-patée	Garter King of Arms (16)
		difference	grant of arms (11)
affronté	aquilated	emblazoner	heraldic emblem (14)
allerion	arraswise	empalement	honour point (11)
armorist	banderole	escalloped	inescutcheon (12)
aversant	blazoning	escutcheon	Lyon King at Arms (14)
barrulet	carbuncle	fesse-point	marshalling (11)
bevilled	cartouche	fleur-de-lis	quarter arms (11)
blazonry	chevronel	fleur-de-lys	Somerset herald (14)
caboched	combatant	king-at-arms	transfluent (11)
caboshed	diapering	knighthood	unscutcheoned (13)
chaperon			

Jewish year

Tishri (6)/Tisri (5)	Nisan (5)/Abib (4)
Heshvan (7)	Iyar (4)/Iyyar (5)
Kislev (6)	Sivan (5)
Tebet (5)	Tammus (6)
Shabat (6)	Ab (2)
Adar (4)/Vendar (6)	Elul (4)

Law sittings

Hilary (6)
Easter (6)
Trinity (7)
Michaelmas (10)

Musketeers

Athos (5)
Porthos (7)
Aramis (6)
D'Artagnan (9)

Names: boys
Including abbreviations, nicknames, and some common foreign names.

3	Len	Algy	Esra	Joey	Otto
	Leo	Ally	Euan	John	Owen
Abe	Mac	Amos	Evan	Josh	Page
Alf	Mat	Andy	Ewen	Juan	Paul
Ali	Max	Axel	Eyre	Jude	Penn
Ben	Ned	Bald	Ezra	Karl	Pery
Bob	Nye	Bart	Fitz	Keir	Pete
Boy	Pat	Beau	Fred	Kemp	Phil
Col	Pip	Bede	Gary	Kent	René
Dai	Ray	Bell	Gene	King	Rhys
Dan	Rea	Bert	Glen	Leon	Rory
Don	Reg	Bill	Glyn	Loel	Ross
Eli	Rex	Boyd	Gwyn	Luke	Saul
Ely	Rod	Buck	Hans	Lyle	Sean
Gus	Ron	Bury	Hope	Lynd	Seth
Guy	Roy	Cain	Hugh	Lyon	Stan
Hal	Sam	Carl	Hugo	Marc	Theo
Hay	Sid	Cary	Hume	Mark	Toby
Hew	Tam	Cass	Hyam	Matt	Tony
Ian	Ted	Ciro	Iain	Mick	Vane
Ira	Tim	Dick	Ifor	Mike	Vere
Ivo	Tom	Dirk	Ikey	Muir	Walt
Jay	Vic	Dion	Iohn	Neil	Will
Jem		Duff	Ivan	Nero	Winn
Jim		Duke	Ivor	Nick	Wynn
Job	*4*	Earl	Jack	Noah	Yule
Joe		Eddy	Jake	Noel	
Jon	Abel	Eden	Jean	Olaf	
Jos	Adam	Emil	Jess	Orme	*5*
Ken	Alan	Eric	Jock	Otho	
Kid	Alec	Esau	Joel	Otis	Aaron

Abdul	Derek	Jonah	Shane	Bryden	Gordon
Abner	Dicky	Jonas	Silas	Bulwer	Graeme
Abram	Drake	Jules	Simon	Caesar	Graham
Alban	Earle	Keith	Speed	Calvin	Gregan
Algie	Eddie	Kenny	Starr	Carlos	Gregor
Allan	Edgar	Kevin	Steve	Caspar	Gunner
Aldred	Edwin	Larry	Storm	Cedric	Gunter
Alroy	Edwyn	Leigh	Tabor	Cicero	Gustav
Alves	Eldon	Lewin	Taffy	Claude	Gwilym
Alwin	Ellis	Lewis	Teddy	Conrad	Hallam
Alwyn	Eliot	Lisle	Terry	Conway	Hamish
Amand	Emery	Llovd	Titus	Crusoe	Hamlet
André	Emile	Louis	Tommy	Curran	Hamlyn
Angus	Enoch	Luigi	Trant	Dallas	Harold
Anson	Ernie	Lyall	Tubby	Damian	Harris
Anton	Ernst	Major	Tudor	Daniel	Hayden
Archy	Evans	Manly	Ulick	Delves	Haydon
Arden	Ewart	Mayor	Usher	Declan	Hector
Athol	Felix	Meyer	Wally	Demian	Hedley
Aubyn	Franc	Micky	Willy	Dennis	Henryk
Aymar	Frank	Miles	Wolfe	Dermot	Herman
Barry	Franz	Monty	Wyatt	Derric	Hervey
Barty	Frith	Moses	Wylie	Dickie	Hilary
Basil	Fritz	Myles	Wynne	Donald	Hilton
Berty	Fulke	Neill	Wyvil	Dougal	Hobart
Bevis	Garry	Nigel	Yorke	Dryden	Holman
Billy	Garth	Oscar		Dudley	Horace
Bobby	Gavin	Osman		Dugald	Howard
Booth	Geoff	Oswyn	**6**	Duggie	Howell
Boris	Giles	Paddy		Duncan	Hubert
Brian	Glynn	Paget	Adolph	Dundas	Hylton
Bruce	Govan	Paton	Adrian	Dunlop	Ignace
Bryan	Grant	Pedro	Aeneas	Edmond	Irvine
Bunny	Guido	Pelan	Albert	Edmund	Israel
Cairn	Harry	Percy	Albion	Eduard	Jackey
Caius	Haydn	Perry	Alexis	Edward	Jackie
Carew	Hebel	Peter	Alfred	Egbert	Jacomb
Carol	Henri	Piers	Alston	Eldred	Japhet
Cecil	Henry	Punch	Andrew	Elliot	Jasper
Clare	Heron	Ralph	Angelo	Ernest	Jeremy
Claud	Hiram	Ramon	Anselm	Erroll	Jerome
Clive	Hyman	Raoul	Antony	Ervine	Jervis
Clyde	Hymie	Remus	Archer	Esmond	Johann
Colet	Iltyd	Renée	Archie	Eugene	Johnny
Colin	Inigo	Rider	Armand	Evelyn	Joseph
Conan	Innes	Robin	Arnold	Fabian	Joshua
Cosmo	Isaac	Roger	Arthur	Fergus	Josiah
Cyril	Jabez	Rolfc	Aubrey	Forbes	Julian
Cyrus	Jacky	Rollo	August	Freddy	Julien
Dacre	Jacob	Romeo	Austin	Garnet	Julius
Damon	Jaime	Rowan	Alymer	Gasper	Justin
Darcy	James	Royce	Aylwin	Gaston	Kersey
D'arcy	Jamie	Rufus	Balbus	George	Kirwan
David	Jason	Rumer	Barney	Gerald	Laddie
Davie	Jemmy	Ryder	Bennie	Gerard	Lawley
Denis	Jerry	Sandy	Bertie	Gideon	Leslie
Denny	Jesse	Saxon	Braham	Giulio	Lionel
Denys	Jimmy	Scott	Brodie	Godwin	Loftus
Derby	Johan	Serge	Brutus	Gonvil	Lucien

Ludwig
Luther
Magnus
Marcel
Marcus
Marten
Martin
Mauris
Melvin
Merlin
Mervyn
Mickie
Milton
Montie
Moritz
Morris
Morvyn
Mostyn
Murray
Napier
Nathan
Nelson
Nevile
Nevill
Ninian
Norman
Norris
Norton
Nowell
Oliver
Osbert
Osmond
Oswald
Pelham
Philip
Pierre
Powell
Prince
Rafael
Ramsay
Randle
Raphel
Rayner
Reggie
Rendle
Reuben
Rhodes
Robbie
Robert
Roddie
Rodger
Roland
Ronald
Rowley
Rowlie
Royden
Rudolf
Rupert
Samson

Samuel
Sefton
Selwyn
Seumas
Shafto
Sidney
Simeon
Simons
Sinbad
Square
Squire
Steven
St. John
Stuart
Sydney
Thomas
Tobias
Trefor
Trevor
Verney
Vernon
Victor
Vivian
Vyvyan
Wallis
Walter
Warren
Watkin
Wesley
Willem
Willie
Wolsey
Xavier
Yehudi

7

Abraham
Aladdin
Alfonso
Alister
Almeric
Alsager
Amadeus
Ambrose
Anatole
Andries
Aneurin
Anthony
Antoine
Antonio
Artemus
Auguste
Baldwin
Balfour
Barclay
Barnaby
Barnard

Beaufoi
Bernard
Bertram
Burnard
Calvert
Cameron
Carlyon
Charles
Charley
Chester
Clayton
Clement
Clinton
Compton
Connell
Crispin
Cyprian
Dalziel
Denison
Derrick
Desmond
Dillwyn
Dominic
Donovan
Douglas
Edouard
Emanuel
Emilius
Ephraim
Etienne
Eustace
Everard
Faraday
Fielder
FitzRoy
Francis
Frankie
Freddie
Gabriel
Gaspard
Geoffry
Geraint
Gervais
Gervase
Gilbert
Gilmour
Gladwyn
Gloster
Godfrey
Goronwy
Grahame
Gregory
Gunther
Gustave
Hadrian
Herbert
Hermann
Hewlett
Hilaire

Hildred
Horatio
Humbert
Humphry
Ibrahim
Isidore
Jackson
Jacques
Jeffrey
Jocelyn
Justice
Kenneth
Lachlan
Lambert
Lennard
Leonard
Leopold
Lindsay
Lindsey
Lorimer
Lucifer
Ludovic
Malcolm
Matthew
Maurice
Maxwell
Maynard
Merrick
Michael
Montagu
Neville
Nicolas
Orlando
Orpheus
Orville
Osborne
Padraic
Paladin
Patrick
Perseus
Phineas
Pierrot
Quentin
Quintin
Randall
Ranulph
Raphael
Raymond
Raymund
Redvers
Reynard
Richard
Roderic
Rodolph
Romulus
Rowland
Rudolph
Rudyard
Russell

Sergius
Seymour
Sheldon
Sigmund
Solomon
Spencer
Spenser
Stanley
St. Aubyn
St. Clair
Stephen
Steuart
Stewart
St. Leger
Terence
Tertius
Timothy
Ughtred
Ulysses
Umberto
Vaughan
Vincent
Wallace
Warwick
Westley
Wilfred
Wilfrid
Wilhelm
William
Winston
Wyndham
Zachary
Zebedee

8

Achilles
Adolphus
Alasdair
Alastair
Algernon
Alisdair
Alistair
Aloysius
Alphonse
Alphonso
Annesley
Antonius
Aristide
Augustus
Aurelius
Barnabas
Bartlemy
Beaumont
Bedivere
Benjamin
Bernardi
Bertrand

Campbell	Lancelot	Valdimar	Peregrine
Carleton	Laurence	Vladimir	Rodriguez
Champion	Lawrance	Wolseley	Rupprecht
Clarence	Lawrence		Sackville
Clemence	Leonhard		Salvatore
Clements	Leonidas	**9**	Sebastian
Clifford	Llewelyn		Siegfried
Crauford	Llywelyn	Abernethy	Sigismund
Crawford	Maitland	Abimeleck	Stanislas
Cuthbert	Marshall	Alaistair	Svlvester
Diarmaid	Meredith	Alexander	Thaddaeus
Dominick	Montague	Alphonsus	Theodoric
Ebenezer	Mortimer	Arbuthnot	Valentine
Emmanuel	Nicholas	Archibald	Valentino
Ethelred	Octavius	Aristotle	Wilbraham
FitzHugh	Oliphant	Armstrong	Zachariah
Florizel	Oughtred	Athelstan	Zechariah
François	Paulinus	Augustine	
Franklin	Perceval	Bartimeus	
Frederic	Percival	Beauchamp	**10** *AND OVER*
Geoffrey	Peregrin	Christian	
Geoffroy	Peterkin	Constable	Athanasius (10)
Giovanni	Philemon	Cornelius	Athelstane (10)
Guiseppe	Randolph	Courtenay	Barrington (10)
Greville	Randulph	Courteney	Bartholomew (11)
Gustavus	Reginald	Creighton	Carmichael (10)
Hamilton	Robinson	Demetrius	Christopher (11)
Harcourt	Roderick	Dionysius	Constantine (11)
Harrison	Ruaraidh	Ethelbert	Fitzherbert (11)
Havelock	Sandford	Ferdinand	Fitzpatrick (11)
Herbrand	Secundus	Fortescue	Hildebrand (10)
Hereward	Septimus	Francisco	Llewhellin (10)
Hezekiah	Sherlock	Frederick	Maximilian (10)
Horatius	Siegmund	Gascoigne	Pierrepont (10)
Humphrey	Sinclair	Glanville	Sacheverel (10)
Ignatius	Spensley	Granville	Somerville (10)
Immanuel	Stafford	Hazledine	Stanislaus (10)
Ironside	St. George	Honoratus	Theodosius (10)
Jeremiah	Sylvanus	Josceline	Theophilus (10)
Jonathan	Thaddeus	Llewellyn	Washington (10)
Joscelyn	Theobald	Mackenzie	Willoughby (10)
Josephus	Theodore	Marmaduke	
Kingsley	Trelawny	Nathaniel	

Names: girls
Including abbreviations, nicknames, and some common foreign names.

3	Dot	Heë	Kay	Pam	Val
	Eda	Ida	Kit	Pat	Viv
Ada	Ena	Ina	Liz	Peg	Yda
Ame	Eva	Isa	Lot	Pen	Zia
Amy	Eve	Ivy	Mai	Ray	Zoë
Ann	Fay	Iza	May	Rio	
Ave	Flo	Jen	Meg	Sue	
Bee	Gay	Joy	Nan	Una	

4

	Jane	Suky	Clare	Innes
	Jean	Susy	Coral	Irene
Aase	Jess	Syme	Daisy	Isold
Aimé	Jill	Tess	Delia	Janet
Alba	Joan	Tina	Della	Janey
Alma	Judy	Vera	Denes	Janie
Alys	June	Vida	Diana	Janny
Anna	Kate	Vita	Diane	Jayne
Anne	Katy	Viva	Dilys	Jenny
Anny	Kaye	Zara	Dinah	Jessy
Avis	Lacy	Zena	Dodie	Joann
Baba	Lala	Zita	Dolly	Joyce
Babs	Leah		Donie	Julia
Bebe	Lena		Donna	Julie
Bess	Lila	## 5	Dorah	Karen
Beth	Lily		Doris	Karin
Caré	Lina	Abbie	Dreda	Katey
Cely	Lisa	Adela	Dulce	Katie
Clea	Lita	Adele	Edith	Kitty
Cleo	Liza	Aggie	Effie	Laila
Cora	Lois	Agnes	Eilsa	Laura
Dawn	Lola	Ailsa	Elena	Lelia
Dido	Lucy	Aimée	Elfie	Letty
Dodo	Lulu	Alice	Elise	Lilia
Dora	Lynn	Aline	Eliza	Lilly
Edie	Maie	Altha	Ellen	Lizzy
Edna	Mana	Angel	Ellie	Lorna
Ella	Mary	Anita	Elsie	Lotte
Elma	Maud	Annie	Emily	Lotty
Elsa	Meta	April	Emmie	Lucia
Else	Mimi	Arbel	Erica	Lucie
Emma	Mina	Ariel	Essie	Lydia
Emmy	Moll	Avice	Ethel	Lynne
Enid	Mona	Avril	Ettie	Mabel
Erin	Muff	Barbi	Faith	Madge
Erna	Muir	Becky	Fanny	Maeve
Esmé	Myra	Bella	Filia	Magda
Etta	Nell	Belle	Fiona	Maggy
Etty	Nena	Berta	Fleur	Mamie
Evie	Neva	Beryl	Flora	Manie
Fifi	Niki	Bessy	Freda	Manon
Gaby	Nina	Betty	Gemma	Marge
Gage	Nino	Biddy	Gerty	Maria
Gail	Nita	Bobby	Gipsy	Marie
Gene	Nora	Budie	Grace	Matty
Gola	Olga	Buena	Greer	Maude
Gwen	Oona	Bunny	Greta	Mavis
Gwyn	Pola	Bunty	Gussy	Megan
Hebe	Puss	Carol	Hazel	Mercy
Hope	Rena	Carré	Hedda	Merry
Ilse	Rita	Caryl	Helen	Milly
Inez	Rosa	Cathy	Henny	Minna
Inge	Rose	Cecil	Hetty	Mitzi
Ioné	Rosy	Celia	Hilda	Moira
Iris	Ruby	Chloe	Honor	Molly
Irma	Ruth	Circe	Hulda	Morag
Isla	Sara	Cissy	Hylda	Moyra
Isma	Sari	Clair	Idina	Myrle
Ivey	Sita	Clara	Ilona	Nancy

Nanny	**6**	Egeria	Lettie	Petula
Naomi		Eileen	Levina	Phoebe
Nelly	Agatha	Elaine	Lilian	Pinkie
Nerys	Aileen	Elinor	Lilias	Poppet
Nessa	Alicia	Emilie	Lillah	Poppie
Nesta	Alison	Esther	Lillie	Popsie
Netta	Almond	Eunice	Lizzie	Portia
Ninie	Althea	Evelyn	Lorina	Psyche
Ninny	Amabel	Fannie	Lottie	Rachel
Niobe	Amanda	Fatima	Louisa	Ramona
Norah	Amelia	Felice	Louise	Regina
Norma	Amelie	Galena	Lucile	Renira
Olive	Anabel	Gerrie	Maggie	Richie
Oriel	Angela	Gertie	Maidie	Robina
Pansy	Anthea	Gladys	Maimie	Rosina
Patsy	Armyne	Glenda	Maisie	Rowena
Patty	Astrid	Gloria	Marcia	Roxana
Paula	Audrey	Glynne	Margot	Sabina
Pearl	Aurora	Godiva	Marian	Sabine
Peggy	Averil	Gracie	Marion	Salome
Penny	Babbie	Gretel	Marnie	Sandra
Phebe	Beatie	Gussie	Martha	Sappho
Pippa	Benita	Gwenda	Marthe	Selina
Pixie	Bertha	Gwynne	Mattie	Seonad
Polly	Bessie	Hattie	Maxine	Serena
Poppy	Bettie	Hannah	Melita	Sharon
Queen	Bibbie	Helena	Mercia	Sheena
Renée	Biddie	Helene	Meriel	Sheila
Rhoda	Billie	Hester	Mignon	Simone
Rhona	Binnie	Hilary	Millie	Sophia
Robin	Birdie	Honora	Mimosa	Sophie
Rosie	Blanch	Honour	Minnie	Stella
Sadie	Blonde	Ileana	Miriam	Sybell
Sally	Bobbie	Imelda	Mollie	Sylvia
Sarah	Brenda	Imogen	Monica	Tamsin
Sonia	Brigid	Ingrid	Moulie	Teresa
Susan	Candis	Ioanna	Muriel	Tertia
Susie	Carmen	Isabel	Murtle	Tessie
Sybil	Carrie	Ishbel	Myrtle	Thalia
Tania	Cecile	Isobel	Nadine	Thelma
Tanya	Cecily	Isolde	Nancie	Tootie
Tanis	Celina	Jackie	Nancye	Trixie
Thora	Cherry	Janice	Nellie	Ulrica
Trudy	Cicely	Jeanie	Nelsie	Ursula
Unity	Cissie	Jeanne	Nessie	Verity
Valda	Claire	Jemima	Nettie	Verona
Venis	Connie	Jennie	Nicola	Violet
Venus	Dagmar	Jessie	Nicole	Vivian
Vesta	Daphne	Joanna	Noreen	Vivien
Vicki	Davina	Joanne	Odette	Vyvyen
Viola	Debbie	Judith	Olivia	Willow
Vivie	Denise	Juliet	Paddie	Winnie
Wanda	Dorcas	Kirsty	Pamela	Yvette
Wendy	Doreen	Lalage	Parnel	Yvonne
Zelda	Dorice	Lallie	Pattie	
Zelia	Dulcie	Lassie	Pegeen	
	Editha	Leonie	Peggie	**7**
	Edwina	Lesley	Pernel	
	Edythe	Leslie	Persis	Abigail

Adeline
Alberta
Alethea
Alfrida
Ameline
Annabel
Annette
Anstice
Antonia
Antonie
Ariadne
Athenia
Augusta
Aurelia
Babette
Barbara
Barbary
Beatrix
Belinda
Bettina
Billy Jo
Blanche
Blodwen
Blossom
Bridget
Camilla
Cecilia
Cherrie
Clarice
Claudia
Colette
Colleen
Coralie
Cynthia
Damaris
Darling
Deborah
Deirdre
Delysia
Diamond
Dolores
Dorinda
Dorothe
Dorothy
Dorrice
Dulcima
Eleanor
Elfreda
Elfrida
Ellenor
Ellinor
Elspeth
Emerald
Emiline
Estelle
Etienne
Eudoxia
Eugenia
Eugenie

Evaline
Eveline
Fayette
Felicia
Fenella
Feodora
Florrie
Flossie
Frances
Georgia
Gertrud
Gillian
Gwennie
Gwenyth
Gwladys
Gwyneth
Gwynnie
Harriet
Heather
Hellena
Horatia
Hypatia
Janette
Janitha
Jessamy
Jessica
Jocelyn
Johanna
Juliana
Lavinia
Leoline
Leonora
Letitia
Lettice
Lettuce
Lillian
Lillias
Lisbeth
Lucilla
Lucille
Mabelle
Margery
Marjery
Marjory
Martina
Matilda
Maureen
Melanie
Melissa
Michèle
Mildred
Minerva
Miralda
Miranda
Myfanwy
Natalie
Natasha
Nigella
Ninette

Octavia
Ophelia
Ottilie
Palmyra
Pandora
Paulina
Pauline
Perdita
Phillis
Phyllis
Queenie
Rebecca
Rhodena
Ricarda
Roberta
Rosalie
Rosella
Rosetta
Rosette
Sidonia
Susanna
Susanne
Suzanne
Suzette
Sybilla
Tabitha
Tatiana
Theresa
Therese
Titania
Tootles
Valerie
Valetta
Vanessa
Venetia
Winsome
Yolande

8

Adelaide
Adrienne
Albertha
Amabelle
Angelica
Angelina
Angeline
Angharad
Arabella
Araminta
Atalanta
Beatrice
Berenice
Carlotta
Carolina
Caroline
Cathleen
Catriona

Christie
Chrystal
Clemency
Clotilde
Consuelo
Cordelia
Cornelia
Dorothea
Dorothie
Drusilla
Dulcinia
Eleanora
Eleanore
Elfriede
Ellaline
Emmeline
Euphemia
Evelinda
Everalda
Felicity
Filomena
Florence
Francine
Georgina
Germaine
Gertrude
Gretchen
Grizelda
Grizelle
Harriett
Hermione
Hortense
Isabella
Jeanette
Jennifer
Jeromina
Julianna
Julietta
Juliette
Katharin
Kathleen
Laburnum
Laetitia
Lavender
Lorraine
Lucretia
Madeline
Magdalen
Marcella
Marcelle
Margaret
Marianne
Mariette
Marigold
Marjorie
Michelle
Mireille
Morwenna
Murielle

Nathalie	*9*	Geraldine	*10* AND *11*
Nathanie		Guglielma	
Patience	Albertine	Guinivere	Alexandrina (11)
Patricia	Alexandra	Gwendolen	Antoinette (10)
Penelope	Ambrosine	Harriette	Bernadette (10)
Petronel	Anastasia	Henrietta	Christabel (10)
Philippa	Annabelle	Henriette	Christiana (10)
Primrose	Britannia	Hortensia	Christobel (10)
Prudence	Cassandra	Hyacinthe	Cinderella (10)
Prunella	Catherine	Iphigenia	Clementina (10)
Raymonde	Celestine	Josephine	Clementine (10)
Rebeccah	Charlotte	Kathailin	Constantia (10)
Reinagle	Christian	Katharine	Desiderata (10)
Reinelde	Christina	Katherine	Ermentrude (10)
Rosalind	Christine	Madeleine	Ethelwynne (10)
Rosamond	Cleopatra	Magdalena	Evangelina (10)
Rosamund	Clothilde	Magdalene	Evangeline (10)
Rosemary	Columbine	Margarita	Fredericka (10)
Samantha	Constance	Melisande	Gwendolene (10)
Sapphire	Corisande	Millicent	Gwendoline (10)
Seabelle	Desdemona	Philomena	Hildegarde (10)
Sheelagh	Eglantine	Pierrette	Irmentrude (10)
Susannah	Elisabeth	Priscilla	Jacqueline (10)
Tallulah	Elizabeth	Rosabelle	Margaretta (10)
Theodora	Ermengard	Stephanie	Margherita (10)
Veronica	Ernestine	Theodosia	Marguerite (10)
Victoria	Esmeralda	Thomasina	Petronella (10)
Violetta	Esperance	Valentine	Philippina (10)
Virginia	Francisca	Winefride	Wilhelmina (10)
Vivienne	Frederica		
Vourneen	Gabrielle		
Winifred	Georgiana		

Nine Muses

Calliope (8) *epic*
Clio (4) *history*
Erato (5) *love songs*
Euterpe (7) *lyric poetry*
Melpomene (9) *tragedy*

Polyhymnia (10) *sacred poetry*
Terpsichore (11) *choral song and dance*
Thalia (6) *comedy and idyllic poetry*
Urania (6) *astronomy*

Nine Virtues

charity (7)
faith (5)
fortitude (9)
hope (4)
justice (7)

love (4) *charity*
modesty (7)
prudence (8)
temperance (10)

Palindromes

3

aba
aga
aha!
ala
ama
ana
asa
ava
bab
bib
bob
bub
dad
did
dod
dud
eke
ere
eve
ewe
eye
gag
gig
gog

hah!
huh!
mam
mim
mum
nan
non
nun
oho!
oxo
pap
pep
pip
pop
pup
s.o.s.
tat
tit
tot
tut!
wow
zuz

4

abba
anna
boob
deed
dood
ecce
keek
ma'am
noon
otto
peep
poop
sees
toot

5

alula
anana
civic
kayak
level
madam

minim
put-up
radar
refer
rotor
sagas
sexes
shahs
sohos
solos
tenet

6 AND OVER

Able was I ere I saw
  Elba (19)
deified (7)
marram (6)
pull-up (6)
redder (6)
reifier (7)
repaper (7)
reviver (7)
rotator (7)
terret (6)

Rivers of Hell

Acheron (7)
Avernus (7)
Cocytus (7)

Lethe (5)
Phlegethon (10)
Styx (4)

Roman emperors

Antoninus Pius (13)
Augustus (8)
Aurelian (8)
Caligula (8)
Caracalla (9)
Claudius (8)
Commodus (8)
Constantine (11)
Diocletian (10)
Elagabalus (10)

Galba (5)
Gordian (7)
Hadrian (7)
Honorius (8)
Jovian (6)
Julian (6)
Lucius Verus (11)
Marcus Aurelius (14)
Maximian (8)
Nero (4)

Nerva (5)
Otho (4)
Pertinax (8)
Probus (6)
Septimius Severus (16)
Titus (5)
Trajan (6)
Valerian (8)
Vespasian (9)
Vitellius (9)

Seven against Thebes

Adrastus (8)
Amphiaraus (10)
Capaneus (8)
Hipomedon (10)

Parthenopaeus (13)
Polynices (9)
Tydeus (6)

Seven deadly sins

accidie (7)
acedia (6)
anger (5)
avarice (7)
covetousness (12)
envy (4)
gluttony (8)

lust (4)
pride (5)
sloth (5)
vainglory (9)
wrath (5)

Seven sages

Bias (4)
Chilon (6)
Cleobonlos (10)
Periander (9)

Pittacus (8)
Solon (5)
Thales (6)

Seven Wonders of the World

The Pyramids of Egypt
The Hanging Gardens of Babylon
The Tomb of Mausolus
The Temple of Diana at Ephesus
The Colossus of Rhodes

The Statue of Zeus by Phidias
The Pharos of Alexandria
or
The Palace of Cyrus (cemented with gold)

Signs of the Zodiac

Aquarius (8), *Water-bearer*
Aries (5), *Ram*
Cancer (6), *Crab*
Capricorn (9), *Goat*
Capricornus (11), *Goat*

Gemini (6), *Twins*
Leo (3), *Lion*
Libra (5), *Balance*
Pisces (6), *Fishes*
Sagittarius (11), *Archer*

Scorpio (7), *Scorpion*
Taurus (6), *Bull*
Virgo (5), *Virgin*

329

Three Fates

Atropos (7)
Clotho (6)
Lachesis (8)

Three Furies

Alecto (6)
Megaera (7)
Tisiphone (9)

Three Gorgons

Eurayale (8)
Medusa (6)
Stheno (6)

Three Graces

Aglaia (6)
Euphrosyne (10)
Thalia (6)

Three Harpies

Aello (5)
Celaeno/Podarge (7)
Ocypete (7)

Typefaces

Baskerville (11)	Doric (5)	Gondy (5)	Propane (7)
Blackface (9)	Elzevir (7)	Gothic (6)	Roman (5)
Bodoni (6)	Ethylene (8)	Ionic (5)	Sans Serif (9)
Caslon (6)	Garamond (8)	Italic (6)	Times (5)
Clarendon (9)	Gill (4)	Old Style (8)	

Index